Delilah Roars Again!

Stoke City – 1984-2009

25 Years of Pain and Glory

DESERT ISLAND HISTORIES OF STOKE CITY FC

DELILAH ROARS AGAIN! STOKE CITY 1984-2009
25 YEARS OF PAIN AND GLORY

STOKE CITY: 101 GOLDEN GREATS

POTTERS AT WAR: STOKE CITY 1939-1947

DELILAH ROARS AGAIN!
STOKE CITY – 1984-2009
25 YEARS OF PAIN AND GLORY

Series Editor: Clive Leatherdale

Simon Lowe

DESERT ISLAND BOOKS

Published in 2009

Earlier editions of this book were published as
Stoke City: The Modern Era – A Complete Record
2000 and 2003

DESERT ISLAND BOOKS LIMITED
7 Clarence Road, Southend-on-Sea, Essex SS1 1AN
United Kingdom
www.desertislandbooks.com

British Library Cataloguing-in-Publication Data
A catalogue record for this book is available from the British Library

ISBN 978-1-905328-47-5

Printed in Great Britain

Photographs in this book are reproduced by kind permission of:
Stoke City FC, Huston Spratt, Andy Peck, Central Office of Information,
Sporting Pictures UK, Action Images, Anthony Brown.
All photographs since 2004 courtesy of the *Stoke Sentinel*

CONTENTS

3. RULE BRITANNIA – 1997-2005

4. RESURRECTION MEN – 2005-09

AUTHOR'S NOTE

Delilah Roars Again! is the third edition of *Stoke City: the Modern Era*. The first appeared, with great success, in November 2000 and covered the period from 1970 to the summer of 2000. This new edition commences in the summer of 1984, just before the club's seemingly terminal decline began, and chronicles the struggle to reinvent Stoke City with a new stadium and Icelandic owners and the controversial, and eventually triumphant, return to the Brit of Peter Coates and Tony Pulis. It brings the story up to date to the end of the successful and incredible first ever season in the Premier League, following promotion in 2008.

In keeping with the 'complete record' format of Desert Island Football Histories, the book comprises two distinct sections. The first is a season-by-season narrative that analyses the changing fortunes of the club. The second presents a statistical game-by-game chronology, incorporating every fact that could possibly be fitted in, including amending the few errors that were found in previous editions. I apologise unreservedly if any remain uncorrected. Every effort is made to cross-check every piece of information, but for such an enormous task it is nigh on impossible to achieve one hundred per cent accuracy.

As with the original book, this edition is not the work of one person alone. Clive Leatherdale of Desert Island Books has guided me in its conception, while photographs are provided by Huston Spratt, for many years the *Sentinel*'s Stoke City photographer, Julian Boodell, Anthony Brown, Andy Peck, the Sentinel themselves and EMPICS. Julian also provided much help with the original research, in allowing me access to his massive programme collection. I would also like to thank my fellow Desert Island author Jim Brown for his assistance and support.

Finally my thanks go to my wife Kath and daughter Evie, whose support has kept me going through the massive task of researching and putting together this third edition.

SIMON LOWE
August 2009

INTRODUCTION

For years the crest of Stoke City Football Club bore the legend 'Founded 1863'. Being the second oldest league club, after Notts County, carried certain kudos. However, Wade Martin's research points to a later year – 1868 – when Henry John Almond, an Old Carthusian, formed a team amongst his fellow apprentices at the North Staffordshire Railway Works.

Known initially as 'the Ramblers' and later as Stoke FC, the club, having merged with the Stoke Victoria Athletics Club, settled into new premises, the athletics stadium, which became known as the Victoria Ground after the nearby Victoria Hotel.

Turning professional in 1885, Stoke were founder members of the Football League in 1888, finishing bottom. Years of struggle to retain First Division status followed, including one season outside the League in 1890-91. The Potters reached the semi-final of the FA Cup in 1899, but lost 1-3 to Derby. However, in 1908, following relegation to Division Two, Stoke announced a crippling £1,100 loss, as a result of which they folded.

A new club rose out of the ashes. AJ Barker, as new secretary-manager, moulded a team which competed in the Birmingham and District League and the Southern League before rejoining the Football League's Division Two after the Great War. Promotion to Division One in 1922 was followed by relegation in 1923 and again in 1926. The club spent 1926-27 in Division Three (North), but at least their stay was brief: they finished the season as champions.

Renamed Stoke City FC in 1925, when Stoke-on-Trent was granted city status, the club returned to the top flight in 1932-33, when they unleashed the legendary Stanley Matthews. This time the club blossomed in the big time. Home attendances trebled. England international Matthews was a star throughout the land. Ground records were regularly broken when Stoke – and Matthews – visited. The largest crowd ever to attend an English domestic club match outside Wembley, 84,569, saw Manchester City defeat Stoke 1-0 in an FA Cup quarter-final in 1934.

Under the stewardship of manager Bob McGrory, Stoke achieved their highest finish in Division One, fourth in 1935-36. West Brom were thrashed 10-3 in February 1937, with centre-forward Freddie Steele scoring five. These halcyon days saw the club provide three

England forwards at Hampden Park in 1937 – Matthews, Steele and Joe Johnson. A record crowd for the Victoria Ground, 51,373, saw Stoke draw 0-0 with Arsenal on Easter Monday.

During the war years, Stoke played in the League North with players such as Frank Bowyer, Tommy Sale, Frank Mountford and Frank Soo sacrificing the best part of their careers to the conflict. The reintroduction of the FA Cup in 1945 saw Stoke travel to Bolton for a two-legged quarter-final. Crush barriers collapsed behind the goal which Stoke were defending. The crush claimed 33 lives and 520 injured in what became known as the Burnden Park disaster, the worst that English football had then suffered.

The 1946-47 season saw Stoke mount their first serious challenge for the championship. The icy winter extended league fixtures into the summer. City's last match was at Sheffield United on 14 June, when a win would secure the title. But tension between Matthews and McGrory erupted, as it had done throughout the previous decade. This time the split was irrevocable and Matthews, despite being a veteran of 32, was sold to Blackpool in May for £11,500. Without their star turn, Stoke went down at Bramall Lane 1-2. Who knows, Matthews might have made all the difference.

Bob McGrory severed his connections with the club in 1952, resigning when the board refused to back his judgement on replacing ageing striker Freddie Steele. The bluff Scot had played as a right-back for Stoke from 1921 to 1935, making a club record 511 appearances, before taking over from Tom Mather as manager. McGrory's replacement was the former Wolves full-back and fitness fanatic, Frank Taylor, but, handicapped by a parsimonious board and an ageing squad, Stoke were relegated the following season.

Eight years in the doldrums followed as Stoke failed to mount a serious challenge for promotion. A record 8-0 win over Lincoln in February 1957, with winger Tim Coleman bagging seven goals, did little to disguise the overall stagnation. New chairman Albert Henshall decided a change at the top was for the best.

Coach Tony Waddington was promoted into the hot seat in June 1960, and discovered that he had a fight on his hands. In 1960-61 attendances fell below an average 10,000 for the first time since 1908. It took a masterstroke to transform the club. Waddington bought back Stanley Matthews, at the princely age of 46, from Blackpool. The maestro made his second Stoke debut at home to Huddersfield on 28 October 1961. The 35,974 crowd quadrupled that of City's previous home game and more than repaid Stan's £3,000 transfer fee. The club was on the up. In 1962-63 Stoke won promotion as Second Division champions, with 48-year-old Matthews scoring the promotion-clinching goal at home to Luton.

1963-64 saw Stoke reach the League Cup final, a two-legged affair against Leicester. After a 1-1 draw at home, the away leg was lost 2-3 in a tight and dramatic contest. On 21 March 1964 Stoke racked up a 9-1 win against Ipswich, which still stands as City's biggest ever margin of victory.

Stoke's centenary was celebrated (prematurely as it turned out!) in 1963 with a prestigious friendly against European Champions Real Madrid. In February 1965 Stanley Matthews finally retired at the age of 50. He bade farewell to Stoke City with a celebratory game against a World XI starring Puskas, Di Stefano, Masopust and Yashin, at the Victoria Ground.

Over this period Waddington cannily signed several experienced players to accompany Matthews. Dennis Viollet from Manchester United, George Eastham (Newcastle), and Jimmy McIlroy (Burnley) were all 30-plus when putting pen to paper. These old-stagers proved useful foils to the promising younger players, such as John Ritchie, who would go on to become the club's record aggregate goalscorer with 176 goals in all competitions. But Waddington's biggest coup came when he signed Gordon Banks, acclaimed as the world's best goalkeeper, in 1967. Playing behind a homegrown defence of Denis Smith, Alan Bloor, Jackie Marsh and Mike Pejic, Banks provided the last line of a redoubtable defence.

The team made itself felt as a cup-fighting force, reaching the FA Cup semi-final, for only the second time, in 1970-71. Despite leading Arsenal 2-0, Stoke could not hold on. A last-minute penalty sunk City's hopes of reaching Wembley and City lost the replay 0-2. The following season gave Stoke a chance to lay that ghost, as they were again paired with Arsenal in the FA Cup's last four. This time after a 1-1 draw Stoke led the replay through Jimmy Greenhoff, but a harsh penalty and a linesman's error – confusing a Goodison Park programme seller's white coat with the Stoke change strip – allowed John Radford to score when offside. Arsenal won 2-1.

Stoke's luck held better in that season's League Cup semi-final, when Gordon Banks saved a late Geoff Hurst penalty in the second leg at Upton Park to keep City in the tie. After four games with West Ham, Stoke finally reached their first major Wembley final, beating the Hammers 3-2 at Old Trafford. Under the Twin Towers, Waddington's policy of mixing old heads and young paid off as Irish international winger Terry Conroy and 37-year-old George Eastham scored the goals which gave Stoke a 2-1 win over Chelsea.

Having now won a cup, Stoke entered European competition for the first time. They were paired with Kaiserslautern in the first round of the UEFA Cup and won the home leg 3-1. Stoke's naivety showed in the second leg, though, as the Germans triumphed 4-0.

Waddington developed his squad by splashing out £240,000 on Chelsea's star midfielder Alan Hudson. Huddy proved the final piece of Stoke's jigsaw and they challenged for the title in two successive seasons, playing skilful, passing football in the process. However, in both seasons the side's inexperience was exposed in the final weeks and Stoke faded to finish fifth. 1974-75 also provided another European excursion when Stoke played Ajax, only losing on away goals scored.

The halcyon days came to a crushing end when, in January 1976, a freak wind blew the roof off the ageing Butler Street Stand. Lack of adequate insurance meant that the board dismantled Waddington's side. Within months Hudson, Greenhoff, Pejic and young striker Ian Moores had been sold to manage the debts incurred by the stand's rebuilding. Waddington quit. An inevitable relegation season in 1976-77 ensued under new boss George Eastham.

After a poor start to life in Division Two, Eastham, too mild-mannered for the cut-throat world of soccer management, resigned in January 1978 and, under caretaker-manager Alan A'Court, Stoke suffered a humiliating 2-3 home defeat to non-league Blyth Spartans in the FA Cup. The board appointed young Shrewsbury manager Alan Durban. Through signing solid professionals, such as midfield veteran Howard Kendall and striker Brendan O'Callaghan, and blending them with exciting, home-produced youngsters such as Garth Crooks, Adrian Heath, Paul Bracewell and Lee Chapman, Durban won the club promotion in 1978-79.

Back in the top division, Stoke began an almost annual flirtation with relegation. Twice City's fate hung on the last match. On the second occasion, Stoke needed to win and hope another of the three teams involved in the relegation scrap dropped points. City hammered Wolves 4-0, with winger Paul Maguire scoring all four goals to earn heroic status. Birmingham slipped into Division Two following a goalless draw at home to Southampton.

Stoke's escape from that 1983-84 relegation battle was improbable in the extreme. Next to bottom with only seventeen points, following a 0-6 hammering at QPR in January, manager Ritchie Barker, who was appointed after Durban departed for Sunderland in 1981, was sacked. Caretaker-manager Bill Asprey persuaded Alan Hudson to return to the club. Despite being 32, the midfielder prompted Stoke to win eight of the next twelve games. The form of winger Mark Chamberlain earned him England caps, while goalkeeper Peter Fox had also been mentioned in international terms. But the majority of the squad was ageing and slow-paced. Asprey would have to pull something equally spectacular out of the hat to avoid another relegation struggle.

This book follows the ups and downs of the club from that seminal 1984-85 campaign, which became known to all Stoke fans who endured it as the 'holocaust' season. From the ashes of the debacle of a record low points-scoring season, Stoke embarked upon a remarkable 23 years of yo-yoing between divisions, clutching disaster from the jaws of safety, failure from the edge of victory and shooting itself in the foot on more occasions than seems possible from a neutral perspective. Often City's story over these years has been likened to a soap opera, except that this script would have been laughed out of town by even the most outlandish producer. Almost every football club lays claim to these faults and foibles, but Stoke City has tested the patience of even its most faithful supporters and it was the pain and agony generally endured over more than twenty years which made the joy of winning promotion in May 2008 all the more exuberant.

Quickly that joy turned to a stunned disbelief before the expectation of a first Premier League season set in. With pundits and 'experts' presenting a united front in predicting an instant return to the Championship, possibly with even fewer points than the hideous 1984-85 season, Tony Pulis's men proved that they were made of sterner stuff. The subsequent joyous, astonishing and successful rise up to a twelfth-placed finish has brought a new emotion to Potters fans when discussing their club – confidence. Alongside that sits a new belief that their club is no longer an under-achieving laughing stock, living on past glories. Stoke City is a club building for a promising future with an exciting, determined team under a manager whose capabilities have yet to reach their limit, despite many believing otherwise.

The only question on Stoke fans' lips now is how far the club can go – and that just makes the journey from humiliation 25 years ago to 2009, as relived in this book, all the more incredible.

1

DECLINE AND FALL 1984-1991

LEAGUE DIVISION 1	**1984-85**
Canon Division 1	22nd (Relegated)
Milk Cup	2nd Round
FA Cup	3rd Round

The improbable escape from relegation had served only to paper over the cracks that were appearing all over the club. A drop in average attendances of seventeen per cent caused more financial hardship, to the extent that the experienced Peter Hampton and four-goal hero Paul Maguire were released on free transfers to ease the burden of the wage bill. Bill Asprey, aside from being confirmed as manager on a permanent basis, was coach and stand-in physiotherapist. One of his first decisions was to revert training to the antiquated facilities at the Victoria Ground. The club had been using Keele University's superb sports facilities, but Asprey felt he needed to be near the stadium to fulfil his onerous duties. It was also cheaper to train at the Vic, which pleased the board.

Asprey spoke of new signings but talk proved cheap. Youngsters Maskery, Heath, Parkin, Bould and Painter started the season at Luton. Nine months later there would be six teenagers in the side, hardly an improvement. Asprey did not believe the youngsters were ready for the First Division. He was right, but with no funds forthcoming from the newly expanded board, City had little choice but to start the new season with a thin squad.

It soon became apparent that the squad was painfully inadequate for First Division football. Five players were tried at left-back, where opponents were causing Stoke endless problems. The midfield, for so long the strongest department, was now looking long in the tooth. McIlroy's industry could not compensate for his loss of pace, while Chamberlain's lack of confidence would have warranted him being dropped – except that there was no one to replace him. An embarrassing home defeat by Third Division Rotherham in the Milk Cup provoked the first protests from fans. The club was falling apart.

DID YOU KNOW?

The Stoke anthem 'Delilah' originated with City fan Anton 'TJ' Booth. Following a bad display at Derby in 1987 he was asked to sing something 'clean' at a Derby pub!

Chairman Frank Edwards tried to raise funds by selling the car park and training pitches – a huge area between the stadium and the A500 artery through Stoke – to supermarket chain Asda, but the deal died. Planning permission was refused in early 1985 and an appeal rejected after more than a year of wrangling. Much hope had been placed upon the £3 million that Stoke expected to receive for the land. Rejection meant there was nowhere else to look for funds. The board could hardly expect to cash in on the players, not when they were associated with such an appalling team.

With the club hamstrung financially, there was no possibility of bringing in new players, as had happened in previous seasons, to stop the rot. Nor was there an Alan Hudson to effect a dramatic escape, as injury restricted him to just seventeen appearances. In desperation Asprey sold the one player who had been performing to anywhere like his potential, Robbie James, for £100,00 to QPR in mid-October to finance the £80,000 purchase of Keith Bertschin, a striker, who had become surplus to requirements at Norwich. The transactions smacked of desperation. Bertschin had only appeared in five of Norwich's games, scoring just twice to add to his poor return of seven the previous season, but, with the transfer market spiralling higher in line with inflation in Britain as a whole, Stoke could not afford a top-drawer striker.

With stalwart keeper Peter Fox injured, Welsh Youth International Stuart Roberts, aged seventeen years 258 days, became the youngest keeper ever to play for Stoke – a record he holds at the time of writing – when he started against Ipswich. His appearance was from desperation, rather than ability. Playing behind a porous back four, Roberts let in eight goals in three games and was traumatised so much that he never played league football again.

From the team that had beaten Liverpool in April to the rabble that picked up only eight points before Christmas was a blink of the eye. The side showed no ideas going forward and confusion at the back. The frustration turned to ill-discipline as Dyson, Hudson, Berry and loanee Tony Spearing were sent off within a few weeks. Each was for dissent, or aggressive behaviour towards the referee or opponents, rather than dangerous challenges. City also gave away five own-goals and nine penalties over the season, a sign that the constant pressure on the defence was too much to withstand. An insurance assessor would have made Stoke a write-off.

After a 2-3 home defeat by Luton in an FA Cup replay in early January Stoke's season was effectively over. Asprey was reduced to talk of 'building for next year', while Chairman Edwards was subjected to much personal abuse as the club lumbered through its most disastrous season ever. There were more calls for his resignation than Asprey's, as it was obvious that it was the dire state of the club that needed addressing rather than any coaching issue.

Stoke's decline was a microcosm of the sea change which football underwent during the 1970s and 80s. Gone was the preeminence of northern traditions. The likes of Blackpool, Burnley, Blackburn and Derby had all fallen down the divisions. Wolves and Sheffield United as low as Division Four. A new order was arising. Watford and Oxford, clubs with small support bases, but backed by sizeable investment by distant sugar daddies from the media and pop music world, were now challenging the established elite of Liverpool, Manchester United, Everton, Tottenham and Arsenal.

But there was no Robert Maxwell or Elton John waiting in the wings to ease Stoke's pain. The board blamed the humiliations on the manager and Asprey, who had suffered ill-health and depression over the preceding months, was relieved of his duties after another abject home defeat – this time by Luton. Tony Lacey, the only other coach employed by Stoke, took charge and was faced with the thankless task of trying to get a team predominantly populated with his youth team players to survive in the First Division. It was, of course, impossible. That it took until Easter for City's relegation to be confirmed was the only surprising aspect of their demise. Dudley Kernick's nous was rewarded by collecting £6,000 from the bookmaker and his P45 from the board, becoming another victim of the internal feuding which riddled the entire club.

By curtain-fall Stoke boasted a host of unwanted records for a 42-game League season – most defeats (31), most home defeats (fifteen), fewest points (seventeen), and fewest goals scored (24). Stoke also set club records for most goals conceded (91), worst goal difference (–67) and fewest home wins (three). The average gate had fallen to below 11,000. The club was in such a parlous state that another relegation the following season seemed probable.

Match of the Season 1984-85

Stoke 0 Coventry 1

Division 1, 17 May 1985

At the end of the worst season in not only their own, but of any club's, history, Stoke faced one final match, postponed until after the conclusion of the regular season due to illness in their opponents' camp earlier in the campaign. Wearied by a run of ten successive defeats, the last thing Stoke needed was one more game, particularly against a team who would come out with their sleeves rolled up. Having narrowly avoided relegation the previous season, Coventry faced an even deeper crisis this time. Perennial bookies' favourites for the drop, the Sky Blues were eight points adrift and faced three games in nine days, all of which had to be won, to avoid joining Stoke in the Second Division.

Coventry had parted with manager Bobby Gould at Christmas following a run of nine wins in 42 games. His replacement was assistant manager Don Mackay. Form had hardly improved and Coventry entered this match having won only two of their previous nine. Brian 'Killer' Kilcline, a muscular centre-half who sported a beard that lent him a gladiatorial air, had joined Coventry earlier in the season from Notts County. Along with left-back Stuart Pearce, completing his first full season in professional football after signing from non-league Wealdstone, and the powerful Cyrille Regis in attack, he formed the backbone of a physical Coventry side.

The game was desperate. Coventry were up-tight, Stoke merely going through the motions. The first half passed without incident. In the second period Coventry began to exert pressure as the lively Dave Bennett had the beating of Chris Hemming down Stoke's left. As usual Stoke wilted. From a corner, Regis headed goalward only for the ball to strike Berry's hand. Referee Neil Midgley blew for a penalty. Stoke protested but the decision stood and new skipper Stuart Pearce nervelessly slotted the spot-kick.

To give Stoke their due, they roused themselves for one final fling at First Division football. A draw would enable them to equal the all-time lowest points total in a 42-game season of eighteen, set by QPR in 1969, rather than set a new record. With Coventry protecting their lead, Stoke found space to attack for the first time in months. On 83 minutes Paul Dyson attempted to get his head to another corner, but as he jumped he was nudged by Regis and another penalty was awarded. Ian Painter, who had already scored four penalties during the season, cracked the ball against the underside of the bar, from where it rebounded to safety. Coventry breathed a collective sigh of relief. They were off the hook.

Coventry would win both their remaining games – including an improbable 4-1 victory over Everton – champions and European Cup-Winners' Cup winners – to stay up, sending Norwich down. Within two years the Sky Blues would be celebrating a Wembley FA Cup triumph with Ogrizovic, Regis and Kilcline becoming heroes. Stoke's players were consigned to posterity for different reasons.

LEAGUE DIVISION 2	**1985-86**
Canon Division 2	10th
Milk Cup	3rd Round
FA Cup	3rd Round

Brendan O'Callaghan had gone to Oldham for £30,000 in February and Sammy McIlroy was freed in the summer. Their departure eased the wage bill but left the squad short of experience. Chairman Frank Edwards died in June, having come under pressure from supporters during the relegation season. Sandy Clubb replaced him. Clubb's first task was to seek a manager capable of putting a club on its knees back on its feet.

Due to the change in the chair, the managerial question was not settled until late June. Clubb plumped for the first player-manager in the club's history. Mick Mills was a former international full-back who had captained England (in the absence of the injured Kevin Keegan) during the 1982 World Cup. He had just been released by Southampton. Stoke hoped that, having worked with the likes of Bobby Robson, Lawrie McMenemy and Ron Greenwood, he would have much to give, and his arrival also filled the problem left-back position. Mills' choice as coach was Cyril 'Sammy' Chung, who had top-flight managerial experience with Wolves. Mills hoped Chung's tactical brain, combined with his own motivational skills, would halt the club's slide. But with an atmosphere of deep gloom permeating the club, that would not be easy.

Clubb also identified a need for improved public relations with the fans. Firstly, the pin-striped kit, now indelibly associated with the club's worst ever season, was ditched, along with the PR people who had introduced it. The club also instituted the 'Lifeline Society' – an appeal for funds to allow Stoke to continue to develop its own youngsters and, it was hoped, keep them. Admission prices rose slightly, to £2.50 for the Boothen End and £5 for a seat. These compared well with the cost of seeing First Division football across the country, especially in London where the average price was £4 to stand on the terrace. A Stoke season ticket cost £50 on the terraces and £100 to sit down.

The prevarication over Mills' appointment meant he had little opportunity to add to the playing staff, even with free transfers. Every chance to liquidise cash had to be taken. The beginning of the season saw Mark Chamberlain return to something like the form which had seen him win the last of his eight full England caps just eleven months earlier. He starred in a 6-2 thrashing of Leeds and was suddenly marketable again. Surprisingly, his dribbling skills caught the eye of Howard Wilkinson, whose Sheffield Wednesday side were renowned as the most physical, long-ball team in the First Division. Wilkinson tempted Chamberlain, but as the clubs could not agree a fee it went to a tribunal. Stoke were aggrieved to receive only £300,000 for a player who a year earlier would have been worth almost a million. Worse, the bank sought to reduce Stoke's overdraft rather than allow reinvestment in players. The outlook was bleak. Stoke were deep in the bottom half and – the 6-2 win aside – scored just four goals in the opening ten games.

Supporters deserted the club in droves. Football was no longer the drug which had seen attendances hit the 40 million mark in the immediate post-war years. 1985-86 saw audiences dip below seventeen million for the first time. There is no telling how many were put off by the yob element. Trouble had been commonplace inside and outside Britain's grounds since the 1960s. Stoke were one of the worst offenders. The Boothen End had a reputation for vociferous support, but those same fans enjoyed nothing more than baiting the opposition team and supporters. At times, this could spill over into violence which ordinary folk wanted no part of. With better transport and higher disposable incomes, the average working man could look elsewhere for his Saturday entertainment. Even in such a predominantly working class area as the Potteries, attractions such as Alton Towers and the new Festival Park, with its cinema complex and bowling alleys, ensured that football slipped down the pecking order. The more so, now that City were in the Second Division. Stoke's average gates hit their lowest for 78 years.

The return of Peter Fox from long-term injury put an end to the goalkeeping torments that marred the previous campaign. Under Mills, George Berry also found himself back in favour. The popular centre-half was reinstated as captain and provided solidity in the middle of the back four. Neil Adams, an 18-year-old apprentice, was the next player to emerge from the youth system. He replaced Chamberlain on the right wing, using his body swerve and pace to beat defenders, while his accurate crossing created chances for the new strikeforce of Bertschin and 18-year-old Graham Shaw. The youngsters, outclassed last season, were finding their feet.

Alan Hudson retired through injury in November. Mills replaced him with Norwich's John Devine on a free transfer. Devine was tempted by the chance of teaming up again with Keith Bertschin and proved an inspired signing. He had played for Arsenal in an FA Cup final and in a memorable European Cup-Winners' Cup semi-final at Juventus, which the Gunners won 1-0. Principally a full-back at Highbury, he converted to midfield during a three-year spell at Carrow Road, but had fallen out of favour the previous season, when the Canaries were relegated alongside Stoke.

Devine's debut coincided with a 4-2 win at Oldham (see Match of the Season) which began a run of four straight wins that propelled Stoke from eighteenth to tenth. His neat passing released Heath and Adams down the wings. City only lost three matches of the fifteen which Devine started, but a hideous tackle by Brighton's Eric Young at the Goldstone Ground ended his career in March and Stoke lost a major midfield influence just as their momentum was mounting.

Mills' full-back partner was Steve Bould, but Mills and Chung, being flank players themselves, believed that the lanky defender was actually better suited to the centre-half role. Bould had a good awareness, a strong physique and was dominant in the air. With a ready-made replacement in Bould, Mills sold the unpopular Paul Dyson to West Brom for £60,000 in March. The cash was earmarked for a playmaker to replace Hudson and Devine.

Mills plumped for Tony Kelly of Wigan for £80,000. Popularly known as 'Zico', Kelly was a portly midfielder, prone to flashes of brilliance, renowned for being among the best free-kick specialists outside the top flight, but with an Achilles heel of food and beer. Clearly unfit, having been dropped by Wigan boss Bryan Hamilton, Kelly still controlled the game on his debut, a 2-0 win over Oldham, providing killer passes for both goals. With the summer in which to get fit, Kelly was seen as the great hope of the future, personifying Mills' positive approach. It had needed a fresh face, from outside the club, to replace Asprey, and Mills' perceived value to the club was such that his contract was extended to the summer of 1989.

Match of the Season 1985-86

Oldham 2 Stoke 4

Division 2, 23 November 1985

Joe Royle's Oldham were one of the best sides outside the top flight throughout the late 1980s. They had vied for promotion each season from 1985-86, bar one, until that goal was finally achieved in 1991. In Micky Quinn and Roger Palmer they had goalscorers who could win any game. They were virtually unbeatable at home, having lost only one game all season.

There were signs that City's confidence was returning after the nightmare of the previous season, but Mills recognised the lack of craft in midfield. Constrained by the dire financial situation, Mills had signed Norwich's experienced midfielder John Devine on a free transfer in midweek. Sometimes new signings take time to settle in. This one made an immediate impact.

DID YOU KNOW?

In May 1967 the Football League Review reported that Stoke striker Gerry Bridgwood was voted the most attractive man in football with over 800 female admirers!

Devine pulled on the No 4 shirt, which had already seen five occupants this season as Mills searched for an answer to his creative problem in midfield. Hudson had retired, and Williams, Parkin, Hemming and Beeston were too young to be able to dictate a game. On a freezing cold day, Devine showed them exactly how it should be done as he pulled the strings and Stoke tore Oldham apart. He set up Bertschin for a coolly taken goal, and once Phil Heath had rounded off a run from the halfway line with a superb strike, Stoke played the ball around confidently on the uneven surface.

After the break Chris Maskery and Bertschin both capitalised on Devine's short passes to put Stoke 4-0 ahead away from home. No one could quite believe what was happening. Oldham were finally stirred and managed to score twice, one a penalty, but their two goals flattered them. City killed the game, with Devine now acting as a midfield spoiler. His all-round performance, as that of the team, had been outstanding.

The game marked the first sign that Stoke were starting the long road to recovery, sparking a run of one defeat in ten games. Sadly John Devine was not able to share in the team's success further than March, when his leg was broken in five places at Brighton. His career in British football was over, but he played on in Norway, for IK Start, and later in India, where he also coached.

Oldham's form slumped and they dropped out of the promotion running, finishing just three points ahead of Stoke in eighth place.

LEAGUE DIVISION 2	**1986-87**
Today Division 2	8th
Littlewoods Cup	2nd Round
FA Cup	5th Round

Central to Stoke's preparations for 1986-87 was the announcement of a sponsorship deal with local ceramics company H & R Johnson. The brand name that adorned the players' shirts was 'Cristal Tiles'. To that £200,000 deal was added the sale of Neil Adams, who had impressed Everton manager Howard Kendall to the extent that he paid £150,000 for a player who had only completed one year as a professional. By the end of the season Adams had won a League championship medal. The decision to sell the young winger upset many Stoke fans who had contributed to the 'Lifeline' appeal in the hope that Stoke would be able to hold onto its young stars, but at least the money allowed Mills to venture into the transfer market for the first time. He proceeded to bring in 22-year-old Lee Dixon from Bury for £50,000 – to fill Bould's place at right-back – and experienced right-sided midfielder Tony Ford from his hometown club, Grimsby, to replace Adams.

There was tentative talk that Stoke might achieve one of the play-off spots, which had been introduced. The teams finishing third, fourth and fifth in the Second Division, together with the side finishing third from bottom of the First, would fight it out for the right to play in the top flight. Despite his pledge to get fit over the summer, Tony Kelly returned to the club palpably overweight and was immediately put on a vigorous training programme. Without Kelly firing on all cylinders, Stoke won just one of their first nine games. Bertschin and Shaw were missing the crosses that Adams once provided, and each managed only one goal from open play, although Shaw did find the net from a penalty. Confidence was so low that both he and Bertschin managed to miss one spot-kick each. Following a 0-1 defeat at Brighton, Stoke were firmly rooted to the bottom of the table and had been dumped out of the Littlewoods Cup by Shrewsbury.

With things going awry, Peter Coates took over from Sandy Clubb as chairman. Coates was a self-made millionaire who ran catering company Stadia Catering. He promised much in providing funds for the redevelopment of the squad. His backing allowed Mills to invest a modest £25,000 in his old Ipswich team-mate, Brian Talbot, who signed from Watford. At 33, Talbot was a combative midfielder who had become the first player to win the FA Cup in consecutive seasons with different clubs, after leaving Ipswich for Arsenal. He was also chairman of the Professional Footballers'

Association, the Players' Union. Talbot's arrival provided a stable base in midfield, allowing Mills to persist with the experiment of playing midfielder Carl Saunders as a striker. Saunders used his pace to make inroads into opposing defences, revelling in the spaces opened up by a fit Kelly's through-passes.

Next to arrive was Nicky Morgan, a striker who had fallen out of favour with Alan Ball at Portsmouth and cost Stoke just £40,000. Although only 5ft 10in, Morgan was an excellent shielder of the ball, allowing the midfield time to support him and take return passes. Morgan proved the perfect foil for the quicksilver Saunders. Stoke embarked upon an unbeaten run of eleven games, racking up 24 goals in eight games in the period around Christmas. Bertschin, Morgan and Saunders all scored hat-tricks. At the height of the run City thrashed Grimsby 6-0 to win only their second FA Cup-tie since 1978. By the end of January Stoke were up to fourth. The fans talked of automatic promotion now. Mills was named Manager of the Month for December and, with City the form team in the division, confidence was sky-high.

Not only were Stoke scoring goals, they had stopped conceding them. Steve Bould adapted well to his switch to centre-half and was improving visibly with every match. At 6ft 3in, and over thirteen stone, his was an imposing bulk for opposing forwards to pass. His presence led to him becoming widely recognised as the best centre-half outside the First Division. George Graham, Arsenal's manager, made no secret of his admiration for Bould. However, a back injury sustained during a defeat by Blackburn truncated his season and quelled the transfer speculation, for now.

George Berry had found a new lease of life after his exclusion from first-team affairs under Bill Asprey. He relished the challenge of pulling together a young, growing team and was a demonstrative captain. Mills respected Berry, relying on him to lift the dressing room when results did not go Stoke's way with his irrepressible sense of humour. He had a distinctive 'Afro' hairstyle which often brought him abuse from opposition fans, but Berry revealed that it was actually a tactic! He deliberately grew his hair so that when he stood at the near post for a corner in the opponents' area, nobody could see past him. If the ball was directed to the near post, as was a favourite ploy at Stoke, the first time the defence and goalkeeper would be able to catch sight of it was when Berry had flicked it on, causing confusion which often led to Stoke goals.

The FA Cup run carried Stoke into the fifth round, where First Division Coventry were waiting. It was a mark of how far the side had come under Mills that there was a real feeling in the Potteries that Stoke could beat their higher-ranked opponents. In the event,

DID YOU KNOW?

Until he resigned in February 1977, Tony Waddington was the longest serving First Division manager at 16 years and 8 months.

Stoke pushed Coventry to the limit, but lost to a Mickey Gynn goal, despite having a good penalty shout turned down when Lee Dixon was felled in the area. On such decisions seasons turn. Coventry went on to Wembley glory, Stoke embarked on a run of one win in ten games to drop out of the play-off picture entirely. But the Cup run confirmed the enormous potential deep within Stoke City FC. The crowds had flocked back: indeed Stoke were one of only six Second Division clubs to record improved gates, including the promoted teams from Division Three and those sides that were challenging for promotion.

No sooner were they out of the Cup than Stoke's form slumped, primarily due to Bould's injury, which cost the team stability at the back and possibly the play-offs. The crowds tapered off once it was clear that City would not make the play-off shake-up. Kelly's form had also dipped as his weight increased. To spice things up, Mills bought veteran midfielder Gerry Daly, who had been instrumental in dumping Stoke out of the Littlewoods Cup, for £15,000 from Shrewsbury. He injured his thigh on his debut and did not play again until the following season. Hindsight is a wonderful thing but, at 32, the gamble on Daly was possibly not worth the risk.

It was a season of three distinct thirds, with a successful spell in the middle sandwiched by periods of relegation form. These directly coincided with the periods when Tony Kelly had been in and out of form. His fitness was the key and he, and his twin Achilles heels of food and alcohol, had proved too frustrating for Mills to deal with. Before the final match Kelly was told he would be leaving and in July Mills took a small loss by selling him to West Brom for £60,000. The question was, could Mills produce the necessary consistency over a whole season to enable what was undoubtedly a talented squad to challenge for promotion?

Match of the Season 1986-87

Stoke 7 Leeds 2

Division 2, 21 December 1986

Eighth-placed Leeds were managed by former midfield firebrand Billy Bremner. Unsurprisingly, he had fashioned a team in his own image. Centre-backs Peter Swan and Jack Ashurst, midfielder David

Rennie and centre-forward Ian Baird were all hard, physical players, who liked to get amongst opponents.

Stoke were in a rich vein of form which had dragged them up from bottom to mid-table inside six weeks, and Mills was able to field an unchanged team for the fourth consecutive game. Despite the recent good form, Mills believed the goals-to-chances ratio could be improved and he asked the team to prove that they had the killer instinct. Leeds, the biggest club in the Second Division, were seen as the litmus test for Stoke's promotion credentials.

Despite it being the weekend before Christmas, the crowd was the biggest of the season so far. As the teams emerged, Stoke fans taunted Leeds' keeper Mervyn Day with the result of the previous season's game – 6-2 to Stoke. He had vowed in the press that no way he was going to concede six this time!

Stoke swarmed forward with accurate and clinical passing and scored three goals in the first twenty minutes, through Morgan, Saunders and a Lee Dixon bicycle-kick. Morgan bagged his second as Leeds were forced back in the face of wave upon wave of attacks. The perfect first half, as far as Stoke fans were concerned, was completed by a cheeky Kelly free-kick. After pointing to Day to tell him that he was going to aim for the right side of the goal, he proceeded to beat the keeper with a delicate chip exactly where he had indicated.

Leeds got among the goals themselves, without ever threatening to match Stoke's scoring spree. Baird and Sheridan, the latter from the penalty spot, found the net, but City also scored twice through Tony Ford and Morgan, who completed his hat-trick with a neat turn and shot from twelve yards. Mills was delighted that Stoke had finally shown what he had always believed they were capable of. The 7-2 win was City's best since Ipswich had been thrashed 9-1 in 1964. Everything seemed to be falling into place for a serious promotion challenge. The turnaround in the eighteen months in which Mills had been in charge was remarkable.

Leeds reached the FA Cup semi-final and the promotion play-off final, losing to Coventry and Charlton respectively. Unlike Stoke, they found the consistency over the season, and it nearly took them into the top flight.

LEAGUE DIVISION 2	**1987-88**
Barclays Division 2	11th
Littlewoods Cup	4th Round
FA Cup	3rd Round

There was huge anticipation that this would finally be Stoke's year. It was misplaced. City conceded the first goal of the new season in the first minute in a 0-2 defeat by Birmingham. Mills was worried about the defence. The unit were separated from the rest of the squad and given an intensive defensive clinic at Keele University. It improved matters little. Cliff Carr, a £45,000 signing from Fulham, had not had the best of starts and was the target of the Boothen End's boo-boys. He benefited from Mills' influence, but the chunky left-back never won over the cynics in the crowd who scorned his one-footedness and poor distribution. Bould's return, following his back problems, added solidity to the centre of the back four, but Mills was reduced to describing the general standard of defending as 'unprofessional'. 24-year-old keeper Scott Barrett was brought in from Wolves, initially on loan, before signing for £10,000. Mills gave him an extended run in the team due to a knee injury to Fox, the first of several opportunities, but Barrett lacked consistency and each time Fox returned to reclaim his place.

Despite the obvious shortcomings in defence, Mills appeared to have misread the situation. It was in attack where Stoke were really struggling. A paltry nine goals in the first sixteen league games told its own story. Carl Saunders, the previous season's goalscoring hero, had his confidence dented by a series of bad misses and he scored only three times all season. Instead of persevering with the talented player, Mills dropped him. His replacement, Graham Shaw, fared little better, finding the net only twice in the League before Christmas.

The problem stemmed from the lack of a credible replacement for Tony Kelly. Mills had signed Ian Allinson, a predominantly left-footed player who had been on the fringes of an average Arsenal side. Allinson had been freed as part of George Graham's summer clear-out, but he proved a flop, losing his place to Phil Heath after only seven starts. It emerged that Allinson did not particularly relish the idea of moving to the north and as a result he was sold to Luton, much nearer to his Hertfordshire home, for £15,000 in October. To cap it all, Nicky Morgan dislocated his collarbone in the 'dead' second round, second leg Littlewoods Cup-tie at Gillingham, as a result of which Mills, with barely enough fit professionals available, was forced to use a palpably unfit Gerry Daly as a makeshift striker for six weeks.

DID YOU KNOW?

The Stoke fanzine 'The Oatcake' is named after a Staffordshire delicacy made of oats and cooked on a griddle. It is best eaten hot with cheese or with a cooked breakfast.

Occasionally, to Mills' frustration, Stoke would get it right. City were drawn at home to struggling First Division Norwich in the third round of the Littlewoods Cup. Stoke thoroughly outplayed the Canaries to win 2-1, with even Daly managing to find the net. In the Simod Cup (a filler competition, designed to compensate clubs denied European competition in the wake of the Heysel ban on English clubs), Stoke were drawn at Alan Ball's Portsmouth, headed for promotion to Division One. City's 3-0 win was described by Mills as 'the best in my time here as manager'. Stoke picked up the Barclays Team of the Week Award for their efforts.

With the squad stretched to the limit, Mills was even forced to pick himself – becoming the third oldest player ever to appear for the club, aged 38 years, 289 days – when filling in for the injured Cliff Carr against Swindon in October. The game was a microcosm of Stoke's season, culminating in Talbot's sending off for retaliation. Frustration was setting in. Mills was on the defensive, both on the field and in the press. He threatened to put the whole team up for sale if results did not improve. If this was intended as shock tactics, it failed. Stoke won only two of the next eight games and went out of the Littlewoods Cup at Arsenal. A dire display at Crystal Palace forced Mills to belatedly dip into the transfer market.

Mills signed Oldham midfielder Tony Henry for £40,000 and QPR's Simon Stainrod for £90,000, believing that they would spark City's sluggish attack into life. He was wrong. Stainrod failed to score until the end of April, and Henry proved to be a one-paced player in an increasingly anonymous midfield. In a bid to inject flair, Mills signed Shrewsbury winger Gary Hackett, splashing out a further £110,000 to bring his total spending for the season to over £300,000. The experienced Hackett was not short on commitment, which had brought him his share of injuries. He made his Stoke debut with a pain-killing injection for a groin injury, broke down within twenty minutes, and did not reappear until the following season.

Mills had proved to be fallible in the transfer market. Perhaps his failure to transform Tony Kelly's career had affected his judgment. He no longer trusted 'flair' players, preferring to rely on consistent ones. The downside was that the team lacked spark and drive. It also lacked personalities, becoming bland, methodical and uninspiring. The club was slipping towards terminal torpor.

The only excitement in a tortuous second half of the season was provided by the visit of Liverpool in the FA Cup (see Match of the Season). Once again the club's potential was shown by the sell-out 31,979 crowd but average league gates were still below 10,000. It seemed to many that the board was happy for the club to idle along in the lower reaches of the Second Division, and there were isolated incidents of protests by groups of concerned supporters. The board rejected the criticism, citing the transfer expenditure as an example of their efforts to turn the club around.

The board's self-espoused philanthropy proved false. Their true colours were revealed in February when they redressed the season's transfer deficit by selling Lee Dixon to Arsenal for £375,000. The financial reality of running a football club in the late 1980s was that players such as Dixon would be groomed by Stoke for elite clubs to enjoy the pick of the crop. Steve Bould had been catching Graham's eye for the past two seasons and it seemed that it was only a matter of time – back-injury permitting – before he would be joining Dixon at Highbury. Brian Talbot also left, signing for West Brom for a nominal £10,000. He joined the Baggies as player-coach to Ron Atkinson, although by the end of the season he would find himself manager at the Hawthorns. With no money to replace the departed players Mills turned to the youth squad. In April, defender Lee Fowler became the third youngest player ever to appear for Stoke, aged sixteen years and 247 days. Paul Ware wasn't far behind, in May, aged just seventeen. Ian Gibbons, Andy Holmes and Kevin Lewis also helped to plug the gaps.

No sooner was the season over than Bould was sold to Arsenal. The fee, set by a tribunal at £390,000, was a travesty for a player who had proved to be the best centre-half outside the First Division for three seasons. That he, alongside Dixon, would form part of Arsenal's most successful defence, playing for eleven seasons for the club, proved that his true value was far higher. Stoke had failed to cash in on one of the few successes of an altogether forgettable season. Some sections of the crowd had begun to call for Mills' head. Such drastic action seemed premature to the majority, and Mills promised improvements for the following season.

Match of the Season 1987-88

Stoke 0 Liverpool 0

FA Cup, 3rd Round, 9 January 1988

Stoke reserved some of their best performances in this season of underachievement for the cup competitions. The third round draw paired them with an all-conquering Liverpool side featuring the creative talents of Peter Beardsley and John Barnes. Many observers felt this to be the best of the Liverpool sides that had dominated English, and European, football over the previous twenty years. The Heysel Stadium disaster of 1985 and the subsequent banning of English clubs from European competition meant that they were denied the opportunity to pit their talents against the best that the continent had to offer, and so prove the pundits right. Liverpool had started the season in blistering form, and were on a run which would see them equal Leeds' feat of 29 games unbeaten from the start of the season.

The cup-tie was a sell-out and there was enormous anticipation that Stoke might just be able to sneak a result. After all, with form as erratic as theirs, wouldn't it be typical for the team to go and win. There was just the smallest chink in Liverpool's armour: with Bruce Grobbelaar injured, second-choice keeper Mike Hooper was in goal.

On a dreadful surface Liverpool struggled to make their passing game tell. Steve Bould policed John Aldridge expertly, barely allowing the First Division's leading scorer a sight of the ball, while Talbot and Henry kept Ronnie Whelan and Ray Houghton quiet. Liverpool held a territorial advantage, while Stoke looked for opportunities to hit them on the break. It was absorbing stuff, but there seemed little chance of a goal at either end until, with under five minutes remaining, Graham Shaw, on as a substitute for Stainrod, was sent clear by Henry's pass from the halfway line. Crucially the young forward stuttered, and glanced across to the linesman to see if he was onside. This delayed his run onto the ball, which allowed Hooper to race out of his goal to block. A chance to win the game and cause the biggest cup upset in years was wasted.

Stoke had played above themselves and fared well in the replay, losing to Beardsley's goal at Anfield. To Mills' eternal frustration City could not reproduce the same form in the League. Liverpool walked away with the League title and also reached the FA Cup final. Strong favourites to beat Wimbledon, their limp performance on the day allowed the Dons to sneak a famous victory and deny Liverpool a second double in three years.

LEAGUE DIVISION 2	**1988-89**
Barclays Division 2	13th
Littlewoods Cup	2nd Round
FA Cup	4th Round

With Bould gone, Mills had to find a centre-half capable of replacing him. The team would undoubtedly miss one of its few quality players. The manager prevaricated, hoping to sign no-nonsense Kevin Moran of Manchester United, who asked for time to consider his options after being freed by Alex Ferguson. Moran eventually decided to chance his luck with Spanish club Sporting Gijon, where the lifestyle and pay packet better suited his idea of winding down his career than three years in Stoke.

The season started with Mills desperately seeking an alternative. He eventually plumped for Bury's Mark Higgins who cost £150,000. Higgins, at nearly 30, was an experienced defender, who had also proved to be injury prone, having been forced to quit Everton due to persistent groin problems. After his experience with the now fit Gary Hackett, for Mills to risk such a sum on yet another injury-plagued player was risky in the extreme. Higgins never approached the form expected of a capable centre-half and, predictably, his injury problems recurred. Was the manager losing his grip?

Two of Mills' other signings adapted better. Chris Kamara was a combative midfielder who was signed from Swindon for £27,500. The nominal fee reflected Swindon's wish to rid themselves of a player whose disciplinary record was little short of disgraceful. The last straw for the Robins came at Shrewsbury, when Kamara had been involved in a fracas which led to a court appearance and heavy fine. Mills wanted him to instil grit into a shambolic midfield. Flair would be provided by Peter Beagrie, recruited from Sheffield United for £215,000. The moustachioed winger was viewed by many as the best creative force outside the First Division and there was surprise that the Blades were prepared to let him go. He replaced Phil Heath on the left, whom Mills had sold to Oxford for £80,000. Beagrie had a trick that allowed him to flummox full-backs. It was a variation of the 'Cruyff turn', which saw him speed down the wing and shape to cross before dragging the ball inside the defender. He then either crossed with his other foot, or took the ball on into the penalty area. Beagrie also scored spectacular goals, evidenced by a superb match winner against Bournemouth, which allowed the fans a first sight of his trademark backflip somersault celebration.

With the new arrivals failing to gel, Stoke found themselves next to bottom with just three points after six games. To make matters worse, City lost at home on penalties to Fourth Division Leyton

Orient in the Littlewoods Cup (see Match of the Season). Things could not get much worse than that. Mills was floundering and the board inactive. The supporters could not stand by and see their beloved club fall apart so humiliatingly. Those dissenting voices of the previous season rallied themselves into groups campaigning to keep the club alive. Several 'fanzines' emerged. Most were one-offs, but one, The Oatcake, the brainchild of Martin Smith – a disaffected supporter who believed the club was headed for a fall – proved so popular that its circulation grew from a few hundred at games in the autumn of 1988 to over 3,000. It soon became the most widely read fanzine in the country. So influential was it that The Oatcake began to dictate the debate over the club's future. For anyone who wanted to know what was happening at Stoke City, it – rather than the club programme – became required reading.

Mills was also finding that discipline was a problem. Stainrod and Ford got themselves stupidly sent off, Stainrod against Chelsea and Ford, uncharacteristically, in a 0-6 mauling at West Brom. Indeed, Stoke ended the season with the second worst disciplinary record in the League. Mills needed to act, and he brought in John Butler, a full-back, from Wigan for £75,000, and Dave Bamber from Watford for £190,000, touting the new arrivals as 'the missing link'. Butler's arrival meant Mills allowed Ford to move to West Brom for £50,000, despite the player believing he was playing the best football of his career. That he earned England B honours as a 30-year-old, proved Mills' judgment was questionable.

Dave Bamber was a lumbering centre-forward with the look and demeanour of Frankenstein's monster. His goalscoring record had never been particularly good, showing that he had only managed double figures in two of his ten seasons in League football. He had only found the net three times in eighteen games for Watford, but Mills now saw him as a player who could capitalise on Beagrie's crosses, previously aimed at the height-impaired Shaw-Stainrod partnership. Bamber proved to be slow, awkward on the ground and prone to missing the easiest of opportunities. He scored just nine goals, despite being provided with a succession of crosses from the boots of Beagrie and Hackett. Part of the problem was that Beagrie liked to over-indulge, loving nothing better than beating his man twice or three times before crossing. This made it hard to judge the timing of runs into the box and often resulted in players – having committed themselves too early – being caught offside, or having the ball fly over their heads. Mills urged Beagrie to be more consistent in his delivery: Beagrie replied that he would have no hold over a full-back if the defender knew that he was always going to try to cross.

Kamara was also proving to be something of a poisoned chalice. The fans loved his commitment, but bridled when Kamara went looking for revenge after being fouled. Too often his heart ruled his head and a silly challenge would lead to a yellow or red card. He missed eight games through suspension, of which Stoke won only two.

Though City skirted around the edges of the play-off pack, there were early exits to Barnsley in the FA Cup and Southampton in the Simod Cup. A dreadful run of one win in the final fourteen League matches meant Stoke's season was effectively over by Easter. Five successive defeats thereafter meant a paltry crowd of 5,841 paid to watch the last game of the season. The life was slowly being strangled out of the club.

The date 15 April 1989 saw a football tragedy that transcended everything. The Hillsborough disaster, which saw the death of 96 fans at an FA Cup semi-final, stunned the nation. Its aftermath had profound implications throughout the football world. Lord Justice Taylor's report into the management of crowds at grounds ushered in a new era of all-seater stadia. For Stoke City, whose antiquated stadium – aside from the relatively new Stoke End Stand – had for years been the butt of complaints from visiting fans, the report spelt the end of an era. Within three years, all grounds in the top two divisions would have to become all-seating. The 'standing terrace culture' was to be eradicated. The intention was to provide a stable environment where football could become a family spectator sport. Football had historically been a sport watched predominantly by white, working-class males, but it was now time for it to grow up and open its arms to women, children and ethnic minorities. Stoke were amongst the worst offenders. Women and, particularly, black people had never felt welcome at the Victoria Ground. The debate commenced about transforming the Vic into an all-seated stadium, suitable for top division football, where the club hoped to be in twelve months' time.

Match of the Season 1988-89

Stoke 1 Leyton Orient 2

Littlewoods Cup, 2nd Round, 2nd leg, 11 October 1988

Leyton Orient were a club going nowhere in the autumn of 1988. A poor start in the League saw them 21st in the Fourth Division, some fifty places below City. Frank Clark, Orient's manager for six years, was under increasing pressure. His team had been expected to be among the promotion challengers after missing out on the play-offs

DID YOU KNOW?

Six players have played 100 consecutive League games for Stoke – Tony Allen, Arthur Turner, Tom Holford, Alan Dodd, Bob McGrory, and Nigel Gleghorn.

by a point the previous season. Stoke were expected to dispose of them easily, but there were signs in the first leg at Orient that all was not going to plan. The O's had applied early pressure and deservedly went ahead thanks to Ian Juryeff's 30-yard strike. Mills read the riot act at half-time and City came out stoked up for the second half. Kamara was in a particularly fiery mood. His goal, coupled with Morgan's header, gave Stoke a 2-1 win.

By the second leg, two weeks later, City's form had improved slightly. They had recovered from two goals down at Oldham to draw 2-2, securing the club's first ever point on an artificial pitch. Orient's away form was atrocious: they had picked up one point and scored one goal on their travels thus far. It looked an obvious home banker, but football is never quite that straightforward. The match turned into a freakish penalty competition, beginning in the first half when Kevin Hales scored from the spot for Orient. Beagrie then skied a penalty over the bar for Stoke, before Stainrod made amends from yet another spot-kick. City, thinking the tie was as good as won, went to sleep and failed to close down Alan Comfort, who lashed in a 30-yarder to send the game into extra-time.

Stoke's dreadful performance got no better in the extra half-hour and the tie went to penalties, an outcome which not even the most diehard O's fan could possibly have contemplated before kick-off. Peter Wells saved two of Stoke's kicks and Simon Stainrod missed a third to hand Orient a morale-boosting victory. While their players celebrated, Stoke's fans reacted angrily, calling for Mills' head. For Stoke to have lost to Orient was unforgivable.

The O's win sent them for the first time in twelve years into the third round, where they lost 0-2 to Ipswich. Buoyed by their win over Stoke, they promptly thrashed Colchester 8-0, a result which sparked a run that saw them scrape into the play-offs by finishing sixth. They duly beat Scarborough and Wrexham to win promotion. The next time they faced Stoke would be in the Third Division.

LEAGUE DIVISION 2	**1989-90**
Barclays Division 2	24th (Relegated)
Littlewoods Cup	2nd Round
FA Cup	3rd Round

Mick Mills' contract with Stoke expired in June and there was doubt about whether he should be offered a new one. He had worked hard to rebuild the club after the trauma of relegation, but the lack of progress over the past two years raised questions about Mills' ability to make an impact on his players. Opinions were divided, but finally his contract was renewed. Simon Stainrod left for Rouen in France for £70,000. More surprisingly, Steve Parkin was also allowed to leave, joining his former midfield mentor, Brian Talbot, at West Brom for £190,000. Having won six England Under-21 caps whilst at Stoke, many were surprised at Mills' decision to let the popular 'Billy' go.

The reason soon became apparent. Having decided that Mills was still their man, the directors produced over £1 million for him to spend to finance a push for promotion. Mills had proved that he sometimes had an eye for a bargain in the transfer market. What could he do now with money to burn? When Ian Cranson arrived from Sheffield Wednesday for £450,000, he became the club's record signing. Mills had played alongside Cranson at Ipswich during the central defender's formative years. Dominant in the air, Cranson sported a headband that added to his imposing appearance. Bolstering the forward line was Wayne 'Bertie' Biggins, a £240,000 signing from Manchester City. Midfielder Ian Scott also arrived from Maine Road for £175,000. Mills was so determined that Scott should join Stoke that he met the player at Manchester Airport on his return from holiday in order to secure his signature. Derek Statham arrived from West Brom for £60,000, with a further £40,000 payable after 40 appearances. Mills' million had all been spent. The board now demanded success to recoup it. The consequences of failure were unimaginable.

Sadly, Mills once again fell victim to signing injured players. Cranson's knee had required surgery whilst at Wednesday and in consequence he had lost pace on the turn. Furthermore, the injury now recurred, at Bournemouth. After just seventeen games for Stoke, Cranson was forced to go under the surgeon's knife and would not re-appear for nearly a year. Statham was also carrying a knee injury, which had been common knowledge, as it had caused the curtailment of both Rangers' and Liverpool's interest in him two seasons earlier. He made only 21 appearances for Stoke before the injury flared up again. The other summer signings did not produce the goods either. Biggins lacked pace and scored just ten goals – although that was enough to make him top scorer – while Scott made just fourteen starts. City failed to win any of their first eleven League games and went out of the Littlewoods Cup at the first hurdle to Millwall. They also lost in the FA Cup at the first time of asking, though their conquerors were the defending champions, Arsenal. In the Full Members' Cup (the Simod Cup had lost its sponsorship and had only two more years to run) Stoke lost on penalties to Leeds in the second round after a 2-2 draw. The early cup exits served to focus attention on Stoke's dreadful League form. Following a 1-1 draw with bottom club Hull, there were demands by supporters for Mills' head. Confidence in the manager, players and the board was zero.

In a bid to bolster players' self-belief, Alan Ball was appointed as first-team coach. He had previously managed Portsmouth for four years before becoming assistant manager at Colchester, and was persuaded by his former England colleague, Mills, that a move to Stoke could bring about a change in fortunes for both himself and the club. It was tantamount to Mills signing his own death warrant. The board now had a ready-made replacement. It was surely a matter of time before Mills was shown the door.

Mills' last desperate act was to sell Peter Beagrie to Everton for £750,000 in October. Beagrie's departure had been on the cards for some time, but it left the side bereft of its one star player. Mills was also victim of the success of near neighbours Port Vale. Stoke fans could not stomach the sight of 'the Fail' – as they are not so affectionately known – rising above them in the League. After decades of languishing in the lower reaches of the League, Vale, under the astute management of John Rudge, had risen through the ranks, joining Stoke in the Second Division this season. To be below Vale in the table confirmed how low Stoke had sunk. Mills' first two seasons had, on the whole, been positive, but since the failed 1986-87 promotion campaign, City had won only 37 out of 122 League games. With only one win in sixteen this term, the club was headed for the abyss. Still the board dithered, and it took a 0-6 thrashing at Swindon to force their hand. Mills was sacked.

There was considerable hope that caretaker manager Ball might be the right man to inject much-needed passion and commitment into Stoke's players. He had been the youngest of England's World Cup winning side of 1966 and as recently as 1982 had finished a highly successful playing career, which had seen him win 72 caps and a League championship medal with Everton. Since moving into management his record was patchy. His first match in charge of Stoke brought a much-needed win over Brighton (see Match of the

Season). Carl Beeston's first-minute goal seemed to signal a change of fortune and perhaps a change of luck under the now permanently appointed new manager.

Ball's first-team coach, Graham Paddon, struggled to make an impact on a constantly changing team as, in a bid to halt the slide, Ball wheeled and dealed to bring in new players. Many wondered if this was wise, as common sense told the average fan that one of the reasons for the team's wretched form was the influx of new players who had yet to gel.

Nonetheless Ball was determined to bring in players he trusted, which meant those that had brought him success at Portsmouth. The board backed his judgment and in came Lee Sandford, Vince Hilaire (on loan) and Chris Male, all recruited from Portsmouth for a combined fee of £140,000. Noel Blake, a hardman centre-half who had also been with Ball on the south coast, arrived from Leeds for £160,000. Ball also signed forwards Nyrere 'Tony' Kelly from non-league St Albans City for £20,000 and Tony Ellis from Preston, who cost £250,000 with Graham Shaw going in the other direction. Dave Kevan and Paul Barnes joined from Notts County for a combined fee of £105,000. To balance the books, Kamara was sold for £150,000 to Leeds, whom he would help to gain promotion. Bamber went to Hull for £130,000 and Hackett joined West Brom for £70,000. Morgan joined Bristol City for £30,000, while his erstwhile partner, Saunders, was sold to the other Bristol club, Rovers, for £70,000. The sale of those strikers left a bitter aftertaste, for both rediscovered their form in teams that came up as Stoke went down.

Such a huge turnover of players ensured there was hardly any understanding in the team. Twenty games with only one win shut the door on Stoke's chances of avoiding the drop. The fans vented their spleen on the manager. Indeed, Ball proved more unpopular than Mills had ever been. Ball retaliated, openly criticising fans for not getting behind the team. He had a point but he had not been at Stoke long enough to realise that they were more worried about the long-term structural decline of the club, rather than any specific games lost. The spirit had vanished from the side well before a 0-3 defeat at Newcastle confirmed relegation.

The board's £1 million gamble had failed catastrophically. Mills should have gone earlier and the choice of Ball as his belated successor was ill-conceived. Stoke would play in the Third Division for only the second time. Their previous experience at that level, in 1926-27, had seen them promoted as Third Division (North) champions at the first attempt. The current financial plight, as the club announced a trading deficit of £377,000 for the year, suggested that any hopes of a repetition were clutching at straws.

DID YOU KNOW?

In a poll of 500,000 football fans, two Stoke players were voted among the top 25 players of the 20th Century. Gordon Banks was 6th and Stanley Matthews 16th.

Match of the Season 1989-90

Stoke 3 Brighton 2

Division 2, 11 November 1989

After Mick Mills' sacking, Alan Ball, who had been first-team coach for six weeks, took charge of the team for the first time – against Brighton. It was understood that improved performances would lead to his position being made permanent. It was crucial that City find some form as they were in danger of being marooned at the foot of the table. Ball was confident, predicting good things.

Barry Lloyd's Brighton were mid-table, although they had lost consecutive home games 1-2 against Blackburn and Swindon. The Seagulls' side was made up of journeyman players who functioned well as a team. Alan Curbishley and Dean Wilkins, brother of England's Ray, formed the engine room in midfield, while Paul Wood and Kevin Bremner provided the firepower in attack.

Ball's managerial career at the Victoria Ground started in stirring fashion. In the first minute Carl Beeston skirted over two tackles to crash the ball past John Keeley. By half-time Stoke led 3-1, Bamber netting a header and Kamara haring in to convert Beeston's cross. Brighton's reply came from Robert Codner but City were dominating a game for the first time in the season.

On the hour Stoke were awarded a penalty for a trip on debutant Vince Hilaire. George Berry, reinstated by Ball in a bid to add some pride to the side, cracked the kick against the post. The confidence visibly drained out of Stoke. The more so, when Kevin Bremner pulled a second goal back. City were on the ropes for the final twenty minutes but somehow clung on. The celebrations at the final whistle were more akin to those surrounding a vital promotion win, indicating the depth of the despair which many fans felt about the club's plight.

The win proved a false dawn. Despite Ball's media bluster that he would lead Stoke clear of the relegation mire, City would win just four more games all season and be ignominiously relegated.

LEAGUE DIVISION 3	**1990-91**
Barclays Division 3	14th
Rumbelows Cup	2nd Round
FA Cup	2nd Round

If last season's horror show had tested Stoke fans' patience to the limit, then this year would see it snap. City considered themselves far too big a club to be languishing in the Third Division. Ball felt he had a squad of players able to climb out of the division at the first attempt. His only summer signing was another former Portsmouth player, Mick Kennedy, who signed from Luton for £180,000 and a reported £70,000 a year in wages, making him the highest paid player in Stoke's history. Kennedy was a well-known midfield hardman who had assisted Luton in their successful battle to avoid relegation from the top flight. Ball appointed him captain, expecting him to add much-needed steel in midfield. Guile would be provided by the return of veteran Mickey Thomas, whose loan period from Leeds was made permanent on a free transfer.

Despite relegation, the board thought it necessary to increase admission prices. To stand on the Boothen End now cost £4.50, an increase of 50p, while seats also went up by 50p to £7.50. The rise sparked protests, spearheaded by The Oatcake, rightly claiming that it was the financial mismanagement of the board that had saddled the club not only with Division Three, but also with another hefty overdraft. To pass on the cost of their malpractice was yet another indignity that could only drive supporters away. It was vital that the club make a quick return to Division Two.

Ball's promises of a quick return seemed to have some foundation when David Webb's table-topping Southend were thrashed 4-0 and, following a 2-0 win over Wigan in early November, Stoke sat comfortably in third place.

But there were signs that all was not well. A 1-3 home defeat by Shrewsbury saw Lee Sandford contrive to score an own-goal and he was targeted by more vocal sections of the fans as a player to abuse. He was seen as 'Ball's man', and his form suffered under a barrage of invective. Poor displays against Grimsby and Cambridge, who were charging up the divisions under the maniacal management of John Beck, rocked the boat further. The fans were not taking to life in Division Three and the defeat at Blundell Park was the cue for demonstrations which quickly turned into fisticuffs with Mariners fans. There would in consequence be bad blood between the clubs for years to come.

Ball's team were starting to be shown up for what they really were, a collection of ill-disciplined cloggers. From Noel Blake, who had been exposed as a limited, if wholehearted centre-half, even at this level, through Mick Kennedy to Tony Ellis, the team lacked skill and mobility. Paul Ware, who had risen through the ranks of the youth team to become a regular in midfield under Ball, had learnt a number of dirty tricks from Kennedy and contributed to getting two opponents sent off before finally being rumbled and dismissed himself. Kennedy was also red-carded and was fortunate that his appalling disciplinary record did not bring him a more hefty suspension than the four games handed down by the League. In attack the team was one-dimensional and the goals dried up for Biggins and Ellis. Seven goals in thirteen games from the pairing was hardly promotion form. Ball had persisted with his favourites and they had failed him. The crowd were not slow in vocalising their feelings, but that did not help steady the ship. Noel Blake was an immensely proud man and disliked the treatment he got from some sections of the crowd. Abuse relating to his colour was rightly derided by everyone at the club.

Stoke lost to West Ham in the Rumbelows Cup second round, having edged past Swansea 1-0 on aggregate in the first, and only squeezed past non-league Telford 1-0 after an FA Cup first-round replay. The second round brought more humiliation in the shape of defeat by Fourth Division Burnley. Mansfield, bottom of the Third, beat Stoke 3-0 in the preliminary round of the Leyland DAF Cup, as the Associate Members Cup was now known. That defeat meant Stoke failed to qualify from a group of three teams, having drawn against Fourth Division Northampton 1-1 at the Vic. A puny crowd of just over 4,000 demonstrated both the low regard with which the competition was held, and also how faith had been sapped in the manager's ability to lead Stoke to promotion.

The supporters no longer trusted Ball's judgment and a stream of vitriol was poured upon the manager, much of it unseemly. He was hounded by angry fans, not just after matches but also arriving at and leaving the ground after training. Ball stuck to his guns, insisting that 'his' players were the right ones for the job. He was plainly wrong. City won two out of thirteen games, which included defeats by Chester, Exeter and Southend. Ball's position was untenable and following an embarrassing 0-4 defeat by Wigan (see Match of the Season) he resigned, claiming that abuse he received from a young fan in the aftermath of the defeat at Springfield Park was the final straw. He left the club in its worst ever position in the Football League, having called upon 42 players in fifteen months. Ball went on to manage Exeter and act as coach and advisor to Graham Taylor during his abortive tenure as England manager. In truth, his record as a manager is indefensible. He has been relegated with each of the five clubs he has managed, aside from Southampton, whom he guided to a creditable tenth-place in the Premiership. Many football fans believe that certain managers suit certain clubs. Ball found his place on the south coast with Pompey and the Saints. It most certainly was not in Stoke.

Graham Paddon was handed the task of seeing Stoke through to the end of the season. The board wished to wait till then before appointing a new manager, when they would have a wider range of options. The truth was that they couldn't afford to lure a contracted manager from another club at this stage of the season and wanted to wait to see who would be out of contract come the summer. Just eighteen months earlier they had lavished £1 million in spending money on a manager whose contract they had nearly decided not to renew. Two ill-judged decisions relating to successive managers had contributed enormously to the plight in which Stoke City now found itself.

A cloud hung over the Victoria Ground and no matter where the dwindling numbers of Stoke fans looked, it was hard to see a silver lining. The club was all but broke, had no manager and a playing staff of run-of-the-mill professionals and barely blooded youngsters. The Oatcake made representations to the board that the situation must be dealt with or there was a danger that the club would actually go under. There had been talk for many years that smaller clubs would start to disappear once television money enhanced the power of the elite. Within a year Aldershot would fold. To suggest that Stoke City might go the same way was almost heretical, but did not go unwhispered in many quarters. It would take something or someone outstanding to lift the club out of its seemingly terminal malaise.

Match of the Season 1990-91

Wigan 4 Stoke 0

Division 3, 23 February 1991

Alan Ball's last match in charge of Stoke City was a desperate affair. Having won only eighteen out of the 67 games in which he was in charge, he was under intolerable pressure from supporters to quit. Stoke's first ever League visit to Springfield Park was an indication of just how far the club had sunk. The ground itself was falling to bits, with the away fans housed under a leaking roof on the top of a grassy bank behind one of the goals. The pouring rain did not help Stoke fans' humour. The mood was black. The supporters wanted heads to roll. Starting with Ball's.

DID YOU KNOW?

The ashes of Sir Stanley Matthews are buried under the centre spot at the Britannia Stadium.

Under Bryan Hamilton, Wigan were having the most successful period in their history. Hamilton had first joined the Latics in 1985 and taken them to within a point of promotion to the Second Division. He had moved on to manage Leicester, returning to Springfield Park after the club had finished in mid-table under Ray Mathias. Hamilton had failed to make the same impact second time around and Wigan lay one position below Stoke, although they had taken First Division Coventry to an FA Cup replay the previous month.

The game started badly for Stoke and got progressively worse. Cliff Carr and Wayne Biggins both missed golden opportunities to open the scoring. Wigan, on the other hand, were not so profligate. Phil Daley put them ahead with a glancing header. It all seemed depressingly familiar and triggered torrents of abuse aimed towards the Stoke dug-out from the outraged fans.

If the team had been poor in the first half, they appeared to lie down and die in the second. Daley chipped Fox from the edge of the area and Darren Patterson and Don Page both rose above City's supposed giant defence to nod home. Stoke's players were happy to wait for the final whistle and disappear from the pitch before the inevitable vitriol-charged invasion by hordes of angry fans baying for Ball's blood.

The news that Ball had finally thrown in the towel came as a relief. However, some of the inflammatory personal abuse hurled in his direction was unforgivable. Ball's departure, although essential, did not divert attention from the appalling state of Stoke City in general. Sixteen years to the day that Stoke had last topped the Football League, the club was at its lowest ebb since 1908, when it had gone out of existence, only to be re-formed by AJ Barker, a local businessman. There were no local millionaires in the 1990s stepping forward to place wads of cash at City's disposal. The next managerial appointment could prove vital to the club's continued existence.

2

SKIP TO MY LOU MACARI 1991-1997

LEAGUE DIVISION 3	**1991-92**
Barclays Division 3	4th
Rumbelows Cup	2nd Round
FA Cup	1st Round

Lou Macari was the man the board chose as the next manager. He had quit Birmingham following a dispute with the Kumar brothers, who had taken control of the club, over money for team-building. Indeed, Macari had not been far from controversy throughout his career. As a 24-year-old forward he was a hot property and chose Manchester United ahead of Liverpool when leaving Celtic, thus becoming one of the few men ever to say no to Bill Shankly. After 311 League games for United, and 24 Scotland caps, Macari became player-manager at Fourth Division Swindon. Sacked by chairman Harry Gregg, he was reinstated six days later after supporters – believing that he cared passionately about their club – petitioned the board. Swindon thrived under his stewardship, winning consecutive promotions. Having achieved success on a shoestring, Macari was then offered the chance to manage West Ham, an altogether different kind of club, who had been relegated to Division Two. After just seven months at Upton Park he became embroiled in a scandal from his Swindon days, relating to non-payment of tax. Macari resigned from West Ham, to prevent his new club being dragged into the affairs of his old. Swindon were eventually denied the place in the First Division they had secured by winning the 1990 play-offs. The threat of legal action still hung over Macari, his chairman, Brian Hillier, and several other Swindon directors.

Macari promised nothing other than to instil an appetite to win into the Stoke team. His frankness endeared him to the fans, who sensed that here was no blustering Ball or meek Mills. He was also a disciplinarian, expecting players to be fit enough to put in 100 per cent effort throughout the 90 minutes of a game. His teams often scored vital goals in the closing stages of matches.

DID YOU KNOW?

When Old Trafford was closed in 1973-74 as punishment for hooliganism, Manchester United played one of their 'home' games at the Victoria Ground.

Macari's choice of No 2 was former Shrewsbury manager Chic Bates, who had been his assistant at Swindon and Birmingham. Macari's appointment convinced a new sponsor, Ansells, to commit £100,000 to the club over a period of two years.

Renowned for a direct style of play, Macari described his system as 'a power game to get the ball into the final third of the pitch. Once there to play incisive, attacking football'. But after a sticky start, which had some fans wondering if Stoke needed 'route one' football at the Vic again, sorting out the ramshackle defence became Macari's priority. Ian Cranson, Stoke's record signing, had finally recovered from injury. Having to cut his cloth, Macari offered the out-of-contract player reduced terms, entitling him to a free transfer. Cranson thought long and hard, weighed up an offer from Hearts, but finally put pen to paper. He had a superb season, showing why Mills had risked nearly half a million pounds on him.

Macari's first buy was Vince Overson, a towering man-mountain of a centre-half, from Birmingham for a tribunal-set fee of £55,000. It proved money well spent. Overson was made captain, as he had been under Macari at St Andrews, and marshalled the new system of three big centre-backs, Overson, Cranson and either Blake or Sandford.

The first sign that Stoke meant business came when Tony Kelly nutmegged Liverpool goalkeeper Bruce Grobbelaar at Anfield to earn City a 2-2 draw in the Rumbelows Cup. The second leg was lost 2-3, but Stoke conceded only eight goals in nine games before Christmas, winning six to find themselves handily placed in fourth position.

Wayne Biggins was having his best season. He was a head-down-and-go type of striker, lacking any pretence at finesse, but possessing a good shot and a cool head from the penalty spot. He also appeared obsessed with his appearance, sporting a perma-tan that belied the weather in the Potteries. Macari's system played to his strengths, but he needed to secure Biggins the right partner. Having toyed with signing Bournemouth's Jimmy Quinn, but lacked the £300,000 fee, Macari unearthed another gem in the tiny form of Mark Stein, who was acquired on loan from Oxford. Stein provided finesse and lightning speed around the box, combining well with Biggins. Stein was signed permanently for £100,000 and repaid Macari's faith by scoring regularly. He had a rapier-like right-foot shot and Macari made him practice with his left so that he became comfortable when shooting with either foot. Stein outscored Biggins over the second half of the season.

The new strike partnership was unable to save Stoke from further FA Cup humiliation. City drew Telford in the first round for the second year running and the 1-2 defeat prompted Macari to seek a new goalkeeper. He chose Ronnie Sinclair from Bristol City, who was initially taken on loan and asked to prove his worth. At only 5ft 9in, Sinclair was short for a keeper and consequently often struggled in the air. The bulky defenders in front of him often took care of matters, but Sinclair was prone to the odd rush of blood, coming for crosses he was never going to reach. Despite this, he convinced Macari that he was worth the £25,000 that Bristol City were asking. Signing permanently boosted his confidence and he was an integral part of a defence which conceded only eight goals in twelve games after Boxing Day.

The system Macari had adopted often meant that the side played straight up and down the pitch in a rather narrow fashion. A 0-2 defeat at promotion rivals Brentford in January prompted Macari to look for more width to boost the team for a final promotion push. He signed right-sided Steve Foley for £50,000, a highly experienced midfielder whom he had previously signed for Swindon, left-winger Kevin Russell from Leicester on loan, and Ashley Grimes, a left-sided midfielder, who was looking to return to this country after a two-year spell with Osasuna in Spain. Grimes was also made coach of the club's youth set-up.

With the season coming to the boil, there were signs that things were getting tense. In February, the game at Birmingham, Macari's old club, boiled over after Paul Barnes scored an injury-time equaliser, precipitating a pitch invasion by angry Blues fans. Referee Roger Wiseman took the players off the pitch and the stadium was cleared, allowing the teams to play out the final 90 seconds of the game at walking pace behind closed doors. The riot made headlines around the world, but, although not initiated by Stoke fans, other incidents were. There was a sizeable element amongst Stoke fans who would just not let Ball's failure at the Vic drop and the former manager was disgracefully spat at and abused, describing his visit to the Vic as Exeter's manager as 'the most harrowing experience of my career'. Despite all this the crowds were streaming back through the turnstiles. No matter that it was the Third Division; City fans had something to sing about. Adapting the old school playground chant the Boothen End's mantra now became 'Lou, Lou, skip to my Lou, Skip to my Lou Macari!' Gates were up by 12.5 per cent and nearly 24,000 saw Stoke knock West Brom off the top on a chilly

February night. Macari was being hailed a hero and a genius in the transfer market.

Added to City's promotion push was a second Wembley final. Stoke beat Walsall and Birmingham in the Autoglass Trophy (as the Leyland DAF Cup was now called) preliminary round group, from which two teams qualified, allowing Stoke the privilege of beating Walsall again in the second round, before defeating Peterborough in a two leg semi-final to earn a place at Wembley.

With eight games to go, Stoke sat atop the League, favourites for promotion. At this crucial stage their form deserted them, failing to beat some of the also-rans of the division. Hull and Bury, both just above the relegation zone, won at the Vic in consecutive matches, before City lost at Torquay, who were next to bottom. The team exposed its old Achilles heel – ill-discipline. Seven players received suspensions during the season, five in April, and Stoke finished bottom of the Third Division fair-play league, devised to assess disciplinary records across the divisions. A pitiful home defeat by another relegation candidate, Chester, condemned Stoke to the end of season play-offs for the first time.

Stockport were City's play-off semi-final opponents. The first leg, at Edgeley Park, was an unmitigated disaster. Carl Beeston was sent off and Stoke lost 0-1 to a Peter Ward free-kick. The second leg did not start much better. Chris Beaumont headed Stockport into a first-minute lead which Stoke never looked likely to retrieve, despite exerting heavy pressure. Stein finally broke through to set up a frantic last ten minutes, but Stoke went out. The club was devastated at missing promotion, though they would be permitted an early opportunity for revenge, as Stockport were their opponents in the Autoglass Trophy final (see Match of the Season).

Macari's arrival had sparked renewed life into the club. The turnaround in the space of a season was testament to his, and the players', hard work. It was an all-round good year for Stoke as the reserves, under Peter Henderson, won the Pontin's League Second Division, often attracting crowds of over 2,000 during their run in. The club was also improving its public relations, having finally constructed a permanent stand for wheelchair-bound supporters in the Butler Street stand. The development was paid for by a £5,000 grant from the Football Trust, a body dedicated to the improvement of football grounds, which had been set up in the aftermath of the Taylor Report. There was also a new, larger club shop, housed in the bottom of the Stoke End stand. To encourage fans to buy its merchandise a club-sponsored credit card was launched, with City receiving a small percentage of each transaction. New life had been breathed into Stoke City.

Match of the Season 1991-92

Stoke 1 Stockport 0

Autoglass Trophy final, 16 May 1992

Danny Bergara's Stockport appeared to be hewn out of rock. Up front they boasted 6ft 7in Kevin Francis, the League's tallest player. He was partnered by 6ft 1in Andy Preece, who had joined County midway through the season from Wrexham and provided thirteen goals in their promotion push. Jim Gannon, a rugged centre-back, had found a new lease of life as a goalscoring midfielder, finishing as leading scorer with 21 goals. This was County's first appearance at Wembley.

The local public had barely responded. Stockport's average gate was below 5,000 and they had only 13,000 fans at Wembley. Stoke had sold more than 34,000 of their 45,000 allocation at the tunnel end. Basic ticket prices were £11 for the lower tier, rising to £21 for the Olympic Gallery. Stoke fans did not mind paying these prices. It meant a modicum of success had come their way and they were going to enjoy it.

Stoke's line-up featured veteran keeper Peter Fox in goal. He had appeared in most of the Autoglass games, as Ronnie Sinclair was cup-tied after appearing on loan for Walsall in the preliminary round, ironically against Stoke.

After two combative League games and the play-off semi-finals, there was sufficient tension between the two teams to ensure that this was no showpiece final. The expected succession of long balls aimed at Francis was capably dealt with by Overson and Cranson. In an untidy first half there were few chances and it was well into the second before Stein and Biggins made inroads into County's defence. On 65 minutes a long ball fell to Stein, who turned sharply on the edge of the area, let the ball drop and whacked a half-volley past Neil Edwards in the County goal. Stoke hung on, as, once Andy Preece was substituted, County's threat subsided.

There was jubilation at the final whistle. It mattered little that it was only the Autoglass Trophy, a competition contemptuously dismissed as the Nissan Cherry Brake Line Fluid Wotsit Cup until Stoke actually won it! The win signalled a change of fortunes of the kind that had hardly been imaginable just twelve months earlier.

Stockport were left to concentrate on winning the promotion play-off final, but lost in the last minute to Peterborough. Stoke toured the Potteries in an open topped bus in glorious sunshine, proudly displaying the first trophy the club had won in twenty years. Promotion was next on the bill.

LEAGUE DIVISION 2	**1992-93**
Barclays Division 2	1st (Champions)
Coca-Cola Cup	2nd Round
FA Cup	1st Round

Even without winning promotion Stoke were back in the Second Division. After the formation of the breakaway Premier League, the Football League had been re-constituted and what had been the Third Division was now renamed the Second. The formation of the FA Premiership seemed just the first step on the way to an inevitable European Super league, which the likes of Manchester United, Barcelona, AC Milan and Bayern Munich craved. That the breakaway coincided with the arrival on the British media scene of Rupert Murdoch's Sky Television Corporation was no accident. Sky's deal, which brought live Premier League football to subscribers on a weekly basis, brought sponsorship money swilling into the game at the top level, changing the face of football forever. For clubs like Stoke, the revolution meant the probability of further financial hardship as the media homed in on the Premier League at the expense of the lower divisions. The change in football's financial climate had already claimed its first victim. Aldershot of the Fourth Division had gone to the wall at the end of the previous season and Barnet had only survived by the skin of their teeth. Maidstone would perish within weeks. It was perverse that, while clubs struggled to stay alive, record transfer fees were being set almost monthly. Duncan Ferguson was the latest to bear the tag of Britain's most expensive player, having signed for Rangers for £4 million. Stoke were still £1.9 million in debt and, to the supporters, the crazy figures commanded by these players was pie in the sky. The only possible means of paying off the overdraft was to win promotion.

In June Lou Macari had been acquitted of all complicity in the tax scandal which had rocked his former club, Swindon. His former chairman was not so fortunate. In October, Macari also stood trial on charges of illegal operation of a bookmakers, in which he held a stake. He was acquitted by magistrates in Devizes, whereupon City fans breathed a huge sigh of relief.

Keeping the players that had taken Stoke so close to promotion was proving tricky. Seven of the squad rejected new contracts and, with trouble brewing, Macari issued an ultimatum: either sign or leave. Most signed, although Cranson procrastinated, refusing until November to sign anything other than a weekly contract. Kevin 'Rooster' Russell signed permanently from Leicester for a tribunal-fixed fee of £95,000, and Macari managed to finally rid himself of Tony Ellis, with whom he had fallen out. Ellis objected to a £100,000 price tag the manager had placed on him, whereupon Macari swapped him for former Stoke forward Graham Shaw, now with Preston, plus £50,000. This reversed the transfer of some two years earlier.

The sense of expectation was intense. Stoke were favourites to win the championship, at 6-1 with Corals. This was to be City's year, but initially the players found the pressures difficult to cope with and won only one of the first seven games, also going out of the Coca-Cola Cup to First Division Cambridge, despite drawing 2-2 at the Abbey Stadium. In the League, a 1-1 draw with Brighton saw City ahead after only 45 seconds, but they failed to win. The team appeared to be losing the winning momentum instilled the previous season. The next visitors were West Brom who, conversely, had shot out of the starting stalls and were top of the table (see Match of the Season). The manner of Stoke's victory spoke volumes about the determination of the team to put matters right. These were now Macari's players, singing from his hymnbook.

Macari reasoned that City's sluggish start was partly down to the unsettling influence of 'Bertie' Biggins, who hankered after a bigger club. Macari also believed that Biggins, who had amassed six cautions in the previous campaign for dissent-related incidents, was a disruptive influence on the pitch. Before the start of the season the club introduced a new disciplinary code aimed at reducing the number of suspensions which had disrupted the team at a crucial stage. Biggins' 'dream' move to Barnsley was completed in October, costing the Tykes a tribunal-fixed fee of £200,000, £100,000 short of Stoke's valuation. Despite scoring on his debut, within a month Biggins was on the phone to Macari asking to return to Stoke. There is no record of the manager's response!

With cash in hand Macari was on the lookout for quality players, not only for this season's promotion bid, but also to establish a firm footing in the First Division the following year. He returned to his former club Birmingham to sign Nigel Gleghorn, a stylish midfielder whose vision and distribution gave the team an added dimension. Gleghorn's fee was a paltry £100,000, with Macari taking advantage of the fact that he knew Birmingham were in serious financial difficulties.

Mark Stein, who by now was known to the fans as 'the golden one', found the net 33 times, earning himself a place in the hearts of Potters fans and acquisitive glances from Newcastle boss Kevin Keegan. Macari was concerned that Stein's pocket-sized partnership with Shaw lacked the necessary muscle to compete over a whole season in a physical league. After enquiring about Blackburn's Steve Livingstone and Notts County's Tony Agana, in October Macari bought 28-year-old Dave Regis from Plymouth for £130,000. At 6ft 3in, Regis – brother of former West Brom, Coventry and England centre-forward Cyrille – was a combative player who was capable of providing more chances for Stein with his knockdowns than could be created with Shaw in the side.

Armed with their new signings, Stoke were head and shoulders above the rest of the Second Division. 25 games separated the 0-0 draw with Bolton on 25 September and the 0-1 defeat at Leyton Orient on 27 February – a club record. Stoke hit the top with a win over Blackpool during a run of seven successive victories. Macari was named manager of the month for October and December amid press rumours that Liverpool and Celtic were keeping tabs on him – incumbents Graeme Souness and Liam Brady were under intense pressure. Macari scotched the gossip by claiming that he would never want to work in 'goldfish bowl environments where every move is examined'.

The season was given added spice by the duels with local rivals Port Vale, relegated from Division One, but now neck and neck with Stoke at the top of Division Two. The season saw five sell-out clashes, with Stoke winning both League meetings. The 2-0 victory at Vale Park in late March was City's most complete performance of the season and all but guaranteed promotion. Vale exacted revenge in the Cups. The clubs were paired in the FA Cup for the first time since 1951, and such was the interest generated that it was switched to a Monday night for Television coverage. With the intense focus on the match it was no surprise that it turned out to be a scrappy affair, necessitating a replay. In diabolical conditions Vale clinched a place in the second round after Dave Regis's shot stuck in the mud on the line, with Stoke trailing 1-2. Vale also won the Autoglass Trophy Southern Area semi-final, when Stein's missed penalty saw Stoke relinquish their hold on the Trophy.

Continuing the previous season's PR initiative under new director Paul Wright, Stoke restricted half of the Boothen Paddock to a Family Membership area, with entrance for adults only if accompanied by at least one child. The 'Lifeline' initiative, launched on City's relegation from the First Division in 1985, was relaunched as the Executive Society, with the promise that half of the weekly £2 members' contribution would go towards purchasing players. The rest was put into a pot, from which cash prizes were handed out via a lucky dip. With the club on a crest of a wave, prizes often totalled over £1,000. One innovation, that proved not so popular, was a ghastly new away kit, featuring two bright shades of purple.

Back on the pitch, battle was rejoined with Stockport, who were also challenging for promotion. Stein and County's Jim Gannon, who had been involved in Carl Beeston's dismissal in the previous season's play-off semi-final, grappled on the pitch after the latter's allegedly racial abuse. The case ended in court, with Stein bound over to keep the peace. For his part, Gannon became a favourite hate victim of the Boothen End, and consequently reserved his best form for visits to the Vic. Stoke had the last laugh, winning at home and drawing away to put County out of the automatic promotion picture.

Slight promotion jitters were not helped by a cruciate ligament injury sustained by goalkeeper Ronnie Sinclair at Bournemouth. Macari brought in 35-year-old Liverpool keeper Bruce Grobbelaar on loan, but when he was recalled to Anfield turned to veteran Peter Fox. His brilliant double save from Plymouth's Steve Castle allowed Stoke to register the vital win that saw them claim promotion and the championship in one fell swoop.

Macari had triumphed in bringing the fans what they most craved – promotion. He was rightly made manager of the season for the Second Division. The difference he had made to the club in the two years of his reign was quite astonishing. It was built on hard work, commitment and self-belief. Simple qualities, but difficult ones to instil in a motley assortment of players who had seemed so disparate under Ball. There was a growing tendency for promoted clubs to return immediately whence they came. This season had seen Brentford make a rapid return to Division Two, having gone up as champions, while fellow promoted club Birmingham only avoided the drop with a last-day win. Getting to the First Division was one thing; staying there quite another. Stoke fans did not care. They had Lou Macari.

Match of the Season 1992-93

Stoke 4 West Brom 3

Division 2, 19 September 1992

Ossie Ardiles' West Brom held an early lead at the top of the Second Division, three points clear of second placed Leyton Orient and twelve ahead of Stoke. In a division dominated by physical, route-one teams, Albion stood out by playing a neat, incisive, short-passing game.

Rivalry between the two clubs was becoming something of a millstone for Albion. Since beating City 6-0 in December 1988, they had not repeated the feat in seven attempts. Stoke, for their part, were finding the burden of expectation weighing heavily on them. One win in seven games meant that the pressure was on.

DID YOU KNOW?

When Stoke played in a 1976 pre-season tournament in Madrid against Atletico and Cruzeiro (Brazil), it was sandwiched between friendlies against Rhyl and Buxton.

Albion dominated the game from the off, with their four-man midfield running rings round City's three. The pitch was greasy from early morning rain and suited the Baggies' neat-passing style. Stoke's goalkeeper, Tony Parks, on loan from West Ham, had been brought in as last-minute cover for Sinclair, who had strained his hamstring in training. Parks was still getting acclimatised when he lost his footing in the process of taking a goal-kick. The ball rolled to Bob Taylor who waltzed around Parks to deservedly give Albion the lead.

That goal acted as an alarm-call to Stoke. Driven forward by Steve Foley, the midfield began to take a hold on the game. Just on half-time Foley broke clear on the left edge of the box to equalise. The balance was swinging towards Stoke, and immediately after the restart City went 2-1 up through Russell. Stoke's three centre-backs were not used to facing strikers as skilled with the ball at their feet as Taylor and Garner. In combination with Hamilton they fashioned two openings in quick succession and scored from both. The game then swung back towards Stoke. Russell carved his way past three players before rounding Stuart Naylor to level the score at 3-3.

City's midfield proved decisive. They ground Albion down and on 83 minutes the Baggies cracked. A right-wing corner was swung across and Ian Cranson crashed a header in off the underside of the bar. He later said that the emotion of that goal in that game was one of the highlights of his career.

Football is not just about talent, it is about application and heart. Stoke proved that they had those qualities in abundance and the result launched a run which took the team to the Second Division title. They were fortunate that they did not face many teams of Albion's class that season. West Brom also made it into the First Division, but by a more circuitous route. Finishing fourth meant they had to endure the agonies of the play-offs where they beat Port Vale 3-0 in the final.

LEAGUE DIVISION 1	**1993-94**
Endsleigh Division 1	10th
Coca-Cola Cup	2nd Round
FA Cup	4th Round

Promotion meant a financial bonanza. Record season-ticket sales of over 8,000 resulted in almost £1 million being banked before a ball was kicked. Supporters carped about the 10 per cent hike in admission prices and the cost of the new replica kit (£48) but, reacting to the first positive season at the club for a decade, Stoke fans happily spent record amounts in the club shop too.

Macari wanted to recruit experienced, quality players and was linked with Leeds' Gordon Strachan, Blackburn's Gordon Cowans and Graeme Hogg of Hearts. Despite the improved financial situation, resources were not available to fund the wages of players who expected Premiership levels of pay. Instead, Macari raided Premier League reserve sides. Striker Martin Carruthers, 21, signed from Aston Villa: he had been top scorer as Villa's reserves won the Pontins League. Icelandic midfielder Thorvaldur 'Toddy' Orlygsson arrived from Nottingham Forest on a free transfer, and Macari swooped for the Birmingham duo, right-back Ian Clarkson, £50,000, and striker Simon Sturridge, £75,000. Goalkeeper Ronnie Sinclair would be out with his cruciate ligament injury until after Christmas, so Macari signed Mark Prudhoe, £120,000 from Darlington and Carl Muggleton, on loan from Leicester.

Stoke started steadily and, following a 3-2 win at Frank Clark's Nottingham Forest, lay seventh, but a 1-4 defeat at early leaders Crystal Palace indicated that City still had some way to go if they wanted to make their mark. Promotion also meant an opportunity to compete in the Anglo-Italian Cup after a gap of 21 years. The competition, now exclusively for teams in the second division of each country, involved initial round-robins of three teams, with the winner of each group progressing. Despite being viewed very much as an early season kick-about, Stoke progressed to the second stage. At the Vic they beat Cosenza 2-1 and drew 0-0 with Fiorentina. But they lost both games in Italy and failed to make it to the semi-final stage.

There was more excitement generated by City's pairing with Manchester United in the second round of the Coca-Cola Cup (see Match of the Season). Stoke matched United for spirit and endeavour, indicating just how far the club had come under Macari in just two years, and held their heads high after narrow defeat.

Macari was losing patience with the lack of money available to him for transfers. This had recently denied him the opportunity of signing Newcastle's Gavin Peacock and Derby's Paul Williams. The fees wanted were around £750,000, and Macari declared publicly that his spending limit had been capped by the board at £500,000. Stoke could not compete in this market. Despite the recent success, the club was still saddled with an overdraft in excess of £2 million. The board were keen to improve the club's footing with the bank and the sale of Kevin Russell, for £140,000, realising a £45,000 profit, hinted at the club's priorities.

Rumours that began circulating back in March were confirmed when Celtic – whose supremo David Smith wanted Lou Macari to spearhead the Bhoys' attempt to knock Rangers from their perch – were given permission to speak to Stoke's manager, provided 'suitable compensation' could be agreed should he decide to leave. Coincidentally, with a profit of over £1.4 million beckoning, the board accepted a £1.5 million bid for hot property Mark Stein from Glenn Hoddle's Chelsea. Within two days Macari had accepted Celtic's offer, explaining his decision to Stoke's distraught fans: 'If you are in any walk of life and *the* job comes up, wouldn't you want it?' But it was the sale of Stein that convinced Macari that his long-term future lay away from the Victoria Ground.

Stoke's backroom staff all resigned to join Macari at Parkhead, while Director Robert Lee also resigned, citing differences of opinion over the appointment of the new manager. Lee required the repayment of a loan that he had made to the club, the effect of which was to compromise financial stability once again. It emerged that each of the remaining four directors had loaned sizeable amounts and that it was only this which had kept the club afloat, despite the record season ticket sales.

Macari's replacement was Joe Jordan, formerly Liam Brady's assistant at Celtic. As an indication of the quicksands which were to beset Macari's reign, 42-year-old Jordan had quit Parkhead after just one day as caretaker manager. He protested that the club had been pursuing other managers while he was taking a training session in the belief that he was a candidate for the job. Jordan brought in former Scotland midfielder Asa Hartford as his assistant and former Leicester and Chelsea full-back Denis Rofe as reserve-team coach. Brian Caswell, a former Walsall and Leeds full-back, was appointed as Youth Team Coach.

Jordan's dour exterior did not endear him to Stoke's fans, although it was a two-way thing. Quite simply Joe Jordan was not Lou Macari – their hero. Abortive terms with Hearts (as manager) and Celtic (as Brady's assistant), meant that Jordan was inclined to take a safety-first approach, and without Stein's firepower Stoke scored only nine goals in fifteen games. Jordan's team produced stale, boring football and the crowd were quick to protest. Jordan's loanee keeper, Gordon Marshall, had a nightmare debut in Stoke's 2-6 hammering by Luton, raising questions about the manager's judgement, but the question which vexed most Stoke fans was why did Jordan not replace Stein?

The reason lay in the board paying off much of the overdraft. By March, Stoke were only £500,000 in debt, having reduced the deficit by £2 million in twelve months. The decision was intended to reduce interest repayments totalling £187,000 in the previous year. The price for this financial prudence was lack of investment in the team, a risky business in the first season after promotion. Jordan did contrive to win an FA Cup-tie for Stoke, the first for four years, albeit against Conference side Bath. Premiership Oldham proved too strong in the next round, winning 1-0 in a Vic replay.

On 29 January the death was announced of former manager Tony Waddington after a short illness. His funeral cortege began its journey from the Victoria Ground and thousands lined the streets to say farewell, braving atrocious weather. His departure did not help the mood of defeatism enveloping the club.

After weeks of begging for time to find new players, a flurry of activity marked deadline day. For £170,000 Jordan signed 'Bertie' Biggins, who returned from unhappy sojourns at Oakwell and Celtic Park, where he had joined Macari. Defender Mickey Adams signed on a free transfer from Southampton. Terms were agreed with Swindon for £250,000 striker Andy Mutch, but his suspect knee killed the deal. The new arrivals made little impact and, after a 2-4 defeat at Derby, the first calls for the manager's head were heard. There was terrace talk that ex-Stoke player Steve Bould was being lined up as player-manager, having been spotted attending several Stoke home games.

Jordan's position was also under threat by director Bob Kenyon's bid to buy out majority shareholders Peter Coates and Keith Humphreys, with the aim of reinstating Macari as manager. Coates and Humphreys refused what would have been a sizeable injection of capital into the club, not wanting to relinquish control.

Over the course of the season rumours had circulated about the viability of redeveloping the ground. This was now becoming a burning issue, as Stoke had only three years to turn the Victoria ground into an all-seated arena compliant with the Taylor Report. Other options included moving to a site a mile from the ground, known as Sideway or Trentham Lakes. This was earmarked for possible development should rebuilding of the Vic prove too expensive. The idea of leaving the Victoria Ground, home to Stoke City since 1878, provoked much heated debate.

DID YOU KNOW?

In September 1975, Lincoln City became the lowest placed opponents ever to knock Stoke out of the League Cup. Lincoln were 9th in Division 4 at the time.

Match of the Season 1993-94

Stoke 2 Manchester United 1

Coca-Cola Cup, 2nd Round, 1st leg, 22 September 1993

Under Alex Ferguson, United were patently the best team in the country, having won the inaugural Premier League with ten points to spare. Their customary line-up featured Frenchman Eric Cantona, whose arrival from Leeds had inspired the Red Devils to their first title since 1967. Cantona, though, was absent as United fielded an 'understrength' side which still included ten full internationals! Heavily involved in Europe, United had made noises about fielding their second team in the Coca-Cola Cup and, when threatened with sanctions by the League, declared several of their first team 'unfit' instead.

United started the better and it took the force of Vince Overson's tackling to bring Stoke into the game. Following his lead was Toddy Orlygsson, who proved a thorn in United's left flank and gave Republic of Ireland international full-back Denis Irwin a torrid night. Orlygsson set up Stein to hammer a shot high past Peter Schmeichel. Once ahead City dominated. Stoke's midfield had such a grip on the game that former England captain Bryan Robson was substituted for winger Lee Sharpe, whose arrival sparked a United fightback. Dion Dublin, starting in place of Cantona, rose to nod home his cross.

Stoke attacked again and Stein wriggled free of three defenders to shoot past Schmeichel. Understandably the ground went berserk, and Stein was booked for celebrating with fans who had encroached onto the pitch. Stoke hung on to record a famous victory. As Macari put it: 'Two years ago we were struggling to beat teams like Wigan. Now we have beaten Manchester United and that's a credit to the players.'

United won the second leg 2-0, scoring the winner three minutes from time. They reached the final of the Coca-Cola Cup, where they lost 1-3 to Aston Villa. United retained the Premier League title and completed the first double in the club's history thanks to a 4-0 hammering of Chelsea, including Mark Stein, in the FA Cup final.

LEAGUE DIVISION 1	**1994-95**
Endsleigh Division 1	11th
Coca-Cola Cup	3rd Round
FA Cup	3rd Round

After the boardroom shenanigans of the spring, City fans were frustrated by a summer of silence. The apparent inability of Chairman Coates to communicate with fans had the effect of casting him in the role of villain. There were demonstrations outside the ground by angry fans demanding a boycott of Stoke's opening games. The objective was to oust Coates and Humphreys and allow Bob Kenyon to take over and inject fresh capital. Coates' blunt response was to call the protests 'absolute nonsense'. Kenyon wanted his fellow directors to match his proposed injection of £500,000 into the club, but Coates refused to comply and Kenyon, along with Paul Wright, was voted off the Board at an EGM in early September. In response, the pair apparently demanded repayment of the interest free loans they had made to the club, as a consequence of which the overdraft was back over £1 million again. Stoke's terrible public image impeded season-ticket sales. It also took a turn for the worse when the club overturned its stated policy of only changing shirts every two years and introduced new Home and Away kits simultaneously. Commercial Manager Mick Cullerton cryptically countered criticism by saying: 'We get more complaints if we don't change the kit than if we do.'

As for the team, signing a proven striker was paramount, but Jordan received a pointed rebuff from Nottingham Forest striker Lee Glover, who chose to sign for Port Vale rather than Stoke, believing Vale had the better prospects of success! Jordan eventually signed £400,000 Paul Peschisolido, who arrived from Birmingham. Pesch, as he became known, was a 5ft 8in forward in the mould of Mark Stein, although not yet as prolific. One of the major reasons for his departure from St Andrews was his relationship with managing director Karren Brady; indeed the couple would wed at the end of the season. The two-way deal included £200,000-rated Dave Regis joining Birmingham and was the largest transfer package that Stoke had ever put together to bring a player to the club. It also allowed the board to crow about the money they were investing in players. Midfielders Ray Wallace from Leeds, Keith Downing from Birmingham, and Luton central defender John Dreyer joined the club on free transfers, a truer indication of the lack of cash Jordan had to contend with.

Jordan did not help his own position by informing club captain Vince Overson that he was surplus to requirements, stripping him of the captaincy and handing the job to Nigel Gleghorn. The rift became public. Now it seemed Jordan had lost the players' respect. Sandford, Ware and Butler all rejected new terms. Ware eventually joined Stockport for £40,000, while Butler and Sandford grumpily re-signed after receiving slightly improved offers. Confidence was hardly improved when the manager declared his aim to be to collect enough points to avoid the drop.

Stoke won just one of their first five League games. With Jordan coming under severe pressure, his resignation was announced on 8 September, after only ten months in the job. His undemonstrative style, defensive tactics, and insistence on using striker Peschisolido wide on the right had cost him dear. The following day Jordan sensationally revealed that he had not quit but had been told to go. 'I was the victim of politics,' he said, hinting that he had been jettisoned to save the hides of certain unnamed directors. Asa Hartford took control for seven games – which saw a dramatic improvement in form – giving time for the board to decide who the next man in the hot seat would be.

It turned out to be a familiar face. Lou Macari had been sacked by new Celtic Chairman Fergus McCann and was only too pleased to accept Stoke's offer to return, filing a £400,000 suit for wrongful dismissal against Celtic in the process. Rumours had been rife that his return would be confirmed over the summer, but it was typical of the board's intransigence that it took consecutive 0-4 defeats and two red cards to prompt Jordan's inevitable departure.

Returning alongside Macari was first-team coach Chic Bates. The players responded well to the restoration of the old order, winning Macari's first match in charge, against West Brom, 4-1 (see Match of the Season). But City struggled to make any impression thereafter. Qualification for the semi-finals of the Anglo-Italian cup – courtesy of beating Udinese 3-1 away and Piacenza 4-0 at the Vic – appeared to affect League form. Stoke twice lost on Saturdays following Anglo-Italian matches. The same quandary faced British clubs in the major European competitions and led to the belief that a rotational squad system was the answer to twice-a-week football. That option was not open to a club in Stoke's position. City lost in the semi-final of the Anglo-Italian Cup 2-3 on penalties after two tedious 0-0 draws with Notts County.

A 1-2 defeat at Liverpool in the Coca-Cola Cup hinted that there was still some spirit left, but defeat by Bristol City in the FA Cup – now managed by a certain Joe Jordan – was hard to take. Over the winter Macari introduced several new faces as he sought to breathe life back into the team. Larus Sigurdsson, signed from Icelandic side Thor Akuyeri, was the cousin of Toddy Orlygsson. He impressed at

DID YOU KNOW?

In 1993 the club had to upgrade the Victoria Ground's floodlights to meet new League standards. Each new bulb cost £850!

centre-half in place of Vince Overson, whose lack of mobility was being exposed at First Division level. New strikers Keith Scott, from Swindon for £300,000, and John Gayle, from Burnley for £70,000, both looked cumbersome players. Gayle proved better in the air for a big man than Scott, who soon became a target for the boo-boys. The jury was out on Macari's other signings – £300,000 midfielder Kevin Keen from Wolves, and centre-half Justin Whittle (bought out of the Army when Macari was at Celtic) on a free transfer. Perhaps Macari was losing his touch in the transfer market. Physiotherapist Richard Gray had also left the club after Jordan's departure and the vacant position had not been filled. When, inevitably, Stoke lost several players through injury, the lack of professional treatment available to them spoke volumes about the deterioration at the club since Macari's departure.

By Easter the situation was becoming a worry. A 2-4 defeat at Southend left Stoke just one place above the relegation zone. There was genuine fear that this might be one crisis too far for Macari. A last bid to inject much-needed goals was dashed when Macari's £450,000 bid for Wolves striker David Kelly was rejected and the board refused to sanction the £650,000 asking price. A few gutsy displays meant relegation was narrowly averted, but the fans' mood was not helped by the AGM announcement that Stoke had made a profit of over £1.5 million in the past year. As ever, the economics of football proved maddening, and, rather than spending the money on improving the team, it had to be reserved to fund Stoke's compliance with the Taylor Report.

The debate raged over whether Stoke should remain at the Victoria Ground or move to a new, purpose-built stadium. The sum needed to revamp the Vic was put at £5 million. Plans were drawn up, but the fact that the canal ran under the south-eastern corner of the ground made the club think again. Port Vale Chairman Bill Bell threw in his tuppence ha'penny, suggesting that a new stadium could be shared between both clubs. Unsurprisingly, a telephone poll in the *Sentinel* revealed that a massive 88 per cent of supporters of *both* clubs were against the move. Stoke's board were not in favour either. They were leaning towards the new stadium option, which although more costly than developing the Vic, would attract more outside investment, particularly from the Football Trust and the City council, whose leader, Ted Smith, was an advocate of the project. Supporters were angry that they had been omitted from the decision-making process. One letter to the *Sentinel* read: 'The most important decision the club have possibly ever faced is in the hands of a board who seem contemptuous of the views of supporters as both stakeholders and as customers – this is no way to run a business.' With the decision all but reached, the board moved to put in place a man to oversee the operation. Jez Moxey, 31, was recruited from Scottish club Partick Thistle to become the club's first Chief Executive. His brief included responsibility for the new stadium and negotiating players' contracts. With the divide between planning for the new ground and investing in players, his job was going to require the finest of balancing acts.

Match of the Season 1994-95

Stoke 4 West Brom 1

Division 1, 2 October 1994

The icing on the cake of Lou Macari's triumphant return to the Victoria Ground was this rout of rivals West Brom. The popular Scot had been confirmed as Stoke manager three days previously, after sorting out legal wrangles over his sacking from Celtic. Albion were struggling, one place off the bottom of the table as they adjusted to life under new boss Alan Buckley, their ninth manager in ten years.

It rained all day until just before kick-off, when as Lou Macari appeared from the tunnel, the skies, as if in reverence, cleared to reveal glorious sunshine. Stoke were clearly wound up from the start, putting Albion under heavy pressure which finally took its toll when Gary Strodder slipped and allowed Martin Carruthers to score. Carl Muggleton returned the compliment six minutes later, when he dropped a cross at the feet of Bob Taylor, who gratefully equalised, but Stoke tore into Albion once again. Five minutes later Ray Wallace played a neat one-two and blasted home his first goal for the club.

Orlygsson kept City on the offensive. Midway through the second period Peschisolido applied the finishing touch in a goal-mouth scramble and Carruthers, having his best game for the club so far, scored the fourth as Stoke cruised to victory. Despite the win, Macari knew there was much work to do in regenerating an ageing squad which had suffered a crisis of confidence under the ineffective Jordan.

LEAGUE DIVISION 1	**1995-96**
Endsleigh Division 1	4th
Coca-Cola Cup	3rd Round
FA Cup	3rd Round

Relegation avoided, Macari conducted major surgery on his squad, letting numerous players go. Wayne Biggins and Keith Downing were released on frees, joining Oxford and Hereford respectively, while John Butler was offered the same terms in the knowledge that that entitled him to a free transfer, as he had been at the club for more than five years. He returned to his former club Wigan. Nigel Gleghorn and Martin Carruthers were offered pay-as-you-play deals, a type of contract Stoke had pioneered the previous season, which allowed players to put themselves in the shop window. Despite the departures, Macari still had no money to spend. He hoped to buy Lee Martin of Celtic, Alan McLoughlin of Portsmouth and Mark Walters of Liverpool, but as their combined fees topped £1 million the moves were not sanctioned.

The reason for the directors' parsimony was the continuing saga over relocation. The decision to press ahead with plans for a new stadium had been taken over the summer and fans now voiced concerns about the design of Stoke's new home. One of the biggest advantages of the Vic was that it was an intimidating place to visit and the testimony of City players through the ages proved how the Boothen End was, in effect, a twelfth man. After an open meeting, where one director's remark that 'fans like big bowls like Old Trafford' brought howls of derision, the worry was that the new ground would be a concrete cavern, devoid of atmosphere. Given the lack of investment in the team, it could even be hosting Second Division football.

More intrigue was afoot when it was revealed that Independent Supporters organisation, SCISA, led by Lester Hughes, had made a bid to invest funds on behalf of Staffordshire businessman Keith Sutherland. Chairman Coates rejected the offer, saying, 'We live within our overdraft and within our means. We can manage our finances and are currently looking at ways to improve our income.' Why then were Sutherland's advances rejected?

Joining the coaching staff was Mike Pejic, Stoke's former left-back of the 1970s. Renowned as a disciplinarian, Pejic replaced Asa Hartford, who departed to Manchester City to partner Alan Ball. Stoke finally filled the vacant physiotherapist's position with Ian Liversage, who had been at Oldham for ten years.

The team was slow to get going. Ian Cranson began the season recovering from a snapped cruciate ligament, which kept him out until late November. Toddy Orlygsson was left in the cold after announcing that he wanted to leave the club. He would eventually sign for Oldham, with the tribunal setting the fee at £180,000. He departed amid much flak, accusing the club of trying to stifle his career. Keith Scott had proved immobile and lackadaisical and was dropped after remonstrating with some Boothen Stand Paddockers as he trudged off after a home defeat by Oldham. He would not last much longer. Poor early form, coming to a head in a dreadful defeat at Watford, was turned around after City were paired with Chelsea in the Coca-Cola Cup. A 0-0 draw at the Vic restored much of the faith of both players and fans. When Stoke returned from Stamford Bridge with a place in the third round draw, the season took off (see Match of the Season).

League form picked up, helped by a 4-1 victory at promotion favourites Wolves. Mark Prudhoe seized his first opportunity in over a year for senior football, turning in a series of consistent displays that added stability at the back. When Peschisolido injured his knee against Luton, Simon Sturridge grabbed his chance, scoring twice as a substitute versus Luton and, working well with John Gayle, notched a hat-trick at Southend the following week. A run of six wins in seven took Stoke into the play-off zone.

Stoke's three draws in the group phase of the Anglo-Italian Cup meant that as the final game, against Reggiana, could not affect qualification, it was cancelled. The competition itself was scrapped, a reflection of public apathy and an unsavoury incident involving Birmingham in Ancona, whose coach, Masimo Cacciatori, was accused of attacking the referee and starting a mass brawl. Macari suggested an Anglo-Scottish Cup might be a better idea!

In November Macari signed striker Mike Sheron from Norwich. He had cost the Canaries £850,000 from Manchester City fifteen months earlier, but two changes of manager inside a year had seen Sheron rusting away in the reserves. At 23, he needed the challenge of regular first-team football and he arrived in a straight swap for Keith Scott, although Stoke were committed to paying £150,000 once Sheron played 30 games. There were rumours that Norwich manager Martin O'Neill, in the midst of an acrimonious parting of the ways with Chairman Robert Chase to join Leicester, sold Sheron in a fit of pique, deliberately lumbering Norwich with misfit striker Scott. Sheron and Sturridge soon struck up a formidable partnership. Once fit, Sheron's close control and expert finishing brought him media attention, but Sturridge contributed greatly to the team's success. His unselfish running and passing provided Sheron with a number of goals, while 'Studger' finished only one behind his partner in the scoring stakes, with fourteen.

DID YOU KNOW?

Lee Sandford's sale to Sheffield United in 1996 for £450,000 realised the only profit on any player that Alan Ball brought to Stoke City.

Stoke outplayed Premier League Nottingham Forest in the FA Cup, but Forest sneaked a draw and won the replay 2-0. Graham Potter, a Joe Jordan signing from Birmingham, shone at the City Ground. Potter was a boyish 20-year-old whose ability to beat full-backs for pace gave Stoke an added dimension on the left wing. His emergence allowed Macari to switch Nigel Gleghorn inside. At 33, Gleghorn relished the role as playmaker, prompting the team forward from midfield. His passing ability benefited the strikers, who liked the ball to feet on the ground, or played into space ahead of them. Alongside Gleghorn, Kevin Keen was proving a shrewd acquisition. Standing only 5ft 7in, the blond midfielder's diminutive stature belied his committed approach to the game. Completing the midfield quartet was Ray Wallace, who worked hard to cover the ground between both penalty areas, regularly winning the ball back outside Stoke's box and feeding either Gleghorn or Keen. At the back, Larus Sigurdsson was proving almost impossible to pass. His positioning allowed him to pull off tackles which he seemed to have no chance of making. His form brought him to the attention of Icelandic national manager Gudjon Thordarsson, and he played for Iceland 'A' against Slovenia in February. With Stoke riding high in fourth, after a 2-0 win over play-off rivals Barnsley in early March, it appeared that Macari had once again made a silken purse from a sow's ear.

On transfer deadline day Peschisolido was controversially sold back to Birmingham for £475,000. Macari claimed he knew nothing of the deal – being on the training pitch when it was struck – and expressed anger at it. But Pesch's contribution had dwindled, partly due to international commitments with Canada. He had not started a Stoke game since the turn of the year. Even so, it seemed a low price to pay for an international forward. Attention was diverted by Mike Sheron's club record run of seven goals in seven League games, one of which was a last-gasp winner as City won their first away match in four months, at Luton. Five wins out of the last seven games put Stoke into the play-offs.

The board finally sought fans' opinion when they took members of the Oatcake's editorial team on a fact-finding mission to Middlesbrough's new Cellnet stadium, upon which Stoke's new ground was to be based. There was debate about a name for the stadium. Many suggested the Stanley Matthews Stadium, in honour of the

Life President, but Stan, as ever, bashfully declined the honour. Permission was granted by the football licensing authority to play at the Vic for one more year, even though Stoke had exceeded the three-year limit on their non all-seated arena.

The new stadium was to be built and owned by the Stoke-on-Trent Regeneration Company, in which both the club and council owned shares, and would cost in the region of £19 million. The council agreed to plough in £4.5 million, £3 million came from the Football Trust, £1 million from the brewers McEwans, which included sponsorship of the main stand, and £2.6 million was raised from a number of banks. This still left Stoke City to find £6 million. The move was officially approved by National Heritage Secretary Virginia Bottomley on 13 May, as City were embroiled in the end of season play-offs against Martin O'Neill's Leicester, whom they had beaten twice in the League. Stoke had the better of a tense 0-0 draw at Filbert Street, but when it came to the crunch Stoke turned in their worst home performance of the season and the Foxes won 1-0. The fact that Leicester made it into the Premiership, where they have remained ever since, rubbed salt into the wounds.

The rewards of winning the play-offs were huge. The difference between just one season in the Premiership (as is the fate of most First Division play-off winners) and another in Division Two was put at £4 million – enough to clear Stoke's debts as the club announced a £1.89 million loss on the financial year. City fans could not understand why, with such riches at the end of a fairly short rainbow, the board did not speculate, investing in quality talent to push for promotion. Furthermore, the Potteries was an area in structural decline, with the traditional pottery and coal-mining industries mere shadows of their former selves. These factors explained why, despite the most successful season in a decade, Stoke's crowds dipped by 10 per cent. Those fans who did turn up made it quite clear that they were supporting the team in spite of the increasingly remote board.

Match of the Season 1995-96

Chelsea 0 Stoke 1

Coca-Cola Cup, 2nd Round, 2nd leg, 4 October 1995

Stoke's poor start to the season saw them languishing two places off the bottom when they were paired with Glenn Hoddle's Chelsea in the Coca-Cola Cup. Just a week earlier Macari had replaced want-away midfielder Orlygsson with inexperienced left-winger Graham Potter, while reinstating Mark Prudhoe in goal in place of Carl

Muggleton. These changes had prompted an improved performance to hold Tranmere to a draw. Chelsea were resurgent under Glenn Hoddle, having reached the semi-finals of the European Cup-Winners' Cup and an FA Cup final. Their lynchpin was former Dutch international midfielder Ruud Gullit, who had started the season impressively as a sweeper in Hoddle's new system.

Stoke had the better of the first leg at the Vic. Vince Overson headed against the bar and Carruthers twice wasted chances to score. Chelsea emerged unscathed with a goalless draw. Between the two legs Stoke's form continued to improve as they beat West Brom and drew at high-flying Crystal Palace. Chelsea beat Arsenal 1-0 but the Blues were still short of goals. Their principal source was veteran Welsh international striker Mark Hughes, whose tally was three in nine games. Former Stoke golden boy Mark Stein rarely got a look in, although he was named as a substitute for the second game.

Stamford Bridge was undergoing huge changes in the mid-1990s and Stoke's fans were housed in a temporary stand at what had been the Shed End, where the new Chelsea Village hotel complex was being built. On a balmy evening all the attacking was done by Chelsea. Their measured, constructive approach created numerous half chances and it only seemed a matter of time before they scored. Stoke's new-found resilience, founded on Vince Overson, allowed the Potters back into the game. A series of crunching tackles cut the supply to strikers Hughes and Paul Furlong. Chelsea's frustration began to show and, with fifteen minutes to go, Hughes, foraging deep to receive the ball, was harried by Wallace into presenting the ball to Peschisolido. Pesch raced into the area, received a lucky bounce off Sinclair and gleefully swept the ball home.

Chelsea poured forward, missing chance after chance. Stein, on for the final few minutes, poked a glorious opportunity wide when, as they say, it seemed easier to score. Sandford headed off the line the one shot to defeat Prudhoe and the final whistle blew on the shock of the round.

The win was Stoke's first against a team from a higher division since Norwich in the Littlewoods Cup in 1987. Lightning could not be expected to strike twice and a 0-4 defeat at home to Kevin Keegan's Premier League leaders Newcastle in the next round was only to be expected.

LEAGUE DIVISION 1	**1996-97**
Nationwide Division 1	12th
Coca-Cola Cup	3rd Round
FA Cup	3rd Round

The valedictory season at the Victoria Ground was one of preparing for the biggest upheaval in the club's history. The all-consuming ground move swallowed cash, severely affecting the team's fortunes on the field. By early October the foundation piles of the steel superstructure had been driven into the soil high on the hill looking down on the city. The project had just ten months to be completed, giving rise to a nervous year for chief executive Jez Moxey and developers St Modwen's. The construction company, Mowlem's, were given a deadline of 1 July, which would then allow six weeks for the start of the new season. Supporters, divided on the issue, either saw the ground as a new start, or a millstone around the club's neck, or both.

The first ramifications of the move became clear in the summer of 1996. Eleven players refused to sign the initial contracts on offer, of which Cranson, Whittle, Keen, Overson and Gleghorn were the highest profile. The latter pair left for Burnley, and Gleghorn, in particular, was outspoken in his criticism of the club, revealing that the difference between what he asked and what he was offered was a mere £50 per week. Cranson, Keen and Whittle eventually re-signed. Funds were generated by the sale of Graham Potter to Southampton for £300,000 and Lee Sandford to Sheffield United for £450,000. The board did permit Macari to spend £200,000 on Birmingham midfielder Richard Forsyth, who became the first signing to cost money since Keith Scott in 1994. Coventry right-back Ally Pickering signed for a tribunal-fixed fee of £300,000. The only other arrival, Leeds' experienced left-back, Nigel Worthington, came on a free. Stoke also bade farewell to Tony Lacey after 24 years' involvement with the youth set-up which had seen him develop the likes of Garth Crooks, Adrian Heath and Paul Bracewell.

With the team losing three of its most consistent performers of recent years, two of them club captains, supporters were downbeat about the club's prospects, so an opening five-match unbeaten run took many by surprise and Stoke to the top of the League. Macari was manager of the month and talk was of starting the following season with a brand new stadium in the Premiership. A 0-3 defeat at Barnsley pulled the wool from the eyes and prompted Macari to sign Spurs' Northern Ireland international winger Gerry McMahon for £250,000 and midfielder Graham Kavanagh, after an initial loan spell, from Middlesbrough, also for £250,000. The chairman claimed that these signings, and Sheron's acceptance of a two-year contract extension, 'demonstrates we are an ambitious club and anxious for Premier League football.' For a moment even some of the sceptics were taken in, until ever-present central defender John Dreyer, in the best form of his career, was sold to Bradford City for £25,000.

The huge upsurge of football fever that accompanied England's performances as hosts of Euro '96 prompted BSkyB to pay a record £674 million over five years for the rights to show live Premiership football. The gap between the haves and have-nots was now a yawning chasm, although Sky also purchased the rights to show Nationwide League football, guaranteeing each First Division club £1 million per season. None of this would be much help to cash-strapped Stoke if they slipped back into the Second. The club's turnover of £5 million was lower than that of many 'smaller' clubs, including Norwich, West Brom, QPR and Bolton. It begged the question of where would Stoke find their share of the money, amounting to £6 million, for the new stadium. Part of the answer came when the Britannia Building Society confirmed a £1.3 million sponsorship deal. The stadium was to be called the Britannia Stadium and the logo would adorn the team's shirts. It was the biggest deal in the club's history, but over a ten-year period it was not as generous as initially thought. The lion's share would still have to be raised in Stoke's traditional manner, the sale of their best players. Prime contender to bring in a sizeable fee was Mike Sheron. He finished as runner-up in the Nationwide Player of the Year awards to Derby's Igor Stimac and was now the most predatory striker in the division. His strikes at Ipswich and Charlton were international class and a bidding war developed, which the club fanned openly, between Harry Redknapp's West Ham, Trevor Francis' Birmingham and QPR's Stewart Houston.

Behind the scenes yet more shenanigans leaked out from time to time, which did the club no credit. Director Mike Moors offered to put funds into the club and resigned when he was rebuffed 'so the board could pursue alternative arrangements'. These proved to be a link-up with Stan Clarke, the owner of developers St Modwen, who agreed to act as guarantor of the sums involved, in return for acquiring first option on buying shares in the club. It then emerged that Clarke, who had turned around the Staffordshire racecourse of Uttoxeter, had five years to decide whether to take up the shares option, putting Stoke in limbo once again. In an era when clubs of comparable size were going public to raise funds for team-building, Stoke were still in the hands of parochial businessmen. That the board then had the temerity to attack supporters in the press for not supporting a team that had gone from promotion contenders to mid-table also-rans under their stewardship merely served to drive more fans away. Average gates were a mere 12,748, a 21 per cent fall in just three years.

Stoke won one game in seven to drop into mid-table and defeats by Arsenal in the Coca-Cola Cup and Second Division Stockport in the FA Cup effectively ended the season.

Macari's squad, often depleted by international call-ups for Sigurdsson, Worthington and McMahon, proved exceptionally thin. Struggling for available players against Portsmouth, Macari blooded Neil Mackenzie and Andy Griffin, despite the two of them having played for the 'A' team four hours earlier. Worthington eventually lost his place at left-back to Griffin, who produced a string of confident performances, earning a call up for England Under-18s. Injury also deprived Stoke of Ian Cranson, who announced his retirement after having to undergo yet another knee operation. Simon Sturridge damaged ligaments at Barnsley, putting him out for the season.

Stoke's away form was appalling. They lost eight of their final nine away games scoring just one goal, an own-goal at that, in the process. Fortunately, home form held up as the landmark games came and went. Stoke won the last evening game and drew the last Saturday match, while Port Vale were soundly beaten 2-0 in the last Potteries derby at the Vic.

Ominously, on the eve of the Vale match, news came that Lou Macari would vacate his position as manager at the end of the season. He initially claimed it was to allow him to concentrate on his £400,000 litigation with Celtic, which was due to come to court early the following season, although prior to the final game Peter Coates announced that Macari had been 'stripped of his responsibilities'. Soon after leaving, Macari launched a lawsuit against Stoke for wrongful dismissal, claiming that 'as soon as I said I might be leaving people were coming up to me with their diaries saying "When are you going then?" I cannot work in an environment like that.' Less of a mystery was the departure of Mike Sheron who signed for QPR for £2.75 million at the end of the season. His fee conveniently matched the deficit required to complete the new stadium. The widely predicted impact on the team of the move to a new ground had struck its most damaging blow.

The season was kept alive by the nostalgia of the Vic, which hosted its last League match on 4 May 1997 (see Match of the Season). Chief Executive Jez Moxey predicted that the move to the Britannia Stadium would mark the beginning of a new, successful era, proving that the club had ambition. Not many shared his optimism.

DID YOU KNOW?

Stoke always lose replayed FA Cup-ties abandoned when they were ahead – Reading (home, 1913, fog), Doncaster (away, 1930, snow) and Oldham (home, 1979, fog).

Match of the Season 1996-97

Stoke 2 West Brom 1

Division 1, 4 May 1997

The last League game at the Victoria Ground was a stomach-churning occasion. The club had set up a special day for the fans. Alan Hudson, Gordon Banks, Eric Skeels and George Berry appeared in a pre-game celebrity kick-about against former West Brom players, among them Jeff Astle. There was also a parade of Stoke heroes from earlier eras, including the likes of Stan Matthews, Johnny King, Jimmy O'Neill and Dennis Wilshaw. To great cheers Sir Stan symbolically scored one last goal at the Boothen End. Fans also competed for prizes for the best fancy dress costume, which attracted a large number of entrants, and best banner.

After a downpour drenched the pitch, the two teams took to the field in blazing sunshine for a re-run of the first League game to be played at the ground, which West Brom had won 2-0 on 8 September 1888. But Stoke won this game thanks to a McMahon diving header and Kavanagh's lob over the advancing Alan Miller. With five minutes left Justin Whittle gave away a penalty, which Andy Hunt converted, to slightly dampen the occasion, but the scenes at the final whistle brought tears to the eyes of hardened supporters. Outpourings of emotion greeted the departing Macari and Sheron as they circled the pitch, but most of the capacity crowd were there to say goodbye to the Victoria Ground which had played such an important part in their lives. Fans lingered for hours after the game to sit quietly and reflect on their favourite matches and moments. Lou Macari bade farewell by saying, 'It has been a humbling experience to have this duty to discharge.'

The Vic was the oldest remaining League football ground in the world, second only to non-league Northwich Victoria's Drill Field, to be in continuous use since 1874. The Boothen End was the largest terrace left in Britain, holding a much reduced capacity of 9,000. The Victoria Ground was demolished at the end of 1997. The pitch's turf sold out in hours at £5 per square half-metre.

3

RULE BRITANNIA
1997-2005

LEAGUE DIVISION 1	**1997-98**
Nationwide Division 1	23rd (Relegated)
Coca-Cola Cup	3rd Round
FA Cup	3rd Round

The dawn of the new era at the Britannia Stadium should have been full of hope, but the departure of Macari – still not fully explained – plus the farcical search for a replacement, left fans wondering exactly what was going on. Many felt the board's delay in naming Macari's successor was just a ruse to boost season ticket sales. Initially the board announced that an appointment would be made by the end of May, as the man they wanted – believed to be Sammy McIlroy, manager of League new boys Macclesfield – was under contract. The ensuing silence was deafening and Chic Bates, in his caretaker capacity, assumed responsibility for developing the squad. It became increasingly obvious that Bates would be named manager and after much prevarication, in late July, he was.

Bates had proved to be an excellent coach, but he was out of his depth in the hot seat. By early September former boss Alan Durban, who had given Bates his first chance in football at Shrewsbury, was invited back as assistant manager to take the weight off Bates' shoulders.

If Stoke had bade farewell to the Victoria Ground in a blaze of glory, then the fiasco surrounding the opening of the new stadium was a pit of despair. From the outset there were problems actually getting there. The plans catered for only one access road from the nearby A50. That meant that spectators arriving from the City and the motorway, the vast majority, had to travel up the A50 for over a mile to a roundabout, then double-back on themselves on the other side of the dual carriageway. This resulted in hideous tail-backs. Those on foot fared equally badly. The footbridge, allowing access from the canalside path that led to the city centre, was barely wide enough to carry the large number of supporters who chose to walk.

Problems emerged after matches, as the area became dangerously crowded. There was also congestion around the ticket office, as tickets could not be bought at turnstiles. With spectators already fed up with the effort of getting to the ground, to ask them to queue up for just seven booths was folly. Congestion was such that many fans missed much of the first half. Although tickets were soon made available on all gates around the stadium, visitors to the club shop discovered that for several months it was not even equipped to take its own credit cards.

The three open corners of the ground meant that the wind buffeted round the stadium, causing a nuisance for fans and the bizarre sight of the four corner flags blowing in different directions. For the opening fixture, against Swindon, pre-match ceremonies included a 'sing-alike' Tom Jones who led the crowd in a dreadfully out of time rendition of 'Delilah'. The crowning glory was to be Sir Stanley Matthews officially declaring the stadium open by scoring at the new 'Boothen End', the North Stand, just as he had done to close the Vic.

Stupidly, the ball was placed on the edge of the penalty area and 82-year-old Stan's 'shot' was whisked away by the wind, coming to rest just outside the six-yard box. This high farce symbolised Stoke's season. Stan declared that watching City at the Brit was 'like watching Stoke play away from home' and he attended only a handful of games at the new ground. While acknowledging the difficulties of a project the size and complexity of the Britannia Stadium, the club brought many of the problems on itself by not listening to supporters' concerns, particularly over the access issue, during the planning stage.

Before long the rumblings turned into actual dissent. In the third home game two fans invaded the pitch at half-time with a banner proclaiming 'Coates out', which precipitated chants of 'Stand up if you want Coates out' from around the ground.

At least Stoke had a new avenue to explore in their quest to find cheap players. Jean-Marc Bosman, a Belgian footballer, had won a test case in the European court of Human Rights which allowed him to leave a club for free at the end of his contract. Stoke took advantage as Paul Stewart (Sunderland), Dutchman Dick Schreuder from JC Roda, Zay Angola, formerly known as Jose Andrade, who had been at the club during the 1994-95 season, and Scottish central defender Steven Tweed, from Greek club Ionikos, all arrived on frees. The only signing to cost money was 24-year-old striker Peter Thorne. He had the onerous responsibility of following in Sheron's footsteps and would cost the club £550,000, after appearances were taken into consideration. Coates' justification of the club's failure to invest in the team – 'some clubs have spent money and failed' – had supporters scratching their heads in disbelief.

City were already in serious trouble. The team failed to adjust to playing at the 'Brit' as it did not feel like home to either players or fans. Visiting teams would be inspired by the superb facilities, including warm-up gymnasium, and the vast acres of empty home seats in the ground. In attack, Thorne and Stewart proved one-paced and lacking in finishing ability. Two goals in the first five games did not bode well, and around Christmas five successive losses, including a first ever defeat by Crewe, set the scene for the second half of the season.

The slump was brought to a head early in the New Year. Nine players discovered via the *Sentinel* that they were no longer required by the club – McMahon, McNally, Andrade, Birch, Woods, Devlin, Nyamah, and Mike and Paul Macari. Six of these faced Birmingham's reserves two days later and were hammered 0-4. Three days later the Blues' first team thrashed Stoke 0-7 at the Brit. The team were effectively striking in support of their unwanted colleagues. There were ugly scenes at the final whistle as 2,000 fans invaded the pitch with some climbing the McEwans stand in an attempt to stampede the directors box. The result was, after all, Stoke's worst ever home defeat, surpassing the 1-6 inflicted by Spurs in 1951.

Early exits in the League and FA Cup – a 1-3 loss at West Brom, which brought to an end Stoke's long unbeaten run against the Baggies stretching back nearly a decade – left morale at an all-time low. For the visit of Bradford City, Stoke fans organised a protest and the watching world, courtesy of Sky TV, saw 2,000 supporters enter fifteen minutes into the game bearing placards with the words 'Coates Out!' The protests stirred the board into action.

Coates resigned as chairman, handing over to Keith Humphreys. Their shareholding was unchanged. Although it was claimed that new investors were sought, the club's record of stone-walling any attempt to inject money, giving the appearance of denying outside interference in a closed-shop, meant that this was taken with a big pinch of salt. The sale of the Vic to St Modwen, the developers of the Britannia Stadium, for £1 million (half the asking price and £6 million less than the value of the stadium in the club's assets column) raised more questions. Once again, fans felt that their club had been undersold. In fact, Stan Clarke insisted he had no interest in taking control of the club, investing in Brighton racecourse in the same week. SCISA staged a meeting at the King's Hall in Stoke, at which motions of no confidence in the board and in chief executive Jez Moxey were carried by over 2,000 fans. They also decided to boycott the club shop, season tickets, and Stadia Catering's produce in an attempt to topple the board. It was felt that such extreme action was necessary to effect change, even though it was likely to damage the club in the short term. Relegation had already been accepted. The board's response was to demote Bates to first-team coach, replacing him with ex-Bradford City manager Chris Kamara. The sideways shuffle convinced no one of anything.

As a player, Kamara had been headstrong and reactionary, and his managerial style was no different. He arrived claiming, 'Stoke is a sleeping monster. We're going to build a squad for the Premier League,' but one of his first acts was to sell the only classy player the club had left. Andy Griffin left for Kenny Dalglish's Newcastle for £1.5 million. Kamara sacked coach Mike Pejic, replacing him with his former Bradford City coach Martin Hunter, and introduced a ghetto-blaster into the dressing room in an effort to pep up the team before games. This innovation had little effect other than to inspire cheeky letters to the *Sentinel*, suggesting that it play 'The Only Way is Up' and 'Heaven Knows I'm Miserable Now'. Kamara used 31 players in his thirteen games in charge and, after winning just once, resorted to slamming his players in the press. On deadline day, appropriately April Fool's Day, he put the entire squad up for sale. No club made an offer for any Stoke player. After a 0-3 home defeat by Tranmere, Kamara quit. His three-month tenure had seen City plummet into the relegation zone. Declaring Kamara's appointment as 'a nightmare for all concerned', Humphreys handed the reigns to Alan Durban, who was given the task of trying to pull Stoke clear of the relegation zone.

So despairing were Stoke fans that during the defeat by Huddersfield they began singing 'Bring on the Hippo', referring to the club mascot, Pottermus! The portly Hippo went on to finish seventh in the club's player of the season awards, won, astonishingly by bit-part player Justin Whittle.

Three wins in four home games gave Stoke hope but a heavy defeat by Manchester City on the last day (see Match of the Season) confirmed what had seemed inevitable all along. Relegation. The perceived arrogance of those at the helm, in the face of the club's total collapse, attracted even more condemnation. At the AGM, Jez Moxey claimed that the club's problems stemmed from the fans' protests which 'let the side down'. Shares in Stoke City traditionally changed hands for a £1. Those at the top were now apparently holding out for £15 per share, and when this became public knowledge there was uproar. A protest group called SOS (Save Our Stoke) was formed by an irate fan, Tim Gallimore, which demanded that the club's affairs be made more public. Stoke were £4.3 million in debt, had no manager, and were back in the Second Division.

DID YOU KNOW?

Peter Dobing, Stoke's skipper in the 1972 League Cup final, once appeared as 12th man for the Lancashire cricket team in a Roses county match against Yorkshire.

Match of the Season 1997-98

Stoke 2 Manchester City 5

Division 1, 3 May 1998

Both teams went into this game knowing that defeat spelled certain relegation and that even a win might not be enough. The other four relegation candidates – Port Vale, QPR, Bury and Portsmouth – had a mixed bag of fixtures. Six clubs were vying to avoid the last two relegation places, Reading being doomed, but Stoke and Man City filled them at start of play and needed favours from others if either was to escape. With their 4,000 allocation sold out, during the week Manchester City fans had driven south in droves to buy tickets from Stoke, despite the policy of strict segregation. This led to problems during the game, the first ever sell-out at the Brit.

Live on Sky, mainly due to the involvement of Man City, the Blues took the game by the scruff of the neck. Goater lobbed the portly Southall from 25 yards to put them 1-0 ahead at the break. Stoke rarely threatened.

The half-time scores were not encouraging, as each of the other four teams involved was winning. Man City scored early in the second half through an unmarked Dickov, before Thorne replied in similar fashion. By this stage it was clear that each of the other four relegation candidates would win easily, leaving Stoke and Man City to play out time. Stoke collapsed and allowed three more goals, while scoring what in other situations might be called a consolation themselves. The Man City fans supported their side to the death while Stoke's fans reacted angrily to another dreadful performance. There were numerous ejections and post-match scuffles as Stoke's hoodlum element chucked bricks at departing Manchester fans. In town that evening, Stoke and Port Vale fans clashed while the Valiants were celebrating their escape from relegation. After viewing closed-circuit TV camera footage, police arrested 28 fans in dawn raids on homes on the Potteries over the summer. Disgraced at all turns, Stoke City was now at its lowest ebb.

LEAGUE DIVISION 2	**1998-99**
Nationwide Division 2	8th
Worthington Cup	2nd Round
FA Cup	2nd Round

Jez Moxey predicted Stoke would lose around £1 million through being in Division Two for just *one* season. Such was the price the board paid for the mismanagement of the previous two years. In a bid to retain fans' interest, a freeze on ticket prices was announced with special deals for children and families introduced. During the summer Keith Humphreys apologised to fans for the 'bloody awful nine months' but pleaded that the season ticket and merchandise bans, spearheaded by Save Our Stoke, should be lifted. SOS leader Tim Gallimore pointed out that the intention was indeed to harry the current board to the point where they would have to sell the club to those prepared to breathe life and, more importantly, money into Stoke City. SOS appeared to hold sway. Just 4,500 season-ticket holders renewed, a drop of nearly 1,000.

It came as a welcome surprise when Humphreys announced that Brian Little would be Stoke's new manager. Little was an experienced manager, having resuscitated Darlington after their demotion from the Football League in 1989 and led them to two successive promotions before being lured to Leicester. The board believed that his record of wheeling and dealing during his time at Darlington made him perfectly suited to Stoke's current situation. Some detractors pointed to his subsequent record of having baled out of both the Leicester and Aston Villa jobs when the pressure mounted. Having walked out of Villa, Little had been recuperating in Mallorca when contacted by Stoke. For once the board had exceeded fans' expectations. Little assembled his own managerial team of assistant manager Tony McAndrew, Allan Evans as coach, and Ian Cranson as reserve-team coach. Durban and Bates were dispensed with, which seemed sensible, given the need for a complete change of direction. There were thirteen departures from the playing staff, including McMahon and Stewart, as Stoke cut its wage-bill, and a new physiotherapist arrived, Rob Ryles.

Accepting the fact that there was no money, Little exploited his knowledge of the lower divisions to sign some experienced players. He lured defenders Chris Short from Sheffield United, Bryan Small from Bury, and Phil Robinson from Notts County, plus midfielder David Oldfield from Luton, all on free transfers. He clung on to star midfielder Graham Kavanagh, despite Moxey confirming that 'every player is available at the right price'. Aberdeen's £450,000 bid was rejected as Stoke were holding out for £1 million.

DID YOU KNOW?

During Stoke's tour of Australasia in 1973, John Ritchie scored all 8 goals in the win over New Zealand side Otago. That remains an individual record for Stoke City.

Little's new-look side set off with a bang, winning seven League games on the trot, a club record from the start of the season, and a manager of the month award for Little in his first month in the job. The run was reward for a tactical switch to a 5-3-2 formation, with Small and Short operating as wing-backs. In attack Dean Crowe and Peter Thorne looked a cut above most Second Division defenders. A 4-3 win at Preston saw Stoke installed as 9-4 favourites for promotion. A rapid exit from the League Cup (now sponsored by Worthington) at the hands of Sammy McIlroy's Macclesfield put things into perspective. It was the first time Stoke had been knocked out in the first round of the competition in its 38-year history, and provided supporters with another glimpse of the behind-the-scenes workings of the club. Jez Moxey divulged that City had budgeted for three cup rounds and thereby lost some £125,000 in anticipated revenue. Given Stoke's appalling record in cup competitions this seemed a crass assumption to make.

As John Cleese's character in the film Clockwise said, 'It's not the despair. Despair I can handle. It's the hope. The hope I can't cope with.' Stoke's good start was too good to last. The reality was that it was impossible to turn around a shambolic club so quickly. Stoke's run came to an end at promotion favourites Fulham where, alarmingly, Chris Short was carried off the pitch having suffered a breathing problem. He was out of action for a month, disrupting the balance of the five-man defence. The mystery condition would eventually end his career. Up front, the goals started to dry up. £500,000 striker Kyle Lightbourne, signed by Kamara, but out for six months due to a blood disorder, was still not fully fit and Simon Sturridge's career had been ended by his cartilage problems. The injuries checked City's progress, while David Oldfield suffered loss of form and became the target of the boo-boys. The experienced midfielder possessed good passing ability but lacked pace and bite in the tackle. This gave an impression of lack of commitment, which Stoke fans will never tolerate.

Stoke won their first away FA Cup-tie in 26 years against League opponents. Their victims were Reading, 1-0, in the first round, but normal service was resumed in the second when Third Division Swansea won 1-0. There was no joy either in the Auto Windscreens Shield, with an embarrassing exit to Rochdale 1-2, which brought new levels of humiliation. Not only did the team muster just one shot against Third Division opposition, but the players were openly squabbling among themselves on the pitch. While promotion rivals Fulham were splashing out £2 million on Bristol Rovers striker Barry Hayles, whose goals would push them to the championship, City had to be content with blooding a number of reserves. Free transfer imports Ben Petty and Lee Collins came from Aston Villa, centre-half Greg Strong arrived on loan from Bolton, while midfielder James O'Connor was promoted from Stoke's second team.

Stoke won one game between Christmas and the beginning of March, dropping out of the play-off scene entirely. The knives were out, particularly after a humiliating 0-2 defeat by nine-man Millwall, about which Little said: 'That was the worst result in my twelve years in management.' During the game at Bloomfield Road, Stoke and Blackpool fans staged the first ever combined protest with 1,000 black balloons being released. At the next home game the Oatcake issued 5,000 red cards to be brandished towards the directors box. Moxey countered by saying that he only saw three cards waved. A 2-3 defeat by Notts County four days later prompted all 5,000 to be displayed simultaneously, as Stoke lost their sixth home game in a row. The board countered by offering seats at £5 per head and £1 for juniors for the game against Bristol Rovers. But in front of a bumper 17,500 crowd, Stoke lost 1-4 (see Match of the Season). The board were hoist by their own petard.

Little's final fling was to sign keeper Gavin Ward from Bolton and Nicky Mohan, a centre-half from Wycombe, on free transfers. They would be the last arrivals. In February the club declared that it had exceeded its overdraft limit and now lacked funds to pay the wages of any further loanees. The AGM revealed that the wage bill had risen to £3.3 million, up £1 million on 1996-97.

With the club seemingly disintegrating, Lester Hughes, chairman of the SCISA, attempted to put together a supporters' buy-out. Through the pages of the *Sentinel*, fans were invited to donate £200 to secure their place in the consortium. Hughes cited the recent example of Bournemouth, where a similar situation had led to a successful takeover and the saving of the club. Stoke replied to this initiative by publicly stating that it would listen to any serious offer. Hughes raised £250,000 in a week, with £6,000 being pledged by the Scandinavian supporters' branch, but the target of £2 million was never close to being achieved.

Brian Little had lost interest long before the season's end, and on his return from holiday he resigned, saying 'I have tried my best and the disappointment is very hard to take. I hope the supporters understand that it's the right time for me to go.' Eleven days before the start of the new season, he was installed as the new manager at

West Brom. That appointment led to Stoke receiving compensation to cover the costs of terminating the contracts of Little's backroom staff, Allan Evans and Tony McAndrew. Speculation about Little's successor started immediately. Among the names canvassed were Adrian Heath, Sammy McIlroy, John Rudge, Steve McMahon, and Tony Pulis.

Match of the Season 1998-99

Stoke 1 Bristol Rovers 4

Division 2, 22 August 1998

A large crowd of 17,823 responded to Stoke's ticket price-slashing for this game. There was still a glimmer of hope of a play-off place, if the team put together a good run, but there had been protests at each of the last five home matches and more were expected should City fail against Rovers. The visitors were angry that Stoke should reduce admission prices for home fans, but not theirs, and Rovers' directors joined Rovers' fans in the South Stand in protest. Stoke could not even get a gesture of goodwill right.

The Pirates, managed by Ian Holloway, enjoyed the blossoming partnership of Jason Roberts (nephew of former Stoke striker Dave Regis) and Jamie Cureton. Brian Little's line-up lacked width and struggled to make an impression from the start. With Robinson playing in midfield, and Strong having a nightmare at centre-half, Stoke fell back under Rovers' pressure. Roberts, in particular, had the beating of Bryan Small on the left. Yet Stoke went ahead against the run of play when Thorne nodded in Kavanagh's cross. A lucky lead at home! Could this be the turning point? Far from it. Rovers stormed forward after the interval and scored four times without reply. Stoke capitulated in the last ten minutes: Foster headed home unmarked and Cureton twice beat Muggleton. Stoke even managed to waste a penalty, when Kavanagh fired wide from the spot.

The manner and scale of defeat sparked noisy protests. Several hundred fans from the North Stand invaded the pitch and some of the players were manhandled, including striker Kyle Lightbourne, who, disgracefully, received a punch to the head. Sick of these humiliations heaped upon them by the board, supporters performed an hour-long sit-down protest on the pitch. There now appeared to be open warfare between supporters and the ruling regime. Stoke City were coming apart at the seams.

LEAGUE DIVISION 2	**1999-2000**
Nationwide Division 2	6th (lost in play-offs)
Worthington Cup	2nd Round
FA Cup	1st Round

For the third consecutive summer, Stoke were hunting for a new manager. This time the club's search took a new and humiliating twist when Tony Pulis, their first choice, joined Bristol City instead, openly admitting that he felt Stoke lacked ambition. Second choice was Gary Megson, a hard-working and honest manager who had previously been in charge at Norwich, his last club as a player, and Stockport. Megson accepted the challenge and brought in former Middlesbrough skipper Nigel Pearson as first-team coach. The final addition to the backroom staff was the surprise appointment as football executive of former Port Vale boss John Rudge. Rudge was renowned as one of the best managers outside the Premiership, but had been sacked five months previously as Vale struggled against relegation. Some Stoke fans felt that his appointment showed just how desperate City had become. In reality it was one of the best appointments the club has ever made. Rudge has always got the best from players he has worked with, allowing Robbie Earle, Mark Bright and Steve Guppy to enjoy careers in the Premiership, not to mention earning Vale a sizeable income in transfer fees. His role was to do precisely that for Stoke.

There was little expectation of anything other than a season of consolidation. A second round defeat by Sheffield Wednesday in the Worthington Cup at least gave Stoke the satisfaction of holding the Premiership's bottom side to a goalless draw at the Brit. There was steady, if unspectacular, progress, but as the team grew in confidence they put together a run of seven wins in nine matches to climb into third place.

As the financial situation grew ever more perilous, Megson was forced to sell Larus Sigurdsson to West Brom for £350,000. This seemed perverse, given that Stoke had rejected Aberdeen's £500,000 bid over the summer, but the club now reasoned that with his contract up the following year it was better to cash in than lose out entirely. It looked as though Kavanagh and Thorne would be the next to go to balance the books. To add to their woes, Stoke were knocked out of the FA Cup at Blackpool before October was out and embarked upon a seeming eternity of 368 minutes without a goal.

Into this arena stepped the club's saviours. An Icelandic-based consortium tabled a bid for Stoke City that could not be ignored. As details emerged it became clear that one of the provisos was the replacement of Megson with former Icelandic national team boss

Gudjon Thordarson, who had led his team to within a whisker of qualification for Euro 2000 – no mean feat for a country that had never qualified for anything. Many fans bridled at this condition, arguing that Megson was doing a creditable job on scant resources. An orchestrated campaign ensued, fuelled by the media, that Megson should stay. It was only later that it emerged that the whole deal was in fact the brainchild of Thordarson himself. He had regularly visited Stoke in his capacity as manager of Iceland to watch Toddy Orlygsson and Larus Sigurdsson, and had observed the potential of the club at first hand. Megson, it appeared, would become a casualty of circumstance.

The takeover was officially completed on 15 November, and at a press conference at the Britannia Stadium more details emerged. The consortium had acquired a 66 per cent holding in Stoke City, now owned by a company called Stoke Holding. The plan was to restructure the club's debts so that the crippling interest payments no longer impeded the club from signing new players. For the first time in years, the people in charge of Stoke City were speaking of how things could be achieved rather than why they couldn't. The new board members included Gunnar Thor Gislason, who became the youngest League club chairman at the age of 34 and 'Sigi' Sigurvinsson, an Icelandic international of the early 1980s, who, in 1984 had been voted Germany's Sportsman of the Year whilst with Stuttgart.

The residual misgivings relating to Megson's sacking were soon cast aside as the team, featuring two new signings brought in by Thordarson, thrashed Wycombe Wanderers 4-0 away from home in his first game in charge. 'It's just like watching Iceland!' sang Stoke's huge travelling support. One of the first actions of the new board was to institute a regular 'fans' forum', where supporters groups could send delegates to air their views about any issue involving the club. In the light of the previous incumbents 'head in the sand' attitude towards supporters, this proved popular and extremely constructive, helping to deal with issues such as the proposed moving of season-ticket holders from their existing seats in the North Stand, which was scrapped after discussion at the forum.

On 23 February arguably the greatest footballer the world has seen, Sir Stanley Matthews, died at the age of 85. Stan's career had spanned a remarkable 33 years during which he had won 54 England caps, played in 734 League games and won the inaugural Footballer of the Year and European Footballer of the Year trophies. Stan's health had been causing concern for several years, but the death of his wife, six years his junior, had hit him hard. It seemed as if football's greatest survivor had died of a broken heart. Pele called him 'the Sport's greatest ambassador'. His pall-bearers included Bobby Charlton, Gordon Banks, Nat Lofthouse and Geoff Hurst. Flowers festooned his statue, which stands in Stoke city centre.

Three days after his death, at Wigan's new JJB Stadium, the club were once again disgraced by the antics of a minority of louts who reacted to the breaking by home fans of the minute's silence in Sir Stan's honour. Fighting spewed onto the pitch and the teams had to be taken off, returning after nine minutes once the huge police presence had restored order. It later emerged that challenges had been issued via the internet between rival factions which had stirred up the prospect of trouble well in advance. The club's stated intention of eradicating the hooligan element through indefinite bans must be strictly adhered to if there is to be any improvement in City's reputation. Figures released at the end of season showed Stoke as the club with the third highest number of fans in the country banned from attending matches. The thugs who besmirch Stoke's name with incessant regularity know no shame and should be added to this list.

This aspect of the season apart, the club went from strength to strength. City sailed through the early rounds of the Auto Windscreens Shield and a 4-1 aggregate victory over Rochdale in the Northern final sent Stoke back to Wembley to face Bristol City in the real final. A near sell-out crowd of 75,000 witnessed an exciting contest. Graham Kavanagh opened the scoring for Stoke with a mazy run and shot. Bristol City fought back, equalised from a corner-kick, and looked the more likely winners until Peter Thorne popped up to ensure Stoke maintained their 100 per cent record under the Twin Towers.

The excitement caused by the Wembley win was increased by an extraordinary run of form in the League. Stoke won nine and drew the other four of thirteen League games. The team was playing exhilarating football, utilising an attacking 5-3-2 formation under Thordarson, whose arrival sparked an influx of other players from Arctic climes. Brynjar Gunnarsson, a 24-year-old Icelandic central defender – also at home in defensive midfield – arrived for £509,000 from Swedish club Orgryte, while Mikael Hansson, a right wingback, arrived from Norkopping on a free. The manager brought in Leicester's Icelandic left-winger, Arnar Gunnlaugsson, on loan and even signed his own son, midfielder Bjarni Gudjonsson, from Genk of Belgium for £250,000.

While the team was on its winning roll, no one player deserved more acclaim than Peter Thorne. He had taken flak during his two years at the Vic for seeming aloof and disinterested. Thordarson had fired him up and he scored sixteen goals in those thirteen League games, plus three more during the Auto Windscreen Shield triumph. He thrived on through balls provided by Kavanagh, who was released by Thordarson's system to play a more advanced play-making role. The other revelation was 19-year-old James O'Connor in midfield. Nicknamed 'little hard man', the ginger-haired Irishman fought tooth and nail for every ball in the middle of the park, earning comparisons with countryman Roy Keane. His zeal often pitched him into trouble with referees, however, and he faced an FA commission for having accumulated fourteen bookings in the season. John Rudge won over any remaining sceptics by pleading the youngster's case, winning a reprieve, subject to further good behaviour.

Stoke qualified for the promotion play-offs on the back of their unbeaten run, losing out to Gillingham, who had lost their grip on an automatic promotion spot on the last day of the season (see Match of the Season).

Despite the play-off defeat, it nevertheless felt as if the club's fortunes were on a definite upturn. Over the summer City became most bookies' favourites to win the Second Division. Would the enormous potential which lurked within the club finally be unleashed?

Match of the Season 1999-2000

Gillingham 3 Stoke 0

Play-off, semi-final, 2nd leg, 17 May 2000

Stoke's fortunes in the play-offs had previously hinged on their making poor starts to the first leg. This time City could not have begun better. Two goals up after eight minutes, Stoke looked set for a quick return to Wembley. They were still two goals ahead, at 3-1, into the sixth minute of injury-time. The Gills, however, under the management of former England international Peter Taylor, were made of stern stuff and their inspirational captain, Andy Hessenthaler, belted a 30-yard shot past the despairing Ward. At 3-2 the Gills were now favourites.

Stoke went into the second leg minus the influential Peter Thorne, who took a knock to his knee during the nerve-jangling last ten minutes at the Brit. The restricted capacity of Gillingham's Priestfield Stadium meant that only 1,800 tickets were available to Stoke fans. A further 7,500 watched the game on a big screen at the Brit.

DID YOU KNOW?

The capacity of the Britannia Stadium is 28,000, with unimpeded views of the pitch. The single-tier 'home' end houses 7,000 spectators. There are 64 executive boxes.

The game soon deteriorated into a series of niggly fouls, which in many senses should have suited Stoke, who merely needed to keep a clean sheet to progress. Crucially, City's players reacted to provocation from their opponents. Clive Clarke, already booked, let his temper get the better of him as he challenged for a ball which went out for a throw in and petulantly threw it away, earning a second yellow inside a minute and an early bath. The players rallied to the cause and repelled waves of Gillingham attacks. Back at the Britannia Stadium, the tension became so great that the fans asked for the commentary over the tannoy to be switched off.

Early in the second half City were reduced to nine. Kavanagh, involved in an off-the-ball incident at a set-piece, was shown the red card, despite the fact that he was the one bleeding from his face. Still the nine men battled on, conceding only one goal in normal time.

Extra-time upped the ante even more. It took a further ten minutes before Gillingham made the vital breakthrough, Onoura's header putting them ahead in the tie. Stoke did not let their heads drop and substitute Paul Connor came agonisingly close to forcing penalties when he hit the inside of the post just before the Gills grabbed their third and clinching goal.

Gillingham went on to beat Wigan 3-2 in the final to earn the right to play in the First Division for the first time in their history. For Stoke, the inevitable talk was of being robbed by a biased referee. True, he had only cautioned one Gillingham player, when a total of four or five may have been more appropriate, but the two dismissals were the result of a loss of cool on Stoke's part. The players had no one to blame but themselves.

LEAGUE DIVISION 2	**2000-01**
Nationwide Division 2	5th (lost in play-offs)
Worthington Cup	4th Round
FA Cup	1st Round

The expectation of promotion led to season ticket sales of 6,000+. A new family area, kitted out with PlayStations for pre-match entertainment, added a further 1,500 family season tickets, although some disquiet arose due to its location – next to the away fans. Former Stoke hero Terry Conroy joined the club full-time as Commercial Executive. His appointment followed the arrival of Jonathan Fuller as Chief Executive, after Jez Moxey moved to Wolves.

Chairman Gunnar Thor Gislason made no bones about the club's ambitions: 'Promotion to the First Division is the main goal for this season and we are firm believers that this goal should be achieved.' Promotion was made all the more pressing by the club's debts, now over £4.5m. Talk centred on the symmetry of Stoke's previous spell in this division, languishing for two seasons before winning promotion in the third, losing in the play-offs and lifting the Auto Windscreens Shield in the middle season. Having replicated the first two years, many believed history would repeat itself.

Yet Stoke's parsimonious board failed to provide significant transfer funds for Thordarson, who would be without striker Peter Thorne for several months, due to a knee injury picked up in the play-off defeat. Arrivals included 34-year-old ex-England left-back Tony Dorigo, who replaced as captain Nicky Mohan, sent off against Akranes during a 'goodwill' pre-season tour of Iceland. Left-footed striker Stefan Thordarson joined from Bayer Uerdingen, and Henrik Risom, a former Danish international midfielder, from Vejle in Denmark, both on frees. Many believed the £200,000 spent on young Torquay centre-back Wayne Thomas would have been better spent on the goalscoring talent of Bristol Rovers' Jamie Cureton, who instead joined rivals Reading.

Thordarson had lined up Icelandic international Rikki Dadason to partner Thorne. Dadason was playing in Norway for Viking Stavager, where he was Norway's second top scorer with fifteen goals and nine assists. He would become available at the end of the Norwegian season unless Stoke paid £120,000 to sign him earlier. The board chose to wait and City fans now had their very own D-Day (Dadason Day) to count down to: 1 November. It was a huge risk, given that Thorne would be out for roughly the same period.

The season got off to a poor start. Lacking strikers, the team predictably lacked goals. And if they did score, Thordarson insisted his players hold what they had. This sent fans apoplectic, as Stoke consistently failed to finish teams off; fingers were bitten to the quick during narrow wins at Wrexham and Wycombe, when City's defence took a battering.

Thordarson's insistence on playing 5-3-2 was based on a belief that Mohan and Thomas were not mobile enough to deal with pacy attackers and needed a third stopper to maintain stability. This infuriated supporters, whose attitude was that, as a team pushing for promotion, Stoke should be making the running, particularly at home. Thordarson's system failed to release the wide players of the back five into attack – veterans Dorigo and Mikael Hansson could not provide the necessary running for a full 90 minutes. Thordarson's tactics, particularly away from home, invited pressure upon the defence, leading to a negative mentality. The frustrated crowd took to chanting '4-4-2' when Stoke lost their way, as they often did, while playing 5-3-2 at home.

Stoke did not reach the play-off places until a good Christmas programme saw them defeat Bury and Bristol City. Despite defeating Premiership Charlton over two legs in the second round of the League Cup, dissent grew amongst the Boothen Enders. The easiest target for the boo-boys was the manager's son, Bjarni Gudjonsson, who suffered unjustified barrages, particularly on occasions when he did not shine, irrespective of other player's failings.

When D-Day arrived, Rikki Dadason burst onto the scene scoring a last-minute winner over First Division Barnsley in the League Cup. But he failed to live up his whirlwind start. As soon as Thorne returned to fitness, it became clear that they were too similar to form an effective pairing. Both were out-and-out goalscorers. Stoke were now so far behind that thoughts of automatic promotion went out of the window. Coupled with the continuing furore over his use of 5-3-2, Thordarson's credibility was mortally damaged.

Stoke teams regularly featured five or six Scandinavians and a joke did the rounds that the next such arrival was a player called 'On-me-head-sson'! While the Norsemen conversed in their native tongues, the three Irishmen – Kavanagh, Clarke and O'Connor – gravitated together, creating the impression of a cliquey dressing room. O'Connor insisted this was not the case: 'To me, it doesn't matter whether someone is white, black or purple, or whether they come from here or the Moon,' but clearly the team was not gelling. Bjarni Gudjonsson gave an insight into a more worrying trait in a newspaper interview: 'Players are nervous and are afraid to make mistakes. We have to get that nervousness out of the dressing room.' Two painful cup defeats in a week, a club record 0-8 home loss to Liverpool in the League Cup and a 0-1 defeat at Conference Nuneaton in the FA Cup, was bad enough. Worse, after defeating

Scarborough, Halifax and Walsall, Stoke lost a much-postponed Auto Windscreens Shield semi-final on a golden goal to Port Vale.

All-season Thordarson continually fell out with his players. In November James O'Connor complained of being 'constantly threatened with being sold'. West Brom bid £750,000 for the Irish Under-21 international, which Stoke seriously considered. In February Clive Clarke demanded a transfer, citing 'a lack of communication with the manager'. Graeme Kavanagh's desire to make the Ireland squad for the 2002 World Cup saw him declare a need for First Division football. A meeting with Thordarson persuaded Kav to see the season out, but his card was marked. In April Nicky Mohan had a training ground bust up with Thordarson; as a result, Mohan walked out on the eve of the crucial game against Walsall.

By February the disputes had spread to the boardroom, where the abrupt Thordarson and the Chairman of Stoke Holding SA, Magnus Kristinsson, clashed. The board questioned Thordarson's judgment on new players for a promotion push, despite offloading striker Paul Connor to Rochdale for £150,000, a club record for the Dale. Thordarson had lost his protected position as broker of the takeover and was now as vulnerable as any manager. He remained phlegmatic: 'Night is always darkest through dawn.'

In an attempt to improve matters Thordarson brought in a sports psychologist. Whether or not by coincidence, City won the game following the first session 3-0 away at Bristol Rovers. The question remained why Thordarson could not elicit this reaction from his players himself. An unbeaten run of fourteen games followed, but City reverted to their inconsistent ways and limped along in fifth place for much of the second half of the season, despite the belated addition of £350,000 Burnley striker Andy Cooke.

Only two players dodged the criticism heading Stoke's way. Record signing Brynjar Gunnarsson, who switched between central defence and midfield, was considered by fans to at least be playing with pride and desire. He netted four in three games as City ended the season with three wins. Also Wayne Thomas's do-or-die attitude won him the Young Player of the Season award.

In March the board introduced a new Stoke badge – a shield with red and white stripes surrounded by sea blue – 'to reflect the Icelandic influence in the club'. In fact, the badge allowed the board to exercise copyright: its predecessor, the City of Stoke-on-Trent crest, did not belong to the club. It made commercial sense, but was introduced without the consultation promised by the setting up of the Fans' Forum. This prompted that body's vocal chairman, Tim Gallimore, to resign, accusing the club of 'undermining the democratic process'.

DID YOU KNOW?

Stoke's fate depended on their final game in each season at the Britannia Stadium from 1997-98 to 2002-03 – with the exception of Brian Little's year in 1998-99.

Stoke earned only eleven points out of the last 30. Bristol City's equally unimpressive form meant Stoke's play-off place was never threatened, while Bournemouth's late run started from too far back. Few fans believed the manager's claim that Stoke would still go up.

Match of the Season 2000-01

Walsall 4 Stoke 2

Play-off, semi-final, 2nd leg, 16 May 2001

Finishing fifth, Stoke again hosted the play-off first leg, but failed to break down Ray Graydon's Walsall. Just as the game was petering out, Walsall's Pedro Matias broke clear. Ben Petty tugged him back, which meant Stoke played the last ten minutes a man short. Walsall piled on the pressure but City held out for a goalless draw.

Walsall were now favourites to reach the Millennium Stadium, where the play-off finals were to be played following Wembley's demolition. At the Bescot Stadium, Thordarson sent out his team to play 5-4-1, with Rikki Dadason at its head, leaving the club's most prolific goalscorer, Peter Thorne, on the bench. Nicky Mohan replaced the suspended Petty, after missing a month following his training ground sulk, while James O'Connor was fielded out of position at right wing-back.

It started well as, after Matias had seen his header come back off the post, Kavanagh lashed home a volley. Dadason then missed a good chance to make it two, firing wide. But, symptomatic of the season, the team self-destructed when defending a single-goal lead away from home. Goalkeeper Gavin Ward, nervous all night, dropped a ball into the net unchallenged from Tom Bennett's corner just before half-time. The clanger changed the face of the game.

Walsall, tails up, tore into Stoke. Within twelve minutes of the restart they had scored three more goals. Matias netted twice, the second after latching onto Thomas's poor back-pass. In between, Dean Keates' free-kick sailed freakishly into Stoke's net. Thorne's belated entry resulted in a goal of scant consolation. The away end all but emptied before the final whistle, while thousands watching on big screens at the Brit left early. The glorious failure of Gillingham was replaced by a much more chilling surrender. History had not repeated itself after all

LEAGUE DIVISION 2	**2001-02**
Nationwide Division 2	5th (promoted in play-offs)
Worthington Cup	1st Round
FA Cup	3rd Round

The fallout after failing to win promotion was of nuclear proportions, with manager Gudjon Thordarson at its epicentre. Rumour had it that the board was split over whether to sack him. Thordarson walked the tightrope, but not the plank, by forcing the issue himself. He offered to alter his contract from its remaining three years to a make-or-break one year. Gudjon announced the deal saying: 'If, at this time next year Stoke City are not in the First Division, I am not going to be here. It's that simple.'

With the club's debt increasing by £30,000 a week, the board opted not to renew the contract of first-team coach Nigel Pearson. David Kevan found himself promoted to fill the position, with Ian Cranson taking over as Academy coach. To aid the club's financial plight, star midfielder Graham Kavanagh joined promotion rivals Cardiff for just under £1 million, sounding off bitter parting shots through the local media in the process. The move seemed slightly strange as he remained in Division Two, foregoing his chance of making the 2002 Irish World Cup squad. Nicky Mohan and Ben Petty joined Hull on frees.

Gudjon brought in several free transfers: Dave Rowson from Aberdeen, Belgian Jurgen Vandeurzen from Turnhout, and Aston Villa reserve keeper Neil Cutler. Stoke also took a risk on former Dutch international winger Peter Hoekstra, out for a year recovering from knee surgery. Belgian right-back Jimmy Smet arrived as cover for Mikael Hansson, whose knee 'went' during a pre-season tour of Austria, but Thordarson eventually chose to convert Wayne Thomas to right-back. The new-look Stoke impressed with a crisp and incisive attacking display in defeating Wacker Berghausen 3-1 in Austria.

Just before the season began Gudjon surprised everyone by placing Bjarni Gudjonsson on the transfer list, citing the abuse he received from a minority of fans as the manager's son as the reason. Bjarni joined on the list James O'Connor, who still had not patched up things with Gudjon.

Thordarson also brought in a new central defensive partnership, spending his entire transfer budget on Sergei Shtaniuk, who arrived from Dinamo Moscow for £200,000. As captain of the Belarus national team, he was a class act, particularly in the air. His partner, Peter Handyside, who joined on a free from Grimsby, took over the club captaincy following Tony Dorigo's retirement. He also took charge of a dressing room committee of senior payers, including Ward, Cooke and Hansson, through which the manager hoped to avoid the disruptions of the previous term.

The injury curse continued and by September Gunnarsson, Dadason, O'Connor and Handyside were crocked. By that time Peter Thorne, who had bagged 80 goals in 172 games in his Stoke career, had also joined Cardiff. He admitted in an article on the club's website that he did not want to leave. Stoke, however, could not afford to reject Cardiff's £1.7 million offer. City fans, including director Phil Rawlins, railed against his sale, while Thordarson went public with his feelings that the rug was being pulled from beneath his feet. The chairman, though, insisted the deal ensured Stoke would make a profit on the season and not have to sell any more players. None of the money from Thorne's sale found its way into Gudjon's hands, so speculation over the imminent arrival of Danny Cadamarteri, Lee Mills or Arnar Gunnlaugsson seemed pointless. Exeter's Christian Roberts guested in a behind-closed-doors friendly, but failed to excite interest.

Just when it seemed as though another disappointing season would ensue, Stoke produced their best display for years to despatch title favourites Reading more comfortably than the 2-0 scoreline suggested. City played smooth, fluid football with Peter Hoekstra, who moved inside to play as a striker, involved in several magical moments. Thorne's departure seemed to have strengthened the resolve among the players, who were keen to prove that they could succeed without him and pocketed 22 points from the next 27. Hoekstra's passing glued Stoke's attack together far more than the predatory goalscoring of Thorne ever had. During the season striker Chris Iwelumo established himself as City's most improved player. At 6ft 3in, his strength lay in the air, but his first touch improved and he began taking chances too. The fans loved him, chanting his name ending with an 'oooooo', which sounded as if he was being booed. This boosted Iwelumo's confidence and he finished as top scorer, albeit with only eleven goals.

Defensively the Handyside and Shtaniuk partnership solidified, earning comparisons with the partnership of Overson and Cranson of a decade earlier. Wayne Thomas adapted well to his new position, but his rash tackling earned him numerous bookings. He ended the season as the second worst disciplined player in the division, behind Swindon's Andy Gurney, and consistently gave away dangerous free-kicks and penalties.

After another in a line of horrendous gaffes cost Stoke a point in the final minute at Brighton, Gavin Ward was dropped. His replacement, Neil Cutler, smashed the club record for minutes played before conceding a goal. It took 453 minutes before Port Vale's Stephen McPhee netted in the first Potteries derby of the season. Having conceded just three goals in ten games, with Stoke boasting the meanest defensive record in the Football League, all the good work went up in smoke as City let in ten in three, including a 1-6 massacre at Wigan.

Encouragingly, the club began to take a strong stand against troublemaking fans. Chief Executive Jonathan Fuller declared that 'anyone convicted of a public order offence at one of our games, home or away, can automatically expect to be given a lengthy ban. In some cases a life ban.' The club's attitude contributed to a much quieter season.

In October, Sir Stanley Matthews was honoured with the erection of a statue behind the Boothen End overlooking the site of the old Victoria Ground. The statue was composed of three figures denoting three stages of Stan's career – youngster, international and veteran.

City lost on penalties to Oldham in the first rounds of the League Cup and – with seven players under the age of 23 – the LDV Vans Trophy 2-3 to Blackpool. The FA Cup, however, traditionally Stoke's Achilles heel, yielded a better return. City defeated Lewes of the Ryman League and bottom of the Third Division Halifax, to earn a home tie with Everton. Stoke had not won consecutive FA Cup-ties since 1987. Many predicted that a Stoke win would see the departure of hounded Toffees boss Walter Smith. Thordarson, however, handed the initiative to Everton by again playing 5-4-1. The Toffees could not believe their luck and cantered to victory. Another opportunity to create a good impression in front of Match of the Day cameras and a huge crowd had gone begging.

The criticism over his tactics, and Stoke's regression into their bad old ways, caused Thordarson to believe the whole world was against him. He grew a beard, which made him look even more dishevelled and wild-eyed than previously. In March his frustration boiled over when he banned the *Sentinel* from speaking to any of the players, accusing the newspaper of having an 'anti-Icelandic agenda'. This was founded on the number of letters criticising both Gudjon and his son which appeared in the letters columns. Many fans, upset at the paper's long-standing apparent pro-Port Vale stance, felt that Gudjon was justified in his outburst and internet polls indicated around 80 per cent were behind him. However, buried beneath the surface, were fears that these were the actions of a man suffering from the pressures of the job.

Injuries bit deep and, at one stage in January, Stoke were without the services of ten players, while Mikael Hansson's long-term knee injury ended the Swede's career at the age of 34. Peter Handyside's return was cut short after a freak accident while chasing his daughter around the living room. Thordarson finally ended his hunt for a striker when he signed Guinea international Souleymane Oulare from Las Palmas. Oulare appeared once as a substitute and then suffered a life-threatening blood clot. Thordarson made two more permanent signings. Icelandic international defender Petur Marteinsson arrived from Stabaek IF in Norway, while goalkeeper Jani Viander cost £150,000 from HJK Helsinki, where he had played Champions League football. To spend that much money seemed odd, as Cutler was in the midst of a run of good form. Viander would actually never play for Stoke's first team.

The collapse of ITV Digital in the spring of 2002 hailed the start of a new era in football with clubs suddenly finding a hole in their income which left many struggling for survival. Stoke, though, having tightened the purse strings considerably over the previous two seasons, were less affected than were others.

Thordarson bade goodbye to any thoughts of automatic promotion after stuttering City self-destructed in losing at Brentford at Easter. The on-loan Gunnlaugsson got himself sent off for kicking an opponent and the Bees' winner came after a comedy of errors in the Stoke defence. City stuttered into a play-off position, and in-form Cardiff posed a barrier which few thought the Potters could overcome. The players, though, produced a stirring display to overturn a first leg deficit to reach the Millennium Stadium (see Match of the Season).

City's players were on a high and expected to rid the Millennium Stadium of its now-renowned hoodoo. Despite the attentions of a feng shui expert and Welsh artist Andrew Vicari, who painted a mural to defeat the 'bad spirits', it could not be denied that the previous twelve cup finals and play-offs had been won by the team occupying the North Stand and dressing room. Stoke had been allocated the South.

But on a beautiful, sunlit May afternoon Stoke totally outplayed Steve Coppell's Brentford during the first half. First the unmarked Deon Burton forced home a corner. Then Gudjonsson fired a low free-kick into the box and Brentford striker Ben Burgess sliced the ball into his own net. City coasted the second half, restricting Brentford to long-range efforts which rarely troubled Cutler. But the celebrations at the final whistle, though long and raucous, were tempered by the thought that Stoke had effectively gained promotion through playing well for barely one and a half games. Nevertheless, surely now Thordarson could count on some support and investment from the board.

DID YOU KNOW?

Millwall's Neil Harris scored the quickest ever goal at the Britannia Stadium, when he netted after just 20 seconds on 21 October 2000. Stoke pulled back to win 3-2.

Match of the Season 2001-02

Cardiff 0 Stoke 2

Play-off, semi-final, 2nd leg, 1 May 2002

Fifth-placed Stoke hosted fourth-placed Cardiff in the semi-final first leg. The portents were bad. The Bluebirds, under controversial chairman Sam Hammam and featuring former Stokies Kavanagh and Thorne, had won ten of their last thirteen league games, drawing the other three. Cardiff had led 2-0 at the Brit, through Robert Earnshaw and Leo Fortune-West. Manager Lennie Lawrence then replaced Earnshaw and Thorne with defenders, while Thordarson threw on loan striker Deon Burton, who netted a vital goal with six minutes left. Cardiff still entered the second leg as heavy favourites, but now only one goal would put Stoke back on level terms.

Given the history of trouble between the two sets of supporters, the police restricted the number of travelling Stoke fans to 700. The game was tight and tense. On-loan Tony Dinning tested Alexander in the Bluebirds' goal, while Cutler twice denied Thorne. As the game wore on, Cardiff fell back seeking to keep a clean sheet, presenting the initiative to Stoke. City's only clear-cut chance fell to Iwelumo, who skied from five yards with the goal gaping. With the tannoy announcer in the process of asking Cardiff fans to keep off the pitch when the celebrations began, Clive Clarke from the left crossed for Gudjonsson to nod back into the centre of the box. O'Connor arrived at pace to slide home an injury-time equaliser.

As away goals don't count double in play-offs, extra-time was necessary. City were now in the ascendancy. The rattled Bluebirds played for penalties. Spencer Prior gave away an innocuous free-kick 22 yards out. O'Connor's effort deflected into the bottom right-hand corner off Souleymane Oulare's backside. It would be his only goal for the club, sparking what has been described by those fans present as the best 'mental' in living memory.

To complete a dismal night for Cardiff, Prior earned a second yellow card after pursuing the referee to protest about the free-kick award. Cardiff's defeat left ex-Stokies Kavanagh and Thorne with the unenviable record of having lost in the play-off semi-final for three seasons running. Stoke had finally produced the grit and determination to win through.

LEAGUE DIVISION 1	**2002-03**
Nationwide Division 1	21st
Worthington Cup	2nd Round
FA Cup	5th Round

On Wednesday, 15 May 2002, three days after Stoke's play-off final victory over Brentford, the club issued a statement: 'Whilst the Board recognise the contribution of Gudjon Thordarson in helping the club to promotion it is felt that the long-term interests of the club will be best served by the appointment of a new manager. The working relationship between the Board and the current manager is untenable. The manager has not always appreciated the financial constraints within which he has had to work and it is felt by the Board that this situation is unlikely to improve especially given the uncertainty regarding future income from TV rights.'

The shock and timing of the announcement caused consternation. The majority of fans felt that as Thordarson had won the club, an admittedly overdue, promotion, he should be allowed a crack at Division One.

Thordarson, distinctly unamused by this turn of events, immediately mobilised his band of protesters, making numerous press appearances looking a haggard and drawn victim. While a sizeable demonstration of supporters outside the Brit demanded Thordarson's reinstatement, the Stoke board identified his successor. Steve Cotterill had brought Cheltenham through three promotions in five years, winning the Third Division play-off final that May. Highly rated in FA circles, Cotterill was studying for his UEFA 'A' coaching licence. It was a brave move to appoint a new, inexperienced manager while simultaneously asking the team to adapt to a higher division. This was particularly so as Cotterill would neither have funds to work with nor his own choice of backroom team: financial restrictions tied the club's hands to existing contracts.

Despite Stoke revealing a profit for the first time since 1988, with turnover up around £2 millon to £7,873,404, salaries amounted to £5,371,000. To ease the wage bill, goalkeeper Gavin Ward joined Walsall, while Dadason signed for Lillestrom. Stefan Thordarson and Oulare had their contracts cancelled. The only summer arrival saw John Rudge, Director of Football, sign prolific Mansfield striker Chris Greenacre during the interregnum between managers. Thus Stoke started the season with a squad depleted by the departures of the loan players who had bolstered the squad through the play-offs. To continue the theme of the previous campaign, Greenacre injured an ankle in a pre-season friendly against West Brom and did not make an appearance until mid-October.

DID YOU KNOW?

Steve Cotterill's 13-game spell in charge does not make him the shortest-serving full-time Stoke manager. In 1923 player-manager Jock Rutherford lasted 10 games.

The price hikes which accompanied Stoke's return to Division One meant attendance levels dropped. Even though the loss of ITV Digital income hit Stoke less hard than many others, director Phil Rawlins saw his chance to acquire a controlling interest in the club. He made two offers to the Icelandic consortium in August, both of which were refused. Tit-for-tat recriminations through the local media followed. At one stage, Chairman Gislason used the club's own website to call for the resignation of Rawlins and his boardroom partners, Coates and Humphries.

Cotterill swept away the festering ill-feeling which had dominated Thordarson's reign. James O'Connor came off the transfer list, while Bjarni Gudjonsson decided, after a trial at German club MSV Duisburg, that he wanted to stay at Stoke and fight for his place. City got off to a less than auspicious start, winning just three of their first twelve games and residing in lower mid-table. The team's lack of goals was symbolised by the absence of a player sporting the No 9 shirt. City also lost to Third Division Bury in the League Cup first round.

Though the situation had been made clear when he took the job, the lack of funds proved too much for Cotterill, who went from diplomatically biting his tongue to pithy comments bemoaning his lot. On 10 October Cotterill announced his resignation after just five months in charge. It soon emerged that he was joining the Premiership's bottom club Sunderland as assistant manager.

Cotterill was vilified for swanning off after just thirteen games in charge, earning the sobriquet 'Quitterill'. There was some hilarity too at his choice of destination. Realistically, Sunderland stood little chance of avoiding the drop and, as number two to the fossilised Howard Wilkinson, Cotterill could only hope he would be groomed for the manager's role at the Stadium of Light.

Peter Taylor, Peter Reid, Lou Macari and Bryan Robson featured heavily as candidates in Stoke fans' internet votes and in media speculation. It looked as if George Burley, whose seven-year reign at Ipswich had recently ended, would become Stoke's new boss, but, after watching the home defeat by Watford, he chose not to accept the position. The next morning the board rushed out their second choice as manager, former Gillingham, Bristol City and Portsmouth boss Tony Pulis. Pulis's appointment did not go down well with many fans who recalled that he had, in the summer of

1999, turned down the Stoke job. Pulis had been out of football for three years, mostly due to his proliferation of court cases. Both former employers Gillingham and Portsmouth had filed claims against him, though Pulis had won each time. His teams were also known for their no-nonsense, physical approach. This may have been exactly what the club needed at this point, as City were being out-muscled on a regular basis.

While the hunt for a manager unravelled over the weeks, the team, under coach David Kevan, capsized on the pitch. Eight successive defeats turned into a run of sixteen games without a win. Looking demoralised, rudderless and out of their depth, a 1-2 home defeat by lowly Grimsby on 9 November sent Stoke into the bottom three for the first time. City developed an alarming fallibility at corner-kicks, while keeper Neil Cutler conceded a number of goals at his near post. With morale rock-bottom, things got tetchy on the pitch. O'Connor and Shtaniuk featured amongst the most cautioned players in the division. Shtaniuk then handed in a transfer request with eighteen months left on his contract. Rumours linked him with a move into the Premiership with either Southampton or Fulham, but the truth proved to be that he sought a move back to Russia, having failed to settle in the UK.

Pulis began to rebuild the team in a slow and methodical manner, starting with the players' faith in themselves. However, it took time to elicit solid 90-minute performances. At both Portsmouth and Leicester, the division's top two sides, Stoke were the better side in the first half, but then found themselves under heavy pressure. City at least held on for a point at Leicester's new Walker's Stadium. An FA Cup run saw Stoke earn a cash windfall from a plumb home fifth round tie with star-studded Chelsea. City performed admirably in a 0-2 defeat.

Outcry greeted the revelation that one of the bidders for neighbours Port Vale – a club, like so many others, now in financial administration – was Stoke's parent company, Stoke Holdings. Despite Chairman Gunnar Thor Gislason's vehement denials, the speculation that Stoke wanted to sell Vale's ground, pocket the cash and close the club down spread like wildfire. After three weeks of rumour and counter-rumour Vale's administrators chose a supporter-based consortium, Valiant 2001, as their preferred bidder, despite Stoke's cash bid being allegedly higher.

In an attempt to curb the continuing hooligan problem, in February the club initiated a scheme to force City's own travelling supporters to carry ID cards. The size of Stoke's travelling support dropped massively, forcing the team to fight against yet more odds. The new measure had the desired effect, though, ending away-day problems and keeping the unwanted Burberry Buffoons, as they were christened by law-abiding fans, away from grounds to which Stoke travelled.

Stoke pulled themselves away from the abyss with two wins over the Christmas period, but the season's blackest moment arrived in a 0-6 thrashing at high-flying Nottingham Forest. Manager Pulis and captain Handyside were visibly shaken by experiencing the worst defeats of either's career. The hammering, though painful at the time, proved a turning point in City's season.

Pulis perked up the the dressing room by bringing in several experienced pros on loan. Marcus Hall, Lee Mills, Paul Warhurst, Ade Akinbiyi, and goalkeeper Mark Crossley added a touch of swagger to the squad and livened things up during training. Crossley, still in the Welsh national squad though relegated to third choice at Middlesbrough, proved to be Pulis's ace in the pack. City's defence had lacked leadership and direction. Crossley soon had them organised and, suddenly, what had been the worst defence in the division had become the best, conceding just three goals in nine games. Crossley also pulled off a series of stunning saves, which earned Stoke numerous points. Much of the team's improvement came after Pulis altered tactics away from home. He signed Mark Williams, a Northern Irish international central defender, on a short-term contract from Wimbledon. Williams played as one of three central defenders as Stoke opted to play for a draw away from home. It worked. Stoke drew 0-0 at Ipswich and Wolves, while sneaking wins at Watford and Coventry. A run of one defeat in the final eight home games boosted survival hopes, while the news of the dismissal of Cotterill and Wilkinson from Sunderland brought a wry smile to many a Stokie's lips.

It proved to be just as well that Stoke's performances improved, as their three foes in the mini-league of four, which intensified at the foot of the table, also had good runs. Favourites to reach safety were Steve Coppell's Brighton, who had recovered from a club record thirteen successive defeats early in the season to overtake Stoke, Grimsby and Sheffield Wednesday. City, however, defeated Brighton at the Brit and two wins over Easter pulled Stoke clear of the pack by six points with two games left. Stoke needed a solitary point to secure survival. Having stoutly defended for 80 minutes at Crystal Palace, Stoke collectively went to sleep to allow Dele Adebola, so often City's tormentor over the years, to clip in a quickly-taken free-kick. The news that Brighton had beaten Norwich 4-0 merely added to the gloom. The only question now remained whether Pulis could raise the players' spirits to produce a display to defeat high-flying Reading. Much depended on the result.

Match of the Season 2002-03

Stoke 1 Reading 0

Division 1, 4 May 2003

Stoke's task was simple. One point would ensure safety. The 1.30pm kick-off allowed Sky's audience to see Stoke and Brighton, who visited already doomed Grimsby, vie for Division One safety.

Alan Pardew's Reading had already secured fourth place in their first season back in Division One. Unlike Stoke and Brighton, the Royals had adapted to the step up and had a worryingly good away record. They were not, however, high scorers, basing their success on sound defence and playing on the break, with the likes of Nicky Forster and Jamie Cureton offering pace and penetration. Pulis reverted to four at the back, swapping Lewis Neal with Mark Williams to make up the four-man midfield. Ade Akinbiyi shook off his groin strain to take Cooke's place in attack, although he only expected to last for an hour or so.

In blinding sunlight Stoke began eagerly. Early chances fell to Greenacre, whose weak efforts failed to trouble Royals' American keeper Marcus Hahnemann. Lewis Neal also had a shot saved. The crowd began premature celebrations after learning that Grimsby had taken an early lead at Blundell Park. As the half wore on Reading took advantage of Stoke's inability to string passes together to gradually claim superiority in terms of possession.

Despite the news that Brighton had equalised, after half-time Stoke began to press Reading back. On 55 minutes O'Connor won a crunching tackle on the left and released Neal into space. His cross found Ade Akinbiyi, who flicked home on the run. The ground erupted. Akinbiyi celebrated in trademark fashion by ripping off his shirt to reveal his muscular physique into Sky TV's Steadicam. The fact that Brighton had now taken the lead had little relevance.

Stoke relaxed, possibly a little too much. Crossley's weak clearance fell directly to Nicky Shorey, who fired inches wide. Steve Sidwell grazed the top of the crossbar from 25 yards. Hoekstra produced a moment of magic wide on the touchline when a deft flick off his left instep left Graeme Murty grounded. But his cross, scuffed behind the onrushing Stoke forwards, summed up Stoke's season – occasional excellence, but overwhelmed by the grim.

Reading conserved energy for the play-offs and eventually Brighton were pegged back. Pulis and his players had pulled off a feat which had seemed implausible in the dark days following the mauling at Nottingham Forest.

LEAGUE DIVISION 1	**2003-04**
Nationwide Division 1	11th
Carling Cup	2nd Round
FA Cup	3rd Round

Having somehow survived the previous season, Tony Pulis cleared out the deadwood, giving free transfers to Peter Handyside (Barnsley), Brynjar Gunnarsson (Forest), Andy Cooke (Busan Icons, South Korea), Bjarni Gudjonsson (Bochum) and Petur Marteinsson (Hammarby). Loanees Ade Akinbiyi and Mark Crossley returned to their clubs, after Pulis had tried to sign both. The one player all Stokies were sad to see leave was giant centre-half Sergei Shtaniuk, who returned to Russia to sign for Shinnik Yaroslavl.

Attracting players to a side which has just avoided relegation to the third tier is a difficult trick. On the eve of the new campaign Stoke could not even make up a full match-day squad. Bookies had the Potters as certs for the drop. Then Pulis signed midfielders Keith Andrews, on loan from Wolves, John Eustace from Coventry on a free, and all-action Darel Russell from Norwich for £125,000. They joined a new free-transfer strike-force of Gifton Noel-Williams from Watford and Carl Asaba from Sheffield United. The big-name addition was Dutch international goalkeeper Ed de Goey, having been released by Chelsea. The former Dutch national keeper, with 31 caps, added stability to a makeshift back four, which lacked a commanding centre-half. The answer was not provided by another of Pulis's early-season signings, 30-year-old Paul Williams, another 'free'. Williams was experienced, having spent eight years in the Premiership at Coventry and then Southampton, but he had neither the personality nor the legs to play the necessary role. He was also becoming error-prone, as exemplified by his poor clearance at the Hawthorns in September, which ended Stoke's 15-year unbeaten league record against the Baggies.

Stoke rampaged to a 3-0 opening-day victory at Derby, with counter-attacking football that slayed the Rams. The following week Stoke sat atop the nascent league table after Wayne Thomas's last-minute header toppled Wimbledon. It was something of a false dawn – there were no wins in the next five games – but it was clear Stoke had enough to steer clear of a relegation battle.

Pulis began to make crucial additions. Last season's hero Ade Akinbiyi signed permanently from Palace on a free transfer, becoming Stoke's best paid player in the process. He and Gifton Noel-Williams formed a bulldozing strike partnership. Noel-Williams had a deft touch and was also good in the air. He would become injury prone, but made a good initial impression and, when paired with

Akinbiyi, they were a sight to behold. Akinbiyi would prove to be a cult hero. His all-action style saw him chase every lost cause. The problem was that his pace and strength were not matched by his finishing. Akinbiyi scored ten goals in 30 games but wasted countless one-on-one chances.

Where Pulis struggled was filling the left-sided midfield berth. Too often the skilful Peter Hoekstra was unavailable through injury. Pulis was reluctant to over-expose starlet Kris Commons, which grated supporters. Pulis preferred more experienced players, such as Asaba and Greenacre playing out of position. Neither grumbled, but it was clearly not ideal as both were goalscorers rather than wide midfielders.

Pulis solved the central defensive conundrum by 'borrowing' right-back John Halls from Arsenal, moving Wayne Thomas to the centre. While Thomas proved the dominant stopper City needed, albeit still prone to the odd rush of blood, Halls was a classy attacking full-back, linking play and providing good crosses.

Initially Pulis partnered Thomas with another combative defender, Clint Hill, who had joined from Oldham for £120,000 after deterring other would-be buyers with his poor injury record. Indeed Hill began the campaign injured, having broken his leg whilst playing for the Latics in December 2002, and only started nine games all season. He would spend much of his Stoke career in the treatment room, mostly because he was a gritty performer who would throw himself bodily in front of shots.

Thomas only found a permanent partner when Pulis made an inspired signing in December – warhorse Gerry Taggart, loaned from Leicester. The Northern Ireland defender brought stability to the defence with his command and organisational abilities. He was undoubtedly the most important signing of the season. Taggart's debut brought Stoke their first victory at high-flying West Ham for 30 years. Another loanee, young Frazer Richardson, scored his first Stoke goal as City escaped from their incessant goalmouth siege.

That result sparked an unbeaten league run of seven wins and two draws. At home to Reading, winger Peter Hoekstra rolled back the years to produce one of the great individual Stoke displays of the modern era with a hat-trick. His first goal saw him race onto Noel-Williams's pass to stroke the ball home. He then lashed in from the edge of the area, and completed his hat-trick with a cheeky chipped penalty after being pushed over by Nicky Shorey. That proved to be Hoekstra's last hurrah in a Stoke shirt as the injuries finally took their toll. The Dutchman announced his retirement at the end of the season, departing to a huge ovation in the final game against Gillingham.

DID YOU KNOW?

Johan Boskamp won the Belgian Golden Shoe in 1975 for the best footballer in the Jupiler League, as voted by reporters and experts from Het Laatste Nieuws.

That winning run, which saw Noel-Williams and Asaba grab vital goals, gave central midfielder John Eustace the chance to shine. The 24-year-old son of former Sheffield Wednesday midfielder Peter had suffered a bad knee injury in 2001 while at Coventry, but he seemed now to be fully recovered, producing neat and incisive passing, harassing defenders and prompting mistakes by opposing defences. Akinbiyi was by now easily the most popular Stoke player since the heyday of striker Mark Stein, with supporters wearing dreadlocked wigs and performing mock bows whilst screaming 'Ade, Ade, Ade!' each time Akinbiyi scored.

The cups once again proved disappointing, with Stoke going out of the League Cup at home to Gillingham and the third round of the FA Cup in a home replay to Wimbledon. Those defeats left many feeling that Pulis preferred league safety to chasing cup glory. Indeed, by the time Stoke visited Crystal Palace in February ambitions were harboured of a play-off spot, but Iain Dowie's team were themselves charging up the table (see Match of the Season).

Despite a further five-match unbeaten run, Stoke could not squeeze into the play-off picture. Pulis prepared for a proper tilt at promotion the following season by trying different combinations. City only conceded eleven goals in their final 15 games.

One option was utilising left-sided Clive Clarke in central midfield. The captain responded well and scored the winner at Sheffield United, City's first win there since December 1985. Clarke's displays saw him called into Brian Kerr's Republic of Ireland squad, and he made his international debut against Nigeria in May 2004, earning a second cap against Jamaica the following month.

With nothing to play for, youngsters were also given their chance. Commons, Gareth Owen, Andy Wilkinson, and Lewis Neal played against already-promoted West Brom, following the Britannia's first postponed game (caused by high winds). City won 4-1. A season without a fraught ending made for an unusual change, but Stoke had established themselves in the second tier.

In the summer it was announced that Tony Pulis had signed a rolling contract, which seemed to reveal discontent between manager and board regarding Pulis's bullish refusal to sign foreign players or overplay the club's budding stars. Many fans shared the board's frustrations in these regards. At this stage it was not a major issue, but it would become so over the coming campaign.

Match of the Season 2003-04

Crystal Palace 6 Stoke 3

Division 1, 14 February 2005

Stoke were on a storming mid-season run of seven wins from eight games and sights were set on the play-offs. Iain Dowie's Palace were also rampaging up the table, having won four successive matches when the sides met at a sunny Selhurst Park on Valentine's Day.

Palace had in-form striker Andy Johnson spearheading their attack and he began the game like a whirlwind. Clive Clarke had already headed an early effort off the line when Johnson raced onto Hudson's through ball to hammer high into the net. Within a minute Jon Eustace had rammed home a low free-kick, but parity would only last three minutes.

For years Stoke's bête noire had been referee Rob Styles, who did not shrink from more controversial decisions in this game. Styles awarded two penalties against Stoke, one debatable, the other outrageous. First, Paul Williams's challenge on Julian Gray was deemed a foul, even though Gray carried on before falling over of his own accord. Then, Johnson collided with Williams and the referee pointed to the spot. Johnson dispatched both spot-kicks to complete a first-half hat-trick.

Stoke got themselves back into contention when Clive Clarke rifled in a shot from the edge of the box. With only seconds remaining before half-time, City should have shut up shop, ready to regroup. But Palace's Michael Hughes, a veteran Northern Ireland international, raced down the pitch, beat three players and forced his way past the last defender to beat De Goey – 4-2.

After the break, Styles failed to spot Tony Popovic's handball, which would have put the Potters back into the game. Ade Akinbiyi, back on his old stomping ground and ridiculed by the home support, wasted two good opportunities when clean through. It obviously wasn't Stoke's day and Shipperley headed in Hughes's cross at the far post to make it 5-2 on 55 minutes.

Stoke did finally win a penalty when Commons was felled by Popovic, although it was another iffy decision. Asaba lashed in the spot-kick, but once again Palace responded by piling forward. Wayne Routledge pirouetted on the ball to beat De Goey with a cross shot – a superb goal to end a superb match.

6-3 made this the highest scoring match involving a Stoke team since the 5-4 home victory over Barnsley in October 1993, and the highest scoring ever of Tony Pulis's managerial career.

CHAMPIONSHIP	**2004-05**
Coca-Cola Championship	12th
Carling Cup	1st Round
FA Cup	3rd Round

With Stoke City re-established in the newly named Championship, the time seemed right for the Icelandic owners to invest in the team. Reaching the Premiership had always been their stated intention, but the net results of Pulis's numerous enquiries, bids and counter offers over the summer were scant indeed.

Pulis did attract a dynamic young goalkeeper – Steve Simonsen from Everton. The 25-year-old joined on a free, having been a record signing for a British teenager at £3.3 million when moving from Tranmere in 1998. Simonsen became de Goey's number two, replacing Neil Cutler, who joined Stockport.

The other notable arrival was dynamic midfielder Dave Brammer from Crewe. A former Port Vale star, who had often given Stoke headaches in the past, Brammer would prove a solid, capable performer, but not one who inspired Stoke fans with either his passing or shooting. He became a first choice, however, as John Eustace's injury problems recurred. This time it was a lower back injury. Eustace started just two games all season and made a handful of substitute appearances when attempting premature comebacks. He clearly wasn't ready, however.

The reason for the paucity of summer arrivals was never truly made clear. Was Pulis's budget restricted? Did the Icelandic owners truly believe in the manager? Were they committed to attempting to propel Stoke up the league? Had their money run out?

One man who would not stick around was starlet Kris Commons, who left to join his boyhood club Nottingham Forest, claiming publicly that they were more ambitious than Stoke. Forest would be relegated, however, and when the blond winger returned to the Britannia he limped off injured to howls of derision.

This was the first full season of the new transfer window, imposed by FIFA, which meant clubs could only permanently sign players from other clubs in July, August, and January. Players who were free agents could still be signed at any time. This innovation led to Sky Sports News ramping up the hype of potential big moves, with correspondents camped outside windswept football grounds and cameras poking into any car passing by. Stoke were hardly on the radar, so many Stokies resorted to hitting the 'Refresh' button on their computers for news of hoped-for arrivals. By 1 September, it was obvious that true ambition was lacking and that mid-table medicocrity was the best that could be expected.

DID YOU KNOW?

Carl Hoefkens, the Belgian international defender brought in by Johan Boskamp in 2005, can speak five languages – Dutch, English, French, German and Italian.

Against expectations, Stoke began the season well with a 2-1 win over Wolves, newly relegated from the Premier League, in the glare of Sky TV's cameras. A 1-2 defeat at Oldham in the League Cup aside, for which Pulis sent out a weak team, City survived August unbeaten with four wins and two draws, going top on Bank Holiday Monday when Marcus Hall's injury-time volley defeated Derby. But as the season settled down it soon became obvious that Stoke – – now that Hoekstra and Commons had departed – lacked quality.

City's battling qualities were not in doubt, though, and the team hit the top again following victory over Ipswich (see Match of the Season). However, Stoke's lack of goals brought just two wins in thirteen games. The defence stayed strong, and a bizarre sequence of 17 games saw only one goal scored for or against Stoke. Fans cottoned on to these 'binary' results, knowing any first goal would win the game. Bookies, slow to respond, were taken to the cleaners because there were only three possible outcomes – 1-0, 0-1 or 0-0.

The term 'binary football' was also applied derisorily to Stoke's style. Ever the pragmatist, Pulis set up his team in military fashion. Four sturdy defenders snuffed out opposing attacks, Russell ran the engine in midfield alongside two defensively-minded flank players, while Brammer propelled balls into channels for Akinbiyi to hare after, nod down, and head for goal. It wasn't pretty and was designed to keep games tight, as Pulis knew he lacked the firepower to outscore teams in an open game. But these tactics were effective in garnering enough points to keep Stoke in mid-table.

City hardly conceded any goals. During a run of 22 league games City let in just 13. Steve Simonsen replaced Ed de Goey in goal, initially due to a recurring thigh injury the bearded Dutchman could not shake off, but eventually on merit.

With another old campaigner, Gerry Taggart, often out injured, Pulis shrewdly recruited Michael Duberry from Leeds to plug the gap. The former Chelsea centre-half was still a quality player, especially at this level, despite being the wrong side of 30. Following Leeds' relegation from the Premiership they needed to get their high wage-earners off the books. Duberry eventually signed permanently for Stoke on a free transfer on a far lower deal than he would have enjoyed at Elland Road.

The one exception to the binary scores was an FA Cup visit to Arsenal. The Premiership champions had only recently lost their long unbeaten record, but Stoke, backed by 5,000 fans at the Clock End in Highbury's final season, scored first when Thomas prodded in after Akinbiyi's header was palmed out by Lehmann. Arsène Wenger had selected a mixture of invincibles and youngsters, such as Fabregas, Reyes, Senderos and van Persie, and after the break Arsenal restored normality with two goals.

In the league, normal service was resumed with four more one-goal games, but the dam finally burst on Tuesday, 22 February. Leicester were the visitors and, in a snowstorm, a cracking match featured a strike from 25 yards by Dave Brammer and one of the misses of the season from Leicester's David Connolly, who skied from two yards with the goal gaping. That kept the score 3-2 in Stoke's favour, which was how it ended.

Despite the drudgery and jokes at City's expense, Stoke retained an outside chance of the play-offs. Victory at high-flying Wigan and 2-0 home wins over Brighton and Sheffield United seemed to offer hope, but a 1-2 loss at lowly Gillingham was followed by a last-gasp equalizer for Wolves at Molineux. When doomed Rotherham nicked a 2-1 victory at the Brit, all hopes were extinguished.

The players seemed to lose heart, and no wonder. Off-field ructions had been bubbling away for months. Akinbiyi thought he had been promised a new deal and, frustrated at the club's inaction, staged a sit-down protest in the office of Director of Football John Rudge. The club responded by selling the player to Burnley for £600,000, a deal which upset Pulis.

The sale came so late that Pulis was unable to replace his star striker, but not for the want of trying. Rob Hulse, out of favour at West Brom, was courted, with a £1.2 million fee agreed between the clubs. Hulse even attended a game at the Brit but signed instead for Leeds. West Ham's Bobby Zamora also refused sign, although Stoke successfully avoided making a public show of their failure to land a major target.

Indeed, Pulis's only permanent January signing was young defender Lewis Buxton from Portsmouth. Shorn of a new frontline striker, Pulis brought in loanees to fill the hole next to Gifton Noel-Williams – ex-England international Michael Ricketts from Leeds, who was a flop, and unknown beanpole Kenwyne Jones from Southampton. Jones was a hit, scoring three goals in 13 games. His goals were celebrated by a flamboyant somersault and his time at Stoke propelled him into the limelight. In time he would sign for Roy Keane's Premiership Sunderland for £6 million.

With promotion out of the window, the season subsided into a mush of more 'binary' play and rumours about Pulis's future. It was obvious that tensions were mounting between board and manager and so it surprised everyone when, before the final home game, it was announced that Pulis had extended his contract again. Yet once more City seized calamity from the jaws of progress when the tension which had been building all season burst into the open.

Match of the Season 2004-05

Stoke 3 Ipswich 2

Championship, 14 September 2004

Ipswich, under Joe Royle, had just been relegated from the Premiership. They had graced the UEFA Cup and still boasted players such as Jim Magilton, Darren Bent and Jason De Vos in the spine of their team. They were now the early leaders of the division.

Stoke came into this midweek fixture in third position, having just lost their first match, 0-3 at Preston. A 23,000 crowd turned out to watch this attractive match and the teams didn't disappoint.

Ipswich's passing game held sway early on, while Stoke played their usual pressure game and looked for mistakes and set pieces. From one of these Noel-Williams headed against the bar. Richard Naylor handled a through ball bound for Akinbiyi, but referee Mike Dean only booked the player for handball, rather than show red for denying a goalscoring opportunity. The home fans howled.

Strangely, it was Ipswich who netted from a set piece when Westlake crossed and De Vos headed in. Within three minutes Thomas had headed home Clarke's inswinging corner and the sides went into the break level at 1-1.

Stoke began the second half the better. Noel-Williams once again hit the bar with a header, but Ipswich broke away and Bent squared for Westlake to slot in easily. City responded. Substitute Steve Guppy curled a cross onto Thomas's head for the burly defender to plant a second header into the net – 2-2.

The tension increased as the minutes ticked away. City picked up three needless bookings – for Clarke, Akinbiyi and right-back John Halls. That was to prove costly as Halls committed a second reckless tackle on Fabian Wilnis and was dismissed with eight minutes remaining.

After play had been held up following a clash of heads between Noel-Williams and De Vos, Taggart took a long free-kick which, with the Ipswich captain still off the pitch, sowed confusion. The ball bounced over the onrushing Davis, leaving Akinbiyi to net the winning goal in front of a delighted Boothen End.

Ipswich would finish third, two points off automatic promotion, but lost the play-off semi-final to eventually promoted West Ham.

4

RESURRECTION MEN 2005-2009

CHAMPIONSHIP	**2005-06**
Championship	13th
Carling Cup	1st Round
FA Cup	5th Round

On 28 June 2005, weeks after Tony Pulis had signed a new contract, he was sacked for 'failing to exploit the foreign transfer market'. Many supporters believed that Chairman Magnus Kristensson, who rarely attended Stoke games, simply wanted a change of scenery.

Pulis bemoaned having to manage with his hands tied behind his back, but his brand of negative, 'binary' football had few admirers. Something had to give, and as ever in these situations, it was the manager who moved on, in Pulis's case, to Plymouth following Bobby Williamson's sacking.

The day following Pulis's dismissal, his successor was named as Johan Boskamp, an affable, if slightly barmy Dutchman, who had a high opinion of himself, and a 'crazy' sense of humour – in one interview he was asked for a secret about himself, to which he replied: 'I'm really a woman!'

Boskamp had been a midfielder of renown, part of Holland's 1978 World Cup squad. He had managed a string of clubs, including Belgian side Anderlecht, where he twice won the League title. He had also been in charge of the Georgian national team and in the Gulf, although he had not stayed for long.

Boskamp was given the kind of money denied to Pulis. He made English-looking signings, including ex-Gillingham striker Mamady Sidibe, who had been wooed by Pulis. A Mali international, 25-year-old Sidibe was 6ft 5ins: his presence leant itself more to Pulis than the flowing football promised by Boskamp. Nor was Sidibe a natural goalscorer – just ten goals in 106 games for the Gills.

Other English arrivals were defender Marlon Broomes (Preston), swapped with Lewis Neal, and winger Luke Chadwick (West Ham), initially on loan. None were thought to be typical Boskamp targets.

DID YOU KNOW?

Luke Chadwick's goal against Walsall in January 2006 was voted 'Goal of the FA Cup Fourth Round'.

Foreign spice was added by the arrival of midfielders Junior and Martin Kolar from Anderlecht on season-long loans, and Belgian international defender Carl Hoefkens from Germinal Beerschot.

Departures included captain Clive Clarke to West Ham for £275,000 (heart trouble would later end his career). Noel-Williams joined Burnley, teaming up with Akinbiyi and a host of other ex-Stokies under ex-manager Steve Cotterill.

Boskamp's era began, improbably, with four red cards in six games, two of them for Stoke. His 4-5-1 formation, with Sidibe as spearhead, in time showed signs of good attacking football. The Potters took Norwich apart 3-1, but in the next home game subsided 0-3 to Watford. Stoke missed chances before capitulating at the back amid poor organisation and individual mistakes.

Boskamp promised to deliver a striking hero to the fans who, needing to believe in their new manager, bought into Boskamp's pronouncements. Hannes Sigurdsson arrived from Viking FK in Norway, but the Icelandic international would only score once in 29 games. Next came Paul Gallagher, on loan from Blackburn, who stayed all season and ended as top scorer with twelve goals. He was a livewire, if lightweight, forward, but Boskamp often put him on the left wing, from where he could cause danger by cutting in.

Finally, amid much fanfare, came Guinea international Sammy Bangoura from Standard Liege for a club record fee of £900,000. The bejewelled Bangoura scored eight goals in his first nine starts. This meant City outscored their opponents more often than not which, when defending kamikaze-style, was a necessity. Stoke won at Crewe, Coventry and Sheffield Wednesday, and staged a terrific fight-back live on Sky TV against Leicester to secure a 3-2 victory. That game saw Stoke rise to sixth in a congested table, and a 3-2 win at Luton lifted City up to fifth.

Several factors combined to scupper Boskamp's plans. Firstly, his ace scorer flew off for the African Cup of Nations in Egypt in January. When Guinea qualified for the quarter-finals, it meant City would lose Bangoura's services for at least another week. Guinea lost 2-3 to Senegal, but that was not the end of the drama for Stokies, following the tournament on BBC. Bangoura was due back by 8 February, in good time to prepare for the visit to Cardiff. However he failed to turn up, refused to reveal his whereabouts, and was fined two weeks wages. When he did return it was as a different player. Perhaps he was scared of Boskamp's threat to kill him, jokingly delivered in a newspaper. Whatever, his form dipped and he scored only once more in the entire campaign. Not only that, Bangoura was arrested upon re-entering the UK for attempting to smuggle another African into the country. He was eventually released and all charges dropped – all a big misunderstanding.

Meanwhile, it had become evident that while Hoefkens was a talented defender, he was not suited to facing the kind of physical attackers who haunt the Championship. Hoefkens' pirouette and drag-back against Sheffield Wednesday to earn a penalty in the opening game had made him an instant hit. Added to which, he wore an Alice-band, had dark curly locks and a stunning girlfriend. He was the glamour and the glitz that fans were told would change the face of Stoke City. However, he was also a wimp. His forte was to bomb forward, ball at his feet: he couldn't win headers against bruising centre-forwards, unlike Gerry Taggart, who was struggling towards retirement, ravaged by knee injuries.

Despite this, Boskamp insisted on using Hoefkens in central defence, rather than at right-back, until February. By that stage City had slumped to 16th. The more combative Clint Hill was put in the middle of defence to help out new captain Michael Duberry, while Hoefkens was a revelation as swash-buckling right-back and would win the Player of the Season award.

The final negative factor was that Boskamp, first-team coach Jan de Koning, and Director of Football John Rudge, had not been on speaking terms for months. The stand-off dated back to Stoke's trip to Coventry in November, when City had conceded yet another early goal. Rudge was in the stands and communicated a tactical change via a note to the bench, which was passed on without consulting the manager. Stoke turned the game around to win 2-1. Boskamp, however, was furious, threatened to quit, and fuelled a dreadful atmosphere. That this was kept quiet for so long in this modern age of internet gossip seemed extraordinary, but when the news broke there was uproar. At Boskamp's insistence, Rudge was placed on 'gardening leave': 'I'm not Adolf Hitler,' said Boskamp, 'but Jan knows I won't work with him again. When the players told me what had happened I knew what I had to do or I would have lost all their respect.' Boskamp then instructed the board to either sack Rudge and de Koning or himself. It was the kind of ultimatum which shreds any team spirit and heralded a run of 15 games with just two wins. Thankfully, City already had enough points to avoid relegation worries, even though home defeats by Palace, Southampton and Coventry ensured Stoke finished with a home record showing eleven defeats and a goal-difference of minus 8.

But then came the hammer blow. The Icelandic board, who had always overseen affairs from afar, put the club up for sale, even though its value had nose-dived. Boskamp also took to making wild pronouncements, and it was obvious he was going. His final match in charge, against Brighton, saw young Adam Rooney become the youngest scorer of a hat-trick in Stoke's history.

Boskamp resurfaced briefly at Standard Liege. John Rudge returned to bring some stability, as the club teetered on the brink.

Match of the Season 2005-06

Luton 2 Stoke 3

Championship, 17 December 2005

Before Christmas Stoke travelled to muddy Kenilworth Road on the back of five wins in seven games. The sides were level on 34 points. City had beaten Mike Newell's promoted Hatters at the Brit back in August, but now started without talisman Bangoura, who was out through suspension, playing Paul Gallagher behind Sidibe.

Luton drew first blood when Kevin Nicholls crossed down the right. Stoke's defence left the ball to each other and Ahmet Brkovic nipped in to score. On half-time Stoke broke away through Luke Chadwick. Sidibe was sent clear, beat stand-in keeper Dean Brill, and pulled the ball back for Gallagher to net.

After the break Buxton and Underwood traded long-range efforts and Steve Howard, Luton's towering striker, headed against the bar. Then, with seven minutes remaining, Stoke struck with Sidibe once again crossing for Gallagher to score. Luton roused themselves immediately. Nicholls picked himself up after being felled by Henry to score the penalty himself.

The pitch, which had cut up badly, played its part in the final drama. A Stoke corner was cleared in injury-time and the ball was played back to the edge of the box. As the ball was played back in, the Luton defence rushed out, except for Chris Coyne, who raced back with Sidibe. In beating the Mali striker to the bobbling ball, Coyne also clipped it past his own goalkeeper, who had raced from goal to snuff out the danger. The goal sealed Stoke's seventh away win before Christmas, but was only Luton's second home defeat.

The result proved to be the zenith of Boskamp's reign, as Stoke took over fifth position from Luton. That would be the high-point of the season and it was all downhill from here. Boskamp had already fallen out with Rudge and de Koning, and the Icelanders would put the club up for sale before the end of the season. The very future of Stoke City was once again in the balance.

CHAMPIONSHIP	**2006-07**
Championship	8th
Carling Cup	1st Round
FA Cup	4th Round

The summer of 2006 was a time of turmoil as the Icelanders sought an escape route. Despite oil-rich sheikhs and billionaire Americans snapping up Premier League clubs, the attractions of this most working-class club, with debts of £10 million, were hard to identify.

The one person keen on buying was the man who had sold the club in the first place, Peter Coates. This complicated negotiations, as personal animosities and egos had to be circumvented. Despite being 68, Coates was determined to right the wrongs inflicted during his previous chairmanship, which had seen the club sink down the divisions. The issue of 'golden shares', put in place for himself and fellow director Keith Humphreys when selling the club to the Icelanders, still rankled. Now, re-purchasing the club on 23 May 2006, Coates paid just £1.7 million, plus a further £3.3 million to effectively cancel the Icelandic debts. Stoke City was back in British, and importantly, local hands.

Coates, aware that there were bridges to rebuild, embarked upon a charm offensive. He struck most fans as sincere in his aspirations for the club, and was now more financially capable than during his earlier spell in charge. In the intervening years Coates had built his online betting company Bet365 into a huge enterprise, and had sold all his high street shops for £40 million.

The downside came in the form of the new manager Coates was determined to appoint. Indeed, that manager was not new at all. Tony Pulis was brought back from his sojourn at Plymouth, and a special relationship between chairman and manager was born. Yet Pulis's return did not go down well with everyone. The takeover had split City fans into five camps: those grateful to see the back of the Icelanders and happy to throw in their lot with the new regime; those who hated Coates and Pulis being back in charge, but prepared to forgive and forget; those who hated Coates but tolerated Pulis; those who derided Pulis's football but could tolerate Coates; and finally those who loathed both men.

More reflective souls noted both men were now in very different situations – with Coates having pots of cash for Pulis to spend – although it was also true that success rarely visits any returning manager, at any level. The furore was amplified by the innovations of radio phone-ins and internet messageboards. They are forums for moaning and speculation by the uninformed, and often degenerate into swear-fests. They serve the fabulous purpose of keeping fans involved round the clock. The Oatcake's messageboard lit up with threats of mass demonstrations or worse at the return of Coates and Pulis, and when City won just one of the first ten league games – and also lost at home to ten-man Darlington in the League Cup – the rebels sniffed blood. One idiot proposed a mass red-card protest at the Preston game, when Stoke were one place above the relegation zone, but the idea was 'shouted down' online.

A fiery Meet The Manager event chaired by BBC Radio Stoke commentator Nigel Johnson in Delilah's bar saw Pulis squirm under the bombardment, but he kept his counsel, choosing, rightly, to do his talking on the pitch.

Initial results had prompted unfavourable comparisons with that final 'binary' season. Pulis had inherited a much-changed squad, and younger players had been given experience that he had denied them. Pulis had also signed centre-half Danny Higginbotham from Southampton for £225,000, striker Ricardo Fuller for £500,000 – who had spent much of the preceding season injured – and Vincent Pericard from Plymouth on a free transfer. He also brought back assistant manager David Kemp.

Stoke's opener at Southend saw a contentious winning penalty, two players hospitalised, and a hatful of chances missed. It was just like under Boskamp. Pulis took two months to get a grip. Having done so, he held a pivotal meeting with his chairman preceding the visit of Preston which changed the course of the season. In view of the transfer window, Coates and Pulis decided to plunder the loan market, focusing on disaffected Premier League players. It paid rich dividends. Aston Villa's Lee Hendrie and Patrick Berger were the first to arrive, and they would be joined by Gabriel Zakuani (Fulham), Jonathan Fortune (Charlton), and Lee Martin (Manchester United). Former starlet Andy Griffin returned from Portsmouth. The full-back had gained Champions League experience with Newcastle but had fallen out of favour under Harry Redknapp at Fratton Park. Finally, Rory Delap and Liam Lawrence arrived from Sunderland, where they had failed to impress Roy Keane. Both would become Stoke heroes, though Delap broke a leg in his second game, ironically against Sunderland. The injection of these players remoulded the team, and began the transformation that would culminate in promotion 18 months later.

Stoke's form showed an immediate upturn. Leeds were thrashed 4-0 away, and Hendrie led the fight-back against Sunderland after a half-time deficit. By Christmas Stoke had nudged into the play-off positions. The success was built as much on a solid defence as on the burgeoning strike partnership of Fuller and Sidibe. Indeed, after losing at Leicester in late October, keeper Steve Simonsen kept seven clean sheets and did not concede again until the second minute at Layer Road, a total of 658 minutes – a club record.

It was Griffin's rocket against Coventry at a befogged Britannia which launched Stoke on that run. By the time they dislodged Dave Jones's Cardiff 3-0 in late November, Stoke lay sixth. Despite December defeats by Colchester and Sheffield Wednesday, City were only four points behind second-placed Preston.

Two league wins in the next ten games (with City also bowing out of the FA Cup at Premier League Fulham), sank Stoke into mid-table. Victory at Derby renewed hopes. At West Brom, Ricardo Fuller's pace created all three goals, one for himself. Fuller laid on the second for new partner Jon Parkin, from Hull. Nicknamed the Beast, Parkin was a chunky centre-forward in the old-fashioned mould. He had character, though, and fitted into Stoke's system. Two days after the win over the Baggies, Parkin swivelled to slam the ball past Gabor Kiraly in the Crystal Palace goal to set up a 2-1 Easter win.

Now only four games remained and the play-offs were in sight. Three play-off spots were up for grabs, as Sunderland, Birmingham and Derby were guaranteed the top three positions. At Cardiff, Stoke took an early lead when Hoefkens lashed home. Near the end the Potters broke away, Fuller squared the ball to tyro striker Martin Paterson, who shot wide. To complete a bad dream, Stoke's rearguard failed in the last minute when Cardiff's Michael Chopra smashed in a loose ball. The following Saturday Stoke conceded another last-gasp equalizer, this time at home to Hull, as City fell back and back, inviting their opponents on. Nicky Barmby's devastating goal meant three points had turned to one for the second weekend in succession.

Despite a 3-1 win over Colchester in the penultimate game, those two late goals had changed everything. Those dropped four points would have guaranteed the play-offs. Now Stoke went into the final game, at QPR, in seventh position. They had an identical goal-difference as Southampton in sixth, but had scored far fewer goals. City had to better Southampton's result to climb above them. However, the scenario was more complex than that. Stoke were a point behind West Brom and Wolves, and one ahead of Preston. Five clubs were vying for three spots.

At Loftus Road, Simonsen was beaten at his near post by Martin Rowlands' sixth-minute free-kick. Lee Martin hit Rangers' post. But when news emerged that West Brom, Wolves and Preston were all winning, the game looked up. Sidibe's late equaliser meant Stoke finished eighth. That disappointment would prove to be the springboard for the incredible scenes that awaited twelve months ahead.

DID YOU KNOW?

Ricardo Fuller's nickname at Crystal Palace was 'Glass Knees'. He failed medicals on his knees at Leeds, Sunderland and Portsmouth before arriving at Stoke.

Match of the Season 2006-07

West Brom 1 Stoke 3

Championship, 7 April 2007

This vital game on Easter Saturday took Stoke to Tony Mowbray's West Brom. Having beaten Leicester 4-2 the previous weekend to climb to ninth, City were brimming with confidence. Pulis brought in Matteo for the more attack-minded Lee Martin, while Hoefkens moved into midfield to replace the injured Darel Russell.

West Brom began to play their passing football, but soon realised that in Stoke they had met a team with resilience and a rapier thrust in attack. City sat back and soaked up Albion's possession, then got the ball forward quickly, where Ricardo Fuller caused havoc. From one such foray, Fuller pressured Sam Sodje into skying a clearance. While Sodje peered around for the ball, Fuller hared off to meet it on the bounce and steer it past Kiely.

Within eight minutes City scored twice more, carbon-copy goals, other than the actual scorer. Fuller sped down the left, past defenders, before crossing. Albion skipper Jonathan Greening prodded the first into the net. Minutes later Jon Parkin joyfully rifled home on the run from near the penalty spot.

Stoke's devastating spell had killed the game, supporters renting the air with Johnny Cash's 'Ring of Fire'. For the rest of the match the Potters played keep-ball, to the joyous and ironic shouts of the 4,000 travelling fans. They had spent years being taunted by Baggies fans that all Stoke did was 'hoof'. Well, now City were three goals to the good on enemy territory, controlling the game to such an extent that, despite making three half-time substitutions, Mowbray's men could not make much impression on Stoke's massed defence. Ellington hit the bar, and Albion did eventually pull one goal back when Jason Koumas's speculative shot deflected up off Higginbotham and flew over the scrambling Simonsen. It was far too little, far too late.

The comprehensive victory served notice that Stoke would be gunning for one of the three play-off places available over the last five games. Late goals and defensive lapses cost Stoke dear, as they drew three and only won two of those matches to miss out agonisingly on the final day of the season.

CHAMPIONSHIP	**2007-08**
Championship	2nd (promoted)
Carling Cup	1st Round
FA Cup	3rd Round

Having nudged the play-off positions, Tony Pulis had the backing of his chairman to invest. Jon Parkin, having spent part of 2006-07 on loan and become something of a cult figure, signed from Hull for £275,000, rising to £450,000 with add-ons. Pulis plucked 6ft 1in centre-half Ryan Shawcross on loan from Manchester United reserves. Young Shawcross began the season partnering Clint Hill, after Player of the Season Danny Higginbotham signed for Premiership Sunderland for an initial £2.5 million. Higginbotham was a class act and Shawcross was stepping into very big shoes.

Right-back was a problem: Andy Griffin opted to sign for Premiership Derby, while Carl Hoefkens, who had fallen out with Pulis for reasons never revealed, went to West Brom. Pulis acquired Stephen Wright (Sunderland) on loan, along with Jody Craddock (Wolves) and Gabriel Zakuani (Fulham). Goalkeeper Russell Hoult joined from West Brom, where an indiscreet video had surfaced on the internet. Tony Pulis's last-chance saloon for waifs and strays had some more inmates.

Richard Cresswell signed from Leeds on a free. Despite having nearly 100 goals from 275 games, he found himself mostly utilised in left-midfield, where he became a victim of supporter barracking. Much of it was unfair, as Cresswell's duties were more defensive than offensive and he still netted eleven goals. But Stoke fans do like a homegrown villain, and Cresswell was certainly limited in his abilities, no matter how hard he tried.

With a settled team, buttressed by loanees, Stoke began well. At Cardiff, Simonsen's wonder save from a Steve Maclean penalty secured a 1-0 win, and victory on Sky Sports over Charlton saw City with a rapid six points on the board.

The Championship had become ultra competitive. What it lacked in quality it made up for with excitement and unpredictability. This season would be one of the tightest ever, with clubs at the bottom shooting up the table, and vice versa. Early leaders Watford and Bristol City were reeled in, and Hull and Crystal Palace, ninth and 20th at the end of November, both reached the play-offs.

Stoke suffered a poor autumn run and were tenth at that same juncture. Home defeats by Sheffield Wednesday and Coventry led to terrace grumblings. Pulis held his nerve, signing loanee Leon Cort, a recipient of the man-management skills of new Palace boss Neil Warnock, who told Cort (Palace's Player of the Season) that as he hadn't been booked in 150 games he was not his kind of defender! Cort was not everyone's cup of tea. On his debut in that defeat by Coventry, he was given the runaround by a player who so often proved Stoke's nemesis, Dele Adebola.

When Cort settled down he formed a solid partnership with Shawcross. At 6ft 3ins, Cort also proved crucial to a tactical innovation which would take the footballing world by surprise over the next year or so. Rory Delap had become something of a forgotten man since shattering his leg on his home debut the previous October. What no one realised when the 30-year-old signed permanently in January 2007 was his prodigious throwing ability – 50 yards into the enemy goalmouth, which created havoc. The key to 'the Delapidator' was keeping the trajectory flat, rather than the looping long throw which was more easily defended. The ball would arrive quickly and just above head-height, perfect for flick-ons to the far post or directly into the net. Cort and Shawcross benefited by netting nine and eight goals respectively from Rory's howitzers and the more traditional corners.

Remarkably, none of Delap's previous managers had spotted that talent. Pulis, who liked to pack his team with giants in any case, spotted an ideal weapon, not least because of the fear induced in opposing defences. Once word got around, Stoke pinned their opponents into their six-yard box whenever the ball went out of play near halfway, and the crowd transformed each throw into a mini-drama by winding up the tension.

While goals flowed regularly from the long throw, a more traditional source was also proving fruitful. Fuller and Sidibe had gelled in attack, and even fans' villain Richard Cresswell was weighing in with his share of goals, scoring in successive victories over QPR, Norwich and Sheffield United. Fuller netted five in two games, including a blistering hat-trick against West Brom.

For many observers, the 2007-08 promotion battle was contested between two contrasting styles. West Brom, under the dour Tony Mowbray, played fluid, passing football, while Stoke, to their detractors, merely lumped the ball forward and played percentage, set-piece football. While true in general, it overlooked Stoke's other attributes – not least a mental strength not seen since the heyday of the early 1970s. Stoke came from behind to win six games this season, more than any other club. West Brom, meanwhile, had a porous defence, disguised by their ability to outscore the opposition. That approach was the antithesis of Pulis's. When the teams squared up at the Brit before Christmas, Stoke ripped Albion apart. Fuller's was the first City hat-trick at the Britannia Stadium since Peter Thorne's against Bury in 2000.

DID YOU KNOW?

In October 2007 Mamady Sidibe escaped with his life when playing for Mali in Togo. During a crowd riot, Sidibe was knocked unconscious and stabbed in his right arm.

That result left Stoke fourth, three points behind leaders Watford, who were on the wane. A run of victories would have carried Stoke clear: instead five draws followed, the first of which came on Boxing Day, 3-3 at Barnsley, where Liam Lawrence's hat-trick meant consecutive Stoke trebles for the first time since 1957.

Lawrence would prove to be the Potters' star over the campaign, earning the Coca-Cola Championship Actim Index Player of the Season. Making the right-midfield slot his own, Lawrence – who had signed permanently from Sunderland in January 2007 for £500,000 – finished as top scorer with 15 goals.

The Times rich list showed Chairman Peter Coates' fortune had risen to £200 million. This gave Stokies hope for the January transfer window. In fact, Stoke broke the club transfer record twice, both for central defenders – Ryan Shawcross (£1 million) and Leon Cort (£1.2 million). True, both players were already at the club, but it was another marker laid down by the chairman to let everyone know the strength of his ambitions. A third arrival was midfielder Glenn Whelan, signed from Sheffield Wednesday for £500,000. The Republic of Ireland 'B' international had the guile to complement the physical hulks around him. Arguably, Stoke needed another striker, too, but Pulis kept faith with what he had.

On the field, January was below par, aside from a first live appearance on the BBC, when Stoke held Sam Allardyce's Newcastle 0-0 in the FA Cup. In the league, Stoke won just once, but that 3-1 victory over Preston was followed by a 0-1 loss at fellow challengers Charlton.

February, though, proved more fruitful. Five consecutive victories propelled City to the top of the table. The biggest crowd of the season so far, 23,563, saw Stoke defeat rivals Ipswich 1-0, thanks to a 30-yard half-volley by Liam Lawrence. Stoke were now on 62 points, two ahead of the pack. Twelve games now remained, during which almost all the contenders embarked on unexpected climbs or slumps. West Brom fared the best, coping with a run to the FA Cup semi-final, while working their way to the top of the pack with five games remaining. Bristol City and Watford were both crumbling, but the biggest surprise of all was Phil Brown's Hull, who won six of their last eight matches.

Premiership fever gripped the Potteries as Stoke ground out result after result to keep pace with West Brom. The Brit finally felt like home, packed to the rafters with rowdy supporters for the last home games. One fan rang Radio Stoke's *Praise and Grumble* and left a whole poem on their ansaphone. An enterprising producer put the piece to music and aired it the following weekend. It became a Potteries and Youtube sensation, complete with Holst's rousing background from *The Planets*. The anonymous poet called himself 'Pottermouth', and here is a taster:

'This is a call to the men in red and white, a heart felt battle cry,
As you enter the crucial fight, a final inspiration to lead you into war
A chance to remind you of what you're fighting for
'Cause as you reach for the Premier League, as you sweat blood and tears
You carry us all on your backs all our hopes and fears
So do it for the Potteries, do it for all of us
Do it for Josiah Wedgwood, and for a PMT bus
Do it for Nigel Johnson, do it for Sir Stan
Do it for singing toddlers and for my old man
Do it for Trentham Gardens, Do it for Mow Cop
Do it for Pat McGarry and his paper shop
Do it for Wrights Pies, do it for oatcakes
Take us to the Prem, whatever it takes.'

Stoke began their run in by stumbling 0-2 at Preston and 0-3 at QPR, where Andy Griffin was wrongly dismissed by referee Andy D'Urso and had his suspension revoked. That hiccup prompted Pulis to take on-loan goalkeeper Carlo Nash to replace Steve Simonsen for the last ten matches. Simonsen had admittedly made errors, but could consider himself unlucky to be miss out on what was to come. However, Pulis was ruthless at the right time, tweaking his side to achieve the specific task of automatic promotion.

Four draws in five games followed, the other bringing victory at Norwich, where Sidibe made the first of two crucial interventions. His looping header from another Delap throw was followed in mid-April by both goals in the crucial 2-1 home victory over Bristol City. Sidibe had been another player picked on by the boo boys, but he was a vital cog in Stoke's team, his height making him a fearsome proposition, not to mention his neat footwork.

Sidibe's brace against the Robins was timely. The game had been selected for Sky, so kicked off when other matches had finished. Hull had lost at Sheffield United, so three points against Bristol City left Stoke needing four more from two remaining games.

Stokies travelled to Layer Road for the penultimate game, with one ear on Hull v Crystal Palace. Relegated Colchester bowed out of their decrepit home of 101 years by surrendering a scrappy winner to Richard Cresswell. Stoke would have been up, there and then, but for Ian Ashbee's late winner for Hull. Now the Potters needed one more point, at home to Leicester.

The Foxes were facing the dreaded drop to the third tier for the first time ever. Manager Ian Holloway and Pulis were old buddies from Bristol Rovers, but on Sunday, 4 May 2009, that was forgotten. Leicester created the better chances and launched a late barrage as results elsewhere went against them. Hull's defeat at Ipswich meant Stoke were up, and would have gone up even had Leicester won. Instead, the Foxes slunk off to contemplate their fate.

The following day Stoke players toured the Potteries on an open-top promotion bus. It was all reminiscent of the 1972 League Cup celebrations, bringing tears to the eyes of grown men.

Match of the Season 2007-08

Coventry 1 Stoke 2

Championship, 12 April 2008

One win in eight games, with four to play. It looked like being one win in nine for Stoke as Chris Coleman's Coventry pinned them back. Kevin Thornton hit Stoke's bar with an early header before Coventry took the lead. Dickinson fouled Thornton in a scramble and Elliott Ward lashed in the penalty. Stoke were lucky to be just one goal behind as referee Uriah Rennie brought the half to a close.

Whatever Pulis said in that dressing room sealed his reputation as a manager who can change a game. Fuller tested Kasper Schmeichel with a low drive before being tripped in the box. Fuller picked himself up to strike the penalty low to the keeper's left. Midway through the half Pulis gambled by sending on Liam Lawrence, despite his iffy groin, which had seen him miss the defeat by Palace. The workaholic midfielder made an immediate impact with a free-kick which was half-cleared.

Eleven minutes from time Richard Cresswell was put through, but was tackled on the edge of the area. The ball rolled across the box and, with Schmeichel having emerged to close down Cresswell, Lawrence nipped in to smash it home. The Republic of Ireland international celebrated by ripping his shirt off and precipitated a tumult amongst the City fans. Stoke held on for a vital three points which took them back to the summit of the table, a point ahead of both West Brom and Bristol City, although the Baggies had a game in hand. The win also maintained their unbeaten record at Coventry's Ricoh Arena, having won two and drawn one of their matches at the Sky Blues' new home.

PREMIER LEAGUE	**2008-09**
Premier League	12th
Carling Cup	Quarter-finals
FA Cup	3rd Round

The summer of 2008 was one of the most exciting in living memory for Stoke fans. Half of all teams promoted to the Premier League had been immediately relegated, so sights were set on staying up!

The new arrivals began with ginger striker Dave Kitson, for an eye-watering £5.5 million from relegated Reading. Kitson could only thrive with service from midfield and the wings, so perhaps Pulis would adopt more expansive tactics. Central defender Ibrahima Sonko (£2 million) also signed from Reading, while £3 million midfielder Seyi Olofinjana joined from Wolves. Danish international goalkeeper Thomas Sorenson arrived on a free transfer from Aston Villa, and was perhaps the most vital signing of all.

In the finals hours of the transfer window Pulis re-signed Danny Higginbotham from Sunderland and took on three starlets from Championship clubs – midfielder Michael Tonge (Sheffield United, £2 million), flank player Tom Soares (Crystal Palace, £1.25 million) and defender Andrew Davies (Southampton, fee undisclosed). Pulis also recruited Gerry Francis to his backroom staff.

The Britannia was given a much-needed revamp. To meet the requirements of the Premier League, Stoke also had to install a new media suite and have LCD replay screens fitted into the press box. In mid-season a giant screen was erected in the empty corner between the family stand and the south stand to offer instant replays and in-game text voting for fans' player of the match. It also spoiled the fun of those cheapskates who gathered to watch City from the bank behind the gap.

At last the curtain rose. At Bolton, City wilted in the first half, conceded three times, and their eventual 1-3 defeat encouraged bookies PaddyPower to pay out on all bets laid on City to be relegated. Such ludicrous behaviour only inspired Pulis and his players. Martin O'Neill's Aston Villa arrived to play incisive football, but three times Stoke scored and only twice could Villa equalise. Ricardo Fuller's strike was voted *Match of the Day's* goal of the month, yet it was Rory Delap's injury-time throw in which changed the face of Stoke's season. Mamady Sidibe's head guided the ball into the far corner. Not only did that win the game, it transmitted the threat of the 'Delap-idator' to all corners of the globe.

The long throw was debated *ad nauseam*. Was it legitimate? Was it football? Sky's Hawkeye analysts even measured velocity, angle, and target range. The bottom line was that it soiled the pants of visiting defences. Spurs keeper Heurelho Gomes knocked out team-mates in his desperation to clear the ball, while Hull keeper Boaz Myhill preferred to concede a corner rather than a throw. Yet Stoke only scored nine goals directly from the tactic all season.

The other vital factor in Stoke's armoury was the vociferous support of sell-out crowds. When City put Spurs to the sword in October, the noise exceeded 100 decibels, the highest in the Premier League. Later in the season, it peaked at 122 decibels.

Of all the giants liable to come unstuck at fortress Britannia, Arsenal were particularly vulnerable. Stoke won 2-1, both goals coming from Delap's long throws. Arsène Wenger complained that City had bullied his team out of the game, citing a 'tackle' on Emanuel Adebayor which referee Rob Styles did not see as a foul, and a trip by Delap on Theo Walcott which brought a yellow card, but saw the winger dislocate his shoulder as he fell awkwardly. In fact, the only player red-carded was Arsenal's van Persie for flattening Sorenson.

A surge to the League Cup quarter-finals was ended by a last-minute home defeat by Derby. That set off a poor sequence in the league – including bad losses at Manchester United, 0-5, and Blackburn, 0-3 – which left Stoke in 14th position. The tensions surfaced at West Ham, when Ricardo Fuller and Andy Griffin came to blows on the field. Referee Mike Jones was obliged to dismiss the Jamaican, who then missed three games suspended. In the event, it was Griffin, not the aggressor Fuller, who was marginalised afterwards, though that had more to do with the 30-year-old's exposed limitations as a top flight full-back.

Pulis chose Andy Wilkinson ahead of Griffin, but the youngster's lunge on Cristiano Ronaldo at the Brit on Boxing Day, which earned a second yellow card, was rash and costly. Up to that moment, Manchester United had seldom looked like breaching the City rearguard. Tevez's late winner was priceless to United.

Wilkinson, though, learned quickly and became one of Stoke's most consistent performers. Indeed City's consistency was based on the solid defence of which Wilkinson became a key part, alongside Ryan Shawcross, who sprouted from 6ft 1in to 6ft 4ins over the season. Danny Higginbotham was dependable at left-back, but the fulcrum of Stoke's defence was man-mountain Abdoulaye Faye. He had signed in August from Newcastle with little fanfare, but it was a masterstroke by Pulis. Faye, unrelated to countryman Amdy Faye, who confusingly joined Stoke on the same day (from Charlton), combined brute force and calm authority to organise City's defence into a miserly unit. 'Abdoulaye, my Lord, Abdoulaye' to the tune of Kum-Bay-Yah, sang the fans. Player of the Season? Who else?

DID YOU KNOW?

Andy Wilkinson and former Port Vale player Chris Birchall used to own Zenn nightclub in Hanley, Stoke-on-Trent, which closed in July 2008.

The January transfer window saw Pulis capture England striker James Beattie from Sheffield United for £3.5 million. Beattie was needed because Kitson had flopped – no goals in 16 games. Kitson was eventually sent back on loan to Reading.

Beattie exploded onto the Stoke scene, netting seven goals in 15 games. More important than the goals were the points they earned. On his remarkable home debut, he headed the only goal as Stoke defeated the multi-billionaires of Manchester City. Beattie's brace earned a point against Portsmouth, and he opened the scoring as Stoke beat Bolton 2-0. He also scored in victories at West Brom and over Wigan at the Brit, as Stoke's surging run carried them clear of the relegation zone.

The other January arrival was £2 million left-winger Matthew Etherington from West Ham. Etherington linked well with Beattie, supplying the final pass for several of his goals. He was also a reformed gambling addict, who had fallen out of favour at Upton Park. Pulis once again welcomed this stray into his flock.

Pulis had assembled a squad full of players of character, who would not wilt, who relished the battles ahead of them and who, as it transpired, were good enough not just to keep their heads above the relegation waters, but to push into mid-table. Indeed, over the second half of the season City were not outplayed by anyone, bar, arguably, FA Cup finalists Everton, and Arsenal on the final day, at the Emirates. In January, Stoke held leaders Liverpool to a second 0-0 draw, this time at the Brit, when Delap hit the underside of the bar from five yards. City then led until the 88th minute at Chelsea, but conceded twice to lose the game in gut-wrenching fashion. A second-string team exited the FA Cup, embarrassingly, 0-2 at Hartlepool, but Pulis did not appear bothered.

The crunch came with four spring fixtures, each of them against other threatened teams. First, Middlesbrough were beaten in a tense game in which Stoke's strength overcame Gareth Southgate's lightweights. Boro didn't have a shot on goal.

At that stage, however, City still hadn't won away. Indeed, Stoke's last top-flight win on the road had come at Luton in May 1984, and so far this season they had nicked just four away draws. A visit to rock-bottom West Brom offered the ideal chance to put that right. The fortunes of the two clubs had mirrored each other's for a prolonged period, even though their styles and ethos clashed.

The Baggies were prone to defensive howlers, which manager Tony Mowbray dismissed as part and parcel of playing open football. In the main, his supporters backed him, but when Fuller outwitted Shelton Martis and fired under keeper Scott Carson to give Stoke a first-minute lead, that backing was put under strain. Beattie added a second after more errors in the Albion defence allowed him to shoot home from twelve yards. It cemented Stoke's sixth win in seven games over West Brom.

Stoke were on a roll. Those two wins were followed by a home draw with struggling Newcastle, under new manager Alan Shearer, and a victory over Blackburn, who had been rescued from a parlous position by Sam Allardyce. When the final whistle sounded, Stoke had racked up ten points from four games and were effectively safe. Abdoulaye Faye raced around the perimeter, wildly clapping and celebrating, rousing the fans into a frenzy.

Safety was mathematically assured when Stoke won 2-1 at the KC Stadium, leaving fellow promoted Hull in the relegation mire, although they would survive on the final day. Pulis's side were now looking up rather than down, which could earn them extra millions in Premier League prize money, not to mention the ability to attract quality players over the summer. Victory over Steve Bruce's Wigan saw the clubs swap places, leaving Stoke eleventh, although defeat at Arsenal on the final day saw the positions revert. Even so, twelfth place was a huge triumph. Before the Wigan game, PaddyPower – the bookmaker who had paid out on City to be relegated after the first match – handed out free ice creams to Stoke fans and took out full-page adverts to say sorry.

Reflecting what had transpired, many fans were as stunned as they were elated – for the second summer in succession. The turn-around since the return of Coates and Pulis to a moribund club was extraordinary. Stoke City had been completely resurrected. The feelgood factor led many local businesses to report their highest productivity levels for decades, despite the recession biting deep into every area of the economy. Football seemed inured to the credit crunch and Stoke were in as good a shape as any, given their chair-men's continuing wealth accumulation.

Stoke would spend the summer of 2009 seeking only the necessary additional quality, offloading deadwood, and fighting off bids for their better players. It was all a long way from the two ignominious relegations which had visited the club in 1985 and 1998. Supporters have tried to avoid the Premier League arrogance which visits so many clubs who survive in it for a couple of seasons, then sink without a trace. The question was, would this be the peak of this glorious era, or just a stepping stone in an even greater story?

Match of the Season 2008-09

Stoke 1 Manchester C 0

Premier League, 31 January 2009

Stoke's Premier League odyssey stood on the cusp in late January 2009. The Potters had gone nine games without a win (ten if we count the FA Cup debacle at Hartlepool). Defeat at Tottenham on 27 January had left Stoke one off the bottom, denied that embarrassment on goal-difference by West Brom.

Manchester City had been bought by the mega-rich Abu Dhabi United Group and Investment Development Co in September 2008 for over £200 million. This had brought untold riches to the club and seen the arrival of Brazilian star Robinho from Real Madrid for a British record transfer fee of £32.5 million. The January transfer window had already seen manager Mark Hughes buy striker Craig Bellamy from West Ham for £10 million, plus offer a cheeky bid for AC Milan's World Player of the Year, Kaka. Even without Kaka, Hughes's team was packed with internationals.

The game kicked off at 12.45pm for Sky TV and, as is often the case with early starts, took a while to get going. Fuller was restored to Stoke's starting line up after his scrap with Griffin at Upton Park and injected much-needed pace. It was the first time he and new signing James Beattie had played together.

The defining moment came when Etherington was chopped down, two-footed, by Shaun Wright-Phillips. Referee Martin Atkinson didn't see it, which prompted Delap to take matters into his own hands, felling Wright-Phillips from behind in the expectation of a booking. But Delap compounded matters by getting to his feet, belting the ball into the winger's face from close range, then bending over him, wagging his finger. An inevitable red card ensued. Wright-Phillips stayed on, although he was also later suspended for three games by an FA video disciplinary committee.

Partly because of injury time for a clash of heads between Nigel de Jong and Amdy Faye, the first half had seven minutes added on, at the end of which Etherington crossed for Beattie to head in.

After the break the visitors dominated possession, but Robinho was a nonentity against Stoke's ten men, who ran themselves into the ground. Indeed, Beattie had the best chance of the second half, firing just over after controlling Wilkinson's clearance. Remarkably, inspired by the tumult of support teaming down from the stands, Stoke clung on and celebrated wildly at the final whistle.

The win moved Stoke up five places to 16th. But it was the result which altered the course of their season.

Barry Siddall claims the ball at Southampton's 'The Dell' as City clinch a rare away point (March 1985)

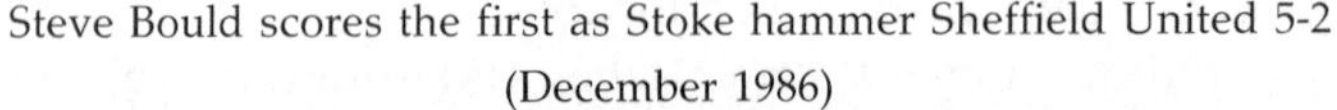

Steve Bould scores the first as Stoke hammer Sheffield United 5-2 (December 1986)

Gary Hackett takes on Sunderland's Reuben Agboola (March 1989)

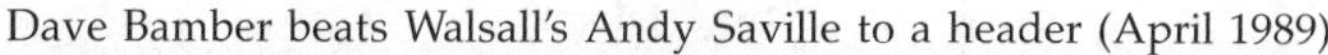

Dave Bamber beats Walsall's Andy Saville to a header (April 1989)

Darren Boughey shoots wide with Blackburn keeper Terry Gennoe looking on (April 1990)

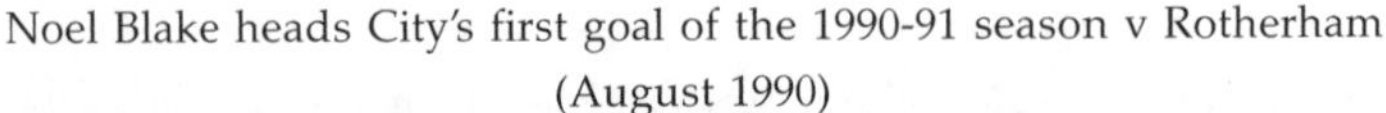
Noel Blake heads City's first goal of the 1990-91 season v Rotherham (August 1990)

'Bertie' Biggins fires past Swansea keeper Lee Bracey (December 1990)

Noel Blake and Tony Gallimore guide Cambridge's Steve Claridge away from goal (April 1991)

Skipper Vince Overson lifts the Second Division trophy (May 1993)

Nigel Gleghorn fires home the winner against Tranmere (August 1994)

Gerry McMahon celebrates scoring in the last match at the Vic, against West Brom (May 1997)

Ade Akinbiyi celebrates in trademark shirtless style after securing Stoke's safety with the winner against Reading (May 2003)

Michael Duberry, a notable free transfer capture from Leeds, tackles Coventry dangerman Dele Adebola (December 2004)

Gifton Noel-Williams shows the hold-up play which was the trademark of his game against Plymouth's Graham Coughlan (April 2005)

Dave Brammer and Michael Duberry attempt to dispossess QPR's Paul Furlong during the tempestuous 1-2 home defeat (December 2005)

Midfielder Dave Brammer never lived up to his reputation during his three years at Stoke. Here he controls the ball at Hillsborough (September 2006)

£500,000 signing from Southampton Ricardo Fuller made quite an impact in the 2006-07 season. Here he leads Luton's defence a merry dance (February 2007)

Darel Russell (left) is about to net the equalising goal against Colchester to begin a dramatic comeback and secure a 3-1 victory (April 2007)

Mali international striker Mamady Sidibe was slow to win admirers amongst the Stoke faithful, although his height and hold-up play was key to Pulis's tactical plan. Here he watches Plymouth's Krisztian Timar clear during a 3-2 home win (September 2007)

Liam Lawrence bundles the ball across goal for Richard Cresswell to score the winner at Colchester in the penultimate game of 2007-08 (April 2008)

Striker Richard Cresswell sinks to his knees to celebrate Stoke's promotion to the Premier League after a goalless draw with Leicester (May 2008)

Ricardo Fuller pressurises Aston Villa's Curtis Davies. Fuller scored *Match of the Day*'s goal of the month for August 2008, outwitting Martin Laursen and lashing the ball across Brad Friedel

Experienced Danish international keeper Thomas Sorensen was snapped up on a free transfer after being released by Aston Villa in the summer of 2008

£5.5 million club record signing Dave Kitson watches Rory Delap challenge Wigan's Mario Melchiot during the goalless draw at the JJB Stadium which saw City pick up their first away point in the Premier League (November 2008)

Rory Delap's long throws became the focus of Stoke's approach to the game – as far the press and opposing fans were concerned. The former junior javelin champion could propel the ball with a flat trajectory into the six-yard box from 50 yards

Seyi Olofinjana chests a Delap long throw past Arsenal keeper Manuel Almunia to secure a famous 2-1 victory (November 2008)

James Beattie, a superb capture from Sheffield United in January 2009, nods the second of his brace in the 2-2 home draw with Portsmouth (February 2009)

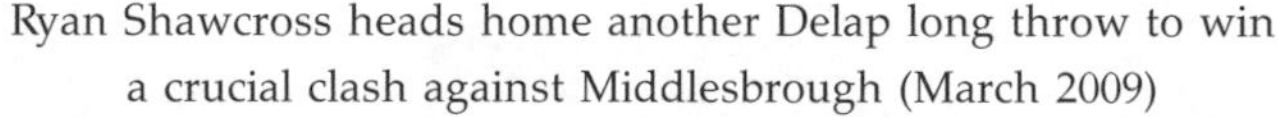

Ryan Shawcross heads home another Delap long throw to win a crucial clash against Middlesbrough (March 2009)

Left-sided utility player Danny Pugh hares after the ball during Stoke's dramatic comeback at Aston Villa (March 2009)

Liam Lawrence hammers the only goal v Blackburn, leaving defender Gael Givet floundering. It gave City yet another home win as they climbed towards a 12th-placed finish (March 2009)

GUIDE TO SEASONAL SUMMARIES

Col 1: Match number (for league fixtures); Round (for cup-ties).
e.g. 2:1 means 'Second round; first leg.'
e.g. 4R means 'Fourth round replay.'

Col 2: Date of the fixture and whether Home (H), Away (A), or Neutral (N).

Col 3: Opposition.

Col 4: Attendances. Home gates appear in roman; Away gates in *italics*.
Figures in **bold** indicate the largest and smallest gates, at home and away.
Average home and away attendances appear after the final league match.

Col 5: Respective league positions of Stoke and opponents after the match.
Stoke's position appears on the top line in roman.
Their opponents' position appears on the second line in *italics*.
For cup-ties, the division and position of opponents is provided.
e.g.:12 means the opposition are twelfth in Division 2.

Col 6: The top line shows the result: W(in), D(raw), or L(ose).
The second line shows Stoke's cumulative points total.

Col 7: The match score, Stoke's given first.
Scores in **bold** indicate Stoke's biggest league win and heaviest defeat.

Col 8: The half-time score, Stoke's given first.

Col 9: The top line shows Stoke's scorers and times of goals in roman.
The second line shows opponents' scorers and times of goals in *italics*.
A 'p' after the time of a goal denotes a penalty; 'og' an own-goal.
The third line gives the name of the match referee.

Team line-ups: Stoke line-ups appear on the top line, irrespective of whether they are home or away. Opposition teams appear on the second line in *italics*.
Players of either side who are sent off are marked !
Stoke players making their league debuts are displayed in **bold**.

Substitutes: Names of substitutes appear only if they actually took the field.
A player substituted is marked *
A second player substituted is marked ^
A third player substituted is marked "
These marks do not indicate the sequence of substitutions.

N.B. For clarity, all information appearing in *italics* relates to opposing teams.

No	Date		Att	Pos	Pt	F-A	H-T	Scorers, Times, and Referees	1	2	3	4	5	6	7	8	9	10	11	12 sub used
1	A	LUTON			L	0-2	0-1		Fox	Bould	Maskery	James	Dyson	O'Callaghan	Painter	McIlroy	Heath	Hudson	Parkin	
	25/8		*8,626*		0			*Elliott 4, Bunn 65*	*Dibble*	*Thomas*	*Grimes*	*Breacker*	*North*	*Donaghy*	*Hill*	*Stein B*	*Elliott*	*Bunn*	*Moss*	
								Ref: T Burns	A controversial goal marks the start of things to come. Peter Fox stops expecting a foul to be given and Steve Elliott prods home. Luton swarm all over Stoke who feature five teenagers. Fox saves superbly from Hill and Stein but cannot keep out Bunn's rasping drive. Heath hits the bar.											
2	H	ASTON VILLA			L	1-3	1-2	Painter 44	Fox	Bould	Maskery	Parkin	Dyson	O'Callaghan	Painter	McIlroy	Heath	Hudson	Hemming	
	27/8		12,605		0			*Walters 15, 43, Withe 90*	*Day*	*Williams*	*Gibson*	*Evans*	*Foster*	*McMahon*	*Bremner*	*Walters*	*Withe*	*Cowans*	*Mortimer*	
								Ref: K Walmsley	Mark Walters finds space in the area to turn and fire two shots past Fox. Ian Painter's reply from Maskery's cross keeps Stoke in it. The Potters put Tony Barton's men under pressure. Painter hits the bar and Heath drives just wide. Peter Withe scores again, forcing home from two yards.											
3	H	SHEFFIELD WED			W	2-1	2-0	McIlroy 35, Heath 44	Fox	**Ebanks**	Maskery	James	Dyson !	O'Callaghan	Painter	McIlroy*	Heath	Chamberlain	Hemming	Parkin
	1/9		13,032		3			*Worthington 80*	*Hodge*	*Sterland*	*Shirtliff**	*Smith*	*Madden*	*Worthington*	*Marwood*	*Blair*	*Varadi*	*Chapman*	*Shelton*	*Pearson*
								Ref: K Barrett	Mark Chamberlain shows his England form providing McIlroy with an easy chance and crossing for Painter to head down for Heath to convert. Dyson walks (65 mins) for butting the provocative Chapman. Despite a midweek flu epidemic City hold out well until Worthington fires home.											
4	H	LEICESTER		18	D	2-2	0-0	Hemming 65, Bould 69	Fox	Ebanks	Maskery	James	Bould	O'Callaghan	Painter	Hudson	Heath*	Chamberlain	Hemming	Saunders
	15/9		13,591	*16*	4			*Lineker 54, Lynex 75p*	*Wallington*	*Wilson*	*Smith R*	*MacDonald*	*Hazell*	*O'Neill*	*Lynex*	*Lineker*	*Smith A*	*Ramsey*	*Peake*	
								Ref: N Wilson	Lineker hits the bar and then slots home Steve Lynex's centre. Carl Saunders appears on 65 mins and his first touch sets up Hemming's diving header. Bould nods in after Wallington fumbles but Maskery trips Lynex who picks himself up to score from the penalty. Two points dropped.											
5	A	NORWICH		18	D	0-0	0-0		Fox	Bould	Hemming	James	Berry	O'Callaghan	Painter	Ebanks	Saunders	Hudson	Chamberlain	
	19/9		*13,591*	*17*	5				*Woods*	*Haylock*	*Van Wyk*	*Mendham**	*Watson*	*Bruce*	*Ordon*	*Farrington*	*Deehen*	*Devine*	*Donowa*	*Goss*
								Ref: J Moules	George Berry plays despite being transfer-listed after a loan spell at Doncaster. Chamberlain produces a great goal-line clearance to deny John Deehan. Wayne Ebanks links well with Hudson in midfield but Saunders is isolated on the left wing. City fail to create a single scoring chance.											
6	A	ARSENAL		18	L	0-4	0-2		Fox	Bould	Maskery	James*	Dyson	Berry	Painter	Ebanks	O'Callaghan	Hudson	Chamberlain	Saunders
	22/9		*26,758*	*2*	5			*Mariner 27, Sans'm 42, Wood' 82, 90p*	*Jennings*	*Anderson*	*Sansom*	*Talbot*	*O'Leary*	*Caton*	*Robson*	*Rix*	*Mariner*	*Woodcock*	*Nicholas*	
								Ref: E Read	Hudson's goal is ruled out for obstruction, then the big guns take over. Mariner beats Fox and fellow England man Kenny Sansom chips Fox expertly. Woodcock's neat finish and penalty, for Bould's trip on him, give the score-line a fair reflection of Terry Neill's team's dominance.											
7	H	SUNDERLAND		18	D	2-2	0-1	Dyson 75, Bould 87	Fox	Bould	Hemming	James	Dyson	Berry	Painter	Ebanks	Saunders	O'Callaghan	Chamberlain	
	29/9		8,882	*12*	6			*Walker 28, Gayle 58*	*Turner*	*Venison*	*Daniel*	*Bennett*	*Chisholm*	*Elliott*	*Berry*	*Gayle*	*Wylde*	*Proctor*	*Walker*	
								Ref: F Roberts	Clive Walker and Howard Gayle profit from defensive lapses. Walker torments Bould all game. An excellent fight-back against Len Ashurst's team sees Dyson power a header into the roof of the net. Chamberlain beats three men to cross for Bould to dive full length amongst the boots.											
8	A	NOTT'M FOREST		18	D	1-1	1-0	Berry 11	Fox	Bould	Hemming	James	Dyson	Berry	Painter	Ebanks	Saunders	O'Callaghan	Chamberlain	
	6/10		*14,129*	*2*	7			*Davenport 87p*	*Sutton*	*Gunn*	*Swain*	*Fairclough*	*Hart*	*Bowyer*	*Wigley*	*Metgod*	*Christie**	*Davenport*	*Hodge*	*Walsh*
								Ref: T Mills	Berry turns the first away goal of the season past Chris Sutton. Stoke deny Forest's midfield space with a great tackling display. Then, in a mad scramble, Saunders handles and Peter Davenport cracks in the penalty for Clough's men. Cruel luck for Stoke who just cannot finish teams off.											
9	H	SOUTHAMPTON		21	L	1-3	1-2	Heath 41	Fox	Bould	Hemming	James	Dyson	Berry	Painter	Ebanks	Heath	O'Callaghan	Chamberlain	
	13/10		9,643	*12*	7			*Curtis 5, Dyson 16 (og), Williams 67*	*Shilton*	*Mills*	*Dennis*	*Williams*	*Wright*	*Bond*	*Holmes*	*Curtis*	*Jordan*	*Moran*	*Wallace*	
								Ref: J Worrall	Lawrie McMenemy's Saints dominate. Alan Curtis fires home and Paul Dyson nods past Fox in a mix-up. Shilton's howler allows Heath a tap-in. Shilton makes amends by saving O'Callaghan's strong header. Steve Williams curls a great free-kick past Fox to complete an easy victory.											
10	H	WEST HAM		21	L	2-4	0-1	Painter 81, Chamberl'n 90 *[Allen 85]*	Fox	Bould	Hemming	Ebanks	Dyson	Berry	Painter	McIlroy*	Heath	O'Callaghan	Chamberlain	Parkin
	20/10		9,945	*7*	7			*Berry 34 (og), Cottee 56, Goddard 73,*	*McAllister*	*Stewart*	*Walford*	*Allen*	*Martin*	*Gale*	*Whitton*	*Goddard*	*Cottee*	*Bonds*	*Pike**	*Orr*
								Ref: K Cooper	Berry dives full length to head past his own keeper. Allen's excellent effort seals the win after Painter and Chamberlain grab close-range strikes against the run of play. John Lyall's men stroll home. Robbie James is sold to QPR for £100,000 and Asprey wants Norwich's Keith Bertschin.											

No	Date	Opponent	Att	Pos	Res	F-A	H-T	Scorers, Times, and Referees	1	2	3	4	5	6	7	8	9	10	11	subs used
11	A	TOTTENHAM		21	L	0-4	0-2		Fox	Bould	Hemming	Ebanks	Dyson	Berry !	Painter	Hudson	Heath	O'Callaghan	Chamberlain	
	27/10		*23,477*	3	7			*Allen 5, 71, Chiedozie 10, Roberts 83p*	*Clemence*	*Stevens*	*Hughton*	*Roberts*	*Miller**	*Perryman*	*Chiedozie*	*Falco*	*Allen*	*Hoddle*	*Galvin*	*Hazard*
								Ref: L Burden	Glenn Hoddle celebrates his 27th birthday by running the show, providing Allen with the first for Keith Burkinshaw's in-form Spurs. Chiedozie picks up a loose pass to round Fox. Berry walks (40 mins) after a tussle with Falco who is then fouled by O'Callaghan for the spot-kick. Dismal.											
12	H	LIVERPOOL		22	L	0-1	0-0		**Corrigan**	Bould	Maskery	Ebanks	Dyson	O'Callaghan	Painter	McIlroy	Heath	Hudson	Chamberlain	
	3/11		20,567	*12*	7			*Whelan 86*	*Grobbelaar*	*Neal*	*Kennedy*	*Lawrenson*	*Whelan*	*Hansen*	*Dalglish*	*Lee*	*Rush*	*Johnston*	*Molby*	
								Ref: P Tyldsley	Stoke give as good as they get in an improved display. Chamberlain causes all sorts of problems cutting in from the wing. Joe Corrigan makes his debut aged 36 and saves brilliantly to deny Ian Rush. Ronnie Whelan produces a superb angled 30-yard volley to finally defeat gallant City.											
13	A	WEST BROM		22	L	0-2	0-1		Corrigan	Bould	Maskery	Saunders	Dyson	O'Callaghan	Painter	McIlroy	Heath	Hudson	Chamberlain	
	10/11		*12,258*	*12*	7			*Hunt 23, Mackenzie 90*	*Godden*	*Nicholl*	*Statham*	*Hunt*	*Bennett*	*Robertson*	*Grealish**	*Thompson*	*Mackenzie*	*Cross*	*Robson*	*Whitehead*
								Ref: D Vickers	Jimmy Nicholl, a Bill Asprey target, chooses Albion instead and lines up for his debut against City. Hunt turns to fire home from 10 yards and then Steve Mackenzie flicks a cross in. Chamberlain and Painter both miss gilt-edged chances as Stoke put Johnny Giles's side under pressure.											
14	A	EVERTON		22	L	0-4	0-2		Corrigan	Maskery	**Spearing**	McIlroy	Dyson	Bould	Painter	**Bertschin**	Heath	Hudson*	Chamberlain	Parkin
	17/11		*26,705*	*1*	7			*Heath 28, 35, Reid 70, Steven 75*	*Southall*	*Stevens*	*V d Hauwe*	*Ratcliffe*	*Mountfield*	*Reid*	*Steven*	*Heath*	*Sharp*	*Bracewell*	*Sheedy*	
								Ref: M Scott	Stoke are easily beaten by Howard Kendall's Everton. Old boy Adrian Heath nips in to poach two close-range goals. Nev Southall saves when Chamberlain is through but Reid fires in Heath's pass and Trevor Steven converts a Stevens cross. City seem to give up once the third goes in.											
15	H	WATFORD		22	L	1-3	0-2	Painter 58p	Corrigan	Bould	Spearing	Maskery	Dyson	O'Callaghan	Painter	McIlroy*	Heath	Bertschin	Chamberlain	Berry
	24/11		10,564	*16*	7			*Reilly 37, Rostron 44, Blissett 52*	*Coton*	*Sinnott*	*Jackett*	*Taylor*	*Terry*	*McClelland*	*Sterling*	*Blissett*	*Reilly**	*Rostron*	*Barnes*	*Gibbs*
								Ref: D Richardson	Graham Taylor's Hornets lay siege and City fail to deal with their route one football. The goals are all scored from eight yards or less. Painter's penalty comes on a rare breakaway when Blissett hauls down Heath. Stoke are lucky to only concede three. The situation is desperate already.											
16	A	NEWCASTLE		22	L	1-2	0-1	McIlroy 55	Corrigan	Bould	Spearing	Maskery	Dyson	Berry	Painter	McIlroy	Heath	Bertschin	Chamberlain	
	1/12		*21,135*	*12*	7			*Anderson 30p, Waddle 85*	*Carr*	*Brown*	*Saunders*	*Heard*	*Anderson*	*Roeder*	*Megson*	*Wharton*	*Waddle*	*Allon**	*McCreery*	*McDonald*
								Ref: J Key	Stoke are competing well when John Key decides that Berry has fouled Wharton and gives a penalty. Anderson lashes in off the bar. City fight back. McIlroy diverts Heath's shot past Kevin Carr. Jack Charlton's Magpies win it when Chris Waddle's curling effort goes in off the upright.											
17	A	QP RANGERS		22	L	0-2	0-1		Corrigan	Bould	Spearing !	Maskery	Dyson	Berry	Painter	Saunders	Heath	Bertschin	Chamberlain	
	4/12		***8,403***	*16*	7			*Bannister 17, Gregory 76*	*Hucker*	*Neill*	*Dawes*	*Waddock*	*Wicks*	*Fenwick*	*Byrne**	*James*	*Bannister*	*Stainrod*	*Gregory*	*Stewart*
								Ref: D Axcell	Tony Spearing is booked twice for not retreating at a free-kick and is cheered off by the small crowd. Bannister strikes after the uneven bounce on the plastic deceives Stoke. Chamberlain misses two chances. Both sets of fans want their manager sacked. At least Rangers go home happy.											
18	H	IPSWICH		22	L	0-2	0-0		**Roberts**	Bould	Spearing	Maskery	Dyson	Berry	Painter	McIlroy	Heath	Bertschin*	Chamberlain	Saunders
	8/12		7,925	*19*	7			*Putney 82, D'Avray 84*	*Cooper*	*Burley*	*McCall*	*Zondervan*	*Osman*	*Butcher*	*Putney*	*Brennan*	*D'Avray*	*Sunderland**	*Gates*	*Cole*
								Ref: D Allison	17-year-old Stuart Roberts is plunged into the relegation battle, spending most of the game as a spectator. McIlroy's free-kick brings a brilliant save from Cooper. Heath also tests the keeper. Out of the blue Trevor Putney's 25-yard shot flies in and D'Avray deflects McCall's shot home.											
19	A	CHELSEA		22	D	1-1	0-0	Dyson 71	Corrigan	Bould	Spearing	Maskery	Dyson	Berry	Heath	McIlroy*	O'Callaghan	Bertschin	Chamberlain	Saunders
	15/12		*20,534*	*6*	8			*Dixon 70*	*Niedzwiecki*	*Wood*	*Rougvie*	*Pates*	*McLaughlin*	*Jones K*	*Nevin*	*Spackman*	*Dixon*	*Davies*	*Canoville**	*Johnstone*
								Ref: J Ashworth	City start with O'Callaghan in his old attacking role. Kerry Dixon gives Dyson a torrid time and finally finds room to head home after Corrigan parries Davies' header. Dyson heads an instant reply but City are penned back by John Neal's men. At least a point gives some encouragement.											
20	A	SHEFFIELD WED		22	L	1-2	1-1	Bould 45	Corrigan	Bould	Saunders	Maskery	Dyson	Berry	Heath	McIlroy	O'Callaghan	Bertschin	Chamberlain	
	22/12		*19,799*	*7*	8			*Varadi 32, Chapman 60*	*Hodge*	*Oliver*	*Shirtliff*	*Madden*	*Lyons*	*Worthington*	*Marwood*	*Blair*	*Varadi*	*Chapman**	*Shelton*	*Sterland*
								Ref: A Saunders	Carl Saunders plays as emergency left-back. Wednesday lay siege. McIlroy clears off the line. Varadi and Marwood both go close. Varadi nods home but then Bould converts Chamberlain's cross. Finally Lee Chapman scores against his old club to clinch it for Howard Wilkinson's men.											
21	H	MANCHESTER U		22	W	2-1	0-1	Painter 70p, Saunders 75	Corrigan	Saunders	Spearing	Maskery	O'Callaghan	Berry	Heath	McIlroy	Painter	Bertschin	Chamberlain	
	26/12		**21,013**	*3*	11			*Stapleton 23*	*Bailey*	*Gidman*	*Albiston*	*Moses*	*McQueen*	*Duxbury*	*Robson*	*Strachan**	*Hughes*	*Stapleton*	*Muhren*	*Brazil*
								Ref: K Baker	United think they can cruise it after Frank Stapleton drives home a rebound. Ron Atkinson's team get the fright of their lives when Stoke press on, forcing Albiston to handle on the line. Chamberlain's corner is flicked on for Saunders to crash into the roof of the net. A glimmer of hope?											

No		Date	Att	Pos	Pt	F-A	H-T	Scorers, Times, and Referees	1	2	3	4	5	6	7	8	9	10	11	12 sub used
22	H	QP RANGERS		22	L	0-2	0-2		Roberts	Saunders	Spearing	Maskery	O'Callaghan	Berry	Heath	McIlroy	Painter*	Bertschin	Chamberlain	Hudson
		29/12	10,811	15	11			James 20, Fillery 26	Hucker	Chivers	Dawes	Waddock	McDonald	Fenwick	James	Fillery	Bannister	Byrne*	Gregory	Robinson
								Ref: H Taylor	Robbie James hits a fierce low drive past Roberts for his first Rangers goal against his old club. All the optimism disappears as QPR have City in turmoil at the back. Only Mike Fillery manages to score again, with Roberts performing heroics to keep out Waddock, Bannister and Byrne.											
23	A	COVENTRY		22	L	0-4	0-3		Roberts	Bould	Spearing	Maskery	O'Callaghan	Berry	Parkin	McIlroy	Heath	Bertschin	Chamberlain	
		1/1	9,829	19	11			Gibson 12, 53, Stephens 30, Hibbitt 33	Ogrizovic	Stephens	Pearce	Bowman	Kilcline	McGrath	Gynn	Hibbitt*	Latchford	Gibson	Adams	Bennett
								Ref: D Hedges	After Bill Asprey's sudden illness, coach Tony Lacey takes charge of demoralised City. They are thrashed by Coventry who are in trouble too. Terry Gibson's second goal is the best as he darts in to head home. Acting manager Don Mackay is not pleased with the way Coventry played!											
24	A	LEICESTER		22	D	0-0	0-0		**Barron**	Bould	Maskery	Hudson	Dyson	Berry	Parkin	McIlroy	Painter	Bertschin	Chamberlain	
		12/1	10,111	15	12				Andrews	Feeley	Wilson	Smith R	Williams	O'Neill	Lynex	Lineker	Smith A	Ramsey	Banks	
								Ref: E Scales	In tricky conditions on-loan Paul Barron is the star, saving point-blank efforts from Alan Smith and Ramsey. Stoke's massed ranks of defenders block efforts by Banks and Ramsey. Barron saves brilliantly from Lineker. Somehow City cling on for a superb point at Jock Wallace's Foxes.											
25	A	SUNDERLAND		22	L	0-1	0-0		**Siddall**	Bould	Maskery	Hudson !	Dyson	Berry	Painter	McIlroy	O'Callaghan	Bertschin*	Dodd	Saunders
		2/2	14,762	18	12			Hodgson 77	Turner	Corner*	Pickerin	Bennett	Agboola	Elliott	Hodgson	Cooke	West	Berry	Cummins	Atkinson
								Ref: T Fitzharris	Alan Hudson gets himself sent off for protesting continually as the referee gives fouls against him. Backs against the wall time. Dave Hodgson glances in a running header that gives ex-Vale keeper Barry Siddall no hope. Bill Asprey, back from illness, re-signs Alan Dodd from Wolves.											
26	A	LIVERPOOL		22	L	0-2	0-2		Siddall	Bould	Maskery	Dodd	Dyson	Berry	Painter	McIlroy	Saunders*	Bertschin	Chamberlain	Heath
		23/2	31,368	5	12			Nicol 14, Dalglish 28	Grobbelaar	Neal	Kennedy	Gillespie	Nicol	Hansen	Dalglish	Whelan	Rush	MacDonald	Wark	
								Ref: M Peck	City battle gamely but are outclassed by Joe Fagan's Reds. Nicol scores when Dalglish's shot rebounds off Siddall then Dalglish accepts a gift after McIlroy miskicks. Liverpool press forward but Stoke are resolute. Siddall saves from Nicol, Dalglish and Rush. Kennedy hits an upright.											
27	H	TOTTENHAM		22	L	0-1	0-0		Siddall	Bould	Maskery	Dodd*	Dyson	Berry	Painter	McIlroy	Saunders	Bertschin	Heath	Parkin
		2/3	12,533	2	12			Crooks 46	Clemence	Stevens	Hughton	Roberts	Miller	Perryman	Chiedozie	Falco	Dick	Hoddle	Crooks	
								Ref: T Simpson	Stoke are competing well until Barry Siddall's howler. He miskicks a straightforward clearance and Garth Crooks nips in to slot home. Keith Burkinshaw's team have the upper hand after that and Siddall tips Hoddle's drive on to the upright. Ray Clemence races out to deny Bertschin.											
28	H	WEST BROM		22	D	0-0	0-0		Siddall	Bould	Maskery	Dodd	Dyson	Berry	Painter	McIlroy	Heath	Bertschin !	Chamberlain*	Parkin
		12/3	6,885	15	13				Godden	Nicholl !	Whitehead*	Hunt	Bennett !	Forsyth	Owen	Thompson	Mackenzie	Cross	Valentine	Grealish
								Ref: N Glover	It's footbrawl rather than football as Bertshin and Martyn Bennett trade blows on 28 mins and are sent off. Jimmy Nicholl follows on 65 mins for swearing at a linesman. The lowest post-war Victoria Ground crowd sees another blank score-sheet. At least this time Stoke don't concede.											
29	A	SOUTHAMPTON		22	D	0-0	0-0		Siddall	Bould	Maskery*	Dodd	Dyson	Berry	Painter	McIlroy	Heath	Bertschin	Parkin	Hemming
		16/3	14,608	5	14				Shilton	Mills	Dennis*	Curtis	Wright	Bond	Whitlock	Baker	Jordan	Armstrong	Wallace	Collins
								Ref: K Miller	City battle well on a pitch covered in early morning snow. Bould goes close with a 15-yard drive. Berry looks for a penalty when he is bundled over. Lawrie McMenemy's Saints drive Stoke back but Berry leaps to clear Danny Wallace's effort off the line. A point gained rather than lost.											
30	H	NOTT'M FOREST		22	L	1-4	1-2	Parkin 10 [Davenport 78p]	Siddall	Bould	Hemming	Dodd*	Dyson	Berry	Painter	McIlroy	Heath	Bertschin	Parkin	**Callaghan**
		23/3	7,453	7	14			Hodge 28, Hart 35, Riley 53,	Segers	McInally	Swain	Fairclough*	Hart	Bowyer	Wigley	Metgod	Riley	Davenport	Hodge	Mills
								Ref: G Courtney	Finally a goal after 745 minutes without scoring! Parkin loops in a gentle shot after Segers and Painter tangle. It doesn't last long. Hodge is left free to rasp home and Segers saves Painter's 41st-minute penalty after Swain handles. Forest plunder three unanswered goals as City lose heart.											
31	A	ASTON VILLA		22	L	0-2	0-0		Siddall	Bould	O'Callaghan	Dodd	Dyson	Berry	Painter	McIlroy	Heath	Hemming	Parkin	
		27/3	10,874	10	14			Berry 71 (og), Six 85	Spink	Williams	Dorigo	Evans*	Ormsby	McMahon	Six	Rideout	Withe	Gibson	Walters	Walker
								Ref: T Bune	City outplay Villa but still manage to lose. Graham Turner admits his Villans could have been two down to Painter's efforts by half-time. But a youthful line-up flounder after Berry unluckily deflects Withe's shot past Siddall. Six finishes off Williams' free-kick to compound the misery.											

No	Date/Venue	Opponent / Att	Pos	Pts	F-A	H-T	Scorers, Times, and Referees	1	2	3	4	5	6	7	8	9	10	11	12
32	H	ARSENAL	22	W	**2-0**	0-0	Painter 55p, Dyson 62	Siddall	Bould	Maskery	Dodd	Dyson	Berry	Painter	McIlroy	Heath	Hudson	Parkin	
	30/3	7,371	*8*	17				*Lukic*	*Anderson*	*Sansom*	*Williams*	*O'Leary*	*Caton*	*Talbot*	*Rix*	*Mariner*	*Meade**	*Nicholas*	*Woodcock*
							Ref: P Willis	At last a win, and against the most unlikely opposition. Ian Painter crashes home a penalty after O'Leary brings down Heath. Dyson dives in to head home McIlroy's cross. Hudson is influential in midfield as Stoke perform for once in front of the BBC cameras. A hard won three points.											
33	A	MANCHESTER U	22	L	**0-5**	0-2	*[Whiteside 89]*	Siddall	Bould	Maskery	Dodd	Dyson	Berry	Painter	McIlroy	Heath	Hudson	Chamberlain*	Bertschin
	6/4	***42,940***	*2*	17			*Hughes 4, 65, Olsen 27, 80,*	*Bailey*	*Gidman*	*Albiston*	*Whiteside*	*McGrath*	*Hogg*	*Robson**	*Strachan*	*Hughes*	*Stapleton*	*Olsen*	*Duxbury*
							Ref: K Redfern	United overwhelm sad City who are nearly down and out. Hughes lashes home from 12 yards and powers home a header but is denied a superb hat-trick by the foot of the post. Olsen also bags a brace and sends Whiteside clear to ram home for Ron Atkinson's side. It's men against boys.											
34	H	LUTON	22	L	0-4	0-1		Siddall	Bould	Maskery	Dodd	Dyson	Bertschin	Painter	McIlroy	Heath	Hudson	Chamberlain	
	8/4	6,951	*19*	17			*Harford 17, 47, Moss 65, Nwajiobi 70*	*Sealey*	*Breacker*	*Grimes*	*Nicholas*	*Turner*	*Donaghy*	*Hill**	*Stein B*	*Harford*	*Nwajiobi*	*Preece*	*Moss*
							Ref: I Hendrick	Chairman Frank Edwards refuses to resign in the face of burgeoning debts and relegation but sacks Bill Asprey after a dismal display. Harford pounces when Dyson's back-pass fails to find Siddall. Moss casually nets the third. Nwajiobi finishes a solo run with a brilliant fourth. Awful.											
35	H	EVERTON	22	L	0-2	0-1		Siddall	Bould	Maskery	Berry	Dyson	Saunders	Painter	McIlroy	Bertschin	Hudson	Heath	
	20/4	18,258	*1*	17			*Sharp 23, Sheedy 46*	*Southall*	*Stevens*	*V d Hauwe*	*Ratcliffe*	*Atkins*	*Reid*	*Steven*	*Sharp*	*Gray*	*Bracewell*	*Sheedy*	
							Ref: H King	Classy Everton send City plummeting into Division Two. Sharp scores from a tight angle. Sheedy cracks home Berry's miscued header. Stoke create little. Everton lay siege and the crowd cheer when City make it over the halfway line! Tony Lacey is in charge after Asprey's dismissal.											
36	H	NORWICH	22	L	2-3	1-2	Bertschin 10, Saunders 90	Siddall	Bould	Maskery	Dodd	Dyson	Berry	Painter	McIlroy	Bertschin	Hudson*	Heath	Saunders
	24/4	**4,597**	*15*	17			*Rosario 4, Gordon 33, Donowa 78*	*Woods*	*Haylock*	*Van Wyk*	*Rigby*	*Mendham*	*Downs*	*Donowa*	*Rosario*	*Deehen*	*Clayton*	*Gordon*	
							Ref: G Tyson	With their fate settled, Stoke relax. Attack-minded Norwich still need the points. Robert Rosario races through to score. Keith Bertschin scores his first goal on his 23rd appearance. Gordon and Donowa score from close range. Saunders grabs a consolation five minutes into injury-time.											
37	A	WATFORD	22	L	0-2	0-1		Siddall	Bould	Maskery	Dodd	Dyson	Berry	Painter	McIlroy	Bertschin	Saunders	Heath	
	27/4	*14,586*	*11*	17			*Blissett 33p, Jackett 52*	*Coton*	*Gibbs*	*Rostron*	*Taylor*	*Sinnott*	*McClelland*	*Callaghan*	*Blissett*	*Johnston*	*Jackett*	*Barnes*	
							Ref: L Burden	In a blustery wind both sides struggle to keep control of the ball. Bertschin fires a free-kick straight at Coton. Bould brings down Barnes for the penalty. Kenny Jackett nets a fierce drive. Sammy McIlroy shoots just wide. Graham Taylor's men comfortably deal with Stoke's blunt attack.											
38	H	NEWCASTLE	22	L	0-1	0-1		Siddall	Bould	Maskery	Dodd	Dyson	Berry	Painter*	McIlroy	Bertschin	Saunders	Chamberlain	Heath
	4/5	7,088	*12*	17			*Dyson 45 (og)*	*Thomas*	*Anderson*	*Wharton*	*McCreery*	*Clarke*	*Roeder*	*Saunders*	*Reilly*	*Waddle*	*Beardsley*	*Heard*	
							Ref: D Allison	Paul Dyson's sliced own-goal drains whatever confidence Stoke have. Reilly hits the post and Chris Waddle runs the show despite being booed by his own fans after announcing his summer transfer to Spurs. Chamberlain has Stoke's only effort saved by Thomas. Another insipid display.											
39	A	IPSWICH	22	L	1-5	0-3	Bertschin 69	Siddall	Bould	Maskery	Dodd	Dyson	Berry	Callaghan*	McIlroy	Bertschin	Saunders	Heath	Hemming
	6/5	*14,150*	*17*	17			*Wils'n 12, 26, 52, Putney 40, Gates 80*	*Cooper*	*Burley*	*Gernon*	*Zondervan**	*Cranson*	*Butcher*	*Putney*	*Brennan*	*D'Avray*	*Wilson*	*Gates*	*Dozzell*
							Ref: D Reeves	The lowest low of the season. City give up as soon as Kevin Wilson scores the first of his unmarked hat-trick. Putney finishes a superb 40-yard run for the best goal of the game. Keith Bertschin becomes the first Stoke forward to score away from home this season netting a 20-yard drive.											
40	H	CHELSEA	22	L	0-1	0-0		Fox	**Williams**	Hemming	Dodd	Dyson	Maskery	Heath	McIlroy	Bertschin*	Saunders	Painter	Callaghan
	11/5	8,905	*6*	17			*Speedie 65*	*Niedzwiecki*	*Lee*	*Jones J*	*Pates*	*McLaughlin*	*Bumstead*	*Nevin*	*Spackman*	*Dixon*	*Speedie**	*Thomas*	*Canoville*
							Ref: G Aplin	Stoke have six teenagers in the team. Fox pulls off two superb saves to deny Dixon and Speedie, who also hits the post. He finally converts Pat Nevin's flighted free-kick. Eddie Niedzwiecki palms away Bertschin's downward header. Terry Williams makes his debut in a better showing.											
41	A	WEST HAM	22	L	1-5	0-3	Painter 63p *[Hilton 90]*	Fox	Bould	Saunders	Maskery*	Dyson	Dodd	Painter	McIlroy	Hemming	Williams	Heath	Callaghan
	14/5	*13,362*	*17*	17			*Bonds 15, 89, Pike 32, Stewart 36p,*	*Parkes*	*Stewart*	*Brush*	*Gale*	*Martin*	*Pike*	*Orr**	*Bonds*	*Barnes*	*Cottee*	*Goddard*	*Hilton*
							Ref: J Martin	Stoke are unlucky at Upton Park where John Martin waves aside a linesman's flag to allow Billy Bonds' opener to stand. He gives John Lyall's men a dubious penalty and then reciprocates for Stoke. West Ham are safe from the drop after a late flurry gives the score-line a lop-sided feel.											
42	H	COVENTRY	22	L	0-1	0-0		Fox	Bould	Hemming	Maskery	Dyson	Berry	Heath	McIlroy	Painter	Saunders*	**Beeston**	Chamberlain
	17/5	6,930	*20*	17			*Pearce 66p*	*Ogrizovic*	*Butterworth*	*Pearce*	*Hibbitt**	*Kilcline*	*Peake*	*Bennett*	*McGrath*	*Regis*	*Gibson*	*Adams*	*Gynn*
	Home	Away					Ref: N Midgley	Stuart Pearce blasts home a penalty after Bould is adjudged to have handled Regis' header. Painter blasts his 83rd-minute spot-kick against the bar to leave the Sky Blues with slim hopes of survival. Stoke say goodbye to the First Division with an unenviable set of 'worst ever' records.											
Average	10,740	17,714																	

Milk Cup			Att			F-A	H-T	Scorers, Times, and Referees	1	2	3	4	5	6	7	8	9	10	11	12 sub used
2:1	H	ROTHERHAM		18	L	1-2	0-1	Saunders 65	Fox	Bould	Maskery	James	Dyson	O'Callaghan	Painter	Ebanks	Saunders	Hudson	Chamberlain	
	26/9		8,221	*3:1*				*Birch 27, Simmons 88*	*Mimms*	*Forrest*	*Mitchell*	*Trusson*	*Johnson*	*Pickering*	*Birch*	*Gooding*	*Dungworth*	*Simmons*	*Kilmore*	
								Ref: A Robinson	The Milk Cup turns sour as City produce a dismal display against George Kerr's merry Millers. Nippy Alan Birch lashes a low drive past Fox. Chamberlain shows glimpses of his old style. Painter sets up Carl Saunders for his first goal but Simmons' late lob is not undeserved. Dreadful.											
2:2	A	ROTHERHAM		18	D	1-1	1-0	Painter 22	Fox	Parkin	Hemming	James	Dyson	Bould	Painter	Ebanks	Saunders*	O'Callaghan	Chamberlain	Heath
	9/10		*6,898*	*3:5*				*Bould 73 (og)*	*Mimms*	*Forrest*	*Mitchell*	*Trusson*	*Johnson**	*Pickering*	*Birch*	*Gooding*	*Dungworth*	*Simmons*	*Kilmore*	*Rhodes*
								Ref: D Scott (Stoke lose 2-3 on aggregate)	Stoke level the tie thanks to Painter's 12-yard finish. James hits a pile-driver which Mimms just reaches. Rotherham win a 60th-minute penalty but Fox saves Birch's kick and the gods seem to be smiling on City. They are just teasing though as Bould deflects Birch's cross-shot past Fox.											

FA Cup																				
3	A	LUTON		22	D	1-1	0-0	Painter 78	Roberts	Bould	Maskery	Hudson	Dyson	O'Callaghan*	Parkin	McIlroy	Painter	Bertschin	Chamberlain	Saunders
	5/1		*7,270*	*21*				*Foster 86*	*Sealey*	*Breacker*	*Thomas*	*Turner*	*Foster*	*Donaghy*	*Hill*	*Stein*	*Harford*	*Daniel*	*Moss**	*Nwajiobi*
								Ref: D Reeves	Painter forces Sealey to save well before beating him in a one on one. Stoke nearly hang on but David Pleat's team equalise when Foster blasts Hill's centre high into the net. Afterwards City Manager Bill Asprey is diagnosed as having suffered complete mental and physical exhaustion.											
3R	H	LUTON		22	L	2-3	0-2	Painter 47p, Chamberlain 68	Roberts	Bould	Maskery	Hudson*	Dyson	O'Callaghan	Parkin	McIlroy	Painter	Bertschin	Chamberlain	Saunders
	9/1		9,917	*21*				*Hill 9, Harford 12, Donaghy 63*	*Sealey*	*Breacker*	*Thomas*	*Turner*	*Foster*	*Donaghy*	*Hill*	*Stein*	*Harford*	*Daniel*	*Parker*	
								Ref: D Reeves	On a snow covered pitch City are knocked out by Ricky Hill's mastery of the conditions. He smashes home from 25 yards and sets up Harford. Foster fouls Parkin for the penalty then Chamberlain scores from 15 yards. Bertschin miscues when well placed. Luton will meet Huddersfield.											

		Home						Away				
	P	W	D	L	F	A	W	D	L	F	A	Pts
1 Everton	42	16	3	2	58	17	12	3	6	30	26	90
2 Liverpool	42	12	4	5	36	19	10	7	4	32	16	77
3 Tottenham	42	11	3	7	46	31	12	5	4	32	20	77
4 Manchester U	42	13	6	2	47	13	9	4	8	30	34	76
5 Southampton	42	13	4	4	29	18	6	7	8	27	29	68
6 Chelsea	42	13	3	5	38	20	5	9	7	25	28	66
7 Arsenal	42	14	5	2	37	14	5	4	12	24	35	66
8 Sheffield Wed	42	12	7	2	39	21	5	7	9	19	24	65
9 Nott'm Forest	42	13	4	4	35	18	6	3	12	21	30	64
10 Aston Villa	42	10	7	4	34	20	5	4	12	26	40	56
11 Watford	42	10	5	6	48	30	4	8	9	33	41	55
12 West Brom	42	11	4	6	36	23	5	3	13	22	39	55
13 Luton	42	12	5	4	40	22	3	4	14	17	39	54
14 Newcastle	42	11	4	6	33	26	2	9	10	22	44	52
15 Leicester	42	10	4	7	39	25	5	2	14	26	48	51
16 West Ham	42	7	8	6	27	23	6	4	11	24	45	51
17 Ipswich	42	8	7	6	27	20	5	4	12	19	37	50
18 Coventry	42	11	3	7	29	22	4	2	15	18	42	50
19 QP Rangers	42	11	6	4	41	30	2	5	14	12	42	50
20 Norwich	42	9	6	6	28	24	4	4	13	18	40	49
21 Sunderland	42	7	6	8	20	26	3	4	14	20	36	40
22 STOKE	42	3	3	15	18	41	0	5	16	6	50	17
	924	237	107	118	785	503	118	107	237	503	785	1279

Odds & ends

Double wins: (0).
Double losses: (11) Luton, Aston Villa, West Ham, Tottenham, Liverpool, Everton, Watford, Newcastle, QP Rangers, Ipswich, Coventry.

Won from behind: (1) Manchester U (h).
Lost from in front: (1) Nott'm Forest (h).

High spots: Beating Manchester U, Arsenal and Sheffield Wed.

Low spots: Lowest average attendances for 24 years.
Worst team ever in any division of the football league.
6 away goals scored.
Losing at home to Rotherham in the League Cup.
Record number of goals conceded/worst goal difference.
Losing last 10 games.
One goal in 10 games after Boxing Day.

Player of the Year: Sammy McIlroy.
Ever-presents: (0).
Hat-tricks: (0).
Leading scorer: (9) Ian Painter.

	Appearances						Goals			
	Lge	*Sub*	LC	*Sub*	FAC	*Sub*	**Lge**	LC	FAC	**Tot**
Barron, Paul	**1**									
Beeston, Carl	**1**									
Berry, George	**31**	*1*					**1**			**1**
Bertschin, Keith	**24**	*1*			2		**2**			**2**
Bould, Steve	**38**		2		2		**3**			**3**
Callaghan, Aaron	**2**	*3*								
Chamberlain, Mark	**27**	*1*	2		2		**1**		1	**2**
Corrigan, Joe	**9**									
Dodd, Alan	**16**									
Dyson, Paul	**37**		2		2		**3**			**3**
Ebanks, Wayne	**10**		2							
Fox, Peter	**14**		2		2					
Heath, Phil	**34**	*2*		*1*			**2**			**2**
Hemming, Chris	**14**	*2*	1		1		**1**			**1**
Hudson, Alan	**14**	*1*	1		1					
James, Robbie	**8**		2		2					
Maskery, Chris	**34**		1		1					
McIlroy, Sammy	**34**				2		**2**			**2**
O'Callaghan, Brendan	**20**		2		2					
Painter, Ian	**38**		2		2		**6**	1	2	**9**
Parkin, Steve	**8**	*5*	1		1		**1**			**1**
Roberts, Stuart	**3**									
Saunders, Carl	**17**	*6*	2			*2*	**2**	1		**3**
Siddall, Barry	**15**									
Spearing, Tony	**9**									
Wiiliams, Terry	**2**									
26 players used	**460**	*22*	**22**	*1*	**22**	*2*	**24**	**2**	**3**	**29**

No	Date		Att	Pos	Pt	F-A	H-T	Scorers, Times, and Referees	1	2	3	4	5	6	7	8	9	10	11	12 sub used
1	H	SHEFFIELD UTD			L	1-3	1-1	Heath 44	Siddall	**Mills**	Maskery	Hudson	Dyson	Berry	Chamberlain	Beeston*	Bertschin	Painter	Heath	Saunders
	17/8		11,679		0			*Cockerill 14, Morris 52p, 78*	*Burridge*	*Eckhardt*	*Kenworthy*	*Thompson*	*Stancliffe*	*McNaught*	*Morris*	*Cockerill*	*Withe*	*Lewington*	*Bolton*	
								Ref: N Wilson	City have a hangover from last season despite new player-manager Mick Mills' presence on the pitch. Hudson hits his clearance at Beeston and it falls for Glenn Cockerill to crack home. Heath buries one from 18 yards but Chamberlain trips Bolton and Morris gets his first from the spot.											
2	A	BARNSLEY		19	D	0-0	0-0		Siddall	Mills	Maskery	Hudson	Dyson	Berry	Chamberlain	Parkin	Bertschin	Painter	Heath	
	24/8		*6,598*	*9*	1				*Baker*	*Joyce*	*Goodison*	*Thomas*	*Burns*	*Futcher*	*Owen*	*Hirst*	*Walsh**	*Jeffels*	*Campbell*	*Plummer*
								Ref: M Peck	Stoke earn their first league point since March in an entertaining game. Bertschin misses City's best chance as Baker makes a fine double save. Chamberlain is also denied. Hirst brings a fine save out of Siddall. Owen has a goal disallowed for offside. Chambo's free-kick whistles over.											
3	H	LEEDS		11	W	**6-2**	1-0	B'rry 15, Bert' 55, 83, Ch'b'rl'n 72, 88,	Siddall	Bould	Mills	Hudson	Dyson	Berry	Chamberlain	Maskery	Bertschin	Painter	Heath	
	26/8		7,047	*20*	4			*Aspin 61, Snodin 70* [Maskery 75]	*Day*	*Irwin*	*Hamson*	*Snodin*	*Linighan*	*Aspin*	*McCluskey**	*Sheridan*	*Baird*	*Lorimer*	*Sellars*	*Wright*
								Ref: P Tyldesley	Mark Chamberlain dazzles as City romp home. Bertschin and Berry convert his crosses to set City on their way but his second goal is the best, curled home from 15 yards. Chris Maskery loses two teeth in a challenge but still scores from Bertschin's cross. First six-goal haul since 1974.											
4	A	BRADFORD C		14	L	1-3	1-1	Painter 18	Siddall	Bould*	Mills	Hudson	Dyson	Berry	Chamberlain	Maskery	Bertschin	Painter	Heath	Saunders
	1/9		*6,999*	*12*	4			*Abbott 10p, 50p, Singleton 56*	*Litchfield*	*Abbott*	*Withe*	*McCall*	*Jackson*	*Evans*	*Hendrie*	*Thorpe*	*Campbell*	*Singleton*	*Graham*	
		(At Elland Road)						Ref: G Tyson	City are seething after the referee awards two dubious penalties. The first seems way outside the area and the second follows Berry's attempted clearance which hits Hudson's arm. Painter deflects home Heath's shot but Stoke wilt when Martin Singleton bursts through to add a solo goal.											
5	H	GRIMSBY		14	D	1-1	0-1	Chamberlain 89	Siddall	Parkin	Mills	Hudson*	Dyson	Berry	Chamberlain	Maskery	Bertschin	Painter	Heath	Saunders
	4/9		7,362	*16*	5			*Lund 2*	*Felgate*	*Robinson*	*Crombie*	*Peake*	*Moore A*	*Moore K*	*Ford*	*Lund*	*Gilligan*	*Bonnyman*	*Hobson*	
								Ref: R Bridges	City are shocked as Tony Ford beats Mills and squares for Gary Lund to score. After that it's the Chamberlain show. He torments Mick Lyons' Mariners despite being double marked. He has two fine efforts saved before lashing the ball high past David Felgate. Steve Parkin hits the bar.											
6	H	MILLWALL		14	D	0-0	0-0		Fox	Saunders	Mills	Parkin	Dyson	Berry	Chamberlain	Maskery	Bertschin	Painter*	Heath	Beeston
	7/9		7,187	*9*	6				*Sansome*	*Hinshelwood*	*Roffey*	*Briley*	*McLeary*	*Nutton*	*Lowndes*	*Wilson*	*Fashanu*	*Lovell*	*Kinsella*	
								Ref: J Key	A physical battle. Briley flattens Saunders and is booked. Bertschin and Painter are injured. Chamberlain rises above the rough-house tactics to weave his magic down the right. Sansome is in brilliant form for George Graham's men. He denies Berry, Painter, Bertschin and Chamberlain.											
7	A	MIDDLESBROUGH		12	D	1-1	0-0	Parkin 80	Fox	Parkin	Mills	Williams	Dyson	Berry	Chamberlain	Maskery	Bertschin	Saunders	Heath	
	10/9		*4,255*	*19*	7			*Rowell 50*	*Pears*	*Laws*	*Heard*	*McAndrew*	*Mowbray*	*Beagrie*	*Gill*	*O'Riordan*	*Stephens*	*Rowell*	*Currie**	*Kernaghan*
								Ref: T Mills	Rowell nets from close in after O'Riordan's knockdown but City are generally organised at the back under new skipper Berry. Carl Saunders is a live-wire all night. Mark Chamberlain bids farewell as he is sold to Sheffield Wednesday. He provides Parkin who fires a 25-yard equaliser.											
8	A	PORTSMOUTH		17	L	0-3	0-0		Fox	Parkin	Mills	Beeston	Dyson	Berry	Williams	Maskery	Bertschin	Saunders	Heath	
	14/9		*13,720*	*1*	7			*Morgan 53, Dillon 65p, Wood 77*	*Knight*	*Tait*	*Swain*	*Dillon*	*Blake*	*Gilbert*	*O'Callaghan*	*Kennedy*	*Morgan*	*Channon**	*Hilaire*	*Wood*
								Ref: A Ward	City, down to the bare bones, keep Alan Ball's Pompey at bay until Nicky Morgan evades Dyson and Fox to finish clinically. Dyson then trips Morgan for the penalty and Paul Wood heads home Kenny Swain's cross. Steve Parkin's last-ditch tackle on Morgan stops any further damage.											
9	A	CHARLTON		19	L	0-2	0-0		Fox	Bould	Mills*	Parkin	Dyson	Berry	Adams	Maskery	Bertschin	Saunders	Heath	Beeston
	21/9		*8,858*	*5*	7			*Stuart 78, Lee 83*	*Johns*	*Humphrey*	*Reid*	*Loveridge*	*Thompson*	*Berry*	*Stuart*	*Shipley*	*Pearson*	*Aizlewood**	*Flanagan*	*Lee*
								Ref: M James	On an emotional day Stoke lose out in the last match played at the Valley before Charlton decamp to Selhurst Park. A sit-down protest by fans dressed in black delays the second half but Charlton are unperturbed. Stuart heads home a rebound and Lee beats the offside trap to slam home.											
10	H	CRYSTAL PALACE		19	D	0-0	0-0		Fox	Bould	Mills	Hudson*	Dyson	Berry	Adams	Maskery	Bertschin	Saunders	Heath	Parkin
	28/9		7,130	*12*	8				*Wood*	*Locke**	*Sparrow*	*Finnigan*	*Droy*	*Cannon*	*Irvine*	*Ketteridge*	*Barber*	*Gray*	*Stebbing*	*Wright*
								Ref: J Worrall	Neil Adams finds space to run at Palace's mean defence but cannot produce the telling pass. Irvine has the clearest chance of the game but fires over with just Fox to beat. Heath stabs just over from close range and City run out of ideas. Alan Hudson makes his final appearance for Stoke.											

No	Venue	Opponent	Att	Pos	Pts	Res	F-A	H-T	Scorers, Times, and Referees	1	2	3	4	5	6	7	8	9	10	11	12
11	A	HULL		17		W	2-0	1-0	Bertschin 10, Saunders 73	Fox	Bould	Mills	Parkin	Dyson	Berry	Adams	Maskery	Bertschin	Saunders	Heath	
	5/10		*6,890*	12	11					*Norman*	*Jobson*	*Pearson**	*Doyle*	*Skipper*	*McEwan*	*Swann*	*Bunn*	*Whitehurst*	*Horton*	*Roberts*	*Flounders*
									Ref: K Redfern	Billy Whitehurst's height causes problems but Stoke are sharper on the deck. Bertschin slides in to finish off Maskery's effort. Fox saves from Swann and Saunders has two headers well stopped by Tony Norman. Saunders then hammers home after wrong-footing Norman. A win at last.											
12	H	BRIGHTON		16		D	1-1	0-1	Maskery 64	Fox	Bould	Mills	Parkin	Dyson	Berry	Adams	Maskery	Bertschin	Saunders	Heath	
	12/10		7,662	*5*	12				*Hutchings 24*	*Digweed*	*Hutchings*	*Pearce*	*Wilson*	*O'Reilly*	*Young*	*Jacobs*	*Saunders*	*Ferguson*	*Biley**	*Mortimer*	*Oliver*
									Ref: T Simpson	Chris Hutchings prods in the rebound when Fox tips Biley's shot onto the bar. City deservedly equalise through Maskery's 30-yard left-footed shot which sails past Perry Digweed. Saunders lobs over and Maskery fires wide. Chris Cattlin's Seagulls force a fourth successive home draw.											
13	A	FULHAM		18		L	0-1	0-1		Fox	Bould	Mills	Parkin	Dyson	Berry	Adams	Maskery	Bertschin	Saunders	Heath	
	19/10		*4,007*	*14*	12				*Pike 38*	*Peyton*	*Cottington*	*Carr*	*Scott*	*Hopkins*	*Parker*	*Marshall*	*Achampong*	*Coney*	*Pike*	*Barnett*	
									Ref: H King	Martin Pike has a goal disallowed before netting a legitimate effort from Dean Coney's pass. Fulham are in charge despite Neil Adams' work-rate on the wing. His crosses cause problems but Heath cannot convert. Fox saves Carr's 80th-minute spot-kick after Parkin handles on the line.											
14	H	WIMBLEDON		18		D	0-0	0-0		Fox	Bould	Mills	Hemming*	Dyson	Berry	Adams	Maskery	Bertschin	Saunders	Heath	Williams
	25/10		6,708	*5*	13					*Beasant*	*Gage*	*Winterburn*	*Galliers*	*Smith*	*Martin*	*Evans*	*Cork*	*Holloway*	*Sanchez*	*Thorn*	
									Ref: K Cooper	Dave Bassett's Wimbledon present their usual long-ball barrage, but Berry dominates. Heath torments Gage but cannot provide the finish as 6ft 4in Dave Beasant deals comfortably with everything Stoke throw at him. Chris Hemming returns after his summer hole-in-the-heart surgery.											
15	H	HUDDERSFIELD		17		W	3-0	2-0	Heath 12, Shaw 43, Bertschin 66	Fox	Bould	Mills*	Hemming	Dyson	Berry	Adams	Maskery	Bertschin	**Shaw**	Heath	Parkin
	2/11		7,291	*14*	16					*Cox*	*Brown*	*Jones J*	*Doyle*	*Webster*	*Jones P*	*Curran*	*Cork*	*Tempest**	*Raynor*	*Cowling*	*Stanton*
									Ref: K Barratt	City end the mini drought by comprehensively outplaying Huddersfield. Heath curls a right-foot shot in from 12 yards then Graham Shaw turns past two players before slotting a debut goal. A linesman needs attention after being flattened by Shaw and Brown slipping on the greasy pitch.											
16	A	CARLISLE		18		L	0-3	0-2		Fox	Bould	Hemming	Parkin	Dyson	Berry	Adams	Maskery	Bertschin	Saunders	Heath	
	9/11		***2,813***	*22*	16				*Halsall 32, Mayes 38, 69*	*Endersby*	*Gorman*	*McCartney*	*Ashurst*	*Saunders*	*Halsall*	*Mayes*	*Cooke*	*Baker*	*Bishop*	*Halpin*	
									Ref: K Walmsley	It looks as though the whole team have been up celebrating the birth of Peter Fox's new son as Carlisle trounce hapless City. Halsall beats Fox from 30 yards before Mayes applies the finish to two deep crosses for Bob Stokoe's men. City never get themselves together in the heavy rain.											
17	H	NORWICH		18		D	1-1	0-0	Bertschin 53p	Fox	Bould	Mills	Williams	Dyson	Berry	Adams	Maskery	Bertschin	Shaw	Heath	
	16/11		6,469	*5*	17				*Drinkell 70*	*Woods*	*Culverhouse*	*Van Wyk*	*Bruce*	*Phelan*	*Watson*	*Barham*	*Drinkell*	*Biggins*	*Mendham*	*Williams**	*Gordon*
									Ref: G Ashby	Heath seems to be brought down just outside the area but Bertschin gladly rams the penalty home against his old team. Kevin Drinkell's header skids off the greasy pitch to beat Fox as Norwich fight back once Dale Gordon appears. Berry grazes the bar with a header from Heath's cross.											
18	A	OLDHAM		16		W	4-2	2-0	Bertschin 35, 60, Heath 44,	Fox	Bould	Mills	**Devine**	Dyson	Berry	Adams	Maskery	Bertschin	Shaw	Heath	
	23/11		*4,817*	*8*	20				*Quinn 67p, 72* [Maskery 49]	*Goram*	*Donachie*	*Ryan*	*McDonough*	*Hoolickin*	*McGuire**	*Palmer*	*Henry*	*Quinn*	*Futcher*	*Atkinson*	*Fairclough*
									Ref: G Aplin	Debutant John Devine is the inspiration as Joe Royle's Oldham are taken apart. Bertschin fires left footed past Goram before Heath rounds off a 40-yard run with a cracking finish. Bertschin rounds it off by side-stepping Andy Goram. Micky Quinn's spot-kick is for Dyson's trip on him.											
19	H	SUNDERLAND		14		W	1-0	0-0	Bertschin 80	Fox	Bould	Mills	Devine	Dyson	Berry	Adams	Maskery*	Bertschin	Shaw	Heath	Saunders
	30/11		9,034	*12*	23					*Bolder*	*Burley*	*Kennedy*	*Venison**	*Bennett*	*Elliott*	*Gray*	*Pickering*	*Swindlehurst*	*Gates*	*Gayle*	*Walker*
									Ref: N Glover	Chris Maskery, subject of interest from Man Utd, cracks a fibula in tackle with Gary Bennett. He is rushed to hospital but is out for the season. Lawrie McMenemy's men are beaten when Bertschin pounces, exchanging passes with Shaw to fire home. Devine again impresses in midfield.											
20	H	MIDDLESBROUGH		11		W	3-2	2-1	Berry 25, Adams 33, Bertschin 55	Fox	Bould	Mills	Devine	Dyson	Berry	Adams	Saunders	Bertschin	Shaw	Heath	
	7/12		7,646	*21*	26				*Stephens 6, O'Riordan 56*	*Pears*	*Laws*	*McAndrew*	*Mowbray*	*O'Riordan*	*Pallister*	*Hamilton*	*Heard*	*Slaven*	*Stephens*	*Rowell**	*Currie*
									Ref: C Trussell	In a superb match George Berry swoops to head home, levelling Stephens' solo opener. Neil Adams angles in a header for his first goal for the club and Bertschin stoops to head past Pears. O'Riordan's shot deflects past Fox. Heard hits a post. Bertschin has a goal disallowed for offside.											
21	A	SHEFFIELD UTD		10		W	2-1	1-1	Adams 7, Shaw 46	Fox	Bould	Mills	Devine	Dyson	Berry	Adams	Saunders	Bertschin	Shaw*	Heath	Williams
	14/12		*12,370*	*5*	29				*Edwards 15*	*Burridge*	*Eckhardt**	*Foley*	*Thompson*	*Stancliffe*	*McNaught*	*Morris*	*Edwards*	*Withe*	*Lewington*	*Arnott*	*Smith P*
									Ref: C Seel	Fox saves point blank from Edwards who then slides in to equalise Neil Adams' far-post header. It takes Stoke just 18 seconds from the restart to win the game when Shaw chips over the advancing Burridge and follows up to head home. Four wins in a row for the first time in 12 years.											

No	Date	Att	Pos	Pt	F-A	H-T	Scorers, Times, and Referees	1	2	3	4	5	6	7	8	9	10	11	12 sub used
22	H BARNSLEY		10	D	0-0	0-0		Fox	Bould	Hemming	Devine	Dyson	Berry	Adams	Saunders	Bertschin	Shaw*	Heath	Williams
	21/12	9,856	*4*	30				*Baker*	*Joyce*	*Gray*	*Goodison*	*May*	*Futcher*	*Owen*	*Thomas*	*Walsh*	*Hirst*	*Plummer*	
							Ref: A Robinson	Stoke make all the running but Allan Clarke's Tykes keep them at bay. Devine has a lob held by Baker and then smashes a free-kick over. The Barnsley defence is well marshalled by Paul Futcher. Mills chases Norwich's Louie Donowa on-loan. Peter Coates is appointed vice-chairman.											
23	A SHREWSBURY		11	L	0-1	0-1		Fox	Bould	Mills*	Devine	Dyson	Berry	Adams	Saunders	Bertschin	Shaw	Heath	Hemming
	26/12	*9,595*	*13*	30			*Dyson 45 (og)*	*Perks*	*Gunn*	*Hughes*	*Cross*	*Pearson*	*Griffin*	*Leonard*	*Hackett*	*Stevens*	*Robinson*	*Daly*	
							Ref: R Guy	5,000 City fans see Ray Guy ruin the flow of the game as he stops play for petty offences. This suits the Shrews after Paul Dyson heads Daly's free-kick high past Fox in trying to clear. Shaw appears to be fouled in the box but no penalty. Shrewsbury don't extend Fox, but don't have to.											
24	H BLACKBURN		13	D	2-2	2-1	Bertschin 33p, Adams 36	Fox	Bould	Hemming	Devine	Dyson	Berry	Adams	Saunders	Bertschin	Shaw	Heath	
	1/1	**11,875**	*10*	31			*Garner 20, Barker 48p*	*Gennoe*	*Branagan*	*Rathbone*	*Barker*	*Fazackerley*	*Mail*	*Miller*	*Lowey*	*Thompson*	*Garner*	*Hamilton*	
							Ref: K Baker	In a tale of disputed penalties Stoke have an obvious one turned down and then are surprised to get one for Gennoe and Bertschin's collision. It is Bertschin's 100th career goal. Adams dives to head in. A bobbling ball hits Berry's hand and another penalty is awarded. City are not happy.											
25	A MILLWALL		11	W	3-2	2-1	Donowa 15, Painter 17, Bertschin 71	Fox	Bould !	Hemming	Devine	Dyson	Berry	**Donowa**	Saunders	Bertschin	Shaw	Painter	
	11/1	*4,611*	*19*	34			*Wilson 31, Lovell 65*	*Sansome*	*Roffey*	*Hinshelwood*	*Briley*	*Walker*	*Nutton*	*Lowndes*	*Wilson*	*Fashanu*	*Lovell*	*Otulakowski*	
							Ref: J Ball	A physical match flares up when Bould and Otulakowski clash. Bould is sent off (44 mins) – Mills has to go down to pitch side to calm furious players. Louie Donowa scores on his debut. City stay on the attack after going down to ten men. Bertschin nods in when Saunders hits the bar.											
26	H BRADFORD C		9	W	3-1	1-0	Shaw 41, Bertschin 48, 82	Fox	Hemming	Mills	Devine	Dyson	Berry	Adams	Saunders	Bertschin	Shaw	Donowa	
	18/1	8,808	*13*	37			*Oliver 68*	*Litchfield*	*Oliver*	*Withe**	*McCall*	*Jackson*	*Evans*	*Hendrie*	*Abbott*	*Campbell*	*Singleton*	*Graham*	*Ellis*
							Ref: R Groves	Shaw has a shot deflected just wide before heading past Peter Litchfield. Bertschin's brace are a brave diving header and a right-foot shot at the second time of asking. Gavin Oliver heads low past Fox for Trevor Cherry's Bantam's consolation goal. Hemming keeps Arthur Graham quiet.											
27	A GRIMSBY		9	D	3-3	3-2	Shaw 10, Bertschin 22, Adams 44	Fox	Hemming*	Mills	Devine	Dyson	Berry	Adams	Saunders	Bertschin	Shaw	Donowa	Painter
	25/1	*4,523*	*14*	38			*Emson 18, Bonnyman 26, Ford 67*	*Batch*	*Robinson*	*Cummings*	*Peake*	*Lyons*	*Crombie*	*Ford*	*Lund*	*Hobson*	*Bonnyman*	*Emson*	
							Ref: J Ashworth	Shaw takes advantage of Nigel Batch's miskick to slot the opener. Bertschin evades Mariners' player-manager Mick Lyons to crack home and Adams follows up his own header to score. Battling Town level through Tony Ford's first-time effort as the temperature drops below freezing.											
28	A LEEDS		9	L	**0-4**	0-1		Fox	Hemming	Mills*	Devine	Dyson	Berry	Adams	Saunders	Bertschin	Shaw	Donowa	Painter
	1/2	*10,425*	*14*	38			*Stiles 33, Baird 52, Swan 59, 85*	*Day*	*Caswell*	*Robinson*	*Snodin*	*Aspin*	*Rennie*	*Ritchie*	*Swan*	*Baird*	*Hamson*	*Stiles*	
							Ref: K Breen	Billy Bremner's Leeds grow in stature once John Stiles' debut goal flies past Fox. Ian Baird unleashes an unstoppable shot from the edge of the area, then Peter Swan nets a pair of stooping headers. Stoke fail to move with any fluency and don't test Day. Mills is unhappy at lack of spirit.											
29	H FULHAM		9	W	1-0	1-0	Devine 9	Fox	Bould	Hemming	Devine	Dyson	Berry	Adams	Saunders	Bertschin	Shaw*	Heath	Callaghan
	18/2	**6,449**	*21*	41				*Peyton*	*Cottington*	*Carr*	*Gore*	*Hopkins*	*Parker*	*Marshall*	*Achampong*	*Caney*	*Donnellan*	*Barnett**	*Pike*
							Ref: J Bray	Stoke's injury list lengthens when Graham Shaw twists knee ligaments. John Devine gets his first goal for the club, firing home off a post with Shaw following in to make sure. City are in charge for the second half with Hemming and Bould using their height to good effect on the wings.											
30	H CHARLTON		9	D	0-0	0-0		Fox	Bould	Hemming	Devine	Dyson	Berry	Adams	Saunders	Bertschin	Painter	Heath	
	22/2	9,297	*3*	42				*Johns*	*Humphrey*	*Reid*	*Curbishley*	*Thompson*	*Pender*	*Shipley*	*Lee*	*Pearson*	*Aizlewood*	*Flanagan*	
							Ref: K Hackett	A tempestuous match as Bertschin is sent hurtling into the paddock wall by the force of Mark Reid's challenge. He retaliates and is cautioned. John Humphrey earns a booking for flattening Heath with a tackle from behind. Bertschin nets but is given offside. Berry heads against the bar.											
31	H HULL		10	L	0-1	0-1		Fox	Hemming	Mills*	Devine	Dyson	Bould	Adams	Saunders	Bertschin	**Curtis**	Heath	Painter
	8/3	9,112	*5*	42			*McEwan 31*	*Norman*	*Swann*	*Pearson*	*Doyle*	*Skipper*	*McEwan*	*Parker*	*Bunn*	*Flounders*	*Askew*	*Roberts*	
							Ref: K Barratt	Alan Curtis makes his debut on-loan from Southampton. Billy McEwan dives headlong to give Hull a hard-earned lead. Hull hound City out of their stride and only Adams, with a header against the bar, threatens in the second half. City rue missed opportunities by Saunders. No spark.											

No	H/A	Opponent	Att	Pos	Pt	F-A	H-T	Scorers, Times, and Referees	1	2	3	4	5	6	7	8	9	10	11	12 sub used
32	A	BRIGHTON		12	L	0-2	0-1		Fox	Saunders	Hemming	Devine*	Bould	Berry	Adams	Painter !	Bertschin	Curtis	Heath	Callaghan
15/3			*8,783*	*7*	42			*Wilson 38, Mortimer 88*	*Digweed*	*Jacobs*	*Hutchings*	*Wilson*	*Young**	*O'Reilly*	*Saunders*	*Penney*	*Biley*	*Connor*	*Mortimer*	*Gatting*
								Ref: D Reeves	City don't compete with physical Brighton. Once Wilson drives home through a crowd there is only one winner. Painter is sent off for claiming a penalty too vehemently (44 mins). Devine's broken leg in a tackle with Eric Young ends his career. Paul Dyson has been sold to West Brom.											
33	A	CRYSTAL PALACE		11	W	1-0	1-0	Bertschin 36	Fox	Callaghan	Hemming	Curtis	Bould	Berry	Adams	Saunders	Bertschin	Painter	Heath	
18/3			*4,501*	*8*	45				*Hardwick*	*Hughton**	*Brush*	*Taylor*	*Nebbeling*	*Cannon*	*Irvine*	*Ketteridge*	*Gray*	*Barber*	*Sparrow*	*Wright*
								Ref: R Hamer	Steve Bould keeps his place at the heart of City's defence as he prefers playing there to full-back. Bertschin darts in to loop a header over Steve Hardwick as Stoke commit daylight robbery. In a bruising game Hughton is taken to hospital with bruised ribs. For once it isn't a Stoke player.											
34	A	BLACKBURN		10	W	1-0	0-0	Saunders 76	Fox	Callaghan	Hemming	Mills	Bould	Berry	Adams	Saunders	Bertschin	**Bonnyman**	Heath	
29/3			*5,408*	*15*	48				*O'Keefe*	*Branagan*	*Rathbone*	*Barker*	*Keeley*	*Mail*	*Miller*	*Hamilton*	*Quinn**	*Patterson*	*Brotherston*	*Garner*
								Ref: R Guy	Phil Bonnyman makes his debut on-loan from Grimsby. Blackburn can't find a way past Bould and Berry. A drab game sees Saunders notch a fabulous goal with a whiplash shot past O'Keefe. He then gets engaged to girlfriend Sherlyn. Mills is interested in Bury right-back Lee Dixon.											
35	H	SHREWSBURY		10	D	2-2	1-1	Bertschin 13p, 63	Fox	Callaghan	Hemming	Bonnyman	Bould	Berry	Adams	Saunders	Bertschin	Shaw	Heath	
31/3			8,988	*17*	49			*McNally 17p, Callaghan 81 (og)*	*Perks*	*Williams*	*Johnson*	*Rees**	*Pearson*	*Griffin*	*McNally*	*Hackett*	*Stevens*	*Robinson*	*Hughes*	*Bates*
								Ref: V Callow	City score another calamitous own-goal against the Shrews. This time Aaron Callaghan lobs a back-pass over Fox. It is the only way Town will get back into a game City control after the teams swap debatable penalties. Bertschin nets after a flick-on. City furiously try to win it but can't.											
36	A	HUDDERSFIELD		10	L	0-2	0-0		Fox	Callaghan	Hemming	Bonnyman*	Bould	Berry	Adams	Saunders	Bertschin	Painter	Heath	Beeston
5/4			*5,750*	*15*	49			*Shearer 66, 68*	*Cox*	*Brown*	*Wilson Paul*	*Doyle*	*Webster*	*Jones J*	*Curran*	*Raynor*	*Shearer*	*Wilson Phil*	*Cowling*	
								Ref: G Aplin	Huddersfield exert pressure on City which finally pays off with two left-foot finishes by Duncan Shearer. England U-21 squad members Heath and Adams test Cox but Stoke never look like getting back level. A statue of Stan Matthews will be erected in Hanley to honour the great man.											
37	H	CARLSILE		11	D	0-0	0-0		Fox	Mills	Hemming	Bonnyman	Bould	Berry	Adams	Saunders	Bertschin	Painter	Heath	
12/4			7,159	*21*	50				*Endersby*	*Haigh*	*McCartney*	*Ashurst*	*Saunders*	*Halsall*	*Hill*	*Cooke*	*Baker*	*Bishop*	*Tolmie**	*Gorman*
								Ref: T Mills	Both sides have chances. Heath hits the bar and Bertschin brings a fine save out of Endersby. Halsall and Baker test Fox. Carlisle are content to hold on as Stoke gain the initiative. Wes Saunders is rock solid. Bertschin scrapes the bar and the ball goes anywhere but in the back of the net.											
38	A	NORWICH		13	D	1-1	0-0	Bertschin 65	Fox	Mills*	Hemming	Bonnyman	Bould	Berry	Adams	Saunders	Bertschin	Painter	Heath	Shaw
19/4			*17,757*	*1*	51			*Gordon 75*	*Woods*	*Culverhouse*	*Van Wyk*	*Bruce*	*Phelan*	*Watson*	*Gordon*	*Drinkell*	*Biggins**	*Deehan*	*Williams*	*Brooke*
								Ref: M Scott	Nearly promoted Norwich start at a furious pace. City cling on and Keith Bertschin heads home against his old side to give them a cheeky lead. Berry heads over but finally Ken Brown's Canaries' pressure tells when Dale Gordon fires in from Dave Watson's flick on. A very good point.											
39	H	PORTSMOUTH		11	W	2-0	2-0	Berry 17, Heath 45	Fox	Mills	Hemming	Bonnyman	Bould	Berry	Painter	Saunders	Bertschin	Shaw	Heath	
22/4			8,529	*3*	54				*Knight*	*Swain*	*Hardyman*	*Dillon*	*Blake*	*Gilbert*	*O'Callaghan*	*Kennedy*	*Quinn*	*Channon**	*Hilaire*	*McGarvey*
								Ref: J Worrall	Stoke outplay Pompey who look scared they may miss promotion after having a great start. Alan Ball screeches encouragement to his men but they are never in it. Berry takes time off from his duel with Mick Quinn to head home Painter's corner and Heath sweeps home Painter's cross.											
40	H	OLDHAM		8	W	2-0	1-0	Shaw 40, Bertschin 47	Fox	Saunders	Hemming	**Kelly**	Bould	Berry	Painter*	Bonnyman	Bertschin	Shaw	Heath	Adams
26/4			8,585	*12*	57				*Goram*	*Bullock*	*Barlow*	*Jones*	*Linighan*	*Gorton*	*Palmer*	*McGuire*	*Colville**	*Futcher*	*Henry*	*Smith*
								Ref: C Downey	City pay Wigan £80,000 for Tony Kelly who is involved in all of the best moves. He passes to Hemming who crosses for Shaw to beat Goram. Shaw provides Keith Bertschin with his 23rd of the season. Stoke test Goram from all sorts of angles. Shaw beats him but hits Jones on the line.											
41	A	WIMBLEDON		9	L	0-1	0-0		Fox	Callaghan	Hemming	Mills	Bould	Berry	Adams	Saunders	Bertschin	Shaw	Heath	
29/4			*5,959*	*3*	57			*Cork 48*	*Beasant*	*Gage*	*Winterburn*	*Galliers*	*Morris*	*Thorn*	*Hodges**	*Cork*	*Fashanu*	*Sanchez*	*Fairweather*	*Downes*
								Ref: B Stevens	Dave Beasant booms long clearances to the edge of City's penalty box as Wimbledon search frantically for the elusive goal. Shaw misses from three yards out. City provide all the finesse but the promotion-chasing Dons snatch a vital three points thanks to Alan Cork's near-post header.											
42	A	SUNDERLAND		10	L	0-2	0-1		Fox	Callaghan*	Hemming	Mills	Bould	Berry	Adams	Saunders	Bertschin	Shaw	Heath	Painter
3/5			***20,631***	*18*	57			*Proctor 2p, Gray 68*	*Dibble*	*Venison*	*Kennedy*	*Gray*	*Bennett*	*Elliott*	*Ford*	*Gayle**	*Wallace*	*Gates*	*Proctor*	*Hodgson*
		Home	Away					Ref: D Hutchinson	Mills fouls Gates for the dubious looking spot-kick. Tempers become frayed after Gayle and Saunders come to blows. Shaw curles a free-kick wide. Sunderland's tension is eased when Gray scores from 12 yards. Mills loses to mentor McMenemy's Rokerites who just escape the drop.											
Average		8,280	8,060																	

Milk Cup	Att			F-A	H-T	Scorers, Times, and Referees	1	2	3	4	5	6	7	8	9	10	11	12 sub used
2:1 A WREXHAM		19	W	1-0	0-0	Bertschin 49	Fox	Bould	Mills	Parkin	Dyson	Berry	**Adams**	Williams	Bertschin	Saunders	Heath	
24/9	*5,241 4:10·*						*Hooper*	*Williams*	*Comstive*	*Jones*	*Keay*	*Cunnington*	*Muldoon*	*Horne*	*Hencher*	*Charles*	*Gregory*	
						Ref: I Hendrick	Saunders is sent clear by Parkin but Hooper makes a fabulous double save. Keith Bertschin is rewarded for a great performance with a stooping header from Heath's deep cross. A large travelling support cheer Stoke's first away win in 28 attempts as Dixie McNeil's men are well beaten.											
2:2 H WREXHAM		17	W	1-0	0-0	Bertschin 80	Fox	Bould	Mills	Parkin	Dyson	Berry	Adams	Maskery	Bertschin	Saunders*	Heath	Williams
9/10	6,784 *4:11*						*Hooper*	*Salathiel*	*Comstive*	*Williams*	*Keay*	*Cunnington*	*Hencher*	*Horne*	*Edwards*	*Charles*	*Gregory*	
						Ref: A Banks (Stoke win 2-0 on aggregate)	The floodlights fuse and City switch off. A dull game is enlivened only by Carl Saunders' reverse pass which wrong-foots the entire Wrexham defence to leave Bertschin clear to race through and score. Wrexham harry Stoke with Horne and Salathiel closing down doggedly in midfield.											
3 A PORTSMOUTH		18	L	0-2	0-0		Fox	Bould	Mills*	Hemming	Dyson	Berry	Adams	Maskery	Bertschin	Parkin	Heath	Saunders
29/10	*13,319 2:1*					*Dillon 46p, 63p*	*Knight*	*Stanley*	*Sandford*	*Dillon*	*Blake*	*Gilbert*	*O'Callaghan*	*Tait*	*Morgan*	*Channon**	*Hilaire*	*McGarvey*
						Ref: A Buksh	Vince Hilaire tumbles over twice in the area to earn Pompey's penalties which Kevin Dillon dispatches past Fox with aplomb. Stoke put up a gutsy show. Heath rolls just wide of the post when through. Alan Knight produces two great saves from Parkin. Seven City players are booked.											

FA Cup	Att			F-A	H-T	Scorers, Times, and Referees	1	2	3	4	5	6	7	8	9	10	11	12 sub used
3 H NOTTS CO		11	L	0-2	0-1		Fox	Mills*	Hemming	Devine	Dyson	Berry	Adams	Bertschin	Saunders	Painter	Shaw	Donowa
13/1	12,219 *3:5*					*Waitt 41, McParland 65*	*Leonard*	*Yates*	*Clarke*	*Benjamin*	*Sims*	*Davis*	*McParland*	*Goodwin*	*Waitt*	*Edge**	*Hunt*	*Robinson*
						Ref: G Napthine	Stoke play all the football with Fox virtually unemployed but Jimmy Sirrel's County ride their luck to win. Mick Leonard is only booked when he flattens Painter who is racing clear. Berry's clearance hits McParland's arm and rebounds for Waitt to score. McParland scores on the break.											

	Home						Away					
	P	W	D	L	F	A	W	D	L	F	A	Pts
1 Norwich	42	16	4	1	51	15	9	5	7	33	22	84
2 Charlton	42	14	5	2	44	15	8	6	7	34	30	77
3 Wimbledon	42	13	6	2	38	16	8	7	6	20	21	76
4 Portsmouth	42	13	4	4	43	17	9	3	9	26	24	73
5 Crys Palace	42	12	3	6	29	22	7	6	8	28	30	66
6 Hull	42	11	7	3	39	19	6	6	9	26	36	64
7 Sheffield Utd	42	10	7	4	36	24	7	4	10	28	39	62
8 Oldham	42	13	4	4	40	28	4	5	12	22	33	60
9 Millwall	42	12	3	6	39	24	5	5	11	25	41	59
10 STOKE	42	8	11	2	29	16	6	4	11	19	34	57
11 Brighton	42	10	5	6	42	30	6	3	12	22	34	56
12 Barnsley	42	9	6	6	29	26	5	8	8	18	24	56
13 Bradford C	42	14	1	6	36	24	2	5	14	15	39	54
14 Leeds	42	9	7	5	30	22	6	1	14	26	50	53
15 Grimsby	42	11	4	6	35	24	3	6	12	23	38	52
16 Huddersfield	42	10	6	5	30	23	4	4	13	21	44	52
17 Shrewsbury	42	11	5	5	29	20	3	4	14	23	44	51
18 Sunderland	42	10	5	6	33	29	3	6	12	14	32	50
19 Blackburn	42	10	4	7	30	20	2	9	10	23	42	49
20 Carlisle	42	10	2	9	30	28	3	5	13	17	43	46
21 Middlesbro	42	8	6	7	26	23	4	3	14	18	30	45
22 Fulham	42	8	3	10	29	32	2	3	16	16	37	36
	924	242	108	112	767	497	112	108	242	497	767	1278

Odds & ends

Double wins: (1) Oldham.
Double losses: (0).

Won from behind: (1) Middlesbrough (h).
Lost from in front: (0).

High spots: Good recovery from last season's debacle.
Keith Bertschin nets the highest goals total for a season for 21 years.
Thrashing Leeds 6-2.
Winning 4-2 at Boundary Park.
A solid start for Mick Mills as manager.

Low spots: Slow start to the season.
Failing to press for the play-offs after a mid-season spurt of good form.
Another disappointing FA Cup exit.
Lowest average home attendance since 1907-08.

Player of the Year: Keith Bertschin.
Ever-presents: (1) Keith Bertschin.
Hat-tricks: (0).
Leading scorer: (21) Keith Bertschin.

	Appearances						Goals			
	Lge	*Sub*	LC	*Sub*	FAC	*Sub*	**Lge**	LC	FAC	**Tot**
Adams, Neil	**31**	*1*	3		1		**4**			**4**
Beeston, Carl	**2**	*3*								
Berry, George	**41**		3		1		**3**			**3**
Bertschin, Keith	**42**		3		1		**19**	2		**21**
Bonnyman, Phil	**7**									
Bould, Steve	**33**		3							
Callaghan, Aaron	**6**	*2*								
Chamberlain, Mark	**7**						**3**			**3**
Curtis, Alan	**3**									
Devine, John	**15**				1		**1**			**1**
Donowa, Louie	**4**					*1*	**1**			**1**
Dyson, Paul	**31**		3		1					
Fox, Peter	**37**		3		1					
Heath, Phil	**38**		3				**4**			**4**
Hemming, Chris	**23**	*1*	1		1					
Hudson, Alan	**6**									
Kelly, Tony	**1**									
Maskery, Chris	**19**		2				**3**			**3**
Mills, Mick	**31**		3		1					
Painter, Ian	**15**	*4*			1		**2**			**2**
Parkin, Steve	**10**	*2*	3				**1**			**1**
Saunders, Carl	**33**	*4*	2	*1*	1		**2**			**2**
Shaw, Graham	**19**	*1*			1		**5**			**5**
Siddall, Barry	**5**									
Williams, Terry	**3**	*3*	1	*1*						
25 players used	**462**	*21*	**33**	*2*	**11**	*1*	**48**	**2**		**50**

No	Date	Att	Pos	Pt	F-A	H-T	Scorers, Times, and Referees	1	2	3	4	5	6	7	8	9	10	11	12 sub used
1	H BIRMINGHAM			L	0-2	0-1		Fox	**Dixon**	Hemming	Kelly	Bould	Berry	**Ford***	Maskery	Bertschin	Shaw	Heath	Saunders
	23/8	11,548		0			*Hemming 43 (og), Whitton 69*	*Hansbury*	*Jones*	*Dicks*	*Hagan*	*Overson*	*Kuhl*	*Bremner*	*Rees*	*Whitton*	*Mortimer*	*Hopkins*	
							Ref: R Groves	Stoke parade new signings Tony Ford and Lee Dixon. A tetchy affair erupts when Hagan seems to foul Shaw but no penalty is given. Five are booked as City lose their young heads. Chris Hemming slices Dicks' cross into his own goal and a mix-up in defence gifts Whitton the second.											
2	A LEEDS			L	1-2	1-1	Saunders 1	Fox	Dixon	Mills*	Kelly	Bould	Berry !	Ford	Maskery	Bertschin	Saunders	Heath	Shaw
	25/8	*13,334*		0			*Sheridan 36, Baird 72*	*Sinclair*	*Aspin*	*Thompson*	*Snodin*	*Ashurst*	*Rennie*	*Stiles*	*Sheridan*	*Baird*	*Edwards*	*Ritchie*	
							Ref: K Redfern	City score from their first corner. Saunders nets after Maskery's shot hits a post. John Sheridan then takes over and curls in a fine equaliser. He crosses for Edwards to head against the bar. Bould slips in the rain leaving Ian Baird clean through. Berry is sent off (87 mins) for two bookings.											
3	A CRYSTAL PALACE		22	L	0-1	0-0		Fox	Dixon	Hemming	Saunders	Bould	Berry	Ford	Maskery	Bertschin	Shaw	Heath*	Kelly
	30/8	*6,864*	*4*	0			*Barber 55*	*Wood*	*Finnigan*	*Brush*	*Taylor*	*Droy*	*Cannon*	*Irvine*	*Ketteridge*	*Barber*	*Wright*	*Otulakowski*	
							Ref: M James	Palace put City under intense pressure and from their 12th corner Phil Barber wallops home from close range. Wright's over-head kick is tipped onto the bar by Fox. Alan Irvine torments Hemming. Micky Droy overshadows Shaw. 'We should have lost by five' says Mills, disconsolately.											
4	H WEST BROM		22	D	1-1	1-0	Berry 29	Fox	Dixon	Hemming	Mills*	Bould	Berry	Ford	Maskery	Saunders	Shaw	Heath	Parkin
	2/9	8,668	*7*	1			*Palmer 62*	*Naylor*	*Whitehead*	*Burrows*	*Bennett*	*Dyson*	*Dickinson*	*Palmer*	*Evans*	*MacKenzie*	*Williamson*	*Thompson*	
							Ref: M Dimblebee	Ford impresses on the right as Stoke produce some stylish football for the first time this season. George Berry characteristically heads home his corner. Fox tips Stuart Evans' header on to the bar. Gangling Carlton Palmer fires home to grab Ron Saunders' Baggies a draw. A point at last.											
5	H MILLWALL		16	W	2-0	2-0	Berry 34, Shaw 37p	Fox	Dixon	Hemming	Parkin	Bould	Berry	Ford	Maskery	Saunders	Shaw	Heath	
	6/9	7,076	*11*	4				*Horne*	*Stevens*	*Coleman N*	*Briley*	*Walker*	*Salman*	*Byrne*	*McLeary*	*Sheringham*	*Marks*	*Mehmet*	
							Ref: T Fitzharris	Saunders moves into a striker's role and looks good as John Docherty's Millwall are totally outplayed. Berry sweeps in his cross. Shaw scores one penalty for a foul on Bould but misses another (46 mins) for a trip on Saunders. Berry vows to wear his new red trousers until Stoke lose.											
6	A OLDHAM		19	L	0-2	0-0		Fox	Dixon	Hemming	Parkin	Bould	Callaghan	Saunders*	Maskery	Bertschin	Shaw	Heath	Williams
	13/9	*6,513*	*1*	4			*Henry 74, Futcher 75*	*Goram*	*Irwin*	*Donachie*	*Jones*	*Linighan*	*Barlow*	*Palmer*	*Henry*	*Ellis**	*Futcher*	*Milligan*	*McGuire*
							Ref: D Allison	City are caught offside continually as they struggle to cope with the 250 tons of sand which have been spread on Boundary Park's plastic pitch. Shaw misses from an acute angle after rounding Goram. Henry and Futcher score for Joe Royle's Oldham who have yet to concede this season.											
7	H PORTSMOUTH		20	D	1-1	0-1	Kelly 58	Fox	Dixon	Hemming	Kelly	Bould	Berry	Ford	Parkin	Bertschin	Shaw	Heath	
	20/9	8,440	*3*	5			*Kennedy 31*	*Knight*	*Swain*	*Hardyman !*	*Dillon*	*Blake*	*Gilbert*	*Tait*	*Kennedy*	*Mariner*	*Quinn**	*Hilaire*	*O'Callaghan*
							Ref: K Baker	Tony Kelly returns after losing a stone in an intensive training programme to score a picture-book free-kick. Knight saves Bertschin's 44th-min penalty. Peter Fox breaks the City goalkeepers appearance record in his 239th game. Paul Hardyman is sent off as he is stretchered off the field.											
8	A SUNDERLAND		21	L	0-2	0-2		Fox	Dixon	Mills*	Kelly	Bould	Berry	Ford	Maskery	Bertschin	Parkin	Heath	Williams
	27/9	*14,394*	*6*	5			*Swindlehurst 18, Armstrong 33p*	*Hesford*	*Burley*	*Kennedy*	*Armstrong*	*Corner*	*Bennett*	*Lemon*	*Doyle*	*Swindlehurst*	*Gray*	*Buchanan*	
							Ref: C Seel	Mills lashes out at City's undisciplined defence after Berry tries to dribble out of a crowded area only to hand possession to Swindlehurst who scores. Dixon's handball is punished by Armstrong. Lawrie McMenemy's team have it won by the break. Tony Ford wastes two good chances.											
9	A BRIGHTON		22	L	0-1	0-1		Fox	Dixon	Hemming	Kelly	Bould	Callaghan*	Ford	Parkin	Bertschin	Williams	Heath	**Crooks**
	4/10	*8,341*	*7*	5			*Wilson 31p*	*Digweed*	*Berry*	*Hutchings*	*Wilson*	*Gatting*	*O'Regan*	*Penney*	*Saunders*	*Armstrong*	*Hughes*	*Jasper*	
							Ref: J Martin	City produce a lamentable performance. Callaghan, Kelly and Bertschin all miss free headers and Williams misses from five yards. Callaghan commits a stupid foul to gift Brighton a penalty and is substituted. Fox makes a wonder save from Hughes. Where are George's trousers now?											
10	H HUDDERSFIELD		22	W	2-0	2-0	Berry 24, Bertschin 29	Fox	Dixon	Parkin	**Talbot**	Bould	Berry	Ford	Kelly	Shaw	Bertschin	Heath*	Maskery
	11/10	7,543	*20*	8				*Cox*	*Trevitt*	*Wilson Paul*	*Banks*	*Webster*	*Jones*	*Raynor**	*Winter*	*Shearer*	*Wilson Phil*	*Cowling*	*Cork*
							Ref: D Scott	Brian Talbot signs from Watford for £25,000. The PFA Chairman gives Stoke stability in midfield allowing Kelly to rove forward. Berry nets a flicked on corner and Bertschin hooks another home. Shaw nets a third but Berry is given offside despite lying prone after running into a post.											

No	Venue	Opponent / Date	Att	Pos	Res / Pts	F-A	H-T	Scorers, Times, and Referees	1	2	3	4	5	6	7	8	9	10	11	12
11	H	BLACKBURN		18	W	1-0	0-0	Shaw 49	Fox	Dixon*	Parkin	Talbot	Bould	Berry	Ford	Kelly	Shaw	Bertschin	Heath	Saunders
		18/10	7,715	*19*	11				*O'Keefe*	*Price*	*Branagan*	*Barker*	*Fazackerley*	*Mail*	*Brotherston*	*Patterson*	*Quinn*	*Garner*	*Rathbone*	
								Ref: L Hamer	Kelly and Talbot run midfield. City waste a host of chances. Bertschin hits the bar and Bould turns the rebound against the post. Don Mackay's men hold out until Shaw cracks home after Vince O'Keefe parries Heath's drive. Kelly hasn't had a beer in six weeks and is down to 13 stone.											
12	A	IPSWICH		20	L	0-2	0-1		Fox	Dixon*	Parkin	Talbot	Bould	Berry	Ford	Kelly	Shaw	Bertschin	Heath	Saunders
		25/10	*11,054*	*6*	11			*Wilson 42, 50*	*Cooper*	*Yallop*	*Zondervan*	*Atkins*	*Dozzell*	*Cranson*	*Gleghorn*	*Brennan*	*Cole*	*Deehan**	*Wilson*	*Atkinson*
								Ref: M Reed	Kevin Wilson plays on Steve Parkin's defensive weaknesses to pinch two goals. City hit the post through Heath and the ball rolls tantalisingly along the goal-line before being cleared. Cooper tips a Berry header over and a Saunders header round. City just cannot score at Mills' old club.											
13	H	DERBY		22	L	0-2	0-1		Fox	Dixon	Parkin	Talbot	Bould	Berry	Ford	Kelly*	Shaw	Bertschin	Heath	Saunders
		1/11	12,358	*7*	11			*Williams 42, Gee 78*	*Wallington*	*Sage*	*Forsyth*	*Williams*	*Hindmarch*	*MacLaren*	*Micklewhite*	*Gee*	*Davison*	*Gregory*	*Harbey*	
								Ref: J Worrall	Stoke slip back to the bottom after Derby survive a furious onslaught. Berry's header is cleared off the line. Wallington touches Shaw's shot on to the bar. Williams and Gee notch breakaway goals for Arthur Cox's disciplined Rams. Mills takes off Kelly (65 mins) who is not best pleased.											
14	A	HULL		19	W	4-0	3-0	Ford 16, McEwan 37 (og), Morgan 41, [Bertschin 64]	Fox	Dixon	Parkin	Talbot	Bould	Berry	Ford	Kelly	**Morgan**	Bertschin	Heath	
		8/11	*5,252*	*14*	14				*Norman*	*Jobson*	*Heard*	*Parker*	*Skipper**	*McEwan*	*Williams*	*Bunn*	*Saville*	*Askew*	*Roberts*	*Flounders*
								Ref: K Lupton	At last City find the right formula with on-loan Nicky Morgan providing the perfect foil for Bertschin. Ford crashes in from six yards and then McEwan lobs over his own keeper under pressure. Morgan scores a debut tap-in. Bertschin rounds off a great show heading in Morgan's flick.											
15	A	SHEFFIELD UTD		20	L	1-3	1-2	Bertschin 19	Fox	Dixon	Parkin	Talbot	Saunders	Berry	Ford	Kelly	Morgan	Bertschin	Heath*	Shaw
		15/11	*11,177*	*5*	14			*Dixon 4 (og), Withe 38, Beagrie 75*	*Tomlinson*	*Barnsley*	*Pike*	*Arnott*	*Stancliffe*	*Glover*	*Daws*	*Wigley*	*Withe*	*Foley*	*Beagrie*	
								Ref: W Flood	City miss Bould (knee) and Talbot is moved into the back four. But the midfield malfunctions without him. Dixon nets trying to keep out Paul Stancliffe's header. Bertschin buries a free header. Peter Withe scores against City yet again. Beagrie heads home after Fox misjudges a cross.											
16	H	READING		18	W	3-0	1-0	Bertschin 12, 58, 79	Fox	Dixon	Parkin	Talbot	Bould	Berry	Ford	Kelly	Morgan	Bertschin	Heath	
		22/11	7,465	*14*	17				*Westwood*	*Williams*	*Richardson*	*Beavon*	*Bailie*	*Crombie*	*Rogers*	*Hurlock*	*Senior*	*Bremner*	*Gilkes**	*Horrix*
								Ref: T Mills	Keith Bertschin's hat-trick of headers is the first treble by a Stoke player for three years. He scores from a flicked-on corner, Heath's cross and after Westwood parries Morgan's effort. Ian Branfoot's third choice central defensive pair struggle. Mills offers to buy Morgan from Pompey.											
17	A	BRADFORD C		16	W	4-1	2-0	Saunders 17, 65, Ford 35, Berry 60p	Fox	Dixon	Parkin	Talbot	Bould	Berry	Ford	Kelly	Morgan	Saunders	Heath	
		29/11 (at Odsal Stadium)	*6,191*	*19*	20			*Hendrie 58*	*Nixon*	*Abbott*	*Withe*	*McCall*	*Oliver*	*Evans*	*Hendrie*	*Goodman*	*Leonard*	*Singleton*	*Ellis**	*Ormondroyd*
								Ref: C Trussell	Stoke outshine the Bantams with stand-in striker Saunders the brightest star. He buries Kelly's cross and then leaps over Ford's shot to deceive Nixon. Saunders is tripped by Hendrie for the penalty and Berry, the new taker, crashes home. Saunders buries Morgan's cross to round it off.											
18	H	PLYMOUTH		12	W	1-0	0-0	Berry 64p	Fox	Dixon	Parkin	Talbot	Bould	Berry	Ford	Kelly	Morgan	Saunders	Heath	
		6/12	10,043	*3*	23				*Cherry*	*Nisbet*	*Cooper L**	*Goodyear*	*Burrows*	*Uzzell*	*Hodges*	*Rowbotham*	*Tynan*	*Clayton*	*Summerfield*	*Nelson*
								Ref: R Wiseman / K Hoare	Substitute ref Mr K Hoare spots Cherry's foul on Morgan, allowing Berry to score from the spot again. Says Mills 'Some of the lads fell about when I handed George the job, but he loves it'. Fox changes direction in mid-air to save Tynan's shot. Parkin is more comfortable at left-back.											
19	A	GRIMSBY		12	D	1-1	0-0	Saunders 88	Fox	Dixon	Parkin	Talbot	Bould	Berry	Ford	Kelly	Morgan	Saunders	Heath	
		13/12	***4,642***	*9*	24			*Rawcliffe 71*	*Felgate*	*Moore D*	*Agnew*	*Robinson*	*Lyons*	*Moore K*	*Turner*	*Walsh*	*Henshaw*	*O'Riordan*	*Grocock**	*Rawcliffe*
								Ref: J Watson	City have to wear Town's damp change kit as Grimsby object to Stoke wearing striped shirts. Saunders' shooting fails to match good approach work as Mick Lyons' men defend in depth. Saunders finally scores after Felgate saves from Morgan. Morgan looks great value for £40,000 fee.											
20	H	LEEDS		11	W	**7-2**	5-0	M'rg'n 5, 35, 72, S'nders 11, Dix'n 21, [K'lly 44, F'rd 62]	Fox	Dixon	Parkin	Talbot	Bould	Berry	Ford	Kelly*	Morgan	Saunders	Heath	Bertschin
		21/12	12,358	*8*	27			*B'rd 51, Sher' 73p*	*Day*	*Aspin*	*Robinson**	*Thompson*	*Ashurst*	*Swan*	*Doig*	*Sheridan*	*Baird*	*Edwards*	*Rennie*	*Ritchie*
								Ref: I Hemley	A magnificent seven for Stoke. Morgan blasts a trio of shots home from inside the box. Lee Dixon's superb overhead kick and Kelly's cheeky free-kick beat Day all ends up. John Sheridan's penalty is for Dixon's handball. 'We've threatened goals for some time.' Says Mills. Fantastic.											
21	A	BARNSLEY		10	W	2-0	1-0	Saunders 30, Kelly 87	Fox	Dixon	Parkin	Talbot	Bould	Berry	Ford	Kelly	Morgan	Saunders	Heath	
		26/12	*7,436*	*21*	30				*Baker*	*Ogley*	*Cross*	*Thomas*	*May*	*Futcher*	*Agnew*	*Foreman*	*Ferry**	*MacDonald*	*Gray*	*Hedworth*
								Ref: N Midgley	Tony Kelly makes Saunders' goal and rounds off a classy Stoke performance by powering a shot past Baker. Saunders also has a goal ruled out for a foul. Allan Clarke's Barnsley put in a lot of hard work but Fox is equal to Gwyn Thomas' headers. Bould is City's most improved player.											

No	Date		Att	Pos	Pt	F-A	H-T	Scorers, Times, and Referees	1	2	3	4	5	6	7	8	9	10	11	12 sub used
22	H	SHEFFIELD UTD		7	W	5-2	2-0	Bould 5, Saunders 17, 55, 82,	Fox	Dixon	Parkin	Talbot	Bould	Berry	Ford	Kelly	Morgan	Saunders	Heath	
	27/12		17,320	*9*	33			*Morris 70p, 87* [Morgan 77]	*Burridge*	*Barnsley*	*Pike*	*Dempsey*	*Stancliffe*	*Smith*	*Morris*	*Wigley*	*Withe **	*Foley*	*Frain*	*Daws*
								Ref: K Breen	United regret playing the offside trap against a rampaging City attack. Berry and Bould combine for the opener from Tony 'Zico' Kelly's free-kick. Saunders' trio of excellent finishes is completed by an exultant header. The penalty is for Berry's foul on Morris. 28 goals in nine games.											
23	H	SHREWSBURY		5	W	1-0	1-0	Saunders 1	Fox	Dixon	Parkin	Talbot	Bould	Berry	Ford	Kelly	Morgan*	Saunders	Heath	Bertschin
	1/1		**19,382**	*15*	36				*Perks*	*Williams*	*Johnson*	*Leonard**	*Pearson*	*Linighan*	*McNally*	*Hackett*	*Brown*	*Robinson*	*Daly*	*Green*
								Ref: D Hedges	Carl Saunders pounces after 52 seconds, slipping the ball to Heath and running on to finish a well-worked move involving Morgan and Talbot. Shrews' good midfield play is spoilt by their woeful crossing. City find it a hard slog on a rain-soaked pitch. Ford blazes wide of an open goal.											
24	A	MILLWALL		6	D	1-1	1-1	Heath 32	Fox	Dixon	Parkin	Talbot	Bould	Berry	Ford	Kelly	Morgan	Saunders	Heath	
	3/1		*6,134*	*9*	37			*Leslie 10*	*Horne*	*Coleman P*	*Coleman N*	*Briley*	*Walker*	*McLeary*	*Byrne*	*Morgan*	*Sheringham*	*Leslie*	*Salman*	
								Ref: G Napthine	City recover from a bout of flu to earn a creditable draw at John Docherty's Millwall. Heath stabs home after Bould flicks on Berry's free-kick to equalise John Leslie's tap-in. Stoke have slightly the better of the second half but tire. Mills is made Manager of the Month on his birthday.											
25	A	BIRMINGHAM		6	D	0-0	0-0		Fox	Dixon	Parkin	Talbot	Bould	Berry	Ford	Kelly	Morgan	Saunders	Heath	
	24/1		*10,641*	*11*	38				*Hansbury*	*Ranson*	*Roberts*	*Williams*	*Dicks*	*Mortimer*	*Bremner*	*Handysides*	*Whitton*	*Rees*	*Kuhl*	
								Ref: H King	Blues boss John Bond reflects that handing Lee Dixon a free transfer while manager at Burnley may not have been a great move. He is superb, both overlapping and defending as Stoke end Birmingham's record of scoring in each home game. Saunders flashes wide as City nearly win it.											
26	H	CRYSTAL PALACE		4	W	3-1	1-0	Ford 2, Dixon 64, Berry 73p	Fox	Dixon	Parkin	Talbot	Bould	Berry	Ford	Kelly	Morgan	Saunders*	Heath	Bertschin
	7/2		13,154	*8*	41			*Ketteridge 65*	*Wood*	*Stebbing*	*Brush*	*Taylor**	*O'Reilly*	*Cannon*	*Gray*	*Ketteridge*	*Bright*	*Wright*	*Barber*	*Finnigan*
								Ref: F Roberts	City start like a whirlwind. Ford takes Morgan's pass in his stride and fires into the far corner, Heath hits a post and Wood makes a great save. Dixon volleys a corner home. O'Reilly fells Bertschin and Berry tucks in the penalty. Berry subdues the famous Wright and Bright strikeforce.											
27	A	WEST BROM		6	L	**1-4**	0-3	Bertschin 80	**Segers**	Dixon	Parkin	Talbot	Bould	Berry	Ford	Kelly	Morgan	Bertschin	Heath !	
	14/2		*12,366*	*11*	41			*Crooks 13, 73, Reilly 14, 20p*	*Naylor*	*Palmer*	*Statham*	*Whitehead*	*Dyson*	*Bradley*	*Hopkins*	*Anderson*	*Reilly*	*MacKenzie*	*Crooks*	
								Ref: R Groves	The wheels come off as ex-Stokie Garth Crooks finishes coolly twice and is tripped by Berry for the pen. Heath walks (42 mins) for a second booking after flattening Hopkins who keeps fouling him. The ten men force seven corners but only Bertschin's close-range finish beats Naylor.											
28	A	PORTSMOUTH		6	L	0-3	0-2		Fox	Dixon	Parkin	Talbot*	Bould	Berry	Ford	Maskery	Morgan	Bertschin	Saunders	Hemming
	28/2		*14,607*	*1*	41			*Quinn 12, 67, Dillon 31p*	*Knight*	*Swain*	*Hardyman*	*Dillon*	*Blake*	*Gilbert*	*O'Callaghan**	*Tait*	*Mariner*	*Quinn*	*Hilaire*	*Collins*
								Ref: A Seville	Suspensions tell as Stoke lose Kelly and Heath for this vital clash. Mick Quinn scorches a drive past Fox. Mariner is upended by Berry for the penalty. Quinn rises to head home Kevin Dillon's free-kick. 'An extra day training next week to make up for the day off here.' grumbles Mills.											
29	A	BLACKBURN		9	L	1-2	0-0	Morgan 83	Fox	Dixon	Hemming*	Maskery	Bould	Berry	Ford	Parkin	Morgan	Saunders	Heath	Bertschin
	14/3		*10,075*	*17*	41			*Price 74, Berry 80 (og)*	*O'Keefe*	*Price*	*Sulley*	*Barker*	*Keeley*	*Mail*	*Miller*	*Ainscow*	*Hendry*	*Patterson*	*Branagan**	*Sellars*
								Ref: G Tyson	A poor display. George Berry has a nightmare deflecting Chris Price's shot inside the far post and then turning a cross past Fox. Nicky Morgan heads home a consolation but Stoke are not worth a point. Mills describes the performance as 'Relegation form'. Where has all the form gone?											
30	H	SUNDERLAND		7	W	3-0	1-0	Berry 21p, Dixon 60, Morgan 89	Fox	Dixon	Parkin	Talbot	Hemming	Berry	Ford	Kelly	Morgan	Shaw	Heath	
	17/3		9,420	*15*	44				*Hesford*	*Agboola**	*Gray*	*Armstrong*	*Hetzke*	*Bennett*	*Lemon*	*Doyle*	*Swindlehurst*	*Proctor*	*Buchanan*	*Atkinson*
								Ref: P Harrison	City splash their way to a comfortable win against struggling Sunderland. Morgan is fouled by Hetzke and after a long delay for protests Berry cracks in. Dixon finishes off Hemming's incisive pass. It is revealed that Chris Hemming will become the first pro player to wear a pacemaker.											
31	A	HUDDERSFIELD		7	D	2-2	0-1	Ford 67, Bertschin 87	Fox	Dixon	Parkin	Talbot	Hemming	Berry	Ford	Kelly	Morgan	Saunders	Heath*	Bertschin
	21/3		*7,222*	*18*	45			*Shearer 25, Cork 61*	*Cox*	*Brown*	*Burke*	*Banks*	*Webster*	*Jones*	*Winter*	*Cork*	*Shearer*	*Wilson Phil*	*Cowling*	
								Ref: D Allison	City do well to fight back after Shearer's quality strike and Cork's bobbling finish. Ford beats the offside trap to score. Bertschin scores a well-taken equaliser. He is set to join Sunderland to bring in cash for deadline day signings. Banks hits the post and Webster hits Parkin on the line.											

No / Date	H/A	Opponent / Att	Pos	Res / Pts	F-A	H-T	Scorers, Times, and Referees	1	2	3	4	5	6	7	8	9	10	11	12 sub used
32 25/3	H	IPSWICH 11,805	7 *4*	D 46	0-0	0-0	 Ref: K Hackett	Fox *Cooper*	Dixon *Yallop*	Parkin *McCall*	Talbot *Atkins*	Hemming *Dozzell*	Berry *Cranson*	Ford *D'Avray*	Kelly *Brennan*	Morgan *Deehan*	Saunders* *Wilson*	Heath *Zondervan*	Maskery
								Stoke, disrupted by injuries, battle all the way to earn a deserved point against Bobby Ferguson's Ipswich. Parkin clears off the line. Fox saves from Brennan. Late City pressure sees Cooper save from Morgan and Ford. D'Avray commits a bad challenge on Lee Dixon, injuring his knee.											
33 28/3	H	BRIGHTON 10,216	8 *22*	D 47	1-1	0-1	Morgan 47 *Wilson 1* Ref: M Bailey	Fox *Digweed*	Dixon *Hutchings*	Parkin *Hughes*	Talbot *Wilson*	Hemming *Isaac*	Berry *Young*	Ford *Crumplin*	Kelly *Gatting*	Morgan *Tiltman*	**Daly*** *Connor*	Heath *Jasper*	Shaw
								Bottom club Brighton are a goal up after 28 seconds when 'constructive' play from the back allows Wilson to seize the ball from Berry and fire past Fox. City never flow and their only chance is Morgan's diving header from Tony Kelly's free-kick. Newcomer Gerry Daly strains a thigh.											
34 4/4	H	HULL 8,146	8 *20*	D 48	1-1	1-0	Talbot 15 *Bunn 84* Ref: A Buksh	Fox ! *Norman*	Dixon *Palmer*	Parkin *Heard*	Talbot *Jobson*	Hemming *Skipper*	Berry *Parker**	Ford *Dyer*	Kelly *Bunn*	Morgan *Saville*	Shaw* *Askew*	Heath *Roberts*	**Gayle** *Payton*
								Talbot's 15-yard finish puts Stoke ahead but Brian Horton's Hull equalise. Fox is sent off (86 mins) for the second time in his career. His foul on Andy Saville is deemed 'professional' by the referee. Stand-in keeper Tony Kelly makes a superb save from Garreth Roberts in injury-time.											
35 11/4	A	DERBY ***19,038***	9 *1*	D 49	0-0	0-0	 Ref: D Hedges	Fox *Steele*	Dixon *Blades*	Parkin *Forsyth*	Talbot *Williams*	Hemming *Hindmarch*	Berry *MacLaren*	Ford *Micklewhite*	Kelly *Gee*	Morgan *Davison*	Shaw *Gregory*	Heath *Callaghan*	
								City expose Derby's weak defence and only Eric Steele stands between them and victory. Steele thwarts Shaw, making two saves with his legs. Heath and Talbot head against the woodwork. Arthur Cox's Rams, on course for promotion, will have to play better than this in the top flight.											
36 18/4	A	SHREWSBURY *6,777*	9 *18*	L 49	**1-4**	0-3	Saunders 88 *[Dixon 85 (og)]* *Robinson 4, Geddis 7, Tester 24,* Ref: H King	**Reece** *Perks*	Dixon *Williams*	Parkin *Johnson*	Talbot *Steele*	Hemming *Pearson*	Berry *Linighan*	Ford *McNally*	Kelly *Hackett*	Morgan *Geddis*	Shaw *Robinson*	Heath* *Tester*	Saunders
								Kick-off is delayed by 10 minutes but Stoke never get started. Poor defending allows Robinson, Geddis and Tester all to find their way through easily. Dixon turns Reece's save past the prone keeper and it just isn't City's day. Saunders taps in but Chic Bates' Shrews are worthy winners.											
37 20/4	H	BARNSLEY 7,263	10 *13*	L 49	1-2	0-1	Morgan 52 *Thomas 29, Clarke 58* Ref: B Hill	Reece *Baker*	Dixon *Joyce*	Parkin *Hedworth*	Talbot *Thomas*	Hemming *Gray*	Berry *Futcher*	Ford *Wylde*	Maskery *Agnew*	Morgan *Dobbin*	Saunders *MacDonald*	Gayle* *Clarke*	Heath
								Stoke miss Steve Bould's influence. Paul Reece saves Stuart Gray's 12th-minute penalty after Hemming fouls Hedworth. Thomas causes panic in the City defence, waltzing through to fire past Reece. Morgan heads in but City's defence parts again to allow MacDonald to supply Clarke.											
38 25/4	A	READING *5,927*	9 *13*	W 52	1-0	1-0	Morgan 12 Ref: M Bodenham	Fox *Francis*	Dixon *Bailie*	Parkin *Richardson*	Talbot *Beavon*	Hemming *Hicks*	Berry *Peters*	Ford *Williams**	Saunders *Taylor*	Morgan *Senior*	Shaw *Bremner*	Heath* *Smillie*	Maskery *Wood*
								Saunders reverts to midfield as Stoke put an end to their poor run. Morgan heads in Talbot's free-kick at the far post. Fox saves Reading's only chance, denying Trevor Senior from six yards. Peters clears off the line and Morgan shoots just wide. City's first visit to Elm Park since 1931.											
39 28/4	H	OLDHAM 7,228	9 *3*	L 52	0-2	0-1	 *Henry 39, Williams 75* Ref: R Milford	Fox *Goram*	Dixon *Irwin*	Parkin *Barlow*	Talbot *McGuire*	Hemming *Hoolickin*	Berry *Moore*	Ford *Palmer*	Kelly *Ormondroyd*	Morgan *Henry*	Saunders *Milligan*	Gayle *Williams*	
								Stoke's play-off dreams are in tatters after another poor home performance. Oldham's five-man midfield takes control and Tony Henry drives a 30-yarder high past Fox. Goram saves well from Saunders' leaping header. Williams heads home after Henry hits the bar. Joe Royle is ecstatic.											
40 2/5	H	BRADFORD C **6,229**	9 *12*	L 52	2-3	0-1	Gayle 81, 86 *Abbott 44p, 71, Hendrie 79* Ref: P Tyldesley	Fox *Litchfield*	Dixon *Graham*	Mills* *Goddard*	Talbot *McCall*	Hemming *Oliver*	Berry *Evans*	Ford *Hendrie*	Parkin *Abbott*	Morgan *Futcher*	Saunders *Palin*	Gayle *Ellis*	Kelly
								Ford fouls Hendrie for the penalty which tips the balance. Stoke go to pieces. At 0-3 angry season-ticket holders throw their books on the track as City lose their third home game in a row. Howard Gayle's late goals are both close-range finishes. Mills makes plans for wholesale changes.											
41 4/5	A	PLYMOUTH *13,774*	8 *6*	W 55	3-1	2-0	Saunders 35, 38, Talbot 46 *Coughlin 55p* Ref: J Deakin	Fox *Cherry*	Dixon *Nisbet*	Mills *Cooper L*	Talbot *Law*	Hemming *McElhinney*	Berry *Matthews**	Ford *Hodges*	Parkin* *Coughlin*	Morgan *Tynan*	Saunders *Evans*	Gayle *Nelson*	Kelly *Summerfield*
								A comprehensive win on the south coast. Saunders finishes off two great moves and nearly bags a hat-trick but Steve Cherry saves well. Mills makes light of his 38 years to turn in a superb performance. Reading's twice-taken penalty is for Gayle's trip. Fox saves but moves too early.											
42 9/5	H	GRIMSBY 6,406	8 *21*	W 58	5-1	3-1	K'ly 6, Talb't 14, B'rry 40p, S'nders 57, *McGarvey 19p* [Ford 76] Ref: M Peck	Fox *Pratt*	Dixon* *Burgess*	Mills *Agnew*	Talbot *Turner*	Hemming *Moore A*	Berry *Crombie*	Ford *McDermott*	Kelly *Halsall**	Morgan *McGarvey*	Saunders *O'Riordan*	Heath *Bonnyman*	Gayle *Henshaw*
Average		Home 9,991 Away 9,604						An end of season romp as City overwhelm the Mariners. Kelly sidesteps two defenders before beating Pratt. Talbot bravely dives in to head in. The penalties are both for fouls. Saunders neatly controls Morgan's pass to slip home. Ford's cross-shot nestles in the corner. Too little too late.											

Littlewoods Cup			Att			F-A	H-T	Scorers, Times, and Referees	1	2	3	4	5	6	7	8	9	10	11	12 sub used
2:1	A	SHREWSBURY		20	L	1-2	1-0	Maskery 17	Fox	Dixon	Hemming*	Kelly	Bould	Berry	Ford	Parkin	Maskery^	Shaw	Heath	Call'/Crooks
	23/9		*5,343*	*17*				*Robinson 60, Waller 78*	*Perks*	*Williams**	*Johnson*	*Hughes*	*Pearson*	*Green*	*McNally*	*Hackett*	*Waller*	*Robinson*	*Daly*	*Tester*
								Ref: R Nixon	City run the first half and should have more than just Maskery's shot from18 yards. They regret sitting back on the lead. Gerry Daly takes over after the break and prompts the Shrews to score through two headers. Ford brings a superb save out of Perks. At least Stoke have an away goal.											
2:2	H	SHREWSBURY		22	D	0-0	0-0		Fox	Dixon	Parkin	Kelly	Bould	Hemming	Ford	Maskery	Shaw	Bertschin	Heath*	Williams
	8/10		6,468	*17*					*Perks*	*Williams*	*Johnson*	*Daly*	*Pearson*	*Green*	*McNally*	*Hackett**	*Waller*	*Robinson*	*Tester*	*Leonard*
								Ref: K Hackett (Stoke lose 1-2 on aggregate)	Stoke hit rock bottom as they fail to find a way past Chic Bates' Shrews. Phil Heath blasts over from 12 yards and Dixon completely misses his kick. Frustration is voiced from the Boothen End at which City have yet to score this season. Kelly is transfer listed after a bust up with Mills.											

FA Cup																				
3	A	GRIMSBY		6	D	1-1	1-0	Saunders 38	Fox	Dixon	Parkin	Talbot	Bould	Berry	Ford	Kelly	Morgan	Saunders	Heath	
	10/1		*7,367*	*13*				*Walsh 60*	*Felgate*	*Burgess*	*Agnew*	*Turner*	*Lyons*	*Moore K*	*Robinson*	*Walsh*	*Bonnyman*	*O'Riordan*	*Cumming*	
								Ref: T Mills	The game goes ahead in a blizzard but Saunders manages to pick the white ball out clearly enough to head home Ford's corner. Walsh snaffles a half chance from Cumming's cross to snatch a draw. Kelly's free-kick is saved by Felgate. Stoke are the better side and Berry curls one wide.											
3R	H	GRIMSBY		6	D	1-1	0-0	Saunders 71	Fox	Dixon	Parkin	Talbot	Bould	Berry	Ford	Kelly	Morgan*	Saunders	Heath	Bertschin
	26/1		14,340	*12*		*aet*		*Moore 82*	*Batch*	*Burgess*	*Agnew*	*Turner*	*Lyons*	*Moore K*	*Robinson*	*Walsh*	*Bonnyman**	*O'Riordan*	*Henshaw*	*Rawcliffe*
								Ref: T Mills	Stoke have so much possession there seems to be only one possible result. After a night of frustration City seem to have won it when Saunders slams home Heath's square pass but the Mariners hit back through Kevin Moore's 20-yard snapshot which beats Fox. Fifth draw in two years.											
3	H	GRIMSBY		6	W	6-0	4-0	Morgan 10, 48, Talbot 17, Heath 22, [Saunders 41, 81]	Fox	Dixon	Parkin	Talbot	Bould	Berry	Ford	Kelly	Morgan	Saunders*	Heath	Bertschin
RR	28/1		12,087	*12*					*Batch*	*Burgess*	*Agnew*	*Turner*	*Lyons*	*Moore K*	*Robinson*	*Walsh*	*Bonnyman*	*O'Riordan*	*Henshaw*	
								Ref: R Bridges	City finally tame Mick Lyons' men. They overwhelm the Mariners in a superb first-half display. Morgan and Talbot both finish Kelly's passes. Berry sets up Heath and Kelly crosses for Saunders and Morgan. Saunders buries Heath's cutback and now has 13 goals in 12 games. Brilliant.											
4	H	CARDIFF		6	W	2-1	1-1	Saunders 33, Heath 70	Fox	Dixon	Parkin	Talbot	Bould	Berry	Ford	Kelly	Morgan	Saunders*	Heath	Bertschin
	31/1		20,423	*4:17*				*Wimbleton 15*	*Moseley*	*Kerr*	*Ford*	*Wimbleton*	*Brignull*	*Boyle*	*Platnauer*	*Bartlett*	*Pike**	*Curtis*	*Marustik*	*Davies*
								Ref: K Hackett	Frank Burrows' Cardiff battle hard and take a shock lead through Paul Wimbleton's left-foot shot. After a spate of corners City's pressure tells when Saunders races on to Kelly's pass. Heath strikes Dixon's cross inside the far post to put Stoke in the fifth round for first time in 11 years.											
5	H	COVENTRY		6	L	0-1	0-0		Fox	Dixon	Parkin	Talbot	Bould	Berry	Ford	Kelly	Morgan*	Saunders	Heath	Bertschin
	21/2		31,255	*1:8*				*Gynn 71*	*Ogrizovic*	*Borrows*	*Downs*	*Gynn*	*Kilcline*	*Peake*	*Bennett**	*Phillips*	*Regis*	*Houchen*	*Pickering*	*Sedgley*
								Ref: R Nixon	In front of the biggest gate for seven years John Sillett and George Curtis' Coventry break swiftly out of defence and Micky Gynn produces an angled finish. Referee Nixon amazingly fails to give Stoke a penalty when Phillips fells Dixon. Bertschin forces Ogrizovic into a brilliant save.											

	P	Home W	D	L	F	A	Away W	D	L	F	A	Pts
1 Derby	42	14	6	1	42	18	11	3	7	22	20	84
2 Portsmouth	42	17	2	2	37	11	6	7	8	16	17	78
3 Oldham	42	13	6	2	36	16	9	3	9	29	28	75
4 Leeds	42	15	4	2	43	16	4	7	10	15	28	68
5 Ipswich	42	12	6	3	29	10	5	7	9	30	33	64
6 Crys Palace	42	12	4	5	35	20	7	1	13	16	33	62
7 Plymouth	42	12	6	3	40	23	4	7	10	22	34	61
8 STOKE	42	11	5	5	40	21	5	5	11	23	32	58
9 Sheffield Utd	42	10	8	3	31	19	5	5	11	19	30	58
10 Bradford C	42	10	5	6	36	27	5	5	11	26	35	55
11 Barnsley	42	8	7	6	26	23	6	6	9	23	29	55
12 Blackburn	42	11	4	6	30	22	4	6	11	15	33	55
13 Reading	42	11	4	6	33	23	3	7	11	19	36	53
14 Hull	42	10	6	5	25	22	3	8	10	16	33	53
15 West Brom	42	8	6	7	29	22	5	6	10	22	27	51
16 Millwall	42	10	5	6	27	16	4	4	13	12	29	51
17 Huddersfield	42	9	6	6	38	30	4	6	11	16	31	51
18 Shrewsbury	42	11	3	7	24	14	4	3	14	17	39	51
19 Birmingham	42	8	9	4	27	21	3	8	10	20	38	50
20 Sunderland *	42	8	6	7	25	23	4	6	11	24	36	48
21 Grimsby	42	5	8	8	18	21	5	6	10	21	38	44
22 Brighton	42	7	6	8	22	20	2	6	13	15	34	39
	924	232	122	108	693	438	108	122	232	438	693	1264

* relegated after play-offs

Odds & ends

Double wins: (2) Plymouth, Reading.
Double losses: (1) Oldham.

Won from behind: (0).
Lost from in front: (1) Leeds (a).

High spots: Scoring seven against Leeds.
28 goals in 9 games leading up to the turn of the year.
Tony Kelly's form after his battle for fitness.
Hat-tricks from three separate players for the first time since 1958.

Low spots: Missing the play-offs by just six points.
Terrible form from February to May.
Being beaten 1-4 at the Hawthorns.
The departure of Tony Kelly.

Player of the Year: Lee Dixon.
Ever-presents: (1) Lee Dixon.
Hat-tricks: (3) Bertschin, Morgan, Saunders.
Leading scorer: (19) Carl Saunders.

	Appearances Lge	*Sub*	LC	*Sub*	FAC	*Sub*	Goals Lge	LC	FAC	Tot
Berry, George	**40**		1		5		**8**			**8**
Bertschin, Keith	**16**	*5*	1			*4*	**8**			**8**
Bould, Steve	**28**		2		5		**1**			**1**
Callaghan, Aaron	**2**			*1*						
Crooks, Paul		*1*		*1*						
Daly, Gerry	**1**									
Dixon, Lee	**42**		2		5					
Ford, Tony	**41**		2		5		**6**			**6**
Fox, Peter	**39**		2		5					
Gayle, Howard	**4**	*2*					**2**			**2**
Heath, Phil	**37**	*1*	2		5		**1**		2	**3**
Hemming, Chris	**21**	*1*	2				**3**			**3**
Kelly, Tony	**32**	*3*	2		5		**4**			**4**
Maskery, Chris	**10**	*3*	2					1		**1**
Mills, Mick	**6**									
Morgan, Nicky	**29**				5		**10**		2	**12**
Parkin, Steve	**37**	*1*	2		5					
Reece, Paul	**2**									
Saunders, Carl	**26**	*5*			5		**14**		5	**19**
Segers, Hans	**1**									
Shaw, Graham	**15**	*3*	2				**2**			**2**
Talbot, Brian	**32**				5		**3**		1	**4**
Williams, Terry	**1**	*2*		*1*						
20 players used	**462**	***27***	**22**	***3***	**55**	***4***	**62**	**1**	**10**	**73**

No	Date		Att	Pos	Pt	F-A	H-T	Scorers, Times, and Referees	1	2	3	4	5	6	7	8	9	10	11	subs used
1	A	BIRMINGHAM			L	0-2	0-1		Fox	Dixon	Parkin	Talbot	Hemming	Berry	Ford	Daly	Morgan	Saunders	**Allinson***	Heath
	15/8		*13,137*		0			*Rees 1, 50*	*Godden*	*Ranson*	*Dicks*	*Overson*	*Williams*	*Handysides*	*Bremner*	*Kennedy*	*Whitton*	*Rees*	*Wigley*	
								Ref: A Buksh	City concede the first goal of the season when Mark Rees turns Bremner's cross past Fox. Rees' second arrives after Dixon's back-pass falls to Whitton. Heath has his shot cleared off the line but Stoke lack conviction at either end. A great start for new Birmingham boss Garry Pendrey.											
2	H	HULL			D	1-1	0-1	Ford 68	Fox	Dixon	Parkin	Talbot^	Hemming	Berry	Ford	Daly*	Morgan	Saunders	Allinson	**Carr**/Heath
	18/8		9,139		1			*Parker 37*	*Norman*	*Palmer*	*Heard*	*Jobson*	*Skipper*	*Parker*	*Roberts*	*Bunn*	*Saville*	*Askew*	*Daniel*	
								Ref: M Reed	Mills is enraged by City's lack of passion. Garry Parker rounds Fox to put Hull ahead but it takes the introduction of two subs to change things. New signing Ian Allinson crosses for Ford to pick his spot. Berry heads against the bar, but Stoke don't deserve to beat Brian Horton's Tigers.											
3	H	MIDDLESBROUGH		11	W	1-0	0-0	Berry 60p	Fox	Dixon	Carr	Talbot	Hemming	Berry	Ford	Daly*	Morgan	Saunders	Allinson	Parkin
	22/8		9,345	*18*	4				*Pears*	*Glover*	*Cooper*	*Mowbray*	*Parkinson*	*Pallister*	*Slaven*	*Stephens*	*Hamilton**	*Kerr*	*Ripley*	*Kernaghan*
								Ref: D Elleray	It's George Berry's day. He blasts home a penalty for Pallister's foul on Saunders and is then fouled as Pallister loops a header into the net and City escape with a free-kick. Cliff Carr is a hit on his full debut after moving from Fulham. Dixon is watched by Liverpool manager Dalglish.											
4	A	IPSWICH		15	L	0-2	0-1		Fox	Dixon	Carr	Talbot	Hemming	Berry	Ford	Parkin	Morgan	Saunders	Allinson*	Heath
	29/8		*11,149*	*6*	4			*Hemming 18 (og), Lowe 82*	*Hamilton*	*Stockwell*	*Harbey*	*Yallop*	*Dozzell*	*Cranson*	*Lowe*	*Brennan*	*D'Avray*	*Zondervan*	*Gleghorn*	
								Ref: C Downey	New Ipswich boss John Duncan sees City take a stranglehold on the game. That is until Chris Hemming over-hits a lobbed back-pass to Fox. His face is as red as his hair. City never recover. David Lowe curls a beauty past Fox. Hemming nearly makes amends but puts a free header wide.											
5	H	LEICESTER		8	W	2-1	2-1	Saunders 4, Heath 45	Fox	Dixon	Carr	Talbot	Hemming	Berry	Ford	Parkin	Morgan	Saunders	Heath	
	31/8		9,948	*20*	7			*McAllister 31*	*Andrews*	*James*	*Venus*	*Osman*	*Horner*	*Ramsey^*	*Ford*	*Moran*	*Reid**	*McAllister*	*Wilson*	*Russell/Morgan*
								Ref: K Cooper	Stoke are lively but profligate. Ford's superb cross finds Saunders unmarked to head home. McAllister rams home the rebound after Fox saves from Moran. Osman nullifies Morgan but Heath races clear to beat Andrews to Hemming's long ball. Mills isn't happy even though Stoke win.											
6	A	SHEFFIELD UTD		10	D	0-0	0-0		**Barrett**	Dixon	Carr	Talbot	Hemming	Berry	Ford	Parkin	Morgan	Saunders	Heath	
	5/9		*10,086*	*19*	8				*Leaning*	*Barnsley^*	*Pike*	*Kuhl*	*Stancliffe*	*Eckhardt*	*Marsden**	*Withe*	*Cadette*	*Dempsey*	*Beagrie*	*Philliskirk/Wilder*
								Ref: V Callow	Mills is happier as the defence seem more of a unit after three days of intense training. On-loan Scott Barrett, from Wolves, replaces Fox, out with a swollen hand. Parkin stars in midfield as City have slightly the better of a very dour game. United's manager Billy McEwan is unhappy.											
7	H	BRADFORD C		13	L	1-2	0-1	Berry 50	Barrett	Dixon	Carr	Talbot	Hemming	Berry	Ford	Parkin	Allinson	Saunders*	Heath	Daly
	12/9		9,571	*3*	8			*Futcher 7, Ellis 80*	*Tomlinson*	*Mitchell*	*Goddard*	*McCall*	*Oliver*	*Evans*	*Hendrie*	*Sinnott*	*Futcher*	*Palin**	*Ellis*	*Abbott*
								Ref: L Shapter	The back four malfunctions again and City are lucky to only concede two. Futcher picks his spot from 10 yards before Barrett saves well twice. Bradford hit bar and post. Berry powers a header home but Terry Dolan's men win through the speedy Mark Ellis who buries Hendrie's cross.											
8	A	READING		12	W	1-0	0-0	Parkin 50	Barrett	Dixon	Carr	Talbot	Bould	Berry	Ford	Parkin	Morgan	Daly	Heath	
	16/9		*5,349*	*17*	11				*Francis*	*Jones*	*Richardson*	*Tait*	*Hicks*	*Peters*	*Smillie*	*Taylor*	*Gordon*	*Joseph**	*Canoville*	*Gilkes*
								Ref: B Stevens	Steve Bould returns early from a back operation to add solidity to City's defence. Steve Parkin glances a header past Steve Francis for his first goal in two years. Barrett makes two superb close-range saves. A much more confident performance. Morgan still needs more support up front.											
9	A	MANCHESTER C		14	L	0-3	0-2		Fox	Dixon	Carr	Talbot	Bould	Berry	Ford	Parkin	Morgan	Daly*	Allinson	Shaw
	19/9		*19,322*	*9*	11			*Varadi 2, 27, 48*	*Nixon*	*Gidman*	*Hinchcliffe*	*Lake*	*Simpson*	*Redmond*	*White*	*Stewart*	*Varadi*	*Scott*	*McNab*	
								Ref: G Tyson	Mills admits he got the tactics wrong as Imre Varadi takes advantage of three defensive errors. Lee Dixon is pulled out of position for the first. Berry kicks the air to allow the ball to run to Varadi for the second. The defence marks each other rather than Varadi who nods home his third.											
10	H	HUDDERSFIELD		15	D	1-1	0-1	Ford 74	Fox	Dixon	Carr	Daly*	Bould	Berry	Ford	Parkin	Morgan	Shaw	Heath	Allinson
	26/9		8,665	*23*	12			*Cooper 22*	*Cox*	*Bray*	*Burke*	*Banks*	*Webster*	*Tucker*	*Barham**	*May*	*Cooper*	*Ward*	*Cork*	*Trevitt*
								Ref: J Deakin	Dixon inexplicably tries to back head to Fox from the halfway line and Graham Cooper races in to score. Dixon atones by curling a cross in for Ford to power a header home, but Stoke's performance is a complete shambles. Mills accuses the team of 'Failing to wear the shirt with pride'.											
11	A	LEEDS		15	D	0-0	0-0		Fox	Dixon	Carr	Parkin	Bould	Berry	Ford	Saunders	Morgan	Shaw	Heath	
	30/9		*17,208*	11	13				*Day*	*Aspin*	*Adams*	*Haddock*	*Ashurst*	*Rennie*	*De Mange*	*Sheridan*	*Melrose**	*Taylor*	*Snodin*	*Pearson*
								Ref: P Vanes	Stoke match Leeds' work-rate and nearly snatch a win when Morgan blasts over from close range. Fox saves Snodin's late drive. Steve Parkin marks the dangerous John Sheridan out of the game. He loses his temper and is booked for kicking out at Parkin. A rare point at Elland Road.											

No	Venue	Opponent / Date	Att	Pos	Pts	F-A	H-T	Scorers, Times, and Referees	1	2	3	4	5	6	7	8	9	10	11	subs used
12	H	BOURNEMOUTH		10	W	1-0	0-0	Ford 77	Fox	Dixon	Carr^	Parkin	Bould	Berry	Ford	Saunders	Morgan*	Shaw	Heath	Daly/Allinson
		3/10	8,104	*21*	16				*Peyton*	*Newson*	*Morrell*	*Brooks*	*Williams*	*Whitlock*	*O'Driscoll*	*Richards*	*Aylott*	*Pulis**	*Cooke*	*O'Connor*
								Ref: K Barratt	Fox saves from Richards, Aylott and Williams. Richards hits the woodwork and Saunders clears off the line from Newson. Tony Ford, City's best player, pops up to clip home Gerry Peyton's punch out. Harry Redknapp cannot believe his Bournemouth team don't have at least a point.											
13	H	PLYMOUTH		9	W	1-0	1-0	Heath 10	Fox	Dixon	Carr	Parkin	Bould	Berry	Ford	Daly*	Saunders^	Shaw	Heath	Allinson /Hemming
		10/10	8,275	*19*	19				*Crudgington*	*Brimacombe*	*Cooper L*	*Tynan*	*Law*	*Smith*	*Hodges*	*Summerfield*	*Clayton*	*Evans*	*Anderson**	*Rowbotham J*
								Ref: N Midgley	Plymouth play an offside game but Heath breaks through bravely heading past Crudgington from Daly's cross. Daly is still troubled by injury and departs after thirty mins but has done enough. Ian Allinson says he is ready to leave. A much better show stretches the unbeaten run to six.											
14	A	BLACKBURN		10	L	0-2	0-1		Fox	Dixon	Carr	Talbot	Bould	Berry	Ford	Parkin	Hemming	Shaw	Heath	
		17/10	*7,280*	*12*	19			*Sellars 28, Garner 52*	*Gennoe*	*Price*	*Sulley*	*Barker**	*Hendry*	*Mail*	*Miller*	*Reid*	*Patterson*	*Garner*	*Sellars*	*Ainscow*
								Ref: G Courtney	Another shoddy performance. Mills is down to just 11 fit pros and introduces a sweeper system but Scott Sellars is allowed to angle a left-foot shot home. Garner rifles in via an upright. With no threat at the other end Mills' patience snaps and he vows to put players on the transfer list.											
15	A	SWINDON		10	L	0-3	0-1		Fox	Dixon	Mills^	Talbot !	Bould	Hemming*	Ford	Parkin	Shaw	Daly	Carr	Berry/Heath
		20/10	*9,160*	*4*	19			*Quinn 1, White 60, 71*	*Digby*	*Hockaday*	*King**	*Kamara*	*Parkin^*	*Calderwood*	*Bamber*	*White*	*Quinn*	*Foley*	*Barnes*	*Barnard/Henry*
								Ref: A Ward	Brian Talbot is sent off for retaliation on 34 mins. Stoke are already one down to Jimmy Quinn's free-kick. Steve White swoops to convert two crosses as City fall apart. Fox makes a great save to deny him a hat-trick. Steve Foley also manages to miss two open goals. A miserable night.											
16	H	ASTON VILLA		10	D	0-0	0-0		Fox	Dixon	Carr	Talbot	Hemming	Berry	Ford	Parkin	Shaw	Daly	Heath	
		24/10	13,494	*4*	20				*Spink*	*Gage*	*Gallacher*	*Lillis*	*Sims*	*Keown*	*Birch*	*Aspinall**	*McInally*	*Hunt D*	*Walters*	*Shaw*
								Ref: I Hemley	Stoke show some pride and passion to hold Villa to a draw. Shaw hits the post, obviously missing his partner Nicky Morgan. Villa's only clear opening comes when Hemming miskicks and McInally fires wide. The match peters out as Villa fail to find the key to City's resolute defence.											
17	A	BARNSLEY		15	L	2-5	0-2	Shaw 62, Ford 75 *[Lowndes 77]*	Fox	Dixon	Parkin	Talbot	Hemming	Berry	Ford	Daly	Morgan	Shaw	Heath	
		31/10	*5,908*	*11*	20			*MacD'ld 30, Wylde 40, 48, Dobbin 70,*	*Baker*	*Joyce*	*Cross*	*Thomas*	*McGugan*	*Futcher*	*Wylde*	*Dobbin*	*Lowndes*	*MacDonald**	*Gray*	*Foreman*
								Ref: T Holbrook	In an enthralling encounter Shaw's close-range finish and Ford's smart turn and shot keep City in the hunt. MacDonald's cracker is the best of Allan Clarke's men's goals. Dobbin heads in unmarked. Barnsley win it as Lowndes and Wylde net from close in. 'Unprofessional' says Mills.											
18	H	WEST BROM		14	W	3-0	2-0	Berry 16p, Heath 45, Parkin 77	Fox	Dixon	Carr	Parkin	Hemming	Berry	Ford	Daly	Morgan	Shaw	Heath*	Saunders
		7/11	9,992	*18*	23				*Naylor*	*Palmer*	*Burrows*	*Hogg*	*Reilly*	*Kelly*	*Lynex*	*Williamson**	*Gray*	*Bradley^*	*Morley*	*Robson/Anderson*
								Ref: L Dilkes	Parkin stars as City finally find some form. Berry converts a penalty after Hogg handles Shaw's cross. Heath races clear to round Naylor. Steve Lynex wastes a penalty for Ron Atkinson's team after Berry's push (58 mins). Parkin blasts home right footed to send the Boothen End wild.											
19	A	CRYSTAL PALACE		14	L	0-2	0-0		Fox	Dixon	Carr	Daly*	Hemming	Berry	Ford	Parkin	Morgan	Saunders	Heath	Talbot
		14/11	*8,309*	*5*	23			*Bright 63, Wright 84*	*Wood*	*Stebbing*	*Burke*	*Pardew*	*Nebbeling*	*O'Doherty*	*Redfearn*	*Thomas*	*Bright*	*Wright*	*Berber*	
								Ref: J Martin	City are beaten by the 27 goal Wright/Bright partnership. Bright admits to nudging Berry before beating him to a header for the opener. Wright arches backwards to angle a header inside the post. Steve Coppell's men easily cope with what little City have to offer. Mills wants new blood.											
20	H	MILLWALL		14	L	1-2	1-0	Heath 36	Barrett	Dixon	Parkin	Talbot	Hemming	Ford	Saunders	Daly	Morgan*	Shaw	Heath	Carr
		21/11	7,998	*7*	23			*Cascarino 57, 83*	*Horne*	*Salman*	*Coleman*	*Stevens*	*Walker*	*McLeary*	*Byrne*	*Briley*	*Sheringham*	*Cascarino*	*Carter*	
								Ref: C Trussell	City start well and Heath races on to Gerry Daly's through-ball to lift over Horne. Tony Ford's inexperience as a stand-in centre-half shows and Cascarino nods in after picking up his weak header. Battling Millwall score a second simple headed goal to continue their charge up the table.											
21	A	SHREWSBURY		14	W	3-0	3-0	Dixon 22, Ford 25, Saunders 32	Barrett	Dixon	Carr	Talbot	Hemming*	Berry	Ford	Daly	Morgan	Saunders	Parkin	**Holmes**
		28/11	***5,158***	*20*	26				*Perks*	*Green*	*Williams B*	*Priest**	*Moyes*	*Linighan*	*Steele*	*McNally*	*Brown*	*Robinson*	*Tester*	*Leonard*
								Ref: M Reeves	1,500 away fans see Dixon glance Ford's corner home. Ford then crashes home a classic volley. Saunders hits his goal so hard it flies back out off the stanchion. McNally hits the bar for managerless Shrews. Andy Holmes is impressive on his debut coming on for the injured Hemming.											
22	H	OLDHAM		14	D	2-2	1-1	Shaw 14, Heath 77	Fox	Dixon	Carr	Talbot*	Holmes	Berry	Ford	Daly	Morgan	Shaw	Parkin	Heath
		8/12	6,470	*20*	27			*Bunn 29, Henry 46p*	*Gorton*	*Irwin*	*Barrett*	*Flynn*	*Linighan*	*Milligan*	*Kelly J*	*Henry A*	*Bunn**	*Wright*	*Ritchie*	*Barlow*
								Ref: V Callow	Stoke are second best but salvage a point. Shaw opens the scoring with a running header but Joe Royle's men doggedly fight back with Bunn's fierce cross-shot and Henry's penalty after Bunn is fouled by Berry. Morgan hits the bar before Heath heads Daly's probing cross past Gorton.											
23	A	MIDDLESBROUGH		15	L	0-2	0-0		Barrett	Dixon	Carr	Talbot*	Bould	Berry	Ford	**Henry**	Morgan	Shaw	Parkin	Heath
		12/12	*12,289*	*1*	27			*Hamilton 46, Slaven 72*	*Pears*	*Glover*	*Cooper*	*Mowbray*	*Laws*	*Pallister*	*Slaven*	*Kernaghan*	*Hamilton*	*Kerr*	*Ripley**	*Parkinson*
								Ref: J Penrose	The referee is the only person not to see Kernaghan knock the ball out of Barrett's hands. Hamilton prods in and a goal is given. Pandemonium as even mild mannered Sammy Chung flies out of the dugout. When it dies down Slaven makes sure with a lucky bounce off the bumpy pitch.											

No	Date		Att	Pos	Pt	F-A	H-T	Scorers, Times, and Referees	1	2	3	4	5	6	7	8	9	10	11	subs used
24	H	READING		14	W	4-2	0-0	Morgan 52, Talbot 72, Henry 82,	Barrett	Dixon	Carr	Parkin	Bould	Berry	Ford	Henry	Morgan	Shaw*	Heath	Talbot
	19/12		6,968	*23*	30			*Moran 59, Gilkes 80* [Ford 85]	*Francis*	*Bailie*	*Gilkes*	*Beavon*	*Hicks*	*Curle*	*Williams*	*Madden**	*Tait*	*Moran*	*White*	*Horrix*
								Ref: S Lodge	In a bruising game Shaw is kicked while on the ground and Dixon is caught badly by Tait. City keep their heads. Morgan heads in and Talbot, influential, sweeps home from 10 yards. Reading peg City back, but Henry buries a spectacular left-foot volley. Ford's fierce drive clinches it.											
25	A	HUDDERSFIELD		14	W	3-0	0-0	Morgan 55, Parkin 75, Shaw 84	Barrett	Dixon	Carr	Parkin	Bould	Berry	Ford	Henry	Morgan	Shaw	Heath	
	26/12		*9,510*	*21*	33				*Martin*	*Trevitt*	*Bray*	*Banks*	*Mitchell*	*Walford^*	*Ward**	*Hutchings*	*Cooper*	*May*	*Cork*	*Shearer/Brown*
								Ref: E Parker	City weather the early storm. Cork miskicks with the goal gaping. Dixon pulls off a last-ditch tackle on Hutchings. Once Morgan heads home Henry's free-kick there is only one winner. Parkin scores with a rasping low drive before Shaw taps in Ford's cross. An excellent performance.											
26	H	MANCHESTER C		15	L	1-3	0-2	Berry 82p	Barrett	Dixon	Carr	Parkin	Bould	Berry	Ford	Henry	Morgan	Shaw	Heath*	Saunders
	28/12		**18,020**	*7*	33			*Stewart 24, 44, Brightwell 55*	*Nixon*	*Brightwell*	*Hinchcliffe*	*Clements*	*Lake*	*Redmond*	*White*	*Stewart*	*Varadi**	*McNab*	*Simpson*	*Scott*
								Ref: J Ashworth	Stoke are never at the races against Mel Machin's talented, young Man City side. The Blues plunder three classy goals. Paul Stewart rounds off two great moves. Ian Brightwell heads home. Berry's penalty, as Shaw is fouled, is academic. Heath breaks his jaw and is out for three weeks.											
27	H	IPSWICH		15	L	1-2	1-1	Morgan 8	Barrett	Dixon	Carr	Parkin	Bould	Berry	Ford	Henry*	Morgan	**Stainrod^**	Shaw	Talbot/Daly
	1/1		9,976	*6*	33			*Lowe 40, D'Avray 52*	*Hamilton*	*Yallop*	*Harbey*	*Atkins*	*Humes*	*Cranson*	*Lowe*	*Brennan*	*D'Avray*	*Dozzell*	*Stockwell*	
								Ref: D Scott	City sit back after Morgan's left-footed finish to Berry's flick-on. Bobby Ferguson's Ipswich play accurate flowing football. Stoke just cannot match them. David Lowe turns in Humes' header. Mich D'Avray hammers home from five yards. Lowe also has a goal disallowed for offside.											
28	A	BRADFORD C		14	W	**4-1**	3-0	Morgan 10, Ford 14, Dixon 39,	Barrett	Dixon	Carr	Talbot	Bould	Berry	Ford	Henry	Morgan	Stainrod	Parkin	
	2/1		*12,223*	*6*	36			*Ormondroyd 69* [Henry 64]	*Tomlinson*	*Mitchell*	*Ormondroyd*	*McCall*	*Oliver*	*Evans*	*Hendrie**	*Sinnott*	*Leonard*	*Palin*	*Ellis*	*Staunton*
								Ref: K Breen	What a difference a day makes! Stoke profit from dreadful Bantams defending. Morgan nips in as the defence stands static then Tomlinson lets Ford's effort slip between his legs. Dixon, inspirational down the right, cuts in to crack home and Tony Henry scores a splendid goal. Brilliant.											
29	H	BIRMINGHAM		14	W	3-1	1-1	Talbot 7, Henry 82, 87	Barrett	Dixon	Carr	Talbot	Bould	Berry	Ford	Henry	Morgan*	Stainrod	Heath^	Shaw/Daly
	16/1		10,076	*15*	39			*Kennedy 10*	*Hansbury*	*Ranson*	*Dicks*	*Roberts*	*Overson*	*Williams*	*Bremner*	*Childs*	*Kennedy**	*Trewick*	*Handysides*	*Rees*
								Ref: R Milford	In a tight game Talbot curls home Heath's cross before Kennedy latches on to Overson's knockdown. Berry has an overhead kick saved. Stoke take their time to break down Birmingham's five-man defence. Tony Henry follows up Stainrod's shot and then heads in Talbot's free-kick.											
30	H	SHEFFIELD UTD		12	W	1-0	0-0	Saunders 63	Barrett	Parkin	Carr	Saunders	Bould	**Beeston**	Ford	Henry	Shaw	Stainrod	Heath	
	6/2		9,344	*18*	42				*Segers*	*Barnsley*	*Pike*	*Todd*	*Stancliffe*	*Smith*	*Duffield*	*Philliskirk^*	*Cadette**	*Frain*	*Beagrie*	*Morris/Downes*
								Ref: T Fitzharris	Carl Beeston wins a two-year battle with glandular fever to play an important role filling in at centre-half. In a tight match Stoke pip the Blades under new boss Dave Bassett. Saunders accepts a return pass from Ford to crack home the decider. Lee Dixon is sold to Arsenal for £300,000.											
31	A	HULL		12	D	0-0	0-0		Barrett	Parkin	Carr	Saunders	Bould	Beeston	Ford	Henry	Shaw	Stainrod	Heath	
	13/2		*6,424*	*8*	43				*Norman*	*Palmer*	*Heard*	*Jobson*	*Skipper*	*Parker*	*Roberts*	*Payton*	*Dyer*	*Askew*	*Williams**	*Saville*
								Ref: M Peck	A dour game with Hull keeping things tight under orders from Brian Horton having just been thrashed at Bournemouth. Tony Norman's goal is never under threat Stoke's midfield struggles for fluidity. Stainrod has an overhead kick saved on the line. Shaw's free-kick whizzes just over.											
32	H	LEEDS		10	W	2-1	1-0	Heath 35, Berry 90	Barrett	Beeston	Carr	Parkin	Bould	Berry	Ford	Henry	Shaw	Stainrod*	Heath	Morgan
	23/2		10,129	*7*	46			*Pearson 55*	*Day*	*Williams*	*Adams*	*Aizlewood*	*Ashurst*	*Haddock*	*Batty*	*Sheridan*	*Pearson*	*Davison*	*Snodin*	
								Ref: A Seville	Heath heads home unmarked at the far post before Pearson beats Barrett to a cross to equalise. Berry, on his return from suspension, stoops to force in Bould's flick-on in added time. 'What a beauty' he grins! Sheridan hits the woodwork. Snodin fires just wide for Billy Bremner's men.											
33	A	BOURNEMOUTH		10	D	0-0	0-0		Barrett	Beeston	Carr	Parkin	Bould	Berry	Ford	Henry	Morgan*	Stainrod	Heath	Shaw
	27/2		*6,871*	*19*	47				*Peyton*	*Langan*	*Morrell*	*Brooks**	*Williams*	*Whitlock*	*O'Driscoll*	*Newson*	*Aylott*	*Cooke*	*Close*	*Armstrong*
								Ref: D Elleray	City dominate but waste the best chances. Stainrod's goalless spell drags on as he freezes when put clean through. Gerry Peyton touches over a great Ford effort. Bournemouth field new record signing £90,000 Shaun Close but he is anonymous. Berry and Bould snuff out Aylott's threat.											
34	H	BLACKBURN		9	W	2-1	1-0	Morgan 14, Shaw 76	Barrett	Beeston	Carr	Parkin	Bould	Berry	Ford	Henry	Morgan	Shaw	Heath	
	5/3		14,098	*2*	50			*Price 50*	*Gennoe*	*Price*	*Sulley*	*Barker*	*Hendry*	*Mail*	*Dawson*	*Reid*	*Archibald*	*Garner*	*Sellars*	
								Ref: K Cooper	City deservedly beat promotion-chasing Rovers. Don Mackay's men have a large following who see Bould foul Price but it is given outside the box. Morgan fires home. Price whips a low shot past Barrett. Parkin's 40-yard run sets up Shaw who curls home brilliantly. 17 points from 21.											

No	Date	Opponent	Att	Pos	Pts	F-A	H-T	Scorers, Times, and Referees	1	2	3	4	5	6	7	8	9	10	11	12
35	A	PLYMOUTH		10	L	0-3	0-2		Barrett	Beeston	Carr	Parkin	Bould	Berry	Ford	Henry	Morgan*	Shaw	**Hackett^**	Heath/Hemming
	12/3		*8,749*	*14*	50			*Tynan 30, 32, Uzzell 85*	*Cherry*	*Brimacombe*	*Uzzell*	*Burrows*	*Marker*	*Smith*	*Hodges^*	*Matthews*	*Tynan*	*Evans**	*Summerfield*	*Clayton/Anderson*
								Ref: J Carter	A disaster from start to end. New signing Gary Hackett plays despite a pain-killing injection and breaks down. Morgan limps off to leave Stoke without a recognised striker. Tommy Tynan pounces twice from close range to reach 200 career league goals for Dave Smith's Plymouth side.											
36	A	LEICESTER		10	D	1-1	0-1	Shaw 72	Barrett	Hemming	Carr	Parkin	Bould	Berry	Ford	Henry	Shaw	Beeston	Heath	
	16/3		*10,502*	*16*	51			*Mauchlen 43*	*Cooper*	*Mauchlen*	*Morgan*	*Osman*	*Walsh*	*Ramsey*	*McAllister*	*Cross*	*Newell*	*Reid*	*Weir*	
								Ref: K Morton	With only one fit striker Stoke play a defensive system and in a physical game Berry and Bould deal well with Leicester's direct approach. The Foxes go ahead when Ally Mauchlen's 25-yarder beats Barrett. Beeston, playing in midfield, sparks the move for Shaw's close-range equaliser.											
37	H	BARNSLEY		9	W	3-1	0-0	Daly 53, Henry 60, Hemming 78	Barrett	Hemming	Carr	Parkin	Bould	Berry*	Ford	Henry	Shaw	Beeston	Heath	Daly
	19/3		8,029	*15*	54			*Rees 69*	*Baker*	*Joyce*	*Cross*	*Thomas*	*McGugan*	*Futcher*	*Currie*	*Blair*	*Lowndes*	*Beresford*	*Rees*	
								Ref: P Harrison	Berry's injury brings the introduction of Gerry Daly who sparks City into life. He picks up Henry's flick to fire low past Clive Baker and then sets up Henry. Hemming coolly finishes after Shaw's shot is blocked. Even with new signing Andy Blair, Allan Clarke's Tykes are never in it.											
38	A	ASTON VILLA		8	W	1-0	0-0	Heath 71	Barrett	Parkin	Carr	Daly*	Bould	Beeston	Ford	Henry	Shaw	**Puckett**	Heath	Stainrod
	26/3		***20,392***	*1*	57				*Spink*	*Gage*	*Gallacher*	*Gray A^*	*Evans*	*Keown*	*Birch*	*McInally*	*Thompson**	*Gray S*	*Platt*	*Daley/Lillis*
								Ref: A Buksh	City are down to the last 11 fit pros after Gerry Daly is carried off on 15 mins. Beeston is superb as a gritty defensive display frustrates leaders Villa. David Puckett hooks off the line from Alan McInally. Heath slides the ball under Nigel Spink to complete a perfect smash and grab raid.											
39	A	WEST BROM		8	L	0-2	0-1		Barrett	Parkin	Carr	Puckett	Bould	Beeston	Ford	Henry	Stainrod*	Shaw	Heath	Hemming
	2/4		*12,144*	*18*	57			*Gray 25, Talbot 90p*	*Naylor*	*Hodson*	*Cowdrill*	*Talbot*	*North*	*Dyson*	*Hopkins*	*Phillips*	*Gray**	*Palmer*	*Anderson*	*Robson*
								Ref: P Foakes	City are always second best against Ron Atkinson's relegation escapees. In the dazzling sunshine Andy Gray, who Carr has lost after bombing forward, sweeps home a Robert Hopkins cross. Ex-Stokie Brian Talbot is delighted to bang home a penalty after Beeston fouls Carlton Palmer.											
40	H	CRYSTAL PALACE		9	D	1-1	1-0	Shaw 43	Barrett	Parkin	Carr	Beeston	Bould	Hemming	Ford	Henry	Shaw*	Puckett	Heath	**Gibbons**
	4/4		9,613	*6*	58			*Bright 58*	*Suckling*	*Finnigan*	*Burke*	*Pennyfather*	*Nebbeling*	*Cannon*	*Redfearn**	*Thomas^*	*Bright*	*Wright*	*Berber*	*Salako/Pardew*
								Ref: F Roberts	Graham Shaw's 30-yard volley rockets past a bemused Perry Suckling. Stoke relax after the break and play-off chasing Palace look dangerous. Mark Bright applies the finishing touch to Thomas' left-wing centre. City drop two more home points. No chance of making the play-offs now.											
41	A	OLDHAM		9	L	**1-5**	1-2	Heath 23 *[Callaghan 90]*	Barrett	Parkin	Carr	Beeston*	Bould	Berry	Ford	Henry	Shaw	Puckett	Heath	**Fowler**
	9/4		*6,505*	*10*	58			*Palmer 3, 71, 83, Ritchie 33,*	*Rhodes*	*Irwin*	*Barrett*	*Flynn*	*Callaghan*	*Barlow*	*Palmer*	*Donachie**	*Bunn*	*Wright*	*Ritchie*	*Kelly N*
								Ref: K Lupton	City capitulate to Roger Palmer's hat-trick of superb left-footed finishes. Ex-Stoke player Aaron Callaghan rubs it in with the last goal. Heath's header after Berry hits the bar is irrelevant. YTS lad Lee Fowler makes his debut replacing the injured Carl Beeston. Stoke hate plastic pitches.											
42	H	SWINDON		8	W	1-0	1-0	Stainrod 16	Barrett	Parkin	Carr	Puckett	Bould	Berry	Ford	Henry	Shaw	Stainrod*	Heath	Hemming
	23/4		**6,293**	*12*	61				*Digby*	*Hockaday*	*King*	*McLoughlin*	*Parkin*	*Gittens*	*Bamber*	*Barnes*	*Quinn*	*Foley*	*Wegerle**	*White*
								Ref: J Deakin	Swindon's shooting is unbelievably bad. Quinn hits the bar. Barrett saves from White, McLaughlin and Quinn. Barrett is even left stranded but the shot still goes wide. Stainrod grabs a long overdue first strike. Lou Macari is furious. Mills says he has never been deflated by a win before.											
43	A	MILLWALL		10	L	0-2	0-0		Barrett	Parkin	Carr*	Puckett	Bould	Hemming	Ford	Henry	Shaw	Stainrod	Heath	**Lewis**
	30/4		*12,636*	*1*	61			*Sheringham 52, O'Callaghan 63p*	*Horne*	*Stevens*	*Coleman*	*Hurlock*	*Wood*	*McLeary*	*Carter*	*Briley*	*Sheringham*	*Cascarino*	*O'Callaghan*	
								Ref: R Gifford	Millwall brush City aside with a dominant display. Sheringham bundles the ball, Carr and himself into the net. Kevin Lewis handles nine mins after coming on for disjointed City. George Graham's Lions roar on to automatic promotion. A summer rebuilding programme is on the cards.											
44	H	SHREWSBURY		11	D	1-1	0-1	Stainrod 59	Barrett	Parkin	Hemming	**Ware**	Bould	Henry	Ford	Puckett	Shaw	Stainrod	Heath	
	2/5		7,452	*19*	62			*Brown 28*	*Perks*	*Green*	*Williams B*	*Priest**	*Pratley*	*Linighan*	*Kasule*	*McNally*	*Geddis*	*Brown*	*Bell*	*Melrose*
	Home	Away						Ref: K Hackett	City, with only ten fit pros, include Paul Ware (aged 16). Michael Brown atones for an earlier miss by heading home Kasule's cross. Stainrod heads home after Perks fumbles Shaw's centre. Ian McNeill's Shrews avoid relegation. A muted finale to a season that never really got going.											
Average	10,469	9,591																		

Littlewoods Cup	Att			F-A	H-T	Scorers, Times, and Referees	1	2	3	4	5	6	7	8	9	10	11	subs used
2:1 H GILLINGHAM		14	W	2-0	1-0	Shaw 18, 65	Fox	Dixon	Carr	Daly	Bould	Berry	Allinson	Ford	Morgan	Shaw	Heath	
22/9	7,198	*3:2*					*Kite*	*Haylock*	*Pearce*	*Quow*	*West*	*Greenall*	*Pritchard*	*Shearer*	*Lovell*	*Elsey*	*Smith**	*Eves*
						Ref: D Hedges	Graham Shaw poaches two close-range goals as his partnership with Morgan develops. Stoke are in third gear after the second goal and cannot press home their advantage. Keith Peacock's Gills fail to test Fox. The boo-boys target new signing Ian Allinson, who looks very disinterested.											
2:2 A GILLINGHAM		10	W	1-0	1-0	Morgan 12	Fox	Dixon	Carr	Parkin	Bould	Berry	Ford	Daly	Morgan*	Shaw	Heath	Allinson
6/10	*5,039*	*3:12*					*Kite*	*Haylock*	*Pearce*	*Quow*	*West*	*Berry*	*Pritchard*	*Shearer^*	*Lovell*	*Elsey*	*Smith**	*Eves/Lillis*
						Ref: R Lewis (Stoke win 3-0 on aggregate)	A Sunday morning meeting has cleared the air and Steve Bould's dominance inspires the team to keep Gillingham at bay. City kill off the Gills through Nicky Morgan's far-post header. On Stoke's first ever visit to Priestfield, Morgan is injured and an x-ray reveals a dislocated shoulder.											
3 H NORWICH		10	W	2-1	2-0	Daly 14, Talbot 17	Fox	Dixon	Carr	Talbot	Hemming	Berry	Ford	Parkin	Shaw	Daly	Heath	
27/10	8,603	*1:18*				*Bruce 76*	*Gunn*	*Culverhouse*	*Elliott*	*Bruce*	*Phelan*	*Ratcliffe*	*Fox*	*Drinkell*	*Biggins*	*Williams**	*Bowen^*	*Crook/Butterworth*
						Ref: J Moules	Stoke threaten to overrun the Canaries as Daly's 25-yard shot zips along the wet turf and in off the post. Talbot perfectly times his run to meet Shaw's centre. Bruce heads home and Daly clears off the line but it is Ken Brown who wants to sell his team rather than Mills after the match.											
4 A ARSENAL		14	L	0-3	0-1		Barrett	Dixon	Parkin	Daly	Hemming	Berry	Ford	Saunders	Morgan	Shaw	Heath	
17/11	*30,058*	*1:1*				*O'Leary 18, Rocastle 48, Richards'n 84*	*Lukic*	*Thomas*	*Sansom*	*Williams*	*O'Leary*	*Adams*	*Rocastle*	*Davis*	*Smith*	*Groves**	*Richardson*	*Hayes*
						Ref: K Hackett	Stoke look comfortable until Barrett drops a corner for O'Leary to score. He makes up for it by saving Thomas' 25th-minute penalty, which is retaken but the shaken Thomas skies it. City battle hard but create little. Richardson rounds off a good Thomas and Hayes move for the third.											

FA Cup	Att			F-A	H-T	Scorers, Times, and Referees	1	2	3	4	5	6	7	8	9	10	11	subs used
3 H LIVERPOOL		14	D	0-0	0-0		Barrett	Dixon	Carr	Talbot	Bould	Berry	Ford	Henry	Morgan	Stainrod*	Parkin	Shaw
9/1	31,979	*1:1*					*Hooper*	*Gillespie*	*Lawrenson*	*Nicol*	*Whelan*	*Hansen*	*Beardsley*	*Aldridge*	*Houghton*	*Barnes*	*McMahon*	
						Ref: T Mills	City throttle the Anfield goal machine. Carr closes down Liverpool's right flank. Barnes and Beardsley both test Barrett. Graham Shaw nearly steals it, but he hesitates when put clean through as he thinks he is offside allowing Hooper to close him down. Best performance of the season.											
3R A LIVERPOOL		14	L	0-1	0-1		Barrett	Dixon	Carr	Talbot	Bould	Berry	Ford	Henry	Morgan	Stainrod*	Parkin	Shaw
12/1	*39,147*	*1:1*				*Beardsley 9*	*Hooper*	*Gillespie*	*Lawrenson*	*Nicol*	*Whelan*	*Hansen*	*Beardsley*	*Aldridge*	*Houghton**	*Barnes*	*McMahon*	*Johnston*
						Ref: T Mills	It's the Scott Barrett show as his wonderful display denies Liverpool time and again. Barnes, Whelan and Aldridge are all denied by wonderful saves. It takes a mis-hit effort from Peter Beardsley to sink brave Stoke. He drives his shot straight into the ground and it bounces over Barrett.											

	Home						Away					
	P	W	D	L	F	A	W	D	L	F	A	Pts
1 Millwall	44	15	3	4	45	23	10	4	8	27	29	82
2 Aston Villa	44	9	7	6	31	21	13	5	4	37	20	78
3 Middlesbro *	44	15	4	3	44	16	7	8	7	19	20	78
4 Bradford C	44	14	3	5	49	26	8	8	6	25	28	77
5 Blackburn	44	12	8	2	38	22	9	6	7	30	30	77
6 Crys Palace	44	16	3	3	50	21	6	6	10	36	38	75
7 Leeds	44	14	4	4	37	18	5	8	9	24	33	69
8 Ipswich	44	14	3	5	38	17	5	6	11	23	35	66
9 Manchester C	44	11	4	7	50	28	8	4	10	30	32	65
10 Oldham	44	13	4	5	43	27	5	7	10	29	37	65
11 STOKE	44	12	6	4	34	22	5	5	12	16	35	62
12 Swindon	44	10	7	5	43	25	6	4	12	30	35	59
13 Leicester	44	12	5	5	35	20	4	6	12	27	41	59
14 Barnsley	44	11	4	7	42	32	4	8	10	19	30	57
15 Hull	44	10	8	4	32	22	4	7	11	22	38	57
16 Plymouth	44	12	4	6	44	26	4	4	14	21	41	56
17 Bournemouth	44	7	7	8	36	30	6	3	13	20	38	49
18 Shrewsbury	44	7	8	7	23	22	4	8	10	19	32	49
19 Birmingham	44	7	9	6	20	24	4	6	12	21	42	48
20 West Brom	44	8	7	7	29	26	4	4	14	21	43	47
21 Sheffield U**	44	8	6	8	27	28	5	1	16	18	46	46
22 Reading	44	5	7	10	20	25	5	5	12	24	45	42
23 Huddersfield	44	4	6	12	20	38	2	4	16	21	62	28
	1012	246	127	133	830	559	133	127	246	559	830	1391

* promoted after play-offs
** relegated after play-offs

Odds & ends

Double wins: (1) Reading.
Double losses: (3) Ipswich, Manchester C, Millwall.

Won from behind: (0).
Lost from in front: (2) Ipswich (h), Millwall (h).

High spots: 7 games without defeat up to February.
Winning at Villa Park for the first time since 1965.
Beating high-flying Norwich in the Littlewoods Cup.
Having the best chance of the game in the first Liverpool match.

Low spots: A tame end of season.
Losing in all three cups to the defeated finalists.
The continuing plastic pitch nightmare.
The lack of a goal-scoring forward after an early injury to Nicky Morgan.

Player of the Year: Steve Parkin.
Ever-presents: (1) Tony Ford.
Hat-tricks: (0).
Leading scorer: (8) Phil Heath, Graham Shaw.

	Appearances						Goals			
	Lge	*Sub*	LC	*Sub*	FAC	*Sub*	Lge	LC	FAC	Tot
Allinson, Ian	**6**	*3*	1	*1*						
Barrett, Scott	**27**		1		2					
Beeston, Carl	**12**									
Berry, George	**35**	*1*	4		2		**5**			**5**
Bould, Steve	**30**		2		2					
Carr, Cliff	**39**	*2*	3		2					
Daly, Gerry	**16**	*5*	4				**1**	1		**2**
Dixon, Lee	**29**		4		2		**2**			**2**
Ford, Tony	**44**		4		2		**7**			**7**
Fowler, Lee		*1*								
Fox, Peter	**17**		3							
Gibbons, Ian		*1*								
Hackett, Gary	**1**									
Heath, Phil	**32**	*7*	4				**8**			**8**
Hemming, Chris	**20**	*4*	2				**1**			**1**
Henry, Tony	**22**				2		**5**			**5**
Holmes, Andy	**1**	*1*								
Lewis, Kevin		*1*								
Mills, Mick	**1**									
Morgan, Nicky	**27**	*1*	3		2		**5**	1		**6**
Parkin, Steve	**42**	*1*	3		2		**3**			**3**
Puckett, David	**7**									
Saunders, Carl	**15**	*2*	1				**3**			**3**
Shaw, Graham	**30**	*3*	4			*2*	**6**	2		**8**
Stainrod, Simon	**11**	*1*			2		**2**			**2**
Talbot, Brian	**19**	*3*	1		2		**2**	1		**3**
Ware, Paul	**1**									
28 Players used	**484**	***37***	**44**	***1***	**22**	***2***	**50**	**5**		**55**

No	Date		Att	Pos	Pt	F-A	H-T	Scorers, Times, and Referees	1	2	3	4	5	6	7	8	9	10	11	subs used
1	H	IPSWICH			D	1-1	1-0	Kamara 43	Fox	**Gidman**	Parkin	**Kamara**	Beeston	Henry	Hackett*	Ford	Shaw	Saunders	**Beagrie**	Morgan
	27/8		8,639		1			*Humes 80*	*Forrest*	*Yallop*	*Hill*	*Zondervan*	*Humes*	*Linighan*	*Lowe*	*Dozzell*	*D'Avray**	*Atkinson*	*Wark*	*Milton*
								Ref: A Seville	Stoke use up a whole season's worth of luck but still only draw. After Kamara's debut glancing header, Parkin clears off the line and Fox saves Zondervan's penalty after Saunders fouls Atkinson. D'Avray has a goal disallowed. Finally Tony Humes heads home unmarked from a corner.											
2	A	BRADFORD C			D	0-0	0-0		Fox	Gidman	Parkin	Kamara*	Beeston^	Henry	Hackett	Ware	Morgan	Saunders	Beagrie	Carr/Shaw
	29/8		*11,918*		2				*Tomlinson*	*Mitchell*	*Goddard !*	*Banks*	*Oliver*	*Evans*	*Thomas*	*Sinnott*	*Ormondroyd*	*Kennedy*	*Jewell**	*Leonard*
								Ref: K Lupton	Stoke again line up without a recognised centre-half and the giraffe-like Ormondroyd causes mayhem in the box. Stand-in skipper Henry flings himself to block Ian Banks' effort on the line. Karl Goddard is sent off (41 mins) for scything down Hackett. Kamara fractures his cheekbone.											
3	A	BARNSLEY		15	L	0-1	0-0		Fox	Parkin	Carr	Kamara	Gidman	Henry	Hackett	Ford	Morgan	Saunders	Beagrie	
	3/9		*5,682*	*6*	2			*Agnew 86*	*Baker*	*Joyce*	*Beresford^*	*Thomas*	*Dobbin*	*Futcher*	*Lowndes*	*Agnew*	*Cooper*	*Currie !*	*Clarke**	*Broddle/MacDonald*
								Ref: E Parker	Baker saves Morgan's overhead free-kick and half-volley as City start on top. Julian Broddle's arrival (50 mins) gives Allan Clarke's Barnsley impetus. Parkin and Carr both make last-ditch tackles. Agnew beats Fox from 18 yards. David Currie walks for foul and abusive. 'Mills out!'											
4	H	BLACKBURN		17	L	0-1	0-1		Fox	Gidman	Carr	Kamara	Beeston	Henry	Hackett	Ford	Shaw	Saunders	Beagrie	
	10/9		8,624	*3*	2			*Hendry 5*	*Gennoe*	*Atkins*	*Millar*	*Finnigan*	*Hendry*	*Mail*	*Miller*	*Hildersley**	*Gayle*	*Garner*	*Sellars^*	*Ainscow/Dawson S*
								Ref: H Taylor	Kamara and Fox leave the ball to each other and Hendry nips in to head in unchallenged. John Millar bicycle-kicks Hackett's cross off the line and also blocks Shaw's shot. Saunders hits the bar. Plenty of high crosses in but no-one to finish them off. Mills needs to spend the money fast.											
5	A	PLYMOUTH		23	L	0-4	0-2		Fox	Gidman*	Carr	Kamara	Beeston	Henry	Hackett	Ford	Stainrod^	Saunders	Beagrie	Morgan/Shaw
	17/9		*7,823*	*9*	2			*Tynan 35, 45, 64, Marker 54*	*Cherry*	*Brown*	*Cooper*	*Burrows*	*Marker*	*Smith*	*Plummer*	*Matthews*	*Tynan*	*McCarthy*	*Brimacombe*	
								Ref: W Burge	Tommy Tynan's hat-trick is assisted by woeful defending. Four players fail to clear before he prods in a corner. Unmarked close-range tap-ins complete his first treble in four years for Ken Brown's team. Nicky Marker is allowed to run 50 yards for the killer third. Mills under pressure.											
6	H	PORTSMOUTH		23	D	2-2	1-1	Stainrod 28, Hackett 90	Fox	Ford	Carr	Kamara	Hemming	Henry	Hackett	Saunders	Morgan	Stainrod	Beagrie	
	20/9		7,025	*4*	3			*Horne 17, Aspinall 85*	*Knight*	*Sandford*	*Hardyman*	*Dillon*	*Hogg*	*Whitehead*	*Chamberlain*	*Horne*	*Aspinall*	*Connor*	*Kelly*	
								Ref: W Flood	Bury centre-half Mark Higgins is seen watching from the stands. Mark Chamberlain returns to the Vic and sets up Barry Horne before his own effort is ruled out for Alan Ball's men. Stainrod powers in after Morgan flattens the keeper. Hackett cashes in when a blunder leaves him clear.											
7	A	WALSALL		19	W	2-1	1-1	Morgan 40, Stainrod 75	Fox	Ford	Carr	Kamara	Hemming	Henry	Hackett	Saunders	Morgan	Stainrod	Beagrie	
	24/9		*7,795*	*15*	6			*Callaghan 23*	*Barber*	*Dornan*	*Taylor M*	*Shakespeare^*	*Forbes*	*Hart*	*Mower*	*Goodwin**	*Taylor A*	*Callaghan*	*Naughton*	*Pritchard/Rees*
								Ref: P Don	City just make it in time due to M6 traffic. Tommy Coakley's men have just hammered Birmingham 5-0. Alex Taylor beats the offside trap to set up Callaghan. Beagrie crosses for Morgan. Stainrod overhead-kicks Morgan's cross in from 12 yards. 3,500 Stokies revel in the first win.											
8	H	BOURNEMOUTH		16	W	2-1	1-0	Shaw 33, Beagrie 69	Fox	Ford	Hemming	Kamara	**Higgins**	Henry	Hackett	Saunders	Morgan*	Stainrod	Beagrie	Shaw
	1/10		7,485	*10*	9			*Brooks 81*	*Peyton*	*Newson*	*Morrell*	*Bond*	*Williams*	*Whitlock**	*Richards*	*Brooks*	*Aylott*	*Bishop*	*O'Connor*	*Close*
								Ref: R Gifford	Shaw gives City good mobility up front and whistles a fierce shot past Peyton from the angle. Beagrie scores an unbelievable goal, beating five players after picking the ball up in his own box and celebrating with a somersault. Kamara and Hackett dominate midfield. Mills is happy now.											
9	H	SHREWSBURY		16	D	0-0	0-0		Fox	Ford	Beeston	Kamara	Higgins	Henry	Hackett	Saunders	Shaw	Stainrod	Beagrie	
	4/10		8,075	*23*	10				*Green Ron*	*Williams W*	*Green Rich'd*	*Moyes*	*Rougvie*	*Finley*	*Bell*	*McNally*	*Geddis*	*Griffiths**	*Thomas*	*Brown*
								Ref: R Bridges	Ian McNeil's five-man defence comfortably nullify Stoke's wing play. Saunders blasts a good chance over. Richard Green clears his own back-pass off the line. Fox foils David Geddis. More bookings, five, than shots on target. Nicky Morgan has knee surgery and is out for four months.											
10	A	OLDHAM		19	D	2-2	0-2	Kamara 57, Stainrod 85	Fox	Ford	Beeston	Kamara	Higgins	Henry	Hackett	Saunders	Shaw*	Stainrod	Beagrie	Gidman
	8/10		*6,600*	*13*	11			*Kelly 10, Bunn 44*	*Litchfield*	*Donachie*	*Blundell*	*Barrett*	*Marshall*	*Williams**	*Palmer*	*Kelly*	*Bunn*	*Ritchie*	*Wright*	*Cecere*
								Ref: F Nixon	Kelly and Bunn score easily and Fox's foot denies Roger Palmer. City's remarkable comeback is sparked by Gidman's arrival (55 mins). Ford moves forward to prompt Kamara to fire home and Stainrod to lash in exultantly in the pouring rain. First point secured on an artificial surface.											
11	A	LEICESTER		20	L	0-2	0-1		Barrett	Ford	Carr	Henry	Higgins	Berry	Hackett	Ware*	Saunders	Stainrod	Beagrie	Shaw
	15/10		*10,312*	*10*	11			*Newell 7, 51*	*Cooper*	*Parris*	*Morgan*	*Groves*	*Walsh*	*Brown*	*Reid*	*Cross*	*Newell*	*McAllister*	*Weir**	*Williams*
								Ref: D Phillips	David Pleat's Foxes snatch the lead against the run of play when Mike Newell cracks in a bobbling loose ball in the box. Beagrie has a dipping 30-yarder tipped over by Cooper. Newell heads in McAllister's centre and Stoke give up. Without Kamara the midfield is clueless. A bad loss.											

12	H	WATFORD	17	W	2-0	1-0	Coton 29 (og), Beagrie 84	Fox	Ford	Carr	Kamara	Higgins	Berry	Hackett	Henry	Saunders	Stainrod	Beagrie	
	22/10	7,878	*2*	14				*Coton*	*Gibbs*	*Rostron*	*Jackett*	*H'worth D'vid*	*McClelland*	*Sterling**	*Wilkinson*	*Blissett*	*Porter*	*Holden*	*Roberts*
							Ref: I Hendrick	Tony Coton's bizarre own-goal sees three of Steve Harrison's Hornets touch the ball after the last Stoke player. Long-ball Watford cannot deal with Kamara and Hackett's bite. Berry polices Luther Blissett. Beagrie's neat sidestep and rapier-like finish round off a splendid team display.											
13	A	BIRMINGHAM	14	W	1-0	0-0	Stainrod 73	Fox	Ford	Carr	Kamara	Higgins	Berry	Hackett	Henry	Shaw	Stainrod	Beagrie	
	25/10	*6,262*	*24*	17				*Thomas*	*Roberts*	*Frain^*	*Atkins*	*Overson*	*Peer*	*Bremner*	*Childs*	*Richards*	*Robinson**	*Wigley*	*Sturridge/Bird*
							Ref: A Buksh	An easy three points against inept Blues. Stainrod dives to head home the impressive Ford's cross. He also misses two other easy chances. Fox superbly saves Robinson's shot. Shaw is the target of the boo-boys and misses badly. Roberts flattens Beagrie and is lucky to stay on the pitch.											
14	H	CRYSTAL PALACE	11	W	2-1	1-0	Shaw 1, Henry 62	Fox	Ford	Carr	Kamara	Higgins	Berry	Hackett	Henry	Shaw	Stainrod	Beagrie*	Gidman
	29/10	9,118	*8*	20			*Bright 46*	*Parkin*	*Pemberton*	*Burke**	*Pardew*	*Hopkins*	*O'Reilly*	*Redfearn*	*Thomas*	*Bright*	*Salako*	*Berber*	*Shaw*
							Ref: D Hedges	Shaw nips in to score when Burke heads against his own bar after only 30 secs. Kamara and Pemberton have a running feud. In a vibrant game Palace level when Berry misjudges a long ball. Ford goes close twice. Henry turns in the winner when Parkin can only smother Stainrod's shot.											
15	A	SUNDERLAND	10	D	1-1	1-0	Shaw 7	Fox	Ford	Carr	Kamara	Higgins	Berry	Hackett	Henry	Shaw	Stainrod*	Beagrie	Gidman
	5/11	*17,923*	*8*	21			*Doyle 52*	*Hesford*	*Gray*	*Agboola**	*Ord*	*MacPhail*	*Doyle*	*Owers*	*Armstrong*	*Gabbiadini*	*Whitehurst*	*Pascoe*	*Bennett*
							Ref: P Tyldesley	Shaw heads home Hackett's deep cross and Denis Smith's Sunderland lay siege. Berry twice heads off the line. Gabbiadini hits the post. Doyle finally cracks in off the bar. Hackett brings a brilliant save from Hesford. Lack of depth in the squad will soon show when suspensions kick in.											
16	H	HULL	8	W	**4-0**	1-0	Henry 20, Beagrie 48, Hackett 65,	Fox	Ford	Carr	Kamara	Higgins	Berry	Hackett	Henry	Saunders	Stainrod*	Beagrie	Shaw
	13/11	10,505	*14*	24			[Carr 74]	*Norman*	*Palmer*	*Jacobs*	*Warren*	*Jobson*	*Terry*	*Roberts**	*De Mange*	*Moore*	*Edwards*	*Jenkinson*	*Payton*
							Ref: K Hackett	Another good performance as Eddie Gray's Hull are torn apart. Henry crashes into the roof of the net and Beagrie dances through to score from 12 yards. Saunders takes a quick free-kick to set up Hackett. Cliff Carr notches his first goal, beating three players and firing home. Great stuff.											
17	H	SWINDON	7	W	2-1	0-0	Berry 50p, Shaw 85	Fox	Ford	Carr	Kamara	Higgins	Berry	Hackett	Henry	Saunders*	Stainrod	Beagrie	Shaw
	19/11	9,339	*19*	27			*Jones 55*	*Digby*	*Hockaday*	*King*	*Jones*	*Parkin*	*Gittens*	*Foley*	*Calderwood*	*Henry*	*White*	*Barnes**	*Shearer*
							Ref: T West	Henry, Stainrod and Hackett all see chances go begging, but Stoke get a penalty when Gittens fouls Stainrod. Berry nets on his birthday! Jones takes time off man-marking Beagrie to fire a superb 20-yard leveller. Carr strikes a post. Shaw heads the winner from Beagrie's perfect centre.											
18	A	LEEDS	8	L	0-4	0-2		Fox	Ford	Carr	Kamara	Higgins	Berry	Hackett*	Henry	Saunders	Stainrod	Beagrie	Shaw
	26/11	*19,933*	*14*	27			*Baird 20, 75, Davison 30, Sheridan 48p*	*Day*	*Aspin*	*Snodin*	*Aizlewood*	*Blake*	*Rennie*	*Whitlow*	*Sheridan**	*Baird*	*Davison*	*Hilaire*	*Batty*
							Ref: M Reed	An atrocious display. Carr and Berry tackle each other to allow Snodin to set up Baird. Higgins stops, expecting offside and Davison nets. Carr palms away a shot but the officials miss his indiscretion. Stoke fans sing 'Oh Maradona'! Fox fouls Davison for the penalty. Baird heads home.											
19	H	CHELSEA	10	L	0-3	0-1		Fox	Ford	Carr^	Kamara	Higgins	Berry*	Hackett	Henry	Shaw	Stainrod !	Beagrie	Saunders/Beeston
	3/12	12,288	*2*	27			*Roberts 6p, Wilson C 52, McAllister 72*	*Freestone*	*Hall*	*Dorigo*	*Roberts*	*Lee*	*Wood*	*Wilson K*	*Nicholas !*	*Dixon*	*McAllister*	*Wilson C*	
							Ref: R Hart	Despite Nicholas's dismissal on five mins for butting Stainrod, Chelsea take the lead when Carr trips Kevin Wilson, although it seems outside the box. Clive Wilson nets after hapless Berry miscues. The frustrated Stainrod is sent off for hacking at McAllister. Stoke totally demoralised.											
20	A	BRIGHTON	12	D	1-1	1-0	Beagrie 26	Fox	Gidman	Carr	Kamara	Beeston	Berry	Ford	Saunders	Beagrie	Stainrod	Hackett	
	10/12	*7,443*	*22*	28			*Gatting 79*	*Keeley*	*Chivers*	*Dublin*	*Wilkins*	*Bissett*	*Gatting*	*Nelson*	*Curbishley*	*Bremner*	*Crumplin*	*Codner*	
							Ref: D Reeves	City survive the Seagulls' onslaught as the ball pings around the area, hits the bar and even goes in, to be given offside. From nowhere Beagrie latches onto a weak clearance to ram in. The defence holds out until Berry and Beeston combine to help on a corner for Steve Gatting to score.											
21	A	WEST BROM	13	L	**0-6**	0-2	*[Paskin 70, 76]*	Fox	Gidman	Carr	Kamara	Henry	Berry	Hackett	Ware	Shaw	Ford !	Beagrie	
	18/12	*17,634*	*4*	28			*Robson 2, 86, Goodman 32, 84,*	*Naylor*	*Hodson*	*Albiston*	*Talbot*	*Whyte*	*North*	*Dobbins*	*Goodman*	*Robson*	*Paskin*	*Anderson*	
							Ref: G Aplin	Stoke are thrashed by Brian Talbot's Baggies. Gary Robson heads in unmarked to start proceedings. Paskin's double includes an acrobatic leap to make it four. Ford is sent off for kicking out after Anderson's vicious foul. Don Goodman also bags a brace. Mills' future is under a cloud.											
22	H	MANCHESTER C	10	W	3-1	0-1	Kamara 48, Bamber 54, Berry 59p	Fox	**Butler**	Carr	Kamara	Beeston	Berry	Hackett	Ware*	**Bamber**	Ford	Beagrie	Henry
	26/12	**24,056**	*5*	31			*Gleghorn 9*	*Dibble*	*Seagraves*	*Hinchcliffe*	*Gayle*	*Brightwell*	*Redmond*	*White^*	*Gleghorn*	*Morley*	*Lake*	*Biggins**	*Beckford/Moulden*
							Ref: K Barratt	New signings John Butler and Dave Bamber inspire Stoke. High-flying Blues, cheered on by several thousand fans carrying inflatable bananas, see Gleghorn score. Bamber heads down for Kamara to blast in and then deflects his shot past Dibble. He is also upended for Berry's penalty.											
23	H	OXFORD	10	W	1-0	1-0	Henry 24	Fox	Butler	Carr	Kamara	Beeston	Berry	Hackett	Henry	Bamber	Ford	Beagrie	
	31/12	10,562	*18*	34				*Judge*	*Bardsley*	*Phillips J*	*Phillips L**	*Lewis*	*Greenall*	*Smart*	*Foyle*	*Hill*	*Shelton*	*Simpson^*	*Heath/Leworthy*
							Ref: P Harrison	An entertaining match sees both teams miss a host of chances. Beagrie's jinking runs torment Mark Lawrenson's Oxford. Phil Heath replaces Les Phillips who dislocates a shoulder and is roundly booed. Henry heads the only goal from Ford's centre. The play-offs are still in reach?											

BARCLAYS DIVISION 2 — Manager: Mick Mills — SEASON 1988-89

No	Date		Att	Pos	Pt	F-A	H-T	Scorers, Times, and Referees	1	2	3	4	5	6	7	8	9	10	11	subs used
24	A	BLACKBURN		13	L	3-4	3-2	S'ders 20, 22, B'grie 44 [Hildersl'y 52]	Fox	Butler	Carr	Kamara	Higgins	Berry	Hackett	Henry	Bamber	Saunders	Beagrie	
	2/1		11,654	3	34			Atkins 17, Gayle 35p, Kennedy 50,	Gennoe	Atkins	Sulley	Finnigan	Hendry	Mail*	Gayle	Hildersley	Kennedy	Garner	Sellars	Ainscow
								Ref: W Flood	City's attacking intentions are signalled by Saunders' first goals for 11 months. The first after Hildersley's back-pass hits his own bar. Beagrie's shot is helped in by Atkins. Gayle's penalty is for Higgins' challenge on Kennedy. The winner is a Hildersley diving header. A pulsating game.											
25	H	BRADFORD C		11	W	2-1	2-1	Hackett 14, Henry 34	Fox	Butler	Carr	Kamara	Higgins	Berry	Hackett	Henry	Bamber	Saunders	Beagrie	
	14/1		9,919	18	37			Banks 38	Tomlinson	Mitchell	Abbott^	Banks*	Jackson	Evans	Palin	Sinnott	Ormondroyd	Kennedy	Leonard	Jewell/Oliver
								Ref: G Ashby	Gary Hackett runs riot. He scores after Bamber's shot is blocked by Abbott and hits the post after beating three defenders. Tomlinson saves his firm header before a neat return pass sets up Henry's goal. Banks heads home unmarked to liven things up but Stoke are well worth the points.											
26	A	IPSWICH		13	L	1-5	0-0	Bamber 74 [Yallop 78]	Fox	Butler	Parkin	Kamara	Higgins	Berry	Ford	Henry	Bamber	Saunders*	Beagrie	Hackett
	21/1		14,692		37			Baltacha 46, Dozzell 50, 79, Kiwomya 63,	Fearon	Yallop	Harbey	Zondervan	Redford	Linighan	Kiwomya	Dozzell	Wark*	Hill	Baltacha	D'Avray
								Ref: A Ward	A travelling army of inflatable Pink Panthers greets Sergei Baltacha, the first Russian to play in England. He responds by opening the scoring. Ipswich walk it. Bamber notches after a prolonged scramble. 'Delilah' bursts forth from dispirited Stokies to applause from Ipswich supporters.											
27	A	SHREWSBURY		12	W	2-1	0-1	Moyes 46 (og), Shaw 82	Barrett	Butler	Carr	Kamara	Higgins	Berry	Hackett	Henry*	Ford	Shaw	Beagrie	Saunders
	4/2		6,646	22	40			Priest 1	Hughes	Green Rich'd*	Williams B	Priest^	Moyes	Pratley	Brown	Kasule !	Griffiths	Irvine	Bell	Kelly/Steele
								Ref: G Pooley	City are a goal down within a minute as Priest taps in unmarked. David Moyes nets his third own-goal in six matches for unlucky Shrews who have won one home game all season. Kasule is sent off for flooring Beagrie who refuses to be subbed. Shaw fires in Beagrie's centre to win it.											
28	H	OLDHAM		10	D	0-0	0-0		Barrett	Butler	Carr	Kamara	Higgins	Berry	Hackett	Ford^	Bamber	Shaw*	Beagrie	Henry/Saunders
	11/2		10,992	21	41				Hallworth	Irwin	Barrett	Kelly J	Marshall	Skipper	Palmer	Ritchie	Wright	Milligan	Adams	
								Ref: A Buksh	An absolutely dreadful match with no attempts at goal to seriously trouble either keeper. Mills is worried that the players have lost the spirit of Christmas time. No new signings are on the horizon due to lack of funds and the Boothen End is restless. 'Coates out!' is the new shout heard.											
29	H	LEICESTER		12	D	2-2	2-2	Beagrie 35, Bamber 37	Barrett	Butler	Carr	Ford	Higgins	Berry	Hackett	Saunders	Bamber	Shaw*	Beagrie	Morgan
	25/2		9,666	16	42			Reid 4, Walsh 32	Hodge	Mauchlen	Spearing	Ramsey^	Walsh	Paris	Reid	Cross	Newell	McAllister	Turner*	Quinn/Groves
								Ref: S Lodge	On a snow-covered pitch Stoke gift Leicester two goals with charitable marking. Beagrie cuts loose and buries one looping effort in the far top corner. Hackett's twice-taken free-kick finds Bamber's head. Butler's rampaging runs are not matched by poor finishing and the Foxes hold on.											
30	H	BIRMINGHAM		9	W	1-0	1-0	Berry 33	Barrett	Butler	Carr	Henry	Higgins	Berry	Hackett	Ford	Bamber	Shaw	Beagrie	
	28/2		7,904	24	45				Thomas	Ashley	Frain	Atkins	Overson	Clarkson	Bremner	Peer*	Whitton	Robinson^	Wigley	Langley/Sturridge
								Ref: D Allison	Stoke fans expect the floodgates to open after the referee rules that Berry's looping header has crossed the line. They don't. Rock-bottom Blues deal easily with the ineffective Bamber. Beagrie and Carr are reduced to firing long-range efforts into the Boothen End. 'Mills out' once again.											
31	A	HULL		7	W	4-1	4-0	Hackett 13, Morgan 20, Beeston 37, 40	Barrett	Butler	Carr	Beeston	Higgins	Berry	Hackett	Saunders	Shaw	Morgan	Beagrie	
	4/3		5,915	17	48			Whitehurst 70	Hesford	Brown	Jacobs	De Mange	Jobson	Buckley	Askew	Roberts	Whitehurst	Edwards	Daniel	
								Ref: G Tyson	Stoke run riot on Humberside again with Carl Beeston the star of the show. He powers two shots past Hesford to firmly put his glandular fever nightmare behind him. Hackett cracks in from 20 yards and Morgan heads home Hackett's centre. Barrett saves Edwards' 53rd-minute penalty.											
32	H	SUNDERLAND		7	W	2-0	1-0	Hackett 30, Beagrie 86	Barrett	Butler	Carr	Kamara	Beeston	Berry	Hackett	Saunders	Bamber	Shaw	Beagrie	
	11/3		12,489	14	51				Norman	Bennett	Gray	Agboola	MacPhail	Doyle	Cullen^	Armstrong	Gates*	Gabbiadini	Pascoe	Hauser/Owers
								Ref: P Wright	City outbattle Denis Smith's Rokerites. New England U-21 cap Gabbiadini misses glaringly before Shaw chips for Hackett to head in at the far post. Shaw has a header disallowed and is booked by the fussy ref for protesting. Beagrie waltzes in when Norman and Bennett get tangled up.											
33	A	PORTSMOUTH		9	D	0-0	0-0		Barrett	Butler	Carr	Kamara	Higgins	Berry	Hackett	Beeston	Bamber	Shaw*	Beagrie	Saunders
	18/3		7,624	13	52				Gosney	Neill	Whitehead	Dillon*	Hogg	Maguire	Chamberlain	Horne	Quinn	Aspinall	Fillery^	Kuhl/Kelly
								Ref: H King	In the face of a gale neither side create much. The match is reduced to a series of offside decisions and the linesman's flag collapses with over-use! Fratton Park is slowly being dismantled for rebuilding and the backdrop reflects the game. Awful. Tony Ford is sold to West Brom (£50k).											
34	H	BARNSLEY		10	D	1-1	1-0	Berry 32p	Barrett	Butler	Carr	Beeston	Higgins	Berry	Hackett	Saunders	Bamber*	Shaw	Beagrie	Morgan
	25/3		10,209	12	53			Currie 85p	Baker	Joyce	Broddle	Dobbin	Tiler	Futcher	Robinson*	Agnew	Lowndes	Currie	MacDonald	Cooper
								Ref: V Callow	Play-off dreams are ended by George Berry's handball, which gifts Barnsley a penalty. Jim Dobbin also handles for City's spot-kick. Kamara is suspended and Stoke miss his drive from midfield. Beagrie has a tremendous shot blocked by Futcher while Barrett tips over Agnew's header.											

No	Venue	Opponent	Att	Pos	Res	Pts	F-A	H-T	Scorers, Times, and Referees	1	2	3	4	5	6	7	8	9	10	11	subs used
35	A	MANCHESTER C		11	L		1-2	0-1	Butler 65	Barrett	Butler	Carr	Kamara	Higgins	Berry	Hackett	Beeston*	Bamber	Shaw^	Beagrie	Henry/Saunders
	27/3		**28,303**	2		53			*Oldfield 22, Hinchcliffe 48p*	*Cooper*	*Lake*	*Hinchcliffe*	*Gayle*	*Megson*	*Redmond*	*White*	*Moulden*	*Oldfield**	*McNab*	*Morley*	*Gleghorn*
									Ref: T Holbrook	Stoke battle hard but after Bamber misses a gilt-edged chance Oldfield nips in to score for Man City. Beeston limps off before Carr trips White and Hinchcliffe buries the penalty. Beagrie also limps off after the second sub is made but Stoke's ten men grab a life-line through John Butler.											
36	H	PLYMOUTH		11	D		2-2	2-0	Bamber 25, Henry 44	Barrett	Butler	Carr	Kamara	Higgins*	Berry	Hackett	Beeston	Bamber^	Saunders	Henry	Shaw/Morgan
	1/4		8,363	17		54			*Tynan 52p, McCarthy 56*	*Wilmot*	*Brown*	*Uzzell*	*Burrows*	*Marker*	*Smith*	*Byrne**	*McCarthy*	*Tynan*	*Matthews*	*Stuart*	*Hodges*
									Ref: R Pawley	Plymouth make April Fools of Stoke. Bamber and Henry both prod in rebounds after Wilmot fails to hold rasping shots. Hackett runs midfield but Stuart is fouled by Barrett and Tynan scores. McCarthy strikes a superb equaliser. Tynan has a second spot-kick saved by Barrett (58 mins).											
37	H	WEST BROM		11	D		0-0	0-0		Barrett	Butler	Carr	Kamara	Higgins	Berry	Hackett	Henry	Bamber	Shaw	Saunders	
	4/4		11,151	3		55				*Naylor*	*Bradley*	*Albiston*	*Talbot*	*Whyte**	*North*	*Ford*	*Bartlett*	*West*	*Robson^*	*Anderson*	*Paskin//Banks*
									Ref: J Key	Kamara welcomes back Chris Whyte from suspension with a sliding tackle, which leaves him needing 10 stitches. In a ferocious match Albion seek reprisals led by player-manager Talbot. Barrett turns over Banks' drive and Stoke fail to trouble Naylor. Tony Ford plays for West Brom.											
38	A	OXFORD		12	L		2-3	1-2	Bamber 37, Henry 73	Barrett	Butler	Carr	Kamara	Higgins	Hemming !	Hackett	Henry	Bamber	Saunders*	Beeston	Shaw
	8/4		**5,297**	15		55			*Hill 9, 55, Durnin 15*	*Hucker*	*Smart*	*Phillips J*	*Shelton*	*Lewis*	*Greenall*	*Briggs*	*Foyle**	*Mustoe*	*Durnin*	*Hill*	*Leworthy*
									Ref: K Morton	Referee Morton sends off Chris Hemming for an innocuous foul on Shelton. Stoke are already 0-2 behind to Hill's free header and Durnin's 20-yard effort. The ten men battle. Bamber drives high past Hucker. Henry heads in Hackett's free-kick. Barrett lets Hill's shot through his hands.											
39	A	WATFORD		12	L		2-3	1-2	Morgan 30, 87	Barrett	Butler	Carr	Kamara	Higgins	Berry	Hackett	Henry	Bamber	Morgan	Beeston	
	11/4		9,086	6		55			*Porter 8, Falconer 18, Hodges 82*	*Coton*	*Gibbs*	*Jackett*	*Falconer*	*Miller*	*McClelland*	*Thomas**	*Wilkinson^*	*Thompson*	*Porter*	*Hodges*	*H'wrth D'n/H'wrth D'd*
									Ref: D Vickers	Stoke are always off the pace in an entertaining game. Gary Porter's wind-assisted shot goes in off the post. Barrett then watches as Falconer's chip sails over him. Morgan heads home Bamber's cross. Glyn Hodges punishes more defensive hesitancy before Morgan bundles in a corner.											
40	A	BOURNEMOUTH		11	W		1-0	0-0	Ware 67	Barrett	Butler	Carr	Kamara	Higgins	Beeston	Hackett	Henry	Bamber	Morgan	Ware	
	15/4		6,834	12		58				*Peyton*	*Newson*	*Morrell*	*Teale*	*Pulis*	*O'Driscoll*	*Barnes^*	*Shearer**	*Aylott*	*Bishop*	*Blissett*	*Brooks/O'Connor*
									Ref: K Cooper	Gerry Peyton gifts Stoke the win after City are outplayed. He drops a mis-hit through-ball over the line to the amusement of City fans who sing 'Gerry is a Stokie'. Harry Redknapp's men hit the post five times. Bamber heads straight at Peyton. This is the day of the Hillsborough tragedy.											
41	H	WALSALL		11	L		0-3	0-2		Barrett	Butler	Carr	Kamara !	Beeston	Berry	Hackett	Henry	Bamber*	Morgan	Beagrie	Ware
	22/4		8,132	23		58			*Rimmer 12, Saville 17, 85*	*Barber*	*Rees*	*Mower*	*Shakespeare*	*Forbes*	*Smith*	*Pritchard*	*Rimmer**	*Saville*	*Hawker*	*Naughton*	*Bertschin*
									Ref: K Lupton	Stoke are outplayed by already relegated Saddlers. Rimmer nets off a post. Saville scores from 20 yards. Ex-Stokie Bertschin sets up Saville's second. Kamara is dismissed for striking Craig Shakespeare. The game kicks off at 3.06pm in remembrance of those who died at Hillsborough.											
42	H	LEEDS		13	L		2-3	2-1	Bamber 22, 33	Barrett	Butler	Carr	Kamara	Higgins	Berry	Hackett	Henry*	Bamber	Beeston	Beagrie	Ware
	29/4		9,051	10		58			*Sheridan 25p, Davison 54, Strachan 74*	*Day*	*Williams A*	*Whitlow*	*Aizlewood^*	*Blake*	*Fairclough*	*Strachan*	*Sheridan*	*Baird**	*Davison*	*Hilaire*	*Haddock/Batty*
									Ref: J Martin	Bamber puts City 2-1 up with two close-range finishes. Sheridan's penalty is for Carr's foul. He then threads a superb pass through to Bobby Davison to equalise. Gordon Strachan scores his first goal since his £300,000 move from Man Utd, chipping over Higgins on the line to win it.											
43	A	CHELSEA		13	L		1-2	1-1	Higgins 12	Fox	Butler	Carr	Kamara	Higgins	Beeston	Hackett	Henry	Bamber*	Ware^	Beagrie	Morgan/Saunders
	1/5		14,946	1		58			*Dixon 43, Roberts 86p*	*Beasant*	*Clarke*	*Dorigo*	*Roberts*	*McLaughlin**	*Bumstead*	*McAllister*	*Wilson C*	*Dixon*	*Hall*	*Wilson K*	*Monkou*
									Ref: R Gifford	Stoke snatch a surprise lead against Bobby Campbell's champions elect. Mark Higgins heads home his first Stoke goal from Ware's flag-kick. Bamber misses a great opportunity just before Kerry Dixon equalises. Higgins turns villain, bringing down Clarke for Roberts' penalty winner.											
44	A	SWINDON		13	L		0-3	0-0		Fox	Butler	Carr^	Ware	Higgins !	Beeston*	Hackett	Henry	Bamber	Saunders	Beagrie	Berry/Morgan
	6/5		9,543	6		58			*Shearer 62, 87, Jones 86*	*Digby*	*Hockaday*	*King*	*Jones*	*Calderwood*	*Parkin*	*Foley*	*Shearer*	*McLoughlin*	*MacLaren*	*White*	
									Ref: P Danson	Stoke hold their own against play-off bound Swindon. Fox makes a string of saves until Shearer beats him at his left-hand post. Higgins is sent off for a bad foul, leaving Stoke with the second worst disciplinary record in the league. Late goals reflect the ten men's desire to chase a point.											
45	A	CRYSTAL PALACE		13	L		0-1	0-1		Fox	Butler	Carr	Ware	Higgins	Berry	Hackett	Henry	Bamber	Morgan	Beagrie	
	9/5		12,159	4		58			*Madden 40p*	*Suckling*	*Hedman*	*Burke*	*Madden*	*Hopkins*	*Nebbeling*	*McGoldrick*	*Pardew*	*Bright*	*Wright*	*Berber*	
									Ref: D Elleray	Higgins is again the villain as he climbs all over Bright and Madden converts the penalty. City's best chance comes when Jeff Hopkins almost slices the ball into his own goal. Fox makes three brilliant saves. His best is from Ian Wright's overhead kick. Where does Mills go from here?											
46	H	BRIGHTON		13	D		2-2	1-1	Morgan 30, Beagrie 53	Fox	Butler	Carr	Ware	Higgins	Berry	Hackett	Henry	Bamber	Morgan	Beagrie	
	13/5		**5,841**	19		59			*Nelson 5, Wilkins 85*	*Keeley*	*Chivers*	*Dublin*	*Wilkins*	*Gatting*	*Chapman*	*Nelson*	*Codner*	*Bremner*	*Curbishley*	*Trusson*	
	Home		Away						Ref: L Dilkes	In the glorious sunshine City contrive to draw with a poor Brighton side. Nelson volleys in before Morgan's flying header and Beagrie's cross-shot lead to the customary acrobatics. Wilkins hits Fox from two yards but the ball rebounds onto him and into the net. Why Why Why Mills?											
Average	9,887		10,958																		

Littlewoods Cup	Att		F-A	H-T	Scorers, Times, and Referees	1	2	3	4	5	6	7	8	9	10	11	subs used
2:1 A LEYTON ORIENT	19	W	2-1	0-1	Morgan 48, Kamara 73	Fox	Ford	Beeston*	Kamara	Henry	Hemming	Hackett	Saunders	Morgan	Stainrod	Beagrie	Gidman
27/9	*3,154 4:21*				*Juryeff 36*	*Wells*	*Howard*	*Dickenson*	*Hales*	*Day*	*Ward*	*Baker*	*Harvey**	*Shinners*	*Juryeff*	*Comfort*	*Ketteridge*
					Ref: M Bodenham	Ian Juryeff cracks a 30-yard shot into the far corner for Frank Clark's lowly Orient. Morgan heads in Stainrod's cross and Kamara prods home when Wells drops the ball from a corner. Orient's pressure dwindles once behind. Stainrod produces some party tricks once victory is assured.											
2:2 H LEYTON ORIENT	19	L	1-2	0-1	Stainrod 86p	Barrett	Gidman^	Beeston	Kamara	Hemming	Henry	Hackett*	Ford	Shaw	Stainrod	Beagrie	Ware/Carr
11/10	5,756 *4:19*				*Hales 41p, Comfort 90*	*Wells*	*Howard*	*Dickenson*	*Hales*	*Day*	*Sitton*	*Baker**	*Ward*	*Hull*	*Juryeff*	*Comfort*	*Harvey*
					Ref: T Fitzharris (Stoke lose 2-3 on penalties)	Stoke contrive to lose even when Stainrod converts from the spot after Beagrie skies an earlier penalty. Hales scores Orient's pen for Barrett's foul on Ian Juryeff. Alan Comfort sends the tie into extra-time. Stainrod then misses the final spot-kick to send Orient through to meet Ipswich.											

FA Cup	Att		F-A	H-T	Scorers, Times, and Referees	1	2	3	4	5	6	7	8	9	10	11	subs used
3 H CRYSTAL PALACE	13	W	1-0	0-0	Shaw 74	Fox	Ware	Carr	Kamara	Higgins	Berry	Hackett	Henry	Bamber	Saunders*	Beagrie	Shaw
271	12,294 *2:8*					*Suckling*	*Pemberton*	*Burke*	*Pennyfather*	*Hopkins*	*Nebbeling*	*Salako*	*Thomas*	*Bright*	*Wright*	*Barber*	
					Ref: J Key	A potteries mist shrouds the Vic as an end-to-end game culminates with Shaw's flick over the onrushing Perry Suckling. Steve Coppell's team lay siege but Stoke cling on with Paul Ware filling in for the cup-tied Butler. Bright and Wright hit the bar. Fox tips over a thunderous header.											
4 H BARNSLEY	13	D	3-3	1-3	Bamber 29, Berry 77, Beagrie 83	Fox	Ford	Carr	Kamara	Higgins	Berry	Hackett	Henry	Bamber	Saunders*	Beagrie	Shaw
28/1	18,592 *2:8*				*Currie 6, 30, MacDonald 24*	*Baker*	*Joyce*	*Beresford*	*Dobbin*	*McGugan*	*Futcher*	*Lowndes*	*Agnew*	*Cooper*	*Currie*	*MacDonald*	
					Ref: P Tyldesley	Taking the field to Henry Mancini's Pink Panther theme seems appropriate as City gift Barnsley three simple goals and only manage Bamber's right-foot shot after having 80% of the play. Berry bullets a header in off the bar. Beagrie salvages a draw with a wonderful sidestep and drive.											
4R A BARNSLEY	13	L	1-2	0-1	Bamber 64	Barrett	Ford	Carr	Kamara	Higgins	Berry	Hackett	Henry	Bamber	Shaw*	Beagrie	Saunders
31/1	*21,086 2:8*				*MacDonald 4, Cooper 70*	*Baker*	*Joyce*	*Beresford*	*Dobbin*	*McGugan*	*Futcher*	*Lowndes**	*Agnew*	*Cooper*	*Currie*	*MacDonald*	*Rees^/Shotton*
					Ref: G Aplin	A cracking game seen by 6,000 Stokies, mostly let in free when the coaches arrive late. Barrett saves well from Joyce but MacDonald slots the rebound. Bamber hits the bar before heading in Beagrie's cross. Cooper slots in and out-somersaults Beagrie as Barnsley go on to face Everton.											

		Home					Away					
	P	W	D	L	F	A	W	D	L	F	A	Pts
1 Chelsea	46	15	6	2	50	25	14	6	3	46	25	99
2 Manchester C	46	12	8	3	48	28	11	5	7	29	25	82
3 Crys Palace *	46	15	6	2	42	17	8	6	9	29	32	81
4 Watford	46	14	5	4	41	18	8	7	8	33	30	78
5 Blackburn	46	16	4	3	50	22	6	7	10	24	37	77
6 Swindon	46	13	8	2	35	15	7	8	8	33	38	76
7 Barnsley	46	12	8	3	37	21	8	6	9	29	37	74
8 Ipswich	46	13	3	7	42	23	9	4	10	29	38	73
9 West Brom	46	13	7	3	43	18	5	11	7	22	23	72
10 Leeds	46	12	6	5	34	20	5	10	8	25	30	67
11 Sunderland	46	12	8	3	40	23	4	7	12	20	37	63
12 Bournemouth	46	13	3	7	32	20	5	5	13	21	42	62
13 STOKE	46	10	9	4	33	25	5	5	13	24	47	59
14 Bradford C	46	8	11	4	29	22	5	6	12	23	37	56
15 Leicester	46	11	6	6	31	20	2	10	11	25	43	55
16 Oldham	46	9	10	4	49	32	2	11	10	26	40	54
17 Oxford	46	11	6	6	40	34	3	6	14	22	36	54
18 Plymouth	46	11	4	8	35	22	3	8	12	20	44	54
19 Brighton	46	11	5	7	36	24	3	4	16	21	42	51
20 Portsmouth	46	10	6	7	33	21	3	6	14	20	41	51
21 Hull	46	7	9	7	31	25	4	5	14	21	43	47
22 Shrewsbury	46	4	11	8	25	31	4	7	12	15	36	42
23 Birmingham	46	6	4	13	21	33	2	7	14	10	43	35
24 Walsall	46	3	10	10	27	42	2	6	15	14	38	31
	1104	261	163	128	884	581	128	163	261	581	884	1493

* promoted after play-offs

Odds & ends

Double wins: (3) Birmingham, Bournemouth, Hull.
Double losses: (3) Blackburn, Chelsea, Leeds.

Won from behind: (3) Manchester C (h), Shrewsbury (a), Walsall (a).
Lost from in front: (3) Blackburn (a), Leeds (h), Chelsea (a).

High spots: Pushing for a play-off spot until March.
Putting eight goals past Hull.
Beating Man City 3-1.
Peter Beagrie's stunning goal against Bournemouth.

Low spots: Losing to Orient in the Littlewoods Cup.
Being thrashed at the Hawthorns.
Not winning a home game after 11 March.
Only scoring one goal in the first five games.
George Berry's early-season injury.
Unrest about the future of manager Mills.

Player of the Year: Chris Kamara.
Ever-presents: (0).
Hat-tricks: (0).
Leading scorer: (9) Dave Bamber, Peter Beagrie.

	Appearances						Goals			
	Lge	*Sub*	LC	*Sub*	FAC	*Sub*	Lge	LC	FAC	Tot
Bamber, Dave	**23**				3		**7**		2	**9**
Barrett, Scott	**17**		1		1					
Beagrie, Peter	**41**		2		3		**8**		1	**9**
Beeston, Carl	**22**	*1*	2				**2**			**2**
Berry, George	**32**	*1*			3		**4**		1	**5**
Butler, John	**25**						**1**			**1**
Carr, Cliff	**40**	*1*		*1*	3		**1**			**1**
Ford, Tony	**27**		2		2					
Fox, Peter	**29**		1		2					
Gidman, John	**7**	*3*	1	*1*						
Hackett, Gary	**45**	*1*	2		3		**5**			**5**
Hemming, Chris	**4**		2							
Henry, Tony	**37**	*3*	2		3		**6**			**6**
Higgins, Mark	**33**				3		**1**			**1**
Kamara, Chris	**38**		2		3		**3**	1		**4**
Morgan, Nicky	**11**	*7*	1				**5**	1		**6**
Parkin, Steve	**4**									
Saunders, Carl	**27**	*6*	1		2	*1*	**2**			**2**
Shaw, Graham	**19**	*9*	1		1	*2*	**5**		1	**6**
Stainrod, Simon	**16**		2				**4**	1		**5**
Ware, Paul	**9**	*2*		*1*	1		**1**			**1**
(own-goals)							**2**			**2**
21 players used	**506**	***34***	**22**	***3***	**33**	***3***	**57**	**3**	**5**	**65**

No	Date		Att	Pos	Pt	F-A	H-T	Scorers, Times, and Referees	1	2	3	4	5	6	7	8	9	10	11	subs used
1	H	WEST HAM			D	1-1	0-1	Biggins 81	Fox	Butler	**Statham**	Kamara	**Cranson**	Beeston	Hackett	**Scott***	Bamber	**Biggins**	Beagrie	Saunders
	19/8		16,058		1			*Keen 28*	*Parkes*	*Potts*	*Parris*	*Gale*	*Martin*	*Keen*	*Ward*	*McAvennie**	*Slater*	*Brady*	*Ince*	*Kelly D*
								Ref: J Aplin	Over £1 million worth of new talent, including record £450,000 Ian Cranson, snatch a deserved late draw. Phil Parkes arches to palm over from Biggins. Keen pokes past Fox in a scramble. Martin shackles Bamber. Kamara breaks McAvennie's ankle. Biggins nips in to poke past Parkes.											
2	A	PORTSMOUTH		15	D	0-0	0-0		Fox	Butler	Statham	Kamara	Cranson	Beeston	Hackett	Scott	Bamber	Biggins*	Beagrie	Morgan
	26/8		*7,433*	*20*	2				*Knight*	*Neill*	*Maguire*	*Fillery*	*Sandford*	*Ball*	*Wigley*	*Chamberlain*	*Kelly**	*Connor*	*Black*	*Whittingham*
								Ref: I Hemley	An entertaining game sees Beagrie sting Knight's fingers with a free-kick. John Gregory's Pompey have a string of corners but City hold firm. Ian Scott knits the midfield together and Derek Statham roams down the left flank. Fox's one save of note is from Kenny Black's 30-yard shot.											
3	H	LEEDS		14	D	1-1	1-0	Cranson 29	Fox	Butler	Statham	Kamara	Cranson	Beeston	Hackett	Scott	Bamber	Saunders*	Beagrie	Morgan
	2/9		14,570	*11*	3			*Strachan 60*	*Day*	*Sterland*	*Whitlow*	*Jones*	*Fairclough*	*Haddock*	*Strachan*	*Batty*	*Baird*	*Davison**	*Hendrie*	*Speed*
								Ref: R Milford	Vinnie Jones is booed by the Boothen but proceeds to prompt Leeds on to the attack. Cranson powers home a free-kick against the run of play. Bamber hits the post. Gordon Strachan chips Fox with a quickly taken free-kick. Butler clears off the line from Hendrie's effort. Another draw.											
4	A	BARNSLEY		16	L	2-3	1-2	Berry 19p, Morgan 58	Fox	Butler	Statham	Kamara	Beeston	Berry	Hackett	Scott	Bamber	Morgan*	Beagrie	Saunders
	5/9		*8,584*	*10*	3			*Agnew 2, Cooper 40, Lowndes 62*	*Baker*	*Shotton*	*Broddle*	*Dobbin*	*Banks*	*Futcher**	*Lowndes*	*Agnew*	*Cooper*	*Currie*	*Robinson*	*Tiler*
								Ref: R Hart	Stoke come unstuck after just 70 secs when Agnew threads in. Berry's penalty is for Agnew's handball. Cooper loops in a header and Morgan replies with a volley. Dobbin nearly heads into his own net. Steve Lowndes wins it and Allan Clarke's men still have the Indian sign over City.											
5	A	WOLVES		19	D	0-0	0-0		Fox	Butler	Statham	Kamara	Cranson	Beeston	Hackett	Scott*	Bamber	Biggins	Beagrie	Ware
	9/9		*15,659*	*23*	4				*Lange*	*Chard**	*Venus*	*Robertson*	*Westley*	*Vaughan*	*Thompson*	*Gooding*	*Bull*	*Mutch*	*Dennison*	*Paskin*
								Ref: P Don	3,500 Stokies witness a half-hearted affair at dilapidated Molineux. Scott is carried off after a tackle by Chard. Cranson hits the bar. Bamber is tripped but Statham hits a poor penalty straight at Tony Lange. Andy Mutch heads wide from four yards. Lange saves from Biggins. Dour fare.											
6	H	OLDHAM		22	L	1-2	0-2	Bamber 65	Fox	Butler	Statham	Kamara	Cranson	Beeston	Hackett	Saunders*	Bamber	Morgan^	Beagrie	Ware/**Boughey**
	16/9		10,673	*13*	4			*Palmer 15, Ritchie 37*	*Rhodes*	*Irwin*	*Barlow*	*Henry*	*Marshall*	*Barrett*	*Palmer*	*Ritchie*	*Bunn*	*Milligan*	*Holden R*	
								Ref: A Ward	The Boothen End make their feelings plain. 'Mills out!' they chant as Joe Royle's Latics snap up two gifts from City's generous defence. Dave Bamber contrives to lob into Andy Rhodes' hands when clean through but then thumps in Beagrie's curling pass as the heavens open. Terrible.											
7	H	PORT VALE		23	D	1-1	0-0	Palin 66	Fox	Butler	Statham	Kamara	Cranson	Beeston	Ware*	**Palin^**	Bamber	Morgan	Beagrie	Saunders/Hackett
	23/9		**27,032**	*18*	5			*Earle 50*	*Grew*	*Webb*	*Hughes*	*Mills*	*Aspin*	*Glover*	*Porter*	*Earle**	*Futcher*	*Beckford^*	*Jefers*	*Walker/Jepson*
								Ref: T Simpson	John Rudge's Valiants take the lead in the first local derby since 1957. A sell-out crowd see Robbie Earle rifle past Fox. Mark Grew saves well from Bamber. Leigh Palin, on-loan from Bradford, volleys home from nine yards. Vale hit the bar and Cranson heads just wide. Honours even.											
8	H	BRADFORD C		22	D	1-1	0-1	Cranson 55	Fox	Butler	Statham	Kamara	Cranson	Beeston	Hackett	Palin	Bamber	Morgan*	Beagrie	Saunders
	26/9		9,346	*19*	6			*Tinnion 2*	*Tomlinson*	*Abbott*	*Tinnion*	*Aizlewood*	*Sinnott*	*Evans D^*	*Megson*	*Duxbury*	*Leonard*	*Quinn*	*Wharton**	*Ellis/Jackson*
								Ref: A Seville	Beeston misjudges the soggy turf and his under-hit back-pass leads to Tinnion converting Leonard's cross. Saunders appears at half-time and is lively. Cranson heads home a free-kick. Bamber misses chance after chance. The team is jeered off for failing to beat Terry Yorath's Bantams.											
9	A	IPSWICH		21	D	2-2	0-2	Palin 47p, Saunders 50	Fox	Butler	Statham	Kamara	Cranson	Beeston	Hackett	Palin	Bamber	Saunders	Beagrie	
	30/9		*10,389*	*16*	7			*D'Avray 11, Dozzell 23*	*Forrest*	*Humes*	*Palmer*	*Zondervan*	*Redford**	*Linighan*	*Lowe*	*Dozzell*	*Wark^*	*D'Avray*	*Stockwell*	*Donowa/Thompson*
								Ref: D Elleray	Stoke fall apart at the back. Kamara's wayward pass allows D'Avray to head in off the post. Fox fails to prevent Jason Dozzell's powerful shot crossing the line. The break sees a turnaround. Bamber is fouled for the penalty. Saunders finishes calmly. Bamber misses again from close in.											
10	A	PLYMOUTH		21	L	0-3	0-1		Barrett	Butler	Statham	Kamara	Cranson	Beeston	Hackett*	Palin	Bamber	Biggins	Beagrie	Saunders
	7/10		*6,940*	*7*	7			*Hodges 44, Tynan 52p, Thomas 74*	*Wilmot*	*Brown*	*Brimacombe*	*Marker*	*Burrows*	*Morrison*	*Byrne*	*Hodges**	*Tynan*	*Campbell*	*Stuart*	*Thomas*
								Ref: R Lewis	Ken Brown's Pilgrims romp home as sorry Stoke register their worst start for years. Beagrie, watched by Chelsea manager Bobby Campbell, forages well. The profligate Bamber wastes three excellent chances. Hackett limps off injured. Statham trips Greg Campbell for the spot-kick.											
11	H	HULL		21	D	1-1	1-0	Biggins 3	Barrett	Butler	Statham	Ware	Cranson^	Beeston	Palin*	Saunders	Bamber	Biggins	Beagrie	Boughey/Higgins
	14/10		9,955	*23*	8			*McParland 59p*	*Hesford*	*Warren*	*Jacobs*	*Swan*	*Terry*	*Jobson*	*Askew*	*Roberts*	*McParland*	*Whitehurst*	*Doyle**	*Jenkinson*
								Ref: D Vickers	Wayne Biggins heads home a brilliant Beagrie cross to give Stoke a great start. Cranson, captain for the day, is troubled by the lively Askew. Ian McParland nets after Roberts' shot is handled on the line. 'Will we ever win a game' drifts down from the Boothen End. Post-match demos.											

12	H	WEST BROM	19	W	2-1	2-0	Hackett 8, Biggins 32	Barrett	Butler	Statham	Scott	Cranson^	Beeston	Hackett*	Palin	Bamber	Biggins	Beagrie	Ware/Higgins
	17/10	11,991	*13*	11			*Bartlett 49*	*Naylor*	*Parkin*	*Burgess*	*Robson**	*Whyte*	*North*	*Ford*	*Goodman*	*Thomas*	*McNally*	*Barham^*	*Talbot/Bartlett*
							Ref: G Tyson	Stoke start with two wingers and one scores when Scott pulls back for Hackett. Biggins turns in the six-yard box to finish Beagrie's cross. Only the second win in 26 league games. Ware has a goal ruled out for offside. Kevin Bartlett scores four minutes after coming on, but City hold out.											
13	A	SHEFFIELD UTD	21	L	1-2	0-2	Palin 67p	Barrett	Butler	Statham	Scott	Cranson	Beeston	Ware*	Palin	Bamber	Biggins	Beagrie	Boughey
	21/10	*16,873*	*1*	11			*Bradshaw 14, Booker 25*	*Tracey*	*Hill*	*Rostron*	*Booker*	*Stancliffe*	*Morris*	*Bradshaw*	*Gannon*	*Agana*	*Deane*	*Bryson**	*Francis*
							Ref: J Lloyd	League leaders United show City how to finish. Carl Bradshaw turns to fire home. The statuesque defence allows Booker to net from 18 yards. Bamber misses from close in but is fouled for the penalty. New team coach Alan Ball urges City forward but Dave Bassett's Blades win easily.											
14	H	SUNDERLAND	21	L	0-2	0-0		Barrett	Butler	Statham	Kamara	Cranson	Beeston	Palin	Scott*	Bamber	Saunders	Hackett	Morgan
	28/10	12,480	*5*	11			*Bracewell 77, Gabbiadini 79*	*Carter*	*Kay*	*Hardyman**	*Bennett*	*MacPhail*	*Owers*	*Bracewell*	*Armstrong*	*Gates*	*Gabbiadini*	*Pascoe*	*Cullen*
							Ref: P Tyldesley	Beagrie is sold to Everton for £750,000. Bamber misses when clean through. Denis Smith's Rokerites take over. Bracewell hits the bar. Gates misses from two yards. Finally Bracewell scores via the underside of the bar. Gabbiadini curles home a beauty. No pride. Mills is clinging on.											
15	A	OXFORD	22	L	0-3	0-1		Barrett	Butler	Statham	Kamara	Cranson	Beeston	Palin	Scott*	Bamber	Saunders	Hackett^	Ware/Morgan
	1/11	***4,375***	*16*	11			*Durnin 6, Foster 65, Mustoe 70*	*Judge*	*Smart*	*Phillips J**	*Lewis*	*Foster*	*Greenall*	*Mustoe^*	*Ford*	*Durnin*	*Stein*	*Heath*	*McClaren/Simpson*
							Ref: R Wiseman	Cranson allows the ball to squeeze under his foot for John Durnin to finish clinically. Judge saves Bamber's header superbly. Foster nudges in from close range and Robbie Mustoe heads in Mark Stein's centre. Foster clears off the line from Bamber. Post-match demos demand changes.											
16	A	SWINDON	23	L	**0-6**	0-2	*[White 68, 86]*	Barrett	Butler	Statham	Kamara	Cranson	Higgins*	Beeston	Palin^	Bamber	Morgan	Saunders	Hackett/Ware
	4/11	*7,825*	*7*	11			*McL'ghlin 7, Sh'rer 23, 78, B'mber 47 (og),*	*Digby*	*Hockaday*	*Bodin*	*McLoughlin*	*Calderwood*	*Gittens*	*Jones*	*Shearer*	*White*	*MacLaren*	*Simpson*	
							Ref: P Alcock	Mick Mills is finally sacked after the most atrocious performance in living memory. The defence is carved to pieces time and again. Bamber's own-goal is the first time he has found the net for seven weeks! Duncan Shearer's 25-yard pile-driver is the best goal for Ossie Ardiles' Robins.											
17	H	BRIGHTON	23	W	3-2	3-1	Beeston 1, Bamber 25, Kamara 30	Fox	Butler	Statham	Kamara	Cranson	Berry	**Hilaire^**	Beeston	Bamber	Biggins*	Hackett	Ware/Saunders
	11/11	10,346	*12*	14			*Codner 13, Bremner 72*	*Keeley*	*Chivers*	*Chapman*	*Curbishley*	*Bissett*	*Dublin*	*Nelson*	*Wood*	*Bremner**	*Codner*	*Wilkins*	*Crumplin*
							Ref: A Wilkie	Caretaker boss Ball reinstates Berry and plays on-loan Vince Hilaire. Beeston, in midfield, waltzes through to score on 35 secs. Bamber nets a header. Kamara flicks in Beeston's cross. Berry puts a 60th-minute penalty wide to set up a nail-biting finish after Kevin Bremner cracks home.											
18	A	BOURNEMOUTH	24	L	1-2	0-1	Hilaire 84	Fox	Butler	Statham	Kamara	Cranson*	Berry	Hilaire	Beeston	Bamber	Biggins	Carr	Ware^/Hackett
	18/11	*6,412*	*13*	14			*Brooks 31, Moulden 53*	*Peyton*	*Bond*	*Coleman*	*Teale*	*Williams^*	*Peacock*	*Lawrence**	*Moulden*	*O'Driscoll*	*Brooks*	*Blissett*	*O'Connor/Miller*
							Ref: A Gunn	Cranson's injury forces Beeston into the back four and weakens the midfield. Fox drops a cross and Shaun Brooks nets. Peyton drops Hilaire's cross over the line. Paul Ware injures himself kicking air rather than ball. Good news. Sir Stanley Matthews is made Life President of the club.											
19	H	LEICESTER	24	L	0-1	0-0		Fox	Butler	Carr	Kamara	Higgins	Berry	Hackett	Beeston	Bamber	Biggins*	Hilaire	Saunders
	25/11	12,264	*22*	14			*Mills 65*	*Hodge*	*Mauchlen**	*Morgan*	*Ramsey*	*Walsh*	*Paris*	*Reid*	*Moran*	*Campbell*	*Mills*	*Wright*	*James*
							Ref: G Ashby	A vital relegation battle and Stoke are unable to score despite Hilaire and Hackett providing numerous chances. Martin Hodge saves well from Biggins and Dave Bamber. Gary Mills cracks home a free-kick from 18 yards. David Pleat's Foxes win their first away match for over a year.											
20	A	WEST HAM	23	D	0-0	0-0		Fox	Butler	Carr	Kamara	Higgins	Berry	Hackett	Beeston	Saunders	Biggins	Hilaire	
	2/12	*17,704*	*7*	15				*Parkes*	*Potts*	*Dicks*	*Strodder*	*Martin*	*Devonshire**	*Brady*	*Slater*	*Keen*	*Ward*	*Fasanu^*	*Kelly D/Foster*
							Ref: B Hill	Fox saves superbly from Kevin Keen after just 15 seconds. Lou Macari's West Ham are below par. Julian Dicks wastes a 55th-minute penalty, saved brilliantly by Fox. Kamara harasses Liam Brady into a rare booking. Saunders has a good strike well saved by Phil Parkes. A good draw.											
21	H	BARNSLEY	24	L	0-1	0-0		Fox	Butler	Carr	Kamara	Higgins	Berry	Hackett*	Beeston	Biggins	Saunders	Hilaire	Palin
	9/12	10,163	*20*	15			*Cooper 72*	*Baker*	*Dobbin*	*Cross*	*Lowndes*	*Shotton*	*Smith*	*McCord*	*Agnew*	*Cooper*	*Currie*	*Archdeacon*	
							Ref: K Morton	A four-day break in Jersey to 'get to know each other' doesn't work. Hackett misses pathetically and Saunders miscues a header. Steve Cooper blasts in after Berry passes straight to Agnew. Stoke are booed off the pitch. Ball is after Luton's Steve Williams and Plymouth's Mark Smith.											
22	H	NEWCASTLE	24	W	2-1	0-1	Biggins 78, Beeston 90	Fox	Saunders	Carr	Kamara	Beeston	Fowler	Hackett*	Palin	**Ellis**	Biggins	**Sandford**	**Holmes**
	26/12	14,878	*6*	18			*Scott 5*	*Burridge*	*Ranson*	*Sweeney*	*Dillon*	*Scott*	*Kristensen*	*Gallacher**	*Brock*	*Quinn*	*McGhee*	*O'Brien*	*Brazil^/Stimson*
							Ref: J Worrall	New coach Graham Paddon sees City fight back after conceding to Kevin Scott's header from a corner. New men Tony Ellis and Lee Sandford add steel. Biggins slides the ball under Burridge. Cliff Carr's superb tackle on Ray Ranson sets up Beeston to crack home an unstoppable shot.											
23	H	WATFORD	24	D	2-2	2-1	Biggins 23, 26p	Fox	Butler	Carr	Kamara	Holmes	Fowler	Saunders*	Beeston	Ellis	Biggins	Sandford	Hackett
	30/12	13,228	*9*	19			*Hodges 21, Penrice 66*	*Coton*	*Gibbs**	*Ashby*	*Richardson*	*H'worth D'vid*	*Roeder*	*Henry*	*Wilkinson*	*Penrice*	*Porter*	*Hodges*	*Thomas*
							Ref: K Redfern	In a cracking game Biggins nets a fantastic goal from Ellis' knockdown to equalise Glyn Hodges' close-range finish. Biggins then slots home a penalty after Ellis is tripped. Steve Harrison's Hornets subject City to a long-ball barrage and Gary Penrice finishes off a flick on. Much better.											

No	Date		Att	Pos	Pt	F-A	H-T	Scorers, Times, and Referees	1	2	3	4	5	6	7	8	9	10	11	subs used
24	A	MIDDLESBROUGH		24	W	1-0	0-0	Ellis 61	Fox	Butler	Carr	Kamara !	Holmes	Fowler*	Palin	Beeston	Ellis	Biggins	Sandford	Saunders
	1/1		*16,238*	*20*	22				*Pears*	*Parkinson*	*Cooper*	*Mowbray*	*Coleman*	*Ripley*	*Slaven*	*Proctor*	*Kernaghan**	*Brennan*	*Davenport*	*Burke*
								Ref: T West	Chris Kamara is sent off in the middle of the first half for a bad retaliatory foul. City resolutely cling on against Bruce Rioch's Middlesbrough. Tony Ellis cracks home to round off the best performance of the season. Ball is confirmed as the new manager with Paddon as his number two.											
25	H	PORTSMOUTH		24	L	1-2	0-2	Sandford 70	Fox	Butler	Carr	Kamara	Holmes*	Fowler	Bamber	Beeston	Ellis	Biggins^	Sandford	Saunders/Hackett
	13/1		12,051	*19*	22			*Whittingham 14, Hazard 40*	*Knight*	*Neill*	*Stevens*	*Fillery*	*Hogg**	*Ball*	*Wigley^*	*Black*	*Whittingham*	*Hazard*	*Chamberlain*	*Fillery/Gilligan*
								Ref: J Watson	Stoke are outplayed by Alan Ball's old team in a vital relegation game. Guy Whittingham nods in a Mickey Hazard cross. On his debut Hazard slams home from close in. Black hits the post with a 38th-minute pen after Chamberlain is felled by Fox but nets the rebound himself. No goal!											
26	A	LEEDS		24	L	0-2	0-0		Fox	Butler	Carr*	Saunders	Holmes	Fowler	Ware^	Beeston	Ellis	Biggins	Sandford	Hackett/Palin
	20/1		***29,318***	*1*	22			*Strachan 68p, Hendrie 74*	*Day*	*Beglin*	*Whitlow*	*Jones*	*Fairclough*	*Haddock*	*Strachan*	*Batty*	*Chapman*	*Davison**	*Hendrie*	*Pearson*
								Ref: G Tyson	Profligate City waste two fine opportunities to kill the game. Biggins sees his penalty saved by Day (48 mins) after Beeston is fouled. Saunders miscues when bearing down on goal. Strachan nets his penalty after ex-Stokie Lee Chapman is fouled. Hendrie forces home from close range.											
27	A	BLACKBURN		24	L	0-3	0-2		Fox	Butler	Statham	Beeston	Holmes	Fowler*	Ware	Ellis	Palin	Biggins	Sandford	Saunders
	27/1		*9,132*	*9*	22			*Kennedy 4, Gayle 37p, Sellars 77*	*Gennoe*	*Atkins*	*Sulley*	*Reid*	*Moran*	*Mail*	*Kennedy*	*Millar*	*Stapleton*	*Gayle*	*Sellars*	
								Ref: C Trussell	Dave Bamber is sold to Hull for £100,000 and Chris Kamara to Leeds for £150,000. City allow Don Mackay's poor Rovers team to look good. Howard Gayle scores from the spot, after Fox saves Atkins' 1st-minute penalty. The other goals are from close in. 'Men against boys' says Ball.											
28	A	PORT VALE		24	D	0-0	0-0		Fox	Butler	Carr	Beeston	Sandford	Berry	**Kelly***	Ellis	Palin	Biggins	**Kevan**	Hackett
	3/2		*22,075*	*10*	23				*Grew*	*Mills*	*Hughes*	*Walker*	*Aspin*	*Glover*	*Porter*	*Earle*	*Cross**	*Beckford*	*Jefers*	*Millar*
								Ref: P Tyldesley	Saunders is sold to Bristol Rovers for £70,000 and replaced by Tony Kelly, signed from St Albans for £20,000. Dave Kevan signs on-loan from Notts County. Lacklustre Stoke cling on to a point at Vale Park. Vale have two goals disallowed for fouls. Ellis blasts over from five yards out.											
29	A	OLDHAM		24	L	0-2	0-0		Fox	Butler	Carr	Beeston	**Blake**	Sandford	Kevan	Ellis	Palin	Biggins	Kelly*	Scott
	10/2		*10,028*	*4*	23			*Palmer 54, Ritchie 64*	*Hallworth*	*Irwin*	*Barlow*	*Henry*	*Marshall*	*Holden A*	*Adams*	*Ritchie*	*McGarvey**	*Milligan*	*Holden R*	*Palmer*
								Ref: M Peck	City lose again on plastic where the Latics remain unbeaten in their last 30 matches. Noel Blake makes his debut after signing from Leeds. Ex-Stokie Neil Adams crosses for Palmer to guide home. Blake allows the ball to run to Ritchie for the clincher. Beeston drives just past the post.											
30	H	WOLVES		24	W	2-0	0-0	Biggins 64, Hackett 75	Fox	Butler	Sandford	Beeston	Blake	Berry	**Smith***	Ellis	Kevan	Biggins	Carr	Hackett
	17/2		17,870	*6*	26				*Kendall*	*Bennett*	*Venus*	*Westley*	*Downing*	*Streete*	*Jones**	*Cook*	*Bull*	*Mutch*	*Dennison*	*McLoughlin*
								Ref: T Lunt	In an exuberant game Gary Hackett replaces the on-loan Mark Smith from Dunfermline to produce a superb show. He sets up Biggins to shoot home from 15 yards and then nets after Ellis robs Streete in the box. Graham Turner's Wolves pile forward. The five-man back-line hold firm.											
31	A	LEICESTER		24	L	1-2	1-0	Biggins 41	Fox	Butler	Sandford	Beeston	Blake	Berry	Hackett	Ellis	Kevan	Biggins	Carr*	Kelly
	24/2		*12,245*	*13*	26			*Oldfield 66, Reid 79*	*Hodge*	*Mauchlen*	*Spearing*	*Mills*	*Walsh*	*James*	*Reid*	*Oldfield*	*Kitson**	*McAllister*	*Wright^*	*Ramsey/North*
								Ref: L Shapter	Biggins' drive hits post and bar before bouncing out but he scores with a cracking free-kick low into the far corner. The ball bobbles in front of Fox and Oldfield profits. Reid pounces when Berry dallies on the ball. Beeston's overhead kick goes wide. Why, why, why are Stoke so poor?											
32	H	BOURNEMOUTH		24	D	0-0	0-0		Fox	Butler	Sandford	Beeston	Blake	Berry	**Brooke**	Ellis	Kevan	Kelly*	Carr	Morgan
	3/3		10,988	*13*	27				*Peyton*	*Bond*	*Morrell*	*Teale*	*Miller*	*Peacock*	*Lawrence**	*Moulden^*	*Shearer*	*O'Driscoll*	*Blissett*	*Brooks/Aylott*
								Ref: J Key	On-loan Gary Brooke becomes City's 30th player this season, a record. In a strong wind City miss Biggins (out with tonsillitis). Morgan hits the upright from three yards. Fox saves well from Lawrence. Noel Blake's header hits a defender on the line as Stoke launch a late cavalry charge.											
33	H	IPSWICH		24	D	0-0	0-0		Fox	Butler	Sandford	Beeston	Blake	Berry*	Brooke	Ellis	Kevan	Biggins	Palin	Fowler
	6/3		10,815	*12*	28				*Forrest*	*Stockwell*	*Thompson*	*Zondervan*	*Gayle*	*Linighan*	*Lowe*	*Dozzell*	*Wark*	*Pennyfather*	*Milton*	
								Ref: I Hemley	John Duncan's Ipswich are as bad as City. Both sides create just one chance each. Gary Brooke contrives to fire over from three yards out after Craig Forrest parries Palin's effort. The whistles from the Boothen End start well before the referee blows his. Five goals in the 1990s so far!											
34	A	BRADFORD C		24	L	0-1	0-0		Fox	Butler	Sandford	Beeston	Blake	Berry	Brooke	Ellis	Kevan	Biggins	Carr*	Morgan
	10/3		*9,269*	*22*	28			*Woods 87*	*Tomlinson*	*Mitchell*	*Tinnion*	*Abbott*	*Sinnott*	*Jackson*	*Aizlewood*	*Davies*	*Leonard*	*Adcock*	*Woods*	
								Ref: G Singh	Managerless Bradford steal the points thanks to a dubious Neil Woods goal. He later admits to handling the ball before firing past Fox. A huge following see Stoke battle hard but Brooke blasts over and Morgan delays too long. Heads drop when the goal goes in. Relegation a certainty.											

No	Date	H/A	Opponent	Att	Pos	Pts	Res	F-A	H-T	Scorers, Times, and Referees	1	2	3	4	5	6	7	8	9	10	11	12
35	17/3	H	PLYMOUTH	9,452	*20*	29	D	0-0	0-0		Fox	Butler	Carr	Beeston	Blake	Sandford	Smith	Ellis*	Kevan	Biggins	Brooke	Morgan
											Wilmot	*Brown*	*Broddle*	*Blacwell*	*Burrows*	*Hodges*	*Morrison*	*McCarthy*	*Tynan*	*Byrne*	*Fiore*	
										Ref: V Callow	City fail to overcome a dire Pilgrims side in an atrocious game. In bright sunshine Mark Smith sets up several chances but Rhys Wilmot is not tested. Tynan scuffs an open goal. McCarthy lobs wide. Ellis sees his goalbound shot hit a defender on the line. Ball is exasperated by ill luck.											
36	20/3	A	HULL	*6,456*	*19*	30	D	0-0	0-0		Fox	Butler	Carr	Palin	Blake	Berry	Brooke*	Morgan	Kevan	Biggins	Fowler	Scott
											Hesford	*Brown*	*Jacobs*	*Jobson*	*Shotton*	*De Mange*	*Roberts**	*Payton*	*Bamber*	*Askew^*	*Atkinson*	*McParland/Hunter*
										Ref: T Mills	Lee Fowler plays as sweeper in a five-man back-line. Stoke start well but Andy Payton is fouled and then hits the bar with the penalty. Brooke needs eight stitches after a collision with Jacobs. De Mange clears off the line from Biggins. Stoke are unbeaten at Boothferry Park since 1960.											
37	24/3	A	WEST BROM	*12,771*	*16*	31	D	1-1	0-1	Ellis 78	Fox	Butler	Carr*	**Thomas**	Blake	Sandford	**Barnes**	Ellis	Kevan	Biggins^	Fowler	Scott/Kelly
										Ford 22	*Naylor*	*Burgess*	*Harbey*	*Shakespeare*	*North*	*Whyte*	*Ford*	*Goodman*	*Bannister*	*Bradley*	*Hackett*	
										Ref: D Phillips	Paul Barnes from Notts Co and the returning Mickey Thomas start against Brian Talbot's Albion featuring ex-Stokies Hackett and Ford. They combine for the Baggies' goal. Thomas' cross allows Ellis to back-head past the startled Naylor. Fox produces four great saves to earn a point.											
38	31/3	H	SHEFFIELD UTD	14,898	*2*	31	L	0-1	0-0		Fox	Butler	Sandford	Beeston	Blake	Berry^	Brooke*	Ellis	Thomas	Biggins	Kevan	Barnes /Fowler
										Deane 81	*Tracey*	*Hill*	*Barnes*	*Todd*	*Stancliffe*	*Morris*	*Wood^*	*Gannon*	*Whitehurst**	*Deane*	*Bryson*	*Agana/Booker*
										Ref: M James	Stoke weather the Blades' long-ball storm. Fox tips over Brian Deane's header. City improve after Barnes arrives. He fires into the side netting from a well-worked opening. Agana's pace proves to be the difference. His cross is headed home by Deane. Fox tips over Ian Bryson's volley.											
39	7/4	A	SUNDERLAND	*17,119*	*5*	31	L	1-2	0-0	Ellis 63	Fox	Butler	Carr	Scott	Blake	Sandford	Kelly*	Ellis	Barnes	Thomas	Kevan	Brooke
										Gabbiadini 46, Armstrong 57	*Norman*	*Kay*	*Hardyman*	*Heathcote*	*MacPhail*	*Owers*	*Bracewell*	*Armstrong*	*Pascoe*	*Gabbiadini*	*Brady**	*Gates*
										Ref: S Lodge	The ageless Thomas is everywhere as City create chances for Ellis and Barnes but both fire wide. Marco Gabbiadini scores after 13 seconds of the second half from 12 yards. Armstrong's header is adjudged to have gone over the line. Ellis turns on a sixpence to half-volley past Norman.											
40	10/4	H	OXFORD	**8,139**	*11*	31	L	1-2	1-0	Sandford 42	Fox	Butler	Carr	Scott	Blake	Sandford	Barnes*	Ellis	Thomas	Biggins	Kevan	Brooke
										Simpson 65p, 89	*Judge*	*Smart*	*Ford*	*Lewis*	*Foster*	*Evans*	*Penney*	*Mustoe*	*Durnin*	*Stein*	*Simpson*	
										Ref: D Allison	At last Stoke have some luck. Sandford scores a soft goal from 10 yards. Ellis is tripped for a 48th-minute penalty and a win seems on the cards, but Biggins hits Judge's trailing legs and collapses to the turf in disbelief. Stein is fouled for Oxford's pen. Simpson shows Biggins what to do.											
41	14/4	H	MIDDLESBROUGH	8,636	*22*	32	D	0-0	0-0		Fox	Butler	Fowler	Scott	Blake	Sandford	Kevan^	Ellis	Thomas	Biggins*	Carr	Berry/Kelly
											Pears	*Parkinson*	*Phillips*	*Kernaghan*	*Coleman*	*McGee**	*Slaven*	*Proctor*	*Baird*	*Brennan*	*Davenport*	*Ripley*
										Ref: J Deakin	Another lame performance as Stoke seem to freeze whenever goal is sighted. Thomas attempts to drive Stoke forward and Coleman misjudges his pass to leave Ellis clear but his effort is parried by Steve Pears. Berry comes on for a cameo role as a centre-forward as things get desperate.											
42	16/4	A	NEWCASTLE	*26,190*	*2*	32	L	0-3	0-2		Fox	Butler	Carr	Sandford	Blake	Berry	Thomas	Ellis*	Barnes	Biggins	Kevan	Scott
										Kristensen 3, 70, Quinn 32	*Burridge*	*Scott*	*Stimson*	*Aitken*	*Anderson*	*Ranson**	*Brock*	*Dillon^*	*Quinn*	*McGhee*	*Kristensen*	*Bradshaw/O'Brien*
										Ref: N Midgely	Relegation is finally confirmed after weeks of waiting. Jim Smith's Toon never get out of second gear. Bjorn Kristensen scores a classy brace. Mick Quinn notches his 35th of the season – more then the entire Potters squad! 'We're not bothered anymore!' opine the small away gathering.											
43	21/4	H	BLACKBURN	9,305	*4*	32	L	0-1	0-0		Fox	Ware	Fowler	Scott	Blake	Sandford !	Boughey	Ellis	Thomas*	Biggins	Kevan	**Gallimore**
										Mail 65p	*Gennoe*	*Atkins*	*Dawson*	*Reid*	*Moran*	*Mail*	*Kennedy*	*Millar*	*Stapleton**	*Garner*	*Sellars*	*Gayle*
										Ref: J Martin	Tony Ellis flings himself dramatically when fouled in the box and nothing is given. Lee Sandford and Kennedy have a running battle. The City player's tackle results in a penalty for Rovers. A second crude challenge earns him a red card. Ball bloods another youngster, Tony Gallimore.											
44	24/4	A	WATFORD	*8,073*	*15*	33	D	1-1	1-1	Biggins 30	Fox	Butler	Fowler	Ware	Blake	Sandford^	Boughey	Ellis	Thomas*	Biggins	Kevan	Kelly/**Farrell**
										Thomas 36	*Coton*	*Gibbs*	*Williams*	*Richardson^*	*H'worth D'vid*	*Roeder*	*Allison**	*Wilkinson*	*Penrice*	*Falconer*	*Thomas*	*Drysdale/Harrison*
										Ref: R Gifford	Peter Fox apologises to his team-mates after criticising them for 'not being 100% behind Stoke City' on live TV. Perhaps his words sting Stoke into action. Biggins opens the scoring, but 19-year-old Rod Thomas nets his 6th of the year for Colin Lee's Hornets. Some hope for next year?											
45	28/4	A	BRIGHTON	*9,614*	*17*	36	W	**4-1**	0-0	Ellis 51, 76, Biggins 70, Scott 80	Fox	Butler	Fowler	Beeston	Blake	Sandford	Boughey^	Ellis	Ware	Biggins	Kelly*	Scott/**Sale**
										Bremner 47	*Digweed*	*Crumplin*	*Chapman*	*Curbishley*	*McCarthy*	*Dublin*	*Gotsmanov*	*Robinson*	*Bremner*	*Codner*	*Wilkins*	
										Ref: P Jones	In a party atmosphere, with many Stokies sporting fancy dress, City produce the best ten-minute spell of the season. Biggins hammers low into the corner. Ellis chips Digweed and turns to fire home. Ian Scott loops a header in. Fox makes a wonder stop from Gotsmanov. Wonderful day.											
46	5/5	H	SWINDON	11,386	*4*	37	D	1-1	1-1	Ellis 12	**Noble**	Butler	Fowler*	Beeston	Blake	**Wright^**	Boughey	Ellis	Ware	Biggins	Scott	Farrell/Sale
										Shearer 12	*Digby*	*Kerslake*	*Bodin*	*McLoughlin*	*Calderwood*	*Gittens*	*Jones**	*Shearer^*	*White*	*MacLaren*	*Foley*	*Simpson/Cornwell*
			Home / Away							Ref: T Holbrook	Ball fields a young team. Danny Noble's handling is sound and Darren Boughey's 40-yard run leads to Ellis sweeping home. Shearer glances a header in before the celebrations have finished. City play three at the back after the break and hold their own against play-off contenders Town.											
Average			12,458 / 12,640																			

Littlewoods Cup		Att			F-A	H-T	Scorers, Times, and Referees	1	2	3	4	5	6	7	8	9	10	11	subs used
2:1 H	MILLWALL		22	W	1-0	1-0	Morgan 32	Fox	Butler	Statham	Kamara	Cranson	Higgins	Palin*	Ware	Bamber	Morgan	Beagrie	Hackett
19/9		8,030	*1:5*					*Horne*	*Stevens*	*Dawes*	*Hurlock*	*Wood !*	*McLeary*	*Carter*	*Briley*	*Sheringham*	*Cascarino*	*Anthrobus**	*Waddock*
							Ref: J Deakin	A win against higher division opposition for once. City cope with the loss of the injured Beeston and Biggins. Morgan exultantly volleys home Bamber's knock-down. Steve Wood is dismissed (66 mins) for stamping on the prone Beagrie. Hurlock hits the post. A brilliant performance.											
2:2 A	MILLWALL		21	L	0-2	0-1		Fox	Butler	Statham	Kamara	Cranson	Higgins*	Hackett	Beeston	Bamber	Palin	Beagrie	Saunders
3/10		*8,637*	*1:5*		*aet*		*Sheringham 42, Cascarino 119*	*Horne*	*Stevens*	*Dawes*	*Hurlock*	*Sparham*	*Thompson*	*Carter*	*Waddock*	*Sheringham*	*Cascarino*	*Anthrobus*	
							Ref: B Stevens (Stoke lose 1-2 on aggregate)	Stoke's five-man defence battle admirably in a bruising match. Carter crosses for Teddy Sheringham to nod in. Stoke have the better chances in extra-time but lose to a clearly offside Tony Cascarino who is allowed to race through and beat Fox. Mills has to be restrained on the touchline.											

FA Cup																			
3 H	ARSENAL		24	L	0-1	0-0		Fox	Butler	Carr	Kamara	Holmes	Fowler	Ware*	Beeston	Saunders	Biggins	Sandford	Hackett
6/1		23,827	*1:3*				*Quinn 74*	*Lukic*	*Dixon*	*Davis*	*Thomas**	*O'Leary*	*Adams*	*Quinn*	*Richardson*	*Groves*	*Bould*	*Merson^*	*Jonsson/Rocastle*
							Ref: N Midgley	Stoke are never in the hunt against George Graham's Gunners. Niall Quinn heads the only goal from a corner. Carr rugby tackles Perry Groves but escapes with a booking. Saunders wastes a glorious chance with two minutes left, failing to make Lukic save. Respectable but out of depth.											

		Home						Away				
	P	W	D	L	F	A	W	D	L	F	A	Pts
1 Leeds	46	16	6	1	46	18	8	7	8	33	34	85
2 Sheffield Utd	46	14	5	4	43	27	10	8	5	35	31	85
3 Newcastle	46	17	4	2	51	26	5	10	8	29	29	80
4 Swindon	46	12	6	5	49	29	8	8	7	30	30	74
5 Blackburn	46	10	9	4	43	30	9	8	6	31	29	74
6 Sunderland *	46	10	8	5	41	32	10	6	7	29	32	74
7 West Ham	46	14	5	4	50	22	6	7	10	30	35	72
8 Oldham	46	15	7	1	50	23	4	7	12	20	34	71
9 Ipswich	46	13	7	3	38	22	6	5	12	29	44	69
10 Wolves	46	12	5	6	37	20	6	8	9	30	40	67
11 Port Vale	46	11	9	3	37	20	4	7	12	25	37	61
12 Portsmouth	46	9	8	6	40	34	6	8	9	22	31	61
13 Leicester	46	10	8	5	34	29	5	6	12	33	50	59
14 Hull	46	7	8	8	27	31	7	8	8	31	34	58
15 Watford	46	11	6	6	41	28	3	9	11	17	32	57
16 Plymouth	46	9	8	6	30	23	5	5	13	28	40	55
17 Oxford	46	8	7	8	35	31	7	2	14	22	35	54
18 Brighton	46	10	6	7	28	27	5	3	15	28	45	54
19 Barnsley	46	7	9	7	22	23	6	6	11	27	48	54
20 West Brom	46	6	8	9	35	37	6	7	10	32	34	51
21 Middlesbro	46	10	3	10	33	29	3	8	12	19	34	50
22 Bournemouth	46	8	6	9	30	31	4	6	13	27	45	48
23 Bradford C	46	9	6	8	26	24	0	8	15	18	44	41
24 STOKE	46	4	11	8	20	24	2	8	13	15	39	37
	1104	252	165	135	886	640	135	165	252	640	886	1491

* promoted after play-offs

Odds & ends

Double wins: (1) Brighton.
Double losses: (7) Barnsley, Blackburn, Leicester, Oldham, Oxford, Sheffield Utd, Sunderland.

Won from behind: (2) Brighton (a), Newcastle (h).
Lost from in front: (2) Leicester (a), Oxford (h).

High spots: Holding Arsenal to only one goal in the FA Cup.
Improved attendances.
The departure of the floundering Mills.
Beating Millwall at home in the League Cup.
Party time at Brighton.

Low spots: Relegation 13 points adrift in bottom position.
Another dreadful start.
Only 6 wins and 35 goals scored.
The 0-6 thrashing at Swindon.
The arrival of the floundering Ball.
Ian Cranson's bad injury.
Just 3 goals in the last 8 home matches.

Player of the Year: Peter Fox.
Ever-presents: (0).
Hat-tricks: (0).
Leading scorer: (10) Wayne Biggins.

	Appearances						Goals			
	Lge	*Sub*	LC	*Sub*	FAC	*Sub*	Lge	LC	FAC	Tot
Bamber, Dave	20		2				2			2
Barnes, Paul	4	*1*								
Barrett, Scott	7									
Beagrie, Peter	13		2							
Beeston, Carl	38		1		1		2			2
Berry, George	15	*1*					1			1
Biggins, Wayne	35				1		10			10
Blake, Noel	18									
Boughey, Darren	4	*3*								
Brooke, Gary	6	*2*								
Butler, John	44		2		1					
Carr, Cliff	22				1					
Cranson, Ian	17		2				2			2
Ellis, Tony	24						6			6
Farrell, Steve		*2*								
Fowler, Lee	13	*2*			1					
Fox, Peter	38		2		1					
Gallimore, Tony		*1*								
Hackett, Gary	18	*8*	1	*1*		*1*	2			2
Higgins, Mark	4	*2*	2							
Hilaire, Vince	5						1			1
Holmes, Andy	5	*1*			1					
Kamara, Chris	22		2		1		1			1
Kelly, Tony	5	*4*								
Kevan, David	17									
Morgan, Nicky	6	*7*	1				1	1		2
Noble, Danny	1									
Palin, Leigh	17	*2*	2				3			3
Sale, Mark		*2*								
Sandford, Lee	23				1		2			2
Saunders, Carl	12	*10*		*1*	1		1			1
Scott, Ian	14	*5*					1			1
Smith, Mark	2									
Statham, Derek	19		2							
Thomas, Mickey	8									
Ware, Paul	9	*7*	1		1					
Wright, Ian	1									
37 players used	**506**	***60***	**22**	***2***	**11**	***1***	**35**	**1**		**36**

BARCLAYS DIVISION 3 — Manager: Alan Ball ⇨ Graham Paddon — SEASON 1990-91

No	Date		Att	Pos	Pt	F-A	H-T	Scorers, Times, and Referees	1	2	3	4	5	6	7	8	9	10	11	subs used
1	H	ROTHERHAM			W	3-1	2-0	Blake 15, Kennedy 44p, Thomas 49	Fox	Butler	Statham	Beeston	Blake	Fowler	**Kennedy**	Ellis	Thomas	Biggins	Kelly*	Ware
	25/8		13,048		3			*Williamson 60*	*O'Hanlon*	*Forrest*	*Scott*	*Goodwin*	*Law*	*Robinson*	*Buckley**	*Spooner*	*Williamson*	*Mendonca*	*Hazel*	*Dempsey*
								Ref: R Lewis	Mick Kennedy, from Luton, is cash-strapped City's only new signing. He slots the penalty when Biggins is fouled. Noel Blake dives to head in a flicked on corner. 'Mad' Mickey Thomas belts in to the far corner to send the crowd, higher than most of the Division two gates, into ecstasy.											
2	A	TRANMERE			W	2-1	2-1	Ellis 36, Kennedy 43p	Fox	Butler	Statham	Beeston	Blake	Sandford	Kennedy	Ellis	Thomas*	Biggins	Ware	Kelly
	31/8		*10,327*		6			*Muir 21p*	*Nixon*	*Mungall*	*McCarrick**	*McNab*	*Hughes^*	*Vickers*	*Morrissey*	*Harvey*	*Steel*	*Muir*	*Thomas*	*Martindale/Irons*
								Ref: E Parker	Paul Ware handles and Ian Muir sends Fox the wrong way from the spot. Ellis' back header creeps into the far corner. Kennedy's spot-kick is courtesy of Vickers' foul. A new yellow and black away kit is christened with six bookings. 'We're going to win the league' chant the Stokies.											
3	H	BIRMINGHAM		7	L	0-1	0-0		Fox	Butler	Statham	Beeston*	Blake	Sandford	Kennedy	Ellis	Thomas	Biggins	Kelly	Ware
	8/9		**16,009**	*2*	6			*Gleghorn 57*	*Thomas*	*Ashley*	*Downs*	*Frain*	*Fox*	*Matthewson*	*Peer*	*Bailey*	*Moran**	*Gleghorn*	*Tait*	*Sturridge*
								Ref: J Deakin	A midfield battle. Stoke hold the upper hand but Moran and Tait threaten on the break. Dean Peer's deep cross falls to Nigel Gleghorn who nets from three yards. Stoke's long-ball game fails to trouble Dave Mackay's Blues. Fox saves Tait's shot well. More creativity needed in midfield.											
4	A	BOURNEMOUTH		6	D	1-1	0-0	Statham 84	Fox	Butler	Statham	Beeston	Blake	Sandford	Kennedy	Ellis*	Kelly^	Biggins	Ware	Thomas /Fowler
	15/9		*6,374*	*20*	7			*Blissett 47p*	*Guthrie*	*O'Driscoll*	*Morrell*	*Teale*	*Shearer*	*Bond*	*Lawrence**	*Peacock*	*Aylott*	*Holmes*	*Blissett*	*Ekoku*
								Ref: P Alcock	Blissett scores from the spot after Butler barges Holmes. Kelly has a goal disallowed for offside even though the referee appears to have played advantage. Stoke push forward in numbers and Statham ghosts into the box to bag his first goal for the club. City are over £1.5 million in debt.											
5	A	CHESTER		8	D	1-1	1-0	Thomas 7	Fox	Butler	Statham	Beeston	Blake	Sandford	Kennedy	Ellis	Ware	Biggins	Thomas	
	18/9		*3,579*	*9*	8			*Ellis 87*	*Stewart*	*Preece*	*Pugh*	*Butler*	*Abel*	*Lane*	*Bennett*	*Barrow*	*Painter**	*Dale*	*Ellis*	*Lightfoot*
								Ref: P Harrison	Over 500 Stokies are locked out. They are the lucky ones as City stumble against Harry McNally's Chester. Thomas nets from a narrow angle. Chester's wind-assisted onslaught sees Fox save well from Dale and Barrow. The midfield disintegrates and Ellis loops a header in. Booed off.											
6	H	SOUTHEND		7	W	**4-0**	2-0	Ware 38, Biggins 41, 49, Cornwell 68 (og)	Fox	Butler	Statham	Beeston	Blake	Sandford	Kennedy	Ellis	Thomas*	Biggins	Ware	Kelly
	22/9		11,901	*2*	11				*Sansome*	*Austin*	*Powell*	*Martin*	*Cornwell*	*Tilson*	*Clark*	*Butler*	*Ansah*	*Benjamin*	*Angell**	*Cook*
								Ref: K Cooper	Southend have won all their games so far but buckle under intense City pressure. Ware cracks home from 15 yards. Biggins rams in exultantly. His second slips through Paul Sansome's grasp. Cornwell heads Ware's centre into his own net. Blake has a header palmed over. More like it.											
7	H	SHREWSBURY		10	L	1-3	1-2	Sandford 26	Fox	Butler	Statham	Beeston*	Blake	Sandford	Kennedy	Ellis	**Evans^**	Biggins	Ware	Thomas/Cranson
	29/9		12,672	*19*	11			*Spink 34, Sandford 40 (og), Worsley 63*	*Perks*	*Worsley*	*Gorman*	*Kelly*	*Heathcote*	*Blake*	*Moore*	*Coughlin*	*Spink*	*Brown**	*Griffiths*	*Wimbleton*
								Ref: P Vanes	Sandford chests down a Kennedy cross to crash in from 15 yards. City sit back and allow ex-Stokie Tony Kelly to run midfield. He crosses for Spink and forces Sandford to turn past Fox. Worsley converts Moore's centre and it is all over bar the booing. Shrews' first win of the season.											
8	A	CREWE		6	W	2-1	1-0	Biggins 42, Ware 77	Fox	Butler	Carr	Ware	Blake	Sandford	Kennedy	Ellis	Evans	Biggins	Thomas	
	2/10		*7,200*	*22*	14			*Foreman 60*	*Greygoose*	*Lennon*	*Carr*	*Smart !*	*Swain*	*Rose*	*Jasper*	*Foreman**	*Hignett*	*Gardiner^*	*Sussex*	*Callaghan/Jones*
								Ref: T Fitzharris	Wayne Biggins scores a superb solo goal, beating two Alex defenders before firing home from outside the box. Foreman prods in after the ball rebounds off the post. Colin Smart is sent off for felling a clean through Ellis. Ware lunges to head in Cliff Carr's resulting left-wing free-kick.											
9	A	BOLTON		4	W	1-0	0-0	Evans 61	Fox	Butler	Carr	Ware	Blake	Sandford	Kennedy	Ellis	Evans	Biggins	Thomas*	Kelly^/Fowler
	6/10		*8,521*	*23*	17				*Felgate*	*Brown*	*Burke**	*Green*	*Seagraves*	*Winstanley*	*Lee*	*Thompson*	*Reeves^*	*Philliskirk*	*Darby*	*Cowdrill/Stevens*
								Ref: P Wright	City dominate but Biggins and Ellis waste golden opportunities. Finally a cushioned Evans header from Kennedy's left-wing cross beats David Felgate. Bolton wobble and City should have more. A late panic sees Fox scrambling when a deflected free-kick loops onto the roof of the net.											
10	H	FULHAM		3	W	2-1	1-0	Ellis 26, 68	Fox	Butler	Carr	Beeston	Blake	Sandford	Kennedy	Ellis	Evans	Biggins	Ware	
	13/10		12,394	*23*	20			*Rosenior 82*	*Stannard*	*Newson*	*Pike*	*Ferney**	*North*	*Morgan*	*Kelly*	*Davies^*	*Rosenior*	*Brazil*	*Marshall*	*Cobb/Milton*
								Ref: T West	Alan Dicks' Fulham, fresh from their first victory of the season, begin brightly. Leroy Rosenior's overhead kick just misses. Ellis cracks home Biggins' flick on. He then drags the ball back to wrong-foot three defenders before slotting past Jim Stannard. Fox makes a superb double save.											
11	H	CAMBRIDGE		3	D	1-1	0-1	Biggins 54	Fox	Butler	Statham	Beeston	Blake	Sandford	Kennedy	Ellis	Evans	Biggins	Ware*	Thomas
	20/10		12,673	*8*	21			*Dublin 14*	*Vaughan*	*O'Shea*	*Kimble*	*Wilkins*	*Chapple*	*Daish*	*Cheetham**	*Leadbitter^*	*Dublin*	*Taylor*	*Philpott*	*Claridge/Bailie*
								Ref: H King	Dion Dublin finishes brilliantly to stun Stoke. He then hits the foot of the post as City fumble for form. Possession means nothing against John Beck's well-organised defence. Biggins heads in Evans' corner to grab a point but puts an easier header wide. U's 20 away matches unbeaten.											

12	A	BRADFORD C		3	W	2-1	0-0	Kelly 58, Thomas 88	Fox	Butler	Statham	Beeston	Blake	Sandford	Kennedy^	Ellis	Thomas	Biggins*	Ware	Kelly/Carr
24/10			8,086	16	24			McCarthy 48	Tomlinson	Mitchell	Babb	James	Oliver	Sinnott	Duxbury	Jewell	McCarthy	Leonard	Stuart	
								Ref: A Flood	Despite a dreadful showing Stoke snatch the win against John Docherty's Bantams. McCarthy nods in after heavy Bradford pressure. Fox pulls off two fantastic saves. The game turns when Mitchell miscues against his own post and Kelly prods in, then Thomas cashes in on Babb's error.											
13	A	GRIMSBY		3	L	0-2	0-0		Fox	Butler	Statham	Beeston	Blake	Sandford	Kennedy^	Ellis	Thomas	Kelly*	Ware	Carr/Kevan
27/10			10,799	2	24			Watson 55, Childs 70	Sherwood	McDermott	Jobling	Tillson	Lever	Cunnington	Childs	Gilbert	Rees	Watson	Woods	
								Ref: P Tyldesley	A bad day as Kelly is crocked by a tackle from behind and City lose to two poor goals emanating from defensive blunders. A post-match pitch invasion is the cue for fights between rival supporters. Director Geoff Manning resigns under the pressure of running the club on a shoestring.											
14	H	READING		3	L	0-1	0-1		Fox	Butler	Statham	Beeston	Blake	Sandford	Scott	Ellis	Thomas	Barnes*	Ware	**Bright**
3/11			12,245	9	24			Moran 2	Burns	Jones	Gilkes	McPherson	Hicks	Williams	Gooding	Taylor	Senior	Conroy	Moran*	Maskell
								Ref: T Simpson	Ball's squad is down to the bare bones. Paul Barnes starts and is replaced by youth starlet David Bright. Ellis blasts a great chance over the bar before Steve Moran prods home. Stoke cannot find the net despite the one-way traffic. Sandford, Ellis, Ware and Statham waste good chances.											
15	H	WIGAN		3	W	2-0	1-0	Biggins 20, Kennedy 68	Fox	Butler	Statham	Beeston	Blake	Sandford	Kennedy	Ware*	**Whitehurst**	Biggins	Thomas	Ellis
10/11			12,756	11	27				Atkins	Parkinson	Tankard	Atherton	Johnson	Langley	Woods	Rimmer	Daley*	Page	Griffiths B	Patterson
								Ref: P Jones	Mickey Thomas is at the centre of everything as Stoke outplay woeful Wigan. Biggins neatly loops a header in. Billy Whitehurst makes a quiet debut but offers another option up front. Thomas is tripped for a penalty after scampering clear. Atkins saves. Kennedy rams home the rebound.											
16	A	BURY		3	D	1-1	0-0	Thomas 47	Fox	**Rennie**	Statham	Beeston	Blake*	Cranson	Kennedy	Ellis	Thomas^	Biggins	Sandford	Fowler/Kelly
14/11			5,118	8	28			McGinlay 77	Kelly	Hill	Stanislaus^	Mauge	Valentine	Knill	Lee*	Parkinson	Robinson	McGinlay	Patterson	Cunningham/Feeley
								Ref: R Shepherd	In pouring rain 3,000 Stokies witness an ill-tempered affair. Biggins and Thomas take punishment but Blake and Kennedy redress the balance. Ellis crosses for Thomas to head home superbly. John McGinlay pounces when Rennie and Cranson get in a mix up. A game City should win.											
17	A	EXETER		3	L	0-2	0-0		Fox	Rennie	Statham	Beeston	Blake	Cranson	Kennedy	Ellis	Whitehurst*	Biggins	Sandford	Thomas
1/12			5,377	18	28			Neville 72, Eshelby 79	Miller	Hiley	Dryden	Cawley	Taylor	Cooper	Marshall	Bailey	Morgan	Neville	Eshelby	
								Ref: R Wiseman	Stoke's first ever visit to the other St James' Park ends in disaster when Steve Neville and Paul Eshelby wrap up the game for Terry Cooper's Grecians. Stoke wilt, the fans boo and the referee books the Exeter trainer who enters the pitch to treat a player without permission! Outplayed.											
18	H	BRENTFORD		5	D	2-2	1-1	Hilaire 10, Sandford 65	Fox	Ware	Statham	Beeston	Blake	Sandford	Kennedy	Thomas	Whitehurst*	Biggins	Hilaire	Ellis
16/12			10,995	6	29			Cadette 44, Smillie 46	Benstead	Ratcliffe	Fleming	Millen	Cousins	Buckle	Jones	Godfrey*	Cadette	Blissett	Smillie	Gayle
								Ref: G Aplin	Vince Hilaire celebrates his permanent transfer from Leeds by riding a tackle and firing past Graham Benstead. Transfer-listed Richard Cadette fires the Bees level and Neil Smillie's deflected shot beats Fox. Ellis' arrival sparks the fightback. Sandford rises to head home from six yards.											
19	A	PRESTON		7	L	0-2	0-1		Fox	Butler	Statham	Beeston	Blake	Sandford^	Kennedy	Ellis	Ware*	Biggins	Hilaire	Kelly/Gallimore
22/12			7,532	17	29			Swann 17, 64	Kelly	Senior	Williams	Flynn	Hughes	Wrightson	Mooney	Bogie	Joyce	Shaw	Swann	
								Ref: S Lodge	Ex-Stokie Shaw sets up Gary Swann to fire low past Fox and then sees his own effort disallowed for offside. Stoke's dislike of the plastic pitch is clear. Ball kicks an advertising hoarding when City foul up a set-piece. The second comes from Blake's mis-hit back-pass. It's 'Ball out' now.											
20	H	SWANSEA		8	D	2-2	1-1	Biggins 44, Thomas 70	Fox	Butler	Statham	Beeston	Cranson	Fowler	Kennedy	Ellis*	Thomas	Biggins	Hilaire	Kelly
26/12			12,534	16	30			Gilligan 17, 89p	Bracey	Hough	Coleman	Walker	Harris	Davies	Raynor^	Coughlin	Gilligan	Connor	Legg*	Hutchison/D'Auria
								Ref: T Lunt	Stoke are awful and concede to Jimmy Gilligan's header. Out of the blue Biggins skips a tackle and drives home. Stoke are galvanised. Hilaire torments the Swans' defence. Thomas heads in Kelly's centre. After dropping a high cross at his feet, Fox brings down Gilligan for the penalty.											
21	H	HUDDERSFIELD		8	W	2-0	1-0	Ellis 15, 48	Fox	Butler	Fowler	Beeston	Cranson	Sandford	Kennedy	Ellis	Thomas	Biggins	Hilaire	
29/12			11,869	14	33				Martin	Trevitt	Parsley*	O'Doherty	Mitchell	Jackson	O'Regan	Donovan	Roberts	Barnett	Onuora	Smith
								Ref: G Aplin	Tony Ellis scores two great goals as Stoke end a terrible year on a bright note. He shrugs off Simon Trevitt to fire past Lee Martin then cleverly clips a first-time shot past the advancing Jackson and Martin. Carl Beeston runs midfield and fires wide after a superb flowing four-man move.											
22	A	LEYTON ORIENT		6	W	2-0	1-0	Ellis 9, Thomas 59	Fox	Butler	Fowler	Beeston	Blake	Sandford	Ware	Ellis	Thomas	Biggins	Hilaire	
1/1			6,371	7	36				Heald	Baker	Howard	Sitton	Whitbread	Pike	Carter	Castle	Nugent	Achampong	Berry*	Harvey
								Ref: M Pierce	Tony Ellis latches onto a long Fox punt to ram home from 15 yards. Frank Clark's O's cause problems with Kenny Achampong prominent on the right. Sandford contains him well. Thomas nips in to notch another brave header as City counter attack. Is form returning at the right time?											
23	H	TRANMERE		7	D	1-1	0-1	Butler 77	Fox	Butler	Statham	Beeston	Blake	Sandford	Kennedy	Ellis	Thomas*	Biggins	Hilaire	Kelly
12/1			13,461	6	37			Brannan 31	Nixon	Higgins	Brannan	Irons	Hughes	Vickers	Morrissey*	Harvey	Steel	Muir	Mungall	Cooper
								Ref: P Taylor	Tempers fray as neither side can get a hold on the match. Hilaire and Hughes have a running battle. Biggins and Vickers lock foreheads. Butler deflects Brannan's shot over Fox before firing a long-range shot past Eric Nixon. Thomas is lucky to stay on after a set to with Steve Mungall.											

No	Date		Att	Pos	Pt	F-A	H-T	Scorers, Times, and Referees	1	2	3	4	5	6	7	8	9	10	11	subs used
24	A	ROTHERHAM		7	D	0-0	0-0		Fox	Fowler	Statham	Ware	Blake	Sandford	Kennedy	Ellis	Thomas	Biggins*	Hilaire	Kelly
	19/1		*6,236*	*24*	38				*O'Hanlon*	*Forrest*	*Russell*	*Thompson*	*Law*	*Robinson*	*Goodwin**	*Dempsey*	*Goater*	*Mendonca*	*Hazel*	*Spooner*
								Ref: I Hendrick	3,000 Stokies bask in the South Yorkshire sun but see little to believe that City will go up. Ellis twice shoots straight at Kelham O'Hanlon and Hilaire does likewise when clean through. Fox's brilliant flying save denies Des Hazel. Billy McEwan's rock-bottom Millers deserve the point.											
25	H	CHESTER		10	L	2-3	0-1	Kelly 60, Hilaire 68	Fox	Butler	Cranson	Ware	Blake	Sandford	Kevan^	Ellis	Thomas*	Kelly	Hilaire	Carr/**Devlin**
	2/2		11,037	*18*	38			*Dale 29, Bishop 52, 54*	*Stewart*	*Butler*	*Painter*	*Lightfoot*	*Abel*	*Pugh*	*Bishop*	*Barrow*	*Morton**	*Dale*	*Croft*	*Bennett*
								Ref: A Bennett	An abysmal performance. Chester are applauded by the Boothen after their third goal. City lack discipline, imagination and heart. Mark Devlin is the honourable exception on his debut as substitute. Kelly and Hilaire convert easy chances but the Potters' lack of commitment is worrying.											
26	A	SOUTHEND		11	L	0-1	0-1		Fox	Butler	Carr	Ware*	Blake	Sandford	Devlin	Ellis	Kelly	**Rice**	Hilaire^	Scott/Cranson
	5/2		*5,164*	*1*	38			*Angell 41*	*Sansome*	*Austin*	*Powell*	*Martin*	*Scully*	*Tilson*	*Clark*	*Butler*	*Ansah*	*Benjamin*	*Angell*	
								Ref: M James	City play without direction and fail to muster a shot in the first half. Brett Angell bundles the ball in for his 22nd of the season as Dave Webb's uncultured Shrimpers stay top. Brian Rice, on-loan from Forest, looks out of place in Div 3. Fox keeps the score down. Blake is booked again.											
27	H	BURY		13	D	2-2	1-0	Biggins 45, 65	Fox	Butler	Carr	Beeston	Blake	Cranson	Devlin*	Ellis	Ware	Biggins	Rice	Thomas
	16/2		9,885	*8*	39			*Hulme 73, 90*	*Kelly*	*Feeley*	*Stanislaus*	*Kearney*	*Valentine*	*Greenall*	*Lee*	*Robinson*	*Cunningham*	*Parkinson*	*Hulme*	
								Ref: R Bigger	Biggins flicks in against the run of play. Roger Stanislaus incredibly fires over from two yards with Fox beaten. Biggins heads the second from Rice's perfect cross but Hulme is left unmarked for two headers and Bury nearly snatch it in added time. Totally inept. Ball's job is on the line.											
28	A	WIGAN		14	L	**0-4**	0-1		Fox	Butler	Carr	Beeston	Blake	Fowler	Kennedy	Ellis	Ware	Biggins*	Rice	Devlin
	23/2		*3,728*	*15*	39			*Daley 36, 52, Patterson 64, Page 88*	*Hughes*	*Patterson*	*Tankard*	*Atherton*	*Johnson*	*Langley*	*Jones*	*Rimmer*	*Daley*	*Page*	*Griffiths B*	
								Ref: V Callow	Alan Ball resigns, leaving Stoke in their worst ever position in the league after taking a fearful hammering from Bryan Hamilton's Latics. Fox has a brilliant game, keeping the score respectable. Carr and Biggins both miss good chances. The team has no confidence left. Truly appalling.											
29	H	BOURNEMOUTH		16	L	1-3	0-0	Biggins 50	Fox	Butler*	Statham	Beeston	Blake	Sandford	Kennedy !	Ellis^	Rice	Biggins	Devlin	Thomas/Barnes
	27/2		7,797	*11*	39			*Jones 61, Lawrence 76, Blissett 84*	*Peyton*	*Mundee*	*Morrell*	*Teale*	*Watson*	*O'Driscoll*	*Wood*	*Holmes**	*Jones*	*Pulis*	*Blissett*	*Lawrence*
								Ref: J Lloyd	Graham Paddon is in charge of the demoralised troops who manage to take the lead through Biggins' header from Rice's centre. The Cherries' rough-house tactics see Butler stretchered off and Mick Kennedy snaps. He is sent off for kicking Matt Holmes. Bournemouth take advantage.											
30	H	EXETER		15	W	2-1	1-1	Biggins 27, 85	Fox	Beeston	Statham	Devlin*	Blake	Sandford	Kennedy	Thomas	Rice	Biggins	Barnes	Ware
	2/3		8,536	*16*	42			*Cooper 29p*	*Miller*	*Hiley*	*Brown*	*McNichol*	*Taylor*	*Cooper*	*Dryden*	*Batty**	*Morgan*	*Neville*	*Marshall*	*Rowbotham*
								Ref: M Peck	Relief as City finally win. Kevin Miller allows a long ball to slip past him and Biggins pounces. Blake handles for the penalty but City manage to put their troubles behind them and dominate the second period. Biggins' deserved second is a superb run and shot. His fifth in four matches.											
31	A	MANSFIELD		15	D	0-0	0-0		Fox	Ware	Statham*	Devlin	Blake	Cranson	Kennedy	Thomas	Rice	Biggins	Barnes^	Carr/Kelly
	5/3		***2,941***	*22*	43				*Beasley*	*Chambers**	*Murray*	*Withe*	*Foster*	*Gray*	*Kent*	*Charles*	*Hathaway*	*Wilkinson*	*Fairclough*	*Christie*
								Ref: J Moules	City revert to type against George Foster's relegation-haunted Stags. Kennedy has a shot cleared off the line and Kelly and Biggins both fail to beat Andy Beasley one-on-one. Ian Cranson is carried off and misses the rest of the season. Forgive us Delilah but Stoke cannot take any more.											
32	A	BRENTFORD		13	W	**4-0**	0-0	Thomas 64, Blake 69, Beeston 86, [Clarke 90]	Fox	Beeston	Carr	Devlin	Blake	Fowler	Kennedy	Thomas	**Clarke**	Biggins	Rice	
	9/3		*7,249*	*6*	46				*Benstead*	*Ratcliffe*	*Carstairs*	*Fleming*	*Evans*	*Buckle^*	*Jones*	*Cockram*	*Holdsworth*	*Cadette**	*Godfrey*	*Gayle/Rostron*
								Ref: G Willard	Stoke run riot in the second half and for once everything that they hit goes in. Thomas glances a header home and Blake lobs Graham Benstead from 10 yards. Beeston twists past two defenders to drive in and Wayne Clarke, on-loan from Man City, taps home from two yards. Fabulous.											
33	H	CREWE		11	W	1-0	0-0	Devlin 90	Fox	Rennie^	Carr	Devlin	Blake	Fowler	Sandford	Thomas	Clarke	Biggins	Rice*	Kelly/Ware
	13/3		15,455	*23*	49				*Beresford*	*Swain*	*Callaghan*	*Smart*	*Carr*	*Lennon*	*Murphy^*	*Hignett**	*Sussex*	*Gardiner*	*Edwards R*	*Doyle/McKearney*
								Ref: R Hamer	A totally forgettable night. Crewe battle tigerishly in their battle to avoid the drop. City rarely threaten. They somehow contrive to score when Devlin nets from Thomas's good approach work. Over 15,000 witness Stoke's undeserved win, almost as many as watch Man Utd at the Dell.											
34	A	SHREWSBURY		12	L	0-2	0-2		Fox	Beeston	Carr	Devlin	Blake	Fowler	Sandford	Thomas	Clarke	Biggins*	Rice^	Ellis/Kelly
	16/3		*6,210*	*22*	49			*Lyne 31, 44*	*Hughes*	*Blake*	*Lynch*	*Kelly*	*Heathcote*	*Clements*	*Brown*	*Spink*	*Summerfield*	*Taylor*	*Lyne*	
								Ref: K Barratt	Neil Lyne, on-loan from Forest, scores twice after Stoke defenders fail to clear. He also hits the post. Shrewsbury's first home league win since 9 Nov. Clarke has an overhead kick cleared off the line. Ellis head-butts Lynch but escapes a red card when he is carried off with concussion.											

No	Date	Venue	Opponent	Att	Pos	Res	Pts	F-A	H-T	Scorers, Times, and Referees	1	2	3	4	5	6	7	8	9	10	11	Subs used
35		A	FULHAM		9	W		1-0	0-0	Biggins 61	Fox	Ware	Carr	Beeston	Blake	Sandford	Devlin	Thomas	Clarke	Biggins	Rice	
	19/3			*3,131*	*22*		52				*Stannard*	*Morgan*	*Thomas*	*Eckhardt*	*North*	*Talbot*	*Milton**	*Scott*	*Stant*	*Brazil*	*Pike^*	*Davies/Cobb*
										Ref: B Hill	A paltry crowd witness a dour match with Stoke just having the edge. Neither side has brought its shooting boots. Blake produces a moment of rare inspiration, breaking free to cross for Biggins to fire in. The Fulham faithful want boss Alan Dicks out. No new manager until the summer.											
36		H	BOLTON		10	D		2-2	0-0	Devlin 47, Kelly 55	Fox	Ware	Carr	Beeston	Blake	Sandford	Devlin	Thomas	Clarke	Kelly	Rice	
	23/3			13,869	*3*		53			*Darby 80, Storer 81*	*Felgate*	*Brown*	*Burke*	*Patterson**	*Seagraves*	*Stubbs*	*Storer*	*Thompson*	*Reeves*	*Philliskirk*	*Darby*	*Green*
										Ref: D Frampton	Yet again Stoke fail to win a match after scoring the first goal. Thomas buzzes around in midfield and sets up Devlin's tap-in and Kelly's close-range header. Stoke self-destruct. Blake loses Darby who fires home and Storer rifles in unchallenged from the edge of the area. Thrown away.											
37		H	MANSFIELD		9	W		3-1	1-0	Clarke 30, 60, Blake 53	Fox	Beeston	Fowler	Devlin	Blake	Sandford	Kennedy	Thomas	Clarke	Kelly	Rice	
	26/3			9,113	*20*		56			*Smalley 46*	*Beasley*	*Chambers*	*Smalley*	*Spooner*	*Kearney*	*Gray*	*Ford*	*Smith*	*Christie**	*Wilkinson*	*Fairclough*	*Stringfellow*
										Ref: N Midgley	The City back four look jittery against Gary Ford's direct running but in attack Stoke move freely. Clarke heads home Kelly's cross to finish a move he begins. Blake heads in Rice's free-kick and Clarke rounds off the scoring from another Rice centre. One defeat in eight since Ball left.											
38		A	SWANSEA		10	L		1-2	0-1	Ellis 88	Fox	Beeston	Fowler	Devlin^	Blake	Sandford*	Kennedy	Thomas	Clarke	Kelly	Rice	Ware/Ellis
	30/3			*4,418*	*19*		56			*Legg 8, Harris 81*	*Bracey*	*Williams*	*Coleman*	*Hough*	*Harris*	*Legg*	*Raynor*	*Davies*	*Gilligan*	*Coughlin*	*Penney*	
										Ref: A Buksh	Newly installed Swans boss Frank Burrows sees his men ride their luck. Legg's shot takes a deflection to beat Fox. Devlin has a header cleared off the line and Kelly hits the bar. Harris picks up a wayward Stoke throw in to shoot past Fox. Ellis buries a snapshot but City run out of time.											
39		H	PRESTON		10	L		0-1	0-0		Fox	Ware	Carr	Beeston^	Blake	Fowler	Kennedy	Hilaire*	Clarke	Biggins	Rice	Kelly/Devlin
	1/4			11,524	*17*		56			*Shaw 85*	*Kelly*	*Senior*	*James*	*Joyce*	*Flynn*	*Wrightson*	*Thompson**	*Bogie*	*Cartwright*	*Shaw*	*Harper*	*Ashcroft*
										Ref: W Flood	Vince Hilaire is brought back into the team despite going AWOL for three days in midweek. He is subbed after 39 mins and never plays again. Predictably ex-Stokie Graham Shaw notches the only goal from Steve Senior's cross. No manager, no play-offs, no hope for Stoke. Dark days.											
40		A	HUDDERSFIELD		13	L		0-3	0-1		Fox	Ware !	Carr	Beeston	Blake	Kelly*	Kennedy	Thomas	Clarke	Biggins	Rice	Ellis
	6/4			*6,520*	*6*		56			*O'Regan 34p, Quinlan 49, Wright 55*	*Hardwick*	*Trevitt*	*Wright*	*Marsden*	*Mitchell*	*Jackson*	*O'Regan*	*Onoura**	*Donovan*	*Quinlan*	*Barnett*	*Edwards*
										Ref: W Burns	A comprehensive defeat against promotion-seeking Town. O'Regan's penalty is for Carr's trip on Donovan. Quinlan beats Fox at his near post. As the rain pours down, Fox drops Mark Wright's cross over the line and Paul Ware is sent off for two yellows. Beeston is lucky not to follow.											
41		H	LEYTON ORIENT		13	L		1-2	1-0	Beeston 27	Fox	Butler	Carr	Beeston	Blake	Fowler^	Devlin	Ellis	Kelly	Biggins*	Rice	Barnes/Gallimore
	13/4			7,957	*14*		56			*Cooper 65, 71*	*Heald*	*Baker*	*Howard*	*Day*	*Whitbread*	*Bart-Williams*	*Carter**	*Castle*	*Nugent*	*Cooper*	*Berry^*	*Harvey/Hales*
										Ref: A Wilkie	Stoke play some football for half an hour. Kelly springs the offside trap and Biggins side-foots home. Kelly fires wide after a great move. Then Orient's physical forwards batter Fowler. Cooper beats him to head in and threads a shot in off a post. The stunned fans depart in total silence.											
42		A	BIRMINGHAM		13	L		1-2	1-2	Ellis 45	Noble	Butler	Carr*	Beeston	Blake	Fowler	Devlin	Ellis	Kelly	Biggins	Rice^	Gallimore/Baines
	16/4			*6,729*	*11*		56			*Matthewson 7, Hopkins 21*	*Thomas*	*Clarkson*	*Frain*	*Yates*	*Overson*	*Matthewson*	*Rodgerson*	*Aylott**	*Robinson*	*Gleghorn*	*Hopkins*	*Gordon*
										Ref: J Key	Stoke take the game to Lou Macari's Blues after Matthewson nets a free header. Kelly's speed troubles the big Birmingham back four. Noble palms Frain's penalty (26 mins) round the post. Hopkins sweeps home a corner. Ellis powers past two defenders to blast past Martin Thomas.											
43		A	CAMBRIDGE		15	L		0-3	0-0		Noble	Butler	Gallimore	Devlin*	Blake	Wright	Kennedy	Ellis	Kelly	Biggins	Baines^	Carr/Barnes
	20/4			*5,743*	*4*		56			*Claridge 51, Cheetham 63, Dublin 71*	*Vaughan*	*Fensome*	*Leadbitter*	*Bailie*	*Chapple*	*O'Shea*	*Cheetham*	*Wilkins^*	*Claridge*	*Taylor**	*Philpott*	*Dublin/Dennis*
										Ref: G Pooley	City's smallest away following of the season witness another debacle. Claridge fires high past Noble. Cheetham shins the ball in from six yards and Dublin scores from close in. Biggins is booked for throwing the ball at an opponent. Kennedy heads off the line twice. Six straight defeats.											
44		H	BRADFORD C		13	W		2-1	2-1	Ellis 17, Butler 45	Fox	Kevan	Butler	Devlin	Blake	Gallimore	Ware	Ellis	Thomas	Kelly	Rice	
	27/4			**6,946**	*12*		59			*Babb 18*	*Tomlinson*	*James*	*Tinnion*	*Duxbury*	*Oliver*	*Sinnott*	*McCarthy*	*Jewell*	*Babb*	*Torpey**	*Reid !*	*Abbott*
										Ref: P Danson	Paul Ware's lunging 8th-minute challenge brings swift retribution from Paul Reid who is promptly sent off. Thomas twists to centre for Ellis to score but no deluge follows. Instead Babb heads a hopeful long punt over Fox. Butler saves Stoke's blushes, firing in after a rare foray upfield.											
45		H	GRIMSBY		14	D		0-0	0-0		Fox	Kevan	Butler	Beeston	Blake	Ware	Devlin	Ellis*	Thomas	Kelly	Gallimore	Biggins
	4/5			11,832	*2*		60				*Sherwood*	*McDermott*	*Jobling*	*Futcher*	*Lever*	*Cunnington*	*Watson*	*Gilbert*	*Birtles**	*Cockerill*	*Woods*	*Smith*
										Ref: K Cooper	Angry City fans invade the pitch with 15 minutes left of a sterile match. The game is held up for 18 mins while the police herd supporters back to the terraces. Mr Cooper blows early as the teams play out time. Demonstrations. Talk of the fences going up again despite the Taylor report.											
46		A	READING		14	L		0-1	0-1		Fox	Kevan	Butler	Beeston	Blake	Ware	Devlin	Ellis*	Thomas	Kelly	Gallimore	Biggins
	11/5			*4,101*	*15*		60			*Senior 15*	*Francis*	*Richardson*	*Conroy*	*McPherson*	*Hicks*	*Bailey*	*Gooding**	*Lovell*	*Senior*	*Maskell*	*Taylor*	*Seymour*
			Home	Away						Ref: R Gifford	Stoke lose to new manager Mark McGhee's Royals, who are on a worse run than City (five defeats in five). City's new boss will have his work cut out to turn a poor side, with no passion, into any kind of team. Senior heads a free-kick in unchallenged. Blake clears off the line. Pathetic.											
Average			11,587	6,150																		

Rumbelows Cup	Att	Pos	Res	F-A	H-T	Scorers, Times, and Referees	1	2	3	4	5	6	7	8	9	10	11	subs used
1:1 H SWANSEA			D	0-0	0-0		Fox	Butler	Statham	Beeston	Blake	Fowler	Kennedy	Ellis*	Thomas	Biggins	Kelly	Boughey
29/8	7,806						*Bracey*	*Raynor*	*Coleman*	*Hough*	*Harris*	*Walker*	*Thornber*	*Davies*	*Gilligan*	*Connor*	*Legg*	
						Ref: C Trusson	In torrential rain Stoke hold the upper hand. Tony Kelly heads straight at Lee Bracey. Kennedy's shot appears to hit the bar and bounce over the line, but no goal is awarded. 36-year-old Thomas runs himself into the ground but Terry Connor fluffs Terry Yorath's Swans' best opportunity.											
1:2 A SWANSEA			W	1-0	0-0	Kelly 86	Fox	Butler	Statham	Beeston	Blake	Sandford	Kennedy	Ellis	Thomas*	Biggins	Ware	Kelly
4/9	*4,464*						*Bracey*	*Raynor*	*Coleman*	*Trick*	*Harris*	*Walker**	*Thornber*	*Davies*	*Gilligan*	*Connor^*	*Legg*	*D'Auria/Watson*
						Ref: K Cooper (Stoke win 1-0 on aggregate)	Stoke escape after Fox brilliantly tips Mark Harris' header over and parries Keith Walker's point-blank effort. Tony Kelly latches on to Trick's back-pass and beats Bracey to spare Alan Ball's blushes. An unimaginative midfield struggle all night and hard-working Swansea are unlucky.											
2:1 A WEST HAM		7	L	0-3	0-1		Fox	Butler	Statham^	Beeston	Blake	Sandford	Kennedy	Evans	Kelly*	Biggins	Ware	Thomas/Fowler
26/9	*15,870*	*2:3*				*Dicks 43p, Keen 64, Quinn 86*	*Miklosko*	*Potts*	*Dicks*	*Foster*	*Martin*	*Keen*	*Bishop*	*Quinn*	*Slater*	*Allen**	*Morley*	*Parris*
						Ref: B Hill	Despite thrashing Southend, Ball makes changes and introduces on-loan Gareth Evans from Hibs. Stoke are never at the races after Morley falls in the box to win a spot-kick. Billy Bonds' Hammers put the tie out of reach through Keen's 30-yarder and Quinn latching onto Fowler's error.											
2:2 H WEST HAM		4	L	1-2	1-0	Evans 37	Fox	Butler	Carr	Ware	Blake	Sandford	Scott	Evans	Ellis	Biggins	Kevan*	Boughey
10/10	8,411	*2:3*				*Allen 64, 79*	*Miklosko*	*Potts*	*Dicks*	*Foster*	*Martin*	*Keen**	*Bishop*	*Parris*	*Quinn^*	*Allen*	*Morley*	*Gale/McAvennie*
						Ref: N Midgley (Stoke lose 1-5 on aggregate)	Evans nips in between Ludo Miklosko and Julian Dicks to lob home. All hope is set aside when Clive Allen clinically plants a pin-point header past Fox and flicks home with the outside of his boot. Hammers run Stoke ragged as the gulf in class between the divisions is clearly visible.											

FA Cup	Att	Pos	Res	F-A	H-T	Scorers, Times, and Referees	1	2	3	4	5	6	7	8	9	10	11	subs used
1 A TELFORD		3	D	0-0	0-0		Fox	Butler*	Statham	Beeston	Blake	Cranson	Kennedy	Ellis	Thomas	Biggins	Sandford	Fowler
17/11	*3,709*						*McDonagh*	*Salathiel*	*Dyson*	*Myers*	*Brindley*	*Humphreys*	*McGinty*	*Grainger*	*Crawley*	*Buxton**	*Nelson^*	*Brown/Bailey*
						Ref: J Lloyd	Stoke face non-league opposition for the first time since Blyth Spartans – and ex-Stokie Paul Dyson. The TV cameras see Stoke out-intimidate Telford. Butler is carried off with a twisted knee. City deal with the Telford threat comfortably. Ian Cranson makes his first start for 12 months.											
1R H TELFORD		3	W	1-0	1-0	Sandford 14	Fox	Rennie^	Statham	Beeston	Blake	Cranson	Kennedy	Whitehurst*	Thomas	Biggins	Sandford	Ellis/Fowler
21/11	11,880						*McDonagh*	*Salathiel*	*Dyson*	*Myers*	*Brindley*	*Humphreys*	*McGinty*	*Grainger*	*Crawley*	*Benbow**	*Nelson^*	*Brown/Daly*
						Ref: J Lloyd	Fox makes good saves from Crawley and Brindley. Biggins has a goal ruled out for offside. Sandford outjumps Dyson to bury Kennedy's cross as City edge past battling Telford. Statham and Myers exchange punches but referee Lloyd only books them. Paul Rennie makes a good debut.											
2 A BURNLEY		3	L	0-2	0-0		Fox	Ware	Statham	Sandford	Blake	Cranson*	Kennedy	Thomas	Whitehurst	Biggins	Hilaire^	Beeston /Ellis
12/12	*12,949*	*4:3*				*Francis 72, White 84*	*Pearce*	*Measham*	*Deakin*	*Deary*	*Pender^*	*Davis*	*White*	*Futcher**	*Francis*	*Jakub*	*Grewcock*	*Mumby/Farrell*
						Ref: K Hackett	Frank Casper's Burnley are caused problems by Biggins and Hilaire but lead through a freak goal when Francis' shot hits the post but rebounds into the net off Ware. City lose their heads. Kennedy is intent on kicking anything that moves. White taps in after Fox tips onto the bar. Awful.											

	P	W	D	L	F	A	W	D	L	F	A	Pts
		Home					Away					
1 Cambridge	46	14	5	4	42	22	11	6	6	33	23	86
2 Southend	46	13	6	4	34	23	13	1	9	33	28	85
3 Grimsby	46	16	3	4	42	13	8	8	7	24	21	83
4 Bolton	46	14	5	4	33	18	10	6	7	31	32	83
5 Tranmere *	46	13	5	5	38	21	10	4	9	26	25	78
6 Brentford	46	12	4	7	30	22	9	9	5	29	25	76
7 Bury	46	13	6	4	39	26	7	7	9	28	30	73
8 Bradford C	46	13	3	7	36	22	7	7	9	26	32	70
9 Bournemouth	46	14	6	3	37	20	5	7	11	21	38	70
10 Wigan	46	14	3	6	40	20	6	6	11	31	34	69
11 Huddersfield	46	13	3	7	37	23	5	10	8	20	28	67
12 Birmingham	46	8	9	6	21	21	8	8	7	24	28	65
13 Leyton Orient	46	15	2	6	35	19	3	8	12	20	39	64
14 STOKE	46	9	7	7	36	29	7	5	11	19	30	60
15 Reading	46	11	5	7	34	28	6	3	14	19	38	59
16 Exeter	46	12	6	5	35	16	4	3	16	23	36	57
17 Preston	46	11	5	7	33	29	4	6	13	21	38	56
18 Shrewsbury	46	8	7	8	29	22	6	3	14	32	46	52
19 Chester	46	10	3	10	27	27	4	6	13	19	31	51
20 Swansea	46	8	6	9	31	33	5	3	15	18	39	48
21 Fulham	46	8	8	7	27	22	2	8	13	14	34	46
22 Crewe	46	6	9	8	35	35	5	2	16	27	45	44
23 Rotherham	46	5	10	8	31	38	5	2	16	19	49	42
24 Mansfield	46	5	8	10	23	27	3	6	14	19	36	38
	1104	265	134	153	805	576	153	134	265	576	805	1522

* promoted after play-offs

Odds & ends

Double wins: (3) Bradford C, Crewe, Fulham.
Double losses: (4) Birmingham, Preston, Reading, Shrewsbury.

Won from behind: (2) Bradford C (a), Tranmere (a).
Lost from in front: (3) Bournemouth (h), Orient (h), Shrewsbury (h).

High spots: A good start, hitting third spot in November.
The good form of Wayne Biggins.
Beating early season leaders Southend 4-0.
Winning on the opening day for the first time since 1982.
7 away victories, most since 78-79.

Low spots: Lowest ever finish in the Football League.
Alan Ball's failure to turn things around.
An abysmal 0-4 defeat at Wigan.
The appalling behaviour of fans towards the departing Alan Ball.
Losing at Burnley in the FA Cup.
Six defeats towards the end of the season.

Player of the Year: Mickey Thomas.
Ever-presents: (0).
Hat-tricks: (0).
Leading scorer: (12) Wayne Biggins.

	Appearances Lge	*Sub*	LC	*Sub*	FAC	*Sub*	Goals Lge	LC	FAC	Tot
Baines, Paul	**1**	*1*								
Barnes, Paul	**3**	*3*								
Beeston, Carl	**37**		3		2	*1*	**2**			**2**
Biggins, Wayne	**36**	*2*	4		3		**12**			**12**
Blake, Noel	**44**		4		3		**3**			**3**
Boughey, Darren				*2*						
Bright, Dave		*1*								
Butler, John	**31**		4		1		**2**			**2**
Carr, Cliff	**15**	*5*	1							
Clarke, Wayne	**9**									
Cranson, Ian	**7**	*2*			3					
Devlin, Mark	**18**	*3*					**2**			**2**
Ellis, Tony	**33**	*5*	3		1	*2*	**9**			**9**
Evans, Gareth	**5**		2				**1**	1		**2**
Fowler, Lee	**14**	*3*	1	*1*		*2*				
Fox, Peter	**44**		4		3					
Gallimore, Tony	**4**	*3*								
Hilaire, Vince	**10**				1		**2**			**2**
Kelly, Tony	**16**	*13*	2	*1*			**3**	1		**4**
Kennedy, Mick	**32**		3		3		**3**			**3**
Kevan, David	**4**	*1*	1							
Noble, Danny	**2**									
Rennie, Paul	**3**				1					
Rice, Brian	**18**						**3**			**3**
Sandford, Lee	**32**		3		3		**2**		1	**3**
Scott, Ian	**1**	*1*	1							
Statham, Derek	**22**		3		3		**1**			**1**
Thomas, Mickey	**32**	*6*	2	*1*	3		**7**			**7**
Ware, Paul	**29**	*5*	3		1		**2**			**2**
Whitehurst, Billy	**3**				2					
Wright, Ian	**1**									
(own-goals)							**1**			**1**
31 players used	**506**	***54***	**44**	***5***	**33**	***5***	**55**	**2**	**1**	**58**

No	Date		Att	Pos	Pt	F-A	H-T	Scorers, Times, and Referees	1	2	3	4	5	6	7	8	9	10	11	subs used
1	A	BRADFORD C			L	0-1	0-1		**Kearton**	Butler	Cranson	Blake	Fowler*	Kevan	Gallimore	Beeston	Kelly	Biggins	Sandford	Ellis
	17/8		*7,556*		0			*Tinnion 17*	*Tomlinson*	*Mitchell*	*Dowson*	*James*	*Oliver*	*Gardner*	*Babb*	*Duxbury L*	*Torpey*	*Tinnion*	*Stuart*	
								Ref: C Trussell	After an on-off saga, Lou Macari is the new manager. He sees a makeshift side beaten by Brian Tinnion's strike from 16 yards, which flies past on-loan Jason Kearton. Despite neat approach play, shot-shy Stoke don't look promotion material. Macari knows the squad needs improving.											
2	H	BOURNEMOUTH		20	D	1-1	1-1	Biggins 17p	Kearton	Butler	Scott*	Kevan	Blake	Sandford	Ellis	Beeston	Kelly	Biggins	Fowler	Gallimore
	24/8		10,011	*18*	1			*Quinn 42*	*Bartram*	*Baker*	*Morrell*	*Morris*	*Watson*	*O'Driscoll*	*Bond*	*Jones^*	*Quinn*	*Case*	*Holmes**	*Cooke/Mundee*
								Ref: S Bell	Bournemouth look the better side before Kelly is brought down by Vince Bartram. Stoke hold the upper hand until Jimmy Quinn nips in to fire past Kearton. City lack midfield bite and the forwards look uninterested without service. Ellis' near-post header is the only other on-goal effort.											
3	A	PETERBOROUGH		20	D	1-1	1-1	Biggins 1	Kearton	**Overson**	Scott	Kevan	Blake	Kennedy	Cranson	Beeston	Kelly*	Biggins	Fowler	Ellis
	31/8		*7,174*	*6*	2			*Kimble 16*	*Barber*	*White*	*Butterworth*	*Halsall*	*Robinson*	*Welsh*	*Sterling*	*Ebdon*	*Gavin*	*Riley**	*Kimble^*	*McInerney/Sterling*
								Ref: J Moules	'Bertie' Biggins turns on the edge of the area to crash home right footed at Chris Turner's newly-promoted Borough. He then has another effort mysteriously disallowed for offside. Gary Kimble pounces when Blake miskicks in the box and Stoke leave with one point not three. Typical.											
4	H	SHREWSBURY		16	W	1-0	0-0	Biggins 53	Kearton	Overson	Scott	Kevan	Blake	Kennedy	Cranson	Beeston	Kelly*	Biggins	Fowler	Ellis
	4/9		10,182	*6*	5				*Hughes*	*Gorman*	*Lynch*	*Henry*	*Heathcote*	*Blake*	*Smith*	*Summerfield*	*Spink**	*Hopkins*	*Lyne*	*O'Toole*
								Ref: K Breen	City beat ex-Stokie Tony Henry's unbeaten Shrews thanks to Biggins' flying header from Kevan's cross. Hughes fingertips his earlier volley over. Biggins, Beeston and Kennedy are booked as City cling on. Solid defending indicates the tactical thinking of Macari. A first win at last.											
5	A	DARLINGTON		7	W	1-0	0-0	Ellis 57	Kearton	Butler	Sandford	Kevan	Blake	Kennedy	Cranson	Beeston	Ellis	Biggins*	Fowler	Kelly^/Scott
	7/9		*4,230*	*17*	8				*Prudhoe*	*Coatsworth*	*Gray**	*Willis*	*Smith*	*Trotter*	*Cook*	*Toman*	*Borthwick^*	*Mardenboro'*	*Tait*	*Cork/Ellison*
								Ref: M Peck	City maul Darlington but the referee fails to spot a blatant handball and doesn't award a penalty. Kevan's free-kick rattles the crossbar. It looks like being another one of those days but Tony Ellis pops up at the far post to drill home. Cranson marshals the defence superbly. Much better.											
6	H	FULHAM		7	D	2-2	1-0	Biggins 25, Cranson 53	Kearton	Butler	Sandford	Kevan	Blake	Kennedy	Cranson	Beeston	Ellis	Biggins*	Fowler^	Kelly/Overson
	14/9		10,567	*11*	9			*Cole 56, Newson 75*	*Stannard*	*Marshall*	*Pike*	*Newson*	*Eckhardt*	*Thomas*	*Kelly**	*Onwere*	*Cole*	*Brazil*	*Scott*	*Georgiou*
								Ref: R Shepherd	Stoke sweep into the lead thanks to Biggins' tap in after Blake beats Stannard and Cranson's header from Kevan's corner; then surrender after Biggins is subbed. Scott hits the bar. Cole and Newson finish well-worked moves. Stoke lose their shape and are lucky to cling on for a point.											
7	H	HARTLEPOOL		6	W	3-2	2-0	Biggins 37, 39, Butler 75	Kearton	Butler	Sandford	Kevan	Blake*	Kennedy	Cranson	Overson	**Stein**	Biggins	Scott	Fowler
	17/9		9,394	*14*	12			*Baker 50, Olsson 65*	*Hodge*	*Nobbs*	*McKinnon*	*Tinkler*	*MacPhail*	*Bennyworth*	*Rush^*	*Olsson*	*Baker*	*Honour**	*Dalton*	*McCreery/Tupling*
								Ref: I Hendrick	Biggins pounces when Hodge fumbles. He then heads Butler's centre in. But another two-goal cushion is let slip. Blake's error gifts Paul Baker his opportunity. Paul Olsson outpaces the back four to smash home a long ball. Grafting City snatch victory thanks to Butler's far post header.											
8	A	PRESTON		8	D	2-2	1-1	Biggins 41, 59	Kearton	Overson	Sandford	Kevan	Butler	Kennedy	Cranson	Beeston	Stein	Biggins	Fowler	
	21/9		*6,345*	*19*	13			*Jepson 7, Swann 60*	*Kelly*	*Senior*	*Wrightson*	*Swann*	*Flynn*	*James J*	*Greenwood**	*Joyce*	*Jepson*	*Shaw*	*James M*	*Thompson*
								Ref: I Cruikshanks	For once Stoke look comfortable on plastic despite Jepson scoring with Les Chapman's Preston's only first-half shot. On-loan Mark Stein links well with Biggins who rounds Alan Kelly. Beeston's cushion header sets up Bertie's second. Sandford's clearance hits Swann and rebounds in.											
9	H	STOCKPORT		8	D	2-2	2-0	Biggins 14p, 28	Kearton	Butler	Sandford	Scott	Overson	Kennedy	Cranson	Beeston	Stein	Biggins	Fowler	
	28/9		12,954	*4*	14			*Lillis 55, Francis 87*	*Edwards*	*Knowles*	*Williams P*	*Thorpe*	*Barras*	*Williams B*	*Gannon*	*Paskin*	*Francis*	*Ward*	*Lillis**	*Kilner*
								Ref: R Poulain	Bertie cracks home a penalty after Stein is felled by Edwards. City look settled and Biggins' second arrives when the County defence stop and leave him free to score. Danny Bergara's County steal a point thanks to debutant Mark Lillis's scrambled shot and giant Kevin Francis' header.											
10	A	CHESTER		10	D	0-0	0-0		Kearton	Butler	Sandford	Scott	Overson	Kennedy	Cranson	Beeston	Stein	Biggins	Blake	
	5/10		*4,212*	*21*	15				*Stewart*	*McGuinness*	*Albiston*	*Pugh*	*Abel**	*Whelan*	*Bishop*	*Barrow*	*Morton*	*Bennett*	*Croft*	*Butler*
		(at Moss Rose)						Ref: A Dawson	Chester, playing at Macclesfield's ground as they wait for a new stadium, reduce Stoke to kick and rush football. Six are booked and the game deteriorates into a series of long balls. Biggins and Stein miss open nets. Vince Overson's tribunal fee is £50k. Cranson signs for another year.											
11	H	BOLTON		6	W	2-0	1-0	Biggins 16, Scott 80	Kearton	Butler	Sandford	Kevan*	Overson	Kennedy	Cranson	Beeston	Stein	Biggins	Fowler	Scott
	12/10		12,420	*9*	18				*Dibble*	*Brown P*	*Burke^*	*Kelly*	*Came*	*Stubbs*	*Brown M*	*Patterson*	*Reeves*	*Green**	*Darby*	*Storer/Seagraves*
								Ref: R Gifford	City's five-man defensive system begins to bear fruit as they shut out Phil Neal's Bolton. Biggins nabs a lucky 13th with a low shot. Scott chips home with his first touch as sub. Stein is superb but hits the bar and is denied by Dibble's fantastic save. Macari is set to sign him from Oxford.											

12	A	SWANSEA		9	L		1-2	0-2	Ellis 88	Kearton	Butler	Sandford	Kevan	Overson	Kennedy	Cranson	Beeston	Ellis	Biggins	Fowler*	Scott
19/10			*3,363*	22		18			*Harris 9, Davies 14*	Freestone	Jenkins	Ford	Coughlin	Harris	Brazil	Bowen	Davies	Gilligan	Raynor	Legg	
									Ref: D Frampton	Stoke lose their way in the swirling wind. Frank Burrows' Swans fly into a two-goal lead as Mark Harris soars above the supposedly strong-in-the-air defence to nod home and then Alan Davies rams home Jimmy Gilligan's neat cross. Ellis fires in Kevan's corner but too late to matter.											
13	H	LEYTON ORIENT		6	W		2-0	1-0	Biggins 36, Cranson 71	Kearton	Butler	Sandford	Kevan	Overson	Kennedy	Cranson	Beeston	Ellis	Biggins	Fowler	
26/10			9,555	10		21				Turner	Howard	Hackett	Achampong	Day	Hales*	Bart-Williams	Jones	Nugent	Castle	Otto	Harvey
									Ref: A Wilkie	Kearton keeps City in it with a brilliant one-handed save from Nugent. Biggins scores from close in after Tony 'Elvis' Ellis's shot is deflected to him. Cranson bullets home a Kevan corner. Turner palms Biggins' shot round the post. The long-ball tactics seem lost without a target man.											
14	H	HUDDERSFIELD		8	L		0-2	0-2		Kearton	Butler	Sandford	Kevan	Overson	Kennedy	Cranson	Beeston	Ellis*	Biggins	Fowler	Kelly
2/11			10,116	4		21			*Roberts 12, 14*	Clarke	Trevitt	Charlton	Marsden	Mitchell	Jackson !	O'Regan	Stapleton	Roberts	Starbuck	Bennett	
									Ref: W Burge	Kearton's howlers allow Iwan Roberts to grab two close-range goals. First he lets a shot through his legs, then he fails to collect a cross to give Roberts a free header. Jackson's second caution is for hauling back Biggins (74 mins). Stoke make no more chances against 10 than 11 men.											
15	A	BURY		6	W		3-1	1-1	Ellis 3, 78, Overson 53	Kearton	Butler	Sandford	Kevan	Overson	Kennedy	Cranson	Beeston	Ellis	Biggins	Fowler*	Ware
5/11			***3,245***	19		24			*Stevens 7*	Kelly	Wilson D	Robertson	Kearney	Valentine	Greenall	Smith	Robinson	Stevens	Cullen	Wilson I*	Parkinson
									Ref: K Redfearn	Stoke murder a poor Shakers team. Ellis heads home a corner. Remarkably Bury level when Stevens turns sharply to fire in. Overson converts another corner and Ellis cuts past two defenders to score. Two shots are cleared off the line. A blatant penalty is turned down. Should be more.											
16	A	EXETER		5	D		0-0	0-0		Kearton	Butler	Sandford	Kevan	Overson	Kennedy	Cranson	Beeston	Stein	Biggins	Fowler	
19/11			*5,309*	6		25				Miller	Hiley	Brown	Williams	Daniels	Whiston	Hilaire*	Wimbleton	Moran	Chapman^	Kelly	Hodge/Dolan
									Ref: M Pierce	Exeter manager Alan Ball is the target of a Stoke hate mob. His team carry out vengeful tackles and are lucky to keep 11 men on. Jon Brown's challenge on Butler is the worst but he escapes with a yellow card. After the whistle, mindless idiots invade the pitch and the police are needed.											
17	H	TORQUAY		5	W		3-0	2-0	Biggins 2, Stein 34, 60	**Sinclair**	Ware	Sandford	Kevan	Overson	Kennedy	Cranson	Beeston	Stein^	Biggins*	Fowler	Ellis/Barnes
23/11			9,124	23		28				Howells	Holmes P	Uzzell^	Compton*	Elliott	Holmes M	Rowbotham	Hall	Joyce	Edwards	Loram	Hodges/Myers
									Ref: P Alcock	Torquay have lost eight in a row away from home. Biggins pounces on a loose ball to sweep home. The Gulls concede Stein's first Stoke goals after his move from Oxford. Howells fails to stop his shot crossing the line and a harmless looking shot deflects wickedly, stranding the keeper.											
18	A	WEST BROM		5	D		2-2	1-1	Overson 40, 52	Sinclair	Ware	Butler	Kevan	Overson	Kennedy	Cranson	Beeston	Stein	Biggins	Kelly*	Barnes
30/11			*17,207*	3		29			*Shakespeare 17, Goodman 83*	Naylor	Parkin	Harbey	Bradley	Strodder^	Burgess	McNally	Goodman	Robson	Shakespeare	White*	Williams/Rogers
									Ref: K Cooper	Stoke are shocked by Craig Shakespeare's cool finish after they have all the early play against Bobby Gould's men. Vince Overson notches his first goals for Stoke. He cracks home Beeston's pass and nods in Ware's corner. Don Goodman turns a cross shot home to save Albion a point.											
19	H	WIGAN		5	W		3-0	2-0	Stein 17, Kelly 43, Biggins 81	Sinclair	Ware	Butler	Kevan	Overson	Kennedy	Cranson	Beeston	Stein	Biggins	Kelly	
14/12			**8,419**	20		32				Adkins	Parkinson	Tankard	Jones	Patterson	Langley	Powell^	Connelly	Pilling	Worthington*	Griffiths	Johnson/Daley
									Ref: M Reed	City romp home against Bryan Hamilton's hapless Latics. Stein fires home his third in three games. Kelly and Biggins both race clear to score coolly. The thick fog prevents many fans arriving or seeing much when they do finally get there. On-loan Ronnie Sinclair looks good in goal.											
20	A	BOURNEMOUTH		4	W		2-1	1-1	Biggins 10, Kelly 76	Sinclair	Ware	Butler	Kevan	Overson	Kennedy	Cranson	Beeston	Stein	Biggins	Kelly	
21/12			*5,436*	12		35			*Wood 5*	Bartram	Bond	Rowland	Morris	Mundee	O'Driscoll	Cooke	Wood^	Quinn	Case	Holmes*	Lawrence/Mitchell
									Ref: G Poll	Paul Wood loops a header in off the far post but Stoke storm back. Bertie turns to drive past Bartram and with the wind at their backs City win thanks to Kelly's header from Stein's clever cut-back. Overson dominates dangerman Quinn. Sinclair saves brilliantly from George Lawrence.											
21	H	PETERBOROUGH		5	D		3-3	2-2	Kevan 7, Stein 30, Biggins 70	Sinclair	Ware	Butler	Kevan	Overson	Kennedy*	Cranson	Beeston	Stein	Biggins	Kelly	Sandford
26/12			14,732	12		36			*Robinson D 17, Halsall 35, Sterling 81*	Barber	Luke	Johnson^	Halsall	Robinson D	Welsh	Sterling	Cooper	Riley	Charlery	Kimble*	Culpin/Robinson R
									Ref: T Lunt	Stoke let Posh off the hook as they present Chris Turner's side with three equalisers. Kevan deflects home Biggins' piledriver. Robinson is left unmarked to head in. Halsall's rocket follows Stein's superb run and shot. Barber lets Biggins' effort wriggle in but Sterling's tap-in squares it.											
22	H	BRADFORD C		5	D		0-0	0-0		Sinclair	Ware	Butler	Kevan	Overson	Sandford	Cranson	Beeston	Stein	Biggins	Kelly*	Barnes
28/12			12,208	19		37				Tomlinson	Mitchell	Williams	Stapleton	Leonard	Babb	McCarthy	Duxbury L	Torpey	McHugh	Jewell	
									Ref: K Barratt	Hampered by a heavy pitch, Stoke struggle against Frank Stapleton's Bantams. Butler and Kelly have poor games – Kelly fouling Torpey for a penalty (55 mins) which Lee Duxbury thankfully blasts over. Tomlinson saves Barnes' deflected effort. Neither keeper is unduly troubled.											
23	A	SHREWSBURY		5	L		0-1	0-1		Sinclair	Ware	Butler	Kevan	Overson	Gallimore	Cranson	Beeston	Stein	Biggins	Kelly	
1/1			*8,557*	11		37			*Summerfield 8*	Perks	Worsley	Lynch*	Henry	Spink	Blake	Donaldson	Summerfield	Griffiths^	MacKenzie	Lyne	Clark/Hopkins
									Ref: P Taylor	Tony Gallimore, on his return from loan at Carlisle, proves ineffective as Macari searches for width. Tony Henry sets up Kevin Summerfield's early goal. Stoke attack all out. Biggins, Ware, Butler and Beeston all go close but Steve Perks stands firm. Kelly misses a glorious open goal.											

No	Date			Att	Pos	Pt	F-A	H-T	Scorers, Times, and Referees	1	2	3	4	5	6	7	8	9	10	11	subs used
24		H	BIRMINGHAM		5	W	2-1	0-0	Ware 52, Biggins 77	Sinclair	Ware	Butler	Kevan	Overson	Sandford	Cranson	Beeston	Stein	Biggins	**Russell**	
	4/1			18,914	*2*	40			*Beckford 49*	*Miller*	*Frain*	*Matthewson*	*Cooper*	*Hicks*	*Mardon**	*Rodgerson*	*Rowbotham*	*Paskin*	*Gleghorn*	*Beckford*	*Okenla*
									Ref: R Milford	Kevin Russell gives Stoke the width Macari wants. The game comes to life when on-loan Jason Beckford fires past Sinclair from Frain's pass. Ware replies with a fine 30-yard shot. Biggins wriggles through to crack a rising shot past Kevin Miller. Steino is felled but no pen is awarded.											
25		A	BRENTFORD		6	L	0-2	0-1		Sinclair	Ware	Butler	Kevan*	Overson	Sandford	Cranson	Beeston	Stein	Biggins !	Russell	Ellis
	11/1			*9,004*	*1*	40			*Luscombe 4, Holdsworth 60*	*Benstead*	*Bates*	*Manuel**	*Millen*	*Evans*	*Ratcliffe*	*Luscombe*	*Booker*	*Holdsworth*	*Blissett^*	*Smillie*	*Godfrey/Gayle*
									Ref: P Scobie	A vital promotion clash. City look lively but Lee Luscombe sets the Bees buzzing with a header from their first chance. Biggins walks (46 mins) for a clash with Billy Manuel. Div 3 leading marksman Dean Holdsworth taps in to seal it. Sinclair's lack of height is giving cause for concern.											
26		H	READING		6	W	3-0	1-0	Jones 24 (og), Butler 64, Stein 71	Sinclair	**Foley**	Butler*	Kevan	Overson	Sandford	Cranson	Beeston	Stein	Biggins	Russell	**Grimes**
	18/1			10,835	*14*	43				*Leighton*	*Jones*	*Dillon !*	*Taylor*	*Williams*	*Streete !*	*Gooding*	*Bailey*	*Senior*	*Lovell**	*Gilkes^*	*Cockram/Gray*
									Ref: B Coddington	A brilliant performance helped by strict refereeing. Mr Coddington sends off Floyd Streete (44 mins) for handball and Kevin Dillon (50 mins) for dissent. Jones helps Biggins' shot over the line after it hits the bar. Butler heads in and Stein rounds Jim Leighton to score easily. Classy.											
27		A	HULL		4	W	1-0	1-0	Russell 20	Sinclair	Foley	Butler	Kevan*	Blake	Sandford	Cranson	Beeston	Stein	Ellis	Russell	Grimes
	25/1			*4,996*	*21*	46				*Fettis*	*Norton*	*Jacobs**	*Mail*	*Wilcox*	*Shotton*	*Palin*	*Stoker*	*Pearson*	*Windass*	*Jenkinson*	*France*
									Ref: P Harrison	Kevin Russell volleys home a beauty to send sorry Hull into the relegation zone. Their fans chant 'sack the board' after failing to score in 480 mins. Biggins and Overson are both suspended but Stoke easily contain Terry Dolan's team. Pearson fires the Tigers' best chances at Sinclair.											
28		H	SWANSEA		3	W	2-1	1-0	Ware 41, Beeston 90	Sinclair	Foley	Ware	Kevan	Blake^	Sandford	Cranson	Beeston	Stein	Ellis*	Russell	Kennedy/Grimes
	1/2			11,299	*15*	49			*Gilligan 61*	*Freestone*	*Agboola*	*Ford*	*Walker*	*Harris*	*Chapple**	*Williams*	*Coughlin*	*Gilligan*	*Raynor*	*Legg*	*Thornber*
									Ref: T Fitzharris	Stoke swarm all over Swansea. Stein is sent sprawling but no penalty is given. Finally Ware latches on to Ellis' pass to fire home. Stoke relax. Jimmy Gilligan exposes Sinclair's lack of height by heading over him. Beeston volleys in a splendid late winner from Kennedy's long throw.											
29		A	LEYTON ORIENT		2	W	1-0	1-0	Beeston 4	Sinclair	Foley	Butler	Kevan	Overson	Sandford	Cranson	Beeston	Stein*	Biggins	Ware	Barnes
	8/2			*9,153*	*7*	52				*Turner*	*Howard^*	*Hackett*	*Burnett*	*Day*	*Whitbread*	*Carter*	*Achampong*	*Jones**	*Nugent*	*Berry*	*Cooper/Castle*
									Ref: G Willard	A dreadful game. The action begins and ends in the fourth minute when Beeston slots home after Adrian Whitbread blocks Steve Foley's shot on the line. Paul Ware's overhead kick sails over. The game deteriorates into a long ball/offside battle. Competent but hardly very entertaining.											
30		H	WEST BROM		1	W	1-0	1-0	Stein 28	Sinclair	Foley	Butler	Kevan	Overson	Sandford	Cranson	Beeston	Stein	Biggins	Ware	
	12/2			**23,645**	*2*	55				*Naylor*	*Hodson**	*Harbey*	*Bradley*	*Shakespeare*	*Burgess*	*Fereday*	*Taylor*	*Robson*	*Roberts*	*Hackett*	*Bannister*
									Ref: I Hendrick	Kick-off is delayed for 15 mins to allow the huge crowd in. Stein pounces to head home a left-wing corner, flicked on by Overson. Stein taunts the Baggies defence, sending the whole back four the wrong way once. He also hits the side netting. Biggins has an effort ruled out for offside.											
31		A	WIGAN		2	L	0-1	0-1		Sinclair	Foley	Butler	Kevan	Overson	Sandford	Cranson	Beeston	Stein	Biggins	Rennie*	Barnes
	15/2			*5,695*	*20*	55			*Griffiths 10p*	*Adkins*	*Parkinson*	*Tankard*	*Johnson*	*Patterson^*	*Langley*	*Jones*	*Collins*	*Daley*	*Taylor*	*Griffiths**	*Worthington/Skipper*
									Ref: C Wilkes	City's best run of victories since 1946-7 comes to an end when Steve Foley handles on the line. Brian Griffiths converts. Stoke pump long balls forward but the strong wind spoils the tactic. The suspended Ware is missed in midfield. Macari still wants to improve the squad for the run in.											
32		H	BRENTFORD		1	W	2-1	1-0	Butler 10, Stein 65	Sinclair	Foley	Butler	Kevan	Overson	Sandford	Cranson	Beeston	Stein	Biggins	**Steele**	
	22/2			16,417	*2*	58			*Blissett 47*	*Benstead*	*Bates*	*Manuel*	*Millen*	*Evans*	*Ratcliffe*	*Finnigan**	*Booker*	*Holdsworth*	*Blissett^*	*Smillie*	*Gayle/Sealy*
									Ref: G Ashby	On-loan Tim Steele, from Wolves, sets up Butler's header. Blissett taps in Bees' only chance. A niggly game turns sour when Beeston is felled and retaliates by dragging his assailant along the ground. Stein atones for earlier misses by mopping up when Benstead parries Overson's shot.											
33		A	BIRMINGHAM		1	D	1-1	0-1	Barnes 89	Sinclair	Foley	Butler	Kevan	Ware	Sandford	Cranson	Beeston	Stein	Biggins	Steele*	Barnes
	29/2			***22,162***	*5*	59			*Frain 20p*	*Miller*	*Clarkson*	*Frain*	*Rennie*	*Hicks*	*Mardon*	*Rodgerson*	*Tait*	*Rowbotham*	*Gleghorn*	*Sturridge**	*Donowa^/O'Neill*
									Ref: R Wiseman	All hell breaks loose when Barnes nets after Biggins pressurises Miller into dropping the ball. Fans run onto the pitch and a full-scale invasion follows Sinclair's save which Blues claim crosses the line. The sides leave the pitch but return to end the game behind closed doors. A sad day.											
34		A	READING		1	W	4-3	2-2	Stein 28, F'ley 30, Ware 60, McP'n 66 (og)	Sinclair	Foley	Butler	Kevan	Ware	Sandford	Cranson	Wright	Stein*	Biggins	Steele	Barnes
	4/3			*4,362*	*16*	62			*Lovell 8, Williams 36, Gooding 58*	*Keeley*	*Jones*	*Richardson*	*McPherson*	*Gooding*	*Streete*	*Dillon*	*Bailey*	*Williams*	*Maskell*	*Lovell**	*McGhee*
									Ref: D Frampton	A superb see-saw game. Biggins sets up Stein with a great cross to level Lovell's header. Foley plays a one-two with Biggins to fire in. Ware's fantastic 25-yard effort equalises Gooding's volley. Keith McPherson finds his own net in trying to clear Biggins' goal-bound header. Brilliant.											

35	H	HULL		1	L	2-3	0-1	Barnes 52, Stein 73	Sinclair	Foley	Butler*	Kevan	Overson	Sandford	Cranson	Ware	Stein	Barnes	Steele	Beeston
		7/3	13,563	*19*	62			*Jenkinson 5, 55, Atkinson 48*	*Fettis*	*Hockaday*	*Brown*	*Mail*	*Wilcox*	*Warren*	*Norton*	*Atkinson*	*Pearson*	*Windass*	*Jenkinson*	
								Ref: J Worrall	Lowly Hull surprise Stoke. Leigh Jenkinson floats the ball into an empty net with Sinclair grounded. Barnes taps in. Alan Fettis saves Beeston's effort. Jenkinson scores the goal of the game, drifting into the area and cracking in. Stein's finish sparks the Alamo but Barnes' header is saved.											
36	H	BURY		1	L	1-2	0-0	Barnes 85	**Pressman**	Foley	Butler	Kevan	Overson	Sandford	Beeston	Ware	Stein	Barnes	Steele*	Ellis
		11/3	12,385	*19*	62			*Stevens 55, 73*	*Kelly*	*Greenall*	*Hughes*	*Flitcroft*	*Valentine*	*Knill*	*Hulme*	*Smith*	*Stevens*	*Kearney*	*Stanislaus*	
								Ref: M Peck	Kevin Pressman is signed on-loan from Sheff Wed. Barnes hits the bar but Ian Stevens snaffles two chances from 12 yards out. Bury shut up shop. City's long ball fails to find the diminutive Stein and Barnes. The pressure tells when Barnes volleys in off the post. Three points wasted.											
37	A	HUDDERSFIELD		1	W	2-1	2-0	Biggins 27, Stein 27	Pressman	Foley	Butler	Kevan	Overson	Beeston	Cranson	Ware	Stein	Biggins	Steele	
		14/3	*10,156*	*7*	65			*Starbuck 55p*	*Clarke*	*Trevitt*	*Charlton*	*McNab*	*Mitchell*	*Jackson*	*O'Regan*	*Kelly**	*Roberts*	*Starbuck*	*Onuora*	*Booth*
								Ref: E Parker	Eoin Hand's Terriers are stunned when Biggins latches onto a wind-assisted goal-kick to score. Direct from the restart Stein pounces to crack home. The referee gives a penalty after Starbuck's cross hits Overson's arm from two yards. Ten mins of injury-time keeps the nerves jangling.											
38	H	EXETER		1	W	**5-2**	3-1	Biggins 16, St'n 33, B'ston 42, Grimes 61,	Pressman	Foley	Butler	Ware*	Overson	Sandford^	Cranson	Beeston	Stein	Biggins	Steele	Grimes/Barnes
		21/3	13,634	*14*	68			*Whiston 45, Th'pstone 72* [St'le 90]	*Miller*	*Brown*	*Cook*	*Williams^*	*Daniels*	*Whiston*	*Thompstone*	*Wimbleton*	*Morris**	*Kelly*	*Hilaire*	*Marshall/Cooper*
								Ref: V Callow	Stoke sweep aside Alan Ball's hapless Exeter. Tim Steele's cross allows Biggins to blast home. Stein nets a fine angled drive. Beeston taps in. Ashley Grimes nets his first from Biggins' cut-back and Steele grabs his first to hand City their biggest win since December 1986. Going up!?											
39	A	TORQUAY		1	L	0-1	0-1		Pressman	Foley	Butler	Ware	Overson	Sandford	Cranson	**Bent^**	Stein	Biggins	Kevan*	Grimes /Barnes
		28/3	*3,260*	*23*	68			*Dobie 17*	*Howells*	*Holmes P*	*Herrera**	*Saunders*	*Curran*	*Compton^*	*Hall*	*Joyce*	*Dobie*	*Myers*	*Trollope*	*Davis/Colcombe*
								Ref: H King	Macari is livid after City lose to Ivan Golac's men. He bans Wayne Biggins from attending the PFA dinner, even though he has been named in the 3rd Division Team of the Season, along with Vince Overson. Macari wants Biggins to concentrate on the crunch midweek game at Fulham.											
40	A	FULHAM		1	D	1-1	0-1	Stein 72	Sinclair	Foley	Butler	Kevan	Overson	Sandford	Cranson	Beeston	Stein	Biggins	**Heath**	
		31/3	*5,779*	*11*	69			*Haag 20*	*Stannard*	*Morgan*	*Pike*	*Marshall*	*Nebbeling*	*Thomas*	*Eckhardt*	*Kelly*	*Byrne*	*Brazil*	*Haag*	
								Ref: G Singh	Stein grabs a vital equaliser after the tall Kelly Haag puts Don Mackay's Fulham ahead. City face stubborn resistance from Jim Stannard, who denies Stein and Biggins. Adrian Heath returns to the club after 10 years away, signing from Manchester City for £50,000. Nerves are jangling.											
41	H	DARLINGTON		1	W	3-0	2-0	Biggins 10p, 20, Stein 69	Sinclair	Foley	Butler	Beeston	Overson	Kevan	Cranson	Grimes	Stein	Biggins	Heath	
		3/4	13,579	*24*	72				*Prudhoe*	*Hinchley*	*Pickering*	*Sunley*	*Gregan*	*Tait**	*Gaughan*	*Toman^*	*Cusack*	*Borthwick*	*Cork*	*Reed/Isaacs*
								Ref: P Don	Biggins, out of contract in June, sends out a 'Come and get me!' message to the big clubs with a fantastic performance capped by two quality finishes. Played on a Friday night to alleviate fixture congestion due to Monday's televised Autoglass Trophy semi-final against Peterborough.											
42	A	HARTLEPOOL		1	D	1-1	1-1	Stein 44	Sinclair	Grimes	Butler	Foley	Kevan	Sandford	Cranson	Beeston	Stein	Barnes*	Heath	Ware
		11/4	*4,360*	*11*	73			*Olsson 39*	*Jones*	*McCreery*	*Cross*	*MacPhail*	*McGuckin*	*Nobbs*	*Southall**	*Olsson*	*Johnrose*	*Fletcher*	*Dalton*	*Thomas*
								Ref: S Lodge	Stoke visit the other Victoria Ground for the first time since 1926. Paul Olsson rams home a weak clearance. Stein's screaming 20-yard volley flies into the back of the net. Lenny Johnrose threatens for Hartlepool. Barnes, Kevan and Ware all test debutant teenage keeper Steven Jones.											
43	H	PRESTON		2	W	2-1	1-1	Stein 44, Biggins 50p	Sinclair	Ware	Butler	Kevan	Overson*	Sandford	Grimes	Beeston	Stein	Biggins	Heath^	Blake/Barnes
		18/4	16,151	*18*	76			*Thompson 20*	*Farnworth*	*Williams*	*James M*	*Cartwright*	*Flynn*	*Greenall*	*Ashcroft*	*Joyce*	*Jepson**	*Shaw*	*Thompson*	*Christie*
								Ref: B Hill	David Thompson stuns Stoke with a neat finish from ex-Stokie Graham Shaw's pass. Ashcroft torments Grimes and only a clinical strike from Stein keeps Stoke in the hunt. Simon Farnworth saves three efforts before Flynn fells Biggins who converts the spot-kick himself. Nearly there.											
44	A	STOCKPORT		2	D	0-0	0-0		Sinclair	Foley	Butler	Kevan	Blake	Sandford	Wright	Beeston	Stein	Biggins	Ware	
		20/4	*8,129*	*4*	77				*Edwards*	*Thorpe*	*Carstairs^*	*Frain*	*Barras*	*Williams B*	*Gannon*	*Ward*	*Francis*	*Beaumont*	*Loram**	*Preece/Miller*
								Ref: J Watson	City stave off the challenge of Danny Bergara's County to ensure it will be either they or Birmingham who go up in the second automatic spot. Stoke keep County quiet with Noel Blake subduing the 6ft 7in Kevin Francis. Biggins goes closest for City. It's all down to the last two games.											
45	H	CHESTER		2	L	0-1	0-0		Sinclair	Foley	Butler	Kevan	Blake	Sandford	Wright*	Beeston	Stein	Biggins	Ware^	Heath/Grimes
		25/4	18,474	*18*	77			*Bennett 59*	*Stewart*	*Preece*	*Albiston*	*Comstive*	*Abel*	*Lightfoot*	*Bennett*	*Barrow*	*Butler*	*Rimmer*	*Pugh*	
								Ref: R Pawley	Relegation-threatened Chester steal the points to leave Stoke short of automatic promotion. Gary Bennett is sent clear to beat Sinclair. Heath's arrival sparks Stoke into life. Despite Sandford playing as centre-forward and three shots cleared off the line, it's the play-offs for the first time.											
46	A	BOLTON		4	L	**1-3**	1-0	Stein 7	Sinclair	Foley	Butler	Kevan	Cranson	Sandford	Heath	Beeston	Stein	Biggins	Grimes	
		2/5	*9,997*	*13*	77			*Patterson 49, Seagraves 69, Walker 90*	*Felgate*	*Spooner*	*Brown P*	*Darby*	*Seagraves*	*Lydiate*	*Green*	*Stubbs*	*Walker*	*Philliskirk*	*Patterson*	
		Home	Away					Ref: K Lupton	Stein's clinical finish seems to give Stoke the upper hand but Bolton fight back to land their first win in ten. Patterson volleys in at the far post. Seagraves nods in a corner. The impressive Walker drives home. A disappointing end to a fabulous first season for Macari. Now for Stockport.											
Average		12,982	7,378																	

Play-offs	Att	Pos		F-A	H-T	Scorers, Times, and Referees	1	2	3	4	5	6	7	8	9	10	11	subs used
SF A STOCKPORT			L	0-1	0-1		Sinclair	Fowler	Butler	Kevan	Blake	Sandford	Cranson	Beeston !	Stein	Biggins	Grimes	
1 10/5	7,537					*Ward 40*	*Edwards*	*Knowles**	*Todd*	*Frain*	*Barras*	*Williams B*	*Gannon*	*Ward*	*Francis*	*Beaumont*	*Preece*	*Wheeler*
						Ref: A Buksh	Carl Beeston lives up to his nickname 'The Beest' and flattens Lee Todd after a bad challenge on Biggins. He is sent off and immediately Peter Ward scores from a free-kick just outside the box. City battle hard to restrict County's chances. A one-goal lead should be assailable at the Vic.											
SF H STOCKPORT			D	1-1	0-1	Stein 81	Sinclair	Foley	Butler	Kevan^	Blake*	Sandford	Cranson	Fowler	Stein	Biggins	Grimes	Kelly/Heath
2 13/5	16,170					*Beaumont 1*	*Edwards*	*Knowles*	*Todd*	*Frain*	*Barras*	*Williams B*	*Gannon*	*Ward*	*Francis*	*Beaumont*	*Preece**	*Wheeler*
						Ref: K Hackett (Stoke lose 1-2 on aggregate)	Disaster as a long ball allows Chris Beaumont to loop a header past Sinclair. Stoke lose their cool and it takes an hour to regain it. Cranson hits the bar. Paul Edwards saves from Butler. Stein lobs Edwards to set up a grandstand finish but County hold on despite exuberant penalty claims.											

Rumbelows Cup	Att	Pos		F-A	H-T	Scorers, Times, and Referees	1	2	3	4	5	6	7	8	9	10	11	subs used
1:1 H CHESTERFIELD			W	1-0	1-0	Ellis 20	Fox	Butler	Cranson	Kevan	Blake	Sandford	Ellis	Beeston	Kelly	Biggins*	Fowler	Barnes
21/8	7,815						*Leonard*	*Dyche*	*Williams*	*Rogers*	*Brien*	*McGugan*	*Gunn*	*Hewitt**	*Morris*	*Benjamin^*	*Grayson*	*Cooke/Evans*
						Ref: H King	Fox plays as Everton do not want Kearton cup-tied. Stoke fail to impose themselves on Chris McMenemy's awful Spireites team. Ellis glances in from Butler's centre but City lose their way. Biggins looks awkward up front and is subbed. Mick Leonard saves well from Kelly and Ellis.											
1:2 A CHESTERFIELD			W	2-1	1-0	Kelly 22, Beeston 68	Fox	Butler	Cranson	Barnes	Blake	Fowler	Kevan	Beeston	Kelly^	Biggins	Scott*	Ellis/Kennedy
27/8	5,391	*4:11*				*Lancaster 58*	*Leonard !*	*Dyche*	*Williams*	*Rogers*	*Brien*	*McGugan*	*Gunn*	*Cooke**	*Lancaster*	*Grayson*	*Morris^*	*Turnbull/Evans*
						Ref: T Fitzharris (Stoke win 3-1 on aggregate)	Stoke are comfortable on their first visit to Saltergate since 1965. Kelly and Beeston pounce after Leonard only parries Biggins effort and then Kennedy's header. Leonard is sent off (69 mins) for bringing down the charging Biggins. Kelly scores but the ref awards a free-kick to Stoke.											
2:1 A LIVERPOOL		8	D	2-2	1-1	Cranson 28, Kelly 88	Fox	Butler	Sandford	Scott	Overson	Kennedy	Cranson	Beeston	Ellis*	Biggins	Fowler	Kelly
25/9	18,389	*1:9*				*Rush 16, 71*	*Grobbelaar*	*Ablett*	*Burrows*	*Nicol*	*Marsh*	*Tanner*	*Saunders**	*McManaman*	*Rush*	*Walters*	*McMahon*	*Rosenthal*
						Ref: K Lupton	A magical night. 6,000 Stokies go wild when Cranson heads Scott's corner past Bruce Grobbelaar. Rush's brace are classic poachers finishes. Record transfer man Dean Saunders is kept quiet by Vince Overson. The hordes are sent silly by Tony Kelly nut-megging Grobbelaar. Superb!											
2:2 H LIVERPOOL		10	L	2-3	0-1	Biggins 75p, 88	Fox	Butler	Sandford	Scott	Overson	Kennedy	Cranson^	Beeston	Kelly*	Biggins	Fowler	Wright/Kevan
9/10	22,335	*1:9*				*McManaman 9, Saunders 56, Walters 84*	*Hooper*	*Harkness*	*Burrows*	*Nicol*	*McManaman*	*Tanner*	*Saunders*	*Houghton*	*Rush*	*Walters*	*McMahon*	
						Ref: A Smith (Stoke lose 4-5 on aggregate)	The biggest crowd for three years sees Tony Kelly's back-pass fall to Ian Rush who squares to Dean Saunders to effectively end the game as a contest. Biggins converts a penalty after Tanner handles Overson's header on the line. He then grabs a consolation header after Walters taps in.											

FA Cup	Att	Pos		F-A	H-T	Scorers, Times, and Referees	1	2	3	4	5	6	7	8	9	10	11	subs used
1 H TELFORD		5	D	0-0	0-0		Fox	Butler*	Sandford	Kevan	Overson	Kennedy	Cranson	Beeston	Stein	Biggins	Fowler	Ellis
15/11	9,974	*C:6*					*Acton*	*Humphreys*	*Brindley*	*Dyson*	*Nelson*	*Whittington*	*Myers*	*Grainger*	*Benbow*	*Langford*	*Parrish*	
						Ref: I Borrett	Stoke's new double strength floodlights are the only bright spot of a dour game. City lack a flank player to unlock a Telford defence headed by ex-Stokie Paul Dyson. Acton saves well from Cranson. Ellis hits the bar with a drive. Gerry Daly's plucky Conference side deserve to cling on.											
1R A TELFORD		5	L	1-2	0-1	Beeston 81	Fox	Ware	Sandford^	Kevan	Overson	Kennedy	Cranson	Beeston	Stein	Biggins	Scott*	Ellis/Blake
26/11	*4,032*	*C:8*				*Benbow 29, 83*	*Acton*	*Humphreys*	*Brindley*	*Dyson*	*Nelson*	*Whittington*	*Myers*	*Grainger*	*Benbow*	*Langford*	*Parrish*	
						Ref: I Borrett	City plumb further depths at Bucks Head. Ian Benbow's intelligently finished opener seems enough as former YTS trainee Darren Acton saves well from Ware and Biggins. Finally Beeston crashes a 30-yarder into the top corner. Relief is short-lived as Benbow finishes Langford's cross.											

		Home					Away					
	P	W	D	L	F	A	W	D	L	F	A	Pts
1 Brentford	46	17	2	4	55	29	8	5	10	26	26	82
2 Birmingham	46	15	6	2	42	22	8	6	9	27	30	81
3 Huddersfield	46	15	4	4	36	15	7	8	8	23	23	78
4 STOKE	46	14	5	4	45	24	7	9	7	24	25	77
5 Stockport	46	15	5	3	47	19	7	5	11	28	32	76
6 Peterborough*	46	13	7	3	38	20	7	7	9	27	38	74
7 West Brom	46	12	6	5	45	25	7	8	8	19	24	71
8 Bournemouth	46	13	4	6	33	18	7	7	9	19	30	71
9 Fulham	46	11	7	5	29	16	8	6	9	28	37	70
10 Leyton Orient	46	12	7	4	36	18	6	4	13	26	34	65
11 Hartlepool	46	12	5	6	30	21	6	6	11	27	36	65
12 Reading	46	9	8	6	33	27	7	5	11	26	35	61
13 Bolton	46	10	9	4	26	19	4	8	11	31	37	59
14 Hull	46	9	4	10	28	23	7	7	9	26	31	59
15 Wigan	46	11	6	6	33	21	4	8	11	25	43	59
16 Bradford C	46	8	10	5	36	30	5	9	9	26	31	58
17 Preston	46	12	7	4	42	32	3	5	15	19	40	57
18 Chester	46	10	6	7	34	29	4	8	11	22	30	56
19 Swansea	46	10	9	4	35	24	4	5	14	20	41	56
20 Exeter	46	11	7	5	34	25	3	4	16	23	55	53
21 Bury	46	8	7	8	31	31	5	5	13	24	43	51
22 Shrewsbury	46	7	7	9	30	31	5	4	14	23	37	47
23 Torquay	46	13	3	7	29	19	0	5	18	13	49	47
24 Darlington	46	5	5	13	31	39	5	2	16	25	51	37
	1104	272	146	134	858	577	134	146	272	577	858	1510

* promoted after play-offs

Odds & ends

Double wins: (3) Darlington, Leyton Orient, Reading.
Double losses: (0).

Won from behind: (4) Birmingham (h), Bournemouth (a), Preston (h), Reading (a).
Lost from in front: (1) Bolton (a).

High spots: The remarkable resurgence under Lou Macari.
Going top of the Division in February.
Winning the Autoglass Trophy at Wembley.
The arrival of Mark Stein and his formidable partnership with Biggins.
Ian Cranson finally having an injury-free season.

Low spots: Only making the play-offs having been top with four games to go.
Conceding in the first minute at home to Stockport in the play-offs.
Losing at home to relegation candidates Chester to miss out on automatic promotion.

Player of the Year: Wayne Biggins.
Ever-presents: (0).
Hat-tricks: (0).
Leading scorer: (24) Wayne Biggins.

	Appearances						Goals			
	Lge	*Sub*	LC	*Sub*	FAC	*Sub*	Lge	LC	FAC	Tot
Barnes, Paul	**3**	*10*	1	*1*			**3**			**3**
Beeston, Carl	**42**	*1*	4		2		**3**	1	1	**5**
Bent, Junior	**1**									
Blake, Noel	**12**	*1*	2			*1*				
Biggins, Wayne	**41**		4		2		**22**	2		**24**
Butler, John	**42**		4		1		**3**			**3**
Cranson, Ian	**41**		4		2		**2**	1		**3**
Ellis, Tony	**9**	*6*	2	*1*		*2*	**4**	1		**5**
Foley, Steve	**20**						**1**			**1**
Fowler, Lee	**15**	*1*	4		1					
Fox, Peter			4		2					
Gallimore, Tony	**2**	*1*								
Grimes, Ashley	**4**	*6*					**1**			**1**
Heath, Adrian	**5**	*1*								
Kearton, Jason	**16**									
Kelly, Tony	**10**	*3*	3	*1*			**2**	2		**4**
Kennedy, Mick	**19**	*1*	2	*1*	2					
Kevan, David	**43**		2	*1*	2		**1**			**1**
Overson, Vince	**34**	*1*	2		2		**3**			**3**
Pressman, Kevin	**4**									
Rennie, Paul	**1**									
Russell, Kevin	**5**						**1**			**1**
Sandford, Lee	**37**	*1*	3		2					
Scott, Ian	**6**	*3*	3		1		**1**			**1**
Sinclair, Ronnie	**26**									
Steele, Tim	**7**						**1**			**1**
Stein, Mark	**36**				2		**16**			**16**
Ware, Paul	**22**	*2*			1		**3**			**3**
Wright, Ian	**3**			*1*						
(own-goals)							**2**			**2**
29 players used	**506**	***38***	**44**	***6***	**22**	***3***	**69**	**7**	**1**	**77**

No	Date		Att	Pos	Pt	F-A	H-T	Scorers, Times, and Referees	1	2	3	4	5	6	7	8	9	10	11	subs used
1	A	HULL			L	0-1	0-0		Sinclair	Butler	**Harbey**	Cranson	Overson	Sandford	Foley	Ware	Stein	Kelly*	**Russell**	**Shaw**
	15/8		*9,088*		0			*Hunter 82*	*Fettis*	*Hockaday*	*Hobson*	*Mail*	*Lund*	*Warren*	*Stoker**	*Atkinson*	*Hunter*	*Windass*	*Jenkinson*	*France*
								Ref: I Cruikshank	4,000 Stokies see another poor start to a season. Paul Hunter's first goal for two years arrives after £95,000 signing Kevin Russell hits the post. City use a 5-3-2 formation but miss the suspended Biggins. Galling news: recent departures Scott, Barnes and Ellis all net for their new clubs.											
2	H	WIGAN		15	W	2-1	1-0	Biggins 7, Foley 70	Sinclair	Butler	Harbey	Cranson	Overson	Sandford	Foley	Devlin	Stein	Biggins	Russell	
	22/8		12,902	*22*	3			*Griffiths 55*	*Adkins*	*Parkinson*	*Tankard*	*Robertson*	*Doolan*	*Langley^*	*Jones*	*Powell*	*Daley*	*Worthington**	*Griffiths*	*Sharratt/Appleton*
								Ref: R Pawley	Biggins heads home a Russell corner after an early flurry. Foley, Stein and Russell all miss good chances. From nowhere Bryan Griffiths waltzes past three tackles to fire home. Livewire Russell crosses for Foley to stoop and head home. Langley clears Biggins' header off the line.											
3	A	EXETER		13	D	2-2	2-1	Stein 23, 25	Sinclair	Butler	Harbey	Cranson	Overson	Sandford !	Foley	Devlin	Stein	Biggins	Russell*	Kevan
	29/8		*4,106*	*21*	4			*Jepson 5, Harris 90*	*Miller*	*Hiley*	*Cooper*	*Kelly*	*Brown*	*Whiston*	*Collins**	*Harris*	*Jepson*	*Chapman*	*Hodge*	*Williams*
								Ref: P Scobie	In the new purple away kit City start badly. Renowned Potters fan Ronnie Jepson fires Exeter ahead. Stein's brace puts Stoke in a comfortable position. Sandford is sent off (70 mins) for a bad tackle and Alan Ball's men storm forward. Stoke hold firm until the 10th minute of injury-time.											
4	A	BRADFORD C		15	L	**1-3**	1-1	Stein 18	Sinclair	Butler	Harbey	Cranson	Overson	Kelly*	Foley	Devlin	Stein	Biggins	Russell	Shaw
	2/9		*5,959*	*8*	4			*Jewell 29, 64, Duxbury L 77*	*Pearce*	*McDonald*	*Heseltine*	*Duxbury L*	*Blake*	*Hoyle*	*Jewell*	*Duxbury M*	*McCarthy*	*Tinnion*	*Reid*	
								Ref: T West	Stoke swarm all over Frank Stapleton's Bradford. Cranson heads inches wide before Stein volleys a sweet left-foot shot home. On a rare attack Paul Jewell hammers his first and then as the balance tips beats Sinclair in a one-on-one. Lee Duxbury pounces after Tony Kelly loses the ball.											
5	H	BOLTON		15	D	0-0	0-0		Sinclair	Butler	Harbey	Cranson	Overson	Sandford	Foley*	Ware	Stein	Biggins	Russell	Kevan
	5/9		14,252	*7*	5				*Branagan*	*Brown P*	*Butler*	*Darby*	*Seagraves*	*Winstanley*	*Green*	*Stubbs*	*Walker*	*Philliskirk**	*Kelly*	*Brown M*
								Ref: A Smith	Free transfer Keith Branagan stonewalls a dominant City. He stops a fierce Stein shot with his legs and palms away Biggins' shot. Alan Stubbs heads Bolton's only chance over the bar. Branagan saves from Biggins, Russell hits the post and Ware's late shot is tipped away spectacularly.											
6	A	PLYMOUTH		16	D	1-1	1-0	Stein 34	Sinclair	Butler	Harbey	Cranson	Overson	Wright	Foley	Ware	Stein	Biggins*	Russell	Kelly
	12/9		*8,208*	*13*	6			*Walker 83*	*Kite*	*Poole*	*Morgan*	*Morrison*	*Walker*	*Marker*	*Skinner*	*McCall*	*Nugent*	*Marshall*	*Evans**	*Adcock*
								Ref: K Cooper	Ex-Stokie Peter Shilton is suspended for Argyle, but his Plymouth team grab a point thanks to Alan Walker's header. A stop-start match is not helped by both sides' offside tactics. Stein profits when Marker and the on-loan Phil Kite get mixed up. Another strong position thrown away.											
7	H	BRIGHTON		17	D	1-1	1-0	Sandford 1	Sinclair	Butler	Harbey	Cranson	Overson	Sandford	Foley	Ware	Stein	Biggins*	Russell	Kelly
	16/9		**10,867**		7			*Wilkins 83*	*Beeney*	*Chivers*	*Chapman*	*Wilkinson**	*Crumplin*	*Foster*	*Edwards*	*Moulden*	*Cotterill*	*Codner*	*Wilkins*	*Macciochi*
								Ref: P Wright	Lee Sandford returns from suspension to net a header after just 45 secs. Stoke press hard but Stein heads over and Biggins, considering a move to Barnsley, heads wide. Graham Wilkins curls a free-kick past the despairing Sinclair. Kelly stubs a golden chance into Mark Beeney's hands.											
8	H	WEST BROM		14	W	4-3	1-1	Foley 45, Russell 46, 76, Cranson 83	**Parks**	Butler	Harbey	Cranson	Overson	Sandford	Foley	Ware	Stein	Biggins	Russell	
	19/9		18,674	*1*	10			*Taylor 27, 71, Garner 74*	*Naylor*	*Coldicott**	*Lilwall^*	*Bradley*	*Raven*	*Shakespeare*	*Garner*	*Hamilton*	*Taylor*	*McNally*	*Robson*	*Hackett/Fereday*
								Ref: E Parker	Loan keeper Tony Parks fluffs a clearance and Bob Taylor nets. Foley nips in to fire home. Russell swoops after Naylor tips away Stein's cross and then neatly sidesteps the keeper. Taylor and Garner finish well for Ossie Ardiles' men. Cranson soars high to bullet a header in off the bar.											
9	A	MANSFIELD		11	W	**4-0**	3-0	Stein 33, 45, Ware 41, Biggins 61	Parks	Butler	Harbey	Cranson	Overson^	Sandford	Foley	Ware	Stein	Biggins	Russell*	Beeston/Kelly
	26/9		*6,826*	*20*	13				*Pearcey*	*Parkin*	*Charles*	*Holland*	*Fee*	*Walker*	*Spooner*	*McCord*	*Stant*	*McLoughlin^*	*Noteman**	*Withe/Wilkinson*
								Ref: I Hemley	Stoke beat George Foster's Stags at a canter. Stein rounds Pearcey to score and Ware follows suit. Stein side-foots 'Rooster' Russell's cross in. Russell is injured and replaced by Beeston who sets up Wayne Biggins to turn and fire his last goal in a Stoke shirt before moving to Barnsley.											
10	A	CHESTER		11	D	1-1	0-0	Beeston 61	**Horne**	Butler	Harbey	Cranson	Overson	Sandford	Foley	Ware	Stein	Shaw	Beeston	
	3/10		*5,237*	*23*	14			*Bishop 69*	*Stewart*	*Preece*	*Goodwin^*	*Butler**	*Abel*	*Garnett*	*Thompson*	*Barrow*	*Rimmer*	*Bishop*	*Kelly*	*Ryan/Whelan*
								Ref: P Harrison	City visit Chester's new Deva Stadium for the first time. Beeston runs the game and hits the post before volleying home sweetly from 12 yards. On-loan Brian Horne misses a corner and Bishop gratefully accepts Harry McNally's men's only chance. A tribunal sets Biggins' fee at £200k.											
11	H	LEYTON ORIENT		10	W	2-1	0-0	Stein 87, 89	Fox	Butler	Harbey*	Cranson	Overson	Sandford	Foley	Ware	Stein	Shaw	Beeston	Kelly
	10/10		12,640	*3*	17			*Otto 53*	*Turner*	*Bellamy*	*Howard*	*Hales*	*Kitchen*	*Whitbread*	*Otto*	*Achampong*	*Jones^*	*Taylor*	*Okai**	*Zoricich/Cooper*
								Ref: E Wolstenholme	Peter Fox appears to have his 400th appearance ruined after Chris Turner saves Stein's 46th-minute penalty following a trip by Bellamy. Ricky Otto scores with a good drive. Stein makes amends, turning home after Beeston hits the bar and then nonchalantly side-footing in Shaw's cross.											

No	Venue	Opponent	Att	Pos	Res	F-A	H-T	Scorers, Times, and Referees	1	2	3	4	5	6	7	8	9	10	11	12
12	A	PRESTON		7	W	2-1	2-0	Butler 13, Sandford 40	Sinclair	Butler	Harbey	Cranson	Overson	Sandford	Foley	Ware	Stein	Shaw*	Beeston	Kelly
17/10			*8,138*	*17*	20			*Callaghan 48*	*Farnworth*	*Davidson*	*Fowler*	*Tinkler*	*Flynn*	*Callaghan*	*Ashcroft !*	*Cartwright*	*Leonard*	*Ellis*	*James**	*Kidd*
								Ref: W Flood	Stoke produce an impressive display to secure a first ever win on a plastic pitch. Butler nods home Harbey's cross. His free-kick is headed in by Sandford. Ex-Stokie Aaron Callaghan nets from Ellis' pass. Lee Ashcroft is sent off for swearing (64 mins). Farnworth saves from Harbey.											
13	H	PORT VALE		4	W	2-1	0-0	Cranson 69, Stein 86p	Sinclair	Butler	**Gleghorn**	Cranson	Overson	Sandford	Foley	Ware*	Stein	Shaw	Beeston	Russell
24/10			**24,459**	*9*	23			*Kerr 68*	*Musselwhite*	*Sandeman*	*Sulley*	*Walker*	*Swan*	*Glover*	*Aspin*	*Taylor*	*Cross*	*Houchen*	*Van der Laan**	*Kerr*
								Ref: J Watson	A capacity crowd see a dour first half. Vale lead through Kerr's strike after Ian Taylor's run, but Ian Cranson rises to head home Russell's free-kick. A clean-though Stein collides with Musselwhite whose lengthy protests earn a caution but don't put off Stein who nets the penalty. Great.											
14	A	BURNLEY		2	W	2-0	2-0	Shaw 21, 37	Sinclair	Butler	Gleghorn	Cranson	Overson	Sandford	Harbey	Ware	Stein*	Shaw	Beeston	Russell
31/10			*16,667*	*14*	26				*Beresford*	*Measham*	*Jakub*	*Davis*	*Monington*	*Farrell*	*Penney**	*Deary*	*Heath*	*Conroy*	*Harper*	*Eli*
								Ref: M Reed	4,500 Stokies witness Burnley' first home defeat of the season. Nigel Gleghorn, £100k Birmingham, leads an inspired midfield who are first to every ball. Jimmy Mullen's much vaunted defence are ripped apart. Shaw beats Beresford at the third attempt and then lashes high into the net.											
15	A	FULHAM		3	D	0-0	0-0		Sinclair	Butler	Harbey	Cranson	Overson	Gleghorn	Foley	Ware*	Stein	Shaw	Beeston	Russell
3/11			*5,903*	*10*	27				*Stannard*	*Morgan**	*Pike*	*Eckhardt*	*Nebbeling*	*Thomas*	*Hails*	*Marshall*	*Farrell*	*Brazil*	*Lewis*	*Onwere*
								Ref: R Gifford	Stoke look lively up front but Shaw fluffs from six yards. Paul Ware has a nightmare and is replaced by Russell who sets up Stein for the best chance of the night but his shot is saved by Jim Stannard. Overson is dominant in a flat back four which snuffs out Don Mackay's men's threat.											
16	H	BOURNEMOUTH		2	W	2-0	0-0	Stein 47p, 52	Sinclair	Butler	Sandford	Cranson	Overson	Gleghorn	Foley	Russell	Stein*	Shaw	Beeston	**Regis**
7/11			15,146	*17*	30				*Bartram*	*Mundee*	*Morrell^*	*Morris*	*Watson*	*Shearer*	*O'Driscoll*	*McGorry**	*Lovell*	*Scott*	*Rowland*	*Murray/Masters*
								Ref: I Hendrick	Tony Pulis' Cherries string eight men across the back but can't contain Stein. He cracks home when Russell is floored in the box and slots past Vince Bartram from a tight angle. Dave Regis, £100,000 from Plymouth, finally makes his debut after being non-playing sub for three games.											
17	A	BLACKPOOL		1	W	3-1	2-1	Russell 19, 46, Stein 26	Sinclair	Butler	Sandford	Cranson	Overson	Gleghorn	Foley	Russell	Stein*	Shaw	Beeston	Regis
21/11			*8,028*	*24*	33			*Ward 15*	*Martin*	*Burgess*	*Harvey*	*Horner*	*Briggs*	*Ward*	*Rodwell*	*Sinclair**	*Mitchell^*	*Gouck*	*Eyres*	*Bonner/Murphy*
								Ref: K Redfern	City hit the top of the League after easing past Billy Ayre's Tangerines. Ashley Ward, on-loan from Leicester, gives Pool the lead but Russell scores twice as the fans rejoice at rain-swept Bloomfield Road. Aussie Ernie Tapei, £60k from Adelaide City, has been granted a work permit.											
18	H	SWANSEA		1	W	2-1	0-0	Shaw 47, Stein 80p	Sinclair	Butler	Sandford	Cranson	Overson	Gleghorn	Foley*	Russell	Stein	Shaw	Beeston	Ware
28/11			13,867	*12*	36			*Cullen 53*	*Freestone*	*Lyttle*	*Jenkins !*	*Agboola*	*Harris*	*Connor*	*Cullen*	*Cornforth*	*Legg*	*West**	*Bowen*	*McFarlane*
								Ref: T Lunt	City roar on at the top despite the midweek Cup exit. Shaw crashes in off the post from Russell's chip. Tony Cullen blasts a 30-yard rocket past Sinclair but Shaw is upended by Reuben Agboola and Stein cracks home another penalty. Steve Jenkins gets himself sent off for two bookings.											
19	H	HUDDERSFIELD		1	W	3-0	0-0	Ware 75, 83, Cranson 87	Sinclair	Butler	Sandford	Cranson	Overson	Gleghorn	Foley	Russell	Stein	Shaw^	Beeston*	Harbey/Ware
12/12			13,377	*23*	39				*Clarke*	*Parsley*	*Charlton*	*Mooney*	*Mitchell*	*Jackson*	*Barnett*	*O'Regan*	*Roberts*	*Dunn*	*Stuart**	*Starbuck*
								Ref: P Taylor	Sub Paul Ware finds a way past Neil Warnock's gritty Terriers after a frustrating afternoon. He latches on to Russell's looping cross to nod over the advancing Tim Clarke. Gleghorn then flicks on a corner for him to head home. Cranson blasts a 20-yard piledriver into the top corner.											
20	A	HARTLEPOOL		1	W	2-1	1-0	Regis 7, Gleghorn 90	Sinclair	Butler	Sandford	Cranson	Overson	Gleghorn	Foley	Russell	Stein	Regis*	Ware	Beeston
19/12			***4,021***	*9*	42			*Honour 71*	*Hodge**	*Cross R*	*Cross P*	*Gilchrist*	*MacPhail*	*Emerson*	*Johnrose*	*Olsson*	*Saville*	*Honour*	*Johnson^*	*Southall/Peverell*
								Ref: J Kirkby	Regis and Gleghorn both open their goalscoring accounts as City steal the points at the other Victoria Ground. Manager Alan Murray, who has led Hartlepool to their highest ever position in the League, cannot believe it when Nigel Gleghorn's shot beats stand-in keeper John MacPhail.											
21	A	READING		1	W	1-0	1-0	Regis 37	Sinclair	Butler	Sandford	Cranson	Overson	Gleghorn	Foley	Russell	Stein	Regis	Beeston	
26/12			*7,269*	*16*	45				*Francis*	*Richardson**	*Hopkins*	*McPherson*	*Williams*	*Parkinson*	*Gilkes*	*Dillon*	*Moody*	*Lambert*	*Jones^*	*Gooding/Lovell*
								Ref: K Cooper	Stoke extend their unbeaten run to 17 league games thanks to Dave Regis' poachers goal. Stein brings a fantastic save out of Steve Francis but Regis prods in. Francis is outstanding, pushing a Russell drive round the post and clutching Overson's header. Stoke are moving into top gear.											
22	H	ROTHERHAM		1	W	2-0	1-0	Beeston 40, Foley 81	Sinclair	Butler	Sandford	Cranson	Overson	Gleghorn	Foley	Russell	Stein	Regis	Beeston	
28/12			21,714	*5*	48				*Mercer*	*Pickering*	*Hutchings*	*Banks*	*Johnson*	*Law*	*Hazel*	*Goodwin*	*Cunningham*	*Howard*	*Barrick**	*Goater*
								Ref: P Vanes	City knock the stuffing out of Phil Henson's Millers. Kevin Russell hits the bar. He then crosses for Beeston to nod home. Regis tees up Foley for a thunderous 20-yard drive. An eighth straight league win ends the year on a high. Lou Macari has taken on a god-like status with the fans.											
23	A	BRIGHTON		1	D	2-2	0-0	Stein 48, Foley 89	Sinclair	Butler	Sandford*	Cranson	Overson	Gleghorn	Foley	Russell	Stein	Regis	Ware	Shaw
9/1			*8,622*	*8*	49			*Nogan 61, Overson 63 (og)*	*Beeney*	*Chivers*	*Gallacher*	*Wilkins*	*Foster*	*Bissett*	*Crumplin*	*Kennedy*	*Nogan*	*Codner*	*Walker*	
								Ref: D Axcell	Sandford's injury means Gleghorn fills in at left-back. His roving runs set up the darting Stein. Brighton, facing a winding-up order, fight back. Nogan beats three men to level. Overson volleys Crumplin's cross past Sinclair. Foley's late strike ensures a club record of 19 games unbeaten.											

BARCLAYS DIVISION 2 Manager: Lou Macari SEASON 1992-93

No	Date		Att	Pos	Pt	F-A	H-T	Scorers, Times, and Referees	1	2	3	4	5	6	7	8	9	10	11	subs used
24	H	MANSFIELD		1	W	**4-0**	2-0	Russell 14, Gray 40 (og), Regis 64,	Sinclair	Butler	Harbey	Cranson	Overson	Gleghorn	Foley	Russell	Stein	Regis	Ware	
	16/1		14,643	*21*	52			[Overson 70]	*Pearcey*	*Peer*	*Gray*	*Foster*	*Walker*	*With*	*Holland*	*Charles*	*Ford*	*Rowbotham**	*Noteman*	*Wilkinson*
								Ref: D Gallagher	Stoke profit from Stags errors. Player-boss Foster lets in Russell to score. Russell's shot is saved by Pearcey but cannons off Gray into the net. Regis holds off Walker to crack in on the turn. Overson swoops to power a short corner home. City steam on. Macari is manager of the month.											
25	A	WEST BROM		1	W	2-1	1-1	Gleghorn 11, Stein 69	Sinclair	Butler	Sandford	Cranson	Overson	Gleghorn	Foley	Russell	Stein	Regis*	Beeston	Shaw
	23/1		***29,341***	*3*	55			*Taylor 22*	*Naylor*	*Fereday*	*Lilwall*	*Bradley*	*Raven*	*Strodder*	*Speedie*	*Hamilton^*	*Taylor*	*McNally*	*Donovan**	*Hackett/Heggs*
								Ref: M Bodenham	Gleghorn heads in a corner but Albion have City on the ropes after Bob Taylor races clear to finish calmly. Foley and Beeston sit back to deny classy Albion space. David Speedie has a quiet debut policed well by Overson. Stein deflects Russell's shot past Naylor. 7,500 Stokies go mad.											
26	H	EXETER		1	D	1-1	1-1	Regis 38	Sinclair	Butler	Sandford	Cranson	Overson*	Gleghorn	Foley	Russell	Stein	Regis	Beeston	Shaw
	27/1		14,181	*15*	56			*Cook 24*	*Miller*	*Hiley*	*Cook*	*Bailey*	*Daniels !*	*Whiston*	*Harris*	*Brown*	*Jepson*	*Tonge*	*Hodge*	
								Ref: S Bell	Having lost 0-5 to Orient on Saturday Alan Ball's men take a shock lead. Regis nets his fifth goal in a month. Scott Daniels sees red (52 mins) for fouling Regis when he is through on goal. Stoke lack the ideas to break down Exeter's ten men. First home points dropped since 6 Sept.											
27	A	WIGAN		1	D	1-1	1-1	Beeston 36	Sinclair	Butler	Sandford	Cranson	Overson	Gleghorn	Foley	Russell	Stein	Regis	Beeston	
	30/1		*4,775*	*20*	57			*Pilling 41*	*Adkins*	*Appleton*	*Tankard*	*Johnson*	*Pilling*	*Langley*	*Skipper*	*Powell**	*Jones*	*Woods*	*Griffiths*	*Robertson*
								Ref: K Hackett	Carl Beeston chips Nigel Adkins exquisitely from 40 yards to put Stoke ahead. City sit back and Bryan Griffiths tricks his way down the wing to cross for Andy Pilling to head in unmarked. Griffiths is a nuisance throughout a poor second half. One of Stoke's worst performances so far.											
28	H	HULL		1	W	3-0	2-0	Ware 5, Foley 43, Stein 86	Sinclair	Butler	Harbey	Cranson	Sandford	Gleghorn	Foley	Russell	Stein	Shaw	Ware	
	6/2		15,341	*18*	60				*Wilson*	*Hockaday*	*Brown**	*Mail*	*Wilcox*	*Abbott*	*Norton*	*Atkinson*	*Lund*	*Windass*	*Jenkinson*	*Millar*
								Ref: R Lewis	Against Terry Dolan's men Ware belts Stein's cross past Steve Wilson. Stein has another goal ruled out and a free-kick awarded on the edge of the box. Foley drives home from Stein's pass and Stein curls a 20-yarder past Wilson for what he describes as his best goal of the season so far.											
29	A	BRADFORD C		1	W	1-0	0-0	Kevan 89	Sinclair	Butler	Sandford	Cranson	Overson	Gleghorn	Ware	Russell*	Stein	Shaw	Kevan	Regis
	20/2		*16,494*	*9*	63				*Tomlinson*	*Williams*	*Heseltine*	*Duxbury L*	*Oliver*	*Hoyle*	*Jewell*	*Duxbury M*	*McCarthy*	*Tinnion*	*Reid*	
								Ref: R Groves	Suspension rules out Foley and Beeston but Overson returns. Stoke find Paul Tomlinson in impressive form. He saves from Sandford, Russell and Stein. Dogged Bradford resist a barrage until Ware sends Stein clear to curl a shot over the keeper and off the bar. Kevan follows up to net.											
30	A	LEYTON ORIENT		1	L	0-1	0-1		Sinclair	Butler	Sandford	Cranson	Overson	Gleghorn	Beeston	Russell	Stein	Shaw*	Foley	Regis
	27/2		*10,798*	*3*	63			*Cooper 43*	*Heald*	*Bellamy*	*Howard*	*Carter*	*Whitbread*	*Ludden*	*Ryan*	*Benstock*	*Hackett*	*Otto**	*Cooper*	*Taylor*
								Ref: D Frampton	A snowstorm swirls as the players pay their respects to the late Bobby Moore with a minute's silence. A hard pitch allows little good football. Heald tips over Russell's shot. Stein squanders two good chances. The glorious 25-match unbeaten run is ended by Mark Cooper's firm header.											
31	H	CHESTER		1	W	**4-0**	2-0	Stein 23, 63, Shaw 41, Foley 66	Sinclair	Kevan^	Sandford*	Cranson	Overson	Gleghorn	Foley	Russell	Stein	Shaw	Beeston	Ware/Regis
	6/3		14,534	*24*	66				*Stewart*	*Whelan**	*Albiston*	*Comstive*	*Abel*	*Lightfoot*	*Kelly*	*Wheeler*	*Rimmer*	*Butler*	*Pugh*	*Thompson*
								Ref: M Peck	Stoke outplay caretaker-boss Graham Barrow's Chester. Stein volleys his first for a month. Shaw heads past Stewart. Stein taps in Gleghorn's cross. Foley bundles in after Stein's lob hits the bar. Gleghorn misses from six yards. Stoke secure their first win over Chester in six attempts.											
32	H	STOCKPORT		1	W	2-1	0-0	Stein 47, Gleghorn 77	Sinclair	**Hockaday**	Sandford	Cranson	Overson	Gleghorn	Foley	Russell	Stein	Shaw	Beeston	
	9/3		17,484	*4*	69			*Francis 48*	*Edwards*	*Todd*	*Williams PR*	*Frain*	*Miller*	*Barras*	*Gannon*	*Ward*	*Francis*	*Beaumount*	*Preece**	*Williams PA*
								Ref: A Dawson	Stein nets when Sandford's header is blocked on the line. Francis sticks out a long leg to level. Gleghorn's shot crosses the line despite County defenders' best efforts. After the final whistle Stein reacts to Gannon's racist abuse by clouting him. Mayhem ensues. The case ends in court.											
33	A	BOURNEMOUTH		1	D	1-1	0-0	Stein 68p	Sinclair*	Butler	Hockaday	Cranson	Sandford	Gleghorn	Foley	Russell	Stein	Shaw^	Beeston	Ware/Regis
	13/3		*7,129*	*15*	70			*Ekoku 89*	*Bartram*	*Mundee*	*Masters*	*Morris*	*Watson*	*McGorry*	*Wood^*	*Shearer*	*Fletcher**	*Ekoku*	*Rowland*	*Murray/O'Driscoll*
								Ref: R Hamer	Overson starts another suspension but Butler returns. Ronnie Sinclair is injured in a scramble. Gleghorn takes over in goal. Stein is tripped for the penalty. Gleghorn performs well but cannot stop the speedy Efan Ekoku who races clear to shoot home. Ware volleys into the side netting.											
34	H	FULHAM		1	W	1-0	0-0	Stein 72p	**Grobbelaar**	Butler	Hockaday	Cranson*	Sandford	Gleghorn	Foley	Russell	Stein	Shaw^	Beeston	Ware/Regis
	20/3		17,935	*14*	73				*Stannard*	*Tucker*	*Pike**	*Onwere*	*Newson*	*Thomas*	*Hails*	*Marshall*	*Farrell*	*Brazil*	*Kelly*	*Ferney*
								Ref: T Lunt	Bruce Grobbelaar pulls out of a Zimbabwe international to rescue Stoke's goalkeeping crisis. His debut is largely untroubled by a poor Fulham side. Mark Stein cracks home another penalty for his 50th goal in a Stoke shirt. 'This is the best run of form we've had in my time' Macari says.											

No	H/A	Date / Opponent	Att	Pos	Pts	Res	F-A	H-T	Scorers, Times, Referees	1	2	3	4	5	6	7	8	9	10	11	subs used
35	A	SWANSEA		1		W	2-1	0-1	Gleghorn 51, Foley 74	Grobbelaar	Butler	Sandford	Hockaday*	Overson	Gleghorn	Foley	Kevan*	Stein	Regis	Beeston	Russell
		23/3	*8,366*	*10*	76				*Legg 17*	*Freestone*	*Lyttle*	*Jenkins*	*Walker*	*Harris*	*Ford^*	*Bowen*	*Coughlin**	*McFarlane*	*Cornforth*	*Legg*	*Wimbleton/Chapple*
									Ref: J Carter	Stoke produce some great football but Andy Legg's superb left-foot volley snatches the lead for Frank Burrows' Swans. Stoke hit back through Gleghorn who heads Dave Hockaday's free-kick home. Beeston supplies Foley with a perfect pass for the winner. Stein has two efforts saved.											
36	H	BLACKPOOL		1		L	0-1	0-0		Grobbelaar	Butler	Sandford	Cranson	Overson	Gleghorn	Foley	Russell	Stein	Regis*	Beeston	Shaw
		27/3	17,918	*20*	76				*Sinclair 89*	*Dickins*	*Bailey*	*Thornber**	*Horner*	*Briggs*	*Gore*	*Leitch*	*Sinclair*	*Bamber*	*Murphy*	*Eyres*	*Stoneman*
									Ref: P Alcock	Promotion jitters as Stoke fail to take advantage of heavy pressure against relegation-threatened Blackpool. Lilleshall graduate Trevor Sinclair scores his first league goal for Billy Ayre's men. Macari has failed to sign Birmingham striker John Gayle after the clubs could not agree a fee.											
37	A	PORT VALE		1		W	2-0	1-0	Stein 4, Gleghorn 64	Grobbelaar	Butler	Sandford	Cranson	Overson	Gleghorn	Foley	Kevan	Stein	Regis*	Ware^	Shaw/Russell
		31/3	*20,373*	*2*	79					*Musselwhite*	*Kent*	*Sulley**	*Walker*	*Swan*	*Glover*	*Slaven*	*Van der Laan*	*Houchen*	*Billing^*	*Kerr*	*Jeffers/Cross*
									Ref: R Milford	Paul Ware produces a magnificent performance as City overpower Vale. Stein lashes home after a scramble to settle early nerves. Macari keeps Vale waiting at the break and Stoke run out to a cacophony of sound. Vale are stunned. Gleghorn bundles a corner past Musselwhite. Delirium.											
38	A	STOCKPORT		1		D	1-1	1-0	Regis 40	Fox	Butler	Sandford	Cranson	Overson	Gleghorn	Foley	Kevan	Stein	Regis	Beeston	
		3/4	*9,402*	*3*	80				*Ward 70*	*Kite*	*Connolly*	*Williams PR*	*Frain**	*Miller*	*Flynn*	*Gannon*	*Ward*	*Francis*	*Beaumont*	*Duffield^*	*James/Williams PA*
									Ref: T Fitzharris	A poor match sees on-loan Phil Kite parry Gleghorn's effort but Regis follows up to fire home the rebound. Amid a succession of niggly fouls Peter Ward curles a free-kick home left footed. Stein and Beeston miss good opportunities. Nearly there as Stockport cannot now catch Stoke.											
39	A	HUDDERSFIELD		1		L	0-1	0-1		Fox	Butler	Sandford	Cranson	Overson	Gleghorn	Foley	Kevan*	Stein	Regis	Beeston	Russell
		7/4	*11,089*	*16*	80				*Dunn 17*	*Clarke*	*Parsley*	*Charlton*	*Robinson*	*Cooper*	*Jackson*	*Barnett*	*O'Regan*	*Roberts*	*Onuora*	*Dunn*	
									Ref: R Hart	Iain Dunn's superb volley gives Fox no chance as it lodges in between the angle of bar and post. Onoura and Roberts prove a handful. Foley wastes the best opportunity, blazing wide when clean through. Russell's cross is turned just past the post by a defender. Seven points clear still.											
40	H	READING		1		W	2-0	1-0	Shaw 35, Gleghorn 69	Fox	Butler	Sandford	Cranson	Overson	Gleghorn	Foley	Kevan	Stein	Shaw^	Beeston*	Russell/Ware
		10/4	6,919	*8*	83					*Francis*	*McDonald**	*Holzman*	*McPherson*	*Hopkins*	*Parkinson*	*Bass^*	*Dillon*	*Quinn*	*Lovell*	*Taylor*	*Lambert/Gray*
									Ref: K Redfern	Stoke are wasteful against the play-off chasing Royals. Cranson rounds Francis but fluffs the chance. Foley heads over from seven yards. Stein miskicks in front of goal. The breakthrough arrives when Francis clears against Shaw and the ball rolls in. Gleghorn rockets a free-kick home.											
41	A	ROTHERHAM		1		W	2-0	1-0	Stein 2, 54	Fox	Butler	Sandford	Cranson	Overson	Gleghorn	Foley*	Kevan	Stein	Regis	Hockaday	Ware
		12/4	*9,021*	*10*	86					*Mercer*	*Pickering*	*Taylor*	*Wilder*	*Law*	*Richardson*	*Hazel*	*Goodwin*	*Cunningham**	*Varadi*	*Barrick*	*Page*
									Ref: R Pawley	Stein swivels brilliantly to wrong-foot the entire Rotherham defence before beating Billy Mercer. He then scores an even better goal, cracking a dipping drive home from 25 yards. A late effort is cleared off the line to deny him his first Stoke hat-trick. 4,500 Stokies party on in the rain.											
42	H	HARTLEPOOL		1		L	0-1	0-1		Fox	Butler	Sandford	Cranson	Overson	Gleghorn	Ware	Kevan*	Stein	Regis^	Foley	Russell/Shaw
		17/4	17,363	*18*	86				*Johnrose 10*	*Hodge*	*Cross R*	*Cross P*	*Gilchrist*	*MacPhail*	*Nobbs*	*Southall**	*Olsson*	*Johnrose*	*Honour*	*Tait*	*Peverell*
									Ref: R Dilkes	Hartlepool haven't won in four months but Lenny Johnrose pounces after Fox parries his shot. Pool shut up shop and lethargic Stoke struggle. Stein volleys over and Hodge saves two flying headers. He also saves Stein's penalty (44 mins) with his legs after Stein is nudged in the box.											
43	H	PRESTON		1		W	1-0	0-0	Stein 55	Fox	Butler	Sandford	Cranson	Overson	Gleghorn	Foley	Kevan	Stein	Shaw	Ware	
		24/4	18,334	*21*	89					*Farnworth*	*Callaghan*	*Lucas*	*Ainsworth*	*Kidd*	*Greenall*	*Cartwright**	*Leonard*	*Watson*	*Burton*	*Ashcroft*	*Tinkler*
									Ref: S Dunn	John Beck's Preston side offer stern resistance. The Boothen End is becoming restless before Stein grabs another opportunist strike to put City three points away from automatic promotion and the championship. Another powerful team performance. Stoke's long wait is close to ending.											
44	H	PLYMOUTH		1		W	1-0	1-0	Gleghorn 4	Fox	Butler	Sandford	Cranson	Overson	Gleghorn	Foley	Kevan	Stein	Shaw^	Ware*	Russell/Regis
		28/4	19,718	*14*	92					*Shilton*	*Poole*	*McCall*	*Adcock*	*Regis*	*Garner*	*Castle*	*Morgan*	*Marshall*	*Spearing*	*Barlow*	
									Ref: D Elleray	The early goal, after Gleghorn chests down Ware's cross and side-foots home, makes City nervous as they fight to cling on. Fox saves superbly from Castle. Marshall threatens up front. City cling on and the celebrations begin. Several rousing Delilah's later Overson collects the trophy.											
45	A	BOLTON		1		L	0-1	0-1		Fox	Butler	Sandford	Cranson	Overson	Gleghorn	Foley	Kevan	Stein	Regis*	Hockaday	Russell
		4/5	*19,238*	*2*	92				*Darby 7*	*Branagan*	*Brown*	*Burke*	*Lee*	*Seagraves*	*Stubbs*	*Kelly*	*McAteer*	*Darby**	*McGinlay*	*Patterson*	*Green*
									Ref: K Lupton	Stoke are greeted by a flurry of red and white ticker tape. Gleghorn's error lets in Julian Darby to score. John Butler revels in his new free role in front of the back four. Hockaday, Stein and Cranson all go close. Bolton go above Vale into second place and everybody goes home happy!											
46	H	BURNLEY		1		D	1-1	0-1	Stein 64	Fox	Butler*	Sandford	Cranson	Overson	Gleghorn	Foley	Kevan	Stein	Russell	Hockaday^	Regis / Shaw
		8/5	21,840	*13*	93				*Randall 40*	*Beresford**	*Farrell*	*Wilson*	*Monington*	*Pender*	*Deary*	*Francis*	*Randall*	*Heath*	*Conroy*	*Harper*	*Painter*
		Home Away Average 15,831 10,613							Ref: D Gallagher	A champions' welcome greets the team who take the field down a tunnel of Burnley players. Adrian Randall beats Fox to give Jimmy Mullen's Clarets the lead. Stein notches his 33rd goal of the season in all competitions. Peter Fox makes his farewell Stoke appearance. A wonderful day!											

Coca-Cola Cup	Att			F-A	H-T	Scorers, Times, and Referees	1	2	3	4	5	6	7	8	9	10	11	subs used
1:1 A PRESTON			L	1-2	1-1	Stein 8	Sinclair	Butler	Harbey	Cranson	Overson	Sandford	Foley	Ware*	Stein	Shaw	Russell	Kelly
8/8	*5,581*					*Tinkler 41, Ellis 51*	*Farnworth*	*Davidson*	*Fowler*	*Tinkler*	*Flynn*	*Callaghan*	*Ashcroft*	*Cartwright*	*Leonard*	*Ellis*	*James*	
						Ref: A Wilkie	Stein latches on to Shaw's flick to finish into the far corner. City are coasting. A first ever win on plastic seems a foregone conclusion. Ashcroft suddenly has the beating of Graham Harbey. His crosses cause panic and Tinkler prods home. Confidence drains, Ellis scores and Stoke slump.											
1:2 H PRESTON		15	W	4-0	0-0	Stein 90, Overson 95, Biggins 102, 105	Sinclair	Butler	Harbey	Cranson	Overson	Sandford*	Foley	Devlin	Stein^	Biggins	Russell	Kelly/Shaw
26/8	9,745			*aet*			*Farnworth*	*Davidson^*	*Fowler*	*Tinkler*	*Flynn*	*Callaghan*	*Ashcroft*	*Cartwright*	*Leonard*	*Ellis**	*James*	*Eaves/Flitcroft*
						Ref: B Coddington (Stoke win 5-2 on aggregate)	Stein, Sandford and Biggins all waste good chances in front of the largest first round crowd. City fall foul of the new back-pass law but Sinclair saves the free-kick. Finally Stein lashes in a great shot. The floodgates open. Overson and Biggins head home corners. Biggins neatly chips in.											
2:1 A CAMBRIDGE		14	D	2-2	1-1	Stein 34, 63	Parks	Butler	Harbey	Cranson	Overson	Sandford	Foley	Ware	Stein	Biggins	Russell	
22/9	*3,426 1:19*					*Philpott 37, Chapple 89*	*Sheffield*	*Fensome*	*Kimble*	*Dennis**	*Chapple*	*Daish*	*Rowett*	*Leadbitter*	*Raynor*	*Cheetham^*	*Philpott*	*Fowler/Francis*
						Ref: P Alcock	In heavy rain City match John Beck's physical Cambridge. Stein pounces from long passes to shoot past Jon Sheffield as Stoke create several good chances. Parks struggles to deal with Cambridge's deep crosses. Philpott scores and Phil Chapple heads a free-kick home at the far post.											
2:2 H CAMBRIDGE		11	L	1-2	0-1	Shaw 68	Horne	Butler	Harbey	Cranson	Wright*	Sandford	Foley	Ware	Stein	Shaw	Beeston	Devlin
7/10	10,732 *1:20*					*Fowler 36, Francis 80*	*Sheffield*	*Clayton*	*Kimble*	*Rowett*	*Chapple**	*Daish*	*Raynor*	*Leadbitter*	*White*	*Cheetham^*	*Philpott*	*Fowler/Francis*
						Ref: T Fitzharris (Stoke lose 3-4 on aggregate)	Injury-hit Stoke fail to deal with Cambridge's long-ball tactics. Phil Chapple is carried off injured and his replacement scores after hesitancy in the City box. Stein's overhead kick is blocked on the line. Shaw nets when clean through but Francis heads Philpott's cross past a static Horne.											

FA Cup	Att			F-A	H-T	Scorers, Times, and Referees	1	2	3	4	5	6	7	8	9	10	11	subs used
1 H PORT VALE		2	D	0-0	0-0		Sinclair	Butler	Sandford	Cranson	Overson	Gleghorn	Foley	Russell	Stein	Shaw	Beeston	
16/11	24,490						*Musselwhite*	*Sandeman*	*Sulley*	*Walker*	*Swan*	*Glover*	*Aspin*	*Kerr^*	*Cross**	*Houchen*	*Taylor*	*Foyle/Jeffers*
						Ref: V Callow	In torrential rain a capacity crowd, and several million on TV, see Stoke swarm all over Vale. John Rudge's team hold firm and Shaw springs to nod Houchen's looping header off the line. A midfield stalemate ensues. Musselwhite tips Gleghorn's late shot round the post as nerves fray.											
1R A PORT VALE		1	L	1-3	1-2	Sandford 24	Sinclair	Butler	Sandford	Cranson	Overson	Gleghorn	Foley	Russell	Stein	Shaw*	Beeston	Regis
24/11	*19,810*					*Foyle 24, 90, Porter 45*	*Musselwhite*	*Sandeman*	*Sulley*	*Walker*	*Swan*	*Glover*	*Aspin**	*Porter*	*Cross*	*Foyle*	*Taylor*	*Jeffers*
						Ref: V Callow	Sandford nets from close in but Vale's quick reply comes courtesy of Martin Foyle. Andy Porter nets a beauty. In dreadful conditions the ball stops on Vale's line after Regis beats Musselwhite to a through-ball. Foyle then nicks the ball past Sinclair after the ball sticks in the mud again.											

		P	W	D	L	Home F	Home A	W	D	L	Away F	Away A	Pts
1	STOKE	46	17	4	2	41	13	10	8	5	32	21	93
2	Bolton	46	18	2	3	48	14	9	7	7	32	27	90
3	Port Vale	46	14	7	2	44	17	12	4	7	35	27	89
4	West Brom *	46	17	3	3	56	22	8	7	8	32	32	85
5	Swansea	46	12	7	4	38	17	8	6	9	27	30	73
6	Stockport	46	11	11	1	47	18	8	4	11	34	39	72
7	Leyton Orient	46	16	4	3	49	20	5	5	13	20	33	72
8	Reading	46	14	4	5	44	20	4	11	8	22	31	69
9	Brighton	46	13	4	6	36	24	7	5	11	27	35	69
10	Bradford C	46	12	5	6	36	24	6	9	8	33	43	68
11	Rotherham	46	9	7	7	30	27	8	7	8	30	33	65
12	Fulham	46	9	9	5	28	22	7	8	8	29	33	65
13	Burnley	46	11	8	4	38	21	4	8	11	19	38	61
14	Plymouth	46	11	6	6	38	28	5	6	12	21	36	60
15	Huddersfield	46	10	6	7	30	22	7	3	13	24	39	60
16	Hartlepool	46	8	6	9	19	23	6	6	11	23	37	54
17	Bournemouth	46	7	10	6	28	24	5	7	11	17	28	53
18	Blackpool	46	9	9	5	40	30	3	6	14	23	45	51
19	Exeter	46	5	8	10	26	30	6	9	8	28	39	50
20	Hull	46	9	5	9	28	26	4	6	13	18	43	50
21	Preston	46	8	5	10	41	47	5	3	15	24	47	47
22	Mansfield	46	7	8	8	34	34	4	3	16	18	46	44
23	Wigan	46	6	6	11	26	34	4	5	14	17	38	41
24	Chester	46	6	2	15	30	47	2	3	18	19	55	29
		1104	259	146	147	875	604	147	146	259	604	875	1510

* promoted after play-offs

Odds & ends

Double wins: (7) Mansfield, Port Vale, Preston, Reading, Rotherham, Swansea, West Brom.

Double losses: (0).

Won from behind: (5) West Brom (h), Leyton Orient (h), Port Vale (h), Blackpool (a), Swansea (a).

Lost from in front: (1) Bradford C (a).

High spots: Promotion as Champions.

The 25-match club record unbeaten run.

Mark Stein becoming the first City player to score 30 goals in a season since John Ritchie in 1963-64.

Peter Fox finally making his 400th league appearance in goal for the club.

Low spots: Losing at Leyton Orient to end the unbeaten run.

A nervous blip at Huddersfield and against Hartlepool to delay winning promotion.

Player of the Year: Mark Stein.

Ever-presents: (1) Mark Stein.

Hat-tricks: (0).

Leading scorer: (30) Mark Stein.

	Appearances Lge	*Sub*	LC	*Sub*	FAC	*Sub*	Goals Lge	LC	FAC	Tot
Beeston, Carl	**25**	*2*	1		2		**3**			**3**
Biggins, Wayne	**8**		2				**2**	2		**4**
Butler, John	**44**		4		2		**1**			**1**
Cranson, Ian	**45**		4		2		**3**			**3**
Devlin, Mark	**3**		1	*1*						
Foley , Steve	**44**		4		2		**7**			**7**
Fox, Peter	**10**									
Gleghorn, Nigel	**34**				2		**7**			**7**
Grobbelaar, Bruce	**4**									
Harbey, Graham	**16**	*1*	4							
Hockaday, Dave	**7**									
Horne, Brian	**1**		1							
Kelly, Tony	**2**	*5*		*2*						
Kevan, Dave	**13**	*2*					**1**			**1**
Overson, Vince	**43**		3		2		**1**	1		**2**
Parks, Tony	**2**		1							
Regis, Dave	**16**	*9*				*1*	**5**			**5**
Russell, Kevin	**30**	*10*	3		2		**5**			**5**
Sandford, Lee	**42**		4		2		**2**		1	**3**
Shaw, Graham	**20**	*9*	2	*1*	2		**5**	1		**6**
Sinclair, Ronnie	**29**		2		2					
Stein, Mark	**46**		4		2		**26**	4		**30**
Ware, Paul	**21**	*7*	3				**4**			**4**
Wright, Ian	**1**		1							
24 players used	**506**	***45***	**44**	***4***	**22**	***1***	**72**	**8**	**1**	**81**

ENDSLEIGH DIVISION 1   Manager: Lou Macari ⇨ Joe Jordan   SEASON 1993-94

No	Date		Att	Pos	Pt	F-A	H-T	Scorers, Times, and Referees	1	2	3	4	5	6	7	8	9	10	11	subs used
1	H	MILLWALL			L	1-2	1-1	McCarthy 28 (og)	**Prudhoe**	Butler	Sandford	Harbey	Overson	**Lowe**	**Orlygsson***	Foley	Stein	**Bannister^**	Gleghorn	**Gynn/Carruthers**
	14/8		18,766		0			*Bogie 14, Murray 55*	*Keller*	*Cunningham*	*Dawes*	*Maguire*	*McCarthy*	*Stevens*	*Roberts*	*Bogie*	*Murray**	*Kerr*	*Dolby*	*Byrne*
								Ref: J Kirkby	A new-look Stoke line-up fail to settle against Mick McCarthy's Millwall. Lowe and Orlygsson tire after a good start in midfield. Bogie's shot finds it way past Prudhoe. The Lions' player-manager lobs the ball over his own keeper. Bruce Murray taps in on his debut. A struggle ahead?											
2	A	BOLTON		20	D	1-1	0-0	Stein 69	Prudhoe	Butler	Sandford	Cranson	Overson	Lowe*	**Williams**	Foley	Stein	Regis^	Gleghorn	Orlygsson/Carruthers
	21/8		*11,328*	*17*	1			*Coyle 48*	*Branagan*	*Brown*	*Phillips*	*Kelly*	*Burke*	*Stubbs*	*Lee*	*McAteer*	*Coyle**	*McGinlay*	*Thompson*	*Patterson*
								Ref: J Watson	Ian Cranson, back from injury, and on-loan Brett Williams bolster the shaky-looking defence. Ex-Stokie Tony Kelly and Jason McAteer have a grip on midfield. Owen Coyle volleys home. Thompson blazes over the bar when clean through. Regis crosses for Stein to nod in the equaliser.											
3	H	WEST BROM		16	W	1-0	0-0	Stein 68	Prudhoe	Butler	Sandford	Cranson	Overson	Lowe^	Gynn	Foley*	Stein	Regis	Gleghorn	Orlygsson/Carruthers
	28/8		17,948	*14*	4				*Lange*	*Fereday*	*Lilwall*	*Bradley*	*Raven*	*Burgess*	*Hunt*	*Hamilton*	*Taylor*	*O'Regan*	*Donovan*	
								Ref: J Lloyd	Baggies threaten through Bob Taylor and new signing Kieran O'Regan. Micky Gynn tests Tony Lange from 20 yards. His free-kick is floated to Cranson whose header is cracked in by Stein. Prudhoe fingertips Paul Raven's volley on to the bar. Darren Bradley also hits the woodwork.											
4	A	PORTSMOUTH		16	D	3-3	1-3	Stein 17, 65, Regis 84	Prudhoe	Butler	Sandford	Cranson	Williams*	Orlygsson^	Gynn	Foley	Stein	Regis	Gleghorn	Carruthers/Lowe
	4/9		*12,552*	*14*	5			*Durnin 3, Walsh 12, Gittens 39*	*Horne*	*Awford**	*Burns*	*McLoughlin*	*Gittens*	*Daniel*	*Neill*	*Blake*	*Durnin*	*Walsh^*	*Butters*	*Price/Powell*
								Ref: A Groves	Walsh is lively for Jim Smith's Pompey. He sets up Durnin and fires in from 20 yards. Stein belts home a free-kick but Gittens' header restores the lead. All change after Brett Williams is subbed at half-time. Stein lashes in after Horne picks up a back-pass. Regis smashes home to level.											
5	H	TRANMERE		21	L	1-2	1-0	Martindale 25 (og)	Prudhoe	Butler*	Sandford	Cranson	Orlygsson	Kevan	Gynn	Foley	Stein	Regis^	Gleghorn	Bannister/Carruthers
	11/9		17,296	*4*	5			*Thomas 70, Muir 72*	*Nixon*	*Higgins*	*Mungall*	*Irons*	*Martindale*	*Garnett*	*Nevin*	*Aldridge*	*Muir*	*Brannan*	*Thomas*	
								Ref: P Jones	City outclass John King's Tranmere but only manage one goal when Stein's header is brilliantly saved by Eric Nixon but rebounds into the net off Martindale. The ref misses a blatant handball and gives a dodgy free-kick for a back-pass. Rovers score and nick it when Muir lobs Prudhoe.											
6	A	MIDDLESBROUGH		14	W	2-1	1-0	Carruthers 42, Foley 84	Prudhoe	**Clarkson**	Sandford	Cranson	Harbey	Orlygsson	Carruthers	Foley	Stein*	Regis	Gleghorn	Lowe
	14/9		*13,189*	*2*	8			*Hignett 86*	*Pears*	*Morris*	*Liburd*	*Pollock*	*Kernaghan*	*Whyte*	*Hendrie*	*Hignett*	*Wilkinson*	*Mustoe**	*Moore*	*Wright*
								Ref: R Poulain	Promotion favourites Boro are well beaten at Ayresome. Stein wastes a great chance having rounded Stephen Pears. Carruthers buries a similar shot. Foley rounds off a superb move by steering past Pears. Craig Hignett's free-kick flies in but City hang on for a great win. Settling in now.											
7	A	NOTT'M FOREST		7	W	3-2	2-0	Regis 16, Stein 25p, 49	Prudhoe	Clarkson	Sandford	Cranson	Overson	Orlygsson	Gynn*	Foley	Stein	Regis	Gleghorn	Lowe
	19/9		***20,843***	*18*	11			*Phillips 50, Pearce 66*	*Crossley*	*Lyttle*	*Pearce*	*Blatherwick*	*Chettle*	*Stone*	*Phillips*	*Glover*	*Roasrio**	*Collymore*	*Woan*	*Gemmill*
								Ref: K Lupton	3,000+ Stokies are present despite this being City's first live league match. Regis rolls the ball past Crossley and inside the post. Stein converts the penalty when Gynn is floored. Stein volleys a beautiful goal. Delilah sounds out. Phillips and Pearce put on the pressure but Stoke cling on.											
8	H	SOUTHEND		9	L	0-1	0-0		Prudhoe	Clarkson	Sandford*	Cranson	Overson	Orlygsson	Gynn^	Foley	Stein	Carruthers	Gleghorn	**Sturridge**/Lowe
	25/9		16,145	*6*	11			*Mooney 84*	*Sansome*	*Poole*	*Powell*	*Jones !*	*Howell*	*Bressington*	*Ansah*	*Payne*	*Lee*	*Otto*	*Allon**	*Mooney*
								Ref: K Leach	Both teams have early goals disallowed. Simon Sturridge is City's tenth debutant this season. Stoke press forward once captain Keith Jones is sent off for swearing (52 mins). Barry Fry's Southend nick the points thanks to Tommy Mooney's strike from a long punt by Paul Sansome.											
9	A	CRYSTAL PALACE		12	L	1-4	0-3	Stein 75	Prudhoe	Clarkson	**Cowan**	Cranson	Overson	Orlygsson	Gynn*	Foley^	Stein	Carruthers	Gleghorn	Shaw/Sturridge
	2/10		*12,880*	*1*	11			*Southgate 24, Salako 31, 44, 88*	*Martyn*	*Humphrey*	*Coleman*	*Southgate*	*Young*	*Thorn*	*Shaw*	*Bowry*	*Whyte*	*Salako**	*Rodger*	*Williams*
								Ref: R Bigger	City attack in the pouring rain but pay for their cavalier approach when Gareth Southgate poaches a rare goal. John Salako notches two tap-ins on his return from a two-year injury lay-off. Stein glances in on-loan Tom Cowan's cross but Salako completes his hat-trick with a neat header.											
10	A	OXFORD		15	L	0-1	0-1		Muggleton	Clarkson	Cowan	Cranson	Overson	Orlygsson	Gynn	Foley*	Stein	Sturridge	Gleghorn	Carruthers
	10/10		*6,489*	*23*	11			*Penney 41*	*Whitehead*	*Collins*	*Ford M*	*Lewis*	*Robinson*	*Rogan*	*Magillton*	*Beauchamp*	*Druce^*	*Penney*	*Allen**	*Wanless/Ford R*
								Ref: D Elleray	Stoke waste chance after chance as Denis Smith's men lead a charmed life. Phil Whitehead saves from Stein and Sturridge. Muggleton saves a Magilton penalty but cannot stop Penney's header. Foley's awful miss sums up a preoccupied Stoke, wondering if Macari and Stein will leave.											
11	H	GRIMSBY		14	W	1-0	0-0	Orlygsson 69	Muggleton	Clarkson	Cowan*	Cranson	Overson	Orlygsson	Gynn^	Carruthers	Stein	Sturridge	Gleghorn	Lowe/Foley
	16/10		14,696	*8*	14				*Crichton*	*McDermott*	*Agnew*	*Futcher*	*Lever*	*Dobbin*	*Childs*	*Gilbert**	*Daws^*	*Mendonca*	*Groves*	*Shakespeare/Jobling*
								Ref: E Wolstenholme	City end their worst sequence since Macari became manager in his last home game. A quiet game is won by a deflected Toddy Orlygsson shot. Crichton saves from Stein and Cranson. Cranson heads off the line with Muggleton beaten. Fans stage 'Macari must stay' demos at the whistle.											

No	Date	Opponent / Att	Pos	Res / Pts	F-A	H-T	Scorers, Times, and Referees	1	2	3	4	5	6	7	8	9	10	11	subs used
12	A	WOLVES	14	D	1-1	1-1	Stein 33	Muggleton	Clarkson	Cowan	Cranson	Overson	Orlygsson*	Foley	Carruthers	Stein	Sturridge^	Gleghorn	Sandford/Butler
	23/10	*20,421*	*17*	15			*Kelly D 23*	*Stowell*	*Simkin*	*Venus*	*Thompson*	*Mountfield*	*Shirtliff*	*Cook*	*Kelly J**	*Regis*	*Kelly D*	*Dennison*	*Keen*
							Ref: P Harrison	Rebuilt Molineux has three complete sides ready to see Stoke frustrate Graham Turner's Wolves. Regis sets up Kelly who scores at the second attempt. Andy Thompson puts a 32nd-minute penalty wide after Sturridge fouls Cook. Stein poaches a simple goal. City shut up shop. Job done.											
13	H	BARNSLEY	11	W	5-4	2-3	Flem'g 23 (og), Bish'p 25 (og), Glegh'n 50,	Muggleton	Butler	Cowan	Cranson	Overson	Orlygsson	Foley	Carruthers	Shaw	Sturridge*	Gleghorn	Lowe
	30/10	14,679	*22*	18			*Redf'rn 6, O'C'nll 7, Brys'n 42, Arch'n 86*	*Butler*	*Fleming*	*Boden*	*Wilson*	*Bishop*	*Anderson^*	*O'Connell*	*Rammell**	*Bryson*	*Redfearn*	*Eaden*	*Archdeacon/Liddell*
							Ref: R Gifford [Overson 55, Carruthers 64]	A crazy week ends with a crazy game. Stoke lack Macari (to Celtic) and Stein (to Chelsea) but score five for the first time in seven years. Two copycat own-goals keep Stoke in the hunt. Gleghorn curls a shot in from 25 yards. Overson flicks a header in. Carruthers strolls around Butler.											
14	H	SUNDERLAND	9	W	1-0	0-0	Orlygsson 86	Muggleton	Butler	Sandford	Cranson	Overson	Orlygsson	Foley	Carruthers*	Shaw	Cowan	Gleghorn	Bannister
	3/11	13,551	*14*	21				*Chamberlain*	*Ball*	*Gray Martin**	*Bennett*	*Melville*	*Owers*	*Atkinson*	*Goodman*	*Gray P*	*Smith*	*Armstrong*	*Gray Michael*
							Ref: T Lunt	A poor crowd reflects the feeling after Macari's departure. No replacement is on the horizon. Caretaker boss Chic Bates keeps to Macari's tried and tested formation. Orlygsson produces a sublime moment to win the game, beating four men to crash the ball into Chamberlain's far corner.											
15	A	WATFORD	8	W	3-1	1-1	Orlygsson 10, Carruthers 53, Regis 84	Muggleton	Butler	Sandford	Cranson	Overson	Orlygsson	Foley	Carruthers	Regis	Cowan	Gleghorn	
	6/11	*7,767*	*14*	24			*Dyer 30*	*Sheppard*	*Lavin*	*Drysdale**	*Hessenthaler*	*Holdsworth*	*Dublin*	*Dyer*	*Soloman*	*Charlery^*	*Porter*	*Nogan*	*Ashby/Harding*
							Ref: G Willard	Orlygsson volleys a beauty past Simon Sheppard. Overson polices Ken Charlery well but Bruce Dyer poaches an equaliser. Carruthers heads in and Regis shrugs off two players to power home and seal a first ever win at Glenn Roeder's Hornets. Still no sign of a replacement for Macari.											
16	H	LEICESTER	9	W	1-0	1-0	Gleghorn 43	Prudhoe	Butler	Sandford	Cranson	Overson	Orlygsson*	Foley	Carruthers	Regis	Cowan	Gleghorn	Gynn
	14/11	15,984	*3*	27				*Ward*	*Grayson*	*Whitlow*	*Mills^*	*Carey*	*Hill*	*Joachim*	*Thompson*	*Speedie*	*Oldfield*	*Gibson**	*Philpott/Smith*
							Ref: J Parker	New manager Joe Jordan presides over an excellent performance as Stoke defeat Brian Little's high-flying Foxes. Sandford and Overson have Speedie and Joachim in their pockets allowing City to attack at will. Gleghorn's swirling 35-yard drive beats Ward. Overson heads off the line.											
17	A	NOTTS CO	8	L	0-2	0-0		Prudhoe	Butler	Sandford	Cranson	Overson	Orlygsson	Foley*	Carruthers	Regis	Cowan	Gleghorn	Bannister
	20/11	*9,815*	*15*	27			*Robinson 50, Turner 82*	*Cherry*	*Gallagher*	*King*	*Robinson*	*Johnson*	*Turner*	*Devlin*	*Draper*	*Lund*	*Wilson*	*Agana*	
							Ref: K Lynch	Stoke dominate and miss three good chances. Carruthers hits Cherry from eight yards. Regis heads over and shoots tamely when clean through. County capitalise when Phil Robinson's overhead kick goes in off the bar. Turner prods home after Prudhoe makes a mess of a long-range shot.											
18	A	LUTON	10	L	**2-6**	2-3	Regis 3, Linton 19 (og) *[Hartson 89]*	**Marshall**	Butler	Sandford	Ware	Overson	Orlygsson	Foley	Carruthers*	Regis	Cowan	Gleghorn	Bannister
	27/11	*7,384*	*15*	27			*Dixon 22, 71, 79, Hughes 32, Oakes 37,*	*Sommer*	*Linton*	*Thomas*	*Harper*	*Peake*	*Campbell*	*Hughes*	*Oakes*	*Dixon*	*Rees^*	*Dickov**	*Hartson/Thorpe*
							Ref: B Hill	An appalling display after being 2-0 to the good sees ex-England striker Kerry Dixon bag a hat-trick and on-loan keeper Gordon Marshall have a nightmare debut. Hughes fires in a free-kick. An ill-tempered game is not helped by ineffectual refereeing. City miss the influential Cranson.											
19	H	WATFORD	6	W	2-0	0-0	Bannister 53, Regis 63	Marshall	Clarkson	Sandford	Cranson	Overson	Orlygsson	Foley	Bannister	Regis	Cowan	Gleghorn	
	4/12	13,465	*22*	30				*Sheppard*	*Lavin*	*Dublin*	*Johnson*	*Holdsworth*	*Watson*	*Dyer*	*Soloman*	*Charlery**	*Nogan*	*McCarthy*	*Willis*
							Ref: J Lloyd	City put the Luton humiliation behind them. Orlygsson crosses for Regis to dummy and Bannister nets his first goal for the Potters. Regis cuts in from the touchline, eludes two defenders and fires in a 20-yard shot. Fantastic stuff. Marshall doesn't have to make a save. An easy victory.											
20	H	MIDDLESBROUGH	7	W	3-1	2-0	Bannister 18, Orlygsson 32, 69	Marshall	Clarkson	Sandford	Cranson	Overson	Orlygsson	Foley	Bannister	Regis	Cowan	Gleghorn	
	11/12	13,777	*15*	33			*Peake 70*	*Pears*	*Fleming**	*Liburd*	*Vickers^*	*Mohan*	*Whyte*	*Peake*	*Hignett*	*Wilkinson*	*Mustoe*	*Moore*	*Hendrie/Gannon*
							Ref: T Holbrook	Stoke profit when Stephen Pears' clearance hits Regis and Bannister pounces. Orlygsson cracks home a beauty on the run and then thrashes the ball in after Regis' shot is saved. Clarkson looks good down the right. Pears saves Regis' drive. Marshall fails to stop Peake's deflected shot.											
21	A	MILLWALL	9	L	0-2	0-0		Marshall	Clarkson	Sandford	Cranson	Overson	Orlygsson	Foley	Bannister	Regis	Cowan	Gleghorn	
	19/12	*8,930*	*3*	33			*Rae 87, Kennedy 90*	*Keller*	*Dolby*	*Barber**	*Roberts*	*Carter*	*Stevens*	*Rae*	*Verveer*	*Mitchell*	*Goodman^*	*Huxford*	*Beard/Kennedy*
							Ref: K Martin	Gordon Marshall continues his atrocious form by gifting Mick McCarthy's men both late goals. City test USA international Keller three times before Marshall starts the Panto season early. New Birmingham boss, Barry Fry, wants to swap his keeper Kevin Miller for striker Dave Regis.											
22	H	BIRMINGHAM	8	W	2-1	1-0	Orlygsson 12, Sandford 69	Marshall	Clarkson	Sandford	Cranson	Overson	Orlygsson	Foley	Bannister	Regis	Cowan	Gleghorn	
	26/12	16,584	*17*	36			*Peschisolido 60*	*Miller*	*Fenwick^*	*Cooper*	*Lowe*	*Dryden*	*Whyte*	*McMinn*	*Wallace**	*Peschisolido*	*Saville*	*Harding*	*Shutt/Barnett*
							Ref: K Cooper	Orlygsson runs half the length of the pitch to crack past Kevin Miller. Blues counter attack well, but the final pass is lacking until Peschisolido beats three players to slot home. Stoke, urged on by a small Xmas crowd, pour forward and Sandford lashes home after Miller drops a corner.											
23	A	CHARLTON	10	L	0-2	0-1		Marshall	Clarkson	Sandford	Cranson	Overson	Orlygsson*	Foley^	Bannister !	Regis	Butler	Gleghorn	Gynn/Carruthers
	29/12	*8,416*	*3*	36			*Leaburn 23, McLeary 80*	*Salmon*	*Brown*	*Minto*	*Pardew*	*McLeary*	*Chapple*	*Robson*	*Pitcher*	*Leaburn*	*Grant**	*Walsh*	*Nelson*
							Ref: R Bigger	A stormy game sees Jordan and Asa Hartford ordered from the bench and Bannister sent off for hitting Pitcher (36 mins). City's ten men chase shadows as the Addicks build on Carl Leaburn's header. McLeary heads a second. Cranson risks a red for fouling Pitcher who is clean through.											

No	Date		Att	Pos	Pt	F-A	H-T	Scorers, Times, and Referees	1	2	3	4	5	6	7	8	9	10	11	subs used
24	H	DERBY		7	W	2-1	1-1	Foley 35, Orlygsson 49	Marshall	Clarkson	Sandford	Cranson	Overson	Orlygsson	Foley	Bannister*	Regis	Butler	Gleghorn	Sturridge
	1/1		20,307	*10*	39			*Gabbiadini 15*	*Taylor*	*Charles*	*Forsyth*	*Kuhl**	*Short*	*Wassall*	*Harkes*	*Ramage^*	*Johnson*	*Gabbiadini*	*Williams*	*Simpson/Kavanagh*
								Ref: G Singh	A mediocre first half is only enlivened by Gabbiadini's close-range finish. Foley scores after Regis beats the offside trap. Roy McFarland's £13 million Rams are ripped apart after the break Orlygsson rounds off a good move by charging down Craig Short's clearance which rebounds in.											
25	A	BRISTOL CITY		8	D	0-0	0-0		Marshall	Clarkson	Sandford	Cranson	Overson	Orlygsson	Foley	Bannister	Regis	Butler*	Gleghorn	Gynn
	3/1		*11,132*	*12*	40				*Welch*	*Munro*	*Scott*	*Shail*	*Bryant*	*Edwards*	*Martin*	*Robinson*	*Baird**	*Allison*	*Tinnion*	*Brown*
								Ref: P Durkin	Bristol City fail to make much impression on Stoke's well-drilled defence. Marshall has his best match so far. Even knocking out Ian Baird in an aerial challenge. Welch saves well from Foley and Gleghorn. Baird rounds Marshall but fires wide. Idle mutterings about the play-offs start!											
26	A	GRIMSBY		8	D	0-0	0-0		Marshall	Butler	Sandford	Cranson	Overson	Orlygsson	Foley	Carruthers*	Regis	**Potter**	Gleghorn	Sturridge
	15/1		*8,577*	*19*	41				*Crichton*	*Ford*	*Croft*	*Futcher*	*Handyside*	*Dobbin*	*Watson**	*Gilbert^*	*Groves*	*Mendonca*	*Shakespeare*	*Agnew/Rees*
								Ref: T Heilbron	A dreadful match with little incident. Jordan reshuffles the defence after the cup debacle v Bath. Youngster Graham Potter makes his debut at left-back. Butler reverts to his favoured right side. Neither Cowan nor Muggleton can be signed up due to lack of funds. No ambition shown.											
27	H	OXFORD		8	D	1-1	1-0	Regis 12	Marshall	Butler	Sandford	Cranson	Overson	Orlygsson	Foley	Carruthers*	Regis	Sturridge^	Gleghorn	Shaw/Gynn
	22/1		14,689	*22*	42			*Beauchamp 85*	*Whitehead*	*Elliott*	*Ford M*	*Lewis*	*Robinson*	*Rogan*	*Magillton*	*Beauchamp*	*Cusack^*	*Byrne*	*Dyer**	*Allen/Saunders*
								Ref: T Lunt	Not for the first time Stoke fade badly after a whirlwind start. Regis runs onto Sturridge's through-ball to beat Whitehead. Denis Smith's Oxford battle back. Only Marshall's superb save denies Magilton. Sandford clears off the line. Finally Beauchamp sees his effort creep past Marshall.											
28	H	WOLVES		9	D	1-1	0-1	Overson 53	Prudhoe	Butler	Sandford	Cranson	Overson	Orlygsson	Foley	Carruthers*	Regis	Potter	Gleghorn	Sturridge
	5/2		**22,579**	*8*	43			*Blades 37*	*Stowell*	*Rankine*	*Thompson*	*Venus*	*Blades*	*Shirtliff*	*Marsden*	*Ferguson*	*Regis*	*Kelly D*	*Keen*	
								Ref: N Barry	A minute's silence is observed for ex-Stoke manager Tony Waddington. Wolves start the brighter and Paul Blades latches onto Marsden's pass to beat Prudhoe. Big Cyrille wins the battle of the Regis brothers after a crunching early tackle. Overson hooks in after Carruthers hits the bar.											
29	A	BARNSLEY		10	L	0-3	0-1		Prudhoe	Butler	Sandford	Cranson*	Overson	Orlygsson	Foley^	Bannister	Regis	**Clark**	Gleghorn	Carruthers/Potter
	12/2		*7,561*	*21*	43			*Rammell 20, Redfearn 58, Taggart 74*	*Butler*	*Eaden*	*Fleming*	*Wilson*	*Taggart*	*Bishop*	*O'Connell*	*Redfearn*	*Rammell*	*Payton*	*Archdeacon*	
								Ref: M Bailey	Stoke are ripped apart by Viv Anderson's confident Tykes. Andy Rammell races through to beat Prudhoe. Cranson is injured and debutant Jon Clark moves to defence from up front as cover. Barnsley take advantage as Redfearn chips Prudhoe. Taggart ferociously heads a corner home.											
30	A	PETERBOROUGH		8	D	1-1	1-1	Gleghorn 45	Prudhoe	Butler	Sandford	Cranson	Overson	Orlygsson	Foley	Carruthers	Regis	Clark	Gleghorn	
	19/2		*7,428*	*23*	44			*Bradshaw 6*	*Barber*	*Bradshaw*	*Carter*	*Greenman*	*Howarth*	*Welsh*	*Williams*	*McGorry*	*Adcock*	*Charlery*	*Brissett*	
								Ref: W Flood	Lowly Posh score when Prudhoe drops a corner and Darren Bradshaw nets. Stoke struggle and are lucky to equalise when Gleghorn beats Fred Barber at his near post for City's first away goal in six games. Disquiet is voiced about not investing in players with the play-offs still in reach.											
31	H	BOLTON		6	W	2-0	1-0	Orlygsson 45, Regis 85	Prudhoe	Butler	Sandford	Cranson	Overson	Orlygsson	Foley*	Carruthers	Regis	Clark	Gleghorn	Sturridge
	23/2		14,257	*11*	47				*Davison*	*Lydiate*	*Phillips*	*Kelly*	*McAteer*	*Seagraves*	*Thompson^*	*Burke*	*Coyle**	*McGinlay*	*Patterson*	*Walker/Lee*
								Ref: J Worrall	The arctic conditions mean an orange ball has to replace the original white one. Orlygsson's left-footed piledriver beats Aidan Davison. Owen Coyle chips just over the bar. Butler and Cranson combine to provide for Regis to slot the clincher, killing off Bruce Rioch's battling Trotters.											
32	H	PORTSMOUTH		5	W	2-0	1-0	Orlygsson 45p , Carruthers 84	Prudhoe	Butler	Sandford	Cranson	Overson	Orlygsson	Foley	Carruthers	Regis	Clark	Gleghorn	
	26/2		14,506	*15*	50				*Knight*	*Stimson^*	*Butters*	*Burns*	*Symons**	*Awford*	*Neill*	*Durnin*	*Creaney*	*Walsh*	*Kristensen*	*Powell/Wood*
								Ref: J Parker	Alan Knight is lucky to stay on the pitch after felling Carruthers in the act of scoring. Carruthers is then tripped for the penalty. Orlygsson slots the kick to become joint top scorer. Carruthers races on to a Regis flick on to score at the second attempt. Pompey are tumbling down the table.											
33	A	WEST BROM		6	D	0-0	0-0		Prudhoe	Butler	Sandford	Cranson	Overson	Orlygsson	Foley	Carruthers	Regis	Clark	Gleghorn	
	5/3		*16,060*	*19*	51				*Naylor*	*Burgess*	*Edwards*	*Bradley*	*Mardon*	*Raven*	*Hunt*	*McNally**	*Naylor*	*Donovan*	*Smith*	*Hamilton*
								Ref: G Pooley	A truly awful game in which neither side can string more than three passes together. The away end is being rebuilt so 2,000 Stokies get soaked to boot. Stoke are reluctant to commit to all-out attack. A point may not be enough when the play-off spots are being decided in May. Dreadful.											
34	H	NOTT'M FOREST		8	L	0-1	0-1		Prudhoe	Butler	Sandford	Cranson	Overson	Orlygsson	Foley	Bannister*	Regis	Clark	Gleghorn	Sturridge
	12/3		20,550	*3*	51			*Webb 40*	*Crossley*	*Lyttle*	*Pearce*	*Cooper*	*Chettle*	*Stone*	*Phillips*	*Bohinen*	*Lee*	*Webb*	*Black*	
								Ref: J Kirkby	Forest are without Collymore and Gemmill but still stroll past subdued City. Steve Stone robs Cranson and squares for the portly Neil Webb to net. Stoke attack but Frank Clark's Forest defend well. Prudhoe saves from Bohinen. Pearce and Orlygsson square up after a crunching tackle.											

No	Venue / Date	Opponent / Att	Pos	Res / Pts	F-A	H-T	Scorers, Times, and Referees												
35	A	TRANMERE	9	L	0-2	0-0		Prudhoe	Butler	Sandford	Cranson	Overson	Orlygsson	Foley	Carruthers	Regis	Clark	Gleghorn	
	15/3	*6,346*	*8*	51			*Aldridge 47, 85*	*Nixon*	*Higgins*	*Nolan*	*Brannan*	*Garnett*	*O'Brien*	*Morrissey*	*Aldridge*	*Jones*	*Nevin*	*Thomas*	
							Ref: G Singh	Another inept away performance. Two corners in the first two mins flatters to deceive. Tranmere take over and Pat Nevin back-heels to set up Aldridge to score easily. Jon Clark hits the post. Aldridge seals it with a looping header from ten yards. 'Jordan out!' is heard for the first time.											
36	A	SOUTHEND	9	D	0-0	0-0		Prudhoe	Butler	Sandford	Cranson	Gynn*	Orlygsson	Foley	Carruthers	Regis	Clark	Gleghorn	Sturridge
	19/3	***4,542***	*12*	52				*Sansome*	*Poole*	*Powell*	*Sussex*	*Scully*	*Edwards*	*Ansah^*	*Payne**	*Beadle*	*Otto*	*Nogan*	*Gridelet/Hunt*
							Ref: P Vanes	Another dull and uninspiring display. The supporters are restless despite a solid defensive display, which snuffs out the threat of Peter Taylor's Southend. Stoke fail to create a worthwhile chance. The frontline has lost all confidence. Is Jordan the man to restore it? Play-offs out of reach.											
37	H	CRYSTAL PALACE	10	L	0-2	0-0		Prudhoe	Butler	Sandford	Cranson	**Adams**	Orlygsson	Foley	Carruthers*	**Biggins**	Clark	**Walters**	Regis
	26/3	18,071	*1*	52			*Gordon 55p, Williams 69*	*Martyn*	*Humphrey*	*Gordon*	*Southgate*	*Young**	*Coleman*	*Rodger*	*Shaw*	*Armstrong^*	*Stewart*	*Dyer*	*Salako/Williams*
							Ref: T Holbrook	A much improved display against the runaway leaders. Three deadline day signings bolster the attack. Biggins apparently sings 'Delilah' all down the M6 from Celtic to sign for City! The penalty is for a dubious foul on the lumbering Paul Stewart. Martyn dominates. Stoke are better.											
38	H	BRISTOL CITY	9	W	**3-0**	1-0	Adams 8, 78, Biggins 59p	Prudhoe	Butler	Sandford	Cranson	Adams	Orlygsson^	Foley	Carruthers	Biggins*	Clark	Walters	Regis/Gleghorn
	30/3	13,208	*16*	55				*Welch*	*Harriott*	*Munro*	*Shail*	*Bryant*	*Scott*	*Hoyland^*	*Hewlett**	*Martin*	*Allison*	*Tinnion*	*Robinson/Milsom !*
							Ref: M Reed	Micky Adams scores Stoke's first goal in March with a diving header. Biggins converts a penalty after Mark Walters is floored. Allison brings a great save out of Prudhoe. Welch saves from Walters. Adams crashes in an unstoppable shot. Paul Milsom is sent off (90) for two bookings.											
39	A	BIRMINGHAM	11	L	1-3	1-1	Carruthers 33	Prudhoe	Butler	Sandford	Cranson	Adams	Gleghorn	Foley	Carruthers	Biggins*	Clark	Walters	Regis
	2/4	*13,568*	*23*	55			*Claridge 35, Ward 57, Willis 59*	*Bennett*	*Hiley*	*Frain*	*Harding*	*Barnett*	*Daish*	*Ward*	*Claridge*	*Saville*	*Willis*	*Doherty*	
							Ref: C Wilkes	Carruthers heads home a Walters cross for Stoke's first away goal for seven weeks. But the defence stand and watch as the ball bobbles around the area. Claridge pounces to level. Walters is lucky to stay on after a bad tackle and Ward blasts the free-kick home. Willis heads in the third.											
40	H	CHARLTON	9	W	1-0	1-0	Orlygsson 31	Prudhoe	Butler	Sandford	Cranson	Overson	Orlygsson^	Foley	Carruthers	Biggins*	Adams	Walters	Regis/Gynn
	4/4	13,569	*8*	58				*Salmon*	*Balmer*	*Minto*	*Garland**	*McLeary*	*Chapple*	*Bennett*	*Sturgess^*	*Gorman*	*Nelson*	*Pardew*	*Grant/Walsh*
							Ref: E Wolstenholme	Easter Monday sees a dreadful game won by Toddy Orlygsson's shot from the edge of the box. The Addicks, under managerial duo Steve Gritt and Alan Curbishley fail to create a chance of note. Hardly a game between two play-off chasing sides dreaming of a place in the Premiership!											
41	A	DERBY	9	L	2-4	0-2	Biggins 77p , Adams 81 *[Kitson 66]*	Prudhoe	Butler	Sandford	Cranson	Overson	Orlygsson*	Foley	Gynn	Biggins	Adams	Walters	Regis
	9/4	*16,593*	*6*	58			*Simps'n 20, P'mbridge 22, Cranson 62(og),*	*Taylor*	*Charles*	*Nicholson*	*Harkes*	*Short*	*Williams*	*Cowans*	*Johnson*	*Kitson*	*Pembridge*	*Simpson*	
							Ref: G Poll	City are simply awful for an hour in the mud. Simpson's corner curls straight in. Pembridge and Kitson both score well-worked goals. Cranson tops a poor display by heading a corner past Prudhoe. Somehow Stoke fight back. Regis is fouled for the penalty. Adams scores at the far post.											
42	H	PETERBOROUGH	8	W	**3-0**	2-0	Regis 14, Biggins 36, Walters 79	Prudhoe	Butler^	Sandford	Cranson	Overson	Orlygsson	Foley	Biggins*	Regis	Adams	Walters	Carruthers/Gynn
	13/4	**10,181**	*24*	61				*Barber*	*Bradshaw*	*Carter*	*Williams*	*Peters*	*Welsh*	*Iorfa^*	*McGlashan*	*Furnell*	*Charlery*	*McGee**	*McGorry/Hackett*
							Ref: K Leach	A deathly atmosphere surrounds the ground as City have nothing to play for. They are still too good for rock-bottom Posh. Barber's howler lets in Regis to score. Gynn crosses for Biggins to head in. Barber saves a brilliant Orlygsson effort. Mark Walters follows up his own shot to net.											
43	A	SUNDERLAND	7	W	1-0	1-0	Walters 28	Prudhoe	Clark	Sandford	Cranson	Overson	Orlygsson	Gynn	Biggins*	Regis	Adams	Walters^	Carruthers/Gleghorn
	16/3	*17,406*	*13*	64				*Chamberlain*	*Kubicki*	*Gray Michael*	*Bennett*	*Ferguson*	*Melville*	*Ball*	*Goodman*	*Gray P*	*Smith*	*Russell*	
							Ref: D Allison	Walters' determination and style allow him time to crack a short free-kick into the far corner of the net. He also hits the post with a thunderous effort. In a swirling wind the defence copes well with Mick Buxton's team's desperate long-ball game. Stoke's first away league win of 1994.											
44	H	NOTTS CO	9	D	0-0	0-0		Prudhoe	Butler*	Sandford	Cranson	Overson	Orlygsson	Gynn	Biggins	Regis	Adams	Foley	Bannister
	23/4	16,470	*7*	65				*Cherry*	*Wilson*	*Yates*	*Turner !*	*Dijkstra**	*Palmer*	*Devlin !*	*Draper*	*Lund*	*Agana*	*McSwegan*	*Johnson*
							Ref: R Poulain	Another sterile match enlivened by County's bizarre turquoise and purple kit! Cherry changes direction to palm a deflected Biggins shot away. McSwegan hits the bar. Paul Devlin elbows Sandford and sees red. Turner follows (85 mins) for yet another foul on Regis. City still can't win.											
45	A	LEICESTER	9	D	1-1	0-0	Regis 48	Prudhoe	Butler	Sandford	Cranson	Overson	Orlygsson	Gynn	Biggins	Regis	Adams	Walters	
	30/4	*19,291*	*4*	66			*Willis 61*	*Poole*	*Grayson*	*Lewis*	*Willis*	*Carey**	*Gibson^*	*Joachim*	*Blake*	*Coatsworth*	*Gee*	*Ormondroyd*	*Philpott/Kerr*
							Ref: K Cooper	A more encouraging performance albeit against an under-strength Foxes side. Coatsworth hits the bar. Regis takes advantage of poor defending to bobble the ball past Kevin Poole. Leicester's goal is just as soft. Prudhoe misjudges a cross and Jimmy Willis beats Cranson to nod past him.											
46	H	LUTON	10	D	2-2	2-0	Biggins 16, Regis 32	Prudhoe	Butler	Sandford	Cranson !	Overson	Gleghorn	Gynn*	Biggins	Regis	Adams	Walters	Orlygsson
	8/5	15,911	*20*	67			*Oakes 47, Telfer 80p*	*Davis*	*Linton*	*James*	*Harper^*	*Peake*	*Greene*	*Telfer*	*Oakes**	*Hartson*	*Hughes*	*Thorpe*	*Campbell/McLaren*
	Home	Away					Ref: J Key	'Bertie' Biggins strokes the ball home after a scramble. Adams is upended in the area but the referee plays advantage for Regis to slot in to an empty net. Oakes' classy volley screams in. Cranson produces a superb one-handed save on the line. He is sent off. Telfer levels from the spot.											
Average	15,965	11,658																	

ENDSLEIGH DIVISION 1 (CUP-TIES) Manager: Lou Macari ⇨ Joe Jordan SEASON 1993-94

Coca-Cola Cup	Att	Pos	Res	F-A	H-T	Scorers, Times, and Referees	1	2	3	4	5	6	7	8	9	10	11	subs used
1:1 H MANSFIELD			D	2-2	1-2	Gleghorn 2, Carruthers 80	Prudhoe	Butler	Sandford	Kevan	Overson !	Lowe	Orlygsson	Foley*	Stein	Regis^	Gleghorn	Gynn/Carruthers
18/8	8,976					*Noteman 18, McLoughlin 28*	*Pearcey*	*Foster S**	*Platnauer*	*Fairclough*	*Gray*	*Clarke*	*Noteman*	*Holland*	*McLoughlin*	*Wilkinson*	*Wilson*	*Stringfellow*
						Ref: D Allison	Gleghorn rams the ball home from six yards. The Stags attack fiercely. Noteman waltzes through a very ill-at-ease defence. McLoughlin cracks a poor clearance home. Overson is sent off (48 mins) for elbowing Lee Wilson in the eye. Carruthers drives in from 20 yards to sighs of relief.											
1:2 A MANSFIELD			W	3-1	1-1	Stein 17, 93, Regis 117	Prudhoe	Butler	Sandford	Cranson	Lowe*	Overson	Gleghorn	Foley	Stein	Orlygsson	Regis	Gynn
24/8	*4,214*			*aet*		*Stant 8*	*Pearcey*	*Foster S*	*Platnauer*	*Fairclough*	*Gray*	*Clarke*	*Noteman*	*Holland*	*Stant**	*Wilkinson^*	*McLoughlin*	*Stringfellow/Wilson*
						Ref: T Holbrook (Stoke win 5-3 on aggregate)	Phil Stant diverts the ball past Prudhoe to give Andy King's Stags a shock lead. Pearcey misses a corner and Stein heads into an empty net. No clear-cut openings are created until extra-time when Stein taps in at the far post. Regis finishes the job, shrugging off three defenders to score.											
2:1 H MANCHESTER U		8	W	2-1	1-0	Stein 32, 74	Prudhoe	Clarkson	Sandford	Cranson	Overson	Orlygsson	Gynn	Foley	Stein	Carruthers	Gleghorn	
22/9	23,327	*P:1*				*Dublin 66*	*Schmeichel*	*Martin*	*Irwin*	*Phelan**	*Kanchelskis*	*Pallister*	*Robson^*	*Ferguson*	*McClair*	*Hughes*	*Dublin*	*Bruce/Sharpe*
						Ref: J Key	City shine against the Champions. Stein turns Mike Phelan inside out before unleashing a raking shot past Schmeichel. Against the run of play United level when Dion Dublin heads in a Sharpe centre. Stein bags another spectacular strike with a low drive that sends the Boothen berserk.											
2:2 A MANCHESTER U		12	L	0-2	0-0		**Muggleton**	Clarkson	Cowan	Cranson	Overson	Orlygsson	Gynn	Foley	Stein	Sturridge*	Gleghorn	Carruthers
6/10	*41,387*	*P:1*				*Sharpe 47, McClair 85*	*Schmeichel*	*Irwin*	*Martin**	*Bruce*	*Sharpe*	*Pallister*	*Robson*	*Kanchelskis*	*McClair*	*Hughes*	*Keane*	*Giggs*
						Ref: K Cooper (Stoke lose 2-3 on aggregate)	City put up stern resistance against a side packed with internationals. Hughes' acrobatic volley is well saved by Carl Muggleton. 9,000 Stokies roar on their heroes but Sharpe volleys in at the far post. Brain McClair wraps it up from 10 yards as United turn on the style. Good team spirit.											

FA Cup	Att	Pos	Res	F-A	H-T	Scorers, Times, and Referees	1	2	3	4	5	6	7	8	9	10	11	subs used
3 H BATH		7	D	0-0	0-0		Marshall	Clarkson	Sandford	Cranson	Overson	Orlygsson*	Foley	Bannister	Regis	Butler	Gleghorn	Sturridge
8/1	14,159	*C:4*					*Mogg*	*Gill*	*Dicks*	*Batty*	*Hedges*	*Cousins*	*Banks*	*Chenoweth**	*Adcock*	*Mings^*	*Brooks*	*Smart/Vernon*
						Ref: P Wright	Stoke lack any semblance of confidence against non-league Bath. Jordan fields a five-man defence which restricts Bath to one shot at goal, but City struggle for ideas against Tony Ricketts' men. To fail to either score or win is embarrassing. Jordan wants to buy Sheff Weds' Phil King.											
3R A BATH		8	W	4-1	2-0	Regis 5, 57, Cranson 38, Orlygsson 83	Marshall	Butler	Sandford	Cranson	Overson	Orlygsson	Foley	Carruthers*	Regis	Sturridge	Gleghorn	Shaw
18/1	*6,213*	*C:6*				*Chenoweth 90*	*Mogg*	*Gill*	*Dicks*	*Batty*	*Hedges*	*Cousins**	*Banks*	*Chenoweth*	*Adcock^*	*Mings*	*Brooks*	*Smart/Vernon*
						Ref: P Wright	Regis and Cranson head home corners to settle the tie. City score a fourth in the pouring rain as Orlygsson races through onto Gleghorn's pass. Marshall's howler from a late free-kick allows Bath some comfort. Lou Macari is present to see City's first away FA Cup victory for 23 years.											
4 A OLDHAM		8	D	0-0	0-0		Prudhoe	Butler	Sandford	Cranson	Overson	Orlygsson	Foley	Carruthers	Regis	Potter	Gleghorn	
29/1	*14,465*	*P:21*					*Hallworth*	*Fleming*	*Makin*	*Pointon*	*Jobson*	*Redmond**	*Adams*	*Bernard*	*Sharp*	*Milligan*	*Holden*	*Palmer*
						Ref: P Jones	Joe Royle's Latics look far from Premier League class. On an awful pitch Stoke dominate. Foley wins the midfield battle and Orlygsson sets up Carruthers to nod wide from close in. Ex-Stokie Adams causes problems on the right but City, backed by massive vocal support, earn a replay.											
4R H OLDHAM		9	L	0-1	0-1		Prudhoe	Butler	Sandford	Cranson	Overson	Orlygsson	Foley	Bannister	Regis	Potter*	Gleghorn	Sturridge
9/2	19,871	*P:20*				*Beckford 3*	*Hallworth*	*Fleming*	*Makin*	*Pointon*	*Jobson*	*McDonald*	*Bernard*	*Beckford*	*Sharp*	*Milligan*	*Holden*	
						Ref: P Jones	An atrocious game decided by a ridiculous goal as Darren Beckford gets in the way of a clearance and the ball loops over Prudhoe's head into the net. City fail to make a decent chance all night. Oldham are as bad. They go on to reach the semi-finals. City's FA Cup curse strikes again.											

	Home						Away					
	P	W	D	L	F	A	W	D	L	F	A	Pts
1 Crys Palace	46	16	4	3	39	18	11	5	7	34	28	90
2 Nott'm Forest	46	12	9	2	38	22	11	5	7	36	27	83
3 Millwall	46	14	8	1	36	17	5	9	9	22	32	74
4 Leicester *	46	11	9	3	45	30	8	7	8	27	29	73
5 Tranmere	46	15	3	5	48	23	6	6	11	21	30	72
6 Derby	46	15	3	5	44	25	5	8	10	29	43	71
7 Notts Co	46	16	3	4	43	26	4	5	14	22	43	68
8 Wolves	46	10	10	3	34	19	7	7	9	26	28	68
9 Middlesbro	46	12	6	5	40	19	6	7	10	26	35	67
10 STOKE	46	14	4	5	35	19	4	9	10	22	40	67
11 Charlton	46	14	3	6	39	22	5	5	13	22	36	65
12 Sunderland	46	14	2	7	35	22	5	6	12	19	35	65
13 Bristol City	46	11	7	5	27	18	5	9	9	20	32	64
14 Bolton	46	10	8	5	40	31	5	6	12	23	33	59
15 Southend	46	10	5	8	34	28	7	3	13	29	39	59
16 Grimsby	46	7	14	2	26	16	6	6	11	26	31	59
17 Portsmouth	46	10	6	7	29	22	5	7	11	23	36	58
18 Barnsley	46	9	3	11	25	26	7	4	12	30	41	55
19 Watford	46	10	5	8	39	35	5	4	14	27	45	54
20 Luton	46	12	4	7	38	25	2	7	14	18	35	53
21 West Brom	46	9	7	7	38	31	4	5	14	22	38	51
22 Birmingham	46	9	7	7	28	29	4	5	14	24	40	51
23 Oxford	46	10	5	8	33	33	3	5	15	21	42	49
24 Peterborough	46	6	9	8	31	30	2	4	17	17	46	37
	1104	276	144	132	864	586	132	144	276	586	864	1512

* promoted after play-offs

Odds & ends

Double wins: (3) Middlesbrough, Sunderland, Watford.
Double losses: (3) Crystal Palace, Millwall, Tranmere.

Won from behind: (2) Barnsley (h), Derby (h).
Lost from in front: (3) Birmingham (a), Luton (a), Tranmere (h).

High spots: Mid-table stability in Division Two.
Beating Manchester United in the home leg of the Coca-Cola Cup.
Winning an away FA Cup-tie for the first time since 1971.
Eight home wins in a row from late October.

Low spots: Mark Stein's record £2.5m transfer to Chelsea.
The departure of Lou Macari.
Falling from 5th in March to 11th by early April to drop out of the play-off picture.
Over-reliance on loan players to bolster the squad.
Crowds dropping by a third once the play-offs are out of reach.

Player of the Year: Ian Cranson.
Ever-presents: (0).
Hat-tricks: (0).
Leading scorer: (13) Dave Regis.

	Appearances						Goals			
	Lge	*Sub*	LC	*Sub*	FAC	*Sub*	**Lge**	LC	FAC	**Tot**
Adams, Micky	**10**						**3**			**3**
Bannister, Gary	**10**	*5*			2		**2**			**2**
Biggins, Wayne	**10**						**4**			**4**
Butler, John	**34**	*1*	2		4					
Carruthers, Martin	**24**	*10*	1	*2*	2		**5**	1		**6**
Clark, Jon	**12**									
Clarkson, Ian	**14**		2		1					
Cowan, Tom	**14**		1							
Cranson, Ian	**44**		3		4				1	**1**
Foley, Steve	**43**	*1*	4		4		**2**			**2**
Gleghorn, Nigel	**38**	*2*	4		4		**3**	1		**4**
Gynn, Micky	**14**	*7*	2	*2*						
Harbey, Graham	**2**									
Kevan, David	**1**		1							
Lowe, Kenny	**3**	*6*	2							
Marshall, Gordon	**10**				2					
Muggleton, Carl	**6**		1							
Orlygsson, Toddy	**42**	*3*	4		4		**10**		1	**11**
Overson, Vince	**39**		4		4		**2**			**2**
Potter, Graham	**2**	*1*			2					
Prudhoe, Mark	**30**		3		2					
Regis, Dave	**33**	*5*	2		4		**10**	1	2	**13**
Sandford, Lee	**40**	*1*	3		4		**1**			**1**
Shaw, Graham	**2**	*2*				*1*				
Stein, Mark	**12**		4				**8**	4		**12**
Sturridge, Simon	**5**	*8*	1		1	*2*				
Walters, Mark	**9**						**2**			**2**
Ware, Paul	**1**									
Williams, Brett	**2**									
29 players used	**506**	***52***	**44**	***4***	**44**	***3***	**52**	**7**	**4**	**63**

No	Date			Att	Pos	Pt	F-A	H-T	Scorers, Times, and Referees	1	2	3	4	5	6	7	8	9	10	11	subs used
1		H	TRANMERE			W	1-0	0-0	Gleghorn 49	**Muggleton**	Clark	Sandford	**Dreyer**	Overson	Orlygsson	Carruthers*	**Wallace**	Biggins	**Peschisolido**	Gleghorn	**Beckford**
	13/8			15,915		3				*Coyne*	*Higgins*	*Mungall*	*Brannan*	*Garnett**	*O'Brien*	*Morrissey*	*Aldridge*	*Irons*	*Nevin*	*Thomas*	*Muir*
									Ref: J Kirkby	The summer boardroom wranglings have released cash for Dreyer and record £600,000 signing Peschisolido. Rumours spread of the imminent return of Macari who has been sacked by Celtic. Jordan's team win thanks to Nigel Gleghorn's right-footed effort through a crowd of players.											
2		A	BURNLEY		6	D	1-1	0-1	Dreyer 90	Muggleton	Clark	Sandford	Dreyer	Overson	Orlygsson*	Carruthers^	Wallace	Biggins	Sturridge	Gleghorn	Butler/Shaw
	20/8			*15,331*	*20*	4			*Davis 42*	*Beresford*	*Parkinson*	*Vinnicombe*	*Davis*	*Winstanley*	*Joyce*	*Harper**	*Gayle*	*Heath*	*Robinson*	*McMinn*	*Deary*
									Ref: W Flood	Steve Davis takes advantage of City's unconvincing defence. His diving header flashes home. Gary Parkinson has his 40th-minute spot-kick for Sandford's handball saved by Muggleton. City get out of jail via John Dreyer's volley from Shaw's cross in the 93rd minute. Worryingly poor.											
3		H	SUNDERLAND		14	L	0-1	0-1		Muggleton	Clark	Sandford	Dreyer	Cranson	**Downing**	Peschisolido	Wallace	Biggins	Sturridge*	Gleghorn	Carruthers
	27/8			13,159	*9*	4			*Gray P 23*	*Norman*	*Owers*	*Kubicki*	*Bennett*	*Ferguson*	*Melville*	*Atkinson*	*Goodman*	*Gray P*	*Gray M**	*Ball*	*Cunnington*
									Ref: G Lunt	Stoke look sluggish despite dominating possession. The excitement generated by winning in Cosenza in midweek is dampened by the brilliant form of 37-year-old Tony Norman. He denies Pesch, Sturridge and Biggins. Phil Gray's great solo goal wins it for Mick Buxton's Wearsiders.											
4		A	READING		18	L	**0-4**	0-0		Muggleton	Clark	Sandford	Dreyer	Overson !	Downing	Peschisolido*	Wallace	Biggins !	Butler	Gleghorn	Carruthers
	30/8			*7,103*	*10*	4			*Lovell 61, Kerr 71, Gilkes 85, Taylor 90*	*Hislop*	*Hopkins**	*Kerr*	*Wdowczyk*	*Williams*	*Parkinson*	*Gilkes*	*Gooding*	*Quinn*	*Lovell*	*Osborn^*	*Taylor/Holsgrove*
									Ref: G Pooley	Nightmare at Elm Park! Biggins and Overson are sent off (55 mins) following a dust up near the corner flag as City are enjoying the best spell of the game. Lovell's first-time volley opens the floodgates as the nine men capitulate. Kerr's brilliant 25-yard strike fizzes into the top corner.											
5		A	BOLTON		22	L	**0-4**	0-1	*[Paatelainen 79]*	Muggleton	Clark*	Sandford	Dreyer	Overson	Downing	Peschisolido	Wallace	Biggins	Beckford	Gleghorn	Butler
	3/9			*11,515*	*9*	4			*McGinlay 41p, McAteer 59, 66,*	*Branagan*	*Lydiate*	*Phillips*	*McAteer*	*Kernaghan*	*Stubbs*	*Fisher*	*Sneekes*	*Paatelainen*	*McGinlay*	*Kelly*	
									Ref: A Dawson	One of the worst performances in years. Bolton outplay the poor Potters in every department. Jason McAteer's second is a great 30-yard drive. Clark trips McGinlay for the pen. Things are no better in the boardroom as Bob Kenyon and Paul Wright have sold their shares amid acrimony.											
6		H	SOUTHEND		16	W	**4-1**	2-0	Orlygsson 10, Edwards 13 (og), Dreyer 47,	Muggleton	Butler	Sandford	Dreyer	Overson	Orlygsson	Beckford^	Downing	Biggins*	Peschisolido	Gleghorn	Carruthers/Wallace
	10/9			11,808	*23*	7			*Butler 67 (og)* [Biggins 62]	*Sansome*	*Hone*	*Powell*	*Jones*	*Edwards*	*Bressington*	*Hunt*	*Whelan*	*Thomson*	*Otto*	*Forrester*	
									Ref: I Cruikshanks	Joe Jordan has left the club. Reportedly pushed rather than of his own doing. City respond with an upbeat display against Peter Taylor's woeful team. Orlygsson beats three players to lash in. Andy Edwards diverts a centre past Sansome. Dreyer heads in. Biggins latches on to a back-pass.											
7		H	CHARLTON		10	W	3-2	2-0	Glegh' 17, Orlygsson 22, Peschisolido 55	Muggleton	Butler	Sandford	Dreyer	Cranson	Orlygsson	Wallace	Downing	Carruthers	Peschisolido	Gleghorn	
	14/9			10,643	*8*	10			*Nelson 72, Whyte 77*	*Ammann*	*Brown*	*Sturgess*	*Walsh*	*Chapple*	*McLeary*	*Newton**	*Nelson*	*Garland^*	*Whyte*	*Robson*	*Grant/Pardew*
									Ref: K Lynch	Caretaker manager Asa Hartford selects Cranson and Wallace for suspended Overson and Biggins. Gleghorn dives to head in Wallace's cross. Orlygsson cracks in a low free-kick. Pesch touches home Dreyer's header. Nelson and Whyte finish off far-post crosses as Stoke get the jitters.											
8		A	NOTTS CO		6	W	2-0	1-0	Peschisolido 31, 70	Muggleton	Butler	Sandford	Dreyer	Cranson	Orlygsson	Wallace	Downing	Carruthers	Peschisolido	Gleghorn	
	17/9			*8,281*	*23*	13				*Cherry*	*Gallagher*	*Emenalo*	*Turner*	*Johnson*	*Yates*	*Jemson**	*Legg*	*Devlin*	*McSwegan*	*Simpson*	*Lund*
									Ref: E Wolstenholme	Pesch wins over some of his critics with two strikers' goals. He nods in after Cherry saves his initial shot, then sidefoots a Carruthers pass into the corner. Dreyer marshals the defence impressively as County retaliate. Asa Hartford rules himself out of the running for the manager's role.											
9		A	DERBY		8	L	0-3	0-2		Muggleton	Butler	Sandford	Dreyer	Cranson	Orlygsson	Wallace	Downing	Carruthers*	Peschisolido	Gleghorn	Biggins
	25/9			*11,782*	*6*	13			*Hodge 22, Gabbiadini 38, Charles 89*	*Taylor*	*Charles*	*Forsyth*	*Hodge*	*Short*	*Williams*	*Cowans*	*Gabbiadini*	*Johnson**	*Pembridge*	*Carsley^*	*Simpson/Harkes*
									Ref: N Barry	Stoke start brightly but Pesch's shot is cleared off the line and Roy McFarland's Rams score when Steve Hodge turns in a rebound off the post. Gabbiadini finishes with aplomb. Downing and Orlygsson toil but City lack a playmaker. Muggers is beaten by an unkind bounce for the third.											
10		H	WEST BROM		7	W	**4-1**	2-1	Carr' 24, 87, Wallace 35, Peschisolido 68	Muggleton	Wallace	Sandford	Dreyer	Cranson	Orlygsson	Butler^	Downing	Carruthers	Peschisolido*	Gleghorn	Biggins/Overson
	2/10			14,203	*23*	16			*Taylor 32*	*Naylor*	*Parsley*	*Lilwall*	*Phelan*	*Strodder*	*Herbert*	*Hunt*	*Ashcroft*	*Taylor*	*McNally**	*Smith*	*Coldicott*
									Ref: I Cruikshanks	Lou Macari is hailed as the saviour after superb Stoke put Alan Buckley's Baggies to the sword. Carruthers pounces on a weak clearance. Bob Taylor taps in. Ray Wallace's first goal for City is a rasping shot after a one-two. Pesch touches home. Carruthers finishes from a tight angle.											
11		H	LUTON		7	L	1-2	0-1	Carruthers 80	Muggleton	Wallace^	Sandford	Dreyer !	Cranson	Orlygsson	Butler	Downing	Carruthers	Peschisolido*	Gleghorn	Overson/Beckford
	9/10			11,712	*18*	16			*Marshall 22, Preece 81*	*Sommer*	*James*	*Johnson*	*Waddock*	*Thomas*	*Peake*	*Telfer*	*Hughes*	*Hartson*	*Preece**	*Marshall*	*Oakes*
									Ref: P Alcock	Stoke start well but Dreyer fluffs a clearance and Dwight Marshall fires home. Dreyer gives away a penalty but Muggleton saves yet again. A horrendous personal afternoon sees Dreyer sent off for hauling down Marshall. Carruthers taps in but Hatters score a neat goal from the restart.											

No Date	Venue	Opponent	Att	Pos	Pts	F-A	H-T	Scorers, Times, and Referees	1	2	3	4	5	6	7	8	9	10	11	subs used
12	A	MILLWALL		7	D	1-1	0-1	Peschisolido 55	Muggleton	Overson	Sandford	Dreyer	Cranson	Orlygsson	Butler	Downing	Carruthers	Peschisolido*	Gleghorn	Wallace
15/10			*7,856*	*21*	17			*Goodman 15*	*Keller*	*Cunningham*	*Thatcher*	*Connor*	*Witter^*	*Roberts*	*Savage*	*Rae*	*Cadette*	*Goodman**	*Kennedy*	*Mitchell/Dawes*
								Ref: T West	City's defence is all over the shop as Cadette and Goodman threaten. John Goodman steals in to bury Thatcher's centre. The Lions should have more. Pesch wins the ball 40 yards out, beats two men, beats Keller and nets via the post. Carruthers and Pesch hit the woodwork. Good draw.											
13	A	OLDHAM		9	D	0-0	0-0		Muggleton	Butler	Sandford	Cranson	Overson	Orlygsson	**Keen**	Potter^	Carruthers	Peschisolido*	Gleghorn	Biggins/Beeston
22/10			*8,954*	*13*	18				*Gerrard*	*Halle*	*Pointon*	*Henry*	*Jobson*	*Redmond*	*Rickers*	*Banger*	*Graham*	*McCarthy*	*Holden*	
								Ref: R Hart	A capable performance as the five-man defence is more organised. Beeston returns from his injury worries to provide midfield bite for the last 30 mins. Muggleton saves Neil Pointon's stinging drive. Oldham force 20 corners but only Sandford comes close, heading against his own bar.											
14	H	WOLVES		11	D	1-1	1-1	Keen 17	Muggleton	Butler	Sandford	Cranson	Overson	Orlygsson	Keen	Beeston	Carruthers	Peschisolido*	Gleghorn	Biggins
30/10			15,928	*1*	19			*Bull 40*	*Stowell*	*Smith^*	*Thompson*	*Emblen**	*Blades*	*Venus*	*Walters*	*Thomas*	*Bull*	*Kelly*	*Froggatt*	*Ferguson/Stewart*
								Ref: J Holbrook	£300,000 signing Kevin Keen stuns his former team-mates by finishing a superb move involving nine City players. Pesch and Carruthers waste chances as City dominate. Steve Bull cracks home for an undeserved draw. The club may build a new ground in response to the Taylor report.											
15	H	SHEFFIELD UTD		11	D	1-1	0-1	Gleghorn 77	Muggleton	Butler	Sandford	Cranson	Overson	Orlygsson	Keen*	Beeston	Carruthers	Peschisolido	Gleghorn	**Wade**
2/11			11,556	*19*	20			*Gage 15*	*Kelly*	*Gage*	*Nilsen*	*Harfield*	*Beesley*	*Marshall*	*Rogers*	*Veart**	*Starbuck*	*Blake*	*Whitehouse*	*Scott*
								Ref: K Lynch	Dave Bassett's Blades dominate from the off. Dane Whitehouse hits the post before Kevin Gage whacks home a well-worked free-kick. Stoke improve in the second half and Keen crosses for Gleghorn to ram home. The pony-tailed Shaun Wade debuts. Beeston is booked once again.											
16	A	BARNSLEY		16	L	0-2	0-1		Muggleton	Clarkson	Sandford	Cranson	Overson	Orlygsson	Keen	Beeston	Carruthers	Peschisolido*	Gleghorn	Sturridge
5/11			*5,117*	*7*	20			*O'Connell 42, Sheridan 77*	*Watson*	*Eaden*	*Fleming*	*Wilson*	*Taggart*	*Davis*	*O'Connell*	*Redfearn*	*Jackson*	*Liddell*	*Sheridan*	
								Ref: P Wright	Dave Watson recovers to save after Orlygsson rounds him. Brendan O'Connell heads in Eaden's cross. Darren Sheridan trips Orylgsson when clear but the ref only books him. He rubs it in by lobbing the advancing Muggers from 30 yards. Macari tries three at the back but to no avail.											
17	H	GRIMSBY		13	W	3-0	2-0	Peschisolido 23, 44, Carruthers 60	Muggleton	Butler	Sandford	Cranson	Overson	Orlygsson	Keen	Beeston	Carruthers	Peschisolido	Gleghorn	
19/11			12,055	*6*	23				*Crichton*	*Croft*	*Jobling*	*Handyside*	*Lever*	*Groves*	*Watson**	*Dobbin*	*Livingstone^*	*Woods*	*Gilbert*	*Childs/McDermott*
								Ref: J Lloyd	Stoke take control against the Mariners who have won their last three under caretaker boss John Cockerill. Pesch steers home from close range. Overson has a header cleared off the line. Pesch taps in Carruthers' cross-shot. Crichton denies Orylgsson but from a corner Carruthers scores.											
18	A	WATFORD		14	D	0-0	0-0		Muggleton	Butler	Sandford	Cranson	Overson	Orlygsson	Keen	Clarkson	Carruthers	Peschisolido*	Gleghorn	Biggins
26/11			*9,126*	*9*	24				*Miller*	*Lavin*	*Johnson*	*Foster**	*Holdsworth*	*Ramage*	*Hessenthaler*	*Nogan*	*Millen*	*Porter*	*Mooney*	*Moralee*
								Ref: P Foakes	A tight game sees Gleghorn crack a right-footed volley just over. Cranson and Clarkson impress as Ramage and Hessenthaler drive the Hornets on. Watford spurn four good chances. Moralee and Mooney both hit the woodwork. The squad needs improving to avoid a season of struggle.											
19	A	PORTSMOUTH		11	W	1-0	0-0	Beeston 74	Muggleton	Butler	Sandford	Cranson	Overson	Orlygsson	**Sigurdsson**	Beeston	Carruthers	Peschisolido	Gleghorn	
30/11			*5,272*	*21*	27				*Knight*	*Gittens*	*Daniel*	*McLoughlin*	*Symons*	*Dobson*	*Pethick*	*Kristensen*	*Powell*	*Creaney*	*Hall**	*Radosavljevic*
								Ref: I Hemley	Stoke survive the woodwork being hit twice. Larus Sigurdsson, Orlygsson's cousin, makes his debut and proceeds to join in battle with Gerry Creaney. Beeston cracks through a crowd of players from the edge of the box for the winner. Chairman Coates wants to move to a new ground.											
20	H	OLDHAM		12	L	0-1	0-0		Muggleton	Clarkson	Sandford	Cranson	Overson	Orlygsson	Keen*	Beeston	Carruthers	Peschisolido	Gleghorn	Biggins
4/12			12,558	*14*	27			*McCarthy 90*	*Gerrard*	*Makin*	*Pointon*	*Henry*	*Jobson*	*Redmond*	*Richardson*	*Ritchie**	*McCarthy*	*Graham*	*Holden^*	*Banger/Brennan*
								Ref: K Leach	Defeat is snatched from the jaws of a bore draw when Muggers blasts a clearance straight at Sean McCarthy. The ball bobbles back to him but he tries to kick rather than pick up the ball and falls over. McCarthy manages to stop his sides splitting to tap the ball in. Hilarious but unfunny.											
21	H	BURNLEY		11	W	2-0	0-0	Orlygsson 68p, 83	Muggleton	Clarkson	Sandford	Cranson	Overson	Orlygsson	Shaw*	Beeston	Carruthers^	Peschisolido	Gleghorn	Biggins/Sigurdsson
10/12			13,040	*18*	30				*Beresford*	*Parkinson*	*Hoyland*	*Davis*	*Winstanley !*	*Randall^*	*Harper**	*Heath*	*Gayle*	*Robinson*	*Eyres*	*Philliskirk/Mullin*
								Ref: C Wilkes	Jimmy Mullen's Clarets have Mark Winstanley sent off for a professional foul and Orlygsson blasts home the penalty. His second is a 25-yard screamer following a one-two with Pesch. Muggers redeems himself after last week's howler to save brilliantly twice from the big John Gayle.											
22	A	TRANMERE		9	W	1-0	0-0	Carruthers 81	Muggleton"	Butler	Sandford	Cranson	Overson	Orlygsson	Clarkson	Beeston*	Carruthers^	Peschisolido	Gleghorn	Dreyer/Biggins/Sinclair
17/12			*7,601*	*4*	33				*Nixon*	*Stevens*	*Brannan**	*McGreal*	*Higgins*	*Irons*	*Morrissey*	*Aldridge*	*Malkin*	*O'Brien*	*Thomas*	*Branch*
								Ref: R Poulain	City inflict a first home defeat of the season on John King's Rovers. Pesch, Cranson, Orlygsson and Gleghorn all miss decent chances. Sinclair replaces the injured Muggleton at the break and is brilliant. Carruthers heads over from five yards but swoops to slide home Pesch's low cross.											
23	H	SWINDON		8	D	0-0	0-0		Muggleton	Butler	Sandford	Cranson	Dreyer	Orlygsson	Clarkson	Keen*	Carruthers	Peschisolido	Gleghorn	**Williams**
26/12			**17,662**	*19*	34				*Digby*	*Robinson*	*Bodin*	*Culverhouse*	*Nijholt*	*Taylor*	*Horlock*	*Beauchamp*	*Fjortoft*	*Ling*	*Scott*	
								Ref: D Allison	Stoke edge a dull first half. Carruthers hits the post and finds Fraser Digby in fine form. Culverhouse is lucky to stay on after a heavy challenge on Pesch. Muggers tips Taylor's header onto the bar. Cranson clears. Stoke are only the second team in 1994 not to score at home to Swindon.											

No	Date		Att	Pos	Pt	F-A	H-T	Scorers, Times, and Referees	1	2	3	4	5	6	7	8	9	10	11	subs used
24	A	BRISTOL CITY		11	L	1-3	0-0	Cranson 83	Sinclair	Butler	Sandford	Cranson	Dreyer^	Orlygsson	Sigurdsson	Clarkson	Biggins*	Williams	Gleghorn	Peschisolido/Shaw
	27/12		*8,500*	*23*	34			*Bryant 66, Allison 78, 80*	*Welch*	*Hansen*	*Munro*	*Shail^*	*Bryant*	*Tinnion*	*Parris*	*Bent*	*Baird**	*Allison*	*Owers*	*Partridge/Dryden*
								Ref: P Vanes	John Williams, on loan from Coventry, makes his first start. A poor surface contributes to a dismal game. It is brought to life by Matt Bryant's 30-yard thunderbolt. Allison nets twice from close in as Stoke capitulate against old boss Joe Jordan's Robins who have lost six on the bounce.											
25	H	MIDDLESBROUGH		12	D	1-1	1-1	Gleghorn 20	Muggleton^	Butler	Sandford	Cranson	Overson	Orlygsson	Clarkson	**Scott**	Carruthers*	Peschisolido	Gleghorn	Williams/Sinclair
	31/12		15,914	*1*	35			*Vickers 9*	*Miller*	*Morris*	*Fleming*	*Vickers*	*Pearson*	*Mustoe*	*Robson*	*Pollock*	*Wilkinson*	*Hendrie*	*Hignett*	
								Ref: U Rennie	Stoke's shaky start sees Steve Vickers powerfully head home Craig Hignett's cross for Bryan Robson's Boro. City recover thanks to Overson's and Orlygsson's solid performances. Gleghorn slides home Carruthers' cross at the far post. Quiet debut for £300k Keith Scott from Swindon.											
26	A	WOLVES		14	L	0-2	0-1		Sinclair	Clarkson	Sandford	Cranson	Overson	Orlygsson	Butler	Dreyer^	Scott*	Peschisolido	Gleghorn	Biggins/Williams
	14/1		***28,298***	*2*	35			*Kelly 17, Dennison 87*	*Jones*	*Blades*	*Venus*	*Emblen*	*De Wolf*	*Law*	*Birch*	*Kelly*	*Mills*	*Cowans*	*Dennison*	
								Ref: J Winter	City are never in the running after David Kelly puts Graham Taylor's Wolves ahead when Rob De Wolf flicks on a corner. Robbie Dennison's late clincher is his fourth strike in six matches. Stoke have appointed their first ever Chief Executive, Jez Moxey, previously at Partick Thistle.											
27	H	PORTSMOUTH		16	L	0-2	0-0		Sinclair	Clarkson^	Dreyer*	Cranson	Sigurdsson	**Allen**	Orlygsson	Peschisolido	Scott	Downing	Gleghorn	Butler/**Leslie**
	4/2		9,704	*18*	35			*Preki 54, Creaney 90*	*Knight*	*Gittens*	*Daniel*	*McLoughlin*	*Symons*	*Butters*	*Pethick*	*Preki**	*Powell*	*Creaney*	*Rees*	*Hall*
								Ref: W Burns	City lack any kind of confidence against managerless Pompey. Preki cracks home left footed from the edge of the area. Gerry Creaney waltzes past Sinclair to net. Scott scoops over from two yards. Most of City's lowest league gate for five years leave early. Stoke are plummeting fast.											
28	A	SHEFFIELD UTD		16	D	1-1	1-1	Peschisolido 26	Sinclair	Clarkson	Butler	Cranson	Sigurdsson	Allen	Orlygsson	Peschisolido	Scott^	Downing*	Gleghorn	Dreyer/**Gayle**
	11/2		*13,900*	*7*	36			*Starbuck 6*	*Kelly*	*Ward*	*Nilsen^*	*Gannon*	*Gayle*	*Beesley*	*Rogers*	*Veart**	*Starbuck*	*Flo*	*Whitehouse*	*Littlejohn/Scott*
								Ref: P Richards	A slightly improved performance despite conceding to Phil Starbuck's early effort. The Blades have most of the play but Pesch's header levels matters. Stoke create good chances after half-time but Pesch and Scott are wasteful. Blades fans leave en masse disgusted at their performance.											
29	A	GRIMSBY		16	D	0-0	0-0		Sinclair	Sigurdsson	Sandford	Cranson	Overson	Orlygsson	Allen	Peschisolido	Scott*	Butler	Gleghorn	Wallace
	21/2		*6,384*	*7*	37				*Crichton*	*Croft*	*Jobling*	*Handyside*	*Rodger*	*Groves*	*Watson*	*Dobbin**	*Woods*	*Mendonca*	*Gilbert*	*Laws*
								Ref: E Parker	Another non-event counts as a moral victory for Stoke over high-flying Grimsby. The Mariners' attack is reduced to long-range pot shots. The best chance falls to Pesch but Crichton saves his flick. Lack of confidence means the Potters settle for an away point. 11 games without a win.											
30	A	WEST BROM		15	W	3-1	1-1	Scott 34, Peschisolido 65, 80	Sinclair	Sigurdsson	Sandford	Cranson	Overson	Orlygsson	Butler	Allen	Peschisolido^	Scott	Gleghorn*	Keen/Sturridge
	25/2		*16,591*	*19*	40			*Hamilton 21*	*Lange*	*Parsley**	*Agnew*	*Bradley*	*Burgess*	*Raven*	*Donovan^*	*Ashcroft*	*Taylor*	*Hunt*	*Hamilton*	*O'Regan/Rees*
								Ref: E Wolstenholme	City run into a side who are even worse than they are. Albion are outplayed. Pesch hits the post. Hamilton's speculative shot flies past Sinclair. Paul Allen runs midfield. Sandford crosses for Scott to slide in his first goal. Pesch heads in from five yards and pokes a long ball past Lange.											
31	H	DERBY		15	D	0-0	0-0		Sinclair	Sigurdsson	Sandford	Cranson	Overson	Orlygsson*	Butler	Allen	Peschisolido^	Scott	Beeston	Gleghorn/Keen
	4/3		13,462	*13*	41				*Hoult*	*Kavanagh**	*Nicholson*	*Trollope*	*Short*	*Yates*	*Harkes*	*Pembridge*	*Mills*	*Gabbiadini*	*Simpson*	*Wassall*
								Ref: E Lomas	Another goalless game. Pesch scores but is controversially given offside. He and Orlygsson are both carried off after fierce clashes. Sigurdsson restricts Marco Gabbiadini to one mis-hit shot. Roy McFarland's Rams best chance falls to Mills but his shot is saved. Four matches unbeaten.											
32	A	SUNDERLAND		18	L	0-1	0-0		Sinclair	Sigurdsson	Sandford	Cranson	Overson	Beeston	Butler	Allen	Carruthers	Scott^	Gleghorn*	Keen/Sturridge
	11/3		*12,282*	*17*	41			*Melville 87*	*Norman*	*Kubicki**	*Scott*	*Ball*	*Ferguson*	*Melville*	*Agnew*	*Russell*	*Howey*	*Smith*	*Armstrong*	*Brodie*
								Ref: J Lloyd	The proverbial relegation six-pointer goes the way of Peter Reid's Sunderland. The two lowest scoring sides in the division struggle in front of goal. Scott hits the bar. Sinclair saves Howey's header. Andy Melville heads home a free-kick for Sunderland's first home win in three months.											
33	A	PORT VALE		18	D	1-1	1-1	Sandford 33	Sinclair	Butler	Sandford	Cranson	Overson	Orlygsson*	Sigurdsson	Beeston	Carruthers^	Allen	Gleghorn	Keen/Scott
	14/3		*19,510*	*15*	42			*Naylor 2*	*Musselwhite*	*Sandeman*	*Tankard*	*Porter*	*Aspin*	*Billing*	*Guppy*	*Van der Laan*	*Glover L^*	*Naylor*	*Walker**	*Kent/Allon*
								Ref: A Dawson	A nearly full Vale Park sees a pulsating encounter. Orlygsson nearly scores but Vale break out and Tony Naylor pounces on a weak clearance. A free-kick for obstruction inside the box is chipped for Sandford to head home. Delilah resounds around the stadium as Stoke glimpse safety.											
34	H	READING		20	L	0-1	0-1		Sinclair	Butler*	Sandford	Cranson	Overson	Orlygsson	Sigurdsson	Beeston	Carruthers	Allen	Scott^	Gleghorn/Sturridge
	18/3		10,006	*6*	42			*Taylor 8*	*Hislop*	*Bernal*	*Kerr*	*Wdowczyk*	*McPherson*	*Holsgrove*	*Gilkes*	*Gooding*	*Quinn*	*Parkinson*	*Taylor**	*Nogan*
								Ref: A Flood	Jimmy Quinn and Mick Gooding's promotion-hunting Royals snatch a win when City's offside trap fails, leaving Scott Taylor free to fire past Sinclair. The profligate Scott, Carruthers and Sturridge all miss clear chances. Shaka Hislop makes two great saves. Just one win in 16 games.											

No	Date	Opponent	Att	Pos	Res	Pts	F-A	H-T	Scorers, Times, and Referees	1	2	3	4	5	6	7	8	9	10	11	subs used
35	A	SOUTHEND		20	L		2-4	0-2	Allen 48, Biggins 59p *[Sussex 78p]*	Sinclair	Butler	Sandford*	Cranson	Overson	Orlygsson	Allen	Sigurdsson	Biggins !	Beeston^	Gleghorn	Sturridge/Gayle
	21/3		***4,240***	*16*		42			*Jones 17, Tilson 26, Edwards 57,*	*Royce*	*Hone*	*Powell*	*Whelan*	*Bodley*	*Edwards !*	*Hails*	*Sussex*	*Jones **	*Tilson*	*Dublin*	*Gridelet*
									Ref: P Alcock	Southend pummel Stoke. Jones heads in. Tilson turns to drive past Sinclair. Allen scores with a low shot but Edwards' header restores the lead. He is then sent off for handball and Biggins nets the spot-kick. He also departs for protesting after the penalty is given for Overson's handball.											
36	H	NOTTS CO		19	W		2-1	1-0	Gleghorn 13, Sturridge 77	Sinclair	Butler	Sigurdsson	Cranson	Overson	Orlygsson	Allen^	Beeston	Peschisolido	Scott*	Gleghorn	Sturridge/Keen
	25/3		10,204	*24*		45			*White 89*	*Cherry*	*Short*	*Forsyth*	*Turner*	*Murphy*	*Hogg**	*Devlin*	*White*	*Emenalo*	*Nicol*	*Legg^*	*Mills/Russell*
									Ref: N Barry	Nigel Gleghorn scores Stoke's first home goal of 1995, sweeping in an Orlygsson corner. Cherry tips over Toddy's thunderous free-kick. Scott fires over from two yards. Sturridge has a shot kicked off the line but rounds Cherry to net Stoke's first goal at the Boothen End since October.											
37	A	CHARLTON		18	D		0-0	0-0		Sinclair	Butler	Sigurdsson	Cranson	Overson	Keen	Allen	Beeston^	Scott	Peschisolido*	Gleghorn	Carruthers/Clarkson
	1/4		*10,008*	*13*		46				*Salmon*	*Brown*	*Mortimer*	*Jones*	*Rufus*	*Balmer*	*Robson^*	*Leaburn*	*Pardew*	*Grant*	*Robinson**	*Whyte/Newton*
									Ref: G Barber	A poor game ends goalless as Stoke shut up shop. Allen is industrious in midfield. Steve Gritt and Alan Curbishley's Addicks have most of the play. Sinclair tips John Robinson's shot onto the post and recovers brilliantly to deny Grant. Pesch looks sharper after his recent injury lay-off.											
38	H	WATFORD		16	W		1-0	1-0	Sigurdsson 43	Sinclair	Butler	Sigurdsson	Cranson	Overson	Keen	Allen	Downing	Peschisolido*	Scott	Gleghorn	Clarkson
	4/4		9,576	*10*		49				*Miller*	*Lavin*	*Foster*	*Holdsworth*	*Millen*	*Ramage**	*Hessenthaler*	*Payne*	*Beadle*	*Gibbs*	*Phillips*	*Johnson*
									Ref: I Cruikshanks	The relief is tangible when Larus Sigurdsson floats a header between Kevin Miller and the far post. With confidence boosted City dominate the second half. Miller saves superbly from Pesch twice. Allen heads Foster's header off the line but Keen's 20-yard cracker tests Miller to the full.											
39	A	MIDDLESBROUGH		18	L		1-2	1-1	Peschisolido 30	Sinclair	Butler	Sigurdsson	Wallace	Clarkson	Downing	Allen	Carruthers	Peschisolido	Gayle*	Gleghorn	**Andrade**
	8/4		*20,867*	*1*		49			*Pearson 13, Moore 69*	*Miller*	*Cox**	*Whyte*	*Vickers*	*Pearson*	*Kavanagh*	*Hignett*	*Pollock*	*Fjortoft*	*Hendrie*	*Moore^*	*Blackmore/Moreno*
									Ref: M Riley	John Gayle makes his first start in a side lacking nine first teamers. Bryan Robson's leaders storm forward. Vickers flicks on for Nigel Pearson to head in. Pesch slams a deserved goal after Carruthers' run and cross. City battle hard but Boro's class tells. Alan Moore cracks in on the run.											
40	H	BARNSLEY		18	D		0-0	0-0		Sinclair	Butler	Clarkson	Cranson	Sigurdsson	Orlygsson	Downing	Allen	Peschisolido	Scott*	Gleghorn	Andrade
	12/4		10,752	*6*		50				*Watson*	*Eaden*	*Fleming*	*Wilson*	*Taggart*	*Shotton*	*O'Connell*	*Bullock*	*Payton*	*Liddell**	*Sheridan*	*Rammell*
									Ref: K Cooper	2,000 travelling fans out-sing a dismal home crowd. Barnsley play neat football but lack penetration. Allen tests Watson from 25 yards. Pesch finishes well but is ruled to have fouled a defender. Jose Andrade (aka Zay Angola) makes his home debut and nearly scores from a loose ball.											
41	H	BRISTOL CITY		16	W		2-1	1-1	Andrade 27, Peschisolido 89	Sinclair	Butler	Sigurdsson	Wallace	Clarkson	Orlygsson	Allen^	Downing*	Peschisolido	Andrade	Gleghorn	Carruthers/Keen
	15/4		10,172	*23*		53			*Shail 17*	*Welch*	*Hansen*	*Munro**	*Shail*	*Dryden*	*Tinnion*	*Martin^*	*Bent*	*Flatts*	*Allison*	*Owers*	*Baird/Edwards*
									Ref: D Allison	Bristol City skipper Mark Shail forces a Gary Owers corner over the line as the Robins look for the win they need to avoid relegation. Andrade nets his first for Stoke against the run of play. Both sides have chances but Pesch's late winner virtually condemns Joe Jordan's team to Div 2.											
42	A	SWINDON		14	W		1-0	1-0	Orlygsson 35	Sinclair	Butler	Sigurdsson	Clarkson	Overson	Orlygsson	Allen	Keen*	Carruthers	Andrade^	Gleghorn	Wallace/Scott
	17/4		*10,549*	*21*		56				*Digby*	*Todd*	*Robinson**	*Viveash*	*Nijholt*	*Taylor*	*Ling^*	*Beauchamp*	*Gooden*	*Thorne*	*McMahon*	*Thomson/O'Sullivan*
									Ref: G Singh	A smash and grab raid at Lou Macari's old club. City are quicker to the ball and grab a scrappy goal thanks to Toddy Orlygsson in a goalmouth melee. Trialist Jose Andrade has his leg broken in a fierce challenge. Steve McMahon's Robins are now in deep trouble at the foot of the table.											
43	H	PORT VALE		17	L		0-1	0-0		Sinclair	Butler	Wallace	Cranson !	Overson	Sigurdsson	Allen	Keen	Peschisolido	Carruthers*	Gleghorn	Gayle
	22/4		20,429	*14*		56			*Foyle 67*	*Musselwhite*	*Sandeman*	*Tankard*	*Porter*	*Aspin*	*Glover D*	*Bogie*	*Van der Laan*	*Foyle*	*Naylor*	*Guppy*	
									Ref: S Dunn	A poor game. Martin Foyle glances home Steve Guppy's inswinging corner at the near post. Pesch hits the foot of Musselwhite's post. Cranson becomes the first player to be dismissed in a derby match, for two bookings. City's first home league defeat by Vale for 67 years. Humiliating!											
44	H	MILLWALL		15	W		4-3	2-2	Scott 15, Gleghorn 39, 65, Keen 90	Sinclair	Butler	Sigurdsson	Cranson	Overson	Orlygsson	Wallace	Keen	Peschisolido	Scott	Gleghorn	
	29/4		**9,111**	*11*		59			*Dixon 22, Webber 42, Oldfield 50*	*Keller*	*Beard*	*Thatcher*	*Roberts*	*Webber*	*Stevens^*	*Savage**	*Rae*	*Dixon*	*Oldfield*	*Van Blerk*	*Taylor/Forbes*
									Ref: J Kirkby / F Stretton	A pulsating game. Gleghorn cracks in two outstanding strikes. Scott scores at the near post and fluffs an easier chance. Mick McCarthy's Lions lead as Oldfield taps in with Sinclair stranded. Linesman Stretton replaces the ref and denies Stoke a penalty but Keen nets the resulting corner.											
45	H	BOLTON		15	D		1-1	1-1	Orlygsson 12p	Sinclair	Butler	Sigurdsson	Cranson	Overson*	Orlygsson	Wallace	Keen	Peschisolido	Scott^	Gleghorn	Sandford/Carruthers
	3/5		15,557	*3*		60			*McGinlay 22*	*Davison !*	*Bergsson*	*Phillips*	*McAteer*	*Seagraves**	*Stubbs*	*Lee^*	*Patterson*	*Paatelainen*	*McGinlay*	*Thompson*	*Green/Shilton*
									Ref: P Wright	A frantic game sees Aidan Davison dismissed for fouling Pesch. Orlygsson nets the penalty against Peter Shilton making his 998th appearance. Ten-man Trotters fight hard. John McGinlay scores at the second attempt after Sinclair makes a great reaction stop. Pesch misses an open goal.											
46	A	LUTON		11	W		3-2	0-1	Orlygsson 52, Peschisolido 79, Scott 87	Sinclair	Butler	Sandford	Sigurdsson	Overson	Orlygsson	Wallace	Keen	Peschisolido*	Scott	Gleghorn	Clarkson
	7/5		*8,252*	*16*		63			*Harvey 43, Waddock 83*	*Davis*	*Johnson*	*Harvey*	*Waddock*	*Thomas*	*Peake*	*Telfer*	*Oakes*	*Taylor*	*Preece*	*Woodsford**	*Marshall*
Average	Home 12,832		Away 11,188						Ref: G Pooley	Fancy dress again. Richard Harvey fires in from 20 yards for Terry Westley's Town. Gleghorn heads against the bar. Wallace hits the post but Keen sets up Pesch. Waddock punishes a defensive error. The woeful Scott hits the bar from two yards but heads home from Gleghorn's cross.											

Coca-Cola Cup			Att			F-A	H-T	Scorers, Times, and Referees	1	2	3	4	5	6	7	8	9	10	11	subs used
2:1	A	FULHAM		6	L	2-3	0-0	Orlygsson 69p, Gleghorn 70	Muggleton	Butler	Sandford	Cranson	Dreyer	Orylgsson	Wallace	Downing	Carruthers	Peschisolido	Gleghorn	
	20/9		3,721	*3:17*				*Moore 60, Haworth 76, Blake 85*	*Stannard*	*Morgan*	*Herrera*	*Hurlock*	*Moore*	*Blake*	*Marshall*	*Jupp*	*Cork*	*Brazil*	*Haworth*	
								Ref: M Bailey	Lou Macari watches from the stand as Pesch is upended for the penalty. Gleghorn's cool finish puts Stoke 2-1 up. The linesman awards a spot-kick, but as Muggers saves wants a retake. Muggers keeps that out too but the rebound is lashed in. Mark Blake heads the winner on his debut.											
2:2	H	FULHAM		8	W	1-0	1-0	Peschisolido 2	Muggleton	Butler	Sandford	Dreyer	Cranson	Orylgsson	Carruthers	Downing	Biggins	Peschisolido	Gleghorn	
	28/9		7,440	*3:15*					*Stannard*	*Morgan*	*Adams*	*Mison*	*Moore**	*Blake*	*Marshall*	*Jupp*	*Bartley^*	*Brazil*	*Thomas*	*Bedrossian/Haworth*
								Ref: J Watson (Stoke win on away goals)	Pesch's early goal allows City to progress thanks to the away goals rule. Ian Branfoot and Mickey Adams' team of journeymen pros fight hard but Stoke are generally in control. Macari is confirmed as next manager. For the first time in a long while everything is rosy. Better days ahead.											
3	A	LIVERPOOL		7	L	1-2	1-1	Peschisolido 41	Muggleton	Butler	Sandford	Cranson	Overson	Orylgsson	Beeston	Clarkson	Carruthers*	Peschisolido	Gleghorn^	Biggins/Potter
	25/10		*32,060*	*P:5*				*Rush 4, 55*	*James*	*Jones*	*Bjornebye*	*Scales*	*Babb*	*Ruddock*	*McManaman*	*Redknapp*	*Rush*	*Barnes*	*Fowler*	
								Ref: J Holbrook	Ian Rush nets and City fans reach for their calculators. To their astonishment Stoke fight back. Babb is lucky not to see red after felling Pesch. Gleghorn hits the post. Pesch fires Carruthers' cross home to spark scenes of delirium. Rush's winner is his 100th cup goal for the Reds. Great!											

FA Cup																				
3	A	BRISTOL CITY		12	D	0-0	0-0		Sinclair	Butler	Sandford	Cranson	Overson	Orylgsson	Clarkson	Downing*	Scott	Peschisolido^	Gleghorn	Sturridge/Sigurdsson
	7/1		*9,683*	*23*					*Welch*	*Hansen*	*Munro*	*Shail*	*Bryant*	*Tinnion*	*Kuhl*	*Bent*	*Baird**	*Allison*	*Owers*	*Partridge*
								Ref: K Cooper	A terrible game on a heavily sanded pitch. Pesch is one of eight booked as he flicks the ball past Welch with his hand before netting. Sandford clears Partridge's shot off the line. Ex-Stoke loanee Junior Bent fires just past the upright. Keith Welch smothers Keith Scott's last-minute shot.											
3R	H	BRISTOL CITY		14	L	1-3	1-0	Scott 17	Sinclair	Clarkson*	Sandford	Cranson	Overson	Orylgsson	Butler	Wallace	Scott	Peschisolido	Gleghorn	Carruthers
	18/1		11,579	*23*			*aet*	*Bent 70, Baird 93, Tinnion 119*	*Welch*	*Hansen*	*Munro*	*Shail*	*Bryant*	*Tinnion*	*Kuhl**	*Bent*	*Baird*	*Allison^*	*Owers*	*Edwards/Partridge*
								Ref: K Cooper	Keith Scott glances a header in from a corner. Welch fumbles and the ball trickles along the line to safety. Bent scores with Bristol's first effort on target. Baird profits after Overson miskicks. Brian Tinnion fires in from 20 yards. Joe Jordan has the last laugh as Bristol will meet Everton.											

	Home						Away					
	P	W	D	L	F	A	W	D	L	F	A	Pts
1 Middlesbro	46	15	4	4	41	19	8	9	6	26	21	82
2 Reading	46	12	7	4	34	21	11	3	9	24	23	79
3 Bolton *	46	16	6	1	43	13	5	8	10	24	32	77
4 Wolves	46	15	5	3	39	18	6	8	9	38	43	76
5 Tranmere	46	17	4	2	51	23	5	6	12	16	35	76
6 Barnsley	46	15	6	2	42	19	5	6	12	21	33	72
7 Watford	46	14	6	3	33	17	5	7	11	19	29	70
8 Sheffield Utd	46	12	9	2	41	21	5	8	10	33	34	68
9 Derby	46	12	6	5	44	23	6	6	11	22	28	66
10 Grimsby	46	12	7	4	36	19	5	7	11	26	37	65
11 STOKE	46	10	7	6	31	21	6	8	9	19	32	63
12 Millwall	46	11	8	4	36	22	5	6	12	24	38	62
13 Southend	46	13	2	8	33	25	5	6	12	21	48	62
14 Oldham	46	12	7	4	34	21	4	6	13	26	39	61
15 Charlton	46	11	6	6	33	25	5	5	13	25	41	59
16 Luton	46	8	6	9	35	30	7	7	9	26	34	58
17 Port Vale	46	11	5	7	30	24	4	8	11	28	40	58
18 Portsmouth	46	9	8	6	31	28	6	5	12	22	35	58
19 West Brom	46	13	3	7	33	24	3	7	13	18	33	58
20 Sunderland	46	5	12	6	22	22	7	6	10	19	23	54
21 Swindon	46	9	6	8	28	27	3	6	14	26	46	48
22 Burnley	46	8	7	8	36	33	3	6	14	13	41	46
23 Bristol City	46	8	8	7	26	28	3	4	16	16	35	45
24 Notts Co	46	7	8	8	26	28	2	5	16	19	38	40
	1104	275	153	124	838	551	124	153	275	551	838	1503

* promoted after play-offs

Odds & ends

Double wins: (3) Notts County, Tranmere, West Brom.
Double losses: (2) Reading, Sunderland.

Won from behind: (4) Bristol City (h), Luton (a), Millwall (h), West Brom (a).
Lost from in front: (0).

High spots: The return of Lou Macari.
Toddy Orlygsson's form in midfield.
Playing so well at Anfield.
Beating Cosenza, Udinese and Piacenza in the Anglo-Italian Cup.
Winning at fellow strugglers Swindon to ensure survival.

Low spots: Losing at home to Bristol City in the FA Cup.
The sacking of Joe Jordan after an awful start.
Poor performances after Christmas leading to a scramble to avoid relegation.
Losing another Potteries derby.

Player of the Year: Larus Sigurdsson.
Ever-presents: (0).
Hat-tricks: (0).
Leading scorer: (13) Paul Peschisolido.

	Appearances						Goals			
	Lge	*Sub*	LC	*Sub*	FAC	*Sub*	Lge	LC	FAC	Tot
Allen, Paul	17						1			1
Andrade, Jose	2	*2*					1			1
Beckford, Jason	2	*2*								
Beeston, Carl	15	*1*	1				1			1
Biggins, Wayne	8	*9*	1	*1*			2			2
Butler, John	38	*3*	3		2					
Carruthers, Martin	26	*6*	3			*1*	5			5
Clark, Jon	5									
Clarkson, Ian	15	*3*	1		2					
Cranson, Ian	37		3		2		1			1
Downing, Keith	16		2		1					
Dreyer, John	16	*2*	2				2			2
Gayle, John	1	*3*								
Gleghorn, Nigel	44	*2*	3		2		6	1		7
Keen, Kevin	15	*6*					2			2
Leslie, Steve		*1*								
Muggleton, Carl	24		3							
Orlygsson, Toddy	38		3		2		7	1		8
Overson, Vince	33	*2*	1		2					
Peschisolido, Paul	39	*1*	3		2		13	2		15
Potter, Graham	1			*1*						
Sandford, Lee	34	*1*	3		2		1			1
Scott, Keith	16	*2*			2		3		1	4
Shaw, Graham	1	*2*								
Sigurdsson, Larus	22	*1*					1			1
Sinclair, Ronnie	22	*2*			2					
Sturridge, Simon	2	*6*				*1*	1			1
Wade, Shaun		*1*								
Wallace, Ray	16	*4*	1		1		2			2
Williams, John	1	*3*								
(own-goals)							1			1
30 players used	**506**	***65***	**33**	***2***	**22**	***2***	**50**	**4**	**1**	**55**

No	Date		Att	Pos	Pt	F-A	H-T	Scorers, Times, and Referees	1	2	3	4	5	6	7	8	9	10	11	subs used
1	H	READING			D	1-1	1-0	Wallace 12	Muggleton	Clarkson	Sandford	Sigurdsson	Overson	Orlygsson	Keen	Wallace	Peschisolido*	Scott	Gleghorn	Sturridge
	12/8		11,932		1			*Williams A 83*	*Sheppard*	*Bernal^*	*Gooding*	*Parkinson*	*Williams A*	*McPherson*	*Gilkes*	*Jones*	*Nogan**	*Lovell*	*Williams M*	*Morley/Wdowczyk*
								Ref: J Kirkby	Work will begin on Stoke's stadium at Sideway next year. The lack of new signings suggests the move is eating deep into the club's resources. Wallace's effort is reward for a bright opening. Adrian Williams nets a soft equaliser to earn an undeserved point for Quinn/Goodings' Royals.											
2	A	LEICESTER		4	W	3-2	3-0	Peschisolido 9, 23, Gleghorn 33	Muggleton	Clarkson	Sandford	Sigurdsson	Overson	Orlygsson	Keen	Wallace	Peschisolido*	Scott^	Gleghorn	Sturridge/Gayle
	19/8		*17,719*	*12*	4			*Walsh 71, Parker 74p*	*Poole*	*Grayson^*	*Whitlow*	*Willis**	*Walsh*	*Parker*	*Joachim*	*Taylor*	*Robins*	*Corica*	*Lawrence"*	*Roberts/Hill/Lewis*
								Ref: R Gifford	Stoke soak up heavy pressure and play on the break. Pesch's shot dribbles in. Willis is lucky not to go after felling the diminutive Canadian. A great move allows Pesch to head in. Gleghorn puts City in control. Sandford's foul on Walsh for the pen is as good as Mark McGhee's men get.											
3	H	PORT VALE		14	L	0-1	0-0		Muggleton	Clarkson	Sandford	Sigurdsson	Overson	Orlygsson*	Keen	Wallace	Peschisolido	Scott^	Gleghorn	Sturridge/Potter
	27/8		14,283	*18*	4			*Bogie 48*	*Musselwhite*	*Hill*	*Tankard*	*Bogie*	*Griffiths*	*Glover*	*McCarthy*	*Porter*	*Mills*	*Glover**	*Guppy*	*Naylor*
								Ref: G Singh	Stoke sport new Broxap sponsored shirts after finally clinching a deal. The lowest ever gate at a Potteries derby sees Vale outplay City for long periods. Ian Bogie turns on a one-man show and beats Muggleton at his near post. Sturridge lobs the keeper but also past the post. Depressing.											
4	A	IPSWICH		18	L	**1-4**	0-1	Peschisolido 83	Muggleton	Clarkson	Sandford	Sigurdsson	Overson	Orlygsson	Keen*	Wallace	Peschisolido	Scott	Gleghorn	Sturridge
	30/8		*10,848*	*12*	4			*Slater 38, 62, Mathie 82, 86*	*Forrest*	*Stockwell*	*Vaughan*	*Sedgley*	*Palmer*	*Williams**	*Uhlenbeek*	*Milton^*	*Mathie*	*Chapman*	*Slater*	*Taricco/Tanner*
								Ref: M Bailey	City perform well with some slick passing moves but George Burley's Ipswich finish brilliantly. Slater's second is a brilliant turn and shot. Ex-Stokie Lee Chapman misses an open goal. Pesch's rounds Forrest. City's passion elicits a standing ovation from the visiting fans at the whistle.											
5	H	OLDHAM		23	L	0-1	0-0		Muggleton	Clarkson	Sandford	Sigurdsson	Overson	Orlygsson	Keen*	Wallace	Peschisolido	Scott	Gleghorn	Sturridge
	2/9		8,663	*8*	4			*Overson 69 (og)*	*Hallworth*	*Makin*	*Pointon*	*Henry*	*Jobson*	*Redmond*	*Halle*	*Bernard*	*McCarthy*	*Banger**	*Brennan*	*Pemberton*
								Ref: K Lynch	An atrocious game is won by Graeme Sharp's Oldham when Vince Overson, Stoke's best player, miskicks the ball past the shocked Muggers. New coach Mike Pejic conducts a 45-min post-match inquest. Amid rumours of a move upstairs Macari is looking at Willie Falconer of Celtic.											
6	A	WATFORD		23	L	0-3	0-2		Sinclair	Clarkson	Sandford*	Sigurdsson	Overson	Orlygsson^	Keen"	Wallace	Peschisolido	Carruthers	Gleghorn	Scott/Dreyer/Devlin
	9/9		*7,130*	*17*	4			*Ramage 27, 54, Mooney 44*	*Miller*	*Gibbs*	*Johnson*	*Foster*	*Holdsworth*	*Ramage*	*Bazeley^*	*Payne*	*Mooney**	*Porter*	*Phillips*	*Moralee/Pitcher*
								Ref: P Rejer	Goalkeeper Ronnie Sinclair has a nightmare of a game. Glenn Roeder's Hornets have two first-half efforts. Both go in. Kevin Phillips balloons a spot-kick over the bar after Overson's foul. Ramage's second is a great free-kick. Macari is close to signing Oldham's winger Rick Holden.											
7	A	BIRMINGHAM		23	D	1-1	0-1	Carruthers 52	Muggleton	Clarkson	Sandford	Sigurdsson	Overson	Potter	Keen*	Wallace	Peschisolido	Scott^	Gleghorn"	Sturridge/Carruthers/**Br'well**
	12/9		*19,005*	*6*	5			*Hunt 30*	*Bennett*	*Poole*	*Johnson*	*Ward*	*Edwards*	*Daish*	*Hunt*	*Claridge*	*Bowen*	*Charlery**	*Cooper^*	*Tait/Otto*
								Ref: I Cruikshanks	The Holden deal has fallen through due to lack of funds. Macari demands action. Contract rebel Orlygsson is omitted after speaking out in the press. Blues boss Barry Fry offers six players in exchange for the in-form Paul Peschisolido. David Brightwell is taken on loan from Man City.											
8	H	TRANMERE		22	D	0-0	0-0		Prudhoe	Clarkson	Sandford	Sigurdsson	Overson	Potter	Keen*	Wallace	Peschisolido	Carruthers	Gleghorn	Orlygsson
	16/9		**8,618**	*13*	6				*Coyne*	*Stevens^*	*Thomas*	*McGreal*	*Teale*	*O'Brien**	*Brannan*	*Aldridge*	*Bennett*	*Irons*	*Nevin*	*Moore/Jones*
								Ref: S Mathieson	The lowest gate for five years see the best performance of the season. Stoke are out of luck when Keen and Overson hit the woodwork. Danny Coyne saves Ian Clarkson's volley brilliantly. Boardroom turmoil as Chairman Peter Coates says he will sell for the right price. £10m anyone?											
9	H	WEST BROM		22	W	2-1	1-0	Peschisolido 14, Keen 51	Prudhoe	Clarkson	Sandford	Sigurdsson	Overson	Potter	Keen	Wallace	Peschisolido	Carruthers*	Gleghorn	Sturridge
	24/9		9,612	*6*	9			*Hunt 62p*	*Naylor*	*Burgess*	*Edwards**	*Coldicott*	*Mardon*	*Raven*	*Donovan*	*Gilbert*	*Taylor^*	*Hunt*	*Hamilton*	*Ashcroft/Rees*
								Ref: T Lunt	Pesch shrugs off two players to beat Naylor. Carruthers thumps a header against the bar from two yards. Keen is booked for taking his shirt off to celebrate his goal. Andy Hunt goes down dramatically in the area for the penalty. 13 matches unbeaten against the Baggies. First home win!											
10	A	CRYSTAL PALACE		21	D	1-1	1-1	Carruthers 36	Prudhoe	Clarkson	Sandford	Sigurdsson	Overson	Potter	Keen	Wallace	Peschisolido*	Carruthers	Gleghorn	Sturridge
	20/9		*14,613*	*18*	10			*Freedman 31*	*Martyn*	*Edworthy*	*Vincent^*	*Hopkin*	*Coleman*	*Shaw*	*Houghton*	*Pitcher**	*Freedman*	*Taylor*	*Gordon*	*Roberts/Launders*
								Ref: A D'Urso	Palace's £2.5m investment pays off when Dougie Freedman lashes home Gareth Taylor's flick on. Carruthers is put through by Pesch to waltz round Nigel Martyn and score in front of Selhurst's impressive new stand. Prudhoe saves Taylor's header. Another solid away performance.											
11	H	NORWICH		21	D	1-1	0-1	Wallace 67	Prudhoe	Clarkson	Sandford	Sigurdsson	Overson	Potter	Sturridge	Wallace	Peschisolido	Carruthers	Gleghorn	
	7/10		12,016	*11*	11			*Akinbiyi 32*	*Gunn*	*Ullathorne*	*Bowen*	*Crook*	*Newsome*	*Prior*	*Adams**	*Fleck"*	*Akinbiyi*	*Johnson*	*O'Neill^*	*Milligan/Polston/Sheron*
								Ref: G Cain	Stoke are down to the bare bones against Martin O'Neill's strong Canaries. Ade Akinbiyi taps in after Prudhoe superbly saves Andy Johnson's effort. 'Razor' Wallace finishes a fine left-wing move by slotting in past Bryan Gunn. More support up front required to win matches like this.											

No	Date	Opponent	Att	Pos	Pts	Res	FT	HT	Scorers, Times, and Referees	1	2	3	4	5	6	7	8	9	10	11	subs used
12	A	WOLVES		16	W		4-1	2-0	Gleghorn 36, Potter 41, Wallace 85, [Carruthers 90]	Prudhoe	Clarkson	Sandford	Sigurdsson	Overson	Potter	Keen	Wallace	Peschisolido	Carruthers*	Gleghorn	Sturridge
	14/10		***26,483***	*19*	14				*Thompson 65p*	*Stowell"*	*Emblen*	*Thompson*	*Atkins*	*Young*	*Richards*	*Wright*	*Goodman*	*Venus^*	*Ferguson**	*Williams*	*Bull/Cowans/Smith*
									Ref: D Allison	City put Graham Taylor's Wolves to the sword after Gleghorn hammers home. Potter stabs in his first for the club. Mike Stowell is injured in a clash with Young. Dean Richards goes in goal. Wallace's shot squirms past him. Pesch has a goal ruled out. First win at Molineux since 1967.											
13	H	DERBY		16	D		1-1	0-0	Keen 66	Prudhoe	Clarkson	Sandford*	Sigurdsson	Overson	Potter	Keen	Wallace	Peschisolido	Carruthers	Gleghorn	Dreyer
	22/10		9,435	*17*	15				*Van der Laan 89*	*Hoult*	*Carsley*	*Nicholson*	*Preece^*	*Yates*	*Rowett*	*Van der Laan*	*Wrack**	*Willems*	*Gabbiadini*	*Trollope*	*Simpson/Flynn*
									Ref: G Furnandiz	Kevin Keen volleys a wonderful goal from Gleghorn's chip but is again booked for taking his shirt off in celebration. Robin Van der Laan runs clear to give Jim Smith's Rams an undeserved draw. Nine without defeat. Stoke report Birmingham to the FA over illegal approaches to Pesch.											
14	A	GRIMSBY		19	L		0-1	0-0		Prudhoe	Clarkson	Sandford	Sigurdsson	Overson	Potter	Keen*	Wallace	Peschisolido	Carruthers	Gleghorn	Gayle
	28/10		***5,477***	*10*	15				*Groves 51*	*Crichton*	*Laws*	*Croft*	*Handyside*	*Lever*	*Groves*	*Childs**	*Dobbin*	*Woods*	*Bonetti*	*Southall^*	*Livingstone/Forrester*
									Ref: T West	Paul Groves slips in to fire past Prudhoe. Gleghorn has a shot blocked on the line. Carruthers slices a great chance wide. Brian Laws' men look dangerous on the break. No win at Blundell Park since 1947. Keith Scott is wanted by old team Wycombe. Bradford are chasing John Dreyer.											
15	H	LUTON		15	W		**5-0**	1-0	Peschisolido 14, Sturridge 73, 87, [Gayle 75, Gleghorn 90]	Prudhoe	Clarkson"	Sandford	Sigurdsson	Overson	Potter	Keen	Wallace	Peschis'lido^	Carruthers*	Gleghorn	Sturridge/Gayle/Cranson
	4/11		9,382	*24*	18					*Feuer*	*Peake*	*Johnson*	*Davis*	*Hughes*	*Vilstrup**	*Alexander*	*Oakes*	*Riseth*	*Marshall*	*Harvey*	*Oldfield*
									Ref: J Lloyd	6ft 7in Ian Feuer is beaten by Pesch. Sturridge comes on for the injured Carruthers at half-time and his direct running sparks the avalanche. He cracks in from 22 yards for his first. Gayle scores the goal of the game from out on the left. The superb Gleghorn robs a defender to fire home.											
16	A	SOUTHEND		13	W		4-2	1-1	Sturridge 32, 63, 75, Gleghorn 65	Prudhoe	Cranson	Sandford	Sigurdsson	Overson	Potter	Keen	Wallace^	Gayle*	Sturridge	Gleghorn"	Carruthers/**Devlin/Whittle**
	11/11		*5,967*	*16*	21				*Belsvik 25, Hails 54*	*Royce*	*Dublin*	*Powell*	*Lapper*	*Bodley*	*Gridelet*	*Marsh*	*Byrne*	*Regis*	*Belsvik**	*Hails^*	*Thomson/Read*
									Ref: M Pierce	Debutant Peter Belsvik glances a header home. Potter is fouled in the area but an indirect free-kick is given. Sturridge turns in Keen's pass. He completes his hat-trick with two superb individual efforts. Gleghorn neatly shoots through Simon Royce's legs. A first ever win at Roots Hall.											
17	A	PORTSMOUTH		14	D		3-3	1-2	Gayle 29, 61, Sturridge 63	Prudhoe	Cranson*	Sandford	Sigurdsson	Overson	Potter^	Keen	Wallace	Gayle	Sturridge	Gleghorn	Devlin/**Sheron**
	18/11		*8,030*	*22*	22				*McLoughlin 16p, 56, Walsh 44*	*Knight*	*Pethick*	*Russell*	*McLoughlin*	*Whitbread*	*Butters*	*Walsh*	*Allen*	*Durnin*	*Hall*	*Carter**	*Burton*
									Ref: C Wilkes	Paul Walsh runs the show. He is tripped for penalty and scores himself after Prudhoe fails to hold his shot. McLoughlin's header puts Pompey in the driving seat. Gayle's brace are from close in. Sturridge turns well to fire home. Ex-Canary Mike Sheron misses a sitter in the last minute.											
18	H	SUNDERLAND		12	W		1-0	1-0	Wallace 21	Prudhoe	Clarkson	Sandford	Sigurdsson	Overson"	Potter^	Keen	Wallace	Gayle	Sturridge*	Gleghorn	Carruthers/Dreyer/Sheron
	22/11		11,754	*4*	25					*Chamberlain*	*Kubicki*	*Scott*	*Bracewell^*	*Ball*	*Melville*	*Gray M*	*Ord*	*Kelly"*	*Gray P*	*Russell**	*Howey/Smith/Aiston*
									Ref: R Harris	Phil Gray and Kevin Russell waste good chances for Peter Reid's Sunderland. Wallace latches on to Keen's header to put Stoke undeservedly in the lead. Prudhoe makes two brilliant saves as the Rokerites pour forward. Gleghorn has a good effort saved. Sunderland's first defeat in 11.											
19	H	MILLWALL		9	W		1-0	0-0	Gleghorn 62	Prudhoe	Clarkson	Sandford	Sigurdsson	Cranson	Potter	Keen^	Wallace	Gayle*	Sturridge"	Gleghorn	Carruthers/ Dreyer/Sheron
	25/11		12,590	*1*	28					*Keller*	*Lavin*	*Thatcher*	*Bowry*	*Webber*	*Stevens*	*Fuchs*	*Rae*	*Dixon**	*Malkin*	*Van Blerk*	*Savage*
									Ref: P Taylor	Ian Cranson, finally fully fit after his long injury lay-off, is superb as Stoke contain league leaders Millwall. Gleghorn's 20-yard effort deflects off Ben Thatcher leaving Kasey Keller stranded. Mick McCarthy's men's first away loss of the season. Five are booked in a competitive game.											
20	A	NORWICH		7	W		1-0	0-0	Gleghorn 53	Prudhoe	Clarkson	Sandford	Sigurdsson	Cranson	Potter^	Dreyer	Wallace	Peschisolido*	Sturridge	Gleghorn	Sheron/Beeston
	2/12		*15,707*	*4*	31					*Gunn*	*Sutch**	*Ullathorne*	*Adams*	*Newsome*	*Prior*	*Bowen*	*Fleck*	*Ward*	*Scott*	*Eadie*	*Akinbiyi*
									Ref: I Hemley	An inspired Stoke display against a Canaries team which would be top with a win. Pesch sets up Gleghorn to win it. Prudhoe stops everything Norwich throw at him. Cranson is brilliant in defence. Macari is censured by the League for remarks about the referee in the Newcastle cup-tie.											
21	A	WEST BROM		5	W		1-0	1-0	Peschisolido 35	Prudhoe	Clarkson	Sandford	Sigurdsson	Cranson	Potter^	Dreyer	Wallace^	Peschisolido*	Sturridge"	Gleghorn	Keen/Carruthers/Sheron
	9/12		*14,819*	*16*	34					*Naylor*	*Burgess*	*Smith*	*Darby*	*Edwards*	*Raven*	*Hamilton*	*Gilbert**	*Taylor*	*Hunt*	*Ashcroft^*	*Donovan/Coldicott*
									Ref: T Helibron	3,000 Stokies see Naylor deny Wallace in almighty goalmouth scramble. Daryl Burgess heads against the bar. Pesch turns to blast past Naylor. Sigurdsson impresses at the back. Kevin Donovan fires wide when clean through. Albion have lost eight in a row. Stoke into the play-off zone.											
22	H	CRYSTAL PALACE		8	L		1-2	0-1	Sheron 87	Prudhoe	Clarkson	Sandford	Sigurdsson	Cranson	Potter	Keen*	Wallace	Sheron	Sturridge	Gleghorn	Peschisolido
	16/12		12,090	*16*	34				*Freedman 24, Taylor 71*	*Martyn*	*Edworthy*	*Gordon*	*Roberts*	*Cundy*	*Vincent*	*Pitcher*	*Houghton*	*Freedman*	*Taylor^*	*McKenzie**	*Dyer/Boere*
									Ref: K Breen	A wonder goal from Sheron can't save City after a poor display. Freedman takes advantage of sloppy defending to ram home. Sturridge rounds Martyn but can't convert. Prudhoe fluffs a cross and Taylor nods in his first goal for Palace. Five without a win against Steve Coppell's Eagles.											
23	H	SHEFFIELD UTD		8	D		2-2	1-1	Gleghorn 27, Sheron 46	Prudhoe	Clarkson	Sandford	Sigurdsson	Cranson !	Potter	Sheron*	Wallace	Peschisolido	Sturridge	Gleghorn	Dreyer
	23/12		12,265	*23*	35				*Patterson 7, White 74*	*Kelly*	*Rogers*	*Fitzgerald*	*Gannon^*	*Vonk**	*Tuttle*	*White*	*Patterson*	*Battersby*	*Holland*	*Ward*	*Hodges/Heath*
									Ref: E Wolstenholme	Howard Kendall's Blades score when new signing Mark Patterson volleys in. Gleghorn deflects Cranson's shot in. Potter has a goal disallowed for Pesch's offside. Sheron flicks in Potter's centre. David White levels with a far-post header. Cranson walks (76 mins) for a second booking.											

No	Date		Att	Pos	Pt	F-A	H-T	Scorers, Times, and Referees	1	2	3	4	5	6	7	8	9	10	11	subs used
24	A	BARNSLEY		9	L	1-3	0-2	Gleghorn 68	Prudhoe	Clarkson*	Sandford	Sigurdsson	Cranson	Potter	Dreyer	Wallace	Peschisolido	Sheron	Gleghorn	Devlin
	26/12		*9,229*	*13*	35			*Redfearn 30, Rammell 43, Liddell 62*	*Watson*	*Eaden*	*Shirtliff*	*Sheridan*	*Davis*	*Moses*	*Liddell*	*Redfearn*	*O'Connell*	*Rammell*	*Archdeacon*	
								Ref: N Berry	The noon kick-off doesn't suit Stoke, neither does the rock-hard surface. City only have studded boots and slide all over the place. Barnsley are astonished to only score three after dominating. Atrocious. Stoke look for £500,000 from the tribunal after Orlygsson finally moves to Oldham.											
25	A	HUDDERSFIELD		8	D	1-1	0-0	Sheron 47	Prudhoe	Clarkson	Sandford	Sigurdsson	Cranson	Potter	Keen	Wallace	Peschisolido*	Sheron^	Gleghorn	Sturridge/Carruthers
	30/12		*15,071*	*6*	36			*Prudhoe 73 (og)*	*Francis*	*Dyson^*	*Cowan*	*Collins*	*Sinnott*	*Gray*	*Dalton**	*Makel*	*Booth*	*Jepson*	*Jenkins*	*Rowe/Turner*
								Ref: I Cruikshanks	A moment of total embarrassment as Prudhoe slices a routine clearance into his own net from a seemingly impossible angle. It wrecks hopes of leaving Town's new McAlpine Stadium with a win thanks to Sheron's volley. Keen hits the bar. Jepson clears off the line. Quite unbelievable!											
26	H	LEICESTER		4	W	1-0	1-0	Sturridge 27	Prudhoe	Clarkson	Sandford	Sigurdsson	Cranson	Potter^	Keen"	Wallace	Sturridge	Carruthers*	Gleghorn	Gayle/Dreyer/Beeston
	13/1		13,669	*5*	39				*Poole*	*Grayson*	*Whitlow*	*Hill*	*Walsh*	*Parker*	*Corica*	*Taylor**	*Robins^*	*Roberts*	*Smith"*	*Joachim/Philpott/Lowe*
								Ref: J Kirkby	Sturridge runs onto Wallace's pass to fire in. Martin O'Neill's Foxes change shape with a triple substitution and look ominous. Prudhoe denies Joachim who also puts a free header just over. Cranson dominates Iwan Roberts and goes close himself. The Orlygsson fee is set at just £180k.											
27	A	READING		6	L	0-1	0-0		Prudhoe	Clarkson	Sandford	Sigurdsson	Cranson	Potter	Keen	Wallace	Gayle*	Sturridge	Gleghorn	Peschisolido
	20/1		*8,082*	*18*	39			*Gooding 67*	*Sutton*	*Bernal*	*Gooding*	*Wdowczyk**	*Williams A*	*Booty*	*Quinn*	*Parkinson*	*Morley^*	*Nogan*	*Holsgrove*	*Gilkes/Lambert*
								Ref: G Pooley	The poor pitch and high winds make for a forgettable match. Sturridge hits the woodwork twice. Gayle rounds the portly Steve Sutton but also hits the post. The midfield, on a rare off day, allows Mick Gooding to run 40 yards, waltz past three players and fire past the helpless Prudhoe.											
28	H	IPSWICH		7	W	3-1	1-0	Sheron 37, 75, Gleghorn 65	Prudhoe	Clarkson	Sandford	Sigurdsson	Cranson	Potter^	Beeston	Wallace	Sheron	Sturridge*	Gleghorn	Peschisolido/Dreyer
	10/2		12,239	*9*	42			*Scowcroft 54*	*Wright*	*Uhlenbeek*	*Taricco*	*Thomsen*	*Mowbray*	*Williams*	*Mason^*	*Sedgley*	*Scowcroft*	*Marshall*	*Milton**	*Stockwell/Slater*
								Ref: G Cain	Carl Beeston returns from his self-imposed contractual exile and sets up Sheron to curl round Richard Wright. Negative Town level when Jamie Scowcroft heads a free-kick in unmarked. Gleghorn bags a rare header. Sheron controls Sturridge's flick on and lashes into the roof of the net.											
29	H	BIRMINGHAM		3	W	1-0	1-0	Sturridge 25	Prudhoe	Clarkson	Sandford	Sigurdsson	Cranson	Potter^	Beeston*	Wallace	Sheron	Sturridge	Gleghorn	Keen/Dreyer
	17/2		15,716	*13*	45				*Griemink*	*Bass*	*Frain*	*Samways*	*Edwards*	*Johnson*	*Hunt"*	*Bowen^*	*Francis*	*Sheridan*	*Donowa**	*Otto/Bull/Breen*
								Ref: T Helibron	The biggest league gate thus far see Stoke pinch the points in a tight affair. Sturridge smashes wide of Bart Griemink after cutting inside. Barry Fry's team force Prudhoe into a great double save. Potter skins Frain at will but Stoke cannot find a finish. Highest league position since 1985.											
30	A	TRANMERE		5	D	0-0	0-0		Prudhoe	Clarkson	Sandford	Sigurdsson	Cranson	Potter	Beeston	Wallace	Sheron*	Sturridge	Gleghorn	Peschisolido
	24/2		*8,312*	*17*	46				*Coyne*	*Stevens*	*Rogers*	*Teale*	*Garnett**	*O'Brien^*	*Brannan*	*Aldridge*	*Bennett"*	*Irons*	*Branch*	*Mungall/Morrissey/Jones*
								Ref: D Allison	A bright start tails off into a midfield slog in the Birkenhead mud. John King's Rovers are denied by Sigurdsson's last-ditch tackle on Aldridge. Sheron's goalbound header is palmed away by Danny Coyne. Pesch heads narrowly over. City settle for a draw rather than looking for the win.											
31	H	WATFORD		5	W	2-0	0-0	Cranson 48, Wallace 62	Prudhoe	Clarkson	Sandford	Sigurdsson	Cranson	Potter	Beeston	Wallace*	Sheron^	Sturridge	Gleghorn	Keen/Peschisolido
	28/2		10,114	*24*	49				*Miller*	*Gibbs*	*Barnes*	*Hessenthaler*	*Holdsworth*	*Millen*	*Penrice^*	*Palmer*	*White*	*Mooney**	*Phillips*	*Bazeley/Ludden*
								Ref: T West	After a woeful first half Cranson buries a loose ball after Kevin Miller saves twice in a scramble. The first goal by a Stoke defender for a year! Watford wilt visibly. A great move ends with Gleghorn stepping over the ball for the onrushing Wallace to blast home. Play-offs here we come.											
32	H	BARNSLEY		4	W	2-0	1-0	Keen 39, Sheron 70	Prudhoe	Clarkson	Sandford	Sigurdsson	Cranson	Potter*	Beeston	Keen	Sheron	Sturridge	Gleghorn	Dreyer
	2/3		12,663	*6*	52				*Watson*	*Eaden*	*Shirtliff*	*Bullock*	*Archdeacon*	*De Zeeuw*	*Liddell*	*Redfearn*	*O'Connell**	*Payton*	*Sheridan*	*Hurst*
								Ref: R Gifford	Keen, returning from injury, nips in to poach a vital goal in a tight game. Danny Wilson's Tykes waste good chances. Liddell and Payton both at fault. Prudhoe palms O'Connell's shot over. Sturridge's cross is converted easily by Sheron. Level on points with third-placed Charlton now.											
33	A	SHEFFIELD UTD		4	D	0-0	0-0		Prudhoe	Clarkson	Sandford	Sigurdsson	Cranson	Potter^	Beeston	Keen	Sheron*	Sturridge	Gleghorn	Peschisolido/Dreyer
	9/3		*14,468*	*17*	53				*Kelly*	*Short*	*Nilsen*	*Cowans*	*Hodgson*	*Ablett*	*White*	*Ward*	*Taylor*	*Hutchison**	*Whitehouse*	*Walker*
								Ref: R Furnandiz	An end-to-end game amazingly ends goalless. The tension shows as chances go begging at both ends. Sturridge is tripped when breaking clear. Keen works tirelessly. Whitehouse and Taylor waste great openings for Howard Kendall's United. Only two goals conceded in eight matches.											
34	A	PORT VALE		5	L	0-1	0-1		Prudhoe	Clarkson	Sandford	Sigurdsson	Cranson	Wallace	Beeston*	Keen^	Sheron	Sturridge	Gleghorn	Potter/Gayle
	12/3		*16,737*	*22*	53			*Bogie 1*	*Musselwhite*	*Hill*	*Stokes*	*Bogie**	*Griffiths*	*Aspin*	*McCarthy*	*Porter*	*Foyle*	*Glover^*	*Guppy*	*Walker/Naylor*
								Ref: E Lomas	Ian Bogie scores with a ferocious cross-shot after just 12 secs without a City player touching the ball. Shell-shocked Stoke battle back. Sheron hits both posts, the ball rebounds into Musselwhite's hands. Potter gees things up when he arrives but Vale withstand the onslaught to cling on.											

No	H/A	Date	Opponent	Att	Pos	Res	Pts	F-A	H-T	Scorers, Times, and Referees	1	2	3	4	5	6	7	8	9	10	11	subs used
35	H	16/3	HUDDERSFIELD	13,157	5 / *6*	D	54	1-1	0-0	Sturridge 66	Prudhoe	Clarkson	Sandford	Sigurdsson	Cranson	Potter	Beeston	Wallace	Sheron	Sturridge	Gleghorn	
										Edwards 88	*Francis*	*Jenkins*	*Cowan*	*Bullock*	*Sinnott*	*Gray*	*Edwards*	*Makel*	*Booth*	*Dunn**	*Thornley*	*Baldry*
										Ref: K Lynch	Brian Horton's Terriers play neat football as the game starts at a furious pace. Stoke gain superiority. Wallace and Sturridge hit the post. Potter heads back a cross for Sturridge to bury and his corner hits the woodwork again. New signing Rob Edwards levels via the underside of the bar.											
36	A	23/3	CHARLTON	*12,770*	5 / *4*	L	54	1-2	1-0	Sheron 41	Prudhoe	Clarkson	Sandford	Sigurdsson	Cranson	Potter*	Beeston	Wallace	Sheron^	Sturridge	Gleghorn	Keen/Carruthers
										Mortimer 83p, Whyte D 89	*Ammann*	*Brown**	*Sturgess*	*Mortimer*	*Rufus*	*Whyte C*	*Newton*	*Leaburn*	*Robinson*	*Grant^*	*Bowyer*	*Robson/Whyte D*
										Ref: A Butler	Stoke are in control after Sheron bravely heads Clarkson's chip past the onrushing Ammann. It is City's first goal away from the Vic in 1996. Gleghorn fires straight at the keeper. Charlton finish strongly. The penalty is for Clarkson's handball. Whyte heads in after Keen fails to clear.											
37	A	30/3	DERBY	*17,245*	6 / *2*	L	54	1-3	1-0	Sheron 22	Prudhoe	Sandford	Keen	Sigurdsson	Cranson	Potter*	Beeston	Wallace	Sheron	Sturridge	Gleghorn	Carruthers
										Sturridge 53, 79, Powell D 58	*Hoult*	*Wassall*	*Powell C*	*Powell D*	*Yates*	*Stimac^*	*Flynn*	*Ward**	*Willems*	*Gabbiadini*	*Carsley*	*Simpson/Sturridge*
										Ref: S Mathieson	Pesch is sold to Birmingham for £475,000 without Macari's knowledge on deadline day. A sell-out crowd see Sheron dive to head City ahead. Once again Stoke fail to hold on. Dean wins the battle of the Sturridge brothers scoring two after appearing as a half-time sub. Rams almost up.											
38	H	1/4	WOLVES	16,361	6 / *11*	W	57	2-0	1-0	Sheron 3, Sturridge 58	Prudhoe	Clarkson	Sandford	Sigurdsson	Cranson	Potter^	Beeston*	Wallace	Sheron"	Sturridge	Gleghorn	Keen/Dreyer/Carruthers
											Stowell	*Smith"*	*Thompson*	*Young*	*Venus^*	*Richards*	*Corica*	*Goodman*	*Bull*	*Froggatt*	*Osborn**	*Rankine/Ferguson/Atkins*
										Ref: M Pierce	The biggest league gate so far sees Sheron delicately flick Gleghorn's drive past the keeper. Wallace fires wide before hitting the post. Sheron blazes the follow up over. Sturridge whips Potter's centre into the corner of the net after the ever-improving Sigurdsson weaves out of defence.											
39	H	6/4	GRIMSBY	12,524	8 / *15*	L	57	1-2	1-0	Sheron 35	Prudhoe	Clarkson	Sandford	Sigurdsson	Cranson	Potter	Keen*	Wallace	Sheron	Sturridge	Gleghorn^	Carruthers/Beeston
										Groves 47, Gallimore 55	*Crichton*	*McDermott^*	*Gallimore*	*Smith*	*Handyside*	*Groves*	*Flatts**	*Shakespeare*	*Woods*	*Mendonca"*	*Childs*	*Southall/Fickling/Forrester*
										Ref: E Wolstenholme	City lead when Sheron's backheel dumbfounds Paul Crichton. Just 194 Grimsby fans witness a smash and grab win. Paul Groves sweeps home after a good move. Ex-Stokie Tony Gallimore fires in from 20 yards. City are well below par. The new ground is granted planning permission.											
40	A	9/4	LUTON	*7,689*	7 / *23*	W	60	2-1	0-1	Sturridge 86, Sheron 90	Prudhoe	Clarkson	Sandford	Sigurdsson	Whittle	Dreyer^	Beeston"	Wallace	Sheron*	Sturridge	Gleghorn	Keen/Potter/Carruthers
										Grant 45	*Feuer*	*Alexander*	*Thomas*	*Waddock*	*Johnson*	*Patterson*	*Guentchev*	*Thorpe^*	*Oldfield**	*Grant*	*Oakes*	*Taylor/Tomlinson*
										Ref: U Rennie	Justin Whittle makes a nervous start to his full debut. Kim Grant gives Lennie Lawrence's Hatters hope of beating the drop. Prudhoe produces three excellent saves as City hang on. Then Sturridge weaves into the box and pokes past Feuer and Sheron heads in a deep free-kick. Bedlam.											
41	H	13/4	PORTSMOUTH	11,471	5 / *21*	W	63	2-1	1-0	Wallace 7, Sheron 90	Prudhoe	Clarkson	Sandford	Sigurdsson	Whittle	Potter	Beeston*	Wallace	Sheron	Sturridge	Gleghorn	Devlin
										Butters 61	*Knight*	*Pethick !*	*Awford*	*McLoughlin*	*Thomson*	*Butters*	*Allen*	*Durnin*	*Burton*	*Hall*	*Carter**	*Igoe*
										Ref: M Bailey	Wallace follows up to score after Sheron causes havoc. Pethick is dismissed for swearing (20 mins) but Pompey fight hard. With Sigurdsson off for treatment Butters heads in unmarked. Sheron nicks it with a cross-shot. Cranson misses the rest of the season after having knee surgery.											
42	H	17/4	CHARLTON	12,969	5 / *4*	W	66	1-0	1-0	Sheron 29	Prudhoe	Clarkson	Sandford	Sigurdsson	Whittle	Potter*	Devlin	Wallace	Sheron	Sturridge	Gleghorn	Dreyer
											Petterson	*Jackson*	*Stuart**	*Jones^*	*Balmer*	*Whyte C*	*Newton*	*Leaburn*	*Robinson*	*Allen*	*Brown"*	*Robson/Whyte D/Nelson*
										Ref: M Riley	Mike Sheron sets a club record of scoring in seven consecutive matches. He dispatches Sturridge's chip into the far corner of the net in front of an ecstatic Boothen End. Play-off certs Charlton are dreadful. 12 cautions in the last seven games means City will not win the fair play award.											
43	A	21/4	SUNDERLAND	*21,276*	4 / *1*	D	67	0-0	0-0		Prudhoe	Clarkson	Sandford	Sigurdsson	Whittle	Potter^	Devlin	Wallace	Sheron*	Sturridge	Gleghorn	Carruthers/Dreyer
											Chamberlain	*Kubicki*	*Scott**	*Bracewell*	*Ball*	*Melville*	*Gray M*	*Ord*	*Russell"*	*Howey*	*Agnew^*	*Hall/Aiston/Bridges*
										Ref: G Singh	Stoke are party poopers as Peter Reid's team celebrate winning the Championship. Sigurdsson and Whittle are superb. Michael Bridges hits the post. Potter's dipping drive is tipped onto the bar by Alec Chamberlain. Devlin slices wide when well placed. Ex-Stokie Bracewell impresses.											
44	A	27/4	MILLWALL	*10,105*	4 / *19*	W	70	3-2	2-0	Sheron 28, Sturridge 32, 70p	Prudhoe	Clarkson	Sandford	Sigurdsson	Whittle	Potter^	Devlin	Wallace	Sheron*	Sturridge	Gleghorn	Carruthers/Dreyer
										Rae 80p, 89	*Keller*	*Connor*	*Thatcher*	*Newman*	*Van Blerk*	*Stevens*	*Weir*	*Rae*	*Malkin*	*Bowry^*	*Gordon**	*Savage/Neill*
										Ref: R Harris	City sport a natty duo-tone blue kit. Sheron cracks in a fierce shot on the run. Sturridge latches onto a long punt to blast home. His penalty, for Thatcher's foul, is Stoke's first of the season. Millwall look doomed to the drop despite Alex Rae's late brace. The pen is for Sigurdsson's foul.											
45	A	30/4	OLDHAM	*10,271*	4 / *19*	L	70	0-2	0-1		Prudhoe	Clarkson*	Sandford	Sigurdsson	Whittle	Potter	Devlin	Wallace	Sheron	Sturridge	Gleghorn	Carruthers
										Richardson 27p, Creaney 72	*Hallworth*	*Makin*	*Serrant*	*Fleming*	*Graham*	*Rickers*	*Richardson*	*Beckford*	*Orlygsson*	*Creaney*	*Redmond*	
										Ref: K Leach	A win ensures a play-off berth but a huge support leaves disappointed as City fail to perform. The inexperienced Whittle trips Beckford for the penalty. Ex-Stokie Orlygsson runs midfield. Creaney flicks in Richardson's cross. Gleghorn hits the bar. Seven without a goal against Oldham.											
46	H	5/5	SOUTHEND	**18,897**	4 / *14*	W	73	1-0	1-0	Sheron 12	Prudhoe	Clarkson	Sandford	Sigurdsson	Whittle	Potter*	Devlin	Wallace	Sheron	Sturridge	Gleghorn	Dreyer
											Royce	*Hails*	*Stimson*	*McNally*	*Bodley*	*Gridelet*	*Marsh*	*Byrne**	*Dublin*	*Rammell^*	*Tilson*	*Lapper/Roge*
			Home	Away						Ref: M Barry	Tentative City are relieved to get the early clinching goal. Sheron's unstoppable shot finds the roof of the net. Cue 'Delilah'. Prudhoe saves in a one-on-one as nerves become frayed. The ref blows three minutes early as he sees the end of season pitch invasion is about to start early. Phew!											
Average			12,279	12,915																		

Play-offs	Att		F-A	H-T	Scorers, Times, and Referees	1	2	3	4	5	6	7	8	9	10	11	subs used
SF A LEICESTER		D	0-0	0-0		Prudhoe	Clarkson	Sandford	Sigurdsson	Whittle	Potter	Devlin	Wallace	Sheron	Sturridge	Gleghorn	
1 12/5	*20,325*					*Poole*	*Grayson*	*Whitlow*	*Watts*	*Walsh*	*Izzet*	*Lennon*	*Taylor*	*Claridge*	*Robins**	*Heskey*	*Parker*
					Ref: W Burns	Stoke pummel Martin O'Neill's team but can't find the back of the net. Sturridge picks up Steve Claridge's back-pass but Poole saves with his legs. Poole's brilliant flying save denies Potter point blank. Clarkson heads off the line from Walsh but the Foxes are poor. Roll on Wembley!											
SF H LEICESTER		L	0-1	0-0		Prudhoe	Clarkson	Sandford	Sigurdsson	Whittle	Potter*	Devlin	Wallace	Sheron	Sturridge	Gleghorn	Carruthers
2 15/5	21,037				*Parker 46*	*Poole*	*Grayson*	*Whitlow*	*Watts*	*Walsh*	*Izzet*	*Lennon*	*Taylor*	*Claridge*	*Parker*	*Heskey*	
					Ref: G Singh (Stoke lose 0-1 on aggregate)	Leicester gradually get the better of an out-of-sorts Stoke who fail to deal with the fans' expectations. Emile Heskey is superb up front, holding off Whittle as Leicester build moves around him. One moment of magic wins it: Parker's superb left-foot volley at the far post. Totally gutting.											

Coca-Cola Cup	Att		F-A	H-T	Scorers, Times, and Referees	1	2	3	4	5	6	7	8	9	10	11	subs used
2:1 H CHELSEA	22	D	0-0	0-0		Prudhoe	Clarkson	Sandford	Sigurdsson	Overson	Potter	Keen	Wallace	Peschisolido	Carruthers	Gleghorn	
20/9	15,574 *P:9*					*Kharine*	*Clarke*	*Minto*	*Gullit*	*Johnsen*	*Sinclair*	*Newton*	*Hughes*	*Spencer**	*Burley*	*Wise*	*Furlong*
					Ref: T West	A stunning performance to hold Glenn Hoddle's all-star team. Ruud Gullit's assured sweeping keeps Chelsea in it. Carruthers wastes two great chances. Overson heads against the post. The start of something good? After the match Macari asks to have out-of-favour Mark Stein on loan.											
2:2 A CHELSEA	21	W	1-0	0-0	Peschisolido 75	Prudhoe	Clarkson	Sandford	Sigurdsson	Overson	Potter	Sturridge	Wallace	Peschisolido	Carruthers	Gleghorn	
4/10	*16,272 P:10*					*Kharine*	*Burley*	*Barness*	*Gullit*	*Johnsen*	*Sinclair*	*Spackman**	*Hughes*	*Furlong*	*Peacock^*	*Wise*	*Stein/Lee*
					Ref: K Cooper (Stoke win 1-0 on aggregate)	A stupendous night is crowned by Pesch's opportunist strike. Delilah resounds around Stamford Bridge as City use up a season's worth of luck against profligate Blues. Sandford heads off the line. Gullit, Furlong and Stein all miss sitters: Stein in the last minute from six yards. Brilliant.											
3 H NEWCASTLE	16	L	0-4	0-2	*[Peacock 73]*	Prudhoe	Clarkson !	Sandford	Sigurdsson	Overson	Potter*	Keen	Wallace	Peschisolido	Carruthers	Gleghorn	Cranson
25/10	23,000 *P:1*				*Beardsley 29, 39, Ferdinand 52,*	*Hislop*	*Barton*	*Elliott*	*Clark*	*Peacock*	*Howey^*	*Lee**	*Beardsley*	*Ferdinand*	*Ginola*	*Gillespie*	*Watson/Albert*
					Ref: G Ashby	A sell-out crowd see a superb performance by Kevin Keegan's Toon. Beardsley's brace puts the game out of reach. Pesch and Carruthers have good chances saved by £1.5m Hislop. Clarkson is sent off (45) for two fouls on the theatrical Ginola. Ferdinand and Peacock net from close in.											

FA Cup	Att		F-A	H-T	Scorers, Times, and Referees	1	2	3	4	5	6	7	8	9	10	11	subs used
3 H NOTT'M FOREST	8	D	1-1	1-0	Sturridge 27	Prudhoe	Clarkson	Sandford	Sigurdsson	Dreyer	Potter	Keen	Wallace	Sturridge	Carruthers	Gleghorn	
6/1	17,947 *P:7*				*Pearce 82*	*Crossley*	*Lyttle*	*Pearce*	*Cooper*	*Chettle*	*Stone*	*Bart-Williams*	*Gemmill*	*Campbell*	*Roy**	*Woan*	*Lee*
					Ref: D Gallagher	A reshuffled City play Forest off the park. Sturridge finishes well but Gleghorn has a header cleared off the line. Potter hits the upright and the ball rebounds to Crossley. Sturridge's shot hits Dreyer with the keeper beaten. Jason Lee miskicks and Pearce buries at the far post. Travesty.											
3R A NOTT'M FOREST	4	L	0-2	0-1		Prudhoe	Clarkson	Sandford	Sigurdsson	Cranson	Potter	Keen	Wallace	Sturridge	Peschisolido*	Gleghorn	Gayle
17/1	*17,372 P:6*				*Campbell 16, Pearce 55p*	*Crossley*	*Lyttle*	*Pearce*	*Cooper*	*Chettle*	*Stone*	*Bart-Williams*	*Gemmill*	*Campbell**	*Roy^*	*Woan*	*Lee/Phillips*
					Ref: D Gallagher	Forest are in control from the start against the strangely subdued Potters. Campbell turns adroitly to blast past Prudhoe. Potter gives Des Lyttle the runaround but Pesch fails to convert any of his crosses. Sandford fells Stone for the penalty. Lee misses an open goal. Forest meet Oxford.											

		Home					Away					
	P	W	D	L	F	A	W	D	L	F	A	Pts
1 Sunderland	46	13	8	2	32	10	9	9	5	27	23	83
2 Derby	46	14	8	1	48	22	7	8	8	23	29	79
3 Crys Palace	46	9	9	5	34	22	11	6	6	33	26	75
4 STOKE	46	13	6	4	32	15	7	7	9	28	34	73
5 Leicester *	46	9	7	7	32	29	10	7	6	34	31	71
6 Charlton	46	8	11	4	28	23	9	9	5	29	22	71
7 Ipswich	46	13	5	5	45	30	6	7	10	34	39	69
8 Huddersfield	46	14	4	5	42	23	3	8	12	19	35	63
9 Sheffield Utd	46	9	7	7	29	25	7	7	9	28	29	62
10 Barnsley	46	9	10	4	34	28	5	8	10	26	38	60
11 West Brom	46	11	5	7	34	29	5	7	11	26	39	60
12 Port Vale	46	10	5	8	30	29	5	10	8	29	37	60
13 Tranmere	46	9	9	5	42	29	5	8	10	22	31	59
14 Southend	46	11	8	4	30	22	4	6	13	22	39	59
15 Birmingham	46	11	7	5	37	23	4	6	13	24	41	58
16 Norwich	46	7	9	7	26	24	7	6	10	33	31	57
17 Grimsby	46	8	10	5	27	25	6	4	13	28	44	56
18 Oldham	46	10	7	6	33	20	4	7	12	21	30	56
19 Reading	46	8	7	8	28	30	5	10	8	26	33	56
20 Wolves	46	8	9	6	34	28	5	7	11	22	34	55
21 Portsmouth	46	8	6	9	34	32	5	7	11	27	37	52
22 Millwall	46	7	6	10	23	28	6	7	10	20	35	52
23 Watford	46	7	8	8	40	33	3	10	10	22	37	48
24 Luton	46	7	6	10	30	34	4	6	13	10	30	45
	1104	233	177	142	804	613	142	177	233	613	804	1479

* promoted after play-offs

Odds & ends

Double wins: (6) Leicester, Luton, Millwall, Southend, West Brom, Wolves.
Double losses: (3) Grimsby, Oldham, Port Vale.

Won from behind: (2) Luton (a), Southend (a).
Lost from in front: (3) Charlton (a), Derby (a), Grimsby (h).

High spots: Making the play-offs.
The Sheron/Sturridge partnership.
Simon Sturridge's hat-trick at Roots Hall.
Beating Ruud Gullit's Chelsea at Stamford Bridge in the Coca-Cola Cup.
Outplaying Nottingham Forest at home in the FA Cup.
The doubling of attendances over the course of the season.

Low spots: Losing to Leicester after having the best of the first leg of the play-offs.
Not winning the home FA Cup-tie with Forest.
Losing both Potteries derbies.
Saying goodbye to Paul Peschisolido.
Being thrashed by Newcastle in the Coca-Cola Cup.

Player of the Year: Ray Wallace and Mark Prudhoe.
Ever-presents: (3) Gleghorn, Sandford, Sigurdsson.
Hat-tricks: (1) Simon Sturridge.
Leading scorer: (15) Mike Sheron.

	Appearances						Goals			
	Lge	*Sub*	LC	*Sub*	FAC	*Sub*	Lge	LC	FAC	Tot
Beeston, Carl	**13**	*3*								
Brightwell, David		*1*								
Carruthers, Martin	**10**	*14*	3		1		**3**			**3**
Clarkson, Ian	**43**		3		2					
Cranson, Ian	**23**	*1*		*1*	1		**1**			**1**
Devlin, Mark	**5**	*5*								
Dreyer, John	**4**	*15*			1					
Gayle, John	**5**	*5*				*1*	**3**			**3**
Gleghorn. Nigel	**46**		3		2		**9**			**9**
Keen, Kevin	**27**	*6*	2		2		**3**			**3**
Muggleton, Carl	**6**									
Orlygsson, Toddy	**6**	*1*								
Overson, Vince	**18**		3							
Peschisolido, Paul	**20**	*6*	3		1		**6**	1		**7**
Potter, Graham	**38**	*3*	3		2		**1**			**1**
Prudhoe, Mark	**39**		3		2					
Sandford, Lee	**46**		3		2					
Scott, Keith	**6**	*1*								
Sheron, Mike	**23**	*5*					**15**			**15**
Sigurdsson, Larus	**46**		3		2					
Sinclair, Ronnie	**1**									
Sturridge, Simon	**30**	*11*	1		2		**13**		1	**14**
Wallace, Ray	**44**		3		2		**6**			**6**
Whittle, Justin	**7**	*1*								
24 Players used	**506**	***78***	**33**	***1***	**22**	***1***	**60**	**1**	**1**	**62**

NATIONWIDE DIVISION 1 — Manager: Lou Macari — SEASON 1996-97

No	Date		Att	Pos	Pt	F-A	H-T	Scorers, Times, and Referees	1	2	3	4	5	6	7	8	9	10	11	subs used
1	A	OLDHAM			W	2-1	2-0	Sheron 27, 43	Prudhoe*	**Pickering**	Dreyer	Sigurdsson	Cranson	**Forsyth**	**Worthingt'n**	Wallace	Gayle	Sheron	Beeston	Devlin^/Keen
	17/8		*8,021*		3			*Redmond 76*	*Hallworth*	*Halle*	*Serrant*	*Fleming*	*Graham*	*Redmond*	*Orlygsson**	*Richardson*	*McCarthy*	*Barlow^*	*Rickers*	*Beresford/Morrow*
								Ref: U Rennie	Sheron pokes in a long punt and nets when Gayle's shot is parried. Latics have goals ruled out for two fouls on Prudhoe. He is injured – Cranson takes over (31 mins). In the sweltering heat Cranson makes two good saves. Redmond buries a short free-kick. First win at Oldham for 9 years.											
2	H	MANCHESTER C		5	W	2-1	2-0	Forsyth 27, Sheron 32	Muggleton	Pickering	Dreyer	Sigurdsson	Cranson	Forsyth	Worthington	Wallace	Sturridge*	Sheron^	Beeston	Gayle/**Macari**
	24/8		21,116	*15*	6			*Rosler 58*	*Immel*	*Brightwell*	*Kernaghan*	*Lomas*	*Symons*	*Brown**	*Summerbee*	*Clough*	*Kavelashvili^*	*Kinkladze*	*Rosler*	*Phillips/Dickov*
								Ref: I Cruikshanks	Stoke open the last ever season at the Vic with a good win over the promotion favourites. Sturridge's effort is only parried and Forsyth taps in. Sheron outpaces Kit Symons to score. Rosler picks up a loose ball to pull one back, but Man C are awful. Alan Ball resigns as their manager.											
3	H	BRADFORD C		2	W	1-0	0-0	Sheron 90p	Muggleton	Pickering	Dreyer	Sigurdsson	Cranson	Forsyth	Sturridge*	Wallace	Gayle	Sheron	Beeston	Keen
	28/8		11,918	*12*	9				*Roberts*	*Liburd*	*Mitchell*	*Cowans*	*Mohan*	*Sas*	*Hamilton*	*Duxbury*	*Shutt*	*Stalard*	*Kiwomya*	
								Ref: E Lomas	City attack from the off. Sheron fires just wide. The much-improved Gayle holds the ball up well. He loops a header just over. Chris Kamara's Bantams threaten via the dangerous Andy Kiwomya. Sheron is tripped by Richard Liburd in the 3rd minute of injury-time and bangs in the pen.											
4	A	READING		1	D	2-2	1-1	Sheron 25, Forsyth 76	Muggleton	Pickering	Dreyer	Sigurdsson	Cranson	Forsyth	Gayle^	Wallace	Sturridge	Sheron	Beeston*	Keen/**Da Costa**
	31/8		*8,414*	*15*	10			*Morley 7p, Holsgrove 79*	*Bibbo*	*Booty*	*Bodin*	*Holsgrove*	*Hopkins*	*Wdowczyk*	*Parkinson^*	*Williams*	*Morley*	*Nogan**	*Gooding*	*Lovell/Gilkes*
								Ref: A Butler	Morley's penalty goes in via a post after Cranson trips Booty. Sheron curls in a superb free-kick. On-loan Hugo Da Costa (Benfica) appears as Macari opts for five at the back. Forsyth cracks in from 20 yards. Paul Holsgrove blazes a volley home. City are top as Bolton have yet to play.											
5	H	CRYSTAL PALACE		3	D	2-2	2-2	Sheron 20, Dreyer 32	Muggleton	Pickering	Dreyer	Sigurdsson	Cranson	Forsyth	Worthington	Wallace	Sturridge*	Sheron	Beeston	Gayle
	7/9		13,540	*12*	11			*Hopkin 13, Freedman 22*	*Day*	*Edworthy*	*Muscat*	*Roberts*	*Tuttle*	*Hopkin*	*Boxall^*	*Houghton*	*Freedman**	*Dyer*	*Veart*	*Ndah/Andersen*
								Ref: K Lynch	Dave Bassett's Eagles take the game to Stoke. Hopkin scores from 20 yards. Sheron beats Day when clean through. Freedman turns to fire past Muggers. Sturridge is fouled, but Sheron's penalty hits the post (26 mins). Dreyer nods in Pickering's centre. Macari is Manager of the Month.											
6	A	BARNSLEY		5	L	0-3	0-1		Muggleton	Pickering	Dreyer	Sigurdsson	Cranson	Forsyth	Worthingt'n^	Wallace	Sturridge*	Sheron	Beeston	Gayle/Macari
	10/9		*11,696*	*1*	11			*Davis 17, Thompson 88, Liddell 90*	*Watson*	*Eaden*	*Appleby*	*Sheridan**	*Davis*	*De Zeeuw*	*Marcelle*	*Redfearn*	*Wilkinson^*	*Liddell*	*Thompson*	*Baosncic/Regis*
								Ref: R Pearson	Danny Wilson's Tykes pull Stoke all over the park. Steve Davis heads in one of numerous corners. The remorseless pressure tells as City snap. Neil Thompson thumps home a great 30-yarder and Andy Liddell finishes with a flourish. Barnsley retain the only 100% record in the division.											
7	A	BIRMINGHAM		7	L	1-3	0-2	Forsyth 66	Muggleton	Pickering	Dreyer	Sigurdsson	Da Costa	Forsyth	Worthingt'n*	Wallace	Gayle	Sheron	Beeston^	Keen/**Kavanagh**
	14/9		*18,612*	*15*	11			*Furlong 2, 65, Legg 32*	*Bennett*	*Poole*	*Ablett*	*Bruce*	*Breen*	*Holland*	*Bowen^*	*Newell**	*Furlong"*	*Horne*	*Legg*	*Devlin/Castle/Donowa*
								Ref: E Wolstenholme	Lack of depth in the squad is exposed. Da Costa starts but will return to Portugal. Muggers' clearance is blocked and Furlong mops up. Players are left unmarked for the other goals. Forsyth scores against his old club. Graham Kavanagh, loaned by Middlesbro', replaces the hurt Beeston.											
8	H	HUDDERSFIELD		4	W	3-2	1-2	Gayle 41, Sheron 77, 85	Muggleton	Pickering	Worthington	Sigurdsson	Dreyer	Devlin*	**McMahon**	Wallace	Gayle	Sheron	Kavanagh	Keen
	22/9		9,147	*14*	14			*Worthington 7 (og), Stewart 36*	*Francis*	*Jenkins*	*Cowan*	*Bullock*	*Sinnott**	*Gray*	*Makel^*	*Burnett*	*Stewart*	*Payton*	*Lawson"*	*Collins/Edwards/Reid*
								Ref: C Wilkes	An amazing comeback in front of the TV cameras. Worthington nets a dreadful own-goal before Stewart scores with Town's first shot on goal. Incessant pressure tells when Gayle turns to fire in. Sheron scores two superb goals to snatch victory. Gerry McMahon (Spurs) signs for £250k.											
9	A	BOLTON		6	D	1-1	0-1	Kavanagh 90	Muggleton	Pickering	Worthington	Sigurdsson	Dreyer	Forsyth	Devlin^	Wallace	Gayle*	Sheron	Kavanagh	Keen/McMahon
	28/9		*16,195*	*1*	15			*Blake 42*	*Branagan*	*Bergsson*	*Phillips*	*Frandsen*	*Taggart*	*Fairclough*	*Johansen^*	*Sellars**	*Blake*	*McGinlay"*	*Thompson*	*Lee/Todd/Taylor*
								Ref: F Stretton	Leaders Bolton dominate. Muggers saves a Frandsen free-kick. Fairclough blasts wide. Nathan Blake picks up Sigurdsson's weak back-pass to score. Colin Todd's Trotters pile on the pressure but Kavanagh grabs a point, put in by Forsyth. Macari is linked with the vacancy at Man City.											
10	A	PORT VALE		8	D	1-1	0-0	Keen 65	Muggleton	Pickering	Worthington	Sigurdsson	Dreyer	Forsyth	Devlin"	Wallace	McMahon*	Sheron^	Kavanagh	Keen/ Macari/Whittle
	13/10		*14,396*	*17*	16			*Mills 90*	*V Heusden*	*Hill**	*Tankard*	*Porter*	*Griffiths*	*Aspin"*	*McCarthy*	*Bogie^*	*Talbot*	*Naylor*	*Guppy*	*Foyle/Mills/Glover*
								Ref: K Leach	Kavanagh's £250,000 fee is confirmed by Boro. Sheron signs for a further two years. He wants premiership football but won't find it with City if they concede more late strikes. Lee Mills heads home a cross in the fifth minute of injury-time after Keen loops a header over Van Heusden.											
11	A	WEST BROM		7	W	2-0	1-0	Wallace 33, Forsyth 72	Muggleton	Pickering	Worthington	Sigurdsson	Dreyer	Forsyth	Devlin*	Wallace	Gayle"	Sheron^	Kavanagh	Keen/Macari/Whittle
	16/10		*16,501*	*14*	19				*Crichton*	*Holmes**	*Nicholson*	*Sneekes*	*Mardon*	*Burgess*	*Hamilton*	*Gilbert^*	*Ashcroft*	*Hunt*	*Groves*	*Taylor/Peschisolido*
								Ref: D Allison	Albion's methodical play is easily snuffed out by Sigurdsson and Dreyer. Wallace is superb in midfield. He starts and ends a move, converting Gayle's cross. Forsyth relieves the mounting pressure with a great strike off the bar. Ten wins and a draw in the last eleven against the Baggies.											

No	Venue	Opponent / Date	Att	Pos	Res	Score	H-T	Scorers, Times, and Referees	1	2	3	4	5	6	7	8	9	10	11	subs used
12	H	SHEFFIELD UTD		10	L	**0-4**	0-3		Muggleton	Pickering	Whittle	Sigurdsson	Dreyer	Forsyth	Devlin^	Wallace	Gayle*	Sheron	Kavanagh	Keen/McMahon
		19/10	13,581	*6*	19			*Vonk 8, 19, Walker 16, Taylor 77*	*Kelly*	*Ward*	*Sandford*	*Hutchison^*	*Vonk*	*Holdsworth*	*White*	*Patterson*	*Katchuro**	*Walker*	*Whitehouse*	*Taylor/Hawes*
								Ref: P Rejer	Three defensive changes allow United to score unmarked headers from their first three corners. City's discipline is in tatters. Muggers fumbles the ball for the third. Sheron has a goal ruled out for offside but Taylor scores on the turn. Macari is linked to Anderlecht full-back Isaac Asare.											
13	H	PORTSMOUTH		7	W	**3-1**	0-1	McMahon 59, 75, Sheron 71	Muggleton	Devlin	Worthington	Sigurdsson	Whittle	Forsyth	McMahon	Wallace^	Keen"	Sheron*	Kavanagh	Macari/**Griffin/Mackenzie**
		26/10	10,259	*20*	22			*Bradbury 37*	*Flahavan*	*Whitbread*	*Russell"*	*McLoughlin*	*Perrett*	*Awford*	*Carter**	*Simpson !*	*Bradbury*	*Durnin*	*Turner^*	*Hall/Igoe/Thomson*
								Ref: W Burns	Stoke play well, but Pompey net from a corner. The tables are turned when Fitzroy Simpson is deservedly sent off (53 mins). City take charge. McMahon's second is a gem. Sheron scores via a deflection. Mackenzie and Griffin come on despite playing for the A-team four hours earlier.											
14	A	OXFORD		9	L	1-4	0-2	Sheron 59	Muggleton	Devlin	Worthingt'n^	Sigurdsson	Whittle	Forsyth	McMahon	Wallace	Keen*	Sheron	Kavanagh	Macari/Griffin
		29/10	*6,381*	*13*	22			*Gray 5, Angel 27, Jemson 78, Aldridge 80*	*Whitehead*	*Robinson*	*Ford M*	*Smith*	*Elliott*	*Purse*	*Angel**	*Gray*	*Aldridge^*	*Jemson*	*Beauchamp*	*Rush/Moody*
								Ref: M Bailey	City's pedestrian full-backs are exposed by Denis Smith's use of nippy wingers. Oxford score their first goals in 592 minutes. Joey Beauchamp crosses for Gray and Angel to finish. Sheron turns in a flash to notch a beauty but City capitulate. The unhappy Dreyer is to move to Bradford.											
15	A	QP RANGERS		9	D	1-1	1-0	Kavanagh 4	Muggleton	Pickering	Worthingt'n^	Sigurdsson	Whittle	Forsyth	McMahon	Wallace	Keen*	Sheron	Kavanagh	Devlin/Griffin
		2/11	7,354	*11*	23			*Sinclair 65*	*Sommer*	*Graham*	*Brevett*	*Barker*	*McDonald*	*Ready*	*Brazier**	*Murray*	*Dichio*	*Slade*	*Sinclair*	*Impey*
								Ref: A D'Urso	City are poor but Kavanagh waltzes through a stunned Rangers' back four to score joyously. Backs to the wall as Stewart Houston's men pour forward. Finally Trevor Sinclair's overhead kick beats Muggers. A battling point. Sturridge's knee operation will keep him out for five months.											
16	A	GRIMSBY		10	D	1-1	1-1	Forsyth 30	Muggleton	Pickering	Devlin	Sigurdsson	Whittle	Forsyth	McMahon"	Wallace	Keen*	Sheron	Kavanagh^	Macari/Griffin/Carruthers
		16/11	*5,601*	*24*	24			*Mendonca 20p*	*Pearcey*	*Jobling**	*Gallimore*	*Smith*	*Rodger*	*Widdrington*	*Childs^*	*Livingstone*	*Mendonca*	*Shakespeare*	*Black*	*Fickling/Forrester*
								Ref: G Pooley	Forsyth makes amends for tripping Childs for the penalty by firing a fine low shot past Jason Pearcey. Kenny Swain is Town's second manager in as many games. Muggers pulls off a great double save. Loanee Mirko Taccola returns to Napoli after the Italians refuse to clear him to play.											
17	H	SOUTHEND		12	L	1-2	0-1	Forsyth 52	Prudhoe	Pickering*	Devlin"	Sigurdsson	Whittle	Forsyth	**Stein**	Wallace	Keen^	Sheron	Kavanagh	Macari/McMahon/Griffin
		23/11	12,821	*17*	24			*Williams 37, Sigurdsson 51 (og)*	*Royce*	*Harris*	*Dublin*	*McNally*	*Lapper**	*Nielsen*	*Gridelet*	*Hails^*	*Rammell*	*Williams*	*Tilson*	*Stimson/Byrne"/Boere*
								Ref: A Leake	Ian Cranson announces his retirement through injury and is given a standing ovation before kick-off. How Stoke miss him as Ronnie Whelan's Southend grab a goal on the break. Then Sigurdsson slices past Prudhoe. On-loan Mark Stein wastes a one-on-one. Forsyth nets from 12 yards.											
18	A	PORTSMOUTH		18	L	0-1	0-1		Prudhoe	Pickering	Devlin"	Sigurdsson	Whittle	Forsyth	Griffin	Wallace	Stein^	McMahon*	Kavanagh	Gayle/Macari/**Stokoe**
		30/11	*7,749*	*11*	24			*Turner 4*	*Flahavan*	*Whitbread*	*Thomson*	*McLoughlin*	*Perrett*	*Igoe*	*Carter**	*Simpson*	*Bradbury*	*Durnin*	*Turner*	*Hall*
								Ref: C Wilkes	Stoke are even worse than dreadful Pompey. Without Sheron, whose wife has given birth, Stoke fail to score away from home for the first time in 10 games. Andy Turner heads in Carter's corner. Dreyer's fee is set at a measly £25k. Carruthers joins Posh. A tribunal to decide the fee too.											
19	H	CHARLTON		15	W	1-0	0-0	Sheron 49	Prudhoe	Pickering	Griffin	Sigurdsson	Whittle	Forsyth	McMahon	Wallace	Stein*	Sheron	Kavanagh^	Macari/Mackenzie
		4/12	**7,456**	*12*	27				*Salmon*	*Poole*	*Barness*	*O'Connell*	*Rufus*	*Chapple*	*Newton**	*Leaburn*	*Robinson^*	*Whyte*	*Kinsella*	*Lisbie/Robson*
								Ref: R Poulain	Both sides revert to route one football. The loudest cheer arrives when Prudhoe bowls the ball out instead of kicking. Sheron celebrates his first child by burying the rebound when Stein's effort is parried. Stein then blazes over. A lucky win in front of the lowest league crowd since 1991.											
20	H	TRANMERE		10	W	2-0	1-0	Sheron 27, Higgins 82 (og)	Prudhoe	Pickering	Griffin	Sigurdsson	Whittle	Forsyth^	McMahon	Wallace	Stein	Sheron	Kavanagh*	Mackenzie/Keen
		7/12	9,931	*6*	30				*Nixon*	*Stevens*	*Irons**	*Higgins*	*Teale*	*O'Brien*	*Brannan*	*Aldridge*	*Thomas*	*Nevin^*	*Cook*	*Morrissey/Jones*
								Ref: R Harris	Sheron outshines the prolific John Aldridge. He stabs home to finish a good right-wing move. Young Andy Griffin impresses at left-back. Stein and Sheron begin to combine well up front. Sheron squares after rounding Eric Nixon and Dave Higgins runs the ball into his own net. Bizarre.											
21	H	SWINDON		7	W	2-0	1-0	Stein 44, 64	Prudhoe	Pickering	Griffin	Sigurdsson	Whittle	Forsyth	Devlin*	Wallace	Stein	Sheron	Kavanagh	Mackenzie
		14/12	10,102	*13*	33				*Digby*	*Kerslake*	*Elkins*	*O'Sullivan^*	*Robinson*	*Darras**	*Culverhouse*	*Watson*	*Cowe*	*Allison*	*Walters"*	*Collins/Smith/McMahon*
								Ref: A Kaye	Steve McMahon's under-strength Swindon struggle. Fraser Digby's clearance hits Stein but he recovers to save. Sigurdsson's overhead kick is touched over. Stein nets two classic goals as he rediscovers his sharpness in front of goal. Prudhoe pulls off a superb stop from Wayne Allison.											
22	A	IPSWICH		8	D	1-1	1-1	Sheron 23	Prudhoe	Pickering	Griffin	Sigurdsson	Whittle	Forsyth	McMahon	Wallace	Stein*	Sheron	Kavanagh^	Macari/Mackenzie
		21/12	*10,159*	*14*	34			*Mason 45*	*Wright*	*Stockwell**	*Taricco*	*Cundy*	*Sedgley*	*Williams*	*Uhlenbeek*	*Sonner*	*Naylor^*	*Scowcroft*	*Mason*	*Tanner/Jean*
								Ref: P Taylor	City start on top. Sheron volleys a brilliant goal from the angle of the penalty box into the far top corner. George Burley's men swarm forward and after a scramble Paul Mason nets. Stein blazes over from two yards after McMahon's mazy run. Wright pulls off a great save from Sheron.											
23	H	BARNSLEY		7	W	1-0	0-0	Sheron 72	Prudhoe	Pickering	Griffin	Sigurdsson	Whittle	Forsyth*	McMahon	Wallace	Stein	Sheron	Kavanagh	Devlin
		26/12	19,025	*3*	37				*Watson*	*Eaden*	*Appleby*	*Bosancic"*	*Davis*	*De Zeeuw*	*Hendrie*	*Jones^*	*Wilkinson*	*Marcelle**	*Sheridan !*	*Liddell/Bullock/Moses*
								Ref: T Heilbron	A frenetic game sees Prudhoe tip over Marcelle's effort. Wallace rampages forward at will. Sheridan loses it and walks for elbowing Kavanagh in front of the referee (52 mins). Sheron belts an angled drive past Watson. Kav hits the bar. Pickering clears off the line with Prudhoe beaten.											

No	Date		Att	Pos	Pt	F-A	H-T	Scorers, Times, and Referees	1	2	3	4	5	6	7	8	9	10	11	subs used
24	A	HUDDERSFIELD		9	L	1-2	1-1	Stein 18	Prudhoe	Pickering*	Griffin	Sigurdsson	Whittle	Forsyth	McMahon	Wallace	Stein	Sheron"	Kavanagh^	Devlin/Macari/Stokoe
	1/1		*12,019*	*12*	37			*Makel 6, Edwards 63*	*Norman*	*Jenkins*	*Cowan*	*Bullock*	*Sinnott**	*Heary*	*Makel*	*Crosby*	*Lawson*	*Payton*	*Edwards*	*Dyson*
								Ref: N Barry	Macari is Manager of the Month again. Prudhoe is cheered by both sets of fans after last year's comic performance and he is soon at it again, allowing Lee Makel to fire the orange ball past him from 35 yards and spilling Edwards' effort which trickles in. Stein cracks home left footed.											
25	H	BIRMINGHAM		7	W	1-0	1-0	Wallace 18	Prudhoe	Pickering	Griffin	Sigurdsson	Whittle	Forsyth	McMahon	Wallace	Stein	Sheron	Kavanagh	
	10/1		10,049	*15*	40				*Bennett*	*Brown*	*Grainger*	*Bruce*	*Johnson*	*O'Connor*	*Devlin*	*Tait*	*Legg**	*Horne*	*Bowen^*	*Furlong/Bass*
								Ref: R Furnandiz	Forsyth's cross-shot finds Wallace who forces the ball home from close in. A tight match becomes trickier as the conditions take an Arctic turn. £4m is needed to finish constructing the new ground. Millionaire Uttoxeter racecourse owner Stan Clarke is reportedly interested in investing.											
26	A	CHARLTON		5	W	2-1	2-0	Sheron 42, 43	Prudhoe	Pickering	Griffin	Sigurdsson	Whittle	Forsyth	McMahon	Wallace	Stein	Sheron*	Kavanagh	Macari
	18/1		*9,901*	*16*	43			*Barness 49*	*Petterson*	*Brown**	*Barness*	*O'Connell*	*Rufus*	*Chapple*	*Newton"*	*Leaburn*	*Robson*	*Whyte^*	*Kinsella*	*Jones/Robinson/Lisbie*
								Ref: D Orr	Prudhoe allows a Kinsella shot to squirm out of his hands but the ball spins past the post. Mike Sheron grabs two brilliant predatorial goals. He flicks in Stein's low cross and fires home with the inside of his foot from Kav's slide rule pass. Barness' swerving shot flies in at the near post.											
27	H	NORWICH		7	L	1-2	1-2	Stein 14	Prudhoe	Pickering^	Griffin	Sigurdsson	Whittle	Forsyth*	McMahon	Wallace	Stein	Sheron	Kavanagh	Macari/Mackenzie
	22/1		10,179	*5*	43			*O'Neill 4, Eadie 11*	*Gunn*	*Newman*	*Jackson*	*Eadie*	*Scott Kevin*	*Sutch*	*Adams*	*Crook^*	*Rocastle*	*Carey*	*O'Neill**	*Scott Keith/Ottosson*
								Ref: M Bailey	O'Neill and Eadie crack home balls over the top and Norwich defend in depth. Stein bids farewell with a tap-in. The new ground will be called the Britannia Stadium as the Building Society will be its sponsor for 10 years. Sheron is runner-up in Sky TV's Nationwide Player of the Year.											
28	H	BOLTON		7	L	1-2	0-1	Macari 84	Muggleton	Pickering*	Griffin	Sigurdsson	Whittle	Forsyth	McMahon	Wallace	Mackenzie	Sheron	Kavanagh	Macari
	29/1		15,645	*1*	43			*Pollock 28, McGinlay 54*	*Ward*	*Bergsson*	*Small*	*Pollock*	*Taggart*	*Fairclough*	*Frandsen*	*Sellars*	*Blake !*	*McGinlay*	*Thompson*	
								Ref: I Cruikshanks	Leaders Bolton give City a footballing lesson. Pollock strokes in to finish a fine move. Blake is sent off (40 mins) for poleaxing Sigurdsson, but TV replays suggest a dive. Ten-man Trotters remain in charge. McGinlay shrugs off Whittle to calmly beat Muggers. Macari swivels to fire in.											
29	A	WOLVES		9	L	0-2	0-1		Muggleton	Pickering*	Griffin	Sigurdsson	Whittle	Forsyth	McMahon	Wallace	Macari	Sheron	Kavanagh	Devlin
	1/4		*27,408*	*2*	43			*Bull 16, 55*	*Stowell*	*Thompson*	*Froggatt*	*Atkins*	*Williams*	*Curle*	*Corica*	*Emblen*	*Bull*	*Goodman**	*Osborn*	*Roberts*
								Ref: R Poulain	Steve Bull is the difference, exposing City's weak defence. He powers in a floated Froggatt free-kick and stoops to head home Emblen's cross. Macari heads just over the bar. West Ham offer £2.7m for Sheron. Mike Moors resigns from the board after his offer to inject funds is refused.											
30	H	OXFORD		7	W	2-1	2-0	Mackenzie 9, Macari 37	Muggleton	Mackenzie	Griffin	Sigurdsson	Whittle	Forsyth	McMahon	Wallace	Macari	Sheron*	Kavanagh	**Nyamah**
	7/2		8,609	*13*	46			*Moody 88*	*Whitehead*	*Robinson*	*Ford M*	*Smith*	*Purse**	*Gilchrist*	*Angel*	*Gray*	*Gabbiadini^*	*Jemson"*	*Beauchamp*	*Ford B/Aldridge/Moody*
								Ref: S Mathieson	A young Stoke side make it three out of three on Sky TV. Sheron's shot is blocked but Neil Mackenzie finishes coolly. His confidence boosted Mackenzie runs midfield and forces Whitehead into a sharp save. Macari cracks in after U's twice hit the bar. Moody nets with his first touch.											
31	A	SOUTHEND		7	L	1-2	0-1	Harris 70 (og)	Muggleton	Devlin	Griffin	Sigurdsson	Whittle	**Rodger^**	McMahon	Wallace*	Macari	Sheron	Kavanagh	Mackenzie/Nyamah
	15/2		***4,625***	*21*	46			*Thomson 34, Rammell 89*	*Royce*	*Harris*	*Dublin*	*McNally*	*Roget*	*Poric*	*Gridelet*	*Byrne*	*Boere"*	*Thomson**	*Hails^*	*Williams/Nielsen/Rammell*
								Ref: M Pierce	Sheron's header hits the bar. McMahon wastes two good chances. Andy Thomson cracks a great shot home. Stoke keep pressing and a Sheron shot rebounds off the keeper and Harris into the net. Andy Rammell fires into the top corner seconds after coming on. Sigurdsson's 100th game.											
32	H	QP RANGERS		10	D	0-0	0-0		Muggleton	Mackenzie	Griffin	Sigurdsson	Whittle	Pickering	McMahon	Rodger*	Macari	Wallace	Kavanagh	Nyamah
	22/2		13,121	*12*	47				*Sommer*	*Yates*	*Brevett*	*Barker*	*McDonald*	*Ready*	*Murray*	*Peacock*	*Hateley*	*Dichio**	*Sinclair*	*Charles*
								Ref: R Pearson	Sheron is out with a neck strain. Simon Rodger, on loan from Palace, makes his home debut. Gavin Peacock's volley skims the bar. Stoke have 17 shots but Jurgen Sommer saves well from Mackenzie and Kav. An absorbing game peters out. John Gayle is sold to Northampton for £25k.											
33	A	TRANMERE		10	D	0-0	0-0		Muggleton	Pickering	Griffin	Sigurdsson	Whittle	Rodger*	McMahon^	Wallace	Macari	Sheron	Kavanagh	Mackenzie/Nyamah
	28/2		*9,127*	*11*	48				*Nixon*	*Thomas*	*Rogers*	*Challinor*	*Higgins*	*O'Brien*	*Brannan*	*Moore*	*Branch^*	*Irons**	*Nevin*	*Aldridge/Mahon*
								Ref: P Rejer	Debutant Dave Challinor introduces City to his incredible long throw which causes panic in the defence. Nevin takes on Griffin but the 17-year-old emerges on top. Muggers saves when Ian Moore is clean through. Sheron muffs an easy chance. Sixth clean sheet in a row against Rovers.											
34	H	GRIMSBY		8	W	**3-1**	0-1	Southall 48 (og), Kavanagh 50, Griffin 78	Muggleton	Pickering	Griffin	Sigurdsson	Whittle	Rodger*	McMahon^	Wallace	Macari	Sheron	Kavanagh	Mackenzie/Nyamah
	5/3		8,621	*23*	51			*Livingstone 25*	*Love*	*Fickling*	*Shakespeare*	*Rodger*	*Southall*	*Widdrington*	*Appleton*	*Livingstone^*	*Woods*	*Mendonca*	*Oster**	*Childs/Lester*
								Ref: E Lomas	The first half is littered with errors. Steve Livingstone steals beyond Whittle to steer a long ball past Muggers. On a heavy pitch Nicky Southall turns Sheron's cross into his own net. Kav rockets a free-kick in and suddenly it's party time. Griffin plays a one-two with Mackenzie to score.											

No	Date	Opponent	Att	Pos	Res	F-A	H-T	Scorers, Times, and Referees	1	2	3	4	5	6	7	8	9	10	11	subs used
35	H	IPSWICH		9	L	0-1	0-1		Muggleton	Pickering	Griffin	Sigurdsson	Whittle	Rodger*	McMahon^	Wallace	Macari	Sheron	Kavanagh	Mackenzie/Nyamah
	8/3		11,933	*6*	51			*Taricco 7*	*Wright*	*Mowbray*	*Taricco*	*Vaughan*	*Swailes*	*Williams*	*Dyer*	*Sonner*	*Naylor^*	*Scowcroft*	*Mason**	*Milton/Gregory*
								Ref: E Wolstenholme	A sterile display. Mauricio Taricco pounces on a loose ball after a free-kick is not cleared. Town are quicker to the ball. Even Ally Pickering's new red boots cannot inspire Stoke. Muggers saves brilliantly from Jamie Scowcroft's flying header. Macari blasts Nyamah's cross over. Poor.											
36	A	SWINDON		12	L	0-1	0-1		Muggleton	Pickering	Griffin	Sigurdsson	Whittle	Forsyth	McMahon*	Beeston	Macari	Sheron	Kavanagh^	Keen/Mackenzie
	15/3		*8,878*	*10*	51			*Thorne 26*	*Digby*	*Robinson*	*Drysdale^*	*Bullock*	*Watson*	*Broomes*	*Culverhouse*	*Cowe"*	*Thorne**	*Allison !*	*Smith*	*Finney/Elkins/Pattimore*
								Ref: B Knight	The Robins react to a 0-7 thrashing at Bolton by stifling jaded City. Justin Whittle misses a clearing header and Peter Thorne slips the ball past Muggleton. Wayne Allison is dismissed for elbowing Whittle (27 mins) but Stoke fail to take advantage despite having 25 shots to Town's six.											
37	H	WOLVES		9	W	1-0	0-0	Forsyth 47	Muggleton	Pickering	Griffin	Sigurdsson	Whittle	Forsyth	McMahon*	Wallace	Macari	Sheron	Beeston	Kavanagh
	18/3		15,683	*2*	54				*Stowell*	*Thompson*	*Venus*	*Atkins*	*Emblen*	*Curle*	*Corica**	*Thomas"*	*Bull*	*Roberts*	*Osborn^*	*Ferguson/Goodman/Dennison*
								Ref: J Kirkby	Corica and Bull miss good chances straight from the kick-off for Mark McGhee's Wolves. A dour game is lit up by Forsyth's left-footed curler beyond the despairing Mike Stowell. Steve Bull hits the post and forces Muggleton into two brilliant saves. The play-offs are still a possibility.											
38	A	MANCHESTER C		9	L	0-2	0-0		Muggleton	Pickering*	Griffin	Sigurdsson	Whittle	Forsyth	McMahon^	Beeston	Wallace	Sheron	Kavanagh	Devlin/Mackenzie
	22/3		***28,497***	*15*	54			*Atkinson 65, Lomas 68*	*Wright*	*Brightwell*	*McGoldrick*	*Lomas*	*Symons*	*Brannan*	*Summerbee*	*Atkinson**	*Horlock*	*Kinkladze*	*Rosler*	*Kavelashvili*
								Ref: T Lunt	The kick-off is delayed due to a small fire. Wallace goes man-to-man on Kinkladze. He is quiet but Stoke rarely threaten. Griffin slices against his own bar. Debutant Dalian Atkinson nods in McGoldrick's cross. Steve Lomas repeats the feat. Stoke give up. QPR offer £2.5m for Sheron.											
39	H	OLDHAM		10	W	2-1	2-0	Sheron 17, Macari 40	Muggleton	Pickering	Griffin	Sigurdsson	Whittle	Forsyth	**Flynn**	Beeston*	Macari	Sheron	Wallace	Kavanagh
	29/3		11,755	*23*	57			*Barlow 87*	*Kelly*	*Duxbury*	*Serrant*	*Snodin*	*Hodgson*	*Fleming*	*Rush^*	*Rickers**	*McCarthy"*	*Barlow*	*Reid*	*Graham/Richardson/Ritchie*
								Ref: P Richards	Oldham are awful. City lack confidence. Sheron sees his penalty, for a foul on Wallace, saved but he nicks in the rebound. Macari scores when put clear by Forsyth. Kav whacks an 89th-min pen against the post. Stan Clarke takes a third share in Stoke, installing Paul Doona on the board.											
40	A	BRADFORD C		11	L	0-1	0-0		Muggleton	Wallace	Griffin	Sigurdsson !	Whittle	Forsyth	**McNally**	Beeston	Macari	Sheron	Flynn*	Mackenzie
	31/3		*13,579*	*21*	57			*Pepper 49*	*Davison*	*Liburd**	*Jacobs*	*Dreyer*	*Mohan*	*O'Brien*	*Murray*	*Kulcsar*	*Newell*	*Edinho*	*Pepper*	*Wilder*
								Ref: G Frankland	Nigel Pepper cracks in a 20-yarder. Controversy as the referee awards a penalty after Sigurdsson and Edinho clash. Siggy is sent off. Muggers saves the feeble kick. Newell stays on the pitch after a terrible foul on new boy McNally. Angry Macari is banished to the stand for protesting.											
41	H	READING		11	D	1-1	0-1	Forsyth 65	Muggleton	Devlin^	Griffin	Sigurdsson	Whittle	Forsyth	Flynn*	Wallace	Macari	McMahon	Beeston	Kavanagh/Mackenzie
	5/4		9,961	*17*	58			*Lambert 1*	*Mautone*	*Bernal*	*Bodin*	*Parkinson*	*Blatherwick*	*McPherson*	*Lambert*	*Williams**	*Quinn^*	*Nogan"*	*Gooding*	*Meaker/Holsgrove/Lovell*
								Ref: W Burns	A cataclysmic start as Whittle and Muggleton mess up a clearance and James Lambert lobs home. Boos all around the ground. Stoke take time to regroup. More inept defending sets up Jimmy Quinn but he blazes wide. McMahon's shot is charged down and Forsyth fires in the rebound.											
42	A	NORWICH		13	L	0-2	0-1		Muggleton	McNally	Griffin"	Sigurdsson	Whittle^	Forsyth	Kavanagh*	Wallace	Macari	McMahon	Mackenzie	Pickering/Beeston/Devlin
	12/4		*13,805*	*7*	58			*O'Neill 1, Eadie 53*	*Marshall*	*Newman*	*Jackson*	*Crook*	*Bradshaw*	*Sutch*	*Adams*	*Fleck^*	*Milligan**	*Eadie*	*O'Neill"*	*Mills/Polston/Broughton*
								Ref: M Bailey	Mike Walker's Canaries stroll to victory after Keith O'Neill rams in Kav's poor back-pass after 12 seconds. Despite having 89 minutes to level, Stoke only trouble Andy Marshall when Forsyth's shot is saved. Norwich pile on the pressure. Eadie runs onto O'Neill's through-ball to score.											
43	A	CRYSTAL PALACE		13	L	0-2	0-2		Muggleton	Flynn	Griffin	Pickering	Whittle	Forsyth	Beeston^	Wallace	Macari	McMahon"	Mackenzie*	Kavanagh/Devlin/Nyamah
	15/4		*11,382*	*7*	58			*Dyer 6, 21*	*Nash*	*Edworthy*	*Gordon*	*Roberts*	*Davies*	*Linighan*	*Hopkin**	*Houghton*	*Shipperley"*	*Dyer^*	*Rodger*	*Muscat/Freedman/McKenzie*
								Ref: U Rennie	The season limps to a conclusion. City fans cheer when the Potters get through the first 60 seconds unscathed. It doesn't last long. Bruce Dyer curls in after skipping past Pickering and nods Shipperley's cross home. Macari has a good shot saved by Carlo Nash. Palace into the play-offs.											
44	H	PORT VALE		13	W	2-0	1-0	Sheron 44, 85	Muggleton	Pickering	Griffin	Sigurdsson	Whittle	Forsyth	Flynn*	Wallace	Macari	Sheron	Beeston^	McMahon/Mackenzie
	20/4		16,246	*6*	61				*Musselwhite*	*Hill*	*Tankard*	*Bogie*	*Aspin*	*Glover*	*McCarthy^*	*Porter*	*Mills*	*Naylor*	*Koordes**	*Talbot/Corden*
								Ref: D Allison	Macari announces he will be stepping down to fight his court case against Celtic at the end of the season. Rumours abound that he was pushed. Beeston's aggression wins the midfield fight. Sheron belts in two corkers, one via an outrageous deflection off Glover, to defeat the arch rivals.											
45	A	SHEFFIELD UTD		13	L	0-1	0-0		Muggleton	Pickering	Griffin	Sigurdsson	Whittle	Forsyth	McNally^	Wallace	McMahon	Sheron	Beeston*	Kavanagh/Mackenzie
	25/4		*25,596*	*4*	61			*Tiler 66*	*Kelly*	*Ward*	*Sandford*	*Hutchison*	*Tiler*	*Holdsworth*	*White*	*Henry*	*Fjortoft*	*Katchuro**	*Whitehouse*	*Scott*
								Ref: I Cruikshanks	Chic Bates and Mike Pejic are in charge. Papers link Dave Webb to the manager's job. United drop admission to £5 and gain their biggest gate all season. Sheron is fouled when clean through but Kelly escapes with a yellow. In a desperate scramble the ball hits Carl Tiler and trickles in.											
46	H	WEST BROM		12	W	2-1	1-0	McMahon 33, Kavanagh 69	Muggleton	Pickering	Griffin	Sigurdsson	Whittle	Forsyth	McMahon	Wallace	Kavanagh	Sheron*	Beeston	Mackenzie
	4/5		**22,500**	*16*	64			*Hunt 85p*	*Miller*	*McDermott*	*Smith*	*Sneekes*	*Murphy*	*Raven*	*Coldicott*	*Butler**	*Peschisolido*	*Hunt*	*Groves^*	*Nicholson/Donovan*
	Home	Away						Ref: R Poulain	In a carnival atmosphere Stoke bid farewell to the oldest league ground in the world. Ex-players including Sir Stan, Jimmy Greenhoff and John Ritchie parade before kick-off. McMahon's flying header and Kav's cheeky lob set the seal on a great day. Whittle trips Hunt, he slots the pen.											
Average	12,748	12,865																		

Coca-Cola Cup	Att		F-A	H-T	Scorers, Times, and Referees	1	2	3	4	5	6	7	8	9	10	11	subs used
2:1 H NORTHAMPTON	7	W	1-0	0-0	Worthington 60	Muggleton	Pickering	Dreyer	Sigurdsson	Devlin	Forsyth*	Worthington	Wallace	Gayle^	Sheron	McMahon"	Keen/Macari/Da Costa
18/9	6,093 *3:20*					*Woodman*	*Clarkson*	*Maddison*	*Sampson*	*Rennie*	*O'Shea*	*Grayson*	*Peer**	*White^*	*Parris*	*Hunter*	*Gibb/Colkin*
					Ref: N Barry	Stoke are second best for most of the match. John Gayle has a nightmare. Andy Woodman denies him well on three occasions. Muggers clears desperately with Jason White bearing down on him and twice denies Grayson. Sheron's shot is saved but falls to Worthington who fires home.											
2:2 A NORTHAMPTON	4	W	2-1	0-0	Sheron 100, 108	Muggleton*	Pickering	Dreyer	Sigurdsson	Devlin	Da Costa^	Worthington	Wallace	Gayle	Sheron	McMahon"	Prudhoe/Macari/Keen
24/9	*5,088 3:20*		*aet*		*Gayle 89 (og)*	*Woodman*	*Clarkson*	*Maddison*	*Sampson*	*Rennie*	*O'Shea*	*Gibb**	*Parrish^*	*Cooper*	*Hunter*	*Colkin"*	*White/Peer/Grayson*
					Ref: G Cain (Stoke win 3-1 on aggregate)	City seem to have survived Ian Atkins' Cobbler's onslaught until Pickering's clearance hits Gayle and rebounds past an astonished Muggleton. Stoke abandon the negative tactics and look good. Sheron flicks the ball over a defender to net before placing Gayle's cross beyond Woodman.											
3 H ARSENAL	10	D	1-1	1-0	Sheron 26	Muggleton	Pickering*	Worthington	Sigurdsson	Dreyer	Forsyth	Whittle	Wallace	Keen	Sheron	Kavanagh	McMahon
23/10	20,804 *P:2*				*Wright 78*	*Seaman*	*Dixon*	*Winterburn*	*Keown*	*Bould*	*Adams*	*Platt*	*Wright*	*Merson*	*Bergkamp**	*Vieira*	*Hartson*
					Ref: K Burge	Arsene Wenger's Gunners are given a stern test by a vibrant Stoke side. Lone striker Sheron is a nuisance to the famed back four. He nips in to turn the ball past David Seaman. Stoke cling on as Arsenal get narked and have five booked. Wright turns well to level with a hint of handball.											
3R A ARSENAL	9	L	2-5	1-1	Sheron 35, 88 *[Merson 73]*	Muggleton	Pickering*	Devlin	Sigurdsson	Whittle	Forsyth	McMahon^	Wallace	Keen"	Sheron	Kavanagh	Griffin/Macari/Carruthers
13/11	*33,962 P:2*				*Wright 41p, 63, Platt 46, Bergkamp 68,*	*Seaman*	*Dixon*	*Winterburn*	*Keown*	*Bould*	*Adams*	*Platt*	*Wright*	*Merson*	*Bergkamp**	*Vieira^*	*Hartson/Morrow*
					Ref: G Willard	Sheron subtly clips the ball past Seaman as Stoke start on top. Bergkamp tumbles theatrically for the pen. Arsenal run riot after half-time. Platt chests in from a yard out. Wright nets from a corner. Bergkamp scores from 20 yards and Merson in a scramble. Sheron flicks in a consolation.											

FA Cup																	
3 H STOCKPORT	7	L	0-2	0-1		Prudhoe	Pickering	Griffin	Sigurdsson	Whittle	Forsyth	McMahon	Wallace	Devlin*	Sheron	Kavanagh^	Macari/Mackenzie
15/1	9,961 *2:5*				*Durkan 25, Armstrong 90*	*Jones*	*Connelly*	*Todd*	*Bennett*	*Flynn*	*Gannon*	*Durkan**	*Marsden*	*Angell^*	*Armstrong*	*Cavaco*	*Dinning/Mutch*
					Ref: A D'Urso	Another atrocious Cup performance sees City lose to lower league opponents yet again. Kieron Durkan turns neatly to fire past Prudhoe. A dire second half sees Stoke fail to put sufficient pressure on David Jones' huge defence. Armstrong's strike ensures this is the last cup-tie at the Vic.											

		Home						Away					
		P	W	D	L	F	A	W	D	L	F	A	Pts
1	Bolton	46	18	4	1	60	20	10	10	3	40	33	98
2	Barnsley	46	14	4	5	43	19	8	10	5	33	36	80
3	Wolves	46	10	5	8	31	24	12	5	6	37	27	76
4	Ipswich	46	13	7	3	44	23	7	7	9	24	27	74
5	Sheffield Utd	46	13	5	5	46	23	7	8	8	29	29	73
6	Crys Palace *	46	10	7	6	39	22	9	7	7	39	26	71
7	Portsmouth	46	12	4	7	32	24	8	4	11	27	29	68
8	Port Vale	46	9	9	5	36	28	8	7	8	22	27	67
9	QP Rangers	46	10	5	8	33	25	8	7	8	31	35	66
10	Birmingham	46	11	7	5	30	18	6	8	9	22	30	66
11	Tranmere	46	10	9	4	42	27	7	5	11	21	29	65
12	STOKE	46	15	3	5	28	22	3	7	13	17	35	64
13	Norwich	46	9	10	4	34	18	8	2	13	35	50	63
14	Manchester C	46	12	4	7	34	25	5	6	12	25	35	61
15	Charlton	46	11	8	4	36	28	5	3	15	16	38	59
16	West Brom	46	7	7	9	37	33	7	8	8	31	39	57
17	Oxford	46	14	3	6	44	26	2	6	15	20	42	57
18	Reading	46	13	7	3	37	24	2	5	16	21	43	57
19	Swindon	46	11	6	6	36	27	4	3	16	16	44	54
20	Huddersfield	46	10	7	6	28	20	3	8	12	20	41	54
21	Bradford C	46	10	5	8	29	32	2	7	14	18	40	48
22	Grimsby	46	7	7	9	31	34	4	6	13	29	47	46
23	Oldham	46	6	8	9	30	30	4	5	14	21	36	43
24	Southend	46	7	9	7	32	32	1	6	16	10	54	39
		1104	262	150	140	872	604	140	150	262	604	872	1506

* promoted after play-offs

Odds & ends

Double wins: (3) Charlton, Oldham, West Brom.
Double losses: (1) Norwich, Sheffield Utd, Southend.

Won from behind: (3) Grimsby (h), Huddersfield (h), Portsmouth (h).
Lost from in front: (0).

High spots: The electric form of Mike Sheron.
A carnival day for the last match at the Vic.
Leading Arsenal 1-0 at Highbury.
The emergence of the talented Andy Griffin.
Having the second best home record in the division.
Keeping up the hoodoo on the Baggies.

Low spots: Falling away from the play-off zone with a poor run in March.
Being thrashed at home by Sheffield United.
Losing at home to Stockport in the FA Cup.
The sale of Sheron to Queen's Park Rangers.
Failure to sign a forward once Sturridge is injured.
Saying an emotional goodbye to the Victoria Ground.
Only winning three away games.
Losing home and away against bottom club Southend.

Player of the Year: Andy Griffin.
Ever-presents: (0).
Hat-tricks: (0).
Leading scorer: (24) Mike Sheron.

	Appearances						Goals			
	Lge	*Sub*	LC	*Sub*	FAC	*Sub*	Lge	LC	FAC	Tot
Beeston, Carl	**17**	*1*								
Carruthers, Martin		*1*		*1*						
Cranson, Ian	**6**									
Da Costa, Hugo	**1**	*1*	1	*1*						
Devlin, Mark	**13**	*8*	3		1					
Dreyer, John	**12**		3				**1**			**1**
Flynn, Sean	**5**									
Forsyth, Richard	**40**		3		1		**8**			**8**
Gayle, John	**8**	*4*	2				**1**			**1**
Griffin, Andy	**29**	*5*		*1*	1		**1**			**1**
Kavanagh, Graham	**32**	*6*	2		1		**4**			**4**
Keen, Kevin	**5**	*11*	2	*2*			**1**			**1**
Macari, Mike	**15**	*15*		*3*		*1*	**3**			**3**
Mackenzie, Neil	**5**	*17*				*1*	**1**			**1**
McMahon, Gerry	**31**	*4*	3	*1*	1		**3**			**3**
McNally, Mark	**3**									
Muggleton, Carl	**33**		4							
Nyamah, Kofi		*7*								
Pickering, Ally	**39**	*1*	4		1					
Prudhoe, Mark	**13**			*1*	1					
Rodger, Simon	**5**									
Sheron, Mike	**41**		4		1		**19**	5		**24**
Sigurdsson, Larus	**45**		4		1					
Stein, Mark	**11**						**4**			**4**
Stokoe, Graham		*2*								
Sturridge, Simon	**5**									
Wallace, Ray	**45**		4		1		**2**			**2**
Whittle, Justin	**35**	*2*	2		1					
Worthington, Nigel	**12**		3					1		**1**
(own-goals)							**3**			**3**
29 Players used	**506**	***85***	**44**	***10***	**11**	***2***	**51**	**6**		**57**

No	Date	Att	Pos	Pt	F-A	H-T	Scorers, Times, and Referees	1	2	3	4	5	6	7	8	9	10	11	subs used
1	A BIRMINGHAM			L	0-2	0-1		Muggleton	Pickering	Nyamah	Sigurdsson	Whittle	Keen*	Forsyth	Wallace	**Thorne**	**Stewart**	Kavanagh	Sturridge
	9/8	*20,608*		0			*Devlin 33, Ndlovu 87*	*Bennett*	*Wassall*	*Grainger*	*Bruce*	*Ablett*	*O'Connor**	*Devlin^*	*Hey"*	*Hughes*	*Robinson*	*Ndlovu*	*Holland/Francis/Johnson*
							Ref: E Wolstenholme	The new era at the Britannia Stadium will start late as building work is not quite ready. Coach Chic Bates is the new manager. At sun-kissed St Andrews, Whittle misses a long ball and Paul Devlin nods over the stranded Muggleton. Thorne rounds Bennett but fires wide of a gaping goal.											
2	A BRADFORD C			D	0-0	0-0		Muggleton	Pickering	Nyamah	Sigurdsson	Tweed	Keen	Forsyth	Wallace	Thorne	Stewart	Kavanagh	
	15/8	*13,823*		1				*Prudhoe*	*Wilder*	*Jacobs*	*Beagrie*	*Youds*	*Dreyer*	*Lawrence"*	*Pepper*	*Steiner**	*Edinho^*	*Murray*	*Blake/Sundgot/Ramage*
							Ref: T Heilbron	Chris Kamara has his Bradford side, with three ex-Stokies in it, fired up. They have the better of a fiercely competitive match. Muggers denies Steiner, Edinho and Beagrie. Mark Prudhoe tips Steven Tweed's header over. Eddie Youds trips Thorne in the area but the ref waves play on.											
3	A MIDDLESBROUGH		12	W	1-0	0-0	Stewart 60	Muggleton	Pickering	Griffin	Sigurdsson	Tweed	Keen	Forsyth	Wallace	Thorne*	Stewart^	Kavanagh	McMahon/Angola
	23/8	*30,122*	*17*	4				*Roberts*	*Liddle*	*Fleming*	*Vickers*	*Festa*	*Stamp*	*Hignett^*	*Mustoe*	*Moore**	*Merson*	*Ravanelli*	*Beck/Freestone*
							Ref: P Barnes	Tweed snuffs out the threat of Ravanelli. Moore and Stamp blaze wide as Boro fail to register a shot on target. A superb move ends with Paul Stewart sweeping into the net. Victory on Stoke's first ever visit to the Cellnet Stadium. Alan Durban has returned to the club to assist Bates.											
4	H SWINDON		13	L	1-2	1-0	Forsyth 34	Muggleton	Pickering	Griffin	Sigurdsson	Tweed	Keen	Forsyth	Wallace	Thorne	Stewart*	Kavanagh	Angola
	30/8	23,000	*4*	4			*Allison 78, Hay 80*	*Digby*	*Darras*	*Drysdale**	*Leitch^*	*Seagraves*	*McDonald*	*Walters*	*Cuervo*	*Hay*	*Allison*	*Gooden*	*Bullock/Smith*
							Ref: G Frankland	City run out of steam in the blazing sun as Steve McMahon's Robins finish strongly. Richard Forsyth nets the first league goal at the Brit, after Stan Matthews sets a hideous precedent by failing to find the net from 12 yards in the opening ceremony. Allison and Hay crack in on the turn.											
5	H WEST BROM		13	D	0-0	0-0		Muggleton	Pickering	Griffin	Whittle	Tweed	Keen	Forsyth	Wallace	Thorne*	Stewart	Kavanagh	Angola
	3/9	17,500	*3*	5				*Miller*	*Holmes*	*Nicholson*	*Sneekes*	*Burgess*	*Raven*	*Flynn*	*Butler*	*Taylor^*	*Hunt**	*Smith*	*Hamilton/Thomas*
							Ref: E Lomas	City lose Sigurdsson but Albion miss Peschisolido on international duty. In atrocious conditions both teams attack but neither can find a finish. Sneekes' volley flies narrowly wide. City fail to hit the target. Sturridge will be out until January with a recurrence of his knee ligament injury.											
6	H STOCKPORT		13	W	2-1	1-0	Wallace 28, Thorne 50	Muggleton	Pickering	Griffin	Sigurdsson	Tweed	Keen	Forsyth	Wallace	Thorne	Stewart^	Kavanagh*	McMahon/Angola
	13/9	11,743	*23*	8			*Mutch 48*	*Nixon*	*Connelly*	*Woodthorpe*	*Bennett*	*McIntosh*	*Gannon*	*Durkan**	*Marsden*	*Angell^*	*Mutch*	*Cooper*	*Richardson/Grant*
							Ref: B Coddington	Wallace pokes home in a scramble. County are poor, but still push City all the way after Andy Mutch heads in a free-kick. Thorne slides home Stewart's cross. Gannon clears off the line. The whole ground rises to protest about Coates' refusal to back Chic Bates with funds for transfers.											
7	A IPSWICH		14	W	3-2	2-0	Thorne 13, 30, Stewart 55	Muggleton	Pickering	Griffin	Sigurdsson	Tweed	Keen	Forsyth	Wallace	Thorne	Stewart	Kavanagh	
	20/9	*10,665*	*22*	11			*Scowcroft 48, Holland 67*	*Wright*	*Stockwell*	*Taricco*	*Williams*	*Venus*	*Swailes*	*Dyer*	*Holland*	*Stein*	*Scowcroft*	*Sonner**	*Cundy*
							Ref: B Knight	Indecision allows Thorne to loop a header over Richard Wright. Keen's corner is not cleared and Thorne nets in the scramble. Town change to 4-4-2. Scowcroft dives to head in. Stewart races clear to score. Stein puts Holland through to beat Muggleton. First win at Ipswich for 15 years.											
8	A NOTT'M FOREST		15	L	0-1	0-0		Muggleton	Pickering	Griffin	Sigurdsson	Tweed	Keen	Forsyth*	Wallace	Thorne	McMahon^	Kavanagh	Crowe/Mackenzie
	27/9	*19,018*	*1*	11			*Campbell 67*	*Beasant*	*Lyttle*	*Rogers*	*Cooper**	*Chettle*	*Armstrong*	*Saunders*	*Gemmill*	*V Hooijdonk*	*Campbell*	*Bart-Williams*	*Johnson*
							Ref: M Fletcher	Keen hits the bar. Tweed allows Van Hooijdonk to cross and Kevin Campbell heads in. Stoke launch a wave of attacks against Dave Bassett's unconvincing Forest. In injury-time Sigurdsson heads against the bar only for Muggleton to mis-hit the rebound against a defender on the line.											
9	H BURY		11	W	3-2	0-0	Angola 63, Forsyth 69, Thorne 73	Muggleton	Pickering	Griffin	Sigurdsson	Tweed	Keen	Forsyth	Wallace	Thorne	**Angola***	Kavanagh	McMahon
	4/10	11,760	*17*	14			*Swan 70, Gray 85p*	*Kiely*	*Hughes^*	*Morgan*	*Daws*	*Lucketti*	*Butler*	*Gray*	*Johnson*	*Swan*	*Johnrose*	*Battersby**	*Randall/Woodward*
							Ref: C Foy	Stan Ternent's Shakers fight all the way after Jose Angola scores on his debut. Wallace misses a sitter. Forsyth nips in to finish in a scramble. Swan collects Griffin's poor back-pass to score. Thorne smashes Keen's centre home. Gray's penalty is for Pickering's foul on David Johnson.											
10	H PORT VALE		7	W	2-1	2-1	Forsyth 5, Keen 34	Muggleton	Pickering	Griffin	Sigurdsson	Tweed	Keen	Forsyth	Wallace	Thorne	Angola*	Kavanagh	Crowe
	12/10	20,125	*11*	17			*Naylor 21*	*Musselwhite*	*Hill^*	*Tankard*	*Talbot*	*Aspin*	*Snijders*	*Ainsworth*	*Porter*	*Mills**	*Naylor*	*Koordes"*	*Foyle/Bogie/Corden*
							Ref: C Wilkes	Keen's cross finds Forsyth who rises to head in unmarked. Tony Naylor glances a header past Muggers despite being only 5ft 7in. Keen accepts Kav's killer pass to fire precisely into the corner. Six wins in seven. Musselwhite claws back a Forsyth header which appears to cross the line.											
11	A CHARLTON		7	D	1-1	0-0	Wallace 51	Muggleton	Pickering	Griffin	Sigurdsson	Tweed	Keen	Forsyth	Wallace	McMahon*	Angola^	Kavanagh	Whittle/Macari
	19/10	*12,345*	*4*	18			*Kinsella 79*	*Petterson*	*Bowen*	*Barness*	*Jones*	*Rufus*	*Chapple*	*Newton**	*Kinsella*	*Robinson*	*Mendonca*	*Jones^*	*Holmes/Allen*
							Ref: R Furnandiz	Siggy tackles Jones brilliantly as he races clear. Wallace races on to Kav's square pass to rocket home from 20 yards. Charlton pour forward as Stoke sit deep. Kinsella fires in via Wallace's knee. Another lead lost. City cannot afford £300k for ex-Stokie Graham Potter from West Brom.											

No Date	Venue	Opponent	Att	Pos	Res Pts	F-A	H-T	Scorers, Times, and Referees	1	2	3	4	5	6	7	8	9	10	11	subs used
12	A	MANCHESTER C		6	W	1-0	0-0	Wallace 63	Muggleton	Pickering	Griffin	Sigurdsson	Tweed	Keen	Forsyth	Wallace	McMahon	Stewart*	Kavanagh	Nyamah
22/10			*25,333*	*21*	21				*Margetson*	*Brightwell*	*Van Blerk*	*McGoldrick*	*Symons*	*Edghill*	*Brannan**	*Horlock*	*Heaney^*	*Kinkladze*	*Dickov*	*Summerbee/Conlon*
								Ref: A Leake	Frank Clark's Blues have Stoke under the cosh. Heaney fires just over. Muggers brilliantly saves Horlock's effort. Dickov gives Tweed a torrid time. Brannan has a header tipped away. Stoke gradually get a grip. Wallace belts in a half-cleared corner. Muggers denies Eddie McGoldrick.											
13	H	SUNDERLAND		9	L	1-2	0-1	Stewart 81	Muggleton	Pickering^	Nyamah	Sigurdsson	Tweed	Keen	Forsyth	Wallace	McMahon	Stewart	Kavanagh*	Whittle/Angola
25/10			14,587	*10*	21			*Clark 40, 70*	*Perez*	*Holloway*	*Gray*	*Clark*	*Ball*	*Craddock*	*Johnston*	*Williams*	*Bridges**	*Phillips*	*Smith^*	*Russell/Mullin*
								Ref: S Baines	£2.3m Lee Clark, who cost Peter Reid more than the entire City team, peppers Muggleton with shots. His first two fly wide, but he cracks in as Wallace slips in the box. McMahon fires at Lionel Perez. Clark's ferocious 25-yard shot from flies in. Stewart hammers in Angola's flick-on.											
14	A	HUDDERSFIELD		12	L	1-3	0-0	Griffin 79	Muggleton	Pickering	Griffin	Sigurdsson	Tweed	Keen	Forsyth	Wallace*	Thorne^	Stewart	Kavanagh	Angola/McMahon
1/11			*10,916*	*24*	21			*Richardson 46, Stewart 80, Dalton 90*	*Bartam*	*Jenkins*	*Edmondson*	*Dyson*	*Morrison*	*Gray*	*Dalton*	*Horne*	*Stewart*	*Richardson*	*Edwards**	*Lawson*
								Ref: K Lynch	The Terriers register their first win of the season against out of sorts Stoke. Kav shaves the post. Richardson hammers in from 25 yards. Griffin weaves through to net from a tight angle. Marcus Stewart nips in. Muggers goes up for a corner but it is cleared and Paul Dalton slots past Kav.											
15	H	OXFORD		12	D	0-0	0-0		Muggleton	Pickering	Griffin	Sigurdsson	Tweed	Keen^	Forsyth	Wallace	Thorne	Stewart*	Kavanagh	Angola/McMahon
4/11			**8,423**	*18*	22				*V Heusden*	*Gilchrist*	*Ford M*	*Robinson*	*Purse^*	*Wilsterman*	*Ford B*	*Smith*	*Banger*	*Jemson**	*Beauchamp*	*Aldridge/Murphy*
								Ref: R Pearson	Griffin's 30-yarder startles on-loan Van Heusden but he recovers to scoop up his parry. Total lack of invention enrages the fans who single out Ally Pickering as a scapegoat. He responds with a gesture which wins him no friends. 'Where has all the money gone?' sing the North Stand.											
16	H	WOLVES		9	W	**3-0**	2-0	Kavanagh 8, 23p, Forsyth 60	Muggleton	Pickering	Griffin	Sigurdsson	Tweed	Keen	Forsyth	Wallace	Thorne	Stewart*	Kavanagh	Angola
8/11			18,490	*8*	25				*Stowell*	*Muscat*	*Froggatt*	*Robinson**	*Willems*	*Curle*	*Keane*	*Ferguson*	*Bull*	*Freedman*	*Simpson*	*Naylor*
								Ref: E Wolstenholme	Bull's rocket pings against the bar with Muggers stranded. Immediately Kavanagh sweetly fires home from the edge of the box. Kevin Muscat handles in a scramble and Kav slots the penalty. Forsyth hits an absolute pearler from 35 yards past the astonished Mike Stowell. Triumphant!											
17	A	QP RANGERS		10	D	1-1	1-0	Forsyth 7	Muggleton	Pickering	Nyamah	Sigurdsson	Tweed	Keen	Forsyth	Wallace	Thorne	Stewart	Kavanagh	
15/11			*11,923*	*13*	26			*Barker 61p*	*Roberts*	*Perry*	*Brazier*	*Barker*	*Ready*	*Yates*	*Spencer*	*Peacock*	*Murray**	*Sheron*	*Sinclair*	*Quashie*
								Ref: M Bailey	Ex-Stokie Sheron is roundly booed. Forsyth leaps to head Kav's far-post cross past Roberts. City absorb heavy pressure. Spencer fires over but referee Bailey spots shirt pulling by Sigurdsson and Simon Barker nets the spot-kick. Muggers produces a great point-blank save from Sinclair.											
18	A	TRANMERE		12	L	1-3	1-1	Kavanagh 35p	Muggleton	Pickering	Griffin	Sigurdsson	Tweed	Keen	Forsyth	Wallace*	Thorne	Stewart	Kavanagh	McMahon
22/11			*8,009*	*16*	26			*Jones L 9, Aldridge 66, O'Brien 87*	*Simonsen*	*Stevens*	*Thompson*	*McGreal^*	*Thorn*	*Irons*	*Mellon*	*Aldridge**	*Kelly*	*O'Brien*	*Jones L"*	*Jones G/Morrissey/Mahon*
								Ref: G Laws	Over 2,200 Stokies see Rovers' ageing side outfight City's lightweight midfield. Lee Jones heads in at the far post. Kav's penalty arrives when Andy Thompson pushes Stewart. Player-manager Aldridge guides a header in. O'Brien lashes in a third. Stoke in tatters. It does not bode well.											
19	H	READING		13	L	1-2	0-1	Thorne 81	Muggleton	Pickering	Griffin	Sigurdsson	Tweed	Keen	Forsyth	Angola^	Thorne	Stewart*	Kavanagh	Mackenzie/**Tiatto**
29/11			11,103	*18*	26			*Morley 32p, 59*	*Hammond*	*Booty*	*Swales*	*Lambert**	*McPherson*	*Primus*	*Parkinson*	*Houghton*	*Asaba"*	*Morley*	*Williams^*	*Hodges/Caskey/Thorp*
								Ref: T Jones	The miserable weather is matched by Stoke's performance. 36-year-old Trevor Morley torments the central defenders. He misses a sitter from six yards before slotting a penalty after Sigurdsson fouls Williams and then side-foots home unmarked. Thorne hammers in Mackenzie's cross.											
20	A	SHEFFIELD UTD		13	L	2-3	1-0	Thorne 8, 63	Muggleton	Pickering	Griffin	Sigurdsson	Tweed	Keen	Forsyth	Mackenzie	Thorne	Tiatto*	Kavanagh	McMahon
2/12			*14,347*	*4*	26			*Taylor 46, Fjortoft 64, Deane 80*	*Tracey*	*Borbokis*	*Nilsen^*	*Hutchison**	*Dallas*	*Holdsworth*	*Patterson"*	*Marker*	*Fjortoft*	*Deane*	*Stuart*	*Taylor/Woodhouse/Ford*
								Ref: G Frankland	On a bitter night City play excellent football. Thorne guides the ball under Simon Tracey. New boy Danny Tiatto looks lively. Nigel Spackman makes three changes at the break. Taylor scores from close in. Fjortoft taps in after Muggers can only parry. Deane turns the ball past Muggers.											
21	A	PORTSMOUTH		14	L	0-2	0-2		Muggleton	Pickering	Griffin	Sigurdsson	Tweed	Keen	Forsyth	Mackenzie*	Thorne	Tiatto	Kavanagh	McMahon
6/12			*7,072*	*24*	26			*Aloisi 31, Svensson 43*	*Knight*	*Pethick*	*Thomson*	*McLoughlin*	*Whitbread*	*Awford*	*Hall*	*Foster**	*Aloisi^*	*Svensson*	*Hillier*	*Igoe/Durnin*
								Ref: P Rejer	Sigurdsson's shot is superbly saved by veteran Alan Knight. Hall finds John Aloisi who spins to fire into the roof of the net. Sigurdsson misses a tackle and Paul Hall sets up Matthias Svensson for a simple tap-in. Stoke are abject. Under-fire Terry Fenwick's first home win since August.											
22	H	CREWE		15	L	0-2	0-1		Muggleton	Pickering	Griffin*	Sigurdsson	Tweed	Keen	Forsyth	Mackenzie	Thorne	Stewart	Kavanagh	Tiatto
13/12			14,623	*20*	26			*Smith 11, Little 75*	*Kearton*	*Bignot*	*Smith*	*Unsworth*	*Foran*	*Lunt**	*Rivers*	*Holsgrove*	*Adebola^*	*Johnson*	*Street*	*Garvey/Little*
								Ref: A Wiley	Stoke lose for the third time this season against the bottom side. Dario Gradi's youthful side revel in the open spaces at the Brit. Captain Shaun Smith fires a free-kick past a static Muggers. Boos ring out. City lack the imagination to carve a chance. Colin Little finishes from close range.											
23	A	NORWICH		15	D	0-0	0-0		Muggleton	Pickering	Griffin	Sigurdsson	Tweed	Keen	Forsyth	Mackenzie	Thorne	Stewart	Kavanagh	
20/12			*12,265*	*13*	27				*Marshall*	*Segura*	*Mills*	*Grant*	*Scott*	*Jackson*	*Forbes*	*Carey**	*Roberts*	*Bellamy*	*Fugelstad*	*O'Neill*
								Ref: R Harris	Mike Walker's Canaries are as bad as Stoke. At least their future is ensured as millionaire cook Delia Smith has taken control. 364 Stokies see a sterile game. Marshall claws Mackenzie's weak shot away. Forsyth nods straight at the keeper. Griffin heads off the line from Victor Segura.											

No	Date	Att	Pos	Pt	F-A	H-T	Scorers, Times, and Referees	1	2	3	4	5	6	7	8	9	10	11	subs used
24	H SHEFFIELD UTD		14	D	2-2	0-0	Forsyth 66, Thorne 86	Muggleton	Pickering	Griffin	Sigurdsson	Tweed	Keen	Forsyth	Mackenzie	Thorne*	Stewart^	Kavanagh	Tiatto/**Gabbiadini**
	26/12	19,723	*4*	28			*Taylor 59, Deane 90*	*Kelly*	*Borbokis^*	*Woodhouse**	*Ford*	*Lee*	*Nilsen*	*Saunders*	*Marker*	*Taylor*	*Deane*	*Stuart*	*Katchouro/Hutchison*
							Ref: S Mathieson	Reserve keeper Alan Kelly produces a fine display to keep the Blades in it. He denies Stewart, Griffin and Keen. Kav hits the post. Taylor nods in. Forsyth finally beats Kelly from six yards. Thorne seems to have won it from close in but Deane loops a header home. Eight without a win.											
25	A WEST BROM		15	D	1-1	0-0	Thorne 47	Muggleton	Griffin	Nyamah*	Sigurdsson	Tweed	Keen	Forsyth	Mackenzie^	Thorne	Stewart"	Kavanagh	Whittle/Wallace/Gabbiadini
	28/12	*17,690*	*7*	29			*Hunt 62*	*Miller*	*McDermott*	*Smith*	*Sneekes*	*Burgess*	*Murphy*	*Butler*	*Hamilton**	*Hughes*	*Hunt*	*Kilbane*	*Coldicott^/Evans*
							Ref: P Danson	Denis Smith's first home game in charge of Albion sees Stewart loop a header against the post. Thorne slots from close range after Mackenzie miscues his shot. Muggers is injured. Stewart, in goal, fails to hold Sneekes' free-kick. Andy Hunt profits. 18 without loss against the Baggies.											
26	H BIRMINGHAM		16	L	**0-7**	0-3	*[McCarthy 65]*	Muggleton	Griffin	Nyamah*	Sigurdsson	Tweed	Keen	Forsyth	Mackenzie	Thorne	Stewart^	Kavanagh	Wallace/Gabbiadini
	10/1	14,940	*8*	29			*H'ghes 4, 9, F'rster 26, Furlong 50, 69, 87,*	*Bennett*	*Bass*	*Charlton*	*Bruce^*	*Ablett*	*Marsden*	*McCarthy*	*O'Connor*	*Furlong*	*Hughes*	*Forster**	*Ndlovu/Johnson*
							Ref: T Helibron	The most appalling defeat in the club's history. It comes soon after nine players discover via the press they are surplus to requirements. Hughes and Forster waltz through. Paul Furlong's hat-trick completes a biggest ever home defeat. Protesters climb into the stand to confront the board.											
27	H BRADFORD C		14	W	2-1	2-1	Forsyth 35p, Thorne 42	Muggleton	Pickering	Griffin	Sigurdsson	Tweed	Keen	Forsyth	Wallace	Thorne	Gabbiadini*	Whittle	McMahon
	16/1	10,459	*11*	32			*McGinlay 21*	*Walsh*	*Wilder*	*Small^*	*Murray*	*Youds*	*O'Brien*	*Lawrence**	*McGinlay*	*Jacobs*	*Blake*	*Beagrie*	*Edinho/Bolland*
							Ref: R Pearson	Peter Coates announces his resignation as Chairman but retains a controlling interest in the club. Keith Humphreys is the new Chair. 2,000 fans register their disgust by arriving 15 mins late only to see McGinlay's header. Forsyth's pen is for handball. Thorne cracks in Keen's fine pass.											
28	A SWINDON		16	L	0-1	0-0		Muggleton	Pickering	Nyamah	Whittle	Tweed	Keen	**Holsgrove**	Wallace	Thorne	**Scully***	Kavanagh^	McMahon/Gabbiadini
	28/1	*6,683*	*10*	32			*Robinson 71*	*Mildenhall*	*Borrows*	*Robinson*	*Thompson*	*Taylor*	*Collins*	*Cuervo*	*Howe*	*Hay*	*Finney*	*Drysdale**	*Leitch*
							Ref: A Hall	Chris Kamara replaces Chic Bates. Andy Griffin is sold to Newcastle for £2.3m. Loan signings Paul Holsgrove and Tony Scully cannot inspire Stoke to find a way past youth keeper Steve Mildenhall. Mark Robinson cracks home. Former Stokie Ian Moores dies of throat cancer aged 44.											
29	H MIDDLESBROUGH		18	L	1-2	1-1	Kavanagh 36p	Muggleton	Pickering	**McKinlay !**	Whittle	Tweed*	Keen	Holsgrove	Wallace	McMahon	Scully	Kavanagh	Gabbiadini
	1/2	13,242	*2*	32			*Pearson 17, Moreno 81*	*Schwarzer*	*Baker*	*Kinder*	*Vickers*	*Pearson*	*Mustoe*	*Hignett*	*Townsend*	*Campbell^*	*Merson*	*Summerbell**	*Beck/Moreno*
							Ref: P Richards	Bryan Robson's Boro are a class above City. Tosh McKinlay, on loan from Celtic, helps Pearson's header past Muggers. Mark Schwarzer tips Kav's shot over. McKinlay is tripped by Baker for the pen, but is sent off for slapping Hignett (84 mins). Jaime Moreno scores from 20 yards.											
30	H IPSWICH		19	D	1-1	1-0	Holsgrove 15	Muggleton	Pickering	McKinlay	Sigurdsson	Whittle	Keen	Holsgrove	Wallace	McMahon^	Scully	Kavanagh*	**Macari**/Gabbiadini
	7/2	11,416	*13*	33			*Holland 78*	*Wright*	*Stockwell*	*Taricco !*	*Williams^*	*Clapham*	*Cundy*	*Uhlenbeek**	*Holland*	*Mathie*	*Scowcroft*	*Dyer*	*Sonner/Johnson*
							Ref: M Pike	The Victoria Ground has finally been demolished. Much like City's season. Holsgrove slides in to convert McKinlay's cross. Muggers makes a fine save from Clapham as George Burley's men fight back. Matt Holland nods in a corner. Taricco walks (86 mins) for a third foul on Scully.											
31	A STOCKPORT		20	L	0-1	0-0		Muggleton	Pickering	McKinlay*	Sigurdsson	Whittle	Gabbiadini"	Holsgrove	Wallace	McMahon^	Scully	Kavanagh	Tweed/Macari/Mackenzie
	14/2	*8,701*	*8*	33			*Grant 82*	*Nixon*	*Connelly*	*Woodthorpe*	*Byrne"*	*Flynn*	*Dinning*	*Gannon*	*Cook^*	*Angell*	*Mutch**	*Cooper*	*Grant/Travis/Phillips*
							Ref: G Laws	Holsgrove skims the bar from 25 yards. Andy Mutch heads just wide. Sean Connelly misses a sitter after Wallace gives possession away. Steve Grant's aimless cross sails over Muggleton and nestles in the bottom corner. The death of long-serving club secretary Mike Potts is announced.											
32	A BURY		20	D	0-0	0-0		Muggleton	Pickering	Tiatto	Sigurdsson	Whittle	Crowe	Holsgrove	Wallace	**Xausa**	Scully	Kavanagh	
	17/2	*5,802*	*23*	34				*Kiely*	*Woodward*	*Small*	*Daws*	*Lucketti*	*Butler*	*Jemson"*	*Patterson*	*Armstrong*	*Johnrose**	*Battersby^*	*Swan/Rigby/Matthews*
							Ref: J Robinson	Kamara's selection smacks of panic. Davide Xausa, on loan from St Johnstone, is awful. Kav hits the keeper when put clear. Crowe strikes the upright. Pickering nods off the line. Sheffield United turn down £750k for striker Gareth Taylor. Lou Macari loses his court case against Celtic.											
33	H NOTT'M FOREST		20	D	1-1	1-0	Crowe 32	Muggleton	Pickering	Tiatto	Sigurdsson	Whittle	Scully*	Holsgrove	Wallace	Crowe	**Lightbourne**	Kavanagh^	Keen/Mackenzie
	21/2	16,899	*2*	35			*Moore 87*	*Beasant*	*Lyttle*	*Rogers*	*Cooper*	*Chettle**	*Johnson A^*	*Johnson D"*	*Gemmill*	*Moore*	*Campbell*	*Bonnalair*	*Armstr'ng/Thomas/B'rt-Wil'ms*
							Ref: D Pugh	£500k man Kyle Lightbourne, from Coventry, starts despite not fully recovering from flu. Dean Crowe nets his first goal from Tiatto's corner. Ian Moore's effort eludes everyone and trickles into the net. Former player Robbie James collapses and dies while playing for Llanelli aged 40.											
34	H CHARLTON		21	L	1-2	1-1	Kavanagh 42	Muggleton	Pickering*	Tiatto	Sigurdsson	Whittle	Scully	Keen^	Wallace	Crowe	Lightbourne	Kavanagh	Tweed/Thorne
	25/2	10,027	*4*	35			*Robinson 17, Barness 73*	*Ilic*	*Brown*	*Bowen*	*Jones*	*Chapple*	*Balmer*	*Barness*	*Kinsella*	*Robinson*	*Mendonca*	*Lisbie**	*Newton*
							Ref: R Furnandiz	John Robinson is tackled in the act of shooting but the ball spoons up and over the stranded Muggers. Kavanagh fires a brilliant short free-kick past Sasa Ilic and celebrates wildly with club mascot Pottermuss! Anthony Barness nets at the second attempt after Robinson carves City open.											

No	Date	Opponent	Att	Pos	Res	F-A	H-T	Scorers, Times, and Referees	1	2	3	4	5	6	7	8	9	10	11	Subs used
35	A	PORT VALE		23	D	0-0	0-0		**Southall**	Pickering	Tiatto	Sigurdsson	Whittle	Tweed*	Forsyth	Wallace	Thorne	Lightbourne	Kavanagh	Crowe
	1/3		*13,853*	*24*	36				*V Heusden*	*Hill*	*Tankard^*	*Bogie*	*Glover*	*Carragher*	*Ainsworth*	*Porter*	*Mills**	*Foyle*	*Jansson*	*Naylor/Snijders*
								Ref: P Rejer	Neville Southall, on loan from Everton, becomes the third oldest player in Stoke's history. A grim derby sees the teams occupy the bottom two places in the division after the awful pitch makes good football impossible. Coach Mike Pejic has been sacked and replaced by Martin Hunter.											
36	A	WOLVES		23	D	1-1	0-1	Crowe 89	Southall	Pickering*	Tiatto	Sigurdsson	Whittle	Holsgrove^	Forsyth	Wallace	Thorne	Lightbourne	Kavanagh	Crowe/McNally
	4/3		*21,058*	*9*	37			*Freedman 22*	*Segers*	*Atkins*	*Naylor*	*Simpson*	*Richards*	*Curle*	*Keane^*	*Robinson*	*Bull*	*Freedman**	*Osborn*	*Paatelainen/Muscat*
								Ref: E Wolstenholme	Whittle allows Freedman's speculative shot under his foot and the ball speeds into the bottom corner. In pouring rain Dean Crowe profits from lackadaisical defending to shoot through a mass of players as Wolves' minds turn to their forthcoming FA Cup quarter-final tie at Elland Road.											
37	H	HUDDERSFIELD		24	L	1-2	0-2	Tiatto 90	Southall	Pickering"	Tiatto	Sigurdsson	Whittle	Holsgrove	Forsyth	Wallace	Thorne	Lightbourne*	Kavanagh^	Keen/Crowe/**Woods**
	7/3		12,594	*21*	37			*Barnes 15, Stewart 18*	*Harper*	*Phillips*	*Jenkins*	*Browning*	*Watts*	*Gray*	*Richardson**	*Barnes^*	*Stewart*	*Allison*	*Johnson*	*Edwards/Baldry*
								Ref: E Lomas	Stoke go to pieces after Peter Jackson's Terriers score two early goals. Ex-Stokie Paul Barnes profits from awful defending. Stewart powers in from 15 yards. 'Bring on the Hippo!' chorus the North Stand. Tiatto's shot finds its way through Steve Harper's arms and legs before rolling in.											
38	A	OXFORD		24	L	1-5	0-1	Crowe 69 *[Beauchamp 87]*	Southall	Pickering	Tiatto^	Sigurdsson	Tweed	Keen*	Forsyth	Wallace	Thorne	**Donaldson**	Kavanagh	Crowe/**Heath**
	14/3		*7,300*	*13*	37			*Murphy 45, 61, Francis 65, 68,*	*Whitehead*	*Robinson*	*Marsh*	*Gray*	*Davis*	*Gilchrist*	*Murphy**	*Smith*	*Francis*	*Cook^*	*Beauchamp*	*Banger/Powell*
								Ref: B Knight	Stoke surrender abjectly. Wallace heads straight to Murphy who nets. Kevin Francis turns in from close range twice. Kamara slams his players. Relegation is edging ever closer. On-loan O'Neill Donaldson (Sheffield Wed) replaces Lightbourne, having blood tests as his illness continues.											
39	H	QP RANGERS		23	W	2-1	1-0	Dowie 21 (og), Crowe 51	Southall	McNally	**Sobiech**	Sigurdsson	Whittle !	Holsgrove	Forsyth	Crowe	Donaldson*	Stewart^	Kavanagh	Wallace/Lightbourne
	21/3		11,051	*18*	40			*Barker 90p*	*Harper*	*Yates"*	*Morrow*	*Kulcsar^*	*Ready*	*Maddix*	*Baraclough*	*Barker*	*Dowie**	*Sheron*	*Scully*	*Gallen/Slade/Heinola*
								Ref: A Leake	The players appeal for fans to be more positive during games. City pour forward. Dowie slices the ball into his own net. Jorg Sobiech, on loan from NEC Nijmegen, sets up Crowe for the second. Whittle is sent off for fouling Mike Sheron in the box. Only the second win in 23 matches.											
40	H	TRANMERE		23	L	0-3	0-2		Southall	McNally"	Sobiech	Sigurdsson	Whittle	Holsgrove*	Forsyth	Crowe	Thorne	Stewart^	Kavanagh	Tiatto/Lightbourne/**Taaffe**
	28/3		16,692	*16*	40			*Jones G 26, Mellon 39, Kelly 60*	*Simonsen*	*Kubicki**	*Thompson*	*McGreal*	*Challinor*	*Irons*	*Morrissey*	*Jones G*	*Kelly*	*O'Brien*	*Jones L*	*Mellon*
								Ref: M Fletcher	The club slash prices to £10 for adults and kids £4. A bumper crowd assembles to witness another abject performance. Challinor's long throw lands at Gary Jones' feet. Micky Mellon profits when Whittle fails to clear twice. Diminutive David Kelly rises above two defenders to nod in.											
41	A	READING		24	L	0-2	0-1		Southall	Pickering	Sobiech	Sigurdsson	McNally	Holsgrove^	Forsyth	Wallace*	Thorne	Crowe	Kavanagh"	Keen/Lightbourne/Tweed
	4/4		*10,448*	*23*	40			*O'Neill 32, Meaker 48*	*Howie*	*Bernal*	*Gray*	*Parkinson*	*Primus*	*Crawford*	*Meaker**	*Caskey*	*McIntyre^*	*O'Neill*	*Lambert*	*Asaba/Fleck*
								Ref: F Stretton	Tommy Burns fields four deadline day signings as Reading halt a run of seven straight defeats. O'Neill outjumps six players to loop his header past Southall. Meaker nets without a defender in sight. Stokies don't know whether to shout 'Kamara out!' or 'Sack the board!' Utterly abject.											
42	H	PORTSMOUTH		23	W	2-1	0-0	Pickering 78, Lightbourne 90	Southall	Pickering	Nyamah	Sigurdsson	Tweed	Keen	Forsyth"	Wallace	Thorne^	Crowe*	Kavanagh	Whittle/Lightbourne/Heath
	11/4		15,569	*22*	43			*Durnin 69*	*Flahavan*	*Pethick*	*Robinson*	*McLoughlin**	*Whitbread*	*Awford*	*Hillier*	*Simpson*	*Aloisi"*	*Durnin^*	*Thomson*	*Hall/Svensson/Allen*
								Ref: R Furnandiz	Chris Kamara has resigned after just 14 games as manager leaving Alan Durban to see the season out. John Durnin puts Alan Ball's relegation-haunted Pompey ahead. Ally Pickering's rocket almost tears the net off the stanchion. Lightbourne finally scores his first goal when he lobs in.											
43	A	CREWE		23	L	0-2	0-1		Southall	Pickering	Nyamah^	Sigurdsson	Tweed	Keen	Heath	Wallace	Lightbourne	Crowe	Kavanagh*	Mackenzie/Taaffe
	13/4		***5,759***	*13*	43			*Westwood 16, Lightfoot 48*	*Kearton*	*Bignot*	*Smith*	*Westwood**	*Walton*	*Lightfoot*	*Street^*	*Whalley*	*Anthrobus"*	*Johnson*	*Little*	*Unsworth/Rivers/Tierney*
								Ref: R Harris	Ashley Westwood prods in after Little flicks on Seth Johnson's rehearsed set-piece. Stoke rock visibly. Little makes a hash of an easy chance. Chris Lightfoot lunges in to poke home Gareth Whalley's flighted free-kick. A thumb injury will keep Muggleton out for the rest of the season.											
44	H	NORWICH		21	W	2-0	1-0	Sigurdsson 19, Lightbourne 50	Southall	Pickering	Tiatto	Sigurdsson	Tweed	Keen	Heath	Wallace	Lightbourne*	Crowe	Kavanagh	Thorne
	18/4		13,098	*17*	46				*Marshall*	*Sutch*	*Fudelstad"*	*Segura^*	*Scott*	*Jackson*	*Adams*	*Bellamy*	*Roberts*	*Fenn**	*Llewellyn*	*Grant/Coote/Polston*
								Ref: G Cain	Stoke pour forward. Kav crosses into a crowded box and Sigurdsson heads inside the near post. Tiatto releases Heath whose inch-perfect centre finds Lightbourne unmarked. Southall pulls off a miracle save from Ex-Stokie Neil Adams. Stoke out of the bottom three – a glimmer of hope?											
45	A	SUNDERLAND		22	L	0-3	0-1		Southall	Pickering	Tiatto"	Sigurdsson	Tweed	Keen	Forsyth*	Wallace	Lightbourne^	Crowe	Heath	Whittle/Thorne/Holsgrove
	25/4		***41,214***	*2*	46			*Williams 6, Phillips 54, 88*	*Perez*	*Holloway*	*Gray*	*Clark*	*Craddock*	*Williams*	*Summerbee*	*Ball*	*Quinn**	*Phillips*	*Johnston*	*Dichio*
								Ref: T Jones	Stoke's first visit to the magnificent Stadium of Light sees them taken apart by Peter Reid's Champions. Darren Williams scores after Ball hits the bar from a corner. Southall is kept busy. Kevin Phillips races clear twice to rack up thirty goals for the season. It all rests on the last match.											
46	H	MANCHESTER C		23	L	2-5	0-1	Thorne 62, 87 *[Horlock 90]*	Southall	Pickering	Heath	Sigurdsson	Tweed	Keen	Forsyth	Wallace	Thorne	Lightbourne*	Kavanagh	Taaffe
	3/5		***26,664***	*22*	46			*Goater 32, 71, Dickov 49, Bradbury 64,*	*Margetson*	*Edghill*	*Horlock*	*Wiekens*	*Symons*	*Vaughan*	*Whitley Jim**	*Pollock*	*Goater^*	*Dickov"*	*Bradbury*	*Br'nnan/Kinkl'dze/Whitl'y Jeff*
	Home	Away						Ref: M Bailey	Stoke fall apart after Shaun Goater chips Southall to put Joe Royle's Blues ahead. The sell-out crowd see dreadful defending punished by close-range finishes by Dickov and Bradbury. Thorne nets twice from six yards. Fighting erupts out as both clubs learn their joint fate. An awful day.											
Average	14,945	14,563																		

Coca-Cola Cup	Att			F-A	H-T	Scorers, Times, and Referees	1	2	3	4	5	6	7	8	9	10	11	subs used
1:1 A ROCHDALE			W	3-1	1-1	Kavanagh 26, Thorne 67, Forsyth 70	Muggleton	Pickering	Nyamah	Sigurdsson	**Tweed**	Keen	Forsyth	Wallace	Thorne	Stewart*	Kavanagh	Sturridge^/McMahon
12/8	*2,509*					*Painter 32*	*Key*	*Fensome*	*Barlow*	*Hill*	*Farrell*	*Gouck*	*Bailey*	*Painter*	*Leonard*	*Carter*	*Stuart*	
						Ref: D Pugh	Kavanagh has his shooting boots on. His 30-yard free-kick whistles into the corner. Robbie Painter is sent clear by a long ball over the top and duly levels. Thorne finishes Keen's whipped cross and City score from a corner for the first time since 1995-6 when Forsyth nods in a flick-on.											
1:2 H ROCHDALE		12	D	1-1	0-0	Kavanagh 85	Muggleton	Pickering	Griffin	Sigurdsson	Tweed*	Keen	Forsyth	Wallace^	Thorne	Stewart	Kavanagh	Whittle/**Schreuder**
27/8	12,768	*3:18*				*Russell 90*	*Key*	*Fensome*	*Bayliss*	*Hill*	*Farrell*	*Gouck*	*Russell*	*Painter*	*Leonard**	*Bailey^*	*Stuart*	*Carter/Smith*
						Ref: S Mathieson (Stoke win 4-2 on aggregate)	A rather quiet first-ever competitive match at the Brit is enlivened by Graham Kavanagh's 25-yard belter which rockets into the top corner for a superb first goal at the new ground. City go to sleep. Alex Russell pounces to net from 12 yards. Dutchman Dick Schreuder makes his debut.											
2:1 A BURNLEY		13	W	4-0	1-0	Thorne 37, 62, Kavanagh 68, 80	Muggleton	Pickering	Griffin	Sigurdsson	Tweed	Keen	Forsyth	Wallace^	Thorne	Angola*	Kavanagh	Whittle/MacKenzie
16/9	*4,175*	*2:24*					*Beresford*	*Weller*	*Brass*	*Williams*	*Blatherwick*	*Moore*	*Matthew**	*Ford*	*Howey^*	*Barnes*	*Eyres*	*Waddle/Little*
						Ref: J Kirkby	City put Chris Waddle's Clarets to the sword. A superb move out of defence allows Thorne to crash the ball home on the run. Pickering's cross falls to Thorne to volley in. Kav slams home from 20 yards and then hits a belter from slightly further out after Thorne's dummy outwits Brass.											
2:2 H BURNLEY		14	W	2-0	1-0	Keen 36, Thorne 71	Muggleton	Pickering	Griffin	Sigurdsson	Tweed*	Keen^	McMahon	Wallace"	Thorne	**Crowe**	MacKenzie	Whittle/Kav'nagh/Schreuder
24/9	6,041	*2:24*					*Beresford*	*Brass*	*Vinnicombe*	*Matthew**	*Gentile*	*Moore*	*Waddle^*	*Creaney*	*Cooke"*	*Cowans*	*Eyres*	*Huxford/Weller/Little*
						Ref: A D'Urso (Stoke win 6-0 on aggregate)	A professional performance. Keen beats keeper Marlon Beresford to a dropped ball in the box to score. Stoke saunter through the motions. An increasingly angry Waddle is the only booking. Thorne swivels adroitly to finish across Beresford. Dean Crowe, on fire in the reserves, debuts.											
3 H LEEDS		7	L	1-3	0-0	Kavanagh 66p	Muggleton	Pickering	Griffin	Sigurdsson	Tweed	Keen	Forsyth	Wallace	McMahon*	Angola^	Kavanagh"	Crowe/Nyamah/Whittle
15/10	16,203	*P:8*		*aet*		*Kewell 69, Wallace 93, 105*	*Martyn*	*Kelly*	*Robertson*	*Haaland*	*Radebe*	*Wetherall*	*Wallace*	*Ribiero**	*Hopkin^*	*Halle*	*Kewell*	*Lilley/Bowyer*
						Ref: P Jones	Stoke's best cup run for 14 years ends at the hands of George Graham's Leeds. Wetherall hits the post before Griffin's run is ended by a pincer tackle and Kav wallops in the pen. Delirium is cut short by Harry Kewell's first Leeds goal from 25 yards. City run out of steam in extra-time.											

FA Cup																		
3 A WEST BROM		16	L	1-3	0-2	Gabbiadini 61	Muggleton	Pickering	Griffin	Sigurdsson	Tweed*	Keen	Forsyth	Wallace	Gabbiadini	Stewart	Whittle	Thorne
13/1	*17,598*	*7*				*Sneekes 28, 32, Kilbane 78*	*Miller*	*Holmes*	*Nicholson*	*Sneekes*	*Murphy*	*Dobson*	*Evans**	*Hamilton*	*Hughes*	*Hunt*	*Kilbane*	*Butler*
						Ref: P Jones	City's FA Cup hoodoo outweighs the unbeaten run against West Brom. Richard Sneekes cracks a free-kick into the unguarded far post. Then a shot is deflected past the helpless Muggers. Stewart has a strike ruled out for offside. Gabbiadini pokes home. £1m Kilbane heads the clincher.											

		P	W	D	L	F	A	W	D	L	F	A	Pts
			Home					Away					
1	Nott'm Forest	46	18	2	3	52	20	10	8	5	30	22	94
2	Middlesbro	46	17	4	2	51	12	10	6	7	26	29	91
3	Sunderland	46	14	7	2	49	22	12	5	6	37	28	90
4	Charlton *	46	17	5	1	48	17	9	5	9	32	32	88
5	Ipswich	46	14	5	4	47	20	9	9	5	30	23	83
6	Sheffield Utd	46	16	5	2	44	20	3	12	8	25	34	74
7	Birmingham	46	10	8	5	27	15	9	9	5	33	20	74
8	Stockport	46	14	6	3	46	21	5	2	16	25	48	65
9	Wolves	46	13	6	4	42	25	5	5	13	15	28	65
10	West Brom	46	9	8	6	27	26	7	5	11	23	30	61
11	Crewe	46	10	2	11	30	34	8	3	12	28	31	59
12	Oxford	46	12	6	5	36	20	4	4	15	24	44	58
13	Bradford C	46	10	9	4	26	23	4	6	13	20	36	57
14	Tranmere	46	9	8	6	34	26	5	6	12	20	31	56
15	Norwich	46	9	8	6	32	27	5	5	13	20	42	55
16	Huddersfield	46	9	5	9	28	28	5	6	12	22	44	53
17	Bury	46	7	10	6	22	22	4	9	10	20	36	52
18	Swindon	46	9	6	8	28	25	5	4	14	14	48	52
19	Port Vale	46	7	6	10	25	24	6	4	13	31	42	49
20	Portsmouth	46	8	6	9	28	30	5	4	14	23	33	49
21	QP Rangers	46	8	9	6	28	21	2	10	11	23	42	49
22	Manchester C	46	6	6	11	28	26	6	6	11	28	31	48
23	STOKE	46	8	5	10	30	40	3	8	12	14	34	46
24	Reading	46	8	4	11	27	31	3	5	15	12	47	42
		1104	262	146	144	835	575	144	146	262	575	835	1510

* promoted after play-offs

Odds & ends

Double wins: (0).
Double losses: (7) Birmingham, Crewe, Huddersfield, Reading, Sunderland, Swindon, Tranmere.

Won from behind: (2) Bradford C (h), Portsmouth (h).
Lost from in front: (2) Sheffield Utd (a), Swindon (h).

High spots: Early season good form.
Winning at Maine Road, Portman Road and the Riverside.
The late season emergence of Dean Crowe.

Low spots: The dismal relegation.
Being thrashed by Birmingham 0-7.
The violence after the last game against Manchester City.
The atrocious home form at the new Britannia Stadium.
Loss of form of quality players such as Sigurdsson and Kavanagh.

Player of the Year: Justin Whittle.
Ever-presents: (0).
Hat-tricks: (0).
Leading scorer: (16) Peter Thorne.

	Appearances Lge	*Sub*	LC	*Sub*	FAC	*Sub*	Goals Lge	LC	FAC	Tot
Angola, Zay	**4**	*8*	2				**1**			**1**
Crowe, Dean	**10**	*6*	1	*1*			**4**			**4**
Donaldson, O'Neill	**2**									
Forsyth, Richard	**37**		4		1		**7**	1		**8**
Gabbiadini, Marco	**2**	*6*			1				1	**1**
Griffin, Andy	**23**		4		1		**1**			**1**
Heath, Robert	**4**	*2*								
Holsgrove, Paul	**11**	*1*					**1**			**1**
Kavanagh, Graham	**44**		4	*1*			**5**	5		**10**
Keen, Kevin	**37**	*3*	5		1		**1**	1		**2**
Lightbourne, Kyle	**9**	*4*					**2**			**2**
Macari, Paul		*3*								
Mackenzie, Neil	**7**	*5*	1	*1*						
McKinlay, Tosh	**3**									
McMahon, Gerry	**7**	*10*	2	*1*						
McNally, Mark	**3**	*1*								
Muggleton, Carl	**34**		5		1					
Nyamah, Kofi	**9**	*1*	1	*1*						
Pickering, Ally	**42**		5		1		**1**			**1**
Schreuder, Dick				*2*						
Scully, Tony	**7**									
Sigurdsson, Larus	**43**		5		1		**1**			**1**
Sobiech, Jorg	**3**									
Southall, Neville	**12**									
Stewart, Paul	**22**		2		1		**3**			**3**
Sturridge, Simon		*1*		*1*						
Taaffe, Steven		*3*								
Thorne, Peter	**33**	*3*	4			*1*	**12**	4		**16**
Tiatto, Danny	**11**	*4*					**1**			**1**
Tweed, Steven	**35**	*3*	5		1					
Wallace, Ray	**36**	*3*	5		1		**3**			**3**
Whittle, Justin	**15**	*5*		*4*	1					
Woods, Stephen		*1*								
Xausa, Davide	**1**									
(own-goals)							**1**			**1**
34 players used	**506**	*73*	55	*12*	11	*1*	**44**	11	1	**56**

No	Date		Att	Pos	Pt	F-A	H-T	Scorers, Times, and Referees	1	2	3	4	5	6	7	8	9	10	11	subs used
1	A	NORTHAMPTON			W	3-1	1-1	Kavanagh 7p, Thorne 63, Crowe 83	Muggleton	Robinson	Small	Sigurdsson	Woods	Whittle*	Keen	Kavanagh	Thorne	Lightbourne^	Oldfield	Short/Crowe
	8/8		6,661		3			Corazzin 17	Woodman	Matthew*	Frain	Bishop	Warburton	Spedding	Gibb	Peer^	Heggs"	Corazzin	Hill !	Clarkson/Freestone/Hunt
								Ref: A D'Urso	New boss Brian Little gets off to the best possible start as Colin Hill handles Sigurdsson's header on the line. He is sent off and Kavanagh slots the pen. Carlo Corazzin belts home a free-kick before City take control. Thorne's header and Crowe's run and shot seal an easy win. Emphatic.											
2	H	MACCLESFIELD		1	W	2-0	2-0	Crowe 25, Thorne 36	Muggleton	Short	Small	Sigurdsson	Robinson*	Woods	Keen	Kavanagh	Thorne	Crowe	Oldfield^	Whittle/Pickering
	15/8		13,981	24	6				Price	Tinson	Ingram	Payne	McDonald	Sodje	Askey	Wood	Tomlinson*	Sorvel	Whittaker	Barclay
								Ref: B Coddington	Little's wing-back system looks impressive against Sammy McIlroy's Silkmen. Crowe heads Keen's centre home emphatically. Thorne cracks in from the edge of the box. Sodje fouls Crowe persistently and is booked but ventures upfield to fire against the crossbar deep in injury-time.											
3	A	PRESTON		1	W	4-3	0-2	Crowe 50, 85, Kavanagh 69, 72p	Muggleton	Short	Small	Sigurdsson*	Robinson^	Woods	Keen	Kavanagh	Thorne	Crowe"	Oldfield	Whittle/Lightbourne/Wallace
	22/8		11,587	7	9			Nogan 6, 63, Eyres 38	Moilanen	Parkinson	Kidd	McKenna	Jackson	Gregan	Appleton	Rankine	Nogan	Macken*	Eyres	Holt
								Ref: T Jones	Kurt Nogan's cross-shot and David Eyres' drive put David Moyes' Preston in charge. Crowe belts home from an acute angle but as City press Nogan races clear to beat Muggers. Small's cross is headed in by Kav. The penalty is for handball. Crowe runs through to win it. Exhilarating.											
4	H	OLDHAM		1	W	2-0	1-0	Keen 22, Lightbourne 90	Muggleton	Short	Small	Sigurdsson	Robinson	Woods	Keen	Kavanagh^	Thorne	Crowe*	Oldfield	Lightbourne/Wallace
	29/8		12,306	21	12				Kelly	McNiven	Holt	Garnett	Graham	Duxbury	Allott	Orlygsson	Littlejohn	Whitehall	Reid	
								Ref: G Cain	Stoke attack from the off. Keen chips a brilliant goal into the far corner from 25 yards. Kelly pulls off a superb save from Keen's header. Andy Ritchie's Latics push City back. Wallace blocks Reid's shot bravely. Lightbourne converts Thorne's pass. Sheffield Utd are chasing Kavanagh.											
5	A	COLCHESTER		1	W	1-0	0-0	Kavanagh 78	Muggleton	Short	Small	Sigurdsson	Robinson	Woods	Keen^	Kavanagh	Thorne	Crowe*	Oldfield	Lightbourne/Wallace
	31/8		4,728	12	15				Emberson	Haydon	Betts	Williams	Greene	Buckle^	Wilkins	Gregory D	Sale	Gregory N	Duguid*	Abrahams/Forbes
								Ref: P Taylor	City miraculously survive U's furious onslaught. 6ft 6in ex-City apprentice Mark Sale causes mayhem. Muggleton produces a string of superb saves to deny both Gregorys and Abrahams. Carl Emberson saves Thorne's header but is beaten by a 25-yard Kav volley which rockets home.											
6	H	BOURNEMOUTH		1	W	2-0	0-0	Thorne 70, Crowe 76	Muggleton	Short	Small^	Whittle	Robinson	Woods	Keen	Wallace"	Thorne	Lightbourne	Oldfield*	Crowe/Tweed/Heath
	5/9		13,443	4	18				Ovendale	Young	Vincent	Howe	Berthe*	Bailey"	Cox	Robinson	Stein	Fletcher	Hughes	Town^/Dean/Tindall
								Ref: P Richards	Stein screws a good chance wide. City rarely threaten. Little brings on Heath and Crowe who turn the game. Thorne nets amid confusion in the area. Crowe prods past Mark Ovendale. Stoke are 9-4 favs to lift the title after their best ever start to a season. Little is manager of the month.											
7	A	FULHAM		1	L	0-1	0-0		Muggleton	Short*	Heath	Sigurdsson	Robinson	Woods	Keen	Kavanagh^	Thorne	Lightbourne	Oldfield	Whittle/Crowe
	8/9		12,055	2	18			Brevett 60	Taylor	Collins^	Brevett	Morgan	Coleman	Symons	Beardsley	Bracewell	Moody*	Hayward	Salako"	Lehmann/Uhlenbeek/Davis
								Ref: C Wilkes	Kevin Keegan's Fulham put City under heavy pressure. Robinson heads off the line. Symons hits the bar. Hayward hits the post. Rufus Brevett beats two players to drive across Muggleton. Kav slips Thorne in but he drills over. Chris Short flakes out and needs oxygen to resuscitate him.											
8	H	MILLWALL		1	W	1-0	0-0	Lightbourne 90	Muggleton	Whittle	Heath*	Sigurdsson	Robinson	Woods	Keen	Kavanagh	Thorne	Lightbourne	Oldfield	Crowe
	12/9		12,307	14	21				Spink	Lavin	Ryan	Bowry	Nethercott	Fitzgerald	Neill	Cahill*	Harris	Shaw	Carter	Bircham
								Ref: F Stretton	Robinson nods off the line. Sigurdsson puts a free header over from six yards. Sigurdsson stands on the ball but Shaw fires straight at Muggers and then blazes high and wide from four yards. Nigel Spink lets Lightbourne's effort slip through his hands. Bolton are watching Dean Crowe.											
9	A	WREXHAM		1	W	1-0	0-0	Wallace 78	Muggleton	Robinson*	Woods	Sigurdsson	Whittle	Oldfield	Keen	Kavanagh	Thorne	Lightbourne	Crowe^	Heath/Wallace
	19/9		7,290	13	24				Cartwright	McGregor	Brace	Russell^	Ridler	Humes	Skinner	Owen	Connolly	Spink*	Ward	Roberts/Thomas
								Ref: W Burns	A scrappy match of few chances. Crowe slices wide when well placed. Muggleton turns Peter Ward's free-kick round the post. A Lightbourne centre eludes Thorne but Ray Wallace races in to bullet a header home. A takeover bid by Derek Dougan's consortium is rejected by the board.											
10	H	BLACKPOOL		1	L	1-3	0-2	Crowe 69p	Muggleton	Robinson	Heath	Sigurdsson	Whittle	Woods	Keen	Kavanagh*	Thorne	Lightbourne	Oldfield	Crowe
	26/9		15,002	3	24			Carlisle 6, Aldridge 35, 86	Banks	Bryan	Shuttleworth	Bardsley*	Carlisle	Ormerod	Hughes	Clarkson	Aldridge"	Bushell	Malkin^	Brabin/Bent/Nowland
								Ref: J Kirkby	City play superbly. Blackpool ride their luck. Three out of four shots nestle in the back of the net. Kav is injured in a tackle with Steve Bushell. Martin Aldridge scores two on the break as the Tangerines withstand intense pressure. Thorne has his shirt tugged and Crowe converts the pen.											
11	A	READING		1	L	1-2	0-1	Whittle 69	Muggleton	Robinson	Small*	Sigurdsson	Woods	Whittle	Keen	Kavanagh	Thorne	Lightbourne	Oldfield	Crowe
	3/10		13,089	18	24			Brebner 44, McIntyre 73	Howie	Crawford	McPherson	Parkinson	Primus	Casper	Brayson*	Caskey	Williams	Glasgow	Brebner	McIntyre
								Ref: P Walton	Kavanagh is sandwiched in the box but the ref waves play on. Tommy Burns' Royals survive as Thorne heads a great chance at Howie. Darren Caskey whips past Small to set up Grant Brebner to net. Whittle heads home a Keen cross. Jim McIntyre nods home unchallenged. Stoke wilt.											

No	Date / Venue	Opponent / Att	Pos	Res / Pts	F-A	H-T	Scorers, Times, Referees	1	2	3	4	5	6	7	8	9	10	11	Subs used
12	H	CHESTERFIELD	1	D	0-0	0-0		Muggleton	Heath	Small	Whittle	Robinson	Woods	Keen	Kavanagh	Thorne*	Lightbourne	Oldfield^	Crowe/Short
	12/10	10,557	*14*	25				*Mercer*	*Hewitt*	*Nicholson*	*Jules*	*Williams*	*Breckin*	*Howard*	*Holland*	*Reeves*	*Ebdon*	*Perkins*	
							Ref: A Hall	A turgid game with few chances. Stoke have over 70% of the possession but John Duncan's Spireites have the best chance. Jon Howard has a shot blocked point blank by Muggers. Lightbourne heads straight at Billy Mercer. Keen's flair is not matched by the rest of the team. Tedious.											
13	A	LINCOLN	1	W	2-1	0-1	Robinson 49, Sigurdsson 52	Muggleton	Short	Small	Sigurdsson	Robinson	Woods	Keen	Kavanagh	Thorne	Lightbourne	Oldfield	
	17/10	*6,159*	*23*	28			*Battersby 8*	*Richardson*	*Barnett*	*Whitney**	*Fleming*	*Holmes*	*Austin*	*Smith*	*Finnigan*	*Battersby*	*Alcide*	*Oatway*	*Gordon*
							Ref: C Foy	Lowly Imps tear into Stoke. Tony Battersby pounces after Steve Holmes heads against the bar. Lincoln pour forward. Finnigan fires wide. Half-time is timely for City. Phil Robinson nods in his first Stoke goal. Keen's next corner is headed home by Sigurdsson. Muggers denies Smith.											
14	A	BRISTOL ROV	2	L	0-1	0-1		Muggleton	Short	Small	Sigurdsson	Robinson	Woods*	Keen	Kavanagh^	Thorne	Lightbourne	Oldfield"	Whittle/Wallace/Crowe
	20/10	*6,752*	*10*	28			*Cureton 8*	*Jones*	*Leoni**	*Challis*	*Zabek*	*Foster*	*Smith*	*Holloway*	*Meaker*	*Ipoua^*	*Cureton*	*Hayles*	*Trees/Penrice*
							Ref: A Leake	On Stoke's first visit to Rovers' Memorial Stadium, Jamie Cureton blazes a loose ball home from the edge of the box. Thorne sends a dipping 30-yarder just over and then hits the bar. Muggleton saves superbly from Barry Hayles. Crowe cuts inside but his cross evades Thorne's lunge.											
15	H	WIGAN	1	W	2-1	0-0	Kavanagh 52, Griffiths 53 (og)	Muggleton	Short	Small	Whittle	Robinson	Woods	Keen	Kavanagh^	Thorne"	Crowe*	Oldfield	Lightb'rne/Wallace/Mackenzie
	24/10	11,480	*17*	31			*Barlow 74*	*Carroll*	*Green*	*Bradshaw*	*Griffiths*	*Balmer*	*Rogers*	*Kilford*	*Greenall**	*Haworth*	*O'Neill*	*Liddell^*	*Lee/Barlow*
							Ref: W Jordan	In monsoon conditions the balance is tipped when the referee spots a shirt tug on Crowe. Kav's spot-kick is saved but Keen picks up the pieces allowing a relieved Kavanagh to score. Gareth Griffiths nods Chris Short's cross past Roy Carroll. Stuart Barlow nets for Ray Mathias' Latics.											
16	A	NOTTS CO	1	L	0-1	0-1		Muggleton	Short	Small	Sigurdsson	Robinson	Whittle	Keen^	Kavanagh	Thorne	Crowe	Oldfield*	Lightbourne/Wallace
	31/10	*8,546*	*15*	31			*Farrell 35*	*Ward*	*Hendon*	*Pearce*	*Redmile*	*Fairclough*	*Finnan*	*Owers*	*Garcia*	*Farrell**	*Devlin*	*Murray*	*Jones*
							Ref: E Lomas	Sam Allardyce's Magpies are in control from the off. Muggers saves well from Devlin, Pearce and Farrell. Robinson blocks a shot on the line. Sean Farrell nets after a static City fail to clear a corner. Stoke receive six yellow cards. Lightbourne hits a feeble shot straight at Darren Ward.											
17	H	LUTON	1	W	**3-1**	2-0	Oldfield 3, Forsyth 37, Lightbourne 90	Muggleton	Short"	Small*	Sigurdsson	Robinson	Woods	Keen	Forsyth^	Thorne	Lightbourne	Oldfield	Whittle/Wallace/Mackenzie
	7/11	12,964	*6*	34			*Douglas 81*	*Davis*	*Alexander !*	*Thomas**	*Spring^*	*Davis*	*Johnson*	*McKinnon*	*Evers*	*Douglas*	*Gray*	*McGowan*	*McLaren/Doherty*
							Ref: M Jones	David Oldfield is roundly booed by Hatters fans but retaliates by netting against his old team. Richard Forsyth volleys home from 12 yards on his first start for six months and scores. Graham Alexander is sent off for two bookings. Lightbourne heads home Steve Woods' precise centre.											
18	A	BURNLEY	1	W	2-0	0-0	Lightbourne 47, Thorne 62	Muggleton	Woods	Small	Sigurdsson	Robinson	Forsyth	Keen	Kavanagh	Thorne	Lightbourne	Oldfield	
	10/11	*10,575*	*18*	37				*Ward*	*Scott*	*Morgan*	*Vindheim**	*Heywood*	*Reid*	*Little*	*Brass*	*Eastwood^*	*Ford*	*O'Kane*	*Henderson/Maylett*
							Ref: G Laws	Stan Ternent's Clarets miss top scorer Andy Payton. Muggers saves well from Glen Little. Lightbourne knocks in Kav's mis-hit effort. Thorne thumps in a header from Kavanagh's delicious centre. Brian Little is in the frame for the vacant job at Wolves. Kav signs a new four-year deal.											
19	H	YORK	1	W	2-0	2-0	Forsyth 30, Oldfield 35	Muggleton	Woods	Small	Sigurdsson	Robinson	Forsyth	Keen	Kavanagh	Thorne	Lightbourne*	Oldfield	Wallace
	21/11	11,795	*18*	40				*Warrington*	*McMillan*	*Hall*	*Tinkler*	*Jones*	*Garratt*	*Connelly*	*Jordan*	*Cresswell*	*Rowe*	*Agnew**	*Reed*
							Ref: M Pike	The battle of the Little brothers sees Brian outwit Alan. Small's centre is flicked on for Forsyth to finish off at the far post. Oldfield lets loose a thunderbolt which flies past Andy Warrington. Sigurdsson subdues £1m-rated Richard Cresswell classily. Little is manager of the month again.											
20	A	WYCOMBE	1	W	1-0	0-0	Kavanagh 79	Muggleton	**Petty**	Small	Sigurdsson	Robinson	Woods	Keen	Kavanagh*	Thorne^	Forsyth	Oldfield	Wallace/Sturridge
	28/11	*6,023*	*23*	43				*Taylor*	*Lawrence*	*Vinnicombe**	*McCarthy*	*Cousins*	*Mohan*	*Simpson*	*Brown*	*McSporran*	*Scott*	*Emblen*	*Bulman*
							Ref: L Cable	Sigurdsson's header crashes off the bar. Muggers produces a great save from a Michael Simpson free-kick. Woods nods McCarthy's header off the line. Kav rifles in a loose ball from the edge of the box but is booked for over-celebrating and receives a second suspension of the season.											
21	H	GILLINGHAM	1	D	0-0	0-0		Muggleton	Short*	Small	Sigurdsson	Robinson	Woods	Keen	Forsyth	Sturridge^	Lightbourne	Oldfield	Wallace/Crowe
	12/12	17,233	*5*	44				*Bartram*	*Southall*	*Butters*	*Smith*	*Bryant*	*Pennock*	*Patterson*	*Hessenthaler*	*Asaba*	*Galloway*	*Taylor**	*Hodge*
							Ref: T Heilbron	A bore draw. Kav and Thorne are suspended. Crowe has a close-range shot well saved by Vince Bartram. 64 Elvis look-alikes watch the match from the Sentinel Stand. Justin Whittle moves to Hull (£25k). Peter Thorne signs on until 2002. Ally Pickering joins Burnley on a free transfer.											
22	A	WALSALL	3	L	0-1	0-1		Muggleton	Forsyth	Small	Sigurdsson	Robinson	Woods"	Keen	Kavanagh	Thorne	Lightbourne*	Oldfield^	Crowe/Wallace/Petty
	19/12	*9,056*	*2*	44			*Rammell 41*	*Walker*	*Marsh*	*Pointon*	*Keates*	*Green*	*Roper*	*Wrack*	*Otta**	*Rammell*	*Larusson*	*Simpson*	*Brissett*
							Ref: E Wolstenholme	City have plenty of possession but lack a cutting edge. Ray Graydon's Walsall soak up the pressure and break well. Andy Rammell hits the bar before heading home Neil Pointon's cross. A new attendance record is set for the Bescot Stadium. Steven Tweed signs for Dundee for £30,000.											
23	H	PRESTON	3	L	0-1	0-1		Muggleton	Petty	Small	Sigurdsson	Robinson	Woods*	Keen	Kavanagh	Thorne	Lightbourne	Oldfield	Crowe
	26/12	**23,272**	*4*	44			*Jackson 7*	*Lucas*	*Parkinson*	*Kidd*	*Murdock*	*Jackson*	*Gregan*	*Cartwright*	*Rankine*	*Macken^*	*Byfield**	*Eyres*	*Nogan/Harris*
							Ref: G Frankland	A swirling wind ruins the game and contributes to an in-swinging corner finding Michael Jackson who nods in from close range. City huff and puff but Preston close down space well. David Lucas tips Thorne's overhead kick over the bar. Lack of punch up front is worrying Brian Little.											

No	Date		Att	Pos	Pt	F-A	H-T	Scorers, Times, and Referees	1	2	3	4	5	6	7	8	9	10	11	subs used
24	A	MANCHESTER C		3	L	1-2	1-0	Sigurdsson 31	Muggleton	Petty	Small	Sigurdsson	Robinson	Woods	Keen	Kavanagh	Thorne	Lightbourne*	Oldfield	Sturridge
	28/12		30,478	7	44			Dickov 47, Taylor 85	Weaver	Crooks	Edghill	Wiekens	Vaughan	Horlock	Brown	Pollock	Taylor	Bishop*	Dickov	Goater
								Ref: A Butler	Sigurdsson leaps to nod Keen's cross beyond Nicky Weaver. Stoke look comfortable sitting on the lead until Joe Royle puts three up front after the break. Shaun Goater causes havoc. Dickov picks up the pieces. Gareth Taylor heads in his first goal since his £400k move from Sheff Utd.											
25	H	NORTHAMPTON		3	W	**3-1**	0-0	Wallace 56, Thorne 74, Lightbourne 84	Muggleton	Petty	Heath	Wallace	Robinson	Woods	Keen	Kavanagh	Thorne^	Mackenzie"	Oldfield*	Lightbourne/Crowe/Forsyth
	9/1		11,180	18	47			Howey 90	Turley	Gibb	Frain	Sampson	Howey	Parrish*	Hunter	Savage"	Wilkinson^	Freestone	Spedding	Peer/Corazzin/Hope
								Ref: D Pugh	The players are booed off at the break after failing to create a chance. Billy Turley makes a mess of Robinson's effort and Wallace prods home. Thorne is gifted a tap-in after Turley fails to clear a long ball. Lightbourne heads home Keen's chip. Howey nods in a corner. First win in five.											
26	H	COLCHESTER		4	D	3-3	3-2	Gregory D 30 (og), Lightb'rne 34, Sig' 42	Muggleton	Wallace*	Small"	Sigurdsson	Robinson	Woods	Keen	Kavanagh	Thorne	Lightbourne^	Forsyth	Oldfield/Crowe/Petty
	23/1		12,507	17	48			Betts 9, Gregory D 45, Dozzell 79	Emberson	Dunne	Betts	Williams	Greene	Buckle	Wilkins	Gregory D	Skelton	Gregory N^	Duguid*	Abrahams/Dozzell
								Ref: T Jones	Simon Betts nets a cool volley. Stoke pour forward. David Gregory deflects Kav's centre past Emberson. Lightbourne powers in Keen's cross. Sigurdsson heads in Kav's cross. Gregory makes amends from close in. City sit back. Jason Dozzell nods in. Little denies he wishes to resign.											
27	H	MANCHESTER C		5	L	0-1	0-1		Muggleton	Heath	Small	Sigurdsson	Robinson !	Woods	Keen	Kavanagh*	Crowe	Lightbourne	Forsyth^	Oldfield/Wallace
	29/1		13,679	8	48			Wiekens 20	Weaver	Crooks"	Edghill	Wiekens	Vaughan	Horlock	Brown	Pollock^	Taylor	Goater	Cooke*	Dickov/Whitley Jim/Bishop
								Ref: C Wilkes	Stoke are totally outplayed and are lucky only to lose by one. Gerard Wiekens cracks in a loose ball. Joe Royle's Blues miss countless chances. Robinson is sent off (40 mins) for an atrocious challenge on Michael Brown. Supporters are uniting to bring together a bid to buy-out the board.											
28	A	BOURNEMOUTH		6	L	**0-4**	0-2		Muggleton	Short"	Small	Sigurdsson	Robinson	Woods^	Keen	Kavanagh !	Crowe	Mackenzie*	Oldfield	Lightbourne/Forsyth/Wallace
	6/2		7,637	4	48			Fletcher 21, 39, Robinson 71, Hayter 76	Ovendale	Young	Vincent"	Howe	O'Neill !	Bailey	Cox	Robinson	Boli*	Fletcher	Hughes	Warren^/Hayter/Jenkins
								Ref: S Bennett	The wheels really come off at Dean Court. Steve Fletcher heads home and then profits when Sigurdsson nods past Muggers on the edge of the box. Kav and John O'Neill walk for fighting (44 mins). Hayter belts home a beauty from 16 yards. Little acknowledges the unrest in the camp.											
29	A	MILLWALL		7	L	0-2	0-1		Muggleton	Short	Small*	**Collins**	Petty	Woods^	Keen	Wallace	Crowe	Forsyth	Oldfield	Lightbourne/Mackenzie
	20/2		7,855	9	48			Harris 39, Cahill 65	Smith	Lavin	Stuart	Cahill	Nethercott	Dolan	Reid*	Bowry !	Harris^	Sadlier !	Neill	Bircham/Ifill
								Ref: R Styles	City cannot even beat nine-man Millwall – Bobby Bowry is dismissed (3 mins) for elbowing Wallace, Richard Sadlier for a second yellow (70 mins). Harris and Cahill score as the defence stands and watches. City cannot beat stand-in keeper Phil Smith. A total and utter embarrassment.											
30	H	WREXHAM		9	L	1-3	0-1	Sigurdsson 82	**Ward**	Short	Small	Sigurdsson	Petty^	Collins	Keen"	Wallace*	Lightbourne	**O'Connor**	Oldfield	Crowe/Forsyth/Taaffe
	27/2		10,765	14	48			McGregor 8, Owen 54, Connolly 67	Wright	McGregor	Hardy	Brammer	Ridler	Carey	Chalk	Russell	Connolly	Owen	Whitley	
								Ref: M Messias	Mark McGregor lobs free-transfer signing Gavin Ward. Connolly sets up Owen to finish before racing clear himself to round Ward. Sigurdsson heads home Short's corner. Stan Clarke has relinquished all interest in the club and sold his shares back to Peter Coates and Keith Humphreys.											
31	A	BLACKPOOL		7	W	1-0	1-0	Lightbourne 34	Ward	Short	Woods	Sigurdsson	**Mohan**	Petty*	Keen	Forsyth	Lightbourne	Crowe^	Oldfield	Small/Wallace
	6/3		5,504	14	51				Banks	Bryan	Hills	Butler	Carlisle	Couzens^	Barnes*	Clarkson	Nowland	Hughes	Ormerod	Bent/Aldridge
								Ref: M Dean	Nicky Mohan, free transfer from Wycombe, steadies the ship. Nigel Worthington's Blackpool put City under intense pressure. Adam Nowland forces Ward into two good saves. Lightbourne heads home Keen's corner as Stoke steal the points. 'Don't write off promotion yet' says Little.											
32	H	READING		8	L	**0-4**	0-0		Ward	Short*	Woods	Robinson"	Mohan	**Kavanagh J**	Keen^	Forsyth	Lightbourne	Crowe	Oldfield	Small/Thorne/Wallace
	10/3		8,218	10	51			McKeever 59, McIntyre 76, 82, Gray 87	Howie	Murty^	Gray	Parkinson	Primus	Bernal	Gurney"	Caskey	McKeever	Houghton	McIntyre*	Brayson/McPherson/Glasgow
								Ref: M Cowburn	Jason Kavanagh, another free transfer, arrives from Wycombe. His debut is a nightmare as the Royals run riot. On-loan Mark McKeever races clear to score. Crowe hits the post and Jim McIntyre is sent clear to score the first of his brace. City fall apart. The team spirit has disappeared.											
33	A	LUTON		7	W	2-1	2-0	Kavanagh G 10p, 17	Ward	Kavanagh J	Woods	Sigurdsson	Mohan	Short	Robinson	Kavanagh G	Forsyth^	Crowe*	Oldfield	Keen/Wallace
	13/3		5,221	14	54			Alexander 47p	Davis	Alexander	Thomas	Spring	White"	Johnson	Harrison*	McKinnon	Douglas	Gray	George^	McLaren/Doherty/Willmott
								Ref: A D'Urso	Lennie Lawrence's atrocious Hatters allow Stoke to take control. Kavanagh cracks home a spot-kick following Johnson's foul, before hitting a speculative shot which deceives Kelvin Davis. Alexander scores a pen after Woods handles. Luton have a goal disallowed for a foul on Ward.											
34	H	FULHAM		8	L	0-1	0-1		Ward	Kavanagh J	Woods	Sigurdsson	Mohan	Short	Robinson^	Kavanagh G	Lightbourne*	Keen	Oldfield	Crowe/Wallace
	16/3		12,298	1	54			Symons 10	Taylor	Finnan	Brevett	Morgan	Coleman	Symons	Hayward	Smith	Horsfield	Trollope	Hayles	
								Ref: P Danson	Runaway leaders Fulham snatch the lead against the run of play when Kit Symons' header creeps in at the far post. Kav urges City forward but the combative Cottagers defend in depth. 10,000 red cards are displayed by disgruntled fans desperate to see money being invested in the club.											

No	Ven	Opponent	Att	Pos	Pt	F-A	H-T	Scorers, Times, and Referees	1	2	3	4	5	6	7	8	9	10	11	subs used
35	H	NOTTS CO		9	L	2-3	0-0	Oldfield 68, Keen 90	Ward	Kavanagh J	Woods	Sigurdsson	Robinson	O'Connor	Keen	Kavanagh G	Wallace	Mackenzie	Oldfield	
	20/3		9,565	*16*	54			*Beadle 54, Liburd 76, Stallard 85*	*Ward*	*Hendon*	*Pearce*	*Liburd*	*Dyer*	*Richardson*	*Creaney*	*Redmile*	*Stallard*	*Beadle**	*Tierney*	*Rapley*
								Ref: G Cain	A chorus of boos ends an inept first half. Magpies score with their first effort. Oldfield rounds Darren Ward. Richard Liburd waltzes through a somnambulant defence and then Mark Stallard repeats the feat. Keen's volley does not appease the protesters. Two wins in the last ten games.											
36	A	WIGAN		8	W	3-2	0-0	Thorne 54, Kavanagh G 80, Strong 88	Muggleton	Kavanagh J	Small	Sigurdsson	Mohan	**Strong**	Keen	Kavanagh G	Thorne^	Oldfield	Lightbourne*	Crowe/Wallace
	27/3		*4,133*	*9*	57			*Liddell 49, Barlow 51*	*Nixon*	*Bradshaw*	*Sharp*	*McGibbon*	*Balmer*	*Rogers*	*Liddell*	*Greenall*	*Jones**	*O'Neill*	*Barlow*	*Kilford*
								Ref: R Furnandiz	Wigan have won eight in a row. A much-improved performance sees City battle back from the brink. Barlow's 30-yarder sails over Muggleton before Thorne challenges Nixon and nets as the ball runs free. Kav's mazy run is ended by a superb shot. Strong scores the winner on his debut.											
37	H	LINCOLN		7	W	2-0	1-0	Thorne 21, 65	Muggleton	Kavanagh J*	Small	Sigurdsson	Mohan	Strong	Keen	Kavanagh G	Thorne^	Lightbourne	Oldfield"	Robinson/Crowe/Wallace
	3/4		12,845	*22*	60				*Richardson*	*Barnett*	*Phillips*	*Fleming*	*Holmes*	*Brown*	*Wilder^*	*Philpott*	*Battersby*	*Gordon**	*Miller*	*Smith/Fenn*
								Ref: E Lomas	Thorne's brace arrive courtesy of a header from Keen's centre and a crisp, low drive from 25 yards. Lightbourne blazes wildly over from close range. A scrappy match peters out. Fans' organisation Save Our Stoke organise a 2,000 strong march to register their protests against the board.											
38	A	CHESTERFIELD		8	D	1-1	1-1	Oldfield 32	Muggleton	Robinson	Small	Sigurdsson	Mohan	Strong	Keen	Kavanagh G	Thorne	Lightbourne	Oldfield	
	5/4		*5,290*	*10*	61			*Blatherwick 26*	*Mercer*	*Hewitt*	*Nicholson**	*Blatherwick*	*Williams*	*Breckin*	*Lee*	*Beaumont*	*Reeves*	*Ebdon*	*Jules*	*Willis*
								Ref: P Taylor	Steve Blatherwick heads one of a succession of corners firmly into the roof of the net. Oldfield is sent clear by Lightbourne to blast home from the edge of the area. Keen heads off the line. City fail to force a win. Little delays contract talks until May. Stoke's first away draw this season.											
39	H	BRISTOL ROV		8	L	1-4	1-0	Thorne 41	Muggleton	Robinson*	Small	Sigurdsson	Mohan	Strong	Keen	Kavanagh G	Thorne	Lightbourne	Oldfield	Crowe
	10/4		17,823	*16*	61			*Roberts 53, Foster 81, Cureton 84, 88*	*Williams*	*Pritchard*	*Challis*	*Foster*	*Thomson*	*Tilson*	*Holloway*	*Hillier*	*Penrice*	*Cureton*	*Roberts*	
								Ref: M Pierce	Thorne arches his neck to nod in Kav's centre beautifully. Muggers saves Cureton's effort well but can't stop Roberts deflecting the follow-up home. Rovers take over. Kav misses from the spot after Small is tripped. Foster heads in from a free-kick. Cureton scores twice when put clear.											
40	H	WYCOMBE		8	D	2-2	1-1	Wallace 38, Oldfield 61	Muggleton	Robinson	Small	Sigurdsson	Mohan	Strong*	Keen	Kavanagh G	Crowe	Forsyth	Wallace	Oldfield
	14/4		**6,569**	*20*	62			*Devine 29, 89*	*Taylor*	*Lawrence*	*Vinnicombe*	*McCarthy*	*Bates*	*Ryan*	*Carroll**	*Simpson*	*Emblen^*	*Devine*	*Baird*	*Brown/McSporran*
								Ref: R Pearson	Nicky Mohan faces his old club. It appears that Stoke are heading towards a hard-earned win once Oldfield prods Crowe's pinpoint chip home to add to Wallace's cool finish. Record-signing Sean Devine turns to crack in his second goal for Wycombe from 12 yards. No play-offs now.											
41	A	YORK		7	D	2-2	1-0	Kavanagh G 10p, 85	Muggleton	Robinson	Small	Sigurdsson	Mohan	Wallace	Keen	Kavanagh G	Thorne	Lightbourne*	Oldfield^	Crowe/Forsyth
	17/4		*4,142*	*20*	63			*Garratt 51, Jordan 67*	*Mimms*	*Dawson*	*Thompson*	*Jordan*	*Jones*	*Fairclough*	*Pouton**	*Tinkler*	*Williams*	*Rowe*	*Garratt*	*Tolson*
								Ref: J Kirkby	Thorne is felled by Bobby Mimms and Kav tucks away the penalty. Managerless York battle back. Martin Garratt intercepts Mohan's dreadful back-pass to score. Scott Jordan cracks home a beauty from a half-cleared corner. Kav fires in Forsyth's pass. No disguising the lack of quality.											
42	H	BURNLEY		8	L	1-4	1-2	Crowe 31	Muggleton	Robinson	Small	Sigurdsson	Mohan	Oldfield*	Keen	Kavanagh G	Thorne	Crowe	Wallace	Connor
	24/4		10,965	*15*	63			*Pickering 5, Payton 11, Little 68, 90*	*Crichton*	*Pickering*	*Cowan*	*Mellon*	*Davis*	*Brass*	*Little*	*Cook**	*Cooke*	*Payton^*	*Armstrong*	*Jepson/Branch"/Johnrose*
								Ref: D Crick	Struggling Burnley romp home. Ex-Stokie Ally Pickering nets a glorious 25-yard volley. Payton profits when Mohan sells Keen short. Crowe heads home from six yards. Glen Little robs Sigurdsson to score then outruns Mohan to fire in a long ball. City's accounts show a £3m deficit.											
43	A	MACCLESFIELD		8	W	2-1	1-1	Oldfield 31, Crowe 50	Muggleton	Kavanagh J	Small	Sigurdsson	Mohan	Robinson	Keen	Wallace*	Thorne	Crowe	Oldfield	Forsyth
	27/4		***3,825***	*24*	66			*Matias 44*	*Price*	*Tinson*	*Hitchen*	*Brown^*	*Wood**	*Sodje*	*Askey*	*Sorvel*	*Tomlinson*	*Matias*	*Durkan"*	*Sedgemore/Davies/Bailey*
								Ref: E Lomas	Condemned Macclesfield force Muggleton into two good stops. Oldfield cracks in from 15 yards. Matias heads home unmarked from a corner. Crowe lobs the keeper when put clear. The depression is temporarily lifted. Kav is called up by Ireland and scores in a friendly versus Sweden.											
44	A	GILLINGHAM		8	L	**0-4**	0-3		Muggleton	Robinson	Small	Sigurdsson	Mohan	Wallace	Keen	Kavanagh G	Thorne	Crowe	Oldfield	
	1/5		*8,289*	*5*	66			*Taylor 30, 45, Butters 43, Smith 69*	*Bartram*	*Southall*	*Ashby*	*Smith*	*Butters*	*Pennock*	*Patterson"*	*Hessenthaler*	*Asaba**	*Galloway^*	*Taylor*	*Hodge/Saunders/Brown*
								Ref: C Wilkes	Stoke are gutless at Tony Pulis' play-off bound Gills. Robert Taylor nips past a static defence to beat Muggers twice but wastes a 44th-min pen for Sigurdsson's foul. Guy Butters nets a free header. Paul Smith also nods in unmarked. Brian Little admits it is the worst performance so far.											
45	A	OLDHAM		8	L	0-1	0-0		Muggleton	Kavanagh J*	**Clarke**	Collins	Mohan	Petty	O'Connor	Heath	**Connor**	Crowe	Oldfield	Taaffe
	4/5		*5,015*	*21*	66			*Beavers 50*	*Kelly*	*Rickers*	*Holt*	*Garnett*	*Thorn*	*Duxbury*	*Innes*	*Sheridan*	*Beavers**	*Allott*	*Reid*	*Tipton^/Salt*
								Ref: J Robinson	Debutant Irish U-18 international Clive Clarke sets up Crowe with a wonderful cross-field ball but Gary Kelly saves at full stretch. Mark Allott hits the post before Stoke's statuesque defence watches Beavers flick in a long throw. Gloom and despondency amongst Stokies at the whistle.											
46	H	WALSALL		8	W	2-0	1-0	Connor 24, 50	Muggleton*	Petty	Clarke	Collins^	Mohan	O'Connor	Taaffe	Oldfield	Connor	Crowe	Small	**Fraser/Wooliscroft**"/Heath
	8/5		12,091	*2*	69				*Walker*	*Marsh^*	*Pointon*	*Larusson**	*Viveash*	*Roper*	*Wrack*	*Steiner*	*Rammell*	*Keates*	*Mavrak*	*Ricketts/Green*
	Home		Away					Ref: K Lynch	Youth is given its chance again and Crowe stings James Walker's fingers with a free-kick. On-loan Paul Connor (Middlesbrough) wants to stay after scoring his first senior goals. He flings himself at Crowe's cross and converts Taaffe's pass for a second win in nine. Some hope perhaps?											
Average	12,728		7,996																	

Worthington Cup	Att			F-A	H-T	Scorers, Times, and Referees	1	2	3	4	5	6	7	8	9	10	11	subs used
1:1 A MACCLESFIELD			L	1-3	1-1	Kavanagh 19	Muggleton	Short	Small	Sigurdsson	Robinson	Woods	Keen	Kavanagh	Thorne	Lightbourne	Oldfield	
11/8	*2,963*					*Wood 2, Askey 76, 85*	*Price*	*Tinson*	*Ingram*	*Payne*	*McDonald*	*Sodje*	*Askey*	*Wood**	*Tomlinson"*	*Sedgemore^*	*Whittaker*	*Sorvel/Durkan/Barclay*
						Ref: M Dean	The clubs' first meeting goes the way of Sammy McIlroy's Silkmen. Steve Wood nets before Thorne's header is inexplicably disallowed. Kav belts home a free-kick from 25 yards. John Askey runs through unchallenged to score and then cheekily back-heels a decisive third. Appalling.											
1:2 H MACCLESFIELD		1	W	1-0	0-0	Thorne 78	Muggleton	Short*	Small^	Whittle	Robinson	Woods	Pickering	Kavanagh !	Thorne	Crowe"	Oldfield	Tweed/Wallace/Sturridge
19/8	6,152	*24*					*Price*	*Tinson*	*Ingram*	*Payne*	*McDonald*	*Sodje*	*Askey**	*Wood*	*Durkan*	*Sorvel*	*Whittaker^*	*Tomlinson/Howarth*
						Ref: D Pugh (Stoke lose 2-3 on aggregate)	City miss Sigurdsson, on duty with Iceland. Town storm forward looking for the killer away goal. Stoke's passing is awful. Kav is sent off for a two-footed challenge (55 mins). Sturridge appears for the first time in nearly a year. Thorne prods past Ryan Price but Macclesfield hold on.											

FA Cup																		
1 A READING		1	W	1-0	1-0	Lightbourne 27	Muggleton	Woods	Small	Sigurdsson	Robinson	Forsyth	Keen	Kavanagh	Thorne	Lightbourne*	Oldfield	Wallace
14/11	*10,095*	*10*					*Howie*	*Bernal*	*McPherson*	*Crawford**	*Primus*	*Casper*	*Glasgow*	*Caskey*	*Williams*	*Brayson^*	*Brebner*	*Roach/Sarr*
						Ref: G Barber	Thorne is robbed by Linvoy Primus in the act of scoring. Lightbourne's fierce low drive beats Scott Howie to hand Stoke a first victory against Reading since 1993 despite the Royals' heavy late pressure. Stoke's first FA Cup win against league opposition away from home for 26 years.											
2 A SWANSEA		1	L	0-1	0-1		Muggleton	Petty*	Small	Sigurdsson	Robinson	Woods	Keen	Kavanagh	Thorne	Forsyth	Oldfield	Sturridge
5/12	*7,460*	*3:13*				*Appleby 41*	*Freestone*	*Jones S*	*Howard*	*Cusack*	*Smith*	*Bound*	*Price*	*Thomas*	*Alsop*	*Bird**	*Appleby*	*Jenkins*
						Ref: K Lynch	An open game with John Hollins' Swans' long-ball game providing Ritchie Appleby with the opening to fire past Muggers from Alsop's knock down. Thorne hits the bar. Appleby hooks off the line. Kav blazes just over. Bound nods Thorne's header off the line. Swans meet West Ham.											

		Home						Away					
		P	W	D	L	F	A	W	D	L	F	A	Pts
1	Fulham	46	19	3	1	50	12	12	5	6	29	20	101
2	Walsall	46	13	7	3	37	23	13	2	8	26	24	87
3	Manchester C*	46	13	6	4	38	14	9	10	4	31	19	82
4	Gillingham	46	15	5	3	45	17	7	9	7	30	27	80
5	Preston	46	12	6	5	46	23	10	7	6	32	27	79
6	Wigan	46	14	5	4	44	17	8	5	10	31	31	76
7	Bournemouth	46	14	7	2	37	11	7	6	10	26	30	76
8	STOKE	46	10	4	9	32	32	11	2	10	27	31	69
9	Chesterfield	46	14	5	4	34	16	3	8	12	12	28	64
10	Millwall	46	9	8	6	33	24	8	3	12	19	35	62
11	Reading	46	10	6	7	29	26	6	7	10	25	37	61
12	Luton	46	10	4	9	25	26	6	6	11	26	34	58
13	Bristol Rov	46	8	9	6	35	28	5	8	10	30	28	56
14	Blackpool	46	7	8	8	24	24	7	6	10	20	30	56
15	Burnley	46	8	7	8	23	33	5	9	9	31	40	55
16	Notts Co	46	8	6	9	29	27	6	6	11	23	34	54
17	Wrexham	46	8	6	9	21	28	5	8	10	22	34	53
18	Colchester	46	9	7	7	25	30	3	9	11	27	40	52
19	Wycombe	46	8	5	10	31	26	5	7	11	21	32	51
20	Oldham	46	8	4	11	26	31	6	5	12	22	35	51
21	York	46	6	8	9	28	33	7	3	13	28	47	50
22	Northampton	46	4	12	7	26	31	6	6	11	17	26	48
23	Lincoln	46	9	4	10	27	27	4	3	16	15	47	46
24	Macclesfield	46	7	4	12	24	30	4	6	13	19	33	43
		1104	243	146	163	769	589	163	146	243	589	769	1510

* promoted after play-offs

Odds & ends

Double wins: (4) Lincoln, Luton, Macclesfield, Wigan.
Double losses: (5) Bristol Rov, Fulham, Manchester C, Notts Co, Reading.

Won from behind: (3) Preston (a), Lincoln (a), Wigan (a).
Lost from in front: (2) Manchester C (a), Bristol Rov (h).

High spots: The best start to a season in the history of the club.
Astute close season signings.
Brian Little's resignation.
The fabulous away record.
Graham Kavanagh's long-range strikes.

Low spots: Failing to even challenge for the play-offs after dominating the first half of the season.
The turn around at Maine Road which sparks the slump.
Over reliance on the club's youngsters as the squad is stretched.
Brian Little's diffidence when things go awry.
The continuation of the shocking form at the Britannia Stadium.

Player of the Year: Kevin Keen.
Ever-presents: (0).
Hat-tricks: (0).
Leading scorer: (12) Graham Kavanagh.

	Appearances						Goals			
	Lge	*Sub*	LC	*Sub*	FAC	*Sub*	**Lge**	LC	FAC	**Tot**
Clarke, Clive	**2**									
Collins, Lee	**4**									
Connor, Paul	**2**	*1*					**2**			**2**
Crowe, Dean	**19**	*19*	1				**8**			**8**
Forsyth, Richard	**13**	*5*			2		**2**			**2**
Fraser, Stuart		*1*								
Heath, Robert	**7**	*3*								
Kavanagh, Graham	**36**		2		2		**11**	1		**12**
Kavanagh, Jason	**8**									
Keen, Kevin	**43**	*1*	1		2		**2**			**2**
Lightbourne, Kyle	**28**	*8*	1		1		**7**		1	**8**
Mackenzie, Neil	**3**	*3*								
Mohan, Nicky	**15**									
Muggleton, Carl	**40**		2		2					
O'Connor, James	**4**									
Oldfield, David	**43**	*3*	2		2		**6**			**6**
Petty, Ben	**9**	*2*			1					
Pickering, Ally		*1*	1							
Robinson, Phil	**39**	*1*	2		2		**1**			**1**
Short, Craig	**19**	*2*	2							
Sigurdsson, Larus	**38**		1		2		**4**			**4**
Small, Bryan	**35**	*2*	2		2					
Strong, Greg	**5**						**1**			**1**
Sturridge, Simon	**1**	*2*		*1*		*1*				
Taaffe, Steven	**1**	*2*								
Thorne, Peter	**33**	*1*	2		2		**9**	1		**10**
Tweed, Steven		*1*		*1*						
Wallace, Ray	**11**	*20*		*1*		*1*	**3**			**3**
Ward, Gavin	**6**									
Whittle, Justin	**9**	*5*	1				**1**			**1**
Woods, Stephen	**33**		2		2					
Wooliscroft, Ashley		*1*								
(own-goals)							**2**			**2**
32 Players used	**506**	***84***	**22**	***3***	**22**	***2***	**59**	**2**	**1**	**62**

No	Date		Att	Pos	Pt	F-A	H-T	Scorers, Times, and Referees	1	2	3	4	5	6	7	8	9	10	11	subs used
1	H	OXFORD			L	1-2	0-1	Kavanagh 59	Ward	Robinson	Small	Mohan	Sigurdsson	Keen*	Oldfield^	Kavanagh G	Taaffe	Lightbourne"	Connor	**Aiston**/Mackenzie/Crowe
	7/8		11,300		0			*Murphy 28, Anthrobus 78*	*Arendse*	*Robinson*	*Powell*	*Watson*	*Gilchrist*	*Murphy*	*Tait*	*Anthrobus*	*Shepheard*	*Lilley**	*Beauchamp*	*Folland*
								Ref: R Furnandiz	Gary Megson is in the hot seat after Brian Little's June departure. Sam Aiston, on loan from Sunderland, is the only new face. The season gets off to a terrible start when Murphy nods home in United's first attack. Kav blasts in from 20 yards but Steve Anthrobus heads home unmarked.											
2	A	PRESTON		22	L	1-2	1-0	Thorne 9	Ward	Robinson	Clarke	Mohan	Sigurdsson	Keen*	Oldfield	Kavanagh G	Taaffe^	Thorne	Connor"	Mackenzie/Jacobsen/Crowe
	14/8		*11,465*	*1*	0			*Nogan 52, Murdock 80*	*Lucas*	*Alexander*	*Jackson*	*Murdock*	*Kidd*	*Appleton*	*Rankine*	*Gregan*	*Eyres^*	*Macken**	*Nogan*	*Basham/McKenna*
								Ref: K Lynch	Battling Stoke grab a surprise lead at David Moyes' promotion favourites. Thorne nets whilst lying prone on the ground in a goalmouth melee. Eventually Preston's pressure tells as Kurt Nogan nips in to head past Ward. City move to three at the back but Murdock nods in from a corner.											
3	H	MILLWALL		15	W	3-1	1-0	Thorne 15, Connor 51, Kavanagh 84p	Ward	Robinson	Clarke"	Mohan*	Sigurdsson	O'Connor	Oldfield	Kavanagh G	Aiston^	Thorne	Connor	Petty/Small/Keen
	22/8		**7,054**	*20*	3			*Bircham 75*	*Warner*	*Neill*	*Ryan*	*Nethercott*	*Dolan*	*Bircham*	*Cahill*	*Livermore**	*Moody^*	*Shaw*	*Harris*	*Reid/Ifill*
								Ref: S Mathieson	City tame Alan McLeary's Lions who have not won in 10 games. Thorne nets after Joe Dolan gifts him the ball. Millwall have a goal ruled out before Connor lunges in to head Thorne's knock-back home. Marc Bircham sweeps home. Kav converts after Connor is mauled over by Dolan.											
4	A	BURNLEY		19	L	0-1	0-0		Ward	Jacobsen	Clarke	Robinson	Sigurdsson	Short"	Keen^	Kavanagh G	O'Connor	Thorne*	Connor	Crowe/Aiston/Oldfield
	28/8		*11,328*	*3*	3			*Payton 75*	*Crichton*	*West*	*Cowan*	*Mellon^*	*Thomas*	*Armstrong*	*Smith*	*Cook"*	*Lee**	*Payton*	*Johnrose*	*Branch/Little/Jepson*
								Ref: T Heilbron	Defences dominate. Anders Jacobsen organises City's back three well. Connor dwells when put through by Clarke and wastes the chance. Stan Ternent's Clarets push forward. Glen Little's direct running worries Robinson. Andy Payton breaks the deadlock with a shot which dribbles in.											
5	H	GILLINGHAM		19	D	1-1	0-0	Sigurdsson 87	Ward	Short	Clarke^	Jacobsen	Sigurdsson	Oldfield"	Aiston*	Kavanagh G	O'Connor	Thorne	Connor	Keen/Small/Crowe
	30/8		8,369	*23*	4			*Taylor 90*	*Williams*	*Patterson*	*Smith"*	*Ashby**	*Southall*	*Hessenthaler*	*Taylor*	*Saunders*	*Lee^*	*Pennock*	*Lewis*	*Miller/Thompson/Hodge*
								Ref: U Rennie	A dull match is sparked into life by a nail-biting last five minutes. A dubious corner is despatched into the back of the net by Sigurdsson. Peter Taylor's Gills pour forward. Bob Taylor loops home a header from a long throw. Megson is booked for encroaching beyond the technical area.											
6	A	CAMBRIDGE		14	W	3-1	1-0	Connor 19, Oldfield 81, Thorne 86	Ward	Short	Small	Mohan	Jacobsen	Oldfield	Keen	O'Connor	Thorne	Lightbourne*	Connor	Robinson
	4/9		***4,007***	*19*	7			*Lightbourne 47 (og)*	*V Heusden**	*Chenery*	*Ashbee*	*Duncan*	*Wanless*	*Butler*	*Benjamin*	*Russell*	*Kyd^*	*Eustace*	*Wilson*	*Marshall/Taylor*
								Ref: L Cable	In glorious sunshine Connor turns the ball home after Thorne's initial shot is saved. United charge forward and Stoke wobble. Eustace's shot is saved by Ward but rebounds against Lightbourne and into the net. Oldfield finishes off a brilliant free-kick routine. Thorne slams in on the run.											
7	A	CHESTERFIELD		12	W	2-0	0-0	Lightbourne 50, 90	Ward	Short^	Clarke	Mohan	Jacobsen	Robinson	Keen	O'Connor	Thorne	Lightbourne	Connor*	Kavanagh G/Oldfield
	11/9		*4,285*	*17*	10				*Leaning*	*Hewitt**	*Blatherwick*	*Breckin*	*Woods*	*Beaumont*	*Curtis*	*Ebdon*	*Carss^*	*Reeves*	*Willis*	*Dudley/Bettney*
								Ref: D Laws	Lowly Spireites put City under pressure. Ex-Stokie Steve Woods is prominent and the dangerous David Reeves tests Ward twice. Lightbourne nods Keen's free-kick past Andy Leaning. City grow in confidence. Lightbourne is tackled when about to tap in but then lofts home on the run.											
8	H	WIGAN		12	D	1-1	0-1	Lightbourne 48	Ward	Short	Clarke	Mohan	Jacobsen	Robinson*	Keen^	O'Connor	Thorne	Lightbourne	Kavanagh G	Oldfield/Aiston
	18/9		11,195	*3*	11			*Mohan 18 (og)*	*Carroll*	*Bradshaw*	*Bowen*	*Balmer*	*De Zeeuw*	*O'Neill*	*Kilford**	*Sheridan*	*Liddell^*	*Haworth*	*Barlow*	*Lee/Martinez*
								Ref: S Baines	An ill-tempered game. Mohan deflects Liddell's shot in. Lightbourne loops a header over Roy Carroll. Robinson is scythed down and requires 24 stitches in a thigh wound. An Icelandic consortium is rumoured to want to buy the club. Larus Sigurdsson is sold to West Brom for £350k.											
9	A	WREXHAM		6	W	3-2	1-1	Thorne 27, Lightbourne 50, Mohan 78	Ward	Short	Clarke	Mohan	Jacobsen	O'Connor	Keen	Connor*	Thorne^	Lightbourne"	Kavanagh G	Robinson/Heath/Oldfield
	25/9		*5,924*	*11*	14			*Carey 6, Lowe 83*	*Dearden*	*McGregor*	*Owen*	*Carey*	*Connolly*	*Ridler*	*Barrett^*	*Ryan**	*Stevens"*	*F'lconbridge*	*Ferguson*	*Hannon/Chalk/Lowe*
								Ref: M Messias	New skipper Mohan allows Brian Carey to nod Brian Flynn's men ahead. Thorne scores from 10 yards during a scramble. Lightbourne's effort is deflected past the helpless Kevin Dearden. Mohan plants a header home to make amends. David Lowe sets up a frenetic finish with a header.											
10	H	SCUNTHORPE		6	W	1-0	0-0	Connor 90	Ward	Short	Clarke	Mohan	Jacobsen	O'Connor	Keen	Oldfield*	Thorne^	Lightbourne	Kavanagh G	Connor/Aiston
	2/10		13,068	*20*	17				*Evans*	*Harsley^*	*Dawson*	*Logan*	*Wilcox*	*Hope*	*Walker*	*Hodges**	*Ipoua*	*Marshall*	*Sparrow*	*Sheldon/Gayle*
								Ref: R Olivier	Megson is manager of the month but speculation suggests he would leave if the proposed takeover goes through. City have the better of a tight game. Kav has a shot kicked off the line. Guy Ipoua causes problems. United hit a post. Connor scores at the second attempt from Keen's pass.											
11	H	READING		3	W	2-1	0-0	Mohan 68, Jacobsen 89	Ward	Short	Small	Mohan	Jacobsen	O'Connor	Robinson*	Keen"	Thorne^	Lightbourne !	Kavanagh G	Connor/Oldfield/Heath
	9/10		9,621	*19*	20			*Forster 52*	*Whitehead*	*Parkinson*	*Primus*	*Casper*	*Caskey**	*Forster*	*Williams*	*Crawford*	*Bernal*	*Hodges^*	*Smith*	*Grant/McIntyre*
								Ref: T Jones	A minute's silence for those killed in the Paddington rail crash. O'Connor's back-pass falls to Nicky Forster who scores. Mohan volleys home Thorne's nod down gloriously as City fight back. Jacobsen nods in his first for the club to steal the points. Lightbourne walks for two yellows.											

No	Date	Opponent	Att	Pos	Pts	Res	FT	HT	Scorers, Times, and Referees	1	2	3	4	5	6	7	8	9	10	11	subs used
12	A	BOURNEMOUTH		4		D	1-1	0-1	Clarke 62	Ward	Short	Small*	Mohan !	Jacobsen	O'Connor	Robinson^	Keen	Thorne	Lightbourne"	Kavanagh G	Clarke/Connor/**Bullock**
	16/10		*5,990*	*11*	21				*Robinson 24*	*Ovendale*	*Young*	*Warren**	*Howe^*	*Cox*	*Broadhurst*	*Mean*	*Robinson*	*Stein*	*Fletcher*	*Jorgensen*	*O'Neill/Huck*
									Ref: A D'Urso	Stoke escape as Mel Machin's Cherries dominate. Mark Stein releases Steve Robinson to rifle past the outstanding Ward. Short and O'Connor combine to set up Clarke who skips past two challenges before cracking home. Mohan is dismissed (81 mins) for lashing out at Steve Fletcher.											
13	A	CARDIFF		2		W	2-1	1-1	Thorne 23, O'Connor 84	Ward	Short	Clarke	Mohan	Jacobsen	O'Connor	Bullock*	Keen^	Thorne	Lightbourne"	Kavanagh G	Robinson/Petty/Connor
	19/10		*6,146*	*18*	24				*Legg 40*	*Hallworth*	*Faerber*	*Legg**	*Perrett*	*Boland*	*Nugent*	*Fowler*	*Hill*	*Eckhardt*	*Thomas*	*Vaughan*	*Brazier*
									Ref: P Danson	Thorne heads home Short's cross. Andy Legg whacks home a superb 25-yard free-kick. Stoke become disjointed but O'Connor sticks out a leg to deflect in a cross. The Icelanders, including former Bundesliga Footballer of the Year Siggy Sigurvinsson, confirm their offer to buy the club.											
14	H	WREXHAM		3		W	2-0	0-0	O'Connor 48, Kavanagh 58	Ward	Short	Clarke	Mohan	Jacobsen	O'Connor	Bullock*	Keen	Thorne	Connor	Kavanagh G	Robinson
	23/10		10,545	*15*	27					*Dearden*	*McGregor*	*Hardy*	*Owen*	*Carey*	*Chalk**	*Connolly*	*Spink*	*Barrett^*	*Roberts*	*Gibson*	*Faulconbridge/Russell*
									Ref: S Lodge	Ward saves brilliantly from Gareth Owen. 18-year-old Matthew Bullock drives forward down the right. O'Connor cracks a short free-kick past Dearden. Kav races on to Keen's pass to shoot inside the far post. Ward saves from Faulconbridge, who also hits a post. 12 games without loss.											
15	H	NOTTS CO		6		L	0-1	0-1		Ward	Short	Clarke	Robinson	Jacobsen	**Dryden**	Bullock"	Keen^	Thorne*	Lightbourne	Kavanagh G	Crowe/Connor/Heath
	3/11		11,619	*1*	27				*Dyer 23*	*Ward*	*Holmes*	*Fenton*	*Redmile*	*Richardson*	*Pearce^*	*Hughes**	*Owers*	*Bolland*	*Ramage*	*Dyer*	*Rapley/Liburd*
									Ref: P Richards	New boss Gary Brazil sees his Magpies team emerge victorious from a battering. The new fluorescent yellow ball just will not find the back of Darren Ward's net. City are on top until Alex Dyer pounces to beat Gavin Ward. Lightbourne has a drive tipped over. Best display this season.											
16	A	BURY		6		D	0-0	0-0		Ward	Short^	Small	Robinson	Jacobsen	Dryden	O'Connor	Keen*	Thorne	Lightbourne"	Kavanagh G	Connor/Bullock/Clarke
	6/11		*4,280*	*11*	28					*Kenny*	*Williams*	*Daws*	*Swailes C*	*Billy*	*Bullock*	*Barnes**	*Reid*	*Redmond*	*Preece*	*Littlejohn*	*Lawson*
									Ref: M Dean	The consortium is to buy 66% of the shareholding from the current board. Stoke dominate but fail to convert numerous chances. Robinson fires just wide. Dryden has a header tipped round the post. Bernard Manning is dropped as an after-dinner speaker at the club's Sportsman's dinner.											
17	H	BRISTOL CITY		7		D	1-1	0-0	Mohan 66	Ward	Short^	Clarke	Mohan	Dryden	O'Connor	Bullock*	Keen"	Thorne	Lightbourne	Kavanagh G	Jacobsen/Robinson/Oldfield
	14/11		10,775	*17*	29				*Tinnion 85*	*Mercer*	*Bell*	*Jones S*	*Holland*	*Tinnion*	*Mortimer*	*Hutchings*	*Beadle*	*Murray**	*Tistimetanu*	*Millen*	*Goodridge*
									Ref: R Beeby	The takeover is confirmed. The new board parades before the kick-off. 'We're here to win' they declare. Gary Megson's swansong is almost a victory as Mohan's header rockets in to end a 368-minute goal drought. Brian Tinnion lashes home a superb dipping volley from over 30 yards.											
18	A	WYCOMBE		7		W	4-0	2-0	Kavanagh 44, Danielsson 45, Thorne 62, [Mohan 71]	Ward	Robinson	Clarke	Mohan	Jacobsen	O'Connor	**Gislason***	Keen	Thorne	Lightbourne^	Kavanagh G	**Danielsson**"/Oldfield/Petty
	23/11		4,345	*13*	32					*Taylor*	*Lawrence*	*Vinnicombe**	*Cousins*	*Bates*	*Carroll*	*Ryan*	*Devine*	*Simpson*	*McSporran !*	*Emblen^*	*Beeton/Bulman*
									Ref: M Ryan	Ex-Iceland national boss Gudjon Thordarson sees his new players rip Wycombe to shreds. Kav lashes in from 20 yards. Danielsson leaves two defenders and the keeper on the ground to slot a wonder goal. Thorne and Mohan head home. McSporran throws the ball at Kav in injury-time.											
19	H	COLCHESTER		7		D	1-1	0-0	Lightbourne 82	Ward	Robinson	Clarke^	Mohan	Jacobsen*	O'Connor	Danielsson	Keen	Thorne	Lightbourne	Kavanagh G	Petty/Crowe
	27/11		14,183	*23*	33				*Skelton 71*	*Vaughan*	*Keith*	*Richard*	*Greene*	*Johnson*	*Dozzell*	*Duguid^*	*McGavin*	*Gregory D*	*Skelton**	*White*	*Farley/Lock*
									Ref: G Frankland	City are awful. Mick Wadsworth's U's score another unchallenged header as Skelton converts Duguid's cross. Crowe has a goal disallowed for a foul. Lightbourne nods in Keen's free-kick. Relief all round. Thordarson notes the difference in performance level. 'We must be consistent.'											
20	A	OXFORD		8		D	1-1	0-1	Thorne 79	Ward	Robinson	Clarke*	Mohan	Jacobsen	O'Connor	Gislason	Keen^	Thorne	Lightbourne	Kavanagh G	**Hansson**/Danielsson
	4/12		*5,700*	*15*	34				*Beauchamp 27*	*Lundin*	*Folland*	*Weatherst'ne*	*Watson^*	*Whelan*	*McGowan*	*Robinson*	*Murphy*	*Beauchamp*	*Lilley**	*Anthrobus*	*Lambert/Fear*
									Ref: D Crick	Malcolm Shotton's Oxford have the better of a poor game. Joey Beauchamp cuts in to curl home left footed. Speedy Swede Mikael Hansson is introduced and provides a spark. His right-wing centre is headed home by Thorne from six yards. Stoke's first ever point at the Manor Ground.											
21	H	BRISTOL ROV		8		L	1-2	0-0	Keen 52	Ward	Hansson	Danielsson*	Mohan	Jacobsen	O'Connor	Gislason	Keen	Thorne	Lightbourne	Kavanagh G	Oldfield
	18/12		10,379	*3*	34				*Roberts 72, Walters 84*	*Jones*	*Pritchard*	*Foster*	*Thomson*	*Tillson*	*Mauge^*	*Hillier*	*Cureton*	*Roberts*	*Pethick**	*Walters"*	*Challis/Ellington/Bennett*
									Ref: M Brandwood	A much better performance. In a physical match Keen is hacked down. Thorne puts himself about, flattening Jones and Thomson. The pressure tells as Keen nets Lightbourne's cross. The Pirates storm back and Roberts converts Cureton's centre. Walters powers a weak clearance home.											
22	A	BLACKPOOL		8		W	2-1	2-0	Robinson 21, Kavanagh 27	Ward	Hansson	Clarke	Mohan	Robinson	O'Connor	Gislason*	**Kippe**	Thorne^	Lightbourne	Kavanagh G	Danielsson/Oldfield
	26/12		*5,274*	*22*	37				*Nowland 57*	*Caig*	*Hills*	*Bardsley*	*Carlisle*	*Bent*	*Clarkson*	*Bushell*	*Nowland*	*Sh'ttlew'rth**	*Beesley*	*Lee^*	*Coid/Garvey*
									Ref: A Kaye	Frode Kippe, on loan from Liverpool, replaces the suspended Jacobsen. Robinson springs the offside trap to slot past Tony Caig. Thorne heads down for Kav to slam home. Mohan is imperious at the back. Nowland scores for Nigel Worthington's Seasiders after Ward saves Bent's shot.											
23	H	OLDHAM		8		D	0-0	0-0		Ward	Hansson	Clarke"	Mohan	Kippe	O'Connor	Keen^	Danielsson*	Connor	Lightbourne	Kavanagh G	Oldfield/Thorne/Gislason
	28/12		13,709	*15*	38					*Kelly*	*McNiven*	*Holt*	*Garnett*	*Duxbury*	*Rickers*	*Sheridan*	*Whitehall^*	*Allott**	*Hotte*	*Adams*	*Dudley/Tipton*
									Ref: T Parkes	Andy Ritchie's Oldham arrive 45 mins late but it affects City more. Despite attacking constantly the Potters cannot beat Gary Kelly. He saves well from Hansson, Connor and Mohan. Ward reacts brilliantly to smother Garnett's effort on the line. Carl Muggleton is loaned to Mansfield.											

No	Date		Att	Pos	Pt	F-A	H-T	Scorers, Times, and Referees	1	2	3	4	5	6	7	8	9	10	11	subs used
24	A	BRENTFORD		7	W	1-0	0-0	Thorne 60	Ward	Hansson	Clarke	Mohan	Kippe	O'Connor	Petty	Jacobsen	Thorne^	Connor*	Kavanagh G	Lightbourne/Danielsson
	3/1		*6,792*	*9*	41				*Woodman*	*Quinn*	*Powell*	*Marshall"*	*Mahon*	*Owusu*	*Partridge^*	*Ingimarsson*	*Theobald*	*Agyemang*	*Clement**	*Anderson/Bryan/Kennedy*
								Ref: R Furnandiz	In torrential rain Stoke soak up pressure and play on the break. The Bees lack any sting. City look dangerous with Hansson tormenting Powell. Thorne scores when Connor is tackled six yards out. Jacobsen nods off the line. Owusu heads over from close in. 10 away games without loss.											
25	H	LUTON		7	W	2-1	1-0	Connor 24, Lightbourne 87	Ward	Hansson	Clarke^	Mohan	Kippe	O'Connor	Petty"	Jacobsen	Thorne*	Connor	Kavanagh G	L'bourne/Dan'sson/**Gunn'sson**
	8/1		10,016	*12*	44			*Spring 59p*	*Abbey*	*Boyce*	*Taylor !*	*Doherty*	*Watts*	*Johnson*	*Spring*	*Locke*	*White^*	*Douglas**	*Gray*	*Fotiadis/George*
								Ref: C Foy	Thorne nods down for Connor to convert. Matthew Taylor walks for striking Hansson (44 mins). The ten men win a penalty for Mohan's shove on Phil Gray. £600,000 club record signing Brynjar Gunnarsson is inspirational. Lightbourne heads in Kavanagh's long throw at the near post.											
26	H	PRESTON		5	W	2-1	1-0	Kippe 3, O'Connor 87	Ward	Hansson	Clarke	Mohan	Kippe	O'Connor	Gunnarsson	Jacobsen	Thorne*	Lightbourne	Kavanagh G	Gislason
	14/1		10,285	*2*	47			*Alexander 84p*	*Moilanen*	*Alexander*	*Edwards*	*Jackson*	*Murdock*	*Gregan*	*Appleton**	*Rankine*	*Nogan*	*Macken*	*Eyres^*	*Gunnlaugsson/Beresford*
								Ref: P Taylor	Kippe rockets a left-footed volley into the roof of the net. Preston provide City's sternest test yet and Ward is superb in denying Appleton and Nogan. Rankine falls dramatically and the penalty is netted by Graham Alexander. O'Connor slams home in a scramble as Stoke pile forward.											
27	A	MILLWALL		6	L	0-1	0-1		Ward	Hansson^	Clarke	Mohan	Kippe	O'Connor	Gunnarsson	Jacobsen"	Thorne*	Lightbourne	Kavanagh G	Connor/Gislason/Oldfield
	22/1		*11,548*	*4*	47			*Gilkes 33*	*Warner*	*Nethercott*	*Fitzgerald*	*Stuart*	*Newman*	*Ifill^*	*Livermore*	*Gilkes*	*Cahill*	*Moody**	*Shaw*	*Sadlier/Reid*
								Ref: C Wilkes	Jacobsen's error allows Shaw to square to Michael Gilkes to score. Tackles fly in but for once the game doesn't boil over. Paul Moody misses an open goal and has a header ruled out for a foul. Clarke's shot pole-axes a Millwall defender. Other promotion challengers should be beaten.											
28	H	BURNLEY		6	D	2-2	0-0	Thorne 68, Davis 71 (og)	Ward	Hansson	Clarke	Mohan	Kippe	O'Connor	Gunnarsson	Jacobsen	Thorne	Lightbourne	Kavanagh G	
	29/1		**15,354**	*5*	48			*Payton 76p, 83*	*Crichton*	*West^*	*Thomas*	*Armstrong*	*Mullin*	*Davis*	*Cook*	*Johnrose"*	*Cooke*	*Payton*	*Branch**	*Smith/Little/Swan*
								Ref: M Fletcher	Thorne flicks home Gunnarsson's cross. Steve Davis heads past his own keeper under pressure from Lightbourne. Andy Payton nets a penalty after Mullin is fouled and then fires past Ward from 20 yards. Swan's handball is penalised but Kav blasts the penalty straight at Paul Crichton.											
29	A	GILLINGHAM		6	L	**0-3**	0-2		Ward	Hansson	Clarke	Mohan*	Kippe	Petty^	Gunnarsson	Jacobsen	Thorne"	Lightbourne	Kavanagh G	Robinson/Connor/Bullock
	5/2		*7,801*	*7*	48			*Onuora 13, Gooden 32, Rowe 73*	*Bartram*	*Southall*	*Ashby*	*Butters*	*Edge*	*Hess'nthal'r^*	*Smith*	*Lewis*	*Gooden*	*Onoura*	*Thomson**	*Rowe/Saunders*
								Ref: K Lynch	City outplay physical Gillingham for the first half-hour but Mohan's header is cleared off the line and Thorne hits the post. Iffy Onoura nods a corner home then flicks on for Ty Gooden to beat Ward. Rowe slots in unmarked. Stoke's heads drop as the Gills squander numerous chances.											
30	A	LUTON		6	L	1-2	1-0	O'Connor 33	Ward	Hansson	Clarke	Mohan*	Kippe	O'Connor	Gunnarsson	Jacobsen	Connor"	Oldfield^	Kavanagh G	Petty/Lightbourne/Thorne
	8/2		*5,396*	*9*	48			*Gray 62, 78*	*Abbey*	*Boyce**	*Watts*	*Doherty*	*Johnson*	*George^*	*Locke*	*Spring*	*Taylor*	*Gray*	*Douglas*	*McGowan/Fotiadis*
								Ref: W Burns	Stoke are all at sea in defence but profit when Clarke beats two players before finding O'Connor who fires home. Kav screws wide when clear as City gain confidence. Kippe hits the bar. Phil Gray poaches two close-range goals as Lennie Lawrence's men fight back. One point from 12.											
31	H	CAMBRIDGE		6	W	1-0	1-0	Connor 31	Ward	Hansson	Clarke	Petty	Kippe	O'Connor	Gunnarsson	Jacobsen	Connor*	Lightbourne	Kavanagh G	Thorne
	12/2		9,662	*24*	51				*Marshall*	*Chenery*	*Wilson*	*McNeil*	*Eustace*	*Mackenzie^*	*Wanless*	*Ashbee*	*Guinan**	*Benjamin*	*Youngs"*	*Kyd/Preece/Taylor*
								Ref: M Dean	Roy McFarland's men have not won away all season. Ward makes a great stop from Trevor Benjamin as City struggle. Lightbourne's header is saved by Shaun Marshall but Connor knocks home the rebound. Petty's header is tipped on to a post. Dean Crowe joins Northampton on loan.											
32	A	COLCHESTER		6	L	0-1	0-0		Ward	Hansson	Clarke*	Petty	Kippe	O'Connor^	Gunnarsson	Jacobsen	Connor	Lightbourne	Kavanagh G	Gislason/Thorne
	19/2		*4,364*	*14*	51			*McGavin 86*	*Brown*	*Dunne*	*Keith*	*Johnson R*	*Wilkins*	*Gregory D*	*Johnson G*	*Dozzell*	*Duguid^*	*Morralee**	*McGavin*	*Tresor Lua Lua/Lock*
								Ref: A Hall	On a poor pitch Stoke press forward. Petty's drive is tipped over. Dozzell squanders an easy header from eight yards. The pressure builds after Tresor Lua Lua is introduced. Gislason loses Pat McGavin who nods in unmarked at the far post. An incensed Ward makes his feelings known.											
33	A	WIGAN		6	W	2-1	1-1	Kavanagh 28, O'Connor 77	Ward	Hansson	Clarke	Mohan	Kippe	O'Connor	Gunnarsson	Petty	Thorne^	Lightbourne*	Kavanagh	Oldfield/Robinson
	26/2		*9,429*	*4*	54			*Green 19*	*Carroll*	*Green*	*Sheridan**	*Balmer*	*De Zeeuw*	*McGibbon*	*O'Neill*	*Martinez*	*Roberts"*	*Peron^*	*Liddell*	*Bradshaw/Haworth/Barlow*
								Ref: K Leach	The world's greatest player, Sir Stanley Matthews, has died aged 85. In disgraceful scenes fans of both clubs clash. The referee takes the teams off. On resumption Scott Green scores. Kav glances in a header. O'Connor cracks home from the edge of the area. Wigan eight without a win.											
34	H	CHESTERFIELD		6	W	**5-1**	3-0	Thorne 8, 18, 41, 61, Jacobsen 90	Ward	Hansson	Clarke"	Mohan*	Kippe	O'Connor	Gunnarsson^	Petty	Thorne	**Gunnl'gsson**	Kavanagh	Jacobsen/Robinson/Small
	4/3		11,968	*24*	57			*Reeves 70*	*Gayle*	*Hewitt*	*Pointon**	*Blatherwick*	*Breckin*	*Beaumont*	*Curtis*	*Carss*	*Williams^*	*Reeves*	*Perkins*	*Payne/Howard*
								Ref: G Cain	Peter Thorne scores the first ever hat-trick at the Brit. Two headers, a tap-in and a sweet half-volley to become the first Potter to score four from open play since 1966. Jacobsen taps in from close range in a frantic scramble. John Duncan's Spireites have never beaten Stoke in 17 attempts.											

No	Date	Opponent	Att	Pos	Res	Pts	F-A	H-T	Scorers, Times, Referees	1	2	3	4	5	6	7	8	9	10	11	Subs used
35	A	NOTTS CO		7	D		0-0	0-0		Ward	Hansson	Clarke	Mohan	Kippe	O'Connor	Gunnarsson	Jacobsen	Thorne*	Gunnl'gsson	Kavanagh	Lightbourne
	11/3		*9,677*	*8*		58				*Ward*	*Holmes**	*Redmile*	*Richardson*	*Dyer*	*Liburd*	*Brough*	*Owers*	*Hughes^*	*Ramage*	*Stallard*	*Farrell/Bolland*
									Ref: P Danson	Classy Arnar Gunnlaugsson, on loan from Leicester, produces a superb performance. He sends in Gunnarsson, who is fouled, but the ref waves play on. Ward pulls off a sensational save from Sean Farrell to secure a draw. Manager's son Bjarni Gudjonsson arrives from Genk for £250k.											
36	H	WYCOMBE		8	D		1-1	0-1	Gunnlaugsson 54p	Ward	Hansson	Clarke	Mohan	Kippe	O'Connor	Gunnarsson	Jacobsen*	Thorne"	Gunnl'gsson^	Kavanagh	**Gudj'nss'n**/L'bourne/**Iwel'mo**
	18/3		9,738	*12*		59			*McSporran 23*	*Taylor*	*Cousins*	*Vinnicombe**	*Carroll*	*Rogers*	*Ryan*	*Simpson*	*Brown*	*Holsgrove*	*McSporran*	*Senda^*	*Bulman/Thompson*
									Ref: F Stretton	Lawrie Sanchez's Chairboys dig in. Thorne has an effort cleared off the line. McSporran races clear to fire through Ward's legs. Gunnlaugsson slams in a penalty after a handball. Frustrated Stoke cannot find the net. The play-offs look a long way off now. Chris Iwelumo signs for £25k.											
37	H	BLACKPOOL		8	W		3-0	0-0	Gunnarsson 62, Mohan 69, Gudjonsson 71	Ward	Hansson	Clarke	Mohan	Dryden*	O'Connor	Gunnarsson	Gudjonsson	Thorne	Lightbourne"	Kavanagh^	Petty/Gunnlaugsson/Iwelumo
	25/3		10,002	*23*		62				*Barnes*	*Couzens^*	*Bardsley*	*Carlisle*	*Hughes*	*Clarkson*	*Newell**	*Gill*	*Richardson"*	*Jaszczun*	*Thomas*	*Murphy/Wellens/Hills*
									Ref: S Baines	Stoke huff and puff but Nigel Worthington's Tangerines keep it tight. Kav urges City forward. Gunnarsson nets after Carlisle heads against his own crossbar. Mohan nods home a corner. Gudjonsson curls in spectacularly from 25 yards. Millionaire Philip Rawlins is set to join the board.											
38	A	BRISTOL CITY		7	D		2-2	2-1	Lightbourne 26, Kavanagh 39	Ward	Hansson	Clarke	Mohan	Dryden*	O'Connor	Gunnarsson	Gudjonsson	Thorne	Lightbourne	Kavanagh	Gunnlaugsson
	28/3		*8,103*	*9*		63			*Thorpe 10, 78*	*Phillips*	*Amanwaah*	*Burnell*	*Taylor**	*Bell*	*Murray*	*Holland*	*Clist^*	*Brown*	*Thorpe*	*Spencer*	*Hill/Tinnion*
									Ref: B Knight	Stoke run the game but concede when Tony Thorpe heads home Shaun Murray's cross. Thorne sets up Lightbourne to tap in and then supplies Kav who fires home. Gunnlaugsson outwits two players and cracks in but a great goal is disallowed for handball. Thorpe rounds Ward to level.											
39	A	BRISTOL ROV		7	D		3-3	1-2	Thorne 10, 62, 79	Ward	Gunnl'gsson	Clarke	Mohan	Dryden	O'Connor	Gunnarsson	Gudjonsson*	Thorne	Lightbourne	Kavanagh	Hansson
	1/4		*9,312*	*3*		64			*Pethick 20, Cureton 32p, Walters 69*	*Jones*	*Pethick*	*Thomson*	*Tillson*	*Andreasson*	*Astafjevs**	*Hillier*	*Challis*	*Roberts^*	*Cureton*	*Walters*	*Ellington/Wolleaston*
									Ref: R Harris	Thorne nets another treble. He turns in Lightbourne's mis-hit effort, bags a great header and dummies past Jones before slotting in to complete the first away hat-trick for 5 years. Mohan gives away a soft penalty. Walters smokes in a free-kick. Two Rovers fans attempt to assault Ward.											
40	A	OLDHAM		7	W		1-0	1-0	Thorne 23	Ward	Gunnl'gsson*	Clarke	Mohan	Dryden	O'Connor	Gunnarsson	Gudjonsson"	Thorne	Lightbourne^	Kavanagh	Hansson/Iwelumo/**Melton**
	4/4		*4,474*	*11*		67				*Kelly*	*Garnett*	*Hotte**	*Jones*	*McNiven*	*Holt*	*Rickers*	*Duxbury*	*Boshell*	*Sugden^*	*Whitehall*	*Tipton/Futcher*
									Ref: K Hill	Both keepers star in an eventful match. Gary Kelly saves brilliantly from Gunnlaugsson, Thorne and Kav. Ward denies Whitehall and Sugden. Thorne heads home after Kav's long throw is allowed to bounce in the area. A glimmer of hope for the play-offs? Crowe is loaned out to Bury.											
41	H	BRENTFORD		6	W		1-0	1-0	Thorne 8	Ward	Hansson*	Clarke^	Mohan	Gunnl'gsson	O'Connor	Gunnarsson	Gudjonsson	Thorne	Lightbourne	Kavanagh	Melton/Dryden
	8/4		9,955	*15*		70				*Woodman*	*Theobald**	*Marshall*	*Powell*	*Anderson*	*Quinn*	*Rowlands^*	*Evans*	*Scott*	*Owusu"*	*Partridge*	*Graham/Pinamonte/James*
									Ref: D Laws	Thorne thumps in after Andy Woodman drops Kav's corner. City play tidy football. Right-back Steve Melton, on loan from Forest, impresses. Graham volleys just wide from thirty yards. Gunlaugsson's free-kick hits the bar. City fans rank 9th in a national survey on supporters' fashions.											
42	H	BOURNEMOUTH		7	W		1-0	0-0	Thorne 81	Ward	Hansson	Clarke*	Mohan	Gunnl'gsson	O'Connor	Gunnarsson	Gudjonsson	Thorne	Lightbourne^	Kavanagh	Dryden/Connor
	22/4		15,022	*14*		73				*Ovendale*	*Young"*	*Fenton*	*Howe*	*Warren^*	*Stock**	*Fletcher C*	*Robinson*	*Jorgensen*	*Fletcher S*	*O'Neill*	*Elliott/Sheerin/Smith*
									Ref: M Messias	City keep up the pressure on the stumbling play-off clubs by grinding out a good victory. Thorne dives full length to head past Mark Ovendale. Stoke employ American David Raney to ensure that the Feng Shui of the Britannia Stadium is maximised. Last home defeat was in December.											
43	A	SCUNTHORPE		7	W		2-0	2-0	Thorne 24, 39	Ward	Hansson	Gunnl'gsson	Mohan	Dryden"	O'Connor	Gunnarsson	Gudjonsson*	Thorne	Lightbourne^	Kavanagh	Melton/Jacobsen/Clarke
	24/4		*5,435*	*23*		76				*Evans*	*Harsley*	*Dawson*	*Logan*	*Hope*	*Walker*	*Hodges*	*Sheldon**	*Torpey*	*Bull^*	*Stanton*	*Quailey/Ipoua*
									Ref: R Furnandiz	Thorne scores from 12 yards after Lightbourne's persistence forces an error. He then volleys in left footed. Brian Laws' Irons push forward in a bid to beat the drop. Gary Bull chips into Ward's hands when clear. Thorne has 16 goals in 13 games including the Auto Windscreen Shield.											
44	H	CARDIFF		7	W		2-1	1-0	Gunnlaugsson 3, O'Connor 69	Ward	Hansson	Clarke	Mohan	Dryden	O'Connor	Gunnarsson	Gunnl'gsson*	Thorne	Lightbourne	Kavanagh	Melton
	30/4		14,192	*21*		79			*Young 71*	*Kelly*	*Faerber*	*Legg*	*Young*	*Boland*	*Bonner*	*Bowen*	*Nugent*	*Brazier*	*Eckhardt*	*Brayson*	
									Ref: G Frankland	Gunnlaugsson belts in a free-kick. O'Connor plays a one-two and fires past Kelly from 15 yards. Young nods home Kevin Nugent's goalbound header. Trouble as Cardiff fans run riot. A heavy police presence quells the violence. The play-offs edge even closer. Cardiff are nearly down.											
45	H	BURY		4	W		3-0	1-0	Thorne 11, 55, 81	Ward	Hansson	Clarke	Mohan	Dryden^	O'Connor	Gunnarsson	Gunnl'gsson*	Thorne	Lightbourne	Kavanagh	Connor/Melton
	3/5		14,792	*15*		82				*Kenny*	*Bryan*	*Swailes C*	*Swailes D"*	*Hill*	*Billy*	*Daws*	*Reid*	*Littlejohn**	*Bhutia^*	*Preece*	*Avdiu/Barnes/Challinor*
									Ref: M Cowburn	Another Thorne hat-trick sees off Neil Warnock's Bury. He nips between Chris Swailes and Kenny to slot home, swivels to fire an unstoppable shot home and heads past Paddy Kenny after Lightbourne flicks on a corner. Bury offer no resistance. Party time at the Brit. 13 without defeat.											
46	A	READING		6	L		0-1	0-0		Ward	Hansson	Clarke	Mohan	Dryden	O'Connor*	Gunnarsson	Jacobsen"	Thorne	Lightbourne^	Kavanagh	Gunnlaugsson/Connor/Keen
	6/5		***13,146***	*10*		82			*Caskey 81p*	*Whitehead*	*Primus*	*Murty*	*Williams A*	*Igoe**	*Forster*	*Williams M*	*Caskey^*	*Smith*	*Robinson*	*Newman*	*Henderson/Evers*
		Home	Away						Ref: J Robinson	City incredibly go into the final game with a chance to go up automatically if results go their way. A nervy match never looks like providing the avalanche of goals City would need. Connor nets but is given offside. Darius Henderson hits a post before Mohan trips Caskey for the penalty.											
Average		11,426	7,140																		

Play-Offs			Att			F-A	H-T	Scorers, Times, and Referees	1	2	3	4	5	6	7	8	9	10	11	subs used
SF	H	GILLINGHAM			W	3-2	2-1	Gunnlaugsson 1, Lightbourne 8, Thorne 67	Ward	Hansson	Clarke	Mohan	Dryden*	O'Connor	Gunnarsson	Gunnl'gsson^	Thorne	Lightbourne	Kavanagh	Jacobsen/Gudjonsson
1	13/5		22,124					Gooden 18, Hessenthaler 90	Bartram	Southall	Edge	Ashby	Pennock	Butters	Smith*	Hessenthaler	Gooden	Onoura	Lewis	Browning
								Ref: M Dean	A superb game. Lightbourne tees up Gunnlaugsson after just 25 seconds before the compliment is returned. Gooden keeps Peter Taylor's team in it. Thorne taps in when Vince Bartram fails to hold O'Connor's header. Hessenthaler's fantastic effort comes as Stoke are trying to kill time.											
SF	A	GILLINGHAM			L	0-3	0-0		Ward	Hansson	Clarke !	Mohan	Gudjonsson	O'Connor	Gunnarsson	Jacobsen	Gunnl'gsson*	Lightbourne^	Kavanagh !	Melton/Connor
2	17/5		10,386			aet		Ashby 55, Onoura 102, Smith 118	Bartram	Southall	Edge*	Ashby	Pennock	Butters	Asaba^	Hessenthaler	Gooden	Onoura"	Lewis	Butler/Smith/Nosworthy
								Ref: R Styles (Stoke lose 3-5 on aggregate)	City are holding on comfortably when Clarke is sent off (43 mins) for two bookings in a minute. Kav sees red in an off the ball incident. Barry Ashby scores from the following corner. At 0-2 Connor hits the post in extra-time. Paul Smith sends the Gills to Wembley from Butler's pass.											

Worthington Cup																				
1:1	A	MACCLESFIELD			D	1-1	1-0	Keen 8	Ward	Kavanagh J	Small^	Mohan	Sigurdsson	Keen	Oldfield	Kavanagh G	Taaffe	Lightbourne*	Connor	Crowe/Clarke
	10/8		2,551					Priest 77	Price	Tinson	Collins	Ingram	Rioch	Sedgemore^	Davies	Priest	Whittaker"	Barker	Tomlinson*	Askey/Wood/Durkan
								Ref: M Riley	A paltry crowd see a poor match. Kevin Keen's headed goal is eclipsed by Priest's header from yet another poorly defended set-piece. Connor beats Ryan Price but the ball is cleared off the line. Taffe misses when well placed. Durkan blazes wide as Sammy McIlroy's team end on top.											
1:2	H	MACCLESFIELD		15	W	3-0	0-0	Connor 59, Thorne 69, O'Connor 75	Ward	**Jacobsen**	Clarke	Robinson^	Sigurdsson	O'Connor	Oldfield*	Kavanagh G	Aiston	Thorne	Connor"	Keen/Short/Crowe
	25/8		5,003	3:13					Price	Abbey	Collins	Rioch"	Wood^	Ware*	Priest	Sedgemore	Davies	Askey	Barker	Whittaker/Tomlinson/Brown
								Ref: J Kirkby (Stoke win 4-1 on aggregate)	Another low gate. City are abysmal. Luckily Macclesfield are worse. Ward pulls off a superb save from Ben Sedgemore. Confidence returns as Keen releases Connor who cracks home. Thorne nods in Kav's corner. O'Connor nets his first for the club after Thorne and Connor set him up.											
2:1	H	SHEFFIELD WED		12	D	0-0	0-0		Ward	Short	Clarke	Mohan	Jacobsen	Robinson	Keen*	O'Connor	Thorne	Lightbourne	Kavanagh G	Connor
	14/9		9,313	P:20					Pressman	Nolan	Thome	Walker	Briscoe	Alex'dersson	Atherton*	Sonner	Rudi	Booth	De Bilde^	Donnelly/Carbone
								Ref: A Leake	Stoke start brightly against Danny Wilson's team. Thorne hits the foot of the post as City dominate the premiership strugglers. Benito Carbone trots on to fire up Wednesday and Ward parries his 25-yard stinger. Thorne's header just drops the wrong side of the post. Much the better side.											
2:2	A	SHEFFIELD WED		12	L	1-3	0-2	Kavanagh G 74	Ward	Short	Clarke	Mohan	Jacobsen	Petty*	Keen	O'Connor"	Thorne^	Lightbourne	Kavanagh G	Oldfield/Connor/Heath
	22/9		10,993	P:20				Alexandersson 5, 68, De Bilde 24	Srnicek	Nolan	Briscoe*	Donnelly	Emerson	Walker	Alex'dersson	Sonnern	Rudi"	Booth	De Bilde^	Haslam/Sibon/Cresswell
								Ref: A Butler (Stoke lose 1-3 on aggregate)	Niclas Alexandersson volleys home on the run to settle Wednesday's nerves. Gilles de Bilde nets a carbon copy as the Owls bounce back from a 0-8 defeat at Newcastle. Alexandersson taps home after Ward saves Donnelly's effort. Kavanagh blasts in a corker left footed from 25 yards.											

FA Cup																				
1	A	BLACKPOOL		3	L	0-2	0-1		Ward	Short	Clarke	Robinson*	Jacobsen	O'Connor	Wooliscroft	Keen	Thorne^	Lightbourne	Kavanagh G	Bullock/Connor
	30/10		4,721	23				Carlisle 5, Nowland 90	Caig	Bryan^	Carlisle	Hughes	Hills	Clarkson	Bushell	Nowland	Robinson	Murphy	Coid*	Forsyth/Bent
								Ref: D Laws	The noon kick-off doesn't suit City. A deluge renders the pitch impossible. Clarke Carlisle lashes in after Ward parries Nowland's effort. Stoke are shocking and it is no surprise when Adam Nowland snaffles up Short's awful back-pass to score. Out of the cup before the clocks go back.											

		Home					Away					
	P	W	D	L	F	A	W	D	L	F	A	Pts
1 Preston	46	15	4	4	37	23	13	7	3	37	14	95
2 Burnley	46	16	3	4	42	23	9	10	4	27	24	88
3 Gillingham *	46	16	3	4	46	21	9	7	7	33	27	85
4 Wigan	46	15	3	5	37	14	7	14	2	35	24	83
5 Millwall	46	14	7	2	41	18	9	6	8	35	32	82
6 STOKE	46	13	7	3	37	18	10	6	7	31	24	82
7 Bristol Rov	46	13	7	3	34	19	10	4	9	35	26	80
8 Notts Co	46	9	6	8	32	27	9	5	9	29	28	65
9 Bristol City	46	7	14	2	31	18	8	5	10	28	39	64
10 Reading	46	10	9	4	28	18	6	5	12	29	45	62
11 Wrexham	46	9	6	8	23	24	8	5	10	29	37	62
12 Wycombe	46	11	4	8	32	24	5	9	9	24	29	61
13 Luton	46	10	7	6	41	35	7	3	13	20	30	61
14 Oldham	46	8	5	10	27	28	8	7	8	23	27	60
15 Bury	46	8	10	5	38	33	5	8	10	23	31	57
16 Bournemouth	46	11	6	6	37	19	5	3	15	22	43	57
17 Brentford	46	8	6	9	27	31	5	7	11	20	30	52
18 Colchester	46	9	4	10	36	40	5	6	12	23	42	52
19 Cambridge	46	8	6	9	38	33	4	6	13	26	32	48
20 Oxford	46	6	5	12	24	38	6	4	13	19	35	45
21 Cardiff	46	5	10	8	23	34	4	7	12	22	33	44
22 Blackpool	46	4	10	9	26	37	4	7	12	23	40	41
23 Scunthorpe	46	4	6	13	16	34	5	6	12	24	40	39
24 Chesterfield	46	5	7	11	17	25	2	8	13	17	38	36
	1104	234	155	163	770	634	163	155	234	634	770	1501

* promoted after play-offs

Odds & ends

Double wins: (7) Blackpool, Brentford, Cambridge, Cardiff, Chesterfield, Scunthorpe, Wrexham.
Double losses: (0).

Won from behind: (3) Reading (h), Wigan (a), Wrexham (a).
Lost from in front: (3) Bristol Rov (h), Luton (a), Preston (a).

High spots: Making the play-offs on the back of a fabulous unbeaten run.
Having the club's future secured by the arrival of the Icelandic consortium.
Peter Thorne's fantastic form in the second half of the season.
Winning the Autoglass Trophy against Bristol City at Wembley.
Scoring in the first minute of the play-offs.

Low spots: One win in six after beating leaders Preston.
Appalling crowds at the start of the season.
Saying goodbye to the popular Gary Megson.
Andy Hessenthaler's superb late goal in the first leg of the play-offs.
Losing in controversial circumstances at Gillingham in the play-offs.

Player of the Year: James O'Connor.
Ever-presents: (1) Gavin Ward.
Hat-tricks: (3) Peter Thorne.
Leading scorer: (25) Peter Thorne.

	Appearances						Goals			
	Lge	*Sub*	LC	*Sub*	FAC	*Sub*	Lge	LC	FAC	Tot
Aiston, Sam	**2**	*4*	1							
Bullock, Matthew	**4**	*3*				*1*				
Clarke, Clive	**39**	*3*	3	*1*	1		**1**			**1**
Connor, Paul	**17**	*11*	2	*2*		*1*	**6**	1		**7**
Crowe, Dean		*6*		*2*						
Danielsson, Einar	**3**	*5*					**1**			**1**
Dryden, Richard	**11**	*2*								
Gislason, Sigursteinn	**4**	*4*								
Gudjonsson, Bjarni	**7**	*1*					**1**			**1**
Gunnarsson, Brynjar	**21**	*1*					**1**			**1**
Gunnlaugsson, Arnar	**10**	*3*					**2**			**2**
Hansson, Mikael	**24**	*3*								
Heath, Robert		*3*		*1*						
Iwelumo, Chris		*3*								
Jacobsen, Anders	**29**	*4*	3		1		**2**			**2**
Kavanagh, Graham	**44**	*1*	4		1		**7**	1		**8**
Kavanagh, Jason			1							
Keen, Kevin	**20**	*3*	3	*1*	1		**1**	1		**2**
Kippe, Frode	**15**						**1**			**1**
Lightbourne, Kyle	**35**	*5*	3		1		**7**			**7**
Mackenzie, Neil		*2*								
Melton, Stephen		*6*								
Mohan, Nicky	**40**		3				**5**			**5**
O'Connor, James	**40**		3		1		**5**	1		**6**
Oldfield, David	**7**	*12*	2	*1*			**1**			**1**
Petty, Ben	**7**	*8*	1							
Robinson, Phil	**14**		2		1		**1**			**1**
Short, Chris	**14**		2	*1*	1					
Sigurdsson, Larus	**5**		2				**1**			**1**
Small, Bryan	**5**	*3*	1							
Taaffe, Steven	**2**		1							
Thorne, Peter	**41**	*4*	3		1		**24**	1		**25**
Ward, Gavin	**46**		4		1					
Wooliscroft, Ashley					1					
(own-goals)							**1**			**1**
34 players used	**506**	*100*	**44**	*9*	**11**	*2*	**68**	**5**		**73**

No	Date		Att	Pos	Pt	F-A	H-T	Scorers, Times, and Referees	1	2	3	4	5	6	7	8	9	10	11	subs used
1	H	WYCOMBE			D	0-0	0-0		Ward*	Hansson	Petty^	**Thomas**	Mohan	Gunnarsson	**Risom**	**Thordarson**	Lightbourne"	Gudjonsson	O'Connor	Muggleton/**Fenton**/Connor
	12/8		14,532		1				*Taylor*	*Rogers*	*Vinnicombe*	*Bulman*	*McCarthy*	*Bates*	*Harkin**	*Simpson*	*McSporran^*	*Jones*	*Brown*	*Castledine/Baird*
								Ref: A Butler	Bad start as Ward collides with Steve Jones and turns his ankle (16). Muggers denies McSporran in his first game for 15 months. Lightbourne nets but the ref gives a free-kick. Thordarson has the best chances. Neither fall kindly. Lawrie Sanchez's physical Wycombe have five booked.											
2	A	BRISTOL CITY		4	W	2-1	0-0	Gudjonsson 76, O'Connor 87	Muggleton	Petty	**Dorigo**	Thomas^	Mohan	Gunnarsson	Risom	Thordarson	Lightbourne*	Gudjonsson	O'Connor	Connor/Fenton
	19/8		***12,590***	*9*	4			*Thomas 65 (og)*	*Miller*	*Testimitanu*	*Bell*	*Holland**	*Lever*	*Carey*	*Murray*	*Dunning*	*Peacock*	*Thorpe*	*Tinnion*	*Spencer*
								Ref: W Jordan	£600,000 Lee Peacock fluffs two great chances. Bell hacks Thordarson's shot clear. Unseen, Thorpe elbows Thomas in the face. As Stoke get on top, the still dazed Thomas mistimes a clearing header. Fenton crosses for Bjarni to net. O'Connor finishes off a swift four-man breakaway.											
3	H	NOTTS CO		12	L	0-1	0-0		Ward	Petty	Dorigo	Thordarson	Mohan	Gunnarsson	Risom^	Kavanagh	Connor*	Gudjonsson	O'Connor	Lightbourne/Fenton
	26/8		13,041	*6*	4			*Stallard 86*	*Ward*	*McDermott*	*Liburd*	*Warren*	*Richardson*	*Dyer*	*Owers*	*Ramage*	*Stallard*	*Joseph**	*Hamilton^*	*Rapley/Hughes*
								Ref: M Pike	City keep the 4-3-3 formation which won at Ashton Gate. Notts' resolute defensive wall restricts Stoke to long-distance efforts, seeing off Kav, Thordarson and Dorigo's shots. Mark Stallard beats the offside trap with a late run to drill home. City's eight-month unbeaten home run ends.											
4	A	READING		11	D	3-3	2-1	Hunter 17 (og), Thordarson 22, Fenton 75	Ward	Petty	Dorigo	Thomas	Mohan	Gunnarsson	Fenton^	Kavanagh	Gudjonsson	Thordarson*	O'Connor	Lightbourne/Connor
	29/8		*10,668*	*18*	5			*Butler 45, Caskey 84p, Cureton 90*	*Whitehead*	*Gurney^*	*Robinson*	*Viveash*	*Hunter*	*Parkinson*	*Butler*	*Caskey*	*Cureton*	*Newman**	*Rougier"*	*Hodges/McIntyre/Igoe*
								Ref: P Taylor	Reading fail to cope with Fenton's impishness. His touch forces Barry Hunter to net. He then chips for Thordarson to head home and nets after Hunter's mishead strikes a post. Limp defending lets long balls bounce in the box for Royals' first and third. Thomas fouls Cureton for the pen.											
5	H	PETERBOROUGH		9	W	3-0	0-0	Lightbourne 53, Thordarson 87, Kav' 90	Ward	Hansson	Dorigo	Thordarson	Mohan	Gunnarsson	Gudjonsson	Kavanagh	Lightbourne*	Fenton^	O'Connor	Connor/Clarke
	9/9		13,011	*11*	8				*Tyler*	*Drury*	*Scott*	*Shields*	*Edwards*	*Green^*	*Farrell*	*Hanlon**	*Clarke*	*Cullen"*	*Jelleyman*	*Forsyth/Oldfield/Whittingham*
								Ref: E Wolstenholme	Posh's industry sees them frustrate Stoke. Lightbourne heads City's first goal in 322 minutes at the Brit from Kav's hanging cross. Stoke grind down Barry Fry's team. Bjarni fizzes wide. Thordarson crashes in Connor's neat header. Kav's grasscutter finds Tyler's bottom right corner.											
6	H	OXFORD		7	W	**4-0**	3-0	Thordarson 22, Gudjonsson 32, [O'Connor 45, Robinson 71]	Ward	Hansson	Dorigo	Thordarson"	Mohan	Gunnarsson	Gudjonsson	Kavanagh*	Lightbourne	**Robinson^**	O'Connor	Risom/Connor/Clarke
	13/9		9,600	*24*	11				*Glass*	*Robertson*	*McGowan^*	*Whitehead*	*Richardson*	*Mcguckin*	*Omoyimni*	*Tait*	*Murphy"*	*Anthrobus**	*Beauchamp*	*Lilley/Jarman/Folland*
								Ref: C Wilkes	City batter Denis Smith's U's, racking up 35 goal attempts, 23 on target. Loanee Marvin Robinson (Derby) runs riot. Thordarson fires in from 15 yards. Bjarni converts Dorigo's cross. O'Connor nods in after Robinson hits the bar. Robinson deserves his header from Lightbourne's chip.											
7	A	PORT VALE		8	D	1-1	1-1	Lightbourne 15	Ward	Hansson	Dorigo	Thordarson*	Mohan	Gunnarsson	Gudjonsson	Kavanagh	Lightbourne^	Robinson	O'Connor	Clarke/Thorne
	17/9		*8,948*	*16*	12			*Bridge-Wilkinson 11*	*Goodlad*	*Tankard**	*Carragher"*	*Brammer*	*Burton^*	*Walsh*	*Beresford*	*Bridge-Wilk'*	*Viljanen*	*Naylor*	*Widdrington*	*Twiss/Cummins/Burns*
								Ref: W Burns	City under-perform badly. Marc Bridge-Wilkinson's stooping header goes in off the post. Goodlad saves Lightbourne's header, but Kyle bangs in the corner after a scramble. Vale's woodwork is hit twice. Stoke lack passion. Passing is woeful. Midfield is outfought. Thordarson is angry.											
8	H	ROTHERHAM		10	D	1-1	0-1	Thorne 81	Ward	Hansson	Dorigo	Thordarson"	Mohan	Gunnarsson	Gudjonsson^	Kavanagh	Lightbourne	Robinson*	O'Connor	Risom/Thorne /Goodfellow
	23/9		13,472	*7*	13			*Artell 26*	*Gray*	*Scott*	*Hurst*	*Garner*	*Artell*	*Branston*	*Watson*	*Talbot**	*Lee*	*Warne*	*Turner^*	*Beech/Monkhouse*
								Ref: R Beeby	Sturdy Millers overpower Stoke. David Artell nods in right on the line. City lack invention. Thorne's header from Bjarni's chip rescues a draw. Robinson's broken leg holds up play for six minutes. Andy Monkhouse is booked for diving at the death. City thought the ref had given a pen.											
9	A	COLCHESTER		8	W	1-0	1-0	Thorne 14	Ward	Hansson	Dorigo	Thomas	Mohan	Gunnarsson	Gudjonsson	Kavanagh	Lightbourne*	Thorne^	O'Connor	Petty/Thordarson
	30/9		***3,758***	*12*	16				*Brown*	*Dunne*	*Keith*	*Skelton*	*White*	*Johnson*	*Keeble*	*Lock**	*McGavin"*	*Stockwell^*	*Dozzell*	*Opara/Tanner/Arnott*
								Ref: L Cable	Thorne's clean strike from Bjarni's bobbling centre comes from one of only five chances in the match. The stalemate is heightened by Stoke's decision to hold the lead, rather than put the game to bed. O'Connor and Lock accidentally clash heads nastily. Keeble's effort whistles over.											
10	A	SWANSEA		10	L	1-2	0-0	Lightbourne 88	Muggleton	Hansson	Dorigo^	Thomas*	**Kippe**	Gunnarsson	Gudjonsson	Kavanagh	Lightbourne	Thorne	O'Connor	Thordarson/Clarke
	14/10		*6,498*	*13*	16			*Savarese 59, 75*	*Freestone*	*Price*	*Howard*	*Romo*	*Smith*	*Bound*	*Coates*	*Jenkins*	*Savarese*	*Watkin*	*Roberts*	
								Ref: P Alcock	Ward's back problem sees Muggers start in goal. City set their stall out for a point. Swans' endeavour allows Venezuela international Giovanni Savarese to head in on debut. He then pokes in a stray ball as Stoke dither. Potters' late onslaught sees Lightbourne nod in Kav's corner. Poor.											
11	A	CAMBRIDGE		11	D	1-1	1-0	Thorne 41	Muggleton	Hansson	Clarke	Kippe	Mohan	Gunnarsson	Gudjonsson^	Kavanagh	Thorne	Thordarson*	O'Connor	Risom/Lightbourne
	17/10		*4,433*	*7*	17			*Taylor 90p*	*Perez*	*Ashbee*	*Cowan*	*Duncan*	*McAnespie*	*Dreyer^*	*Wanless*	*Axeldal"*	*Abbey*	*Russell**	*Youngs*	*Taylor/Slade/Joseph*
								Ref: R Harris	Thorne runs on to Hansson's inviting cross to net. Under Thordarson's orders, Muggers performs heroics as Stoke drop back to defend like the Alamo. Rob Harris awards U's a bizarre penalty as Lightbourne's clearance whacks Paul Wanless in the testicles! The frustration is building.											

No	Venue	Opponent	Att	Pos	Res	F-A	H-T	Scorers, Times, and Referees	1	2	3	4	5	6	7	8	9	10	11	Subs used
12	H	MILLWALL		10	W	3-2	2-2	Thorne 8, 13, Iwelumo 90	Muggleton	Hansson	Dorigo	Thomas^	Mohan	Gunnarsson	Gudjonsson	Kavanagh	Lightbourne"	Thorne	O'Connor*	Petty/Goodfellow/Iwelumo
	21/10		13,758	*6*	20			*Harris 1, 44*	*Warner*	*Lawrence*	*Bull*	*Cahill*	*Nethercott*	*Dyche*	*Livermore*	*Sadlier**	*Harris*	*Neill*	*Ifill*	*Parkin*
								Ref: M Jones	The 'must win' game crackles in a volatile atmosphere. Neil Harris rockets home on 20 secs. Thorne sweeps in and nods a floating cross home. Trouble flares in the away end. Harris levels with a 25 yarder, then is denied by Muggers' flying save. Big Chris heads in his first league goal.											
13	A	WALSALL		11	L	**0-3**	0-0		Muggleton	Hansson*	Dorigo	Thomas^	Mohan	Gunnarsson	Gudjonsson	Kavanagh	Lightbourne"	Thorne	O'Connor	Petty/Goodfellow/Iwelumo
	24/10		*6,996*	*1*	20			*Leitao 47, Gunnarsson 61(og), Hall 66*	*Emberson*	*Brightwell*	*Aranalde*	*Tillson*	*Barras*	*Burkan"*	*Hall^*	*Bennett*	*Leitao**	*Byfield*	*Matias*	*Angell/Keates/Wright*
								Ref: M Ryan	The floodlights fail twice. City wish they'd stay off. Leitao nets from close in. Mohan hits the bar. Gunnarsson tackles Byfield but prods home. Paul Hall nips in as the defence stands still. Mikael Hansson dislocates his shoulder. O'Connor admits 'We went to pieces'. The knives are out.											
14	H	BOURNEMOUTH		8	W	2-1	2-1	Gudjonsson 9, O'Connor 13	Muggleton	Risom*	Dorigo	Thomas	Mohan	Gunnarsson	Gudjonsson	Kavanagh	Thorne	Thordarson^	O'Connor	Petty/Connor
	28/10		11,572	*21*	23			*Defoe 45*	*Stewart*	*Cummings**	*Purches*	*Howe*	*Tindall*	*Fletcher C*	*Jorgensen*	*Hayter^*	*Defoe*	*Fletcher S*	*Hughes*	*Eribenne"/Elliott/Huck*
								Ref: H Webb	Bjarni cracks in on the run. O'Connor steers home. Stoke relax. Debutant Jermain Defoe, on loan from West Ham, nods in. Bjarni is clattered. The angry Gudjon is sent off for abusing the ref. Gunnarsson fouls Jorgensen. Muggers saves Hughes' pen (56) at the second attempt. Relief.											
15	A	WREXHAM		7	W	2-1	2-0	Thorne 16, Thordarson 27p	Muggleton	Petty	Dorigo	Thordarson*	Mohan	Gunnarsson	Gudjonsson	Kavanagh	Thorne^	Dadason"	O'Connor	Thomas/Risom/Lightbourne
	4/11		*6,447*	*14*	26			*Ferguson 66p*	*Dearden*	*McGregor*	*Roche*	*Bouanane*	*Mardon*	*Barrett*	*Chalk*	*Ferguson*	*Killen**	*Edwards*	*Faulc'bridge*	*Sam*
								Ref: R Pearson	Thorne nods in Thordarson's free-kick. Bjarni is felled by Bouanane. Thordarson puts the pen low to Dearden's left. City sit back. The Robins' pen is for Thomas's silly foul on Faulconbridge. Ferguson forces Muggers to save twice. Dorigo clears off the line six mins into stoppage time.											
16	A	NORTHAMPTON		8	D	2-2	2-2	Kavanagh 10, O'Connor 24	Muggleton	Petty	Dorigo	Thomas !	Mohan	Gunnarsson	Gudjonsson	Kavanagh	Thorne*	Thordarson^	O'Connor	Lightbourne/Dadason
	7/11		*5,475*	*6*	27			*Forrester 13, Howard 45*	*Welch*	*Savage*	*Hughes*	*Hunt*	*Green**	*Hope*	*Hodge*	*Howard*	*Forrester*	*Gabbiadini*	*Hargreaves*	*Dryden*
								Ref: K Hill	Kav fires in from 20 yards. Forrester finds space to drill in. O'Connor's pot-shot spins in off Hope. Howard's header hits Muggers and goes in off Mohan. Thomas' rash foul on Forrester (46) earns red. Thordarson hits the bar. Fisticuffs on the bench between Gudjon and Kevin Wilson.											
17	H	OLDHAM		9	L	0-1	0-1		Muggleton	Hansson*	Dorigo	Thordarson"	Mohan	Gunnarsson	Gudjonsson	Kavanagh^	Thorne	Dadason	O'Connor	Petty/Risom/Goodfellow
	11/11		12,503	*19*	27			*Duxbury 15*	*Kelly*	*McNiven*	*Innes*	*Garnett*	*Rickers*	*Duxbury*	*Adams^*	*Carss*	*Dudley**	*Corazzin*	*Eyres*	*Jones/Allott*
								Ref: T Jones	Strong winds make for a bitty game. Kav's free-kick is saved by Kelly. Lee Duxbury rifles home a loose ball. Bjarni hits the bar. Stoke fail to pressure poor opponents. The high hopes for the Thorne/Dadason partnership look way off the mark. The Icelandics celebrate a year in charge.											
18	A	SWINDON		6	W	3-0	2-0	Dryden 8 (og), Lightbourne 11, 78	Muggleton	Hansson	Dorigo	Kippe	Mohan	Gunnarsson	Risom"	Kavanagh*	Lightbourne	Thorne^	Gudjonsson	Petty/Thordarson/Clarke
	25/11		*4,904*	*22*	30				*Griemink*	*Robinson^*	*Davis*	*O'Halloran*	*Reeves*	*Willis*	*Invincible*	*Howe"*	*Williams**	*Dryden*	*Woan*	*Alexander/Grazioli/Duke*
								Ref: J Robinson	O'Connor is left at home after a reported spat with Gudjon. Kippe replaces the suspended Thomas. He flicks on a corner and debutant Dryden nets in trying to clear. Stoke swamp hapless Town. Lightbourne nods in Risom's corner and scores after Hansson blocks Griemink's clearance.											
19	H	LUTON		7	L	1-3	1-1	Mohan 35	Muggleton	Hansson	Dorigo"	Kippe	Mohan	Gunnarsson^	O'Connor	Kavanagh	**Cooke***	Thorne	Clarke	Dadason/Thordarson/Risom
	2/12		12,389	*23*	30			*McLaren 15, Thomson 50, 61*	*Abbey*	*Helin*	*Taylor*	*Locke*	*Watts*	*Johnson*	*George^*	*McLaren*	*Thomson**	*Whitbread*	*Spring*	*Fotiadis/Karlsen*
								Ref: B Curson	O'Connor is reinstated after the Liverpool debacle. £300,000 Andy Cooke debuts. McLaren's 30 yarder stuns City. Mohan converts Hansson's pull back. Kav heads off the line. Loud jeers as Peter Thomson hooks in and floats home a cheeky shot. Luton's first away win of the season.											
20	A	BRISTOL ROV		7	W	3-0	3-0	Thorne 3, 19, 40	**Kristinsson**	Hansson	Dorigo	Kippe	Mohan	Gunnarsson	Gudjonsson	Kavanagh	Cooke"	Thorne^	O'Connor*	Petty !/Risom/Dadason
	16/12		*6,838*	*18*	33				*Culkin*	*Bignot*	*Challis**	*Foster*	*Foran^*	*Jones !*	*Astafjevs*	*Hillier*	*Ellington*	*Evans*	*Thomson*	*Walters/Barrett*
								Ref: A Hall	Thorne notches his second hat-trick in successive appearances at the Memorial Ground. A far-post volley, 15-yard shot and close-range header. Cooke provides two and Bjarni the third. Solid debut for Birkir Kristinsson. Of the eight yellows Petty (81) and Scott Jones (85) both see two.											
21	A	WIGAN		7	D	1-1	0-0	O'Connor 65	Kristinsson	Hansson	Dorigo	Kippe	Mohan	Gunnarsson	Gudjonsson	Kavanagh	Thorne	Dadason*	O'Connor	Lightbourne
	23/12		*16,859*	*4*	34			*Gunnarsson 90 (og)*	*Stillie*	*Bradshaw*	*Sharp*	*Bidstrup"*	*McGibbon*	*De Zeeuw*	*Kilford*	*Sheridan*	*Haworth^*	*Liddell*	*Gillespie**	*Green/Ashcroft/Roberts*
								Ref: D Laws	Kristinsson smothers bravely when Kilford is twice clean through. O'Connor's header rounds off a tasty seven-man move. Bjarni hits the bar, Thorne goes close twice and Kav produces a flying save from Derek Stillie. Cruel luck sees Gunnarsson slice a near-post clearance into the net.											
22	H	BURY		7	W	2-1	1-1	Dadason 39, Gunnarsson 84	Kristinsson	Hansson	Dorigo*	Kippe^	Mohan	Gunnarsson	Gudjonsson	Kavanagh	Thorne	Dadason"	O'Connor	Lightbourne/Clarke/Cooke
	26/12		16,499	*17*	37			*Barnes 19*	*Kenny*	*Collins*	*Forrest*	*Daws*	*Swailes C*	*Redmond^*	*Billy*	*Reid*	*Barnes**	*Jarrett !*	*Littlejohn"*	*Unsworth/Prece/James*
								Ref: M Dean	Littlejohn and Barnes unnerve Stoke's defence. Barnes deflects in Redmond's shot. Dadason heads his first league goal. Jason Jarrett sees red for hauling down a clean through Thorne (75). Gunnarsson loops a header home. Stoke's desperate defending almost gifts Bury an equaliser.											
23	H	BRISTOL CITY		5	W	1-0	0-0	Gudjonsson 82	Kristinsson	Hansson*	Dorigo^	Thomas	Mohan	Gunnarsson	Gudjonsson	Kavanagh	Thorne	Cooke"	O'Connor	Risom/Clarke/Dadason
	30/12		14,629	*7*	40				*Phillips*	*Hill*	*Bell*	*Clist**	*Millen*	*Carey*	*Murray*	*Brown*	*Spencer^*	*Thorpe*	*Tinnion*	*Testimitanu/Odejayi*
								Ref: P Richards	Kippe's knee injury means Thomas returns to star. Phillips lunges to save Kav's deflected free-kick. Kristinsson tips Clist's curling shot round. Stoke press Danny Wilson's men back but seem fated not to score. Bjarni's flighted cross eludes everyone and drifts in. Has the luck changed?											

No	Date		Att	Pos	Pt	F-A	H-T	Scorers, Times, and Referees	1	2	3	4	5	6	7	8	9	10	11	subs used
24	A	NOTTS CO		5	D	2-2	1-1	Gudjonsson 1, Cooke 80	Kristinsson	Petty	Clarke^	Thomas	Mohan	Gunnarsson	Gudjonsson*	Kavanagh	Cooke	Thorne	O'Connor	Risom/Dadason
	1/1		*9,125*	*9*	41			*Liburd 17, Richardson 57*	*Ward*	*Holmes*	*Liburd^*	*Fenton**	*Richardson*	*Jacobsen*	*Owers*	*Stallard*	*Allsopp*	*Hughes*	*Brough*	*Warren/Joseph*
								Ref: G Laws	A 1pm start sees 3,400 fans travel. Stoke score the first goal of the New Year when Bjarni shoots and Darren Ward spills the ball. Liburd sinks Stallard's cross. Richardson powers home a header. Clarke causes mayhem with his crosses. Thorne hits the bar. Cooke bags an overhead kick.											
25	H	READING		5	D	0-0	0-0		Kristinsson	Hansson	Dorigo	Thomas	Mohan*	Gunnarsson	Gudjonsson	Kavanagh	Cooke	Thorne^	O'Connor	Thordarson/Dadason
	13/1		14,154	*6*	42				*Whitehead*	*Newman*	*Gray*	*Viveash*	*Hunter*	*Parkinson*	*Murty*	*Caskey*	*Cureton"*	*McIntrye**	*Rougier^*	*Hodges/Butler/Jones*
								Ref: R Furnandiz	The North Stand is renamed as the Boothen End after months of fan pressure. Little for its occupants to cheer as both teams cancel each other out. Kristinsson denies Tony Rougier low down. Tempers fray as Kav fouls Darren Caskey. 12 players get involved as the match ends messily.											
26	H	BRENTFORD		5	W	1-0	1-0	Dadason 22	Kristinsson	Hansson	Dorigo	Thomas	Mohan	Gunnarsson	Gudjonsson	Kavanagh	Cooke*	Dadason	O'Connor	Thorne
	17/1		**9,350**	*11*	45				*Gottskalks'n*	*Lovett"*	*Dobson*	*Mahon^*	*Powell*	*Marshall*	*Ingimarsson*	*Evans*	*Owusu**	*Rowlands*	*Partridge*	*McCam'n/Williams/O'Connor*
								Ref: T Leake	Thorne is dropped for Dadason as Gudjon shakes things up. Stoke play their best possession football of the season. Bjarni crosses for Dadason to nod home. Gottskalkson saves from both strikers and Kav. City fail to kill of the game. Youngster Karl Henry is called up to England U18s.											
27	H	WIGAN		5	W	2-0	1-0	Cooke 18, Thorne 60	Kristinsson	Hansson	Dorigo"	Thomas	Mohan	Gunnarsson	Gudjonsson^	Risom*	Cooke	Thorne	O'Connor	Petty/Thordarson/Clarke
	27/1		16,859	*3*	48				*Stillie*	*McGibbon**	*Padula"*	*Nicholls^*	*Balmer*	*De Zeeuw*	*Kilford*	*Sheridan !*	*Roberts*	*Ashcroft*	*Martinez*	*Green/Bradshaw/McLaughlin*
								Ref: R Styles	City lack the suspended Kav and four injured, but produce their best display so far. Cooke slams home. Darren Sheridan sees red for elbowing Bjarni (53). Thorne cashes in on De Zeeuw's slip. Kristinsson confounds Roberts when clean through. Gudjon claims 'The puzzle is complete'.											
28	H	NORTHAMPTON		5	D	1-1	0-0	Cooke 59	Kristinsson	Hansson	Dorigo^	Thomas	Mohan	Gunnarsson	Gudjonsson	Kavanagh	Cooke	Thorne*	O'Connor	Dadason/Goodfellow
	3/2		13,235	*8*	49			*Howard 74*	*Welch*	*Frain*	*Spedding*	*Sampson*	*Green*	*Hope*	*Savage*	*Hunt*	*Forrester*	*Gabbiadini**	*Hargreaves*	*Howard*
								Ref: S Mathieson	Cobblers keep things tight. Welch denies Kav. Cooke's overhead kick looks to have won it for lacklustre City. Kristinsson lets Steve Howard's 25-yard bobbler trickle through his legs. First goal conceded at the Brit for 505 mins. A £150,000 statue to honour Sir Stan is commissioned.											
29	A	PETERBOROUGH		5	W	**4-0**	2-0	Thorne 2, Gudjonsson 45, Dadason 72, [O'Connor 89]	Kristinsson	Hansson	Dorigo	Thomas	Mohan	Gunnarsson	Gudjonsson	Kavanagh	Cooke^	Thorne*	O'Connor	Dadason/Kippe
	10/2		*7,568*	*18*	52				*Tyler*	*Scott**	*Gill*	*Shields"*	*Rae*	*Edwards*	*Farrell*	*Oldfield*	*Clarke*	*Williams^*	*Hanlon*	*Lee/Hooper/Forinton*
								Ref: T Jones	Thorne converts Kav's corner. Hansson hits a post. Bjarni's long-range shot whistles home. He then centres for Dadason to nod in. O'Connor beats two to net. Victory tainted by Thorne's knee injury (37) suffered in a challenge with Mark Tyler. Kristinsson denies Farrell and Hanlon.											
30	H	PORT VALE		4	D	1-1	0-0	O'Connor 55	Kristinsson	Hansson*	Dorigo	Thomas	Mohan	Gunnarsson	Gudjonsson	Kavanagh	Cooke^	Dadason	O'Connor	Kippe/Goodfellow
	17/2		**22,133**	*20*	53			*Brammer 81*	*Goodlad*	*Tankard*	*Carragher*	*Brammer*	*Walsh*	*Brisco*	*Bridge-Wilk'*	*Cummins*	*Naylor*	*Lowe**	*Smith*	*Brooker*
								Ref: P Danson	The largest crowd of the Division Two season sees a poor match disrupted by strong winds. O'Connor stoops to nod in from Dorigo's swirling cross. Vale outpass City. A breakaway ends with Dave Brammer firing a 25-yarder into the top corner. Thomas hits the bar. Distinctly average.											
31	A	OXFORD		4	D	1-1	0-1	Cooke 69	Kristinsson	Mohan^	Dorigo	Thomas	Kippe	Gunnarsson	Gudjonsson	Kavanagh	Cooke	Dadason*	O'Connor	Thordarson/Hansson
	20/2		*4,856*	*24*	54			*Patterson 7*	*Cutler*	*Robertson*	*Hatswell*	*Patterson*	*Quinn*	*Richardson*	*Hackett*	*Gray*	*Murphy^*	*Scott*	*Beauchamp*	*Tait*
								Ref: P Durkin	This dire display shows the players have settled for the play-offs. Patterson nods home a free-kick. Mohan has a header ruled out for pushing. Dadason fluffs twice. Cooke taps in Kav's deflected long-range shot. David Kemp's U's have lost 23 of 29 games. Unbeaten in 15, but awful.											
32	A	ROTHERHAM		6	L	1-2	0-0	Thorne 53	Kristinsson	Hansson	Dorigo^	Thomas	Mohan	Gunnarsson*	Gudjonsson	Kavanagh	Thorne	Dadason	O'Connor	Kippe/Thordarson
	24/2		*8,211*	*3*	54			*Robins 54, 64*	*Pettinger*	*Scott*	*Hurst*	*Garner*	*Artell*	*Branston*	*Watson*	*Robins^*	*Barker*	*Warne*	*Talbot**	*Bryan/Sedgwick*
								Ref: M Fletcher	Ronnie Moore's Millers hit the bar after 10 seconds. Gunnarsson's ankle injury (51) looks serious. Thorne returns from injury to nod in Kav's cross sending the visiting 2,500 delirious. City think they've won it, but Mark Robins hooks in unchallenged and scores with a firm cross-shot.											
33	H	COLCHESTER		6	W	3-1	2-1	Thorne 9, 40, Kavanagh 88	Kristinsson	Hansson	Dorigo	Thomas	Mohan	Kippe	Gudjonsson*	Risom	Cooke"	Thorne	Gunnarsson^	Kavanagh/Petty/Goodfellow
	3/3		11,714	*17*	57			*Skelton 4p*	*Woodman*	*Dunne*	*Keith*	*Johnson R^*	*White*	*Fitzgerald*	*Skelton*	*Johnson G*	*Conlon**	*Stockwell*	*Duguid*	*McGavin/McGleish*
								Ref: M Cowburn	Skelton nets after Thomas trips Gavin Johnson. The officials lose control. City coach Nigel Pearson is sent off for protesting. Thorne smashes Risom's free-kick home. His second, racing clear onto Mohan's pass, is his 36th in 12 months. Kav heads Hansson's cross inside the far post.											
34	H	SWANSEA		6	L	1-2	0-2	O'Connor 81	Kristinsson	Hansson*	Dorigo	Thomas	Kippe^	Gunnarsson	Gudjonsson	Kavanagh	Thorne	Dadason	O'Connor	Risom/Thordarson
	7/3		10,091	*23*	57			*Price 18, O'Leary 31*	*Freestone*	*Appleby*	*Howard*	*Cusack*	*Smith^*	*Bound*	*Price*	*O'Leary*	*Fabiano*	*Watkin**	*Verschave*	*Jenkins/Romo*
								Ref: G Cain	John Hollins' Swans have just one win in 21. Price drills into the corner. O'Leary's low shot sends his 144 fans wild. O'Connor nods Risom's cross in. Stoke have just three efforts on target. Reports of a dressing room dust up between angry players. Automatic promotion impossible.											

No	Venue	Opponent	Att			F-A	H-T	Scorers, Times, and Referees	1	2	3	4	5	6	7	8	9	10	11	Subs used
35	A	BRENTFORD		6	D	2-2	1-0	Cooke 17, Dadason 90	Kristinsson	Hansson*	Dorigo	Thomas	Mohan	Gunnarsson	Risom	Kavanagh	Cooke^	Thorne"	O'Connor	Petty/Thordarson/Dadason
10/3			5,518	12	58			Williams 72, Owusu 79	Gottskalks'n	Gibbs	Lovett^	Mahon	Powell	Theobald	Ingimarsson	Evans	McCammon*	Rowlands	Charles	Owusu/Williams
								Ref: C Foy	Gottskalksson foils O'Connor, Kav and Mohan acrobatically. But Cooke beats him one-on-one. City drop back again. Williams whacks a long ball home on the run. Owusu streaks clear to net. Dadason saves Stoke's blushes by poking in after Gunnarsson's effort is blocked on the line.											
36	A	WYCOMBE		5	W	1-0	1-0	Kavanagh 11p	Kristinsson	Petty	Clarke^	Thomas	Mohan	Gunnarsson	Gudjonsson	Kavanagh	Cooke*	Thorne"	O'Connor	Risom/Thordarson/Dadason
13/3			5,385	16	61				Taylor	Townsend^	Vinnicombe	McCarthy	Cousins	Bates	Bulman	Simpson	Clegg	Essandoh	Brown*	Lee/Phelan
								Ref: F Stretton	A clear the air meeting between players may have done the trick. City cling on agonisingly after Kav lashes in his pen, for a trip on Cooke. Far from saving themselves for their FA Cup semi-final, Wycombe pile on pressure. Simpson blazes over. Mohan heads Phelan's chip off the line.											
37	H	CAMBRIDGE		5	L	2-3	0-2	Kavanagh 56p, Dadason 87	Kristinsson	Petty*	Clarke^	Thomas	Mohan	Gunnarsson	Gudjonsson	Kavanagh	Cooke"	Thorne	O'Connor	Hans'n/Thordarson/Dadason
17/3			11,939	19	61			Riza 10, Wanless 33, Richardson 90	Marshall	Ashbee	Cowan	Duncan	Joseph	Dreyer	Wanless	Taylor"	Youngs^	Riza*	Fleming	Oakes/Richardson/Kitson
								Ref: M Clattenburg	Stoke creak as Omar Riza fires home from 25 yards and Paul Wanless heads in unopposed. Gudjon switches to 4-4-2 and City come back from the dead. Kav nets when Bjarni is fouled. Dadason's header should earn a point. But City go to sleep. Marcus Richardson rounds Kristinsson.											
38	A	BURY		6	L	0-1	0-0		Ward	Hansson	Dorigo	Thomas	Mohan*	Gunnarsson	Gudjonsson	Kavanagh^	Thorne"	Dadason	O'Connor	Kippe/Thordarson/Lightb'ne
27/3			4,224	10	61			Kavanagh 62 (og)	Kenny	Billy	Armstrong	Hill	Swailes C	Redmond	Daws	Reid	Newby	Cramb	Forrest	
								Ref: P Jones	Ward returns from his five-month layoff. City start 4-4-2 and look the part. After the break Bury press hard. City begin to panic. Ward fumbles Newby's header and Kavanagh rockets his clearance into the top corner. Chris Swailes claims the goal. Stoke revert to lumping it forward.											
39	H	BRISTOL ROV		6	W	4-1	2-0	Hansson 4, 15, Thorne 71, 86	Ward	Hansson	Clarke	Thomas	Gudjonsson^	Gunnarsson	Thordarson"	Kavanagh	Thorne	Dadason*	O'Connor	Risom/Lightbourne/**Neal**
31/3			12,274	21	64			Gall 88	Culkin	Partridge"	Wilson	Foster	Thomson	Jones	Bryant	Owusu*	Ellington	Lee^	Plummer	Astafjevs/McKeever/Gall
								Ref: D Pugh	City kill the game with Hansson's salvo, a lob from Dadason's flick on, and cool finish to O'Connor's slide-rule pass. Both sides have penalty claims refused. Ellington hits the bar. Thorne pokes Bjarni's cross under Culkin and nods in Risom's flick. Kevin Gall drills in from a corner.											
40	A	MILLWALL		6	L	0-2	0-1		Ward	Hansson	Clarke	Thomas	Gudjonsson	Gunnarsson	Thordarson^	Kavanagh	Thorne	Dadason"	O'Connor*	Risom/Dorigo/Lightbourne
3/4			11,639	1	64			Sadlier 6, Cahill 78	Warner	Lawrence	Ryan	Cahill	Dyche	Nethercott	Livermore	Sadlier	Claridge*	Reid	Ifill	Cottee
								Ref: S Dunn	Mark McGhee's Lions have won only one of their last six and lack top-scorer Neil Harris. Thommo's mis-kick allows Richard Sadlier to net. Warner keeps out Kav's shot and Gunnarsson's flying header. Millwall nick a second on the break as Gunnarsson's clearance falls to Cahill.											
41	A	LUTON		5	W	2-1	2-1	Kavanagh 30, 40	Ward	Hansson	Clarke	Thomas	Mohan	Gunnarsson	Gudjonsson^	Kavanagh	Cooke*	Thorne	O'Connor	Risom/Lightbourne
7/4			6,456	22	67			Mansell 4	Abbey	Helin	Taylor	McLaren	Boyce	Dryden	Howard	Mansell	Stein*	Rowland^	Spring	George/Douglas
								Ref: W Burns	Back to 5-3-2 as Mohan returns. Hansson sees his shot palmed onto a post. Teenager Lee Mansell streaks clear to lob Ward. Kav hits a cross-shot, which cannons in off Matt Taylor, then cracks a peach of a volley from 20 yards. City defend stoutly. George wastes when clean through.											
42	H	WALSALL		5	D	0-0	0-0		Ward	Hansson	Clarke	Thomas	Kippe	Gunnarsson	Risom	Kavanagh	Cooke^	Thorne*	O'Connor	Thordarson/Dadason
14/4			16,603	4	68				Walker	Brightwell	Aranalde	Tillson	Roper	Barras	Simpson	Bennett^	Leitao	Goodman*	Burkan	Hall/Horne
								Ref: R Pearson	Cooke is tripped by Brightwell. Kav whacks the pen down the middle, but Jimmy Walker palms over. Barras heads just wide. City lack width. Walsall's well-stocked defence holds firm. Thordarson overhead-kicks just over. Derision greets Gudjon's strange substitutions. 4-4-2 please!											
43	A	BOURNEMOUTH		5	L	0-1	0-1		Ward	Hansson	Dorigo*	Thomas^	Kippe	Gunnarsson	Petty"	Kavanagh	Cooke	Thorne	O'Connor	Clarke/Dadason/Thordarson
17/4			5,373	7	68			Defoe 38	Stewart	Broadhurst	Elliott	Howe	Tindall	Fletcher C	Jorgensen	Hayter*	Defoe^	Fletcher S	Hughes	Purches/Feeney
								Ref: P Joslin	Gudjon is intent on avoiding defeat to avert Sean O'Driscoll's men's late run for the play-offs. Dorigo's 30 yarder is Stoke's best effort. Ward badly misjudges a headed clearance outside his box. Defoe taps home. Stewart foils Hansson's run on goal. Dadason's free header sails wide.											
44	H	WREXHAM		5	W	3-1	2-0	Hardy 6 (og), Gunnarsson 44, 56	Ward	Hansson"	Clarke*	Thomas	Kippe	Gunnarsson^	Dadason	Kavanagh	Cooke	Thorne	O'Connor	Dorigo/Risom/Gudjonsson
21/4			12,687	10	71			Ferguson 86p	Walsh	McGregor	Roche	Williams^	Hardy	Carey	Blackwood*	Ferguson	Russell	Edwards	Faulc'bridge	Chalk/Thomas
								Ref: P Richards	Stoke's nerves are calmed when Hardy heads Hansson's cross past Walsh. Brian Flynn's Robins find gaps behind City's full-backs. Playing in midfield, Gunnarsson rockets a 20 yarder in off the bar. He then slots home Cooke's cut-back. The pen is for Thomas's foul on Faulconbridge.											
45	A	OLDHAM		5	W	2-1	0-1	Gunnarsson 73, Dadason 84	Ward	Hansson	Clarke	Thomas^	Kippe	Gunnarsson	Gudjonsson	Kavanagh	Cooke	Thorne*	O'Connor	Petty/Dadason
28/4			9,359	12	74			Parkin 17	Kelly	McNiven	Prenderville	Garnett	Rickers	Duxbury	Adams	Salt	Tipton"	Parkin*	Carss^	Allott/Corazzin/Futcher
								Ref: S Baines	On-loan Sam Parkin sweeps in a long throw, flicked on by Thorne. Gunnarsson urges City on. He slots Cooke's knockback. Thorne twice nods just over. Dadason stabs home in a scramble. Oldham's best gate of the season includes BNP activists who mix with Stokies, causing trouble.											
46	H	SWINDON		5	W	4-1	4-0	O'Halloran 1 (og), Gunnarsson 13,	Ward	Hansson*	Clarke	Thomas	Kippe	Gunnarsson	Gudjonsson	Kavanagh^	Cooke"	Thorne	O'Connor	Petty/Risom/Dadason
5/5			20,591	20	77			O'Halloran 55p [Cooke 23, Kav' 38p]	Mildenhall	Williams"	Duke	Heywood	Willis	O'Halloran	Robinson	V d Linden*	Bakalli^	Grazioli	Invincible	Reeves/Alexander/Mills
	Home		Away					Ref: T Parkes	Any nerves are steadied when Keith O'Halloran miscues a clearance after just 21 seconds. Gunnarson surges through to whack in a hard drive. Cooke beats the offside trap to slot past Mildenhall. Thorne's shirt is pulled. Kav buries the pen. O'Halloran nets after Hansson nudges Reeves.											
Average	13,767		7,140																	

Play-offs	Att		F-A	H-T	Scorers, Times, and Referees	1	2	3	4	5	6	7	8	9	10	11	subs used
SF H WALSALL		D	0-0	0-0		Ward	Hansson^	Clarke	Thomas*	Kippe	Gunnarsson	Gudjonsson	Kavanagh	Thorne	Cooke	O'Connor	Dadason/Petty !
1 13/5	23,689					*Walker*	*Brightwell*	*Aranalde*	*Tillson*	*Barras*	*Bennett*	*Hall**	*Simpson^*	*Leitao*	*Goodman*	*Matias*	*Gadsby/Keates*
					Ref: U Rennie	Gordon Banks is revealed as new Club President. Ray Graydon's Walsall have the better of it. Don Goodman proves a thorn in Stoke's central defence. He nods just over. Walker foils Thorne. Petty sees red (82) for tugging Matias. Kippe tackles Goodman rashly, the ref waves play on.											
SF A WALSALL		L	2-4	1-1	Kavanagh 31, Thorne 85	Ward	Thomas*	Dorigo^	Mohan"	Kippe	Gunnarsson	Gudjonsson	Kavanagh	Dadason	Clarke	O'Connor	Thorne/Thordarson/Cooke
2 16/5	*8,993*				*Ward 42 (og), Matias 47, 61, Keates 50*	*Walker*	*Brightwell*	*Aranalde*	*Tillson*	*Barras*	*Keates*	*Hall**	*Bennett*	*Leitao^*	*Goodman"*	*Matias*	*Gadsby/Angell/Byfield*
					Ref: E Wolstenholme (Stoke lose 2-4 on aggregate)	Gudjon bottles it, fielding a defensive 5-4-1. Kav's spectacular opener looks to justify his decision, but Ward drops a clanger, and the ball, over the line from a corner. Matias fires in and nets Thommo's bad back-pass. Keates' free-kick sails into the net. Thorne's shot is no consolation.											

Worthington Cup	Att		F-A	H-T	Scorers, Times, and Referees	1	2	3	4	5	6	7	8	9	10	11	subs used
1:1 A YORK	4	W	5-1	1-0	Heath 10, Connor 47, 59, Iwelumo 70,	Muggleton	Petty	Dorigo*	Heath	Gunnarsson	Mohan	Risom	Thordarson^	Connor	Fenton	O'Connor	Iwelumo/Clarke
22/8	*2,035 3:24*				*Jones 49* [O'Connor 80]	*Howarth*	*Edmonson**	*Potter^*	*Sertori*	*Jones*	*Hobson*	*McNiven*	*Hulme*	*Duffield*	*Agnew*	*Hall*	*Bullock/Conlon*
					Ref: U Rennie	Rob Heath nets his first goal when Howarth drops a cross. Connor converts two Fenton passes. Barry Jones' 25-yard strike is goal of the night. Iwelumo heads his first goal from a corner with his first touch. O'Connor steers home a 20 yarder. City's first away five-goal haul in 45 years.											
1:2 H YORK	11	D	0-0	0-0		Ward	Hansson	Dorigo*	Clarke	Mohan^	Gunnarsson	Fenton	Kavanagh	Gudjonsson	Thordarson	O'Connor"	Iwelumo/Thomas/Risom
6/9	3,478 *3:24*					*Fettis*	*Edmonson*	*Potter*	*Hocking*	*Jones*	*Thompson**	*Bullock*	*Hulme*	*Williams J^*	*Alcide"*	*Hall*	*Sertori/McNiven/Conlon*
					Ref: F Stretton (Stoke win 5-1 on aggregate)	The huge lead provides no motivation. Only point of note sees Mr Stretton move the ball 10 yards forward due to Mohan's yellow for dissent. Described by one hack as 'the worst game I have ever seen'. City fail to score in the first three home games of a season for the first time ever.											
2:1 H CHARLTON	8	W	2-1	1-1	Thordarson 45p, Goodfellow 86	Ward	Hansson	Clarke	Thomas	Mohan	Gunnarsson	Gudjonsson*	Kavanagh	Lightbourne^	Thordarson"	O'Connor	Risom/Thorne/**Goodfellow**
20/9	9,388 *P:8*				*Johansson 41*	*Kiely*	*Kishishev**	*Powell*	*Shields*	*Todd*	*Parker*	*Newton*	*Jensen*	*Lisbie*	*Johansson^*	*Robinson"*	*Konchesky/MacD'ld/Salako*
					Ref: R Olivier	Charlton's Alan Curbishley fields a below-strength side. Jonatan Johansson nets from Lisbie's pass. Hansson is felled for the pen, although the Addicks claim he dived. Debutant Marc Goodfellow races clear to score the winner on his 19th birthday. First Stoke giant-killing in five years.											
2:2 A CHARLTON	10	L	3-4 *aet*	1-1	O'Con' 36, Gun'son 87, Thordarson 107	Ward	Hansson*	Clarke	Thomas	Mohan !	Gunnarsson	Gudjonsson	Petty	Lightbourne^	Thorne"	O'Connor	Kav'/Thordarson/Connor
26/9	*10,037 P:5*				*Lisbie 25, 111, Johansson 75, 81*	*Ilic*	*Konchesky**	*Brown*	*Shields*	*Parker*	*Todd*	*Newton^*	*Jensen*	*Lisbie*	*Johansson"*	*Salako*	*Powell/MacD'nald/Robinson*
					Ref: R Olivier (Stoke win on away goals)	O'Connor's errant backpass lets in Lisbie. He makes amends with a storming goal. Johansson nets a header and clinical shot. Mohan walks for two yellows (80). Gunnarsson nets a far-post header. Thordarson's left-foot exocet wins goal of the season. Lisbie's shot cannot save Addicks.											
3 H BARNSLEY	8	W	3-2	1-1	Gudjonsson 8, 56, Dadason 90	Muggleton	Petty*	Clarke	Thomas	Mohan	Gunnarsson	Gudjonsson	Kavanagh	Thorne	Thordarson	O'Connor	**Dadason**
1/11	10,480 *1:12*				*Corbo 33, Jones 85*	*Miller*	*Regan*	*Barker*	*Morgan*	*Chettle*	*Ward*	*McClare**	*V d Laan*	*Sheron*	*Dyer^*	*Corbo"*	*O'Callaghan/Thomas/Jones*
					Ref: M Fletcher	Bjarni clips home Thomas's cross-field pass. Corbo curls in a free-kick against the run of play. Bjarni cracks home from a short-corner routine, but gifts Tykes an equaliser when he passes back blind. Enter the conquering hero, Rikki Dadason, who bullets home a header from a corner.											
4 H LIVERPOOL	6	L	0-8	0-4	*[Fow' 39,82, 85p, Hyypia 59, Murphy 65]*	Muggleton	Hansson*	Dorigo	Clarke	Mohan	Gunnarsson	Risom	Kavanagh	Lightbourne^	Thorne"	Gudjonsson	Petty/Thordarson/Goodfell'w
29/11	27,109 *P:5*				*Ziege 6, Smicer 26, Babbel 28,*	*Arphexad*	*Babbel**	*Ziege*	*Carragher*	*Henchoz*	*Hyypia*	*Murphy*	*Smicer^*	*Fowler*	*Partridge"*	*McAllister*	*Wright/Hamann/Barmby*
					Ref: A D'Urso	Thorne hits the post with the net gaping. Gerard Houllier's men cut loose. Gary McAllister runs the game. Fowler's trio are a header, cool shot, and pen for Muggers' foul on him. Reds only have nine shots. At 0-7 the North End drown 'You'll never walk alone' with a rousing 'Delilah'.											

FA Cup	Att		F-A	H-T	Scorers, Times, and Referees	1	2	3	4	5	6	7	8	9	10	11	subs used
1 H NUNEATON	9	D	0-0	0-0		Muggleton	Hansson"	Petty	Thomas	Mohan	Gunnars'n !	Gudjonsson	Kavanagh	Lightbourne*	Thorne	Thordarson^	Dadason/Clarke/O'Connor
18/11	8,437 *VC:16*					MacKenzie	Sykes	Love	Crowley	Weaver	Angus	Wray*	Charles	McGregor^	King	Francis	Taylor/Williams B
					Ref: C Foy	Gunnarsson is wrongly sent off (42) for a second yellow for encroaching at a free-kick actually taken by a Nuneaton player. The entertainment is provided by Pottermus who steals the head from Borough mascot Norris the Hound and parades it down the Sentinel Stand. Desperate stuff.											
1R A NUNEATON	9	L	0-1	0-0		Muggleton	Hansson*	Dorigo^	Clarke	Mohan	Risom	Gudjonsson	Kavanagh	Thorne	Thordarson	Petty	Goodfellow/Collins
21/11	*4,477 VC:16*				*McGregor 90*	MacKenzie	Sykes	Love	Crowley	Weaver	Angus	Wray	Charles*	McGregor	*King*	*Francis*	*Taylor*
					Ref: C Foy	City make no headway on a heavy Manor Park. MacKenzie's save from Thorne is voted save of the month by Sky's viewers. Clarke tackles as McGregor rounds Muggers. Sykes hits the bar. Goodfellow fluffs when clear. McGregor slots a carbon copy chance. Another embarrassment.											

		Home					Away					
	P	W	D	L	F	A	W	D	L	F	A	Pts
1 Millwall	46	17	2	4	49	11	11	7	5	40	27	93
2 Rotherham	46	16	4	3	50	26	11	6	6	29	29	91
3 Reading	46	15	5	3	58	26	10	6	7	28	26	86
4 Walsall*	46	15	5	3	51	23	8	7	8	28	27	81
5 STOKE	46	12	6	5	39	21	9	8	6	35	28	77
6 Wigan	46	12	9	2	29	18	7	9	7	24	24	75
7 Bournemouth	46	11	6	6	37	23	9	7	7	42	32	73
8 Notts Co	46	10	6	7	37	33	9	6	8	25	33	69
9 Bristol City	46	11	6	6	47	29	7	8	8	23	27	68
10 Wrexham	46	10	6	7	33	28	7	6	10	32	43	63
11 Port Vale	46	9	8	6	35	22	7	6	10	20	27	62
12 Peterborough	46	12	6	5	38	27	3	8	12	23	39	59
13 Wycombe	46	8	7	8	24	23	7	7	9	22	30	59
14 Brentford	46	9	10	4	34	30	5	7	11	22	40	59
15 Oldham	46	11	5	7	35	26	4	8	11	18	39	58
16 Bury	46	10	6	7	25	22	6	4	13	20	37	58
17 Colchester	46	10	5	8	32	23	5	7	11	23	36	57
18 Northampton	46	9	6	8	26	28	6	6	11	20	31	57
19 Cambridge	46	8	6	9	32	31	6	5	12	29	46	53
20 Swindon	46	6	8	9	30	35	7	5	11	17	30	52
21 Bristol Rov	46	6	10	7	28	26	6	5	12	25	31	51
22 Luton	46	5	6	12	24	35	4	7	12	28	45	40
23 Swansea	46	5	9	9	26	24	3	4	16	21	49	37
24 Oxford	46	5	4	14	23	34	2	2	19	30	66	27
	1104	242	151	159	842	624	159	151	242	624	842	1505

* promoted after play-offs

Odds & ends

Double wins: (6) Bristol City, Bristol Rovers, Colchester, Peterborough, Swindon, Wrexham.

Double losses: (1) Swansea.

Won from behind: (6) Bristol City (a), Bury (h), Colchester (h), Luton (a). Millwall (h), Oldham (a).

Lost from in front: (1) Rotherham (a).

High Spots: Defeating Premiership Charlton and Division One Barnsley in the Worthington Cup.
Peter Thorne's recovery from two injuries to top score again.
The 15-match unbeaten run which guaranteed a play-off spot.

Low spots: Failing to challenge for automatic promotion once again.
Failure to deliver of the much-vaunted Rikki Dadason.
Club record 0-8 home defeat by Liverpool in the Worthington Cup.
Losing yet again to a non-league club in the FA Cup.
Thordarson's infuriating persistence with 5-3-2 tactics.

Player of the Year: Brynjar Gunnarsson.
Ever-presents: (1) Brynjar Gunnarsson.
Hat-tricks: (1) Peter Thorne.
Leading Scorer: (16) Peter Thorne.

	Appearances						Goals			
	Lge	*Sub*	LC	*Sub*	FAC	*Sub*	Lge	LC	FAC	Tot
Clarke, Clive	**12**	*9*	5	*1*	1	*1*				
Collins, Lee						*1*				
Connor, Paul	**1**	*6*	1	*1*				2		**2**
Cooke, Andy	**21**	*1*					**6**			**6**
Dadason, Rikki	**13**	*15*		*1*		*1*	**6**	1		**7**
Dorigo, Tony	**34**	*2*	3		1					
Fenton, Graeme	**2**	*3*	2				**1**			**1**
Goodfellow, Marc		*7*		*2*		*1*		1		**1**
Gudjonsson, Bjarni	**41**	*1*	5		2		**6**	2		**8**
Gunnarsson, Brynjar	**46**		6		1		**5**	1		**6**
Hansson, Mikael	**36**	*2*	4		2		**2**			**2**
Heath, Robert			1					1		**1**
Iwelumo, Chris		*2*		*2*			**1**	1		**2**
Kavanagh, Graham	**42**	*1*	4	*1*	2		**8**			**8**
Kippe, Frode	**15**	*4*								
Kristinsson, Birkir	**18**									
Lightbourne, Kyle	**11**	*11*	3		1		**5**			**5**
Mohan, Nicky	**37**		6		2		**1**			**1**
Muggleton, Carl	**11**	*1*	3		2					
Neal, Lewis		*1*								
O'Connor, James	**44**		5			*1*	**8**	2		**10**
Petty, Ben	**10**	*12*	3	*1*	2					
Risom, Henik	**9**	*16*	2	*2*	1					
Robinson, Marvin	**3**						**1**			**1**
Thomas, Wayne	**33**	*1*	3	*1*	1					
Thordarson, Stefan	**15**	*15*	4	*2*	2		**4**	2		**6**
Thorne, Peter	**35**	*3*	3	*1*	2		**16**			**16**
Ward, Gavin	**17**		3							
(own-goals)							**4**			**4**
28 players used	**506**	***113***	**66**	***15***	**22**	***5***	**74**	**13**		**87**

No	Date	Opponent	Att	Pos	Pt	F-A	H-T	Scorers, Times, and Referees	1	2	3	4	5	6	7	8	9	10	11	subs used
1	A	QP RANGERS			L	0-1	0-1		Ward	Thomas	Clarke*	**Handyside**	**Shtaniuk**	**Vandeurzen**	Gudjonsson	O'Connor	Cooke^	Thorne	**Hoekstra**	**Rowson**/Iwelumo
	11/8		*14,357*		0			*Thomson 23*	*Day*	*Forbes*	*Bruce*	*Palmer*	*Ben Askar*	*Perry*	*Bignot*	*Bonnot*	*Thomson*	*Wardley**	*Connolly"*	*Griffiths^/Koejoe/Warren*
								Ref: E Wolstenholme	Andy Thomson causes havoc between new City's central defenders. He escapes the offside trap to rifle past Ward. Thorne has a shot ruled out for handball. Thommo booked for dissent. Thorne scraps with Palmer. Day denies Bjarni. A melée follows Shtaniuk's bodycheck on Thomson.											
2	H	NORTHAMPTON		9	W	2-0	0-0	Cooke 52, Thorne 54	Ward	Thomas	Vandeurzen	Handyside	Shtaniuk	Rowson	Gudjonsson	O'Connor	Cooke*	Thorne	Hoekstra^	Goodfellow/Thordarson
	18/8		12,845	*24*	3				*Welch*	*Lavin*	*Spedding*	*Frain*	*Evatt*	*Hope*	*Hunt*	*Parkin^*	*Forrester*	*Gabbiadini"*	*Hargreaves**	*Wol'ston/Asamoah/McGrego*
								Ref: M Cowburn	Forrester is the sharp edge of Cobblers' three-pronged attack. Ward denies him twice. Cooke drags wide. Wolleaston hits the inside of the post. Hoekstra leaves Lavin sprawling to centre for Cooke. Thorne nods across Welch from Bjarni's cross. Welch claws away Cooke's late header.											
3	A	CAMBRIDGE		7	W	2-0	0-0	Thorne 48, Cooke 51	Ward	Thomas	Vandeurzen	Handyside	Shtaniuk !	Rowson	Gudjonsson	O'Connor	Cooke"	Thorne^	Hoekstra*	Clarke/Thordarson/Goodfell'
	25/8		***3,336***	*21*	6				*Perez*	*Fleming*	*Byrne !*	*Walling*	*Angus*	*Ashbee*	*Wanless*	*Richardson^*	*Kitson*	*Alcide**	*Youngs"*	*Cowan/Traore/Duncan*
								Ref: P Danson	In sizzling sun City produce a professional display after Shtaniuk walks for two yellows (40). Thorne nods in Rowson's centre. Cooke swivels to bury. Ward saves Kitson's header. Perez denies Cooke with his shins. John Beck's side reduced to 10 after Des Byrne's second yellow (77).											
4	H	TRANMERE		10	L	1-2	0-1	Thorne 90p	Ward	Thomas	Clarke	Handyside	Shtaniuk	Vandeurzen	Gudjonsson	O'Connor	Cooke^	Thorne	Hoekstra*	Iwelumo/Thordarson
	27/8		12,031	*15*	6			*Hill 13, Flynn 89*	*Murphy*	*Yates*	*Roberts*	*Flynn*	*Challinor*	*Hill*	*Mellon*	*Parkinson*	*Barlow**	*Allison*	*Koumas*	*Hume*
								Ref: S Baines	Clint Hill nods in a corner. Hoekstra blasts at Murphy when through. The keeper then denies JVD. City besiege Rovers' goal, but lack subtlety. Dave Watson's men keep their composure. Flynn's free header seals the win. Cardiff's £1.3m target Peter Thorne slots a pen, given for a push.											
5	H	HUDDERSFIELD		14	D	1-1	0-1	Thorne 90	Ward	Thomas	Clarke	**Henry***	Gunnarsson	Vandeurzen	Gudjonsson	O'Connor	Cooke	Thorne	Hoekstra^	Iwelumo/Thordarson
	8/9		13,319	*3*	7			*Schofield 32*	*Margetson*	*Heary*	*Evans*	*Clarke*	*Moses*	*Gray*	*Beech**	*Holland*	*Hay^*	*Schofield*	*Thorrington*	*Irons/Mattis*
								Ref: C Webster	Lou Macari's men take control after a sterile first half-hour. Danny Schofield races through to beat Ward. Gudjon argues with Terriers assistant Joe Jordan. Ward denies Beech. Iwelumo heads inches wide. Peter Thorne bids adieu by netting a crisp half-volley in a crowded penalty area.											
6	H	READING		9	W	2-0	2-0	Gudjonsson 25, Cooke 30	Ward	Thomas	Clarke	Handyside	Shtaniuk	Gunnarsson	Gudjonsson	O'Connor	Cooke*	Vandeurzen	Hoekstra	Thordarson
	15/9		11,752	*10*	10				*Whitehead*	*Murty*	*Robinson*	*Whitbread*	*Williams*	*Parkinson*	*Igoe**	*Harper*	*Cureton"*	*Butler*	*Smith A^*	*Forster/Henderson/Jones*
								Ref: E Wolstenholme	Lacking the departed Thorne, City outclass Alan Pardew's Royals. The passing is breathtaking. Hoekstra, switched inside, carves huge holes. He crosses for Bjarni to net, then hits the post. Cooke fires in O'Connor's pass. Ward denies Butler twice. First game since Sep 11th atrocities.											
7	A	BRIGHTON		14	L	0-1	0-0		Ward	Thomas	Clarke	Handyside	Shtaniuk	Gunnarsson	Gudjonsson	O'Connor	Cooke*	Vandeurzen	Hoekstra	Thordarson
	18/9		*6,627*	*1*	10			*Watson 90*	*Kuipers*	*Watson*	*Mayo*	*Morgan*	*Cullip*	*Carpenter*	*Rogers*	*Oatway**	*Steele^*	*Zamora*	*Pitcher"*	*Jones/Hart/Brooker*
								Ref: P Jones	City create good chances, but lack a goalscoring predator. Micky Adams' Seagulls hump it towards Bobby Zamora who is expertly marked by Shtaniuk. In the fifth minute of added time, Ward's howler, as he mis-punches on the edge of his box, allows Watson to slot into an empty net.											
8	A	BURY		10	W	1-0	1-0	Vandeurzen 32	Cutler	Thomas	Clarke	Handyside	Shtaniuk	Gunnarsson"	Gudjonsson	O'Connor	Cooke	Vandeurzen	Hoekstra*	Iwelumo^/Thordarson/Henry
	22/9		*4,727*	*24*	13				*Kenny*	*Unsworth*	*Armstrong*	*Syros*	*Swailes*	*Jarrett*	*Billy**	*Reid*	*Newby*	*Lawson*	*Singh*	*Seddon*
								Ref: G Cain	Gudjon has lost patience with Ward. Paddy Kenny denies Bjarni three times. The third save falls to JVD, who nets with aplomb. Newby strikes the post. Syros nods over. Hoekstra magically flicks the ball over a defender's head while facing the other way. Bury's eighth straight defeat.											
9	H	COLCHESTER		7	W	3-0	1-0	Vandeurzen 45, Thordarson 57, 90	Cutler	Thomas	Clarke	Handyside	Shtaniuk	Gunnarsson*	Gudjonsson	O'Connor	Cooke	Vandeurzen	Thordarson	Henry
	26/9		**9,515**	*9*	16				*Woodman*	*Duguid*	*Johnson G*	*Pinault**	*White*	*Clark*	*Izzet*	*Gregory*	*Rapley*	*Stockwell^*	*McGleish*	*Bowry/Morgan*
								Ref: R Pearson	Hoekstra is crocked in the warm up. Thordarson deputises. He is tripped by Woodman for a pen (17), but Bjarni's kick is saved. JVD nods in Cooke's centre. Thordarson lashes home on the run and rifles an angled drive. Gudjon targets Mansfield's Chris Greenacre to replace Thorne.											
10	H	BOURNEMOUTH		5	W	2-0	1-0	Maher 11 (og), Thomas 47	Cutler	Thomas	Clarke	Handyside	Shtaniuk	Gunnarss'n^	Gudjonsson	O'Connor	Cooke*	Vandeurzen	Thordarson	Iwelumo/Henry
	29/9		14,803	*20*	19				*Stewart*	*Ford^*	*Purches*	*Howe*	*Tindall*	*Maher*	*Feeney**	*Holmes*	*Hayter"*	*Fletcher C*	*Elliott*	*Eribenne/O'Connor/Huck*
								Ref: M Clattenburg	Kid for a Quid boosts the gate. Clarke hooks off the line. Shaun Maher skews Bjarni's cross into his own net. Stewart parries Sergei's header, Thommo lunges to prod in. Cutler saves Feeney's penalty (71), given for JVD's foul on him, low to his left. Stewart denies Cooke one-on-one.											
11	H	NOTTS CO		5	W	1-0	0-0	Hoekstra 47p	Ward	Thomas	Clarke	Handyside	Shtaniuk	Gunnarsson	Gudjonsson	O'Connor	Cooke*	Vandeurzen	Hoekstra	Iwelumo
	13/10		13,220	*16*	22				*Mildenhall*	*Richardson*	*Baraclough*	*Caskey*	*Warren*	*Grayson*	*Owers*	*Cas*	*Stallard*	*Allsopp**	*Brough^*	*Hackworth/Nicholson*
								Ref: B Curson	Cutler's back problem means Ward returns. City play tidy football. Steve Mildenhall blocks Cooke's header. Cas pushes O'Connor for the pen. *Tulips from Amsterdam* over the tannoy greets Hoekstra's first Stoke goal. JVD's shot is deflected over. Six yellows as the game deteriorates.											

No	Venue	Opponent	Att	Pos	Res	FT	HT	Scorers, Times, and Referees	1	2	3	4	5	6	7	8	9	10	11	subs used
12	A	PORT VALE		4	D	1-1	0-0	Iwelumo 78	Cutler	Thomas	Clarke	Handyside	Shtaniuk	Gunnarsson	Gudjonsson	O'Connor	Cooke	Vandeurzen^	Hoekstra*	Iwelumo/Neal
21/10			10,344	*17*	23			*McPhee 63*	*Goodlad*	*Cummins*	*Ingram*	*Carragher*	*Burns*	*Burton*	*Dodd**	*Brisco*	*Brooker*	*McPhee*	*Armstrong*	*McClare*
								Ref: P Richards	John Rudge's 57th birthday sees his former club overcome a slow start. Thommo clears as Brooker is poised to net. Cutler flies to deny Dodd. Handyside clears desperately. McPhee lashes home Brooker's cross. The subs work. Cooke steps over Neal's cross for Iwelumo to glide home.											
13	A	CHESTERFIELD		5	W	2-1	0-0	Hoekstra 67, 90p	Cutler	Thomas^	Clarke	Handyside	Shtaniuk	Gunnarsson	Gudjonsson	O'Connor	Iwelumo	Vandeurzen*	Hoekstra	Cooke/Henry
23/10			5,141	*19*	26			*Reeves 64p*	*Abbey*	*Booty*	*Edwards*	*Jones**	*Breckin*	*Payne*	*Ebdon*	*D'Auria*	*Reeves*	*Beckett*	*Richardson*	*Willis*
								Ref: C Wilkes	Stoke pummel Nicky Law's men. Nathan Abbey produces several fine stops. JVD hits the post. Shtaniuk fouls Beckett. Reeves nets. Hoekstra scores after his free-kick rebounds off the wall. Iwelumo nets, but is given offside. O'Connor is felled by Abbey. Hoekstra buries the penalty.											
14	H	BRISTOL CITY		3	W	1-0	0-0	Gunnarsson 88	Cutler	Thomas^	Clarke"	Handyside	Shtaniuk	Gunnarsson	Gudjonsson	O'Connor	Iwelumo*	Vandeurzen	Hoekstra	Cooke/Henry/Neal
27/10			16,828	*4*	29				*Stowell*	*Burnell*	*Bell*	*Hill*	*Lever*	*Carey**	*Murray !*	*Brown A*	*Jones^*	*Thorpe*	*Tinnion*	*Doherty/Peacock*
								Ref: H Webb	The Matthews statue is unveiled by Kevin Keegan. Iwelumo nets twice, but is offside. Danny Wilson's men change shirts from white to green at half-time. Robins settle for the draw. Gunnarsson swivels to crash home in a melee. Scott Murray receives a second yellow (88) for diving.											
15	A	SWINDON		3	W	3-0	1-0	Gunnars'n 28, Iwelumo 65, O'Connor 86	Cutler	Thomas^	Clarke	Handyside	Shtaniuk	Gunnarsson	Gudjonsson	O'Connor	Iwelumo	Neal	Hoekstra*	Cooke/Henry
3/11			7,981	*14*	32				*Griemink*	*Invincible*	*Duke^*	*Heywood*	*Ruddock*	*Gurney*	*Carlisle*	*Howe*	*Edwards P*	*Grazioli**	*Hewlett*	*Sabin/Osei-Kuffour*
								Ref: P Alcock	JVD pulls a muscle in warm-up. Neal starts. Roy Evans' Robins worry Stoke. Gunnarsson follows up Griemink's save to lash in. Culter denies Howe. Carlisle rattles the bar. Iwelumo fluffs, then buries Thommo's cross. O'Connor sidesteps his marker to crash home. Seven wins in eight.											
16	A	BLACKPOOL		3	D	2-2	0-0	Iwelumo 63, 64	Cutler	Henry*	Clarke	Handyside	Shtaniuk	Gunnarsson	Gudjonsson	O'Connor	Cooke	Vandeurzen	Iwelumo	Rowson
6/11			4,921	*15*	33			*Ormerod 73, 79*	*Pullen*	*Coid*	*Jaszczun*	*O'Kane*	*Caldwell*	*Reid^*	*Milligan**	*Simpson*	*Ormerod*	*Marshall*	*Bullock*	*Wellens/Hills*
								Ref: N Barry	Stoke lack Thommo suspended. Cooke's effort is cleared off the line. Iwelumo towers in a header and steers in Cooke's cross. Pool press hard. O'Connor fails to clear. Brett Ormerod bangs in. His brace gives him 18 for the season. Cooke hits the bar. Dean Crowe joins Luton on a free.											
17	H	BRENTFORD		3	W	3-2	1-1	Gunnars'n 32, Iwelumo 49, Shtaniuk 80	Cutler	Thomas	Clarke	Handyside	Shtaniuk	Gunnarsson	Gudjonsson	Neal*	Iwelumo^	Vandeurzen	Hoekstra	Cooke/Rowson
10/11			17,953	*2*	36			*Burgess 45, Owusu 55*	*Gottskalks'n*	*Dobson*	*Anderson^*	*Ingimarsson*	*Powell*	*Hutchinson**	*Sidwell*	*Mahon*	*Owusu*	*O'Connor"*	*Burgess*	*Williams/McCam'n/Rowlands*
								Ref: D Pugh	O'Connor is out suspended. Gunnarsson nods in. Burgess hooks the first away goal at the Brit for 553 mins. Iwelumo prods in Hoekstra's pass. Lloyd Owusu chips Cutler from 25 yards after Handyside mis-controls. Shtaniuk's towering header knocks Steve Coppell's Bees off top spot.											
18	A	WIGAN		3	L	**1-6**	1-3	Van' 6 [*Dalg' 49, Ashc'ft 61p, Kenna 88*]	Cutler	Thomas	Clarke	Handyside	Shtaniuk	Rowson*	Gudjonsson	O'Connor	Iwelumo	Vandeurzen	Hoekstra	**Smart**
13/11			7,047	*18*	36			*Dinning 4, Liddell 14, De Zeeuw 35,*	*Stillie*	*Green*	*Kenna*	*Dinning*	*Jackson*	*De Zeeuw*	*Brannan*	*Dalglish^*	*Ashcroft*	*Liddell*	*McCulloch**	*Roberts/Mitchell*
								Ref: J Winter	City kick-start Wigan's slumbering season. Dinning fires in from 25 yards. JVD nods in Bjarni's cross. Liddell nets easily. De Zeeuw buries a header. Dalglish slams in a peach. Jeff Kenna's strike is his first goal since 1995. JVD and Bjarni hit the post. 3,003 Stokies watch in silence.											
19	H	OLDHAM		3	D	0-0	0-0		Ward	Thomas^	Clarke	Handyside	Shtaniuk	Gunnarsson	Gudjonsson	O'Connor	Iwelumo	Vandeurzen*	Hoekstra"	Cooke/Neal/Smart !
21/11			11,031	*14*	37				*Miskelly"*	*Holden*	*Armstrong*	*McNiven^*	*Balmer*	*Duxbury*	*Beharall*	*Sheridan J*	*Sheridan D*	*Corazzin**	*Eyres*	*Tipton/Eyre/Kelly*
								Ref: G Frankland	New boss Iain Dowie ensures Latics keep it tight. Miskelly denies Bjarni and Shtaniuk. Loanee Allan Smart strikes John Sheridan and sees red (85). Ward's save from Eyres earns Stoke a point. Petur Marteinsson signs from Stabaek in Norway, although he is injured with a broken foot.											
20	A	WREXHAM		2	W	1-0	0-0	Cooke 67	Ward	Thomas	Clarke	Handyside	Shtaniuk	Neal	Gudjonsson	O'Connor	Cooke	Vandeurzen*	Hoekstra	Rowson
24/11			5,477	*22*	40				*Rogers*	*Whitley*	*Holmes*	*Sharp^*	*Roberts*	*Hill*	*Gibson"*	*Ferguson*	*Faulc'bridge*	*Trundle*	*Chalk**	*Thomas/Blackwood/Sam*
								Ref: P Armstrong	Cooke is restored up front. Below-par City defend for long periods. Shtaniuk's mountainous presence earns him the first of nine yellows. Ward clatters Faulconbridge, but Ferguson fluffs the penalty wide (20). Cooke nods over, then nets when Hoekstra's dummy leaves him free. Lucky.											
21	H	WYCOMBE		1	W	5-1	3-1	Gunnarsson 19, 44, Iwelumo 30,	Cutler	Thomas	Clarke*	Handyside	Shtaniuk	Gunnarsson	Gudjonsson	O'Connor	Cooke	Iwelumo^	Vandeurzen	Goodfellow/Dadason
15/12			12,911	*8*	43			*McSporran 24* [Cooke 58, Goodfell' 85]	*Taylor*	*Senda*	*Vinnicombe*	*Bulman"*	*Rogers*	*McCarthy*	*Roberts^*	*Simpson*	*Currie**	*McSporran*	*Emblen !*	*Brown/Ryan/Cousins*
								Ref: R Beeby	Ward is out (knee ligament) after a training collision with Rowson. Gunnarsson nods in a corner and clinically slots. Iwelumo cracks in. Cooke and McSporran bag headers. Goodfellow sidesteps a tackle to net. Paul Emblen sees red for striking Bjarni (32). Sanchez calls Bjarni a cheat.											
22	H	CARDIFF		2	D	1-1	0-0	Gabbidon 77 (og)	Cutler	Thomas	Clarke	Handyside	Shtaniuk	Gunnarsson	Gudjonsson	O'Connor	Cooke	Iwelumo^	Vandeurzen*	Goodfellow/Dadason
19/12			14,331	*6*	44			*Gordon D 83*	*Alexander*	*Gabbidon*	*Gordon D*	*Bonner"*	*Prior*	*Young**	*Bowen^*	*Kavanagh*	*Gordon G*	*Earnshaw*	*Boland*	*Weston/Brayson/Fort'-West*
								Ref: A Leake	Kav's return is greeted by jeers. Earnshaw's shot whistles past the post. Gunnarsson's stinger sees Neil Alexander tip round. Goodfellow drills in a cross and Gabbidon turns into his own net. Dadason drags wide. Shtaniuk clambers on Fortune-West. Dean Gordon curls in the free-kick.											
23	A	TRANMERE		2	D	2-2	1-1	Cooke 19, Dadason 90p	Cutler	Henry	Clarke	Handyside	Thomas	Gunnarsson	Gudjonsson	O'Connor	Cooke	Iwelumo^	Neal*	Goodfellow/Dadason
26/12			12,201	*11*	45			*Price 42, 72*	*Achterberg*	*Yates*	*Roberts*	*Henry*	*Allen*	*Hill*	*Flynn*	*Mellon**	*Price*	*Allison*	*Koumas*	*Barlow*
								Ref: M Fletcher	Cooke's header from Clarke's cross pings in off the bar. Price beats Cutler at the near post, then drills home. Goodfellow's volley hits a Rovers hand. Tranmere try to out-psyche Dadason, but he keeps his cool. Guinea international Souleymane Oulare arrives from Las Palmas on a free.											

No	Date		Att	Pos	Pt	F-A	H-T	Scorers, Times, and Referees	1	2	3	4	5	6	7	8	9	10	11	subs used
24	A	HUDDERSFIELD		2	D	0-0	0-0		Cutler	Thomas	Clarke	Handyside	Shtaniuk	Gunnarss'n^	Gudjonsson	O'Connor	Cooke"	Iwelumo	Vandeurzen*	Goodfellow/Henry/Dadason
	29/12		*16,041*	*9*	46				*Margetson*	*Jenkins*	*Evans*	*Irons**	*Moses*	*Gray*	*Thor'ington^*	*Knight*	*Booth*	*Schofield*	*Mattis*	*Heary/Hay"/Wijnhard*
								Ref: P Danson	O'Connor shoots feebly when clear. Cutler denies Knight twice and Hay. Snow falls as Iwelumo's shot is saved. Cooke's shot deflects wide. A 95th-minute let-off as Wijnhard fires wide when clear. Handyside and Gunnarsson break bones in their feet. Robert Heath is released by Stoke.											
25	H	BLACKPOOL		1	W	2-0	1-0	Shtaniuk 13, O'Connor 82	Cutler	Henry	Clarke	Thomas	Shtaniuk	Vandeurzen	Gudjonsson	O'Connor	Cooke*	Iwelumo^	Goodfellow	Rowson/Dadason
	1/1		16,615	*14*	49				*Barnes*	*Wellens**	*Jaszczun*	*Thompson"*	*Hughes*	*Marshall*	*Collins*	*Bullock*	*Walker*	*Payton^*	*Hills*	*Simpson/MacKenzie/Day*
								Ref: G Frankland	Shtaniuk rises to nod home Bjarni's corner. Goodfellow runs at Steve McMahon's defence and causes havoc. Henry's backpass falls to Payton. His shot is deflected wide by Cutler. Iwelumo's diving header is pouched by Barnes. Goodfellow races away to cross for O'Connor to head in.											
26	A	NORTHAMPTON		3	D	1-1	1-0	Goodfellow 36	Cutler	Rowson	Vandeurzen	**Flynn**	Shtaniuk	Henry*	Gudjonsson	O'Connor	Goodfellow	Iwelumo	Dadason^	Neal/**Oulare**
	13/1		*5,636*	*24*	50			*Parkin 82*	*Sollitt*	*Dempsey^*	*Hunter*	*Sampson*	*Burgess*	*Hunt*	*McGregor**	*Parkin*	*Forrester*	*Gabbiadini*	*Hargreaves*	*Asamoah/Hodge*
								Ref: G Salisbury	Goodfellow and O'Connor waste golden chances when sent clear. Sollitt gifts a goal, allowing Goodfellow's drive to bobble in. Town improve after the break and pressurise. City cling on until a cross finds Sam Parkin's head. New signing Oulare impresses with a spin and vicious shot.											
27	H	QP RANGERS		3	L	0-1	0-0		Cutler	Rowson	Clarke	Flynn	Shtaniuk	Vandeurzen*	Gudjonsson	O'Connor	Cooke	Goodfellow	Dadason	Iwelumo
	19/1		16,725	*5*	50			*Peacock 81*	*Digby*	*Forbes*	*Murphy*	*Palmer*	*Rose*	*Shittu*	*Bignot*	*Peacock*	*Doudou**	*Griffiths*	*Pacqueete^*	*Connolly/Thomson*
								Ref: M Ryan	Oulare is in hospital recovering from the blood clot which nearly killed him. City struggle for any rhythm. Ian Holloway's Hoops cope easily. Digby pouches Cooke's header. Cutler denies Rose. Shtaniuk blazes over. Thomson hits the post. Gavin Peacock waltzes through to fire home.											
28	A	CARDIFF		4	L	0-2	0-1		Cutler	Thomas	Clarke	Flynn	Shtaniuk	Henry	Gudjonss'n^	Rowson	Cooke	Iwelumo	Vandeurzen*	Goodfellow/**Wilson**
	22/1		*11,771*	*10*	50			*Gudjonsson 19 (og), Legg 71*	*Alexander*	*Hamilton**	*Legg*	*Weston*	*Young*	*Gabbidon*	*Bowen*	*Kavanagh*	*Gordon G"*	*Earnshaw^*	*Bonner*	*Low/Brayson/Fortune-West*
								Ref: U Rennie	City lack eight through injury. The patched-up team hold out well until Bjarni nods in a cross inadvertently. Iwelumo misses from two yards to huge jeers. Bowen fires wide. Bjarni's personal nightmare is complete as he allows Legg to nod home. Alan Cork's Bluebirds worthy winners.											
29	H	WIGAN		4	D	2-2	1-2	Goodfellow 37, Dadason 67p	Cutler	Thomas	Clarke	Flynn	Shtaniuk	Rowson*	Gudjonsson	Dadason	Goodfellow	Vandeurzen^	Hoekstra"	Iwelumo/Henry/Neal
	26/1		13,361	*14*	51			*Green 20, Dinning 45*	*Filan*	*Green*	*Croft**	*Dinning*	*McGibbon*	*De Zeeuw*	*Teale^*	*Brannan*	*McCulloch*	*Liddell*	*McMillan*	*Kilford/Dalglish*
								Ref: P Rejer	Scott Green trades passes and fires home. Goodfellow races onto JVD's pass to slot. Teale crosses low for Dinning to sweep home. Hoekstra's ankle goes again. Dadason mis-controls when through and is booed. He turns the jeers to cheers with the pen after being tripped by De Zeeuw.											
30	A	PETERBOROUGH		3	W	2-1	1-1	Dadason 21, Goodfellow 90	Cutler	Thomas	Clarke	Flynn	Shtaniuk	Neal^	Gudjonsson	O'Connor	Goodfellow	Dadason*	**Marteins'n"**	Cooke/Iwelumo/Henry
	29/1		*5,173*	*16*	54			*Farrell 2*	*Tyler*	*Joseph*	*Cowan^*	*Forsyth**	*Rae*	*Edwards*	*Bullard*	*Williams*	*Clarke*	*Fenn"*	*Farrell*	*Danielsson/Green/Forinton*
								Ref: P Taylor	Petur Marteinsson makes a surprise debut. Barry Fry's Posh rattle the bar before Dave Farrell rounds Cutler. Stoke overcome the 'worst pitch in the League'. Cutler performs heroics. Dadason nods in a corner. Goodfellow finally takes one of a succession of chances, burying a volley.											
31	A	BOURNEMOUTH		3	L	1-3	0-2	Dadason 63p	Cutler	Thomas^	Clarke	Flynn	Shtaniuk	Neal*	Gudjonsson	O'Connor	Goodfellow	Dadason	Marteins'n"	Cooke/Vandeurzen/Henry
	2/2		*6,027*	*19*	54			*Purches 6, Hughes 43, Feeney 56*	*Stewart*	*O'Connor**	*Purches*	*Howe*	*Tindall*	*Maher*	*Feeney*	*Holmes^*	*Hayter"*	*Fletcher C*	*Hughes*	*Elliott/Foyewa/Stock*
								Ref: S Bennett	Warren Feeney sets up two. Purches fires across Cutler and Hughes strokes in when put clear. Feeney adds his own with a low drive. Stewart fells Cooke for the penalty. Stewart saves Neal's header and Henry's shot. Dadason blazes wide. 'We defended like children.' moans Gudjon.											
32	H	CAMBRIDGE		3	W	**5-0**	2-0	Cooke 22, Gudjons'n 27, Thordarson 61, [Tann 71 (og), Goodfellow 89]	Cutler	Thomas	Clarke	Flynn	Shtaniuk	Vandeurzen"	Gudjonsson*	O'Connor	Cooke	Iwelumo^	Goodfellow	Henry/Thordars'n/Marteins'n
	6/2		9,570	*24*	57				*Marshall*	*Fleming*	*Murray*	*Tann*	*Angus*	*Ashbee**	*Austin*	*Tudor*	*Kitson^*	*Chil'gworth"*	*Guttridge*	*Wanless/Traore/Scully*
								Ref: R Olivier	John Taylor's U's have won five games all season. Cooke slides in Thommo's cross. Bjarni drills home. Shtaniuk nods wide. Thordarson nods in a corner. Bjarni's cross is turned in by Adam Tann. Henry twists and chips for Goodfellow to nod in. Stoke's biggest win under Thordarson.											
33	H	PORT VALE		3	L	0-1	0-1		Cutler	Thomas	Clarke	Flynn*	Shtaniuk	Vandeurzen^	Gudjonsson	O'Connor	Cooke	Dadason"	Goodfellow	Iwelumo/Henry/Thordarson
	10/2		**23,019**	*12*	57			*Cummins 36*	*Goodlad*	*Cummins*	*Rowland*	*Carragher*	*Walsh*	*Burns*	*Bridge-Wilk'*	*Durnin*	*Brooker*	*McPhee*	*Brisco*	
								Ref: G Laws	Stoke fail to get out of the starting blocks. Brooker forces a flying save from Cutler. Gudjon rages when Rowland and Carragher escape after clattering Goodfellow. Cummins' back-header from a long throw drifts in. Total surrender. Division Two's highest league crowd of the season.											
34	A	NOTTS CO		4	D	0-0	0-0		Cutler	Henry	Clarke	Handyside	Shtaniuk	Vandeurzen*	Gudjonsson	O'Connor	Cooke	Goodfellow^	Flynn	Iwelumo/Thordarson
	16/2		*7,501*	*23*	58				*Garden*	*Richardson*	*Baraclough*	*Caskey**	*Warren*	*Ireland*	*Liburd*	*Cas*	*Allsopp^*	*Hackworth*	*Bolland*	*Owers/Stallard*
								Ref: P Richards	Bill Dearden's County have lost their last six. Both sides hit the underside of the bar. Cooke and Liburd the unlucky men. Danny Allsopp skies from five yards. Cooke fires inches wide and sees a shot blocked on the line. Garden produces three fine saves. Cutler denies Allsopp late on.											

No	Venue / Date	Opponent / Att	Pos	Res / Pts	F-A	H-T	Scorers, Times, and Referees	1	2	3	4	5	6	7	8	9	10	11	Subs used
35	A	READING	5	L	0-1	0-0		Cutler	Thomas	Clarke	Handyside	Shtaniuk !	Flynn^	Gudjonsson	O'Connor	**Burton***	Gunnlaugs'n"	Henry	Cooke/Hoekstra/Iwelumo
	23/2	***21,032***	*1*	58			*Cureton 52*	*Whitehead*	*Murty*	*Shorey*	*Viveash*	*Mackie*	*Parkinson*	*Igoe*	*Hughes*	*Cureton**	*Forster^*	*Salako*	*Henderson/Smith N*
							Ref: S Dunn	Gudjon bottles it again and goes 5-3-2. The presence of Jani Viander on the bench spurs Cutler to fine saves from Forster, Cureton and Salako. He harangues his entire defence after saving their blushes again. Cureton nets after Cutler denies Forster. Shtaniuk gets a second yellow (63).											
36	H	BURY	4	W	4-0	1-0	Iwelumo 45, 56, Vandeurzen 73, [Thordarson 84]	Cutler	Thomas	Clarke	Handyside"	Shtaniuk	Vandeurzen	Gudjonsson	O'Connor	Burton	Gunnlaugs'n*	Iwelumo^	Hoekstra/Thordarson/Flynn
	26/2	9,635	*19*	61				*Kenny*	*Unsworth^*	*Smart*	*Nelson*	*Collins*	*Redmond"*	*Forrest*	*Clegg*	*Newby*	*Jarrett**	*Borley*	*Reid/Preece/Seddon*
							Ref: P Walton	Bury player-boss Andy Preece sees City attack like fiends from the start. Gunnlaugsson the orchestrator. Iwelumo fluffs after charging down a clearance. He makes amends from close range and bags a second off the post. JVD dives to head in. Thordarson converts Flynn's knock-down.											
37	H	BRIGHTON	3	W	3-1	1-0	Iwelumo 29, Gunnlaugs'n 58p, Clarke 86	Cutler	Thomas	Clarke	Handyside	Shtaniuk	Vandeurzen	Gudjonsson	O'Connor	Burton^	Gunnlaugs'n*	Iwelumo"	Hoekstra/Gun'son/Thordarson
	1/3	16,092	*2*	64			*Steele 54*	*Kuipers*	*Pethick"*	*Mayo**	*Morgan*	*Cullip*	*Carpenter*	*Hart^*	*Lewis*	*Steele*	*Brooker*	*Watson*	*Jones/Melton/Webb*
							Ref: W Burns	Brighton lack Zamora, the Division's top scorer, suspended. Iwelumo beats Kuipers to nod home. Steele is seen by ITV Digital viewers to dive to win a pen (53). Cutler saves low to his left. Steele nets the resulting corner. Cullip elbows Bjarni for City's pen. Clarke cracks his first goal.											
38	A	COLCHESTER	4	W	3-1	2-0	Gudjonsson 42, Burton 45, 80	Cutler	Thomas	Clarke^	Handyside	Shtaniuk	Vandeurzen	Gudjonsson	O'Connor	Burton	Gunnlaugs'n*	Iwelumo"	Gunnars'n/Flynn/Thordarson
	5/3	*3,866*	*15*	67			*Duguid 54*	*Brown*	*Duguid*	*Johnson R*	*Pinault*	*Fitzgerald*	*White*	*Izzet*	*Bowry^*	*Barrett*	*Stockwell**	*McGleish*	*Gregory/Morgan*
							Ref: D Crick	A fast-flowing game throbs with excitement. Cutler's flying one-handed save denies McGleish. Bjarni lets rip from 30 yards. Karl Duguid fires in from 15 yards. Deon Burton nets a header and slots past Brown. A glimmer of hope? Karl Henry wins an England U20 cap against Finland.											
39	A	WYCOMBE	4	L	0-1	0-0		Cutler	Thomas	Clarke	Flynn	Gunnarsson	Vandeurzen	Gudjonsson	O'Connor	Burton	Gunnlaugs'n*	Iwelumo"	Cooke^/Goodfel'/Thordarson
	9/3	*7,344*	*11*	67			*McSporran 83*	*Taylor*	*Senda*	*Vinnicombe*	*Bulman*	*Rogers*	*Ryan*	*Currie*	*Simpson*	*McSporran*	*Devine**	*Brown*	*Roberts*
							Ref: B Knight	Bjarni clatters Currie. Brown exacts revenge. Cutler twice denies McSporran and saves Brown's shot. Simpson should see red not yellow when he butts Bjarni. Cutler is relieved to stay on when he trips Devine. McSporran touches home at the near post. Stoke's first defeat by Wycombe.											
40	H	PETERBOROUGH	4	W	1-0	1-0	Gunnlaugsson 10	Cutler	Thomas	Clarke	Rowson^	Gunnarsson	Vandeurzen	Gudjonsson	O'Connor	Burton*	Gunnlaugs'n"	Iwelumo	Goodfel'/Henry/Thordarson
	16/3	12,983	*18*	70				*Tyler*	*Gill*	*Kimble*	*Danielsson*	*Rea*	*Edwards*	*Bullard*	*Oldfield*	*McKenzie**	*Green*	*Farrell*	*Forinton*
							Ref: R Furnandiz	Shtaniuk serves the second of his four-match ban. Gunnlaugsson cracks home a volley after Burton's dummy-run leaves him space. Burton and O'Connor clash heads. Iwelumo wastes two chances. Thommo's lunge on McKenzie concedes a pen (70). Jimmy Bullard drags it wide. Relief.											
41	H	CHESTERFIELD	4	W	1-0	1-0	Gunnlaugsson 23	Cutler	Thomas	Clarke	Handyside	Gunnars'n*	Henry	Gudjons'n"	O'Connor	Burton	Gun'laugs'n^	Thordarson	Vandeurzen/Hoekstra/Iwelumo
	23/3	14,841	*17*	73				*Abbey*	*Booty*	*O'Hara*	*Howson*	*Breckin*	*Payne*	*Hurst*	*Ebdon*	*Allott*	*Burt*	*Buchanan*	
							Ref: M Spike	Gunnarsson limps off. A replica volley from Gunnlaugsson repeats last week's result. He deflects Vandeurzen's effort onto a post. O'Connor's header flies wide. Burt tests Cutler from distance. Stoke get edgy when a second fails to appear. Vandeurzen misses a glorious chance to kill it.											
42	A	BRENTFORD	4	L	0-1	0-0		Cutler	**Brightwell^**	Clarke	Handyside	Thomas	**Dinning**	Gudjonsson	O'Connor	Burton	Gunnlaugs'n!	Hoekstra*	Thordarson/Goodfellow
	30/3	*8,837*	*3*	73			*Sidwell 67*	*Smith*	*Dobson*	*Anderson*	*Ingimarsson*	*Theobald*	*Sidwell*	*Evans*	*Rowlands^*	*Owusu*	*Burgess**	*Hunt"*	*O'Connor/Hutchinson/Boxall*
							Ref: A Butler	On-loan Dinning (Wigan) sets Burton clear but he fluffs. Gunnlaugsson kicks out at Rowlands after he is fouled and walks (29). Stoke defend well until Handyside and Cutler mess up a clearance. Sidwell slots into the empty net. Gudjon confesses automatic promotion is beyond Stoke.											
43	H	SWINDON	4	W	2-0	0-0	Thomas 60, Iwelumo 68	Cutler	Thomas	Clarke	Handyside	Shtaniuk	Dinning	Gudjonsson	O'Connor	Burton"	Gun'laugs'n^	Hoekstra*	Iwelumo/Goodfel'/Thordarson
	1/4	13,530	*14*	76				*McKinney*	*Willis*	*Edwards N*	*Heywood*	*Reeves"*	*Gurney*	*Howe*	*Edwards P**	*Sabin^*	*Invincible*	*Hewlett*	*Duke/Young/Cobian*
							Ref: G Frankland	Shtaniuk returns from suspension. Stoke start sluggishly. Bjarni nets but is given offside. Hoekstra lobs into Smith's arms when clear. Thomas heads in Gunnlaugsson's free-kick. Gunnarsson nets, but handball is given against Iwelumo. He makes amends with a header from 12 yards.											
44	A	OLDHAM	4	L	1-2	0-1	Holden 63 (og)	Cutler	Thomas !	Clarke*	Handyside	Shtaniuk	Dinning	Gudjonss'n^	O'Connor	Burton	Vandeurzen"	Iwelumo	Th'rson/Goodfel'/Brightwell
	6/4	*6,548*	*9*	76			*Carss 25, Hall 88*	*Miskelly*	*Holden*	*Armstrong*	*McNiven*	*Hall*	*Duxbury"*	*Murray**	*Carss*	*Adebola^*	*Corazzin*	*Eyres*	*Rickers/Smart/Haining*
							Ref: D Gallagher	A lunchtime kick-off stops any repeat of last year's BNP trouble. Tony Carss nods in a corner. Thomas gets two yellows for tackles either side of half-time. Dean Holden diverts in Iwelumo's cross. Fitz Hall nods home from another corner. Defeat allows Bristol City a chink of daylight.											
45	H	WREXHAM	5	W	1-0	1-0	Cooke 30	Cutler	Brightwell	Clarke*	Handyside	Shtaniuk	Dinning"	Gudjonsson	O'Connor	Cooke	Burton^	Goodfellow	Vandeurzen/Iwelumo/Henry
	13/4	14,298	*23*	79				*Rogers*	*Whitley*	*Holmes*	*Bennett*	*Pejic*	*Lawrence"*	*Phillips^*	*Ferguson**	*Morrell*	*Sam*	*Barrett*	*Edwards/Thomas/Morgan*
							Ref: A Kaye	Already relegated Wrexham make life hard. Cooke calms nerves as he fires in Goodfellow's pass. Iwelumo forces a flying save from Rogers. Pejic tackles O'Connor when put clean through. Shtaniuk slams a free-kick just over. Uninspiring. Bristol City lose 0-4. Stoke in the play-offs.											
46	A	BRISTOL CITY	5	D	1-1	1-0	Cooke 16	Cutler	Brightwell*	Vandeurzen	Handyside	Shtaniuk	Dinning	Gudjons'n"	O'Connor	Cooke^	Iwelumo	Goodfellow	Henry/Burton/**Miles**
	20/4	*11,277*	*7*	80			*Brown A 68*	*Phillips*	*Murray*	*Woodman*	*Jones*	*Lever*	*Carey*	*Doherty*	*Brown A**	*Peacock*	*Roberts*	*Burnell^*	*Brown M/Rosenior*
	Home 13,455	Away 8,911					Ref: D Pugh	City start brightly in their new all-white kit. Cooke nets when Iwelumo's flick puts him through. Iwelumo elects to pass instead of shoot when clear. Goodfellow cracks against Phillips' legs. Cutler saves Doherty's 25 yarder. Aaron Brown is teed up by Rosenior to finish with aplomb.											

Average

Play-offs	Att		F-A	H-T	Scorers, Times, and Referees	1	2	3	4	5	6	7	8	9	10	11	subs used
SF H CARDIFF		L	1-2	0-1	Burton 84	Cutler	Thomas	Clarke	Handyside	Shtaniuk	Dinning	Gudjonsson*	O'Connor	Cooke	Iwelumo^	Goodfellow"	Vandeurzen/Dadason/Burton
1 28/4	21,245				*Earnshaw 12, Fortune-West 59*	*Alexander*	*Weston*	*Croft*	*Bonner*	*Young*	*Prior*	*Earnshaw**	*Kavanagh*	*Fort'-West*	*Thorne^*	*Boland*	*Campbell/Collins*
					Ref: A Leake	Thomas returns from suspension. Earnshaw races clear to put favourites Cardiff ahead. Bjarni wastes a golden chance. Leo Fortune-West nets after Cutler tips a close-range shot onto the post. Deon Burton climbs off the bench to bring down JVD's far-post cross and net a stinging shot.											
SF A CARDIFF		W	2-0	0-0	O'Connor 90, Oulare 115	Cutler	Thomas	Clarke	Handyside	Shtaniuk	Dinning*	Gudjonsson	O'Connor	Burton	Gun'laugs'n^	Iwelumo"	Vandeurzen/Cooke/Oulare
2 1/5	*19,367*		*aet*			*Alexander*	*Weston*	*Croft*	*Bonner**	*Young*	*Prior !*	*Earnshaw^*	*Kavanagh*	*Fort'-West*	*Thorne"*	*Boland*	*Maxwell/Campbell/Bowen*
					Ref: M Dean (Stoke win 3-2 on aggregate)	Cardiff think the tie is sewn up. While they are edgy, O'Connor drives City on. Bjarni knocks back Clarke's cross and O'Connor's shot nestles in the corner. O'Connor's free-kick deflects in off Oulare's arse sparking a mental amongst 650 Stokies. Prior walks for a second yellow (118).											
F N BRENTFORD		W	2-0	2-0	Burton 16, Burgess 45 (og)	Cutler	Thomas	Clarke	Handyside	Shtaniuk	Dinning*	Gudjonsson	O'Connor	Burton	Gu'nlaugs'n^	Iwelumo"	Brightwell/Vandeurzen/Cooke
11/5	42,523					*Smith P*	*Dobson*	*Anderson*	*Ingeimars'n*	*Powell*	*Sidwell*	*Evans*	*Rowlands**	*Owusu*	*Burgess^*	*Hunt*	*O'Connor/McCammon*
(Millennium Stad)					Ref: G Laws	Burton slots in from a corner as the Bees' defence watches motionless. Ben Burgess slices Bjarni's free-kick into his own net. Only Sidwell's two efforts from distance tests Cutler. Stoke's defence mops up the pressure, with Shtaniuk and Handyside imperious. What South Stand jinx?											

Worthington Cup																	
1 H OLDHAM	9	D	0-0	0-0		**Cutler**	Thomas	Vandeurzen	Handyside !	Shtaniuk	Rowson*	Gudjonsson	**Henry**	Goodfellow^	Thordarson"	Hoekstra	Clarke/Cooke/Iwelumo
22/8	5,636 *15*		*aet*			*Kelly*	*McNiven*	*Sheridan D*	*Prenderville*	*Balmer*	*Duxbury*	*Rickers**	*Carss*	*Tipton*	*Eyre^*	*Eyres"*	*Hotte/Dudley/Innes*
					Ref: A Kaye (Stoke lost 5-6 on penalties)	Mick Wadsworth's Latics play for a draw. Stoke fail to capitalise. Thordarson blazes an easy chance wide. Handyside is denied a blatant pen. Handyside bundles Carss and sees red (103). In a shoot-out, Thommo misses a chance to win it. 18-year-old Karl Henry skies the vital pen.											

FA Cup																	
1 A LEWES	3	W	2-0	1-0	Handyside 19, Gunnarsson 57	Ward	Thomas	Clarke*	Handyside	Shtaniuk	Gunnarsson	Gudjonss'n^	O'Connor	Iwelumo"	Vandeurzen	Hoekstra	Goodfellow/Neal/Cooke
18/11	*7,081 RL2:4*					*Standen*	*Harris**	*Johnson C*	*McCallum*	*Hack*	*Cable*	*Venables^*	*Thomsett*	*Stokes*	*Dicker"*	*Francis*	*Beeston/Shepherd/Johnson A*
(at Stoke City)					Ref: J Ross	As home team Lewes forget the matchball! Groundsman Derek Hartley supplies them with two. Sloppy City misplace passes. Handyside nods his first Stoke goal. Gunnarsson bullets home JVD's corner. Lewes's comedy free-kick routine sees three players leave the ball to each other.											
2 A HALIFAX	2	D	1-1	1-0	Cooke 27	Cutler	Thomas*	Clarke	Handyside	Shtaniuk	Gunnarsson	Gudjonsson	O'Connor	Cooke	Vandeurzen	Hoekstra^	Rowson/Iwelumo
8/12	*3,335 3:24*				*Harsley 85*	*Butler*	*Harsley*	*Mitchell*	*Woodward*	*Clarke M*	*Clarke C*	*Ludden**	*Redfearn^*	*Kerrigan*	*Fitzpatrick*	*Midgley"*	*Herbert/Wright/Jones*
					Ref: S Mathieson	Bjarni bursts forward to set up Cooke for a neat finish. O'Connor, Cooke and Bjarni all go close. Stoke wilt after Alan Little's Town go 4-3-3. Kerrigan and Woodward test Cutler. Hoekstra carried off with a bad ankle injury (83). A right-wing centre is headed on for Phil Harsley to net.											
2R H HALIFAX	2	W	3-0	2-0	Gudjonsson 22, Iwelumo 27, [Gunnarsson 47]	Cutler	Henry	Neal*	Handyside	Shtaniuk	Gunnarsson	Gudjonsson	O'Connor^	Cooke	Iwelumo"	Vandeurzen	Goodfel'/Rowson/Dadason
12/12	4,356 *3:24*					*Butler*	*Harsley*	*Jules**	*Woodward*	*Clarke M*	*Clarke C*	*Mitchell*	*Redfearn^*	*Kerrigan*	*Fitzpatrick*	*Midgley"*	*Wright !/Herbert/Jones*
					Ref: S Mathieson	Gudjon rests Clarke and Thommo as both near five yellows. Bjarni's 25-yard free-kick flies in. City's first direct free-kick goal for 18 months. He makes the other two. Iwelumo guides in his cross. Gunnarsson's flying header seals it. Wright sees red (90) for two-footed tackle on JVD.											
3 H EVERTON	1	L	0-1	0-0		Cutler	Rowson	Clarke	Thomas	Shtaniuk	Vandeurzen	Gudjonsson	O'Connor	Goodfellow*	Iwelumo^	Henry"	Hoekstra/Cooke/Dadason
5/1	28,218 *P:13*				*Stubbs 53*	*Simonsen*	*Unsworth*	*Naysmith*	*Stubbs*	*Weir*	*Xavier*	*Blomqvist*	*Gascoigne*	*Moore*	*Ferguson*	*Gemmill*	
					Ref: E Wolstenholme	A record Brit crowd sees Gudjon fail to go for the jugular. He plays 5-4-1 and lets Walter Smith's Toffees off the hook. Thommo thumps two headers from corners wide. Ferguson and Blomqvist go close. Gazza twice forces Cutler to save. Alan Stubbs' free-kick flies in from 20 yards.											

	P	Home W	D	L	F	A	Away W	D	L	F	A	Pts
1 Brighton	46	17	5	1	42	16	8	10	5	24	26	90
2 Reading	46	12	7	4	36	20	11	8	4	34	23	84
3 Brentford	46	17	5	1	48	12	7	6	10	29	31	83
4 Cardiff	46	12	8	3	39	25	11	6	6	36	25	83
5 STOKE *	46	16	4	3	43	12	7	7	9	24	28	80
6 Huddersfield	46	13	7	3	35	19	8	8	7	30	28	78
7 Bristol City	46	13	6	4	38	21	8	4	11	30	32	73
8 QP Rangers	46	11	10	2	35	18	8	4	11	25	31	71
9 Oldham	46	14	6	3	47	27	4	10	9	30	38	70
10 Wigan	46	9	6	8	36	23	7	10	6	30	28	64
11 Wycombe	46	13	5	5	38	26	4	8	11	20	38	64
12 Tranmere	46	10	9	4	39	19	6	6	11	24	41	63
13 Swindon	46	10	7	6	26	21	5	7	11	20	35	59
14 Port Vale	46	11	6	6	35	24	5	4	14	16	38	58
15 Colchester	46	9	6	8	35	33	6	6	11	30	43	57
16 Blackpool	46	8	9	6	39	31	6	5	12	27	38	56
17 Peterborough	46	11	5	7	46	26	4	5	14	18	33	55
18 Chesterfield	46	9	3	11	35	36	4	10	9	18	29	52
19 Notts Co	46	8	7	8	28	29	5	4	14	31	42	50
20 Northampton	46	9	4	10	30	33	5	3	15	24	46	49
21 Bournemouth	46	9	4	10	36	33	1	10	12	20	38	44
22 Bury	46	6	9	8	26	32	5	2	16	17	43	44
23 Wrexham	46	7	7	9	29	32	4	3	16	27	57	43
24 Cambridge	46	7	7	9	29	34	0	6	17	18	59	34
	1104	261	152	139	870	602	139	152	261	602	870	1504

* promoted after play-offs

Odds & ends

Double wins: (7) Bury, Cambridge, Chesterfield, Colchester, Peterborough, Swindon, Wrexham.
Double losses: (1) QPR.

Won from behind: (2) Chesterfield (a), Peterborough (a).
Lost from in front: (0).

High Spots: Winning the Play-off final to return to Division One
Defeating Cardiff on their own ground to reach the Millennium Stadium.
The 3-2 win over Brentford in November which confirmed Stoke's heart for the promotion battle.
The arrivals of central defender Sergei Shtaniuk and left-winger Peter Hoekstra – both quality internationals.

Low spots: Failure to secure automatic promotion again.
Being hammered 1-6 by Wigan three days after beating Brentford.
The sale of Peter Thorne and the lack of a goalscorer to replace him.
Gudjon Thordarson's increasing tetchiness.

Player of the Year: Wayne Thomas.
Ever-presents: (1) Bjarni Gudjonsson.
Hat-tricks: (0).
Leading Scorer: (11) Chris Iwelumo.

	Appearances Lge	*Sub*	LC	*Sub*	FAC	*Sub*	Goals Lge	LC	FAC	Tot
Brightwell, David	**3**	*1*								
Burton, Deon	**11**	*1*					**2**			**2**
Clarke, Clive	**42**	*1*		*1*	3		**1**			**1**
Cooke, Andy	**26**	*9*		*1*	2	*2*	**9**		1	**10**
Cutler, Neil	**36**		1		3					
Dadason, Rikki	**6**	*5*				*2*	**4**			**4**
Dinning, Tony	**5**									
Flynn, Mike	**11**	*2*								
Goodfellow, Marc	**11**	*12*	1		1	*2*	**5**			**5**
Gudjonsson, Bjarni	**46**		1		4		**3**		1	**4**
Gunnarsson, Brynjar	**21**	*2*			3		**5**		2	**7**
Gunnlaugsson, Arnar	**9**						**3**			**3**
Handyside, Peter	**34**		1		3				1	**1**
Henry, Karl	**9**	*15*	1		2					
Hoekstra, Peter	**20**	*4*	1		2	*1*	**3**			**3**
Iwelumo, Chris	**22**	*16*		*1*	3	*1*	**10**		1	**11**
Marteinsson, Petur	**2**	*1*								
Miles, John		*1*								
Neal, Lewis	**6**	*5*			1	*1*				
O'Connor, James	**43**				4		**2**			**2**
Oulare, Souleymane		*1*								
Rowson, Dave	**8**	*5*	1		1	*2*				
Shtaniuk, Sergei	**40**		1		4		**2**			**2**
Smart, Allan		*2*								
Thomas, Wayne	**40**		1		3		**2**			**2**
Thordarson, Stefan	**3**	*18*	1				**4**			**4**
Thorne, Peter	**5**						**4**			**4**
Vandeurzen, Jurgen	**37**	*3*	1		4		**4**			**4**
Ward, Gavin	**10**				1					
Wilson, Brian		*1*								
(own-goals)							**4**			**4**
(30 players used)	**506**	***105***	**11**	***3***	**44**	***11***	**67**		**6**	**73**

No	Date	Opponent	Att	Pos	Pt	F-A	H-T	Scorers, Times, and Referees	1	2	3	4	5	6	7	8	9	10	11	subs used
1	A	SHEFFIELD WED			D	0-0	0-0		Cutler	Gunnarsson	Clarke	Handyside	Shtaniuk	Henry	Gudjonsson*	O'Connor	Iwelumo	Goodfellow	**Commons**^	Wilson B/Vandeurzen
	10/8		*26,746*		1				*Pressman*	*Bromby*	*Soltvedt*	*Burrows*	*Geary*	*Donnelly*	*Quinn*	*Armstrong*	*Beswether'k*	*Kuqi*	*Sibon*	
								Ref: N Barry	Stoke lack five injured, Terry Yorath's Owls two. Kris Commons shines on his debut. He spies Pressman off his line and a 40-yard effort just misses. He then hits the bar. Cutler denies Sibon at fingertips. 5,934 Stokies clamour for a pen when Iwelumo is bundled over but none ensues.											
2	H	LEICESTER		17	L	0-1	0-1		Cutler	Gunnarsson	Clarke	Handyside	Shtaniuk	Henry"	Gudjonsson*	O'Connor	Cooke	Goodfellow^	Commons	Wilson B/Iwelumo/Neal
	14/8		14,028	*1*	1			*Scowcroft 7*	*Walker*	*Sinclair*	*Rogers*	*Elliott*	*Taggart*	*Summerbee**	*Izzett*	*Scowcroft*	*McKinlay*	*Deane*	*Dickov^*	*Stewart/Stevenson*
								Ref: G Cain	Stoke look pedestrian from the off. Jamie Scowcroft nods in Summerbee's deep cross. Micky Adams' men dominate and deal with City's pale threat comfortably. Walker saves Shtaniuk's header on the line. Iwelumo skies when sent clear. Neal finds the side-netting with Walker to beat.											
3	H	BRADFORD C		12	W	2-1	2-0	Cooke 3, Marteinsson 34	Cutler	Wilson B^	Clarke	Marteinsson	Shtaniuk	Gunnarsson	Henry	O'Connor	Iwelumo*	Cooke	Commons	Goodfellow/Gudjonsson
	17/8		12,424	*18*	4			*Gray 90*	*Walsh*	*Uhlenbeek*	*Myers*	*Emanuel*	*Atherton*	*Gray*	*Lawrence**	*Evans*	*Kearney*	*Ward*	*Tod^*	*Molenaar/Cadamarteri*
								Ref: R Olivier	Cooke pounces as Gary Walsh miscontrols a backpass. Marteinsson, deputising for Handyside (tonsilitis), dives to nod in Commons' free-kick. Atherton clears Cooke's shot off the line. Ward nods wide from close in. Cadamarteri is denied by the flag. Gray swivels to net from 15 yards.											
4	A	PRESTON		14	L	3-4	1-2	Clarke 7p, 65p, Cooke 90	Cutler	Thomas	Clarke	Handyside	Shtaniuk	Gunnarss'n^	Henry*	O'Connor	Goodfellow	Cooke	Commons"	Gudjonsson/Neal/Vandeurzen
	24/8		*15,422*	*10*	4			*Healy 11, 24, Fuller 60, Cresswell 90*	*Moilanen*	*Alexander*	*Edwards*	*Lucketti*	*Murdock*	*Rankine*	*McKenna*	*Etuhu^*	*Healy**	*Cresswell*	*Fuller*	*Cartwright/Keane*
								Ref: G Frankland	Clarke's pens, one in either corner, arrive as Lucketti upends Commons and Etuhu handles. Alexander drags a pen wide after Handyside fouled Cresswell (9). Healy clinically nets his first since March. Fuller prods home. Cooke bullets in a near-post header. Cresswell flies clear to win it.											
5	H	NORWICH		15	D	1-1	0-0	Commons 74	Cutler	Thomas	Clarke	Handyside	Shtaniuk	Gunnarsson	Henry*	O'Connor	Goodfellow^	Cooke	Commons	Gudjonsson/Iwelumo
	26/8		13,931	*3*	5			*Drury 46*	*Green*	*Kenton*	*Drury*	*Nedergaard*	*Fleming*	*Rivers"*	*Mulryne*	*Easton**	*Roberts*	*Holt*	*McVeigh^*	*Heckingbot'm/Nielsen/Notman*
								Ref: C Wilkes	Cooke fires over from close in. Drury converts a slick ten-pass move. Clarke's 30 yarder deflects past. Cutler's clearance finds McVeigh but he misses an open goal from 40 yards. Commons beats three, swaps passes with Goodfellow and fires in. Cotterill publicly bemoans lack of cash.											
6	A	DERBY		19	L	0-2	0-0		Cutler	Thomas	Clarke	Handyside	Shtaniuk	Gunnarsson	Henry	O'Connor	Goodfellow	Cooke	Commons*	Gudjonsson
	31/8		*21,723*	*10*	5			*Christie 81, 83*	*Poom*	*Barton*	*Jackson*	*Higginboth'm*	*Riggott*	*Bolder*	*Lee*	*Murray**	*Christie^*	*Strupar*	*Boertien*	*Kinkladze/Evatt*
								Ref: S Mathieson	Cutler denies Strupar and Lee. Christie hits bar and post. Shtaniuk and Handyside block desperately. Goodfellow hits side-netting after picking up Riggott's backpass. City's thin ice breaks when Christie nicks in and converts Kinkladze's pass. Stoke fans are subjected to rough policing.											
7	A	BURNLEY		22	L	1-2	0-0	Gudjonsson 73	Cutler	Thomas	Clarke	Handyside	Shtaniuk	Gunnarsson"	Gudjonsson	O'Connor	**Mooney !**	Cooke*	Vandeurzen^	Goodfel'/Commons/Hoekstra
	14/9		*14,244*	*20*	5			*Gnohere 75, Papadopoulos 8*	*Beresford*	*West*	*McGregor**	*Gnohere*	*Cox*	*Johnrose*	*Little*	*Grant*	*Briscoe*	*Blake^*	*Moore I"*	*Moore A/Taylor/Papadop'los*
								Ref: D Pugh	Handyside blocks Briscoe's effort. Beresford spectacularly denies Mooney. Blake hits one post and Taylor nods against the other. Bjarni nets a volley, but Stoke wilt. Gnohere heads in a corner. Papadopolous flies to nod home. Tommy Mooney sees red for stamping on Tony Grant (85).											
8	A	BRIGHTON		19	W	2-1	1-0	Mooney 17p, Cooke 75	Cutler	Thomas	Clarke	Handyside	Shtaniuk	Gunnarsson	Gudjonss'n^	O'Connor	Mooney	Cooke	Vandeurzen*	Iwelumo/Henry
	17/9		*6,369*	*23*	8			*Carpenter 79*	*Petterson*	*Pethick**	*Watson*	*Cullip*	*Butters*	*Marney*	*Oatway"*	*Carpenter*	*Wilkinson*	*Hart*	*Melton^*	*Jones/McPhee/Hammond*
								Ref: G Hegley	Watson handles Bjarni's chip. Mooney slots the pen. City defend resolutely. Cutler denies Wilkinson and Pethick. JVD hits a 30-yard screamer just over. Cooke nets a loose ball. Carpenter's 30 yarder screams in. In injury-time Shtaniuk's challenge on Hart looks a pen, but none is given.											
9	H	IPSWICH		15	W	2-1	1-0	Shtaniuk 16, Cooke 79	Cutler	Thomas	Clarke	Handyside	Shtaniuk	Gunnarsson	Gudjonsson	O'Connor	Mooney	Cooke	Vandeurzen*	Commons^/Henry
	22/9		14,587	*19*	11			*Holland 67*	*Marshall*	*McGreal*	*Clapham*	*Venus"*	*Hreidarsson*	*Wilnis*	*Holland*	*Ambrose*	*Armstrong**	*Counago*	*Miller^*	*Bent D/Magilton/Brown*
								Ref: A Butler	Stoke take the game to George Burley's Ipswich. Cooke's early goalbound effort is blocked. Shtaniuk's header from Bjarni's free-kick flies in. Ipswich wake up after Darren Bent's arrival. Holland nods in Ambrose's cross. Commons injures his knee ligament in setting up Cooke to net.											
10	H	NOTT'M FOREST		14	D	2-2	1-2	Shtaniuk 13, Goodfellow 71	Cutler	Thomas	Clarke	Handyside	Shtaniuk	Henry	Gudjonsson	O'Connor	Mooney^	Cooke"	Vandeurzen*	Goodfel'/Hoekstra/Iwelumo
	25/9		14,554	*7*	12			*Dawson 34, Johnson 45*	*Ward*	*Louis-Jean*	*Brennan*	*Dawson*	*Walker*	*Williams*	*Bopp*	*Jess^*	*Johnson**	*Harewood"*	*Prutton*	*Lester/Reid/Hjelde*
								Ref: M Pike	Gunnarsson starts a three-match ban. Prutton and Brennan argue when a free-kick is given. JVD whips it in for Shtaniuk to nod home. Dawson heads his first ever goal from Bopp's corner. Johnson nods home from close in. Goodfellow races onto Bjarni's clever ball to flick over Ward.											
11	A	READING		14	D	1-1	1-1	Vandeurzen 38	Cutler	Thomas	Clarke	Handyside	Shtaniuk	Henry	Gudjonsson	O'Connor	Hoekstra^	Cooke"	Vandeurzen*	Neal/Goodfellow/Iwelumo
	28/9		*13,646*	*11*	13			*Rougier 11*	*Hahnemann*	*Mackie*	*Murty*	*Upson*	*Williams*	*Hughes*	*Watson^*	*Newman*	*Rougier**	*Cureton*	*Salako*	*Forster/Tyson*
								Ref: R Styles	Rougier turns to fire low past Cutler. JVD's speculative shot cannons in off Williams, leaving Hahnemann wrong-footed. He makes amends as he denies O'Connor. Handyside clears off the line as Hughes waltzes through. Cutler saves Henry's misdirected header. Cureton lobs just over.											

No	Venue	Opponent	Pos	Res	F-A	H-T	Scorers, Times, and Referees	1	2	3	4	5	6	7	8	9	10	11	Subs used
12	H	CRYSTAL PALACE	15	D	1-1	0-0	Iwelumo 85	Cutler	Thomas	Clarke	Handyside	Shtaniuk	Henry	Gudjonsson	O'Connor	Hoekstra	Cooke^	Vandeurzen*	Goodfellow/Iwelumo
5/10		14,214	*17*	14			*Adebola 76*	*Michopoulos*	*Fleming*	*Powell*	*Popovic*	*Granville*	*Butterfield"*	*Derry^*	*Mullins*	*Adebola*	*Freedman*	*Johnson**	*Gray/Riihilahti/Black*
							Ref: M Warren	Derry is sent clear but Cutler saves his weak shot. Cooke blazes over. Trevor Francis' tough-tackling Palace cope better with the blustery wind. Dele Adebola outpaces Handyside and blazes low past Cutler at his near post. The subs combine and Iwelumo cracks home from 16 yards out.											
13	H	WOLVERHAMPTON	19	L	0-2	0-0		Cutler	Thomas	Clarke	Handyside	Shtaniuk	Gunnarsson	Gudjonsson*	O'Connor	Hoekstra^	Cooke	Vandeurzen"	Goodfellow/**Greenacre**/Neal
19/10		16,885	*12*	14			*Cameron 78, Blake 90*	*Murray*	*Edworthy*	*Irwin*	*Ince*	*Lescott*	*Clyde*	*Newton**	*Rae*	*Blake*	*Miller^*	*Cameron*	*Ndah/Sturridge*
							Ref: M Halsey	Dave Kevan takes charge after Cotterill defects. Defences are on top. Cooke scrambles in, but is offside. Cutler's reaction save denies Miller. Wolves wear Stoke down. Cameron beats two men to net a deflected shot. Blake cuts inside and beats Cutler at his near post with the last kick.											
14	A	SHEFFIELD UTD	19	L	1-2	0-0	Greenacre 84	Cutler	Thomas	Clarke	Handyside	Shtaniuk	Gunnarsson	Gudjonss'n^	O'Connor	Mooney	Cooke*	Hoekstra	Greenacre/Goodfellow
23/10		*15,163*	*4*	14			*Handyside 62 (og), Brown 70p*	*Kenny*	*Kozluk*	*Murphy*	*Yates*	*Page*	*McGovern^*	*Brown*	*Jagielka*	*Allison*	*Asaba**	*Tonge"*	*Ndlovu/Boulding/McCall*
							Ref: G Poll	In the rain Cutler denies Asaba low down. Allison heads wide with goal gaping. Stoke seem to have weathered the storm until Ndlovu's effort cannons off a post, then off Handyside and in. Brown's penalty is for Thomas' foul on Tonge. Greenacre nets his first from Goodfellow's pass.											
15	A	ROTHERHAM	20	L	0-4	0-2		Cutler	Thomas	Clarke	Handyside	Shtaniuk	Gunnarsson	Gudjonsson	O'Connor	Mooney"	Cooke^	Hoekstra*	Goodfel'/Vand'zen/Greenacre
26/10		*7,078*	*8*	14			*Barker 15, 53, Lee 39, Swailes 87*	*Pollitt*	*Scott*	*Hurst*	*Swailes*	*McIntosh*	*Sedgwick**	*Daws*	*Garner^*	*Barker"*	*Lee*	*Monkhouse*	*Warne/Byfield/Bryan*
							Ref: J Winter	Alan Lee rampages through Stoke's defence. He outpaces Clarke and Barker finishes. Next Lee lobs Cutler. Ronnie Moore's Millers run riot. Barker beats Cutler one-on-one. He nets again but his push denies him a treble. Swailes scores amid mayhem after a free-kick. Total surrender.											
16	H	WATFORD	21	L	1-2	0-2	Mooney 72	Cutler	Henry	Clarke	Thomas	Shtaniuk	Gunnarsson	Neal"	O'Connor	Mooney	Cooke^	Goodfellow*	Gudjons'n/Iwelumo/Greenacre
30/10		11,215	*4*	14			*Helguson 18, Cox 37*	*Chamberlain*	*Cox*	*Robinson*	*Dyche*	*Doyley*	*Ardley*	*Glass^*	*Hyde*	*Helguson*	*Smith**	*Nielsen*	*Foley/Johnson*
							Ref: H Webb	Manager-in-waiting George Burley watches City's kamikaze defending allow Helguson to nod home a corner and hand Cox the freedom of the box to sweep in a free-kick. Mooney's five-yard header is no consolation. Burley clearly isn't impressed. Tony Pulis will be the new manager.											
17	A	WALSALL	21	L	2-4	0-0	Cooke 77, Greenacre 80	Cutler	Thomas	Clarke	Handyside	Shtaniuk	Gunnarsson	Gudjonsson*	O'Connor	Iwelumo^	Mooney	Neal	Cooke/Greenacre
2/10		*6,391*	*16*	14			*Leitao 51, 57, Junior 66, Aranalde 84p*	*Ward*	*Bazeley*	*Aranalde*	*Wrack*	*Hay*	*Roper*	*Sonner*	*Simpson*	*Corica"*	*Junior**	*Leitao^*	*Matias/Zdrilic/Barras*
							Ref: M Ryan	In pouring rain Stoke collapse after the break. Leitao twice nets easily from 12 yards. Junior slides in. Gunnarsson hits the post. The subs make an impact. Cooke and Greenacre score from close in. The comeback is thwarted when Thomas stupidly pushes Zdrilic. Aranalde slots the pen.											
18	H	GRIMSBY	22	L	1-2	0-2	Mooney 50p	Cutler	Thomas	Clarke	Handyside	Shtaniuk	Gunnarsson	Gudjonss'n^	O'Connor	Mooney	Greenacre*	Hoekstra	Iwelumo/Cooke
9/11		11,488	*21*	14			*Livingstone 14, Campbell 22*	*Coyne*	*Ward*	*Gallimore*	*Ford*	*Gavin*	*Coldicott*	*Campbell*	*Groves*	*Livingstone*	*Mansaram**	*Oster*	*Barnard*
							Ref: C Penton	Stoke self-destruct. Cutler denies Campbell, then Livingstone chips home. Campbell's quickly taken free-kick catches Cutler sleeping. Coyne produces three fabulous saves from Mooney. The pen arrives from Gavin's blatant handball. Coyne denies Gunnarsson. Into the bottom three.											
19	A	PORTSMOUTH	22	L	0-3	0-0		Cutler	Thomas	Clarke	Handyside	Marteins'n*	Gunnarsson	Gudjonss'n^	O'Connor	Mooney	Henry	Hoekstra"	Greenacre/Iwelumo/Vand'zen
16/11		*18,701*	*1*	14			*Burchill 49, Pericard 87, Todorov 90*	*Hislop*	*Primus*	*Harper^*	*Diabate*	*De Zeeuw*	*Foxe*	*Quashie*	*Merson*	*Todorov"*	*Burchill**	*Taylor*	*Pericard/Crowe/O'Neil*
							Ref: P Taylor	No Shtaniuk (suspended). Pulis deploys five at the back. Mooney, alone up front, wins everything, bringing the midfield into play. Hislop tips Mooney's header over. Pompey's pace takes its toll. Harper crosses for Burchill. JVD fires wide before Pericard nods in. Todorov lobs home.											
20	H	MILLWALL	22	L	0-1	0-1		Cutler	Thomas^	Clarke	Handyside	Shtaniuk	Gunnarsson	Gudjonsson	O'Connor	Iwelumo*	Mooney	Hoekstra	Greenacre/Cooke
23/11		13,776	*13*	14			*Reid 2*	*Warner*	*Johnson*	*Ryan*	*Nethercott*	*Dolan*	*Ifill*	*Livermore*	*Wise*	*Claridge*	*Harris*	*Reid*	
							Ref: M Messias	Visiting fans are banned due to Millwall's own policy. Reid glances in Wise's floated free-kick (70 secs). Mark McGhee's men sit back. Stoke lack luck. Hoekstra and Gunnarsson, from close in, hit the bar. Warner denies O'Connor and Mooney. Worst run since the awful 84-85 season.											
21	A	GILLINGHAM	22	D	1-1	0-0	Clarke 56	**Crossley**	Thomas	Clarke*	Handyside	Shtaniuk	Gunnarsson	Gudjonsson	O'Connor	Iwelumo	Greenacre	Marteinsson	Henry
30/11		*8,150*	*17*	15			*Shaw 52*	*Brown*	*Nosworthy*	*Edge*	*Smith*	*Johnson L*	*Hope*	*Saunders*	*Shaw*	*King*	*Johnson T**	*Sidibe^*	*James/Wallace*
							Ref: J Ross	Shtaniuk plays despite his transfer request. Shaw's 20-yard shot slips under Crossley. He makes amends by tipping over Shaw's header. Clarke rockets in a 25-yard free-kick. After tackling Nosworthy, he is stretchered off (knee) and will be out for four months. First point in nine games.											
22	H	COVENTRY	22	L	1-2	1-2	Hoekstra 35	**Banks**	Thomas !	**Hall**	Handyside	Shtaniuk	Gunnars'n !	Gudjonsson	O'Connor	Iwelumo^	Greenacre	Hoekstra*	Goodfellow/Cooke
7/12		12,760	*14*	15			*Bothroyd 16, 21*	*Hyldgaard*	*Caldwell*	*Quinn*	*Konjic*	*Shaw*	*Safri*	*McAllister*	*Partridge*	*Holdsworth*	*Hignett**	*Bothroyd*	*Pead*
							Ref: A Hall	Referee Andy Hall starts the pantomime season early as he produces 13 yellow cards. Marcus Hall allows ex-roommate Jay Bothroyd to ghost in from the right to bury twice. Hoekstra's 20-yard free-kick deflects wickedly in. Gunnarsson walks as he is announced as Man of the Match!											
23	H	PORTSMOUTH	22	D	1-1	1-0	Gunnarsson 34	Banks	Thomas	Hall	Handyside	Shtaniuk	Gunnarsson	Gudjonsson	Henry^	Cooke	Greenacre"	Neal*	Marteins'n/Goodfel'/Mooney
14/12		13,330	*1*	16			*Crowe 74*	*Hislop*	*Primus*	*Ritchie**	*Diabate*	*De Zeeuw*	*Foxe*	*Quashie*	*Merson*	*Todorov*	*Burton*	*Robinson^*	*Harper/Crowe*
							Ref: P Walton	Harry Redknapp admires City's flowing football. Hislop tips away Cooke's header and Greenacre's shot. Shtaniuk nods back for Gunnarsson to head in. Pompey fight back. Crowe taps Primus' effort in. Banks turns over Harper's shot. Gordon Banks is inducted into the Hall of Fame.											

No	Date	Att	Pos	Pt	F-A	H-T	Scorers, Times, and Referees	1	2	3	4	5	6	7	8	9	10	11	subs used
24	A WIMBLEDON		22	D	1-1	0-0	Iwelumo 88	Banks	Henry	Hall	Handyside	Shtaniuk	Marteinsson	Gudjonsson	O'Connor	Cooke*	Hoekstra^	Neal"	Iwelumo/Vand'zen/Greenacre
	21/12	***1,687***	*14*	17			*Connolly 82*	*Davis*	*Darlington**	*Hawkins*	*Leigertwood*	*Williams*	*Andersen*	*McAnuff*	*Francis*	*Shipperley*	*Connolly*	*Reo-Coker*	*Agyemang*
							Ref: S Baines	Lowest league gate to see Stoke since 1907 looks even barer. Darlington cause problems. Neal nods Shipperley's header off the line. Connolly rifles home his 14th goal in ten games. Iwelumo flicks JVD's centre over Davis. Cooke damages ankle ligaments and is out for three months.											
25	A BRADFORD C		22	L	2-4	2-1	Marteins'n 9, Henry 23 *[Jorgensen 70]*	Banks	Thomas	Hall	Handyside	Shtaniuk	Henry	Marteins'n*	O'Connor	Iwelumo	Greenacre	Neal^	Gudjonsson/Hoekstra
	26/12	*14,575*	*20*	17			*Gray 20p, 89, Handyside 67 (og),*	*Davison*	*Jacobs*	*Emanuel*	*Bower**	*Molenaar*	*Jorgensen*	*Lawrence*	*Atherton*	*Uhlenbeek*	*Gray*	*Tod*	*Standing*
							Ref: G Laws	On a slippy pitch Marteinsson slides home. Shtaniuk is harshly adjudged to have fouled Tod. Gray nets the pen. Henry slots Neal's cross. City collapse after Handyside deflects in Emanuel's cross. Jorgensen nods in. Gray nets from 15 yards. Hall skies wastefully. Three points from 39.											
26	H SHEFFIELD WED		22	W	3-2	1-1	Iwelumo 16, 66, Gunnarsson 90	Banks	Thomas	Hall	Handyside	Shtaniuk	Gunnarsson	Gudjonsson*	O'Connor	Iwelumo	Greenacre	Hoekstra	Marteinsson
	28/12	16,042	*24*	20			*Sibon 23, Proudlock 72*	*Stringer*	*Haslam*	*Monk*	*Crane*	*Geary*	*McLaren*	*Soltvedt*	*Johnston*	*Bradbury*	*Proudlock*	*Sibon**	*Morrison*
							Ref: K Townsend	Thomas nods back a corner for Iwelumo. Sibon slots Johnston's cross. Stringer tips Greenacre's header onto a post and denies Gunnarsson, but Iwelumo steps in to score. Proudlock spins to fire in from 20 yards. Gunnarsson sends the crowd wild after Greenacre's stepover sets him free.											
27	H PRESTON		22	W	2-1	2-0	Gunnarsson 43, Hoekstra 45	Banks	Thomas	Hall	Handyside	Shtaniuk	Gunnarsson	Gudjonsson	O'Connor	Iwelumo	Greenacre	Hoekstra*	Neal
	1/1	14,862	*18*	23			*Abbott 90*	*Lucas^*	*Alexander*	*Barry-Murphy*	*Lucketti*	*Broomes*	*Lewis*	*McKenna*	*Etuhu"*	*Healy*	*Cresswell**	*Rankine*	*Abbott/Moilanen/Mears*
							Ref: M Jones	Bjarni cleverly leaves Iwelumo's flick for Gunnarsson to net. Hoekstra slots Iwelumo's pass. Banks produces a save reminiscent of namesake, Gordon, against Pele, to deny Healy. Abbott's side-footed finish from Barry-Murphy's left-wing centre provides hope for Craig Brown's men.											
28	A LEICESTER		22	D	0-0	0-0		Banks	Thomas	Hall	Handyside !	Shtaniuk	Gunnarsson	**Richardson**	O'Connor	Iwelumo	Greenacre^	Hoekstra*	Marteinsson/Goodfellow
	11/1	*25,038*	*2*	24				*Walker*	*Impey*	*Rogers*	*Elliott*	*Sinclair*	*Summerbee^*	*McKinlay*	*Jones*	*Stewart**	*Deane*	*Dickov*	*Taggart ! /Benjamin*
							Ref: J Robinson	Foxes have been rescued by Gary Lineker's consortium. City attack with pace. 'What's it like to be outpassed?' enquire 2,000 Stokies. Dickov fires just wide. Handyside and Taggart walk for two yellows. Goodfellow blazes over when clear. First League clean sheet since opening day.											
29	H DERBY		22	L	1-3	0-0	Greenacre 63	Banks	Thomas	Hall	Handyside	Shtaniuk	Gunnarsson	Gudjonsson*	O'Connor	Iwelumo^	Greenacre	Richardson	Goodfellow/**Mills**
	18/1	17,308	*15*	24			*Christie 50, Zavagno 74, Morris 90*	*Grant*	*Jackson*	*Evatt*	*Higginboth'm*	*Zavagno*	*Bolder*	*Burley*	*Kinkladze"*	*Christie^*	*Morris**	*Boertien*	*McLeod/Tugday/Murray*
							Ref: A Kaye	Christie's overhead from Kinkladze's corner flies in. Bjarni miscontrols, but it falls to Greenacre who scores. Zavagno bullets in a header from another corner. Goodfellow nods straight at Grant from nine yards. Christie breaks upfield to relieve pressure. Lee Morris blasts home his pass.											
30	A NORWICH		21	D	2-2	0-2	Gunnarsson 63, Mills 88	Banks	Thomas	Hall	Handyside	Shtaniuk	Gunnarsson	Richardson	O'Connor	Iwelumo*	Greenacre^	Hoekstra	Mills/Marteinsson
	1/2	*20,186*	*7*	25			*Roberts 2, Mackay 23*	*Green*	*Kenton*	*Drury**	*Mackay*	*Fleming*	*Rivers^*	*Russell*	*Healy"*	*Roberts*	*Holt*	*McVeigh*	*Llewellyn/Briggs/Abbey*
							Ref: R Olivier	Roberts forces in when Hall stops Healy's shot on the line after 80 seconds. Mackay dives to nod Kenton's cross home. Russell runs the game. Stoke look down and out. Gunnarsson nods in Hoekstra's chipped cross. Lee Mills controls, swivels and wallops in right-footed from 22 yards.											
31	A GRIMSBY		22	L	0-2	0-2		Banks	Thomas	Hall	Handyside	Shtaniuk !	Gunnarsson	Richardson*	O'Connor	Iwelumo^	Mills	Hoekstra	Gudjonsson/Greenacre
	8/2	*5,657*	*21*	25			*Boulding 4, Thompson 40*	*Coyne*	*McDermott*	*Gallimore*	*Ford*	*Santos*	*Pouton^*	*Cooke*	*Groves*	*Campbell*	*Thompson**	*Boulding"*	*Soames/Bolder/Rowan*
							Ref: C Wilkes	Boulding's header fails to wake up City. Thomas scythes down Thompson to cause a scrap on the bench between Cutler and Grimsby assistant boss Graham Rodger, which sees Rodger dismissed. Thompson gains revenge by sliding past Banks. Shtaniuk walks for pulling back Soames.											
32	A NOTT'M FOREST		24	L	**0-6**	0-4	*[Jess 85]*	Banks	Thomas	Hall	Handyside	Marteins'n !	Henry	Richardson	O'Connor	Mills	Greenacre^	Hoekstra*	Neal/Gudjonsson
	22/2	*24,085*	*4*	25			*Harewood 13, 24, 28, 45p, Johnson 53,*	*Ward*	*Louis-Jean*	*Brennan*	*Dawson*	*Hjelde*	*Scimeca*	*Thompson**	*Williams*	*Johnson^*	*Harewood"*	*Reid*	*Oyen/Westcarr/Jess*
							Ref: U Rennie	O'Connor's 200th game for City is ruined as Marlon Harewood bags four. His second is a peach as Johnson backheels for Harewood to smash in. Marteinsson handles for the pen. His red is later rescinded. Johnson nods in. Jess taps Louis-Jean's cross home. Pulis has to work a miracle.											
33	H WALSALL		23	W	1-0	1-0	Mills 19	Banks	Thomas	Hall	Handyside	Shtaniuk	O'Connor	Gunnarsson	Gudjonsson	Mills*	Greenacre^	Hoekstra	Iwelumo/Neal
	26/2	**10,409**	*20*	28				*Walker*	*Roper*	*Aranalde*	*Wrack^*	*Barras*	*Robinson*	*Zdrilic*	*Simpson**	*Corica"*	*Junior*	*Bazeley*	*O'Connor/Matias/Birch*
							Ref: P Armstrong	Walker produces one flying save to deny Mills and another to deny Bjarni. Mills knocks in Thomas' shot which was going well wide. Banks easily saves Corica's shot, Walsall's only effort on target, though Barras skies from ten yards. Walker tips Iwelumo's long-range effort round.											
34	H BURNLEY		23	L	0-1	0-0		Banks	Thomas	Hall	Handyside	Shtaniuk	Gunnarsson	Gudjonsson	O'Connor	Mills*	Greenacre^	Hoekstra	Iwelumo/Cooke
	1/3	12,874	*10*	28			*West 56*	*Beresford*	*West*	*Branch*	*Diallo*	*Cox*	*Cook^*	*Moore A**	*Grant*	*Taylor*	*Briscoe*	*Moore I*	*Weller/McGregor*
							Ref: P Joslin	Over 2,000 Clarets fans brave the driving sleet. Greenacre slots, but Lee Mills is penalised for a foul. Hoekstra torments Branch. A dour, tight match is won by a powerful 20 yarder from Dean West, after Stoke fail to clear a corner fully. Heads drop and the ball is flung long to no avail.											

No	Date	Opponent	Att	Pos	Res	F-A	H-T	Scorers, Times, and Referees	1	2	3	4	5	6	7	8	9	10	11	subs used
35	H	BRIGHTON		21	W	1-0	0-0	Greenacre 83	Banks	Thomas*	Hall	Handyside	Shtaniuk	Gunnarsson	Gudjonsson	O'Connor	Mills"	Greenacre	Hoekstra^	Richardson/Neal/Iwelumo
	5/3		**21,023**	22	31				*Beasant*	*Ingimarsson*	*Watson**	*Cullip*	*Blacwell*	*Carpenter^*	*Brooker*	*Rodger*	*Mayo*	*Zamora*	*Rougier*	*Barrett/Oatway*
								Ref: M Messias	A huge crowd take advantage of the Board's £5 ticket offer and spur City on. Peter Taylor's languid men fail to muster a shot on target, though Rougier nods wide and has a goal disallowed for offside. Greenacre slots home Neal's cross to send the huge crowd wild. A glimmer of hope?											
36	A	IPSWICH		22	D	0-0	0-0		Crossley	Richardson	Hall	Handyside	Shtaniuk	Gunnarsson	Marteins'n^	O'Connor	Mills*	Greenacre"	Clarke	Cooke/Neal/Iwelumo
	8/3		*24,547*	*7*	32				*Marshall*	*Wilnis*	*Makin*	*Gaardsoe*	*Hreidars'n**	*Wright*	*Holland*	*Magilton*	*Bent D*	*Bent M*	*Miller^*	*Richards"/Reuser/Naylor*
								Ref: L Mason	Mills limps off (2). Shtaniuk and Clarke have to be parted after Holland fires wide. Crossley pulls Hreidarsson back on the blind side of the ref and escapes. He denies Hreidarsson, Darren Bent and Naylor as Joe Royle's team up the pace. Gunnarsson and O'Connor waste on the break.											
37	H	SHEFFIELD UTD		22	D	0-0	0-0		Crossley	Thomas	Hall	Handyside	Shtaniuk	Gunnarsson	**Wilson M**^	O'Connor	Iwelumo*	Cooke	Hoekstra	Gudjonsson/Greenacre
	15/3		14,449	*4*	33				*Kenny*	*Kozluk*	*Jagielka*	*Murphy*	*Page*	*Curtis*	*Ndlovu^*	*Brown*	*Windass**	*Kabba"*	*Tonge*	*Allison/Morrson/Peschisolido*
								Ref: E Wolstenholme	Fresh from defeating Leeds to reach the FA Cup semi-final, Blades play a spoiling game. Tonge and Brown both fall theatrically to earn Stoke players bookings. The blustery wind offers up few chances. Ndlovu blazes wide from eight yards and Kabba somehow over the bar from three.											
38	A	WOLVERHAMPTON		23	D	0-0	0-0		Crossley	Thomas	Hall	Handyside	Shtaniuk	Gunnarsson	**Williams**	O'Connor	Cooke*	Wilson M	Clarke	Greenacre
	18/3		*25,235*	*5*	34				*Murray*	*Irwin*	*Naylor*	*Ince*	*Lescott*	*Butler*	*Newton"*	*Rae^*	*Sturridge**	*Miller*	*Kennedy*	*Proudlock/Cameron/Cooper*
								Ref: J Winter	City's courageous back five stifle Dave Jones' play-off bound Wolves. Miller is booked for diving as their frustration shows. Gunnarsson races through but stops when faced by the flying Matt Murray. Crossley saves Proudlock's shot. Cotterill and Wilkinson are sacked by Sunderland!											
39	A	WATFORD		21	W	2-1	1-0	Hoekstra 34p, 49	Crossley	Thomas	Clarke	Handyside	Shtaniuk	Gunnarsson	Williams	O'Connor	Cooke^	Wilson M"	Hoekstra*	G'dfellow/Iwelumo/Mart'ns'n
	22/3		*12,570*	*17*	37			*Helguson 67*	*Chamberlain*	*Cox*	*Ardley*	*Gayle**	*Fisken^*	*Mahon*	*Glass*	*Hyde"*	*Helguson*	*N'l-Williams*	*Cook*	*Brown/Smith/McNamee*
								Ref: D Crick	Marcus Hall's wife goes into labour, so Hoekstra plays. He slots a pen given for Hyde's handball. Hyde hits the post from 22 yards. Handyside clears off the line. Hoekstra volleys in from 30 yards. Helguson's header is City's first concession in 461 mins. Goodfellow wastes when clear.											
40	H	GILLINGHAM		22	D	0-0	0-0		Crossley	Thomas	Clarke	Handyside	Shtaniuk	Gunnarsson	**Warhurst**	Wilson M*	Iwelumo^	**Akinbiyi"**	Hoekstra	Gudjonsson/Hall/Mills
	5/4		12,746	*9*	38				*Bartram*	*Nosworthy*	*Edge*	*Ashby"*	*Southall*	*Hope*	*Smith*	*Osborn**	*Shaw*	*Wallace^*	*Sidibe*	*Spiller/Johnson T/Johnson L*
								Ref: A Kaye	The minute silence for Corporal Allbutt, killed in Iraq, leaves a lump in the throat. Stoke look lethargic. Iwelumo fails to connect on the volley. Southall blasts wide and puts a free effort over. Akinbiyi pulls a hamstring. Nosworthy fires over. Ashby throws himself to block Mills' shot.											
41	H	ROTHERHAM		21	W	**2-0**	2-0	Warhurst 21, Cooke 40	Crossley	Thomas	Hall	Handyside	Shtaniuk	Gunnarsson	Warhurst	Neal*	Cooke	Greenacre	Hoekstra	Clarke
	9/4		19,553	*12*	41				*Pollitt*	*Barker*	*Branston*	*Swailes*	*McIntosh*	*Sedgwick**	*Mullin !*	*Daws*	*Robins^*	*Lee"*	*Farrelly*	*Warne/Byfield/Barker*
								Ref: G Cain	Warhurst flicks in Neal's corner. Barker hits the post and Lee the angle. Crossley pulls off a stunning save from Branston's volley. Cooke turns to fire in a pearler from 25 yards. Swailes clears Greenacre's effort off the line. Mullin walks after fouling Thomas then attempting to butt him.											
42	A	MILLWALL		21	L	1-3	0-1	Shtaniuk 73	Crossley	Thomas	Hall	Handyside	Shtaniuk	Gunnarsson	Warhurst"	O'Connor	Cooke	Akinbiyi^	Williams*	Hoekstra/Mills/Clarke
	12/4		*8,725*	*10*	41			Harris 19, Roberts 49, Livermore 55	*Warner*	*Lawrence*	*Ryan*	*Nethercott*	*Ward*	*Ifill^*	*Roberts*	*Wise*	*McCammon**	*Harris*	*Livermore*	*Claridge/Braniff*
								Ref: P Walton	No Stokies allowed, so over 3,000 watch a screen at the Brit. They see a woeful City display. Harris nods in. Roberts dispossess Gunnarsson to fire home. Livermore dips one over Crossley from 25 yards. Clarke crosses for Shtaniuk to head in. Pulis decrees: 'It's up to the players now.'											
43	H	WIMBLEDON		21	W	2-1	2-0	Gunnarsson 29, Akinbiyi 45	Crossley	Thomas	Hall	Handyside	Shtaniuk	Gunnarsson	Warhurst*	O'Connor	Cooke	Akinbiyi^	Hoekstra"	Clarke/Gudjonsson/Williams
	19/4		12,587	*12*	44			*Shipperley 51*	*Davis*	*Holloway**	*Hawkins*	*Leigertwood*	*Gier*	*Tapp*	*Nowland*	*Agyemang^*	*Shipperley*	*Connolly*	*Reo-Coker*	*Chorley/Gray*
								Ref: R Pearson	Darren Holloway breaks a leg (5) in a tackle with Hall. Crossley survives fouling Connolly. Gunnarsson flicks home a header. Akinbiyi ghosts past two with a slinky stepover to net. Crossley flies to deny Chorley and Tapp. Shipperley finishes a slick passing move. Just 52 visiting fans.											
44	A	COVENTRY		21	W	1-0	0-0	Montgomery 57 (og)	Crossley	Thomas	Hall	Handyside	Shtaniuk	Gunnarsson	Clarke	O'Connor	Mills*	Hoekstra^	Williams	Iwelumo/Greenacre
	21/4		*12,675*	*20*	47				*Montgomery*	*Caldwell*	*Konjic*	*Davenport*	*Whing*	*Pead*	*Eustace*	*Engonga^*	*McSheffrey*	*Yulu**	*Gordon*	*Pipe/Mackey*
								Ref: J Robinson	Gunnarsson is fouled. Iwelumo sends Montgomery the wrong way from the spot, but hits the post. The ball rebounds in off the prone keeper's legs. Crossley wondrously saves Gordon's wicked dipping volley. Konjic strikes the post. Stoke's luck is in as Brighton and Sheff Wed draw.											
45	A	CRYSTAL PALACE		21	L	0-1	0-0		Crossley	Thomas	Hall	Handyside	Shtaniuk	Gunnarsson	Williams^	O'Connor	Cooke"	Greenacre*	Clarke	Iwelumo/Goodfel'/Warhurst
	26/4		*16,064*	*12*	47			*Adebola 82*	*Kolinko*	*Routledge*	*Powell**	*Popovic*	*Mullins*	*Butterfield*	*Derry*	*Watson*	*Whelan^*	*Freedman*	*Black*	*Thomson/Adebola*
								Ref: T Parkes	City opt to defend. Cooke and Greenacre run tirelessly to close down acting manager Steve Kember's men. Crossley claws away headers from Whelan and Freedman. Just as safety beckons, Stoke go to sleep. Adebola nips home a quickly taken free-kick. Brighton win 4-0. Devastating.											
46	H	READING		21	W	1-0	0-0	Akinbiyi 55	Crossley	Thomas	Hall	Handyside	Shtaniuk	Gunnarsson	Neal^	O'Connor	Akinbiyi*	Greenacre	Hoekstra	Cooke/Clarke
	4/5		20,477	*4*	50				*Hahnemann*	*Nurty*	*Shorey*	*Viveash*	*Mackie*	*Sidwell*	*Harper"*	*Chadwick^*	*Forster*	*Little*	*Salako**	*Henderson/Cureton/Watson*
		Home	Away					Ref: C Webster	Greenacre finishes weakly when clear. Reading stroke the ball around without expending much effort. Neal is denied by Hahnemann. Akinbiyi ghosts in at the near post to power a header in from Neal's cross. Sidwell grazes the bar. Grimsby's equaliser against Brighton confirms safety.											
Average		14,588	14,986																	

Worthington Cup			Att			F-A	H-T	Scorers, Times, and Referees	1	2	3	4	5	6	7	8	9	10	11	subs used
1	A	BURY		19	L	0-1	0-0		Cutler	Thomas	Clarke"	Handyside	Shtaniuk	Gunnars'n !	Gudjonss'n^	O'Connor	Iwelumo	Cooke*	Commons	Hoekstra/Goodfellow/Henry
		10/9	*2,581*	*3:6*				*Stuart 56*	*Garner*	*Woodthorpe*	*Nelson*	*Swailes*	*Unsworth**	*Clegg*	*Forrest*	*Dunfield*	*Abbott"*	*Newby*	*Stuart^*	*Billy/Redmond/Preece*
								Ref: G Salisbury	Twice Abbott nods Shtaniuk headers off the line. Newby's cross eludes Cutler. Stuart heads home. Swailes nods against the bar. Gunnarsson's two-footed lunge on Nelson sparks a melée and earns him an early bath (76). Cotterill's first defeat by lower league opposition as a manager.											

FA Cup																				
3	H	WIGAN		22	W	3-0	2-0	Greenacre 21, 67, Iwelumo 31	Cutler	Thomas	Hall	Handyside	Shtaniuk	Gunnarsson	Gudjonsson"	O'Connor^	Iwelumo	Greenacre*	Hoekstra	Goodfellow/Henry/Neal
		4/1	9,618	*2:1*					*Filan*	*Green**	*Eaden*	*Jackson*	*Breckin*	*Kennedy*	*Jarrett*	*Mitchell*	*Liddell*	*Roberts^*	*Teale*	*McCulloch/Ellington*
								Ref: A Butler	Paul Jewell's runaway Second Division leaders rest key players. Greenacre squeezes in from close range, then nods in Hall's cross. Jarrett puts his close-range header straight at Cutler. Iwelumo's stunning right-footed volley wins Goal of the Season. First clean sheet since opening day.											
4	H	BOURNEMOUTH		22	W	3-0	1-0	Iwelumo 45p, 52, Hoekstra 84	Banks*	Henry	Hall	Thomas	Marteinsson	Gunnarsson	Gudjonss'n^	O'Connor	Iwelumo	Greenacre	Hoekstra"	Cutler/Neal/Goodfellow
		26/1	12,004	*3:9*					*Tardiff !*	*Tindall*	*Purches*	*Fletcher C*	*Stock*	*O'Connor*	*Thomas**	*Buxton*	*Hayter^*	*Fletcher S"*	*Elliott*	*Stewart/Holmes/Feeney*
								Ref: M Ryan	Stoke have a virus in the camp. Elliott cracks against the inside of a post. Tardiff brings down Gunnarsson and is dismissed. Iwelumo slots the retaken penalty. Banks departs with an upset tum. Iwelumo turns in Greenacre's cross at the second attempt. Hoekstra dances inside to lash in.											
5	H	CHELSEA		22	L	0-2	0-0		Banks	Thomas	Hall	Handyside	Shtaniuk	Gunnarsson	Henry*	O'Connor	Iwelumo	Greenacre"	Neal^	Gudjons'n/Marteins'n/Goodfel'
		16/2	26,615	*P:5*				*Hasselbaink 52, Gronkjaer 76*	*Cudicini*	*Melchiot*	*Le Saux*	*Terry*	*Gallas*	*Stanic"*	*Lampard*	*De Lucas**	*Hasselbaink*	*Gudjohnsen*	*Petit^*	*Gronkjaer/Huth/Cole*
								Ref: R Styles	Chelsea's pocket magician Zola, is injured. City lack Hoekstra suspended, but look the more likely in the first half. O'Connor wastes two good chances, over the bar, before Hasselbaink slides home a loose ball and Gronkjaer races clear to score from a tight angle on the right on the run.											

			Home					Away					
		P	W	D	L	F	A	W	D	L	F	A	Pts
1	Portsmouth	46	17	3	3	52	22	12	8	3	45	23	98
2	Leicester	46	16	5	2	40	12	10	8	4	32	27	91
3	Sheffield Utd	46	13	7	3	38	23	10	4	9	34	29	80
4	Reading	46	13	3	7	33	21	12	1	10	28	25	79
5	Wolves *	46	9	9	4	39	18	11	6	6	41	25	75
6	Nott'm Forest	46	14	7	2	57	23	6	7	10	25	27	74
7	Ipswich	46	10	5	8	49	39	9	8	6	31	25	70
8	Norwich	46	14	4	5	36	17	5	8	10	24	32	69
9	Millwall	46	11	6	6	34	32	8	3	12	25	37	66
10	Wimbledon	46	12	5	6	39	28	6	6	11	37	45	65
11	Gillingham	46	10	6	7	33	31	6	8	9	23	34	62
12	Preston	46	11	7	5	44	29	5	6	12	24	41	61
13	Watford	46	11	5	7	33	26	6	4	13	21	44	60
14	C Palace	46	8	10	5	29	17	6	7	10	30	35	59
15	Rotherham	46	8	9	6	27	25	7	5	11	35	37	59
16	Burnley	46	10	4	9	35	44	5	6	12	30	45	55
17	Walsall	46	10	3	10	34	34	5	6	12	23	35	54
18	Derby	46	9	5	9	33	32	6	2	15	22	42	52
19	Bradford C	46	7	8	8	27	35	7	2	14	24	38	52
20	Coventry	46	6	6	11	23	31	6	8	9	23	31	50
21	STOKE	46	9	6	8	25	25	3	8	12	20	44	50
22	Sheffield Wed	46	7	7	9	29	32	3	9	11	27	41	46
23	Brighton	46	7	6	10	29	31	4	6	13	20	36	45
24	Grimsby	46	5	6	12	26	39	4	6	13	22	46	39
		1104	247	142	162	844	666	162	142	247	666	844	1511

Odds & ends

Double wins: (1) Brighton.
Double losses: (4) Burnley, Derby, Grimsby. Millwall.

Won from behind: (0).
Lost from in front: (3) Bradford C (a), Burnley (a), Preston (a).

High Spots: The return of some spirit to the dressing room under Pulis.
The signing of quality players on loan.
Big crowds responding to the board's £5 ticket offers.
The defensive tightening after the Forest debacle.

Low spots: Eight straight defeats in the autumn.
The manner of Steve Cotterill's defection to Premiership Sunderland.
Being publicly embarrassed when George Burley turns down the manager's job.
The 0-6 hammering at Nottingham Forest which left City's position seemingly irreversible.
Being the lowest scoring team in the division.

Player of the Year: Sergei Shtaniuk.
Ever-presents: (0).
Hat-tricks: (0).
Leading Scorer: (7) Chris Iwelumo.

	Appearances						Goals			
	Lge	*Sub*	LC	*Sub*	FAC	*Sub*	**Lge**	LC	FAC	**Tot**
Akinbiyi, Ade	**4**						**2**			**2**
Banks, Steve	**14**				2					
Clarke, Clive	**27**	*4*	1				**3**			**3**
Commons, Kris	**6**	*2*	1				**1**			**1**
Cooke, Andy	**24**	*7*	1				**6**			**6**
Crossley, Mark	**12**									
Cutler, Neil	**20**		1		1	*1*				
Goodfellow, Marc	**6**	*14*		*1*		*3*	**1**			**1**
Greenacre, Chris	**18**	*12*			3		**4**		2	**6**
Gudjonsson, Bjarni	**25**	*11*	1		2	*1*	**1**			**1**
Gunnarsson, Brynjar	**40**		1		3		**5**			**5**
Hall, Marcus	**23**	*1*			3					
Handyside, Peter	**44**		1		2					
Henry, Karl	**15**	*3*		*1*	2	*1*	**1**			**1**
Hoekstra, Peter	**26**	*4*		*1*	2		**4**		1	**5**
Iwelumo, Chris	**15**	*17*	1		3		**4**		3	**7**
Marteinsson, Petur	**7**	*5*			1	*1*	**2**			**2**
Mills, Lee	**7**	*4*					**2**			**2**
Mooney, Tommy	**11**	*1*					**3**			**3**
Neal, Lewis	**7**	*9*			1	*2*				
O'Connor, James	**43**		1		3					
Richardson, Frazer	**6**	*1*								
Shtaniuk, Sergei	**44**		1		2		**3**			**3**
Thomas, Wayne	**41**		1		3					
Vandeurzen, Jurgen	**7**	*5*					**1**			**1**
Warhurst, Paul	**4**	*1*					**1**			**1**
Williams, Mark	**5**	*1*								
Wilson, Brian	**1**	*2*								
Wilson, Mark	**4**									
(own-goals)							**1**			**1**
(29 players used)	**506**	***104***	**11**	***3***	**33**	***9***	**45**		**6**	**51**

No	Date	Att	Pos	Pt	F-A	H-T	Scorers, Times, and Referees	SQUAD	NUMBERS	IN	USE								subs used
1	A DERBY			W	3-0	2-0	Noel-Will'ms 15, Greenacre 20, Neal 90	**De Goey***	Thomas	Clarke	**Eustace**	Marteinsson	Hall	**Russell**	**Asaba**	**Noel-Wil's"**	Greenacre^	**Andrews**	Cutler/Neal/Iwelumo
	9/8	*21,517*		3				*Oakes*	*Elliott*	*Mills*	*Taylor*	*Costa*	*Morris"*	*Jackson*	*McLeod^*	*Hunt**	*Huddlestone*	*Caldwell*	*Tome/Boertien/Bolde*
							Ref: H Webb	In 90 degree heat TP's new-look 3-4-3 formation tears Rams apart. After 50 secs De Goey survives a pen appeal. Andrews centres for GNW to bundle in. Greenacre slots Asaba's classy touch-off. Neal volleys in Iwelumo's cross. First win at Pride Park and first at Derby since 1975.											
2	H WIMBLEDON		1	W	2-1	1-0	Asaba 25p, Thomas 90	Cutler	Thomas	Clarke	Eustace	Marteins'n^	Hall	Russell	Asaba	Noel-Willi'ms	Greenacre*	Andrews	Commons/Goodfellow
	16/8	12,550	*9*	6			*Agyemang 56*	*Banks*	*Darlington*	*Chorley*	*Reo-Coker*	*Leigertwood*	*Tapp*	*Geir*	*Gordon**	*Holdsworth*	*Agyemang*	*Nowland^*	*McAnuff/Holloway*
							Ref: P Robinson	Stoke lack De Goey (leg muscle). Russell is sandwiched for the pen, but Mr Robinson denies City two other clear-cut shouts. Agyemang slots a through ball from Reo-Coker. Banks tips Eustace's header onto the bar. Thomas heads home in a melee in injury-time. Just 33 visiting fans.											
3	A WALSALL		3	D	1-1	1-0	Asaba 33	De Goey	Thomas	Hall	Eustace	Marteins'n*	**Williams**	Russell	Asaba^	Noel-Willi'ms	Clarke	Andrews	Commons/Henry
	23/8	*9,033*	*6*	7			*Merson 85*	*Walker*	*Hay*	*Aranalde*	*Roper*	*Bazeley*	*Emblen**	*Merson*	*Samways !*	*Leitao*	*Corica^*	*Osborn"*	*Matias/Birch Gary/Oakes*
							Ref: P Taylor	New signing Paul Williams from Southampton slots in as TP reverts to 4-4-2. Roper's clearance hits Eustace and Asaba nets. Asaba misses a great chance to kill it. Merson escapes Eustace to ram home Birch's header. Nine booked. Samways walks (90) after a skirmish with Eustace.											
4	H MILLWALL		4	D	0-0	0-0		De Goey	Thomas	Hall	Eustace	Williams	Clarke	Russell	Asaba	Noel-Willi'ms	Greenacre*	Andrews	Commons
	26/8	13,087	*5*	8				*Warner*	*Roberts*	*Craig*	*Nethercott*	*Ward*	*Hearn"*	*Cahill*	*Wise*	*Juan**	*Peeters^*	*Whelan*	*Dunne/Harris/Sadlier*
							Ref: J Winter	Stoke take the initiative. GNW swivels twice to blast straight at Warner. Ward blocks Eustace's shot. Andrews fires over from eight yards. Millwall hit back for the last 15 mins of each half. De Goey pouches Peeters header. TP is sent off after a toe-to-toe ruck with Mark McGhee.											
5	A PRESTON		10	L	0-1	0-1		De Goey	Thomas	Hall	Eustace^	Williams"	Clarke	Russell	Asaba	Noel-Willi'ms	Greenacre*	Andrews	Goodfellow/Iwelumo/Neal
	30/8	*12,965*	*18*	8			*McKenna 19*	*Gould*	*Alexander*	*Lucketti*	*Davis^*	*Broomes*	*McKenna*	*O'Neil*	*Keane**	*Cresswell"*	*Fuller*	*Lewis*	*Etuhu/Jackson/Healy*
							Ref: P Walton	Craig Brown's Preston are without a win but dominate. DeGoey denies Cresswell, but McKenna turns in the rebound. Debutant Claude Davis picks up a groin strain. Etuhu nods against the bar. City lay siege in last 15 mins. Andrews' last-gasp free-kick falls to Thomas who stabs wide.											
6	H BURNLEY		13	L	1-2	0-2	Asaba 53	De Goey	Thomas	Hall	Eustace	Williams^	Clarke	Russell	Asaba !	Noel-Willi'ms	Greenacre*	Andrews	Goodfellow/Iwelumo
	6/9	14,876	*10*	8			*May 17, Chadwick 27*	*Jensen*	*West*	*Camara*	*Todd*	*May*	*Farrelly**	*Chadwick*	*Grant*	*Facey^*	*Blake*	*Branch*	*Weller/Moore I*
							Ref: M Cooper	Burnley's former Man U men bag the all-too-easy goals. May bundles in from a corner. Chadwick slots home Branch's slick pass. Stoke rally. Asaba nods in Clarke's cross, but then sees a second yellow for smashing David May's nose (53). GNW twice hits Jensen's legs when through.											
7	A COVENTRY		15	L	2-4	1-2	Asaba 45, Thomas 78 *[Morrell 75]*	De Goey	Thomas	Hall	Eustace	Williams*	Clarke	Russell	Asaba	Noel-Willi'ms	Greenacre^	Andrews	Neal/Iwelumo
	13/9	*13,982*	*18*	8			*Suffo 5, Barrett 10, Adebola 58,*	*Shearer*	*Whing*	*Konjic*	*Staunton*	*Warnock^*	*Barrett*	*Safri*	*McAllister**	*Adebola*	*Suffo"*	*Doyle*	*Mor'l/Shaw/Mansouri*
							Ref: L Mason	Gary McAllister's Sky Blues have won one of their last 25 games. Cameroon international Suffo prods past De Goey. Barrett lashes in from 25 yards. Asaba lobs Shearer. Adebola nets against City again. Morrell nods in his first Coventry goal. Thommo half-volleys Eustace's corner.											
8	H SUNDERLAND		11	W	3-1	3-0	Noel-Williams 24, Russell 37, 39	De Goey	Thomas	Hall	Eustace	Williams	Clarke	Russell	Asaba	Noel-W'ms^	Greenacre*	Andrews	Neal/**Akinbiyi**
	16/9	15,005	*8*	11			*Kyle 52*	*Poom*	*McCartney*	*Healy*	*Breen**	*James^*	*Thirlwell*	*Arca*	*Thornton*	*Kyle*	*Stewart*	*Oster*	*Bjorklund/Butler*
							Ref: M Pike	GNW fires Hall's cross home left-footed from six yards. Russell twice races through to convert Asaba's passes. De Goey saves Kyle's header, but Kyle nods in the rebound. Thornton is sent off (74) for a second yellow for a foul on Eustace. New signing Ade Akinbiyi debuts as sub.											
9	H NORWICH		11	D	1-1	1-0	Noel-Williams 36	De Goey	Thomas	Hall	Eustace	Williams	Clarke	Russell	Akinbiyi	Noel-Willi'ms	Greenacre	Andrews	
	20/9	10,672	*8*	12			*Huckerby 66*	*Green*	*Edworthy*	*Fleming*	*MacKay*	*Drury*	*Holt*	*Harper"*	*Francis**	*Crouch*	*Huckerby*	*Easton^*	*Mulryne/McVeigh/Roberts*
							Ref: P Joslin	5.35pm kick-off for Sky Sports. Nigel Worthington fields three loanees, Huckerby, Harper and 6ft 7in Crouch. GNW flicks in Akinbiyi's cross. Mulryne's half-time introduction changes things. Huckerby stabs in a loose ball. De Goey makes a super save from Mulryne's free-kick.											
10	A WEST BROM		14	L	0-1	0-0		De Goey	Thomas*	Hall !	Eustace !	Williams	Clarke^	Russell	Henry	Noel-Willi'ms	Iwelumo"	Andrews	Commons/Neal/Akinbiyi
	27/9	*24,297*	*3*	12			*Dobie 59*	*Hoult*	*Haas*	*Clement*	*Gilchrist*	*Gaardsoe*	*Gregan**	*O'Connor*	*Johnson !*	*Koumas*	*Hulse*	*Dobie*	*Sakiri*
							Ref: G Laws	Eustace and Johnson see red for a fracas at a corner (4). 10 v10 means an open game. Koumas hits the bar. Dobie misses a sitter from 3 yards. Williams fails to clear and Hulse sets up Dobie to score. Hall pulls down Dobie and walks (74). First league defeat by Baggies since 1988.											
11	A ROTHERHAM		15	L	0-3	0-1		De Goey	Thomas	Hall	Eustace^	Williams	**Commons**	Russell	Henry"	Noel-Willi'ms	Iwelumo*	Andrews	Akinbiyi/Neal/Goodfellow
	30/9	*5,450*	*22*	12			*Byfield 44p, Butler 51, 90*	*Pollitt*	*Scott*	*Swailes*	*McIntosh*	*Hurst*	*Sedgwick*	*Baudet*	*Robinson*	*Warne*	*Byfield**	*Butler^*	*Barker R/Robins*
							Ref: C Boyeson	Ronnie Moore's Millers have scored only three League goals all season. They double their tally thanks to Byfield's penalty for Williams' foul on Butler and a Butler double. He dispossess Thomas to poke home and converts Byfield's cross which Williams misses. Stoke wilt. Pathetic.											

No	Venue	Opponent / Att	Pos	Res / Pts	FT	HT	Scorers, Times, Referees	1	2	3	4	5	6	7	8	9	10	11	Subs used
12	H	NOTT'M FOREST	13	W	2-1	2-0	Thomas 6, Asaba 31	De Goey	Russell	Hall	Eustace	Thomas*	Halls	Clarke	Asaba	Noel-Willi'ms	Andrews	Commons^	Neal/Akinbiyi
4/10		13,755	*9*	15			*Williams 90*	*Ward*	*Louis-Jean*	*Dawson*	*Thompson*	*Morgan**	*Stewart*	*Williams*	*Jess*	*Harewood*	*McPhail^*	*Reid*	*Taylor/Robertson*
							Ref: N Barry	John Halls (on loan from Arsenal) plays at right-back. Thomas heads in a corner. Asaba and Wes Morgan come to blows with the Forest man forced off injured. De Goey denies lively Harewood. Asaba nods in Clarke's near-post cross. Williams nets from 15 yards with the last kick.											
13	A	WIGAN	14	L	1-2	1-0	Noel-Williams 39	De Goey	Russell	Clarke	Williams	**Hill^**	Halls	Asaba	Henry*	Noel-Willi'ms	Neal	Commons	Akinbiyi/Owen
14/10		*7,678*	*2*	15			*Horsfield 55, 69*	*Filan*	*Eaden*	*Jackson*	*Breckin*	*McMillan*	*Bullard*	*Dinning*	*Liddell*	*Horsfield*	*Ellington**	*McCulloch*	*Roberts*
							Ref: S Mathieson	Eustace, Hall and Andrews serve bans. GNW lashes in Commons' pass to shake Paul Jewell's unbeaten frontrunners. Recent £1m arrival from Birmingham Geoff Horsfield buries both his chances, holding off tiring debutant Hill's challenge to net. Russell hits the bar with a late volley.											
14	A	IPSWICH	17	L	0-1	0-1		Cutler	Russell	Clarke"	Williams	Hill*	Halls	Asaba	Henry	Noel-Willi'ms	Akinbiyi^	Andrews	Owen/Commons/Greenacre
18/10		*22,122*	*6*	15			*Richards 42*	*Davis*	*Wilnis*	*Richards*	*Naylor*	*Santos*	*Bart-Wil'ams*	*Wright*	*Magilton^*	*Counago*	*Kuqi*	*Mahon**	*Westlake/Miller*
							Ref: P Armstrong	De Goey has flu. The three strikers start for the first time but with GNW on the right wing and Asaba the left. Cutler produces a string of fine saves to deny Counago and Kuqi. Matt Richards volleys in his first senior goal. Andrews' rocket hits both posts before nestling in Davis' arms.											
15	H	CREWE	18	D	1-1	0-0	Greenacre 88	De Goey	Russell	Clarke*	Williams	Hill	Halls	Asaba	Henry"	Noel-Willi'ms	Akinbiyi^	Andrews	Commons/Greenacre/Neal
25/10		17,569	*11*	16			*Jones S 52*	*Ince*	*Wright*	*Walker*	*Lunt*	*Foster*	*Sorvel*	*Jones S**	*Ashton*	*Vaughan*	*Cochrane*	*Barrowman*	*Tonkins*
							Ref: R Beeby	A scrappy first half sees Asaba fire wide and De Goey deny Ashton's header. Clarke limps off (30) which leaves City unbalanced. Steve Jones puts Dario Gradi's men ahead after De Goey palms out Ashton's shot. Commons crosses for Asaba to shoot and Greenacre turns in the rebound.											
16	H	SHEFFIELD UTD	19	D	2-2	2-0	Noel-Williams 2, Akinbiyi 17	De Goey	Halls"	Hall	Thomas !	Hill*	Henry	Russell	Andrews	Noel-Willi'ms	Akinbiyi	Commons^	Williams/Greenacre/Hoekstra
1/11		14,217	*4*	17			*Kozluk 52, Lester 90p*	*Gerrard*	*Kozluk*	*Wright^*	*Jagielka*	*Morgan*	*Montgom'y**	*Tonge*	*Ndlovu"*	*Ward*	*Lester*	*McCall*	*Armstrong/Parkinson/Allison*
							Ref: B Knight	GNW nods in a corner and Akinbiyi heads Commons' cross in off the bar. Thomas walks for a second yellow (46). Kozluk's low cross-shot screws in. City weather a storm with De Goey saving from Lester and Ward. In injury-time Lester is felled by Greenacre. He lashes in the pen.											
17	A	CARDIFF	19	L	1-3	0-1	Commons 59	De Goey	Richardson	Hall	Thomas	Hill	Eustace	Russell^	Andrews*	Noel-Willi'ms	Akinbiyi	Commons	Greenacre/Neal
8/11		*15,227*	*8*	17			*Earnshaw 24, 71 Gabbidon 81*	*Alexander*	*Barker*	*Croft*	*Vidmar*	*Gabbidon*	*Gray**	*Kavanagh*	*Bonner^*	*Earnshaw*	*Gordon*	*Robinson*	*Langley/Boland*
							Ref: D Crick	Defensive crisis sees on-loan Frazer Richardson start at right-back. Division top scorer Earnshaw takes his tally to 19 with a 25-yard volley and neat finish from Robinson's pass. Commons levels with a jinking run and shot from an angle. Gabbidon slots after Kav's corner is not cleared.											
18	H	BRADFORD	19	W	1-0	1-0	Eustace 11	De Goey	Richardson	Hall	Halls	Hill	Eustace	Russell	Neal*	Noel-Willi'ms	Akinbiyi^	Commons"	Hoekstra/Asaba/Clarke
22/11		11,661	*23*	20				*Combe*	*Gavin*	*Francis*	*Bower*	*Heckingb'm*	*Atherton**	*Edds*	*Summerbee*	*McHugh^*	*Branch*	*Gray*	*Muirhead/Kearney*
							Ref: P Crossley	Managerless Bradford wilt under a barrage of pressure. Neal ends a sweeping move with a cross for Eustace to nod in. The expected avalanche fails to materialise. Akinbiyi puts a free header at Combe. Eustace's volley hits a post. De Goey's one save is a stunner from Gray's drive.											
19	H	CRYSTAL PALACE	20	L	0-1	0-1		De Goey	Thomas	Hall	Halls	Hill	Eustace	Russell	Richardson^	Noel-Wil's*	Akinbiyi"	Hoekstra	Asaba/Iwelumo/Commons
25/11		10,277	*19*	20			*Johnson 26*	*Myhre*	*Fleming*	*Borrowdale*	*Popovic*	*Edwards*	*Butterfield*	*Derry*	*Hughes*	*Black**	*Johnson"*	*Freedman^*	*Routledge/Symons/Watson*
							Ref: M Clattenburg	Richardson's shot deflects over off Popovic. Andy Johnson nods in Fleming's cross. Russell hits the side netting. Myhre turns over Hoekstra's point-blank header. Halls stabs wide. Commons weaves his way through but Myhre saves again. First win for Kit Symons' men in eight games.											
20	A	GILLINGHAM	21	L	1-3	0-2	Eustace 76	De Goey	Richardson	Hall	Halls	Hill"	Eustace	Russell	Clarke	Iwelumo^	Asaba	Hoekstra*	Commons/Akinbiyi/**Johnson**
29/11		*7,888*	*14*	20			*Shaw 26, Hope 45, Sidibe 84*	*Brown*	*Nosworthy*	*Cox*	*Hope*	*Hills*	*Southall*	*Hes'nthaler^*	*Smith*	*Sidibe*	*Johnson**	*Shaw"*	*James/Perpetuini/Saunders*
							Ref: G Hegley	Gills have sold star striker Marlon King to Forest for £950,000. City start brightly but Shaw nets from 18 yards. In lashing wind and rain Stoke allow Hope a free header. Eustace turns in Asaba's low cross. Hall loses the ball in the box and Sidibe scores. Eight successive away defeats.											
21	H	CARDIFF	22	L	2-3	1-2	Eustace 38, Akinbiyi 74	De Goey	Richardson"	Clarke	Halls	Thomas	Eustace	Russell	Johnson^	Noel-Wil'ms"	Asaba	Hoekstra	Commons/Akinbiyi/Greenacre
6/12		12,208	*7*	20			*Thorne 34, 40, 72*	*Alexander*	*Croft*	*Vidmar*	*Gabbidon*	*Barker*	*Boland*	*Robinson^*	*Langley*	*Thorne*	*Earnshaw**	*Gray"*	*Campbell/Bonner/Prior*
							Ref: A Leake	Hill out for six weeks after ankle surgery. Halls signs from Arsenal. Lennie Lawrence's Bluebirds miss six injured. Old boy Thorne poaches a close-range treble including two headers. Eustace slots GNW's cross. Akinbiyi leathers in from 12 yards. Great entertainment but no points.											
22	A	WEST HAM	20	W	1-0	1-0	Richardson 33	De Goey	Halls	Hall	**Taggart**	Thomas	Eustace	Russell	Clarke	Noel-Wil'ms^	Akinbiyi*	**Richardson**	Asaba/Johnson
9/12		*24,365*	*9*	23				*James*	*Repka**	*Dailly*	*Pearce*	*Stockdale*	*Quinn*	*Mullins*	*Carrick*	*Deane^*	*Harewood*	*Connolly*	*Horlock/Hutchison*
							Ref: B Curson	Loanee Taggart (Leicester) adds strength. James parries Akinbiyi's shot. Richardson side-foots past England's keeper for his first senior goal. Stoke outpass Hammers until Hutchison arrives. He fires wide but City hang on. Eustace chips onto the bar. First win at West Ham for 30 years.											
23	H	READING	19	W	3-0	2-0	Hoekstra 18, 26, 87p	De Goey	Halls	Clarke	Taggart	Thomas	Eustace^	Russell	Neal	Noel-Willi'ms	Akinbiyi*	Hoekstra"	Asaba/Johnson/Hall
13/12		11,212	*7*	26				*Hahnemann*	*Murty*	*Shorey*	*Ingimarsson*	*Mackie*	*Watson*	*Sidwell*	*Harper**	*Forster*	*Salako*	*Murray^*	*Savage/Tyson*
							Ref: C Foy	Hoekstra produces a magical one-man show. He streaks onto GNW's pass to net. Then his sublime 18-yarder flies in and Shorey pushes him and Hoekstra cheekily chips in to complete his first ever hat-trick. First treble by a Potter for 4 years (Thorne). Has TP found the right formula?											

No	Date		Att	Pos	Pt	F-A	H-T	Scorers, Times, and Referees	SQUAD	NUMBERS	IN	USE								subs used
24	A	WATFORD		16	W	3-1	1-1	Taggart 15, Akinbiyi 55, 72	De Goey	Halls !	Hall	Taggart	Thomas	Eustace^	Russell	Clarke	Noel-Willi'ms	Akinbiyi"	Hoekstra*	Johnson/Neal/Asaba
	20/12		*13,732*	*21*	29			*Helguson 4*	*Pidgley*	*Kelly*	*Hand**	*Gayle*	*Cox*	*Brown^*	*Ardley*	*Vernazza*	*Helguson*	*Devlin*	*Fitzgerald"*	*Cook/Hyde/Dyer*
								Ref: A Butler (replaced by Mr Whitestone)	Helguson nets after a defensive mix-up. Taggart nods in a free-kick unchallenged. Akinbiyi twice beats Pidgley when sent clear. Helguson flattens Russell and sub ref Mr Whitestone shows Halls red for retaliation (90), later rescinded as a mistake. First win from behind in two years.											
25	H	PRESTON		16	D	1-1	0-0	Eustace 90p	De Goey	Halls	Clarke	Taggart	Thomas	Eustace	Russell	Neal^	Noel-Wil'ms*	Akinbiyi	Hoekstra	Asaba/Commons
	26/12		**20,126**	*7*	30			*Healy 66*	*Gould*	*Alexander*	*Davis*	*Jackson !*	*Lucketti*	*O'Neil*	*McKenna*	*Lewis*	*Cresswell**	*Healy*	*Fuller^*	*Abbott/Etuhu*
								Ref: E Evans	In wind and rain, City dominate with Akinbiyi and GNW both firing wide. PNE fight back. Cresswell heads against the post. Healy fires home from 25 yards. In injury-time Jackson and Akinbiyi tangle off the ball. The assistant gives Stoke a pen. Chaos. Jackson walks. Eustace slots in.											
26	A	BURNLEY		14	W	1-0	0-0	Akinbiyi 53	De Goey^	Halls	Hall	Taggart*	Thomas	Eustace	Russell	Clarke	Noel-Willi'ms	Akinbiyi	Johnson	Commons"/Cutler/Henry
	28/12		*12,812*	*21*	33				*Jensen*	*West*	*Camara^*	*May*	*Grant*	*Chaplow*	*Branch*	*Weller*	*Moore*	*Blake*	*Chadwick**	*McEveley/O'Neill*
								Ref: D Gallagher	Moore nods against a post early on. City lose Taggart (24) and De Goey (50) through injury. Thomas deflects Chaplow's shot wide. Eustace's threaded pass finds Akinbiyi, who pokes in. Hall receives a second yellow (67) but Stoke hold on after Clarke denies Blake with a super tackle.											
27	H	DERBY		13	W	2-1	1-1	Akinbiyi 29, Taggart 53	De Goey	Halls	Clarke	Taggart	Thomas	Eustace	Russell	Neal^	Noel-Willi'ms	Akinbiyi*	Hoekstra"	Asaba/**Svard**/Commons
	10/1		16,402	*22*	36			*Morris 1*	*Grant*	*Edwards*	*Zavagno*	*Johnson*	*Mawene*	*Bolder**	*Huddlestone*	*Taylor*	*Manel*	*Bradbury^*	*Morris*	*Tudgay/Costa*
								Ref: A Kaye	It's Elvis Day with over 100 fans dressed up and a soundalike singer pre-match. De Goey and Halls leave a high ball to each other and Morris pokes in. Stoke's defence looks all shook up. Akinbiyi hooks home on the run. Taggart nods in Eustace's free-kick. Derby hit the post twice.											
28	A	WIMBLEDON		12	W	1-0	0-0	Noel-Williams 52	De Goey	Halls	Clarke	Taggart	Thomas	Eustace	Russell	Johnson !	Noel-Willi'ms	Akinbiyi*	Hoekstra^	Asaba/Commons
	17/1		*3,623*	*24*	39				*Banks*	*Darlington*	*Lewington*	*Gier*	*Liegertwood*	*Tapp**	*McAnuff*	*Chorley*	*Holdsw'rth"*	*Small*	*Gray^*	*Harding/Mackie/Kamara*
								Ref: L Probert	A scrappy affair until City take control either side of half-time. Akinbiyi has a shot tipped onto a post. GNW volleys in Clarke's cross. Mackie fouls Taggart then whacks the ball at his head to spark a brawl. Four yellows later Johnson sees red, thanks to fourth official Chittendon (87).											
29	H	WALSALL		12	W	3-2	2-2	Russell 8, Asaba 36, 56	Cutler	Halls"	Clarke	Taggart	Williams	Svard	Russell	Neal^	Noel-Willi'ms	Asaba	Hoekstra*	Commons/Wilkinson/Wilson
	31/1		18,305	*17*	42			*Leitao 14, Taylor 41*	*Petterson*	*Bazeley*	*Aranalde*	*Carbon*	*Ritchie*	*Birch*	*Wrack*	*Taylor**	*Leitao*	*Merson*	*Samways^*	*Wales/lawrence*
								Ref: P Armstrong	Heavy rain means it's all-action. Russell's 25-yarder slips through Petterson's fingers. Walsall's goals are down to Halls. Asaba nets his 100th career goal after Petterson parries Commons' effort, then deliberately deflects in GNW's shot. Leitao has injury-time goal ruled out for offside.											
30	A	MILLWALL		13	D	1-1	1-1	Clarke 4	De Goey	Halls	Hall	Thomas	Williams	Svard	Russell	Clarke	Noel-Willi'ms	Asaba	Hoekstra	
	7/2		*9,034*	*10*	43			*Dichio 23*	*Marshall*	*Muscat*	*Lawrence*	*Wise*	*Ward*	*Livermore"*	*Cahill*	*Roberts**	*Dichio*	*Harris*	*Sweeney^*	*Ifill/Elliott/Ryan*
								Ref: L Cable	Asaba's lob hits post and bar. He later claims it went in for a 'phantom goal'. Clarke hammers in a curling drive. Danny Dichio rounds off his loan spell from WBA by nodding in Sweeney's cross. De Goey holds Harris' drive. Halls hooks Dichio's header off the line. Professional.											
31	A	CRYSTAL PALACE		13	L	3-6	2-4	Eust' 6, Clarke 45, Asaba 83p *[Rout' 90]*	De Goey	Halls	Hall*	Thomas	Williams	Svard	Russell	Eustace^	Akinbiyi	Asaba	Clarke	Commons/Noel-Williams
	14/2		*16,715*	*8*	43			*J'son 5, 9p, 33p, Hughes 45, Ship' 55,*	*Berthelin*	*Butterfield*	*Granville*	*Hudson*	*Popovic*	*Riihilati**	*Routledge*	*Hughes^*	*Shipperley*	*Johnson"*	*Gray*	*Leigertw'd/Derry/Freedman*
								Ref: R Styles	Johnson nets a header and two debatable pens. Eustace and Clarke hammer in 25-yard grass-cutters. From the restart Hughes zips through the defence to flick past De Goey. Shipperley nods in unmarked. Asaba nets another debatable pen. Routledge spins on the ball to toe-poke home.											
32	H	WIGAN		13	D	1-1	1-0	Akinbiyi 45	Cutler	Halls	Clarke"	Thomas	Williams	Eustace	Russell	Asaba	Noel-Wil'ms*	Akinbiyi	Hoekstra^	Svard/Commons/Hill
	21/2		14,927	*3*	44			*Ellington 84*	*Filan*	*Eaden^*	*McMillan*	*De Vos*	*Breckin*	*Bullard*	*Jarrett*	*Teale**	*Roberts !*	*Ellington*	*Mahon*	*Liddell/McCulloch*
								Ref: P Prosser	Latics pummel City, who somehow survive. Teale and Mahon both fire wide. Cutler saves from Roberts and Bullard. Eustace twice releases Akinbiyi. He slots the second low past Filan. Roberts kicks Halls and sees red (75). After the ball ricochets around the box Ellington lashes in.											
33	H	IPSWICH		13	W	2-0	1-0	Hoekstra 37p, Akinbiyi 68	De Goey	Halls	Hall	Thomas	Taggart	Svard*	Clarke	Russell	Noel-Wil'ms"	Akinbiyi	Hoekstra^	Wilson/Williams/Asaba
	2/3		11,435	*6*	47				*Davis*	*Wilnis*	*Richards*	*McGreal^*	*Santos*	*Magilton"*	*Miller*	*Wright*	*Bent*	*Kuqi**	*Westlake*	*Naylor/Diallo/Counago*
								Ref: P Walton	De Goey denies Westlake and Kuqi as Joe Royle's play-off contenders start strongly. Santos fells on loan Svard (Arsenal) trying to retrieve his own wayward backpass. Hoekstra strokes in the pen. Akinbiyi rounds Davis to slot then muffs a great chance from Wilson's cross. Play-offs?											
34	H	WATFORD		12	W	3-1	3-1	Akinbiyi 18, 44, Noel-Williams 21	De Goey^	Halls	Hall	Thomas	Taggart	Svard	Clarke	Russell	Noel-Willi'ms	Akinbiyi*	Hoekstra"	Asaba/Cutler/Henry
	6/3		13,108	*17*	50			*Helguson 36*	*Pidgley*	*Ardley*	*Smith"*	*Dyche*	*Cox**	*Hyde*	*Mahon*	*Ifil*	*Helguson*	*Devlin*	*Cook^*	*Vernazza/Fitzgerald/Doyley*
								Ref: E Ilderton	Ray Lewington's Hornets start brightly. GNW squares for Akinbiyi to tap in, then nods in Hoekstra's cross. Helguson nets unmarked. Akinbiyi drives in his 100th league goal. Cutler replaces De Goey, denies Fitzgerald after Hall's hospital pass and is carried off. Halls takes over in goal.											

No	Venue	Opponent	Pos	Res	F-A	H-T	Scorers, Times, and Referees	1	2	3	4	5	6	7	8	9	10	11	subs used
35	A	READING	13	D	0-0	0-0		De Goey	Halls	Hall	Thomas	Taggart	Svard^	Clarke	Russell	Noel-Wil'ms*	Akinbiyi	Hoekstra	Asaba/Henry
	13/3	*14,132*	*8*	51				*Hahnema'n**	*Murty*	*Shorey*	*Williams*	*Ingimarsson*	*Hughes*	*Sidwell*	*Harper*	*Owusu^*	*Goater*	*Salako"*	*Young/Kitson/Brooker*
							Ref: G Hegley	City defend in depth. Owusu muffs a hat-trick of chances. Most notably after rounding De Goey, hitting the post. After saving Taggart's volley and GNW's shot, Royals' Marcus Hahnemann departs with a dead leg. Sub Jamie Young somehow tips over Asaba's header from a corner.											
36	A	SUNDERLAND	12	D	1-1	1-0	Svard 12	De Goey	Halls	Hall	Thomas	Taggart	Svard	Clarke	Russell	Asaba	Akinbiyi	Hoekstra*	Henry
	16/3	*24,510*	*7*	52			*Byfield 67*	*Poom*	*McCartney*	*Wright*	*Breen*	*Babb*	*Oster*	*Thirlwell*	*Whitley**	*Kyle*	*Thornton*	*Smith^*	*Piper/Byfield*
							Ref: M Ryan	Mick McCarthy's men are unbeaten at home for six months. City soak up heavy pressure. Svard nets from 16 yards after Russell's break. 12 minutes after coming on Piper crosses for new signing Darren Byfield to head into the corner. Babb flashes a half-chance from a corner wide.											
37	A	CREWE	14	L	0-2	0-1		De Goey	Halls	Hall	Thomas	Taggart	Svard^	Clarke	Russell	Asaba	Akinbiyi	Hoekstra*	Commons/Gunnarsson
	23/3	*10,014*	*15*	52			*Lunt 25, 61*	*Williams*	*Jones B*	*Vaughan*	*Foster*	*McCready*	*Lunt*	*Cochrane*	*Sorvel*	*Jones S*	*Ashton*	*Hignett**	*Moses*
							Ref: D Gallagher	Hall stretches to block Lunt's shot and redirects it past De Goey. With Halls imperious City lay siege in the second half. Akinbiyi twice hits the post after beating Williams. City have 22 shots to Alex's 6, most are from long-range. Lunt's 20 yarder flies in to seal Alex's second win in 11.											
38	A	NORWICH	14	L	0-1	0-1		De Goey	Halls	Clarke	Thomas	Taggart	Henry	Gunnars'on*	Russell	Asaba	Akinbiyi	Hoekstra^	Commons/Wilkinson
	27/3	*23,565*	*1*	52			*Svensson 45*	*Green*	*Edworthy*	*Drury*	*Fleming*	*Mackay*	*Holt*	*McVeigh*	*Francis*	*McKenzie**	*Svensson^*	*Huckerby*	*Cooper/Roberts*
							Ref: M Riley	Stoke are tenacious but fail to clear Francis' cross. Svensson taps in. Russell bundles over Gary Holt for a controversial spot-kick. De Goey dives to save Huckerby's pen (49). The home fans get very nervous. Green denies Taggart point blank and earns himself an England call up.											
39	H	COVENTRY	13	W	1-0	1-0	Commons 41	De Goey*	Halls	Hall	Thomas	Taggart	Clarke	Russell	Henry	Asaba	Akinbiyi^	Commons	Cutler/Noel-Williams
	3/4	*12,855*	*11*	55				*Shearer*	*Dolomeaux*	*Staunton*	*Konjic*	*Davenport*	*Kerr^*	*Gudjonsson**	*Doyle"*	*Warnock*	*Joachim*	*McSheffrey*	*Barrett/Whing/Olszar*
							Ref: M Dean	The wind threatens to ruin the game. De Goey departs after clashing with McSheffrey (2). The one moment of quality comes when Commons nearly bursts the net with a short free-kick. City retreat to defend the lead. Warnock rattles the woodwork. Eric Black's play-off hopes dashed.											
40	A	NOTT'M FOREST	14	D	0-0	0-0		Cutler	Halls	Hall	Thomas	Taggart	Clarke	Russell	Henry	Noel-Willi'ms	Asaba	Commons	
	10/4	*28,758*	*15*	56				*Gerrard*	*Louis-Jean*	*Doig*	*Dawson*	*Morgan*	*Williams^*	*Impey*	*Evans*	*Taylor*	*King**	*Reid*	*Johnson/Jess*
							Ref: M Cowburn	Without Akinbiyi (back) City lack penetration as GNW still looks unfit. Cutler impresses in denying King three times. Taggart blocks Impey's shot. In a tepid game Commons hits first time volley inches wide. Gerrard saves from Asaba six yards out. TP mutters: 'We should have won.'											
41	H	ROTHERHAM	14	L	0-2	0-1		Cutler	Halls	Hall	Thomas	Taggart"	Clarke	Russell	Hoekstra*	Noel-Wil'ms^	Asaba	Commons	Henry/**Palmer**/Hill
	12/4	11,978	*18*	56			*Morris 22, Butler 68*	*Pollitt*	*Stockdale*	*Minto*	*Swailes*	*Gilchrist*	*Sedgwick**	*Barker*	*Morris*	*Butler*	*Proctor*	*Mullin*	*Warne*
							Ref: R Olivier	Jody Morris fires just over from six yards before cracking in left-footed from 18 yards. Pollitt parries Commons' volley and tips over Russell's 30-yard drive. Asaba misses a hat-trick of chances, hitting the ball at the keeper with the goal gaping. Butler cracks in from 20 yards. Lethargic.											
42	A	SHEFFIELD UTD	12	W	1-0	1-0	Clarke 45	Cutler	Halls	Hall	Thomas	Taggart	Clarke	Russell	Henry	Noel-Willi'ms	Asaba	Commons*	Hoekstra
	17/4	*19,372*	*8*	59				*Kenny*	*Kozluk*	*Wright*	*Page*	*Morgan*	*Montgom'y**	*McCall"*	*Ndlovu^*	*Gray*	*Lester*	*Tonge*	*Allison/Forte/Shaw*
							Ref: A Butler	Neil Warnock's play-off chasers fail to chime. Asaba fires wide. Commons forces Kenny into a flying save. Clarke dances forward from half-way to rifle in from 22 yards. Thomas and Lester tangle. Lester nets but Taggart is fouled in the process. First win at Bramall Lane since 1985.											
43	H	WEST HAM	13	L	0-2	0-1		Cutler	Halls	Hall^	Thomas	Taggart	Clarke	Russell"	Henry	Noel-Willi'ms	Hoekstra*	Commons	Svard/Palmer/Gunnarsson
	24/4	18,227	*6*	59			*Connolly 38, Harewood 58*	*Bywater*	*Mullins*	*Ferdinand*	*Dailly*	*Melville*	*Carrick*	*Lomas*	*Etherington**	*Harewood*	*Connolly^*	*Zamora*	*Cohen/Hutchison*
							Ref: N Barry	In glorious sunshine City start brightly. Clarke fires wide. Bywater tips over GNW's header. West Ham slowly gain control. Connolly turns on a sixpence to net. TP rearranges at half-time but fails to combat Carrick's mastery. Harewood nods in Etherington's chip. City run out of steam.											
44	A	BRADFORD	13	W	2-0	1-0	Noel-Williams 2, 46	De Goey	Halls	Hall	Thomas	Taggart*	Clarke	Russell	Henry	Noel-Willi'ms	Hoekstra^	Commons"	Hill/Svard/Palmer
	1/5	*10,147*	*23*	62				*Combe*	*Gavin*	*Emanuel*	*Atherton^*	*Wetherall*	*Penford*	*Summerbee*	*Wolleaston"*	*Branch**	*Cadamarteri*	*Sanasy*	*Forrest/Kearney/Windass*
							Ref: L Mason	Stokies observe a minute's silence in memory of the Bradford fire victims admirably. GNW glances home Commons' free-kick across Combe. City are not troubled by Bryan Robson's already relegated men. Sanasy's shot is their only effort. GNW lashes in a loose ball to kill the game.											
45	H	WEST BROM	11	W	4-1	1-0	Russell 45, Commons 61, 72, Noel-W' 85	Cutler	Halls	Clarke	Wlikinson	Hill^	Owen	Russell	Henry	Noel-Willi'ms	Commons	Svard*	Neal/Williams
	4/5	18,352	*2*	65			*Dobie 49*	*Hoult*	*Haas*	*Robinson*	*Gaardsoe*	*Moore*	*Gregan*	*Kinsella**	*Koumas !*	*Dobie*	*Hughes^*	*Dyer*	*Clement/Sakiri*
							Ref: K Hill	Due to injuries Pulis throws in the kids. Already-promoted Baggies have plenty of ball but Russell rams in from 20 yards. In heavy rain Hoult lets Commons' 25 yard free-kick to slip through his fingers. Commons and GNW convert crosses. Koumas sees red for kicking Russell (87).											
46	H	GILLINGHAM	11	D	0-0	0-0		De Goey	Halls	Hall	Thomas	Taggart	Clarke	Russell	Henry*	Noel-Willi'ms	Commons^	Asaba	Neal/Hoekstra
	9/5	19,240	*21*	66				*Banks*	*Cox*	*Hope*	*Ashby*	*Hills*	*Southall*	*Hes'enthaler*	*Poulton**	*Saunders*	*Agyemang"*	*Wales^*	*Spiller/Sidibe/Jarvis*
	Home	Away					Ref: G Cain	Andy Hessenthaler's Gills are in danger of the drop. Asaba's 78th-minute header crosses the line, but Banks claws it back and the officials fail to spot it. Agyemang falls over with the goal gaping. Banks saves Halls' near-post shot to ensure the Gills' safety. Walsall bid farewell instead.											
Average	14,437	15,258																	

Carling Cup			Att			F-A	H-T	Scorers, Times, and Referees	SQUAD	NUMBERS	IN	USE								subs used
1	H	ROCHDALE			W	2-1	1-0	Iwelumo 13, Goodfellow 90	De Goey	Thomas	Clarke	Eustace^	**Wilkinson**	Hall	Russell"	Goodfellow	Iwelumo	Greenacre*	Henry	Commons/Neal/Wilson
	19/8		4,687					*Townson 76*	*Gilks*	*Evans*	*Burgess*	*Grand*	*Simpkins*	*Bertos**	*McClare*	*Doughty"*	*Connor*	*Shuker*	*Beech^*	*Townson/Betts/McCourt*
								Ref: S Mathieson	Pulis prefers youngster Andy Wilkinson to Paul Williams. Iwelumo nods home Thomas' cross then heads against the bar. Alan Buckley's men fight back. Former Stokie Paul Connor crosses for Kevin Townson to stab in. Commons hits the post and Goodfellow rolls home the rebound.											
2	H	GILLINGHAM		11	L	0-2	0-1		Cutler	Russell	Clarke	Eustace	Williams	Hall !	Asaba^	Goodfellow*	Noel-Wil'ms"	Neal	Hoekstra	Commons/Akinbiyi/Iwelumo
	23/9		4,607	*13*				*Saunders 23, King 51*	*Brown*	*Nosworthy*	*Cox*	*Hope*	*Hills*	*Saunders*	*Smith*	*Spiller**	*King^*	*Perpetuini*	*Sidibe*	*Crofts/Johnson T*
								Ref: M Ryan	Saunders nods in Perpetuini's cross. Sidibe's header smacks the bar. Asaba fails to connect with Neal's cross. King curls in from 30 yards. Hall goes for two yellows (64), the second for kicking the ball away. Brown makes a double save to deny Commons and Iwelumo. 'Garbage' rants TP.											

FA Cup																				
3	A	WIMBLEDON		14	D	1-1	1-0	Eustace 12	Cutler	Halls	Hall	Eustace	Thomas	Clarke	Russell	Johnson^	Noel-Willi'ms	Akinbiyi*	Asaba	Greenacre/Hoekstra
	3/1		*3,609*	*24*				*Nowland 72*	*Banks*	*Darlington*	*Lewington*	*Leigertwood*	*Geir*	*McAnuff*	*Reo-Coker*	*Small*	*Agyemang*	*Mackie**	*Nowland*	*Gray*
								Ref: I Williamson	With Taggart cup-tied Clarke plays in central defence. Eustace slots Akinbiyi's knockback. Russell hits the post. Stuart Murdoch's 'Franchise FC' fight back. Nowland fires in from 25 yards on the run. Cutler's fine saves thwart Small and Agyemang. Greenacre nods just over late on.											
3R	H	WIMBLEDON		13	L	0-1	0-1		Cutler	Russell	Clarke	Eustace	Thomas	Halls	Svard"	Neal*	Asaba	Greenacre^	Hoekstra	Commons/Iwelumo/Johnson
	13/1		6,463	*24*				*Nowland 32*	*Banks*	*Darlington*	*Lewington*	*Leigertwood*	*Geir*	*Tapp^*	*McAnuff*	*Nowland*	*Holdsw'rth"*	*Small**	*Gray*	*Gordon/Chorley/Mackie*
								Ref: I Williamson	De Goey, Akinbiyi & GNW are injured. Despite selling leading scorer Patrick Agyemang to Gillingham, Dons push forward. Nowland hits the post, before ramming home a free-kick with Cutler badly positioned behind his wall. City fail to spark. Dons to face Premiership Birmingham.											

	P	W	D	L	F	A	W	D	L	F	A	Pts
		Home					Away					
1 Norwich	46	18	3	2	44	15	10	7	6	35	24	94
2 West Brom	46	14	5	4	34	16	11	6	6	30	26	86
3 Sunderland	46	13	8	2	33	15	9	5	9	29	30	79
4 West Ham	46	12	7	4	42	20	7	10	6	25	25	74
5 Ipswich	46	12	3	8	49	36	9	7	7	35	36	73
6 Crys Palace*	46	10	8	5	34	25	11	2	10	38	36	73
7 Wigan	46	11	8	4	29	16	7	9	7	31	29	71
8 Sheff Utd	46	11	6	6	37	25	9	5	9	28	31	71
9 Reading	46	11	6	6	29	25	9	4	10	26	32	70
10 Millwall	46	11	8	4	28	15	7	7	9	27	33	69
11 STOKE	46	11	7	5	35	24	7	5	11	23	31	66
12 Coventry	46	9	9	5	34	22	8	5	10	33	32	65
13 Cardiff	46	10	6	7	40	25	7	8	8	28	33	65
14 Nott'm For	46	8	9	6	33	25	7	6	10	28	33	60
15 Preston	46	11	7	5	43	29	4	7	12	26	42	59
16 Watford	46	9	8	6	31	28	6	4	13	23	40	57
17 Rotherham	46	8	8	7	31	27	5	7	11	22	34	54
18 Crewe	46	11	3	9	33	26	3	8	12	24	40	53
19 Burnley	46	9	6	8	37	32	4	8	11	23	45	53
20 Derby	46	11	5	7	39	33	2	8	13	14	34	52
21 Gillingham	46	10	1	12	28	34	4	8	11	20	33	51
22 Walsall	46	8	7	8	29	31	5	5	13	16	34	51
23 Bradford	46	6	3	14	23	35	4	3	16	15	34	36
24 Wimbledon	46	3	4	16	21	40	5	1	17	20	49	29
	1104	247	145	160	816	619	160	145	247	619	816	1511

* promoted after play-offs

Odds & ends

Double wins: (4) Bradford, Derby, Watford, Wimbledon.
Double losses: (3) Cardiff, C Palace, Rotherham.

Won from behind: (2) Derby (h), Watford (a).
Lost from in front: (1) Wigan (a).

High spots: The flying start.
The emergence of youngsters Commons, Henry, Wilkinson and Clarke.
The signing of Ade Akinbiyi.
Established as mid-table First Division side.

Low spots: Insistence on defending leads with ten men behind the ball.
Out of the cups early again.
Falling crowds once safety had been assured.

Ever-presents: (1) Darel Russell.
Hat-tricks: (1) Hoekstra v Reading (h).
Leading Scorer: (10) Ade Akinbiyi and Gifton Noel-Williams.
Player of the Year: Ade Akinbiyi.

	Appearances						Goals			
	Lge	*Sub*	LC	*Sub*	FAC	*Sub*	Lge	LC	FAC	Tot
Akinbiyi, Ade	**23**	*7*		*1*	1		**10**			**10**
Andrews, Keith	**16**									
Asaba, Carl	**26**	*11*	1		2		**8**			**8**
Clarke, Clive	**41**	*1*	2		2		**3**			**3**
Commons, Kris	**14**	*18*		*2*		*1*	**4**			**4**
Cutler, Neil	**11**	*4*	1		2					
De Goey, Ed	**35**		1							
Eustace, John	**26**		2		2		**5**		1	**6**
Goodfellow, Mark		*4*	2					1		**1**
Greenacre, Chris	**8**	*5*	1		1	*1*	**2**			**2**
Gunnarsson, Brynjar	**1**	*2*								
Hall, Marcus	**34**	*1*	2		1					
Halls, John	**34**				2					
Henry, Karl	**14**	*6*	1							
Hill, Clint	**9**	*3*								
Hoekstra, Peter	**20**	*4*	1		1	*1*	**4**			**4**
Iwelumo, Chris	**3**	*5*	1	*1*		*1*		1		**1**
Johnson, Richard	**3**	*4*			1	*1*				
Marteinsson, Petur	**3**									
Neal, Lewis	**6**	*12*	1	*1*	1		**1**			**1**
Noel-Williams, Gifton	**40**	*2*	1		1		**10**			**10**
Owen, Gareth	**1**	*2*								
Palmer, Jermaine		*3*								
Richardson, Frazer	**6**						**1**			**1**
Russell, Darel	**46**		2		2		**4**			**4**
Svard, Sebastian	**9**	*4*			1		**1**			**1**
Taggart, Gerry	**21**						**2**			**2**
Thomas, Wayne	**39**		1		2		**3**			**3**
Wilkinson, Andy	**1**	*2*	1							
Williams, Paul	**16**	*3*	1							
Wilson, Brian		*2*		*1*						
(own-goals)										
31 players used	**506**	***108***	**22**	***6***	**22**	***5***	**58**	**2**	**1**	**61**

No	Date		Att	Pos	Pt	F-A	H-T	Scorers, Times, and Referees	SQUAD	NUMBERS	IN	USE								subs used
1	H	WOLVERHAMPTON			W	2-1	0-0	Russell 55, Clarke 70p	De Goey	Halls	Hall	**Brammer**	Taggart	Thomas	Russell	Clarke	N'l-Wil'ams"	Akinbiyi^	Neal*	Henry/Asaba/Greenacre
	8/8		17,066		3			*Miller 87p*	*Jones*	*Clyde*	*Naylor^*	*Olofinjana*	*Craddock*	*Bjorklund"*	*Newton*	*Cameron*	*Miller*	*Sturridge**	*Kennedy*	*Clarke L/Edwards/Cooper*
								Ref: A Kaye	Sky viewers see Stoke dominate. Wolves' Miller and Newton come to blows after a poorly defended corner. City waste five clear-cut chances. Russell drills in off the post. Clyde pulls down Akinbiyi and Clarke nets low to Jones' left. GNW handles a corner. Miller rifles in, but too late.											
2	A	SHEFFIELD UTD		4	D	0-0	0-0		De Goey	Halls	**Barker**	Brammer"	Taggart	Thomas	Russell	Clarke	N'l-Wil'ams !	Akinbiyi	Hall*	Asaba/Henry
	10/8		*19,723*	*16*	4				*Kenny*	*Bromby*	*Wright*	*Morgan*	*Jagielka*	*Montgom'y"*	*Tonge*	*Gray*	*Liddell^*	*Hayles**	*Harley*	*Ward/Quinn/Forte*
								Ref: P Danson	Another tetchy encounter. Akinbiyi and Neil Warnock exchange angry words on the touchline. Akinbiyi's shot is headed off the line. Wright and Gray fire wide. On 53 GNW and Morgan tangle. As they fall a boot catches the Blade in the face. Danson waves a red, but it's overturned.											
3	A	ROTHERHAM		4	D	1-1	0-0	Akinbiyi 84	De Goey	Halls	Barker	Brammer"	Taggart	Thomas	Russell	Clarke	N'l-Williams	Akinbiyi^	Hall*	Asaba/Neal/Henry
	14/8		*5,925*	*18*	5			*Shaw 55*	*Pollitt*	*Stockdale*	*Minto*	*Swailes*	*Gilchrist*	*Sedgwick*	*Garner*	*Mullin*	*Shaw*	*Proctor*	*Barker*	
								Ref: K Hill	GNW's header is saved by Pollitt. De Goey denies Proctor. Shaw scores from 20 yards after Taggart blocks Sedgwick's initial effort. Neal and Asaba liven things up. Pollitt claws away Neal's header but Akinbiyi nets. A draw, but City's Millmoor hoodoo continues. No win in 11 years.											
4	H	GILLINGHAM		3	W	**2-0**	1-0	Noel-Williams 43, Akinbiyi 72	De Goey	Halls	Barker	Brammer	Taggart	Thomas	Russell	Clarke	N'l-Wil'ams"	Akinbiyi^	Neal*	Asaba/Henry/Greenacre
	21/8		13,234	*11*	8				*Banks*	*Hills*	*Hope*	*Ashby*	*Rose"*	*Smith*	*Hes'enthaler*	*Spiller*	*Agyemang**	*Roberts*	*Byfield^*	*Jarvis/Southall/Sidibe*
								Ref: A Leake	Stoke coast to victory. Thomas has a header cleared off the line. Russell's volley flies just wide. GNW scuffs an easy chance but rams home Akinbiyi's cross. Hills has Gills' only effort on target. Akinbiyi curls the ball home from 22 yards. Only Banks keeps the Gills from a hiding.											
5	A	CARDIFF		2	W	1-0	1-0	Noel-Williams 37	De Goey	Halls	Clarke	Brammer	Taggart	Hill	Russell	Henry*	N'l-Williams	Akinbiyi^	Hall	Neal/Asaba
	28/8		*12,929*	*22*	11				*Warner*	*Weston*	*Collins*	*Page*	*Gabbidon*	*Robinson^*	*McAnuff*	*Kavanagh*	*Lee*	*Campbell*	*Boland**	*Parry/Bullock*
								Ref: H Webb	An open match only produces one goal. GNW side-foots in Akinbiyi's pass from 12 yards. Akinbiyi hits a post. Lee heads wide from 8 yards. De Goey tips over Kav's drive and clings on to Lee's header. McAnuff makes a nuisance of himself. Neal's late drive is blocked on the line.											
6	H	DERBY		2	W	1-0	0-0	Hall 90	De Goey	Halls	Clarke	Brammer	Taggart	Thomas	Russell	Neal^	N'l-Wil'ams*	Akinbiyi	Hall	Greenacre/Asaba
	30/8		18,673	*14*	14				*Camp*	*Kenny*	*Huddlestone*	*Johnson*	*Vincent*	*Bisgaard**	*Taylor*	*Idiakez*	*Tudgay^*	*Smith*	*Bolder*	*Peschisolido/Junior*
								Ref: N Barry	On a balmy evening all hell breaks loose when Akinbiyi nets and, as City players celebrate, the ref disallows it. From the quickly taken free-kick Tudgay nets, but that is also ruled out as the ball did not leave the box from the restart. Hall slams in Russell's cross deep into injury-time.											
7	A	PRESTON		3	L	**0-3**	0-1		De Goey	Halls	Hall	Brammer	Taggart	Thomas	Russell^	Clarke	N'l-Williams	Akinbiyi"	Barker*	Greenacre/Asaba/Henry
	11/9		*12,759*	*9*	14			*Cresswell 27, 79, Healy 80*	*Lonergan*	*Alexander*	*Curtis*	*Mawene*	*Lucketti*	*McKenna*	*Etuhu*	*O'Neil B^*	*Cresswell*	*Healy"*	*Lynch**	*Smith/Skora/Jackson*
								Ref: M Atkinson	Hall fires over from 8 yards. GNW has good pen claims waved away. PNE take over. Richard Cresswell twice finds space in the box to fire in. Russell hits Asaba with a shot. Healy's deflected shot sails in. Shell-shocked Stoke see Halls' overhead flies wide and Asaba waste criminally.											
8	H	IPSWICH		1	W	3-2	1-1	Thomas 45, 75, Akinbiyi 85	De Goey*	Halls !	Clarke	Brammer"	Taggart	Thomas	Russell	Henry	N'l-Williams^	Akinbiyi	Hall	**Simonsen**/Asaba/Guppy
	14/9		**23,029**	*3*	17			*De Vos 41, Westlake 62*	*Davis*	*Wilnis^*	*Diallo*	*De Vos*	*Naylor*	*Miller*	*Magilton*	*Horlock*	*Bent*	*Kuqi**	*Westlake*	*Counago/Bowditch*
								Ref: M Dean	Drama aplenty as Joe Royle's leaders are toppled. De Vos plants a header. Westlake slots past Simo. Thommo heads in two right-wing corners. Naylor escapes with a yellow for fouling Akinbiyi. Halls' second yellow is for a tackle on Wilnis (82). Akinbiyi nets after a defensive mix up.											
9	H	NOTT'M FOR		3	D	0-0	0-0		Simonsen	Thomas	Clarke	Brammer^	Taggart	Hill	Russell	Henry*	N'l-Williams	Akinbiyi	Hall	Asaba/**Guppy**
	18/9		21,115	*22*	18				*Gerrard*	*Perch*	*Morgan*	*Doig*	*Rogers*	*Impey*	*Evans*	*Jess*	*Johnson*	*Taylor*	*Commons**	*Robertson*
								Ref: M Thorpe	A tight game sees Thommo head wide. Simo smothers Doig's effort. The returning Kris Commons has a nightmare and is subbed to cheers. Akinbiyi heads straight at Gerrard. City pile on the pressure but Simo denies Rogers as Forest break away. First sign that goals are drying up.											
10	A	BURNLEY		4	D	2-2	1-2	Akinbiyi 34, 50	De Goey	Halls	Clarke	Hill"	Taggart	Thomas	Russell	Brammer^	N'l-Williams	Akinbiyi*	Hall	Asaba/Henry/Guppy
	25/9		*12,981*	*14*	19			*Moore 3, Blake 19p*	*Coyne*	*Duff !*	*Camara*	*Sinclair*	*McGreal*	*Hyde*	*Chaplow*	*Grant**	*Branch*	*Moore*	*Blake*	*Duffy*
								Ref: M Jones	Moore toe-pokes in Blake's free-kick. Hill tumbles Blake and he smashes in the penalty. Stoke fight back. Coyne saves Thommo's header but Akinbiyi bundles in. Duff walks for a second yellow (43) for handball. GNW frees Akinbiyi to beat Coyne. Thommo and Henry miss chances.											
11	A	LEEDS		5	D	0-0	0-0		De Goey	Halls	Clarke	Hill	Taggart	Thomas	Russell	Brammer	N'l-Wil'ams*	Akinbiyi^	Hall	Asaba/Greenacre
	28/9		*25,759*	*15*	20				*Sullivan*	*Kelly*	*Crainey*	*Butler*	*Carlisle*	*Richardson**	*Wright*	*Gregan*	*Deane*	*Ormerod*	*Pugh*	*Joachim*
								Ref: L Mason	A solid rearguard action frustrates Kevin Blackwell's men. Hill stars at left-back. Akinbiyi ploughs a lone furrow up front. Ormerod screws wide when clear. De Goey tips over from Crainey. Akinbiyi clears off the line. Deane nods wide from 5 yards. First point at Leeds in 17 years.											

No	Venue	Opponent	Att	Pos	Res	F-A	H-T	Scorers, Times, and Referees	1	2	3	4	5	6	7	8	9	10	11	subs used
12	H	QP RANGERS		6	L	0-1	0-0		De Goey	Halls	Clarke	Brammer^	Taggart !	Thomas	Russell	Neal"	N'l-Wil'ams*	Akinbiyi	Hall	Asaba/Henry/Hill
	2/10		16,877	*3*	20			*Gallen 69*	*Day*	*Bignot*	*Rose*	*Shittu*	*Santos*	*Cook**	*Bircham^*	*Rowlands"*	*Gallen*	*Furlong*	*Cureton*	*Branco/McLeod/Bean*
								Ref: E Evans	The ref fails to give a pen when Akinbiyi is barged by Santos, having rounded Day. Taggart sees red after Marc Bircham throws himself to the floor when shrugged off by the big Irishman (38). Turmoil ensues. Furlong should walk for a tackle on Thomas, but doesn't. Awful refereeing.											
13	H	READING		7	L	0-1	0-1		De Goey	Halls	Hall	Brammer	Hill	Thomas	Russell	Neal*	N'l-Williams	Akinbiyi	Henry^	Asaba/Guppy
	16/10		15,574	*2*	20			*Shorey 41*	*Hahnemann*	*Murty*	*Shorey*	*Ingimarsson*	*Sonko*	*Little*	*Harper*	*Hughes*	*Goater**	*Kitson"*	*Brooker^*	*Newman/Convey/Owusu*
								Ref: A D'Urso	Clarke and Taggart suspended. Akinbiyi volleys over. Brooker is released by Little but fires at De Goey. Hill whacks against his own bar in clearing. GNW back-heels against a post at the other end. Nicky Shorey's free-kick zips into the top corner. Stoke fail to break down Royals.											
14	A	WEST HAM		9	L	0-2	0-1		De Goey	Halls	Clarke	Hill	Duberry	Thomas	Russell	Henry*	N'l-Williams	Akinbiyi	Hall^	Brammer/Asaba
	19/10		*29,808*	*14*	20			*Harewood 31, Sheringham 59*	*Bywater*	*Mullins*	*Brevett*	*Repka*	*Mackay*	*Lomas*	*Chadwick^*	*Reo-Coker*	*Harewood*	*Zamora"*	*Etherington**	*Sheringham/Fletcher/Rebrov*
								Ref: L Probert	Stoke try bravely but are outclassed by the quick-passing Hammers. Lomas and Reo-Coker run the show. Thommo denies Harewood, but the big striker shoots low to score. Hall wastes City's only opportunity, shooting straight at Bywater. Sheringham flicks home classily to clinch it.											
15	A	LEICESTER		10	D	1-1	1-1	Asaba 37	De Goey	Halls	Clarke	Hill	Duberry	Thomas	Russell	Brammer	Asaba^	Akinbiyi	Hall*	Neal/Noel-Williams
	23/10		*22,882*	*13*	21			*Halls 21 (og)*	*Pressman*	*Makin*	*Stewart*	*Keown**	*Heath*	*Scowcroft*	*Gemmill*	*Nalis*	*Connolly*	*Dublin^*	*Tiatto*	*Elliott/Benjamin*
								Ref: C Webster	In heavy rain Foxes press forward. A Nalis screamer hits Dublin when goalbound. Tiatto's 12-yard shot loops over De Goey off Halls. Asaba ends the 437-minute goal drought by volleying in Akinbiyi's knock-down. Pressman denies Akinbyi and Asaba. A sodden pitch kills the game.											
16	H	MILLWALL		8	W	1-0	0-0	Greenacre 86	De Goey	Thomas	Clarke	Hill	Duberry	Taggart	Russell	Brammer"	Asaba	Akinbiyi^	Neal*	N'l-Williams/Henry/Gr'nacre
	30/10		14,125	*11*	24				*Stack*	*Lawrence*	*Dunne^*	*Ward*	*Elliott*	*Livermore*	*Wise*	*Morris*	*Harris**	*Tessem*	*Hayles*	*Simpson/McCammon*
								Ref: U Rennie	Pulis' 100th game in charge. Hayles is a thorn in City's side as Colin Lee's men have the upper hand. Neal brings a save from Stack. Wise and Taggart square up and see yellow. Asaba and Akinbiyi hit the bar. With stalemate likely Greenacre slides in to convert Akinbiyi's pull-back.											
17	H	WIGAN		10	L	0-1	0-0		De Goey	Thomas	Clarke	Hill^	Duberry	Taggart	Russell	Brammer	Asaba*	Akinbiyi	Greenacre	Noel-Williams/Henry
	2/11		15,882	*1*	24			*McCulloch 87*	*Filan*	*Wright*	*Baines*	*Jackson*	*Breckin*	*Graham*	*Mahon*	*Bullard*	*Ellington**	*Roberts*	*McCulloch*	*Flynn*
								Ref: N Barry	Paul Jewell's unbeaten runaway league leaders are matched by Stoke's work ethic. Filan keeps out a rasper from Russell. Ellington blasts over. Mahon hits the post with an overhead. Another tight game is decided by a late goal. This time McCulloch's 25-yarder swerves into the corner.											
18	A	READING		12	L	0-1	0-1		De Goey*	Halls	Clarke	Brammer	Duberry	Thomas	Russell	Greenacre	N'l-Williams	Akinbiyi	Asaba^	Simonsen/Neal
	6/11		*14,831*	*3*	24			*Kitson 23*	*Hahnemann*	*Murty*	*Shorey*	*Ingimarsson*	*Sonko*	*Little*	*Harper*	*Sidwell*	*Owusu*	*Kitson*	*Morgan**	*Brooker*
								Ref: G Laws	Hill and Taggart are injured. Halls returns. Russell and Asaba test Hahnemann. Brammer has a 30-yarder turned over. De Goey limps off with a groin strain. Royals snuff out City. Greenacre's shot is blocked by the prone Hahnemann and Akinbiyi. Steve Coppell's men merit the points.											
19	H	CREWE		9	W	1-0	0-0	Noel-Williams 64	Simonsen	Halls	Clarke	Brammer	Duberry	Thomas	Russell	Greenacre	N'l-Williams	Akinbiyi	Hall	
	13/11		17,640	*21*	27				*Ince*	*Otsemobor*	*Sorvel*	*Jones B*	*Foster*	*Tonkin*	*Lunt*	*Cochrane**	*Vaughan*	*Rivers*	*Ashton^*	*Varney/Jones S*
								Ref: P Crossley	Both sides waste chances. Duberry and Thomas dominate in defence. GNW nips in front of Jones to nod in Hall's cross. Ashton fires just wide. Ince tips round a GNW shot as City get on top after the break. Hall curls wide. Thommo blocks a late shot. First win over Crewe for 13 years.											
20	A	PLYMOUTH		10	D	0-0	0-0		Simonsen	Thomas	Clarke	Brammer	Duberry	Hill	Russell	Greenacre*	N'l-Williams	Akinbiyi	Asaba^	Neal/Henry
	20/11		*15,264*	*13*	28				*Larrieu*	*Worrell*	*Gilbert*	*Doumbe*	*Coughlan*	*Norris*	*Wotton*	*Friio**	*Evans*	*Crawford*	*Capaldi*	*Makel*
								Ref: P Taylor	An injury ravaged line-up steal a point. Thommo almost marks his 200th game for Stoke, but Larrieu turns away his header, who then saves at Akinbiyi's feet. Simo parries Paul Wotton's pile-driver. Matthias Doumbe nets a header from a corner but the goal is disallowed for pushing.											
21	H	SUNDERLAND		14	L	0-1	0-0		Simonsen	Halls	Clarke	Thomas	Duberry	Hill^	Russell	Brammer	N'l-Williams	Asaba	Greenacre*	Neal/Palmer
	27/11		16,980	*3*	28			*Bridges 83*	*Myhre*	*Wright*	*McCartney*	*Caldwell*	*Breen*	*Lawrence"*	*Whitehead*	*Carter*	*Elliott^*	*Stewart**	*Arca*	*Brown/Bridges/Lynch*
								Ref: U Rennie	Defences dominate as both sides lack a cutting edge. Myhre tips round from Greenacre. Simo saves Elliott's deflected effort. Clarke slips when well placed. Michael Bridges' first goal since May 2000 is a near-post header from a corner. Halls' last-minute header is clawed away. Sterile.											
22	A	WATFORD		9	W	1-0	1-0	Noel-Williams 24	Simonsen	Halls	Clarke	Thomas	Duberry	Hill	Russell	Brammer	N'l-Williams	Akinbiyi*	Asaba^	Henry/Greenacre
	4/12		*12,169*	*16*	31				*Lee*	*Doyley**	*Darlington*	*DeMerit*	*Dyche*	*Chambers*	*Gunnarsson*	*Mahon*	*Young"*	*Dyer^*	*Helguson*	*Devlin/Fitzgerald/Gayle*
								Ref: A Kaye	Another physical encounter with Ray Lewington's League Cup semi-finalists. Halls' shot is saved by Lee. GNW swivels to slot home during a scramble in the box against his old club. Halls has a goal ruled out for offside. Simo saves Darlington's rocket. City quash Hornets' late surge.											
23	H	COVENTRY		9	W	1-0	1-0	Akinbiyi 21	Simonsen	Henry	Clarke	Neal*	Duberry	Hill	Russell	Greenacre	N'l-Williams	Akinbiyi	Asaba"	Owen^/**Dickinson**/Eustace
	11/12		15,744	*21*	34				*Steele*	*Carey*	*Williams**	*Shaw*	*Staunton*	*Doyle*	*Morrell*	*Hughes*	*Adebola*	*Johnson^*	*McSheffrey*	*Laville/John*
								Ref: C Penton	Halls, Thomas and Hall are injured. Hill starts despite a virus and is the hero, bodily throwing himself in front of a succession of goalbound shots. Akinbiyi heads in GNW's knockback and the ball deflects in off Shaw. John's last-minute effort is given offside. Huge test of character.											

No	Date		Att	Pos	Pt	F-A	H-T	Scorers, Times, and Referees	SQUAD	NUMBERS	IN	USE								subs used
24	A	BRIGHTON		6	W	1-0	0-0	Akinbiyi 85	Simonsen	Halls	Clarke	Thomas	Duberry	Hill	Russell	Brammer	N'l-Williams	Akinbiyi	Asaba*	Hall
	17/12		***6,208***	*20*	37				*Kuipers*	*Reid*	*Harding^*	*Hinshelwood*	*Butters*	*Oatway*	*Carpenter*	*Nicolas**	*McCammon*	*Knight*	*Virgo*	*Hammond/Jones*
								Ref: G Salisbury	Simonsen twice thwarts the lively Knight, who is also booked for diving. Asaba heads wide from six yards with the net gaping. Kuipers turns aside Clarke's 20-yarder. Akinbiyi muscles Harding off the ball, cuts in and lashes a left-foot shot in off the post. Back in the play-off places.											
25	H	PRESTON		9	D	0-0	0-0		Simonsen	Halls"	Clarke	Thomas	Duberry	Hill	Russell	Brammer	N'l-Wil'ams*	Akinbiyi	Asaba^	Henry/Greenacre/**Buxton**
	26/12		20,350	*13*	38				*Lonergan*	*Alexander*	*Davidson**	*Mawene*	*Davis*	*McKenna*	*Oliveira"*	*O'Neil B*	*Cresswell*	*Agyemang*	*Lewis*	*Broomes^/Etuhu/Daley*
								Ref: P Robinson	The game starts late due to M6 congestion. It is about as entertaining. The sides cancel each other out. Tackles lack seasonal goodwill. Oliveira heads wide, Duberry smacks a 25 yarder but Lonergan saves at the second attempt. The keeper also turns aside an Akinbiyi header. Anaemic.											
26	A	IPSWICH		9	L	0-1	0-1		Simonsen	Buxton	Clarke	Thomas	Duberry	Hill	Russell"	Brammer*	N'l-Williams^	Akinbiyi	Asaba	Henry/Greenacre/Eustace
	28/12		*26,217*	*1*	38			*Kuqi 34*	*Davis*	*Wilnis*	*Richards*	*De Vos*	*Naylor*	*Miller*	*Magilton**	*Currie*	*Bent*	*Kuqi*	*Westlake*	*Horlock*
								Ref: L Mason	Town dominate the first half, but only have Kuqi's neat goal following a one-two with Westlake to show for it. Miller sees two shots blocked by Thomas. Magilton skies one. City grind their way into the game. Simo tips over from Bent but City again fail to make a clear cut opening.											
27	A	NOTT'M FOR		11	L	0-1	0-0		Simonsen	Buxton	Clarke !	Thomas	Duberry	Hill !	Russell	Henry	Greenacre^	Akinbiyi	Asaba*	Noel-Williams/Eustace
	1/1		*22,051*	*23*	38			*Bopp 67*	*Gerrard*	*Thompson*	*Morgan^*	*Dawson*	*Rogers*	*Doig*	*Bopp*	*Derry*	*Harris**	*Taylor*	*Reid*	*King/Louis-Jean*
								Ref: M Jones	Akinbiyi's scissor-kick is tipped over. Ade has a goal controversially ruled out for offside. On a flooded pitch Forest have a good 15 minutes after half-time. Bopp converts Reid's cross from 8 yards. Hill walks for over-reacting to Thompson's tackle. Clarke sees red after the whistle.											
28	H	BURNLEY		12	L	0-1	0-0		Simonsen	Buxton	Clarke*	Thomas	Duberry	Henry	Russell	Eustace^	N'l-Williams	Akinbiyi	Hall	Neal/Greenacre
	3/1		15,689	*11*	38			*Cahill 79*	*Jensen*	*Duff*	*Camara*	*Sinclair*	*McGreal*	*Cahill*	*Hyde*	*Grant*	*O'Connor*	*Branch*	*Moore*	
								Ref: P Joslin	Eustace's first start for 10 months. Burnley defend in depth and restrict Stoke, with former Potter James O'Connor industrious. Steve Cotterill also receives a hostile welcome. Clarke's shot deflects wide. Henry misses by 6 inches. Gary Cahill pokes in a near-post corner in a scramble.											
29	A	QP RANGERS		14	L	0-1	0-1		Simonsen	Buxton	Clarke	Thomas	Taggart	**Jarrett"**	Russell	Brammer	Greenacre*	Akinbiyi	Hall^	Noel-Wil'ms/Asaba/Eustace
	14/1		*13,559*	*13*	38			*Cook 18*	*Royce*	*Edghill*	*Padula*	*Davies**	*Shittu*	*Cook"*	*Ainsworth*	*Santos*	*Gallen*	*Furlong*	*Cureton^*	*Rose/Bean/McLeod*
								Ref: R Styles	Friday night kick-off for Sky. Neither team is in form. A dreadful game is decided by Lee Cook's left-footed drive on the run. The one moment of class. QPR hold on and Stoke fail to break the packed defence down. Eustace nets a header but it's ruled offside. Greenacre lobs wide.											
30	H	LEEDS		16	L	0-1	0-0		Simonsen	Buxton	Clarke	Thomas	Taggart	Hill*	Russell	Brammer"	N'l-Williams^	Akinbiyi	Jarrett	Asaba/Greenacre/Eustace
	22/1		18,372	*11*	38			*Thomas 72 (og)*	*Sullivan*	*Kelly*	*Wright*	*Butler*	*Carlisle*	*Richardson*	*Lennon**	*Gregan*	*Deane^*	*Healy*	*Pugh*	*Joachim/Ricketts*
								Ref: I Williamson	Leeds arrive with Ken Bates their new financial saviour. 4,000 visiting fans roar them on. City fail to convert heavy pressure. Sullivan denies Clarke. Akinbiyi screws wide. A Stoke player finally hits the net but at the wrong end as Thomas volleys in Healy's cross while trying to clear.											
31	A	WIGAN		13	W	1-0	1-0	Noel-Williams 39	Simonsen	Buxton	Clarke	Eustace*	Taggart	Hill	Greenacre	Brammer	N'l-Williams	Asaba	Hall	Henry
	5/2		9,938	*2*	41				*Filan*	*Eaden*	*Baines^*	*Jackson*	*Thome*	*Teale**	*Mahon*	*Bullard*	*Ellington*	*Roberts*	*McCulloch*	*Johansson/Graham*
								Ref: M Clattenburg	At last a goal, after 584 minutes. And a good one, too, as Eustace looks one way and slips the ball to Clarke who in turn finds Hall to square for the transfer-listed GNW to net. Simonsen denies Ellington with a super save and fingertips Thome's drive aside in the final minute. Good win.											
32	A	MILLWALL		12	W	1-0	1 -0	Jones 15	Simonsen	Buxton	Hall	Henry	Hill	**Harper^**	Russell	Brammer	**Jones^**	N'l-Williams	Greenacre	Neal/Wilkinson"/Owen
	19/2		*11,035*	*9*	44				*Marshall*	*Lawrence*	*Dunne*	*Ward*	*Phillips*	*Craig^*	*Serioux*	*Robinson**	*Dobie*	*Hayles*	*Dichio*	*Sweeney/Quigley*
								Ref: A Kaye	On a bitter afternoon, City defend their early lead like tigers. On-loan Kenwyne Jones (Southampton) converts Harper's cut-back. Hill is a rock and Russell tireless. Wilkinson cuts his head nastily in a challenge with Hayles. 16th consecutive league game with no more than one goal.											
33	H	LEICESTER		11	W	3-2	2-1	Brammer 24, N'l-Wil'ms 34, Taggart 59	Simonsen	Henry	Buxton	Harper*	Hill	Taggart	Russell	Brammer	Jones^	N'l-Williams	Greenacre	Asaba/**Ricketts**
	22/2		14,076	*18*	47			*Williams 15, Gudjonsson 86*	*Walker*	*Stewart*	*Maybury^*	*Dabizas*	*Dublin*	*Tiatto*	*Gudjonsson*	*Hughes**	*Williams*	*Connolly*	*Gillespie*	*De Vries/Heath*
								Ref: M Halsey	A glut of goals in a snowstorm ends the run of 'binary' results. Williams stabs home from close in. Brammer hammers in from 20 yards. GNW nods in Harper's perfect cross. Taggart nods in a corner. Gudjonsson hammers in a free-kick. Foxes should level but Connolly misses badly.											
34	A	COVENTRY		11	D	0-0	0-0		Simonsen	Buxton	Clarke	Harper	Hill	Taggart	Russell	Brammer	Jones^	N'l-Williams	Greenacre*	Neal/Ricketts"/**Gudjons'on**
	28/2		*13,871*	*21*	48				*Bennett !*	*Whing*	*Williams*	*Duffy*	*Staunton*	*Doyle*	*Jorgensen*	*Hughes*	*Benjamin*	*John**	*McSheffrey*	*Johnson*
								Ref: J Singh	Last visit to crumbling Highfield Road. Simonsen makes three top saves as Coventry pile forward. Bennett walks for handling outside his area. Stand in Stephen Hughes saves from Neal. Taggart upends McSheffrey. Simo saves his pen low to the right. Stoke can't make extra man pay.											

No	Venue	Opponent	Att	Pos	Pts	Res	H-T	Scorers, Times, and Referees	1	2	3	4	5	6	7	8	9	10	11	Subs used
35	H	BRIGHTON		10	W	**2-0**	2-0	Noel-Williams 39p, 44p	Simonsen	Thomas	Clarke^	Hill	Duberry	Taggart	Russell	Brammer	Jones	N'l-Wil'ams"	Harper*	Henry/Greenacre/**Clark**
	5/3		14,906	*16*	51				*Shabaan*	*Reid*	*Harding*	*Hinshelwood*	*Butters*	*Hart*	*Carpenter*	*Nicolas"*	*McCammon^*	*Knight*	*McPhee**	*Oatway/Jones/El-Abd*
								Ref: R Booth	City dominate throughout, but only net through two GNW pens when McCammon upends Duberry and Taggart has his shirt pulled at a corner. Harper's trickery bemuses Brighton and only Shabaan's saves deny GNW and Clarke from his crosses. Jones skews wide from six yards out.											
36	H	SHEFFIELD UTD		8	W	**2-0**	0-0	Noel-Williams 57, 59	Simonsen	Thomas	Clarke	Hill	Duberry	Taggart	Russell	Brammer	Jones^	N'l-Wil'ams"	Harper*	Henry/Greenacre/Ricketts
	12/3		17,019	*9*	54				*Kenny*	*Bromby*	*Harley*	*Morgan*	*Geary*	*Jagielka*	*Thirlwell*	*Gray*	*Cadermart'ri*	*Francis*	*Quinn*	
								Ref: S Mathieson	Stoke survive as Harley's dipping volley cracks the bar and bounces off Simo's neck onto a post. Neil Warnock's Blades look dangerous. Hill takes a quick free-kick and GNW cuts in from the right to curl home. He then heads in Thommo's cross. Just three points from the play-offs.											
37	A	GILLINGHAM		10	L	1-2	0-1	Jones 54	Simonsen	Thomas	Clarke*	Hill	Duberry	Taggart^	Russell	Brammer	Jones	N'l-Wil'ams"	Harper	Greenacre/Buxton/Ricketts
	15/3		*7,766*	*22*	54			*McEveley 2, Smith 70*	*Banks"*	*Nosworthy*	*McEveley*	*Cox*	*Hope*	*Smith*	*Southall*	*Flynn*	*Henderson^*	*Sidibe*	*Douglas*	*Byfield/Bossu*
								Ref: R Styles	Stan Ternent's strugglers dominate. McEveley's whipped free-kick creeps in. Jones' towering header beats Banks and he turns a somersault in celebration. Smith lashes in from 20 yards with Taggart off the field receiving treatment for a gash. A hopeful travelling support trudge home.											
38	A	WOLVERHAMPTON		11	D	1-1	1-0	Noel-Williams 41	Simonsen	Thomas	Clarke	Hill	Duberry	Taggart	Russell	Brammer	Jones*	N'l-Williams^	Henry	Harper/Ricketts
	19/3		*28,103*	*13*	55			*Cort 90*	*Oakes*	*Clyde*	*Naylor*	*Olofinjana*	*Craddock*	*Bjorklund*	*Newton*	*Cameron*	*Miller*	*Cort*	*Kennedy**	*Ricketts*
								Ref: C Foy	Wolves have one defeat in 17, but City are the better side. Brammer hits the bar and forces Oakes to save. GNW nets a low left-foot shot. He then misses an easier chance. Stoke hold on manfully in the gleaming sunshine. Cort heads home Naylor's free-kick. Terrible disappointment.											
39	H	ROTHERHAM		11	L	1-2	0-1	Noel-Williams 83	Simonsen	Thomas	Clarke*	Hill	Duberry !	Taggart	Russell	Brammer"	Ricketts^	N'l-Williams	Harper	Neal/Asaba/Henry
	2/4		16,552	*28*	55			*Butler 23, Noel-Williams 90 (og)*	*Pollitt*	*Scott*	*Hurst*	*Swailes*	*McIntosh*	*Mullin*	*McLaren*	*Keane**	*Camp'-Ryce*	*Butler*	*Thorpe^*	*Barker/Hoskins*
								Ref: G Salisbury	Alan Knill's Millers are bottom by miles. Swailes denies on-loan Ricketts (Leeds). Simo palms away McLaren's rasper. Buter nods in. Stoke struggle. GNW nods in late on, but Simo palms a McIntosh shot onto his knees which rebounds in. Duberry sees a second yellow. Season over.											
40	H	CARDIFF		11	L	1-3	1-1	Hill 40	Simonsen	Buxton	Hill	Neal*	Thomas	Taggart	Russell	Brammer	Jones"	N'l-Williams	Harper^	Asaba/Henry/Gudjonsson
	5/4		**12,785**	*17*	55			*Jerome 26, 58, Thorne 60p*	*Alexander*	*Vidmar*	*Barker*	*Collins*	*Gabbidon*	*Ardley*	*McAnuff*	*Ledley*	*Thorne**	*Jerome^*	*Langley*	*Lee/Boulding*
								Ref: A Hall	Stoke have nothing to fight for. It shows. Jerome pounces on Taggart's error. Hill fires in a 25-yarder. Neal nods against the post. GNW misses when trying to finish off a goalbound Jones header. Jerome races clear to chip in. Buxton brings down McAnuff. Thorne slots the pen coolly.											
41	A	DERBY		12	L	1-3	1-2	Taggart 7	Simonsen	Buxton	Clarke	Hill	Thomas*	Taggart	Russell	Brammer	Greenacre"	N'l-Williams^	Asaba	Neal/Ricketts/Clark
	9/4		*27,640*	*5*	55			*Raziak 8, Bisgaard 45, Idiakez 79*	*Camp*	*Makin*	*Kenna*	*Johnson*	*Konjic*	*Bisgaard*	*Hud'lestone^*	*Idiakez*	*Tudgay*	*Smith*	*Raziak**	*Peschisolido/Bolder*
								Ref: M Halsey	Taggart glances in Brammer's free-kick. George Burley's play-off bound Rams hit back when Raziak twists to fire in. Bisgaard sweeps home from a quick corner. City get on top. Neal twice stings Camp's hands. Somehow Idiakez's corner eludes everyone and creeps in. Game over.											
42	H	PLYMOUTH		11	W	**2-0**	2-0	Jones 28, Russell 41	Simonsen	Buxton	Clarke*	Duberry	Hill	Taggart	Russell	Brammer	Jones^	N'l-Williams	Greenacre"	Neal/Henry/**Paterson**
	16/4		13,017	*15*	58				*McCormick*	*Worrell*	*Dodd*	*Aljofree*	*Coughlan*	*Norris*	*Wotton"*	*Buzsacky*	*Taylor**	*Evans^*	*Blackstock*	*Capaldi/Chadwick/Lasley*
								Ref: C Boyseon	A bizarre start sees Argyle miss two open goals and City one before Jones nods home Brammer's cross. Russell nets a deflected shot. GNW fires over from 12 yards after beating four players superbly. Simo palms away Worrell's pile-driver. Greenacre shoots straight at McCormick.											
43	H	WEST HAM		11	L	0-1	0-0		Simonsen	Buxton^	Clarke	Duberry	Hill	Taggart	Russell	Brammer	Jones"	N'l-Williams	Greenacre*	Neal/Henry/Ricketts
	19/4		14,534	*7*	58			*Zamora 76*	*Walker*	*Repka**	*Powell*	*Ferdinand*	*Ward*	*Newton*	*Mullins^*	*Reo-Coker*	*Harewood"*	*Sheringham*	*Etherington*	*Zamora/Fletcher/Chadwick*
								Ref: G Laws	Alan Pardew's Hammers are desperate to make the play-offs. Walker saves point blank from Jones and Harewood skies over from 5 yards in the first minute. End to end, both sides waste a hatful of chances. Zamora taps in Harewood's knockback from 5 yards. GNW twice fires over.											
44	A	CREWE		10	W	**2-0**	0-0	Neal 79, Noel-Williams 89	Simonsen	Henry	Clarke	Neal	Duberry	Taggart	Russell	Brammer	Jones*	N'l-Williams	Greenacre	Ricketts
	23/4		*9,166*	*21*	61				*Ince*	*Moss*	*McCready*	*Murdock**	*Tonkin*	*Sorvel*	*Lunt*	*Varney*	*Vaughan*	*Rivers*	*White^*	*Walker/Higdon*
								Ref: R Beeby	Crewe level on points with Brighton in relegation zone. Dario Gradi's men play possession football, but Stoke have the cutting edge. Vaughan fires inches wide. GNW heads Ricketts' cross just past the post. Greenacre nods back for Neal to fire in. GNW turns ten yards out to lash in.											
45	H	WATFORD		12	L	0-1	0-0		Simonsen	Henry	Clarke*	Neal^	Duberry	Taggart	Russell	Brammer	Jones"	N'l-Williams	Greenacre	Halls/Ricketts/Paterson
	30/4		15,229	*16*	61			*Helguson 51*	*Chamberlain*	*Doyley*	*Chambers*	*DeMerit^*	*Cullip*	*Blizzard*	*Bouazza"*	*Mahon**	*Young*	*Dyer*	*Helguson*	*Bangura/Cox/McNamee*
								Ref: M Atkinson	Helguson scores again, his 5th goal in 6 games against City. Stoke, in next season's all-black away kit, fail to trouble Watford's 40-year-old keeper. Greenacre clips the bar. Stoke end with four strikers. Just 22 home goals all season. The club is put up for sale by the Icelanders.											
46	A	SUNDERLAND		12	L	0-1	0-0		Simonsen	Buxton	Clarke	Henry*	Duberry	Taggart	Russell	Brammer	Jones^	N'l-Wil'ams"	Greenacre	Halls/Ricketts/Paterson
	8/5		**47,350**	*1*	61			*Robinson 57*	*Alnwick*	*Wright*	*McCartney*	*Caldwell*	*Breen^*	*Lawrence*	*Whitehead*	*Robinson*	*Brown**	*Stewart"*	*Arca*	*Elliott/Collins/Welsh*
Average	Home 16,455		Away 17,728					Ref: A Leake	Mick McCarthy's champions celebrate promotion. Simonsen, back in his home town, denies Whitehead and McCartney. Henry shoots over. Greenacre fires wide. Lawrence's free-kick is converted by Carl Robinson. City fail to make any chances. Uncertainty reigns at the Brit.											

Carling Cup		Att		F-A	H-T	Scorers, Times, and Referees	SQUAD	NUMBERS	IN	USE								subs used
1 A OLDHAM			3	1-2	1-0	Asaba 25	Simonsen	Halls	Hall	Thomas !	Hill	Henry	Russell	Clarke	Asaba^	Greenacre*	Neal"	Brammer/N'l-Wil's/Akinbiyi
24/8		2,861	*1:20*			*Eyres 72, 75p*	*Pogliacomi*	*Holden*	*Haining**	*Arber*	*Griffin*	*Eyre*	*Bushell*	*Bonner*	*Killen^*	*Johnson*	*Eyres*	*Beherall/Barlow*
						Ref: T Parkes	Asaba nets clinically from 16 yards. Referee Parkes books Thommo twice, keeper Pogliacomi writhing as if pole-axed when barely touched for the second. 40-year-old David Eyres heads in Beherall's cross. Johnson's overhead hits Hill on the arm for a pen. Out in the first round again.											

FA Cup																		
3 A ARSENAL			12	1-2	1-0	Thomas 45	Simonsen	Buxton	Clarke*	Thomas	Taggart	Halls"	Russell	Greenacre^	Akinbiyi	Jarrett	Hall	Eustace/Henry/Asaba
9/1		36,579	*P:2*			*Reyes 52, van Persie 70*	*Lehmann*	*Eboue**	*Clichy*	*Vieira*	*Toure*	*Senderos*	*Pennant*	*Fabregas*	*Reyes*	*van Persie*	*Pires*	*Hoyte*
						Ref: N Barry	A huge travelling support rouses the Highbury library in its final season. City look sound against Wenger's second string. Thomas prods in to great joy after Lehmann saved Akinbiyi's header. Reyes rounds off a fine move. Van Persie guides in a right-wing cross to nick it. Good effort.											

		Home						Away					
		P	W	D	L	F	A	W	D	L	F	A	Pts
1	Sunderland	46	16	4	3	45	21	13	3	7	31	20	94
2	Wigan	46	13	5	5	42	15	12	7	4	37	20	87
3	Ipswich	46	17	3	3	53	26	7	10	6	32	30	85
4	Derby	46	10	7	6	38	30	12	3	8	33	30	76
5	Preston	46	14	7	2	44	22	7	5	11	23	36	75
6	West Ham*	46	12	5	6	36	24	9	5	9	30	32	73
7	Reading	46	13	7	3	33	15	6	6	11	18	29	70
8	Sheff Utd	46	9	7	7	28	23	9	6	8	29	33	67
9	Wolves	46	9	11	3	40	26	6	10	7	32	33	66
10	Millwall	46	12	5	6	33	22	6	7	10	18	23	66
11	QP Rangers	46	10	7	6	32	26	7	4	12	22	32	62
12	STOKE	46	11	2	10	22	18	6	8	9	14	20	61
13	Burnley	46	10	7	6	26	19	5	8	10	12	20	60
14	Leeds	46	7	10	6	28	26	7	8	8	21	26	60
15	Leicester	46	8	8	7	24	20	4	13	6	25	26	57
16	Cardiff	46	10	4	9	24	19	3	11	9	24	32	54
17	Plymouth	46	9	8	6	31	23	5	3	15	21	41	53
18	Watford	46	5	10	8	25	25	7	6	10	27	34	52
19	Coventry	46	8	7	8	32	28	5	6	12	29	45	52
20	Brighton	46	7	7	9	24	29	6	5	12	16	36	51
21	Crewe	46	6	8	9	37	38	6	6	11	29	48	50
22	Gillingham	46	10	6	7	22	23	2	8	13	23	43	50
23	Nott'm For	46	7	10	6	26	28	2	7	14	16	38	44
24	Rotherham	46	2	7	14	17	34	3	7	13	18	35	29
		1104	235	162	155	762	580	155	162	235	580	762	1494

* promoted after play-offs

Odds & ends

Double wins: (3) Brighton, Crewe, Millwall.
Double losses: (4) QPR, Reading, Sunderland, West Ham.

Won from behind: (2) Ipswich (h), Leicester (h).
Lost from in front: (1) Arsenal FAC (a), Derby (a), Oldham LC (a).

High Spots: Another flying start after defeating Ipswich with ten men.
Taking the lead at Highbury against Arsenal in the FA Cup.
Getting to within three points of the play-off positions in mid-March.
The signings of Clint Hill, Michael Duberry and Johnny Halls.

Low spots: Only 22 home goals scored and 14 away.
The monotony of half a season of 'binary' results.
Out of the cups early again.
The late season slump with home defeats by Rotherham and Cardiff.
The stand-off between manager and board over signing foreign players.
Akinbiyi's sitdown protest and eventual departure.

Ever-presents: (0).
Hat-tricks: (0).
Leading Scorer: (13) Gifton Noel-Williams.
Player of the Year: Clint Hill.

	Appearances						Goals			
	Lge	*Sub*	LC	*Sub*	FAC	*Sub*	Lge	LC	FAC	Tot
Akinbiyi, Ade	**29**			*1*	1		7			7
Asaba, Carl	**14**	*19*	1			*1*	1	1		2
Barker, Chris	**4**									
Brammer, Dave	**42**	*1*		*1*			1			1
Buxton, Lewis	**14**	*2*			1					
Clark, Chris		*2*								
Clarke, Clive	**42**		1		1		1			1
De Goey, Ed	**17**									
Dickinson, Carl		*1*								
Duberry, Michael	**25**									
Eustace, John	**2**	*5*				*1*				
Greenacre, Chris	**18**	*14*	1		1		1			1
Gudjonsson, Toddi		*2*								
Guppy, Steve		*4*								
Hall, Marcus	**18**	*1*	1		1		1			1
Halls, John	**20**	*2*	1		1					
Harper, Kevin	**8**	*1*								
Henry, Karl	**13**	*20*	1			*1*				
Hill, Clint	**31**	*1*	1				1			1
Jarrett, Jason	**2**				1					
Jones, Kenwyne	**13**						3			3
Neal, Lewis	**11**	*13*	1				1			1
Noel-Williams, Gifton	**41**	*5*		*1*			13			13
Owen, Gareth		*2*								
Palmer, Jermaine		*1*								
Paterson, Martin		*3*								
Ricketts, Michael	**1**	*10*								
Russell, Darel	**45**		1		1		2			2
Simonsen, Steve	**29**	*2*	1		1					
Taggart, Gerry	**31**				1		2			2
Thomas, Wayne	**35**		1		1		2		1	3
Wilkinson, Andy		*1*								
32 players used	**506**	***112***	**11**	***3***	**11**	***3***	**36**	**1**	**1**	**38**

No	Date		Att	Pos	Pt	F-A	H-T	Scorers, Times, and Referees	SQUAD	NUMBERS	IN	USE								subs used
1	H	SHEFFIELD WED			D	0-0	0-0		Simonsen	Halls	**Broomes**	**Hoefkens**	Taggart !	**Junior"**	**Chadwick**	Brammer	**Sidibe**	Russell*	**Kolar^**	Buxton/Harper/Henry
	6/8		18,744		1				*Lucas*	*Simek*	*Hills*	*Lee*	*Wood*	*Eagles^*	*Rocastle*	*Whelan*	*Peacock*	*Best**	*Brunt*	*Proudlock/Partridge*
								Ref: M Clattenburg	Pulis has gone. Forced out. New boss Dutchman Johan Boskamp has six new signings on show. One of them, Carl Hoefkens, pirouettes on the ball to win a pen. Harper skies it (75). Taggart is unlucky to see red (13) for a tackle on Best. City play 4-5-1 with giant Mama Sidibe up front.											
2	A	LEICESTER		21	L	2-4	0-1	Broomes 64, Halls 89	Simonsen	Halls	Broomes	Hoefkens	Duberry	Junior !	Chadwick	Brammer	Sidibe	Russell*	Kolar	**Dyer**
	9/8		*20,519*	*12*	1			*De Vries 14, Connolly 66, 82, 90*	*Douglas*	*Gilbert*	*Maybury*	*Johansson*	*McCarthy*	*Sylla**	*Gudjonsson*	*Williams*	*Connolly*	*De Vries*	*Wilcox*	*Hammond*
								Ref: P Taylor	A second red of the season as Junior walks for an off-the-ball scuffle with Gudjonsson (61). That sparks a mad 5 mins in which Broomes nets acrobatically and then Connolly begins his finishing masterclass for a treble. Halls finished coolly but in vain. Russell tears a hamstring.											
3	A	MILLWALL		14	W	1-0	1-0	Halls 38	Simonsen	Halls	Broomes	Hoefkens	Duberry	Henry	Chadwick	Brammer	Sidibe	Dyer*	Kolar	Harper
	13/8		*8,668*	*24*	4				*Marshall*	*Lawrence*	*Phillips*	*Vincent*	*Elliott^*	*Dunne*	*Livermore*	*Hutchison"*	*Hayles*	*Morris*	*Simpson**	*Fangueiro/Peeters/Igoe*
								Ref: P Walton	Hayles shoots narrowly wide. Dyer nets from Sidibe's quick free-kick, but is offside. That's the end of the action after 2 mins. Halls rounds off a sweeping move to lash in. Few other chances created as defences dominate. First win for the new boss who's off to Europe to find a striker.											
4	H	LUTON		9	W	2-1	0-1	Broomes 63, Brammer 90	Simonsen	Halls	Broomes	Hoefkens	Duberry	Henry	Chadwick	Brammer	Sidibe	Dyer	Kolar*	Harper
	20/8		18,653	*6*	7			*Morgan 9*	*Beresford*	*Foley*	*Underwood*	*Davies*	*Heikkinen*	*Nicholls*	*Brkovic"*	*Robinson*	*Howard !*	*Feeney^*	*Morgan**	*Davies/Showumni/Edwards*
								Ref: A D'Urso	Newly promoted Luton are bright. Dean Morgan hammers home a left-foot shot after being left unmarked. The game is changed when Howard sees red for spitting (26). Simo denies Feeney. Broomes' volley squirms through Beresford's hands. Brammer hammers in a 30-yard special.											
5	A	CRYS PALACE		13	L	0-2	0-1		Simonsen	Buxton	Broomes	Hoefkens	Duberry	Henry	Chadwick"	Brammer	Sidibe	Junior^	Kolar*	Harper/Dyer/Wilkinson
	27/8		*17,637*	*12*	7			*Johnson 44, 85*	*Kiraly*	*Boyce*	*Borrowdale*	*Hall*	*Ward*	*Watson**	*Leigertwood*	*Soares*	*Johnson*	*Macken"*	*McAnuff^*	*Hughes/Riihilahti/Morrison*
								Ref: M Atkinson	Andy Johnson proves the difference, netting his 4th and 5th of the season. He also hits the post. Sidibe brings the first save from Kiraly on 54 mins. He also heads wide when well placed. Kolar and Hoefkens go close. Boskamp needs a new striker before the window closes on Weds.											
6	H	NORWICH		7	W	3-1	2-1	Kolar 9, Harper 45, Sidibe 69	Simonsen	Buxton	Broomes	Hoefkens	Duberry	Junior*	Chadwick"	Brammer	Sidibe	Harper^	Kolar	Henry/**Gallagher**/Dyer
	29/8		14,249	*23*	10			*Ashton 38*	*Green*	*Colin*	*Charlton*	*Fleming*	*Shackell*	*Marney*	*Huckerby !*	*Safri*	*Brennan*	*McKenzie**	*Ashton^*	*McVeigh/Doherty*
								Ref: M Pike	The first sign of the promised attacking football. City outpass and outplay Nigel Worthington's men. Kolar nets from close range. Harper curls in a left-footed pearler. Huckerby walks for bad language (51). Sidibe smashes in a half-cleared corner – first goal by a City striker this season.											
7	H	WATFORD		10	L	**0-3**	0-1		Simonsen !	Buxton	Broomes	Hoefkens	Duberry	Junior	Chadwick"	Brammer	Sidibe	Harper*	Kolar^	Gallagher/De Goey/Dyer
	10/9		14,565	*3*	10			*Devlin 24, Young 67, King 72*	*Foster*	*Chambers*	*Stewart^*	*Mackay*	*Carlisle*	*Devlin**	*Blizzard"*	*Spring*	*King*	*Young*	*McNamee*	*Doyley/Bouazza/Bangura*
								Ref: N Miller	Sidibe misses a sitter. Buxton hits the bar. Devlin bullets in a header. Young's free-kick curls in untouched. Yet another dismissal as Simo fells Young inside the box (70). De Goey cannot save the penalty. City miss Taggart's organisation. Aidy Boothroyd's men are worthy winners.											
8	A	HULL		6	W	1-0	0-0	Gallagher 74	De Goey	Buxton	Broomes	Hoefkens	Duberry	Henry*	Gallagher	Brammer	Sidibe	Harper^	Kolar"	Russell/Dyer/Junior
	13/9		*18,692*	*14*	13				*Myhill*	*Coles*	*Edge*	*Cort*	*Delaney*	*France**	*Woodhouse"*	*Elliott*	*Welsh*	*Barmby*	*Brown^*	*Price/Green/Burgess*
								Ref: C Webster	First visit to the KC Stadium. Delaney heads against the bar. Broomes fells Barmby but no pen given. Sidibe hits the bar. Duberry wins a great tackle to start a move which ends in Gallagher netting his first from 8 yards. The defence holds firm as Hull go 4-3-3 with Duberry impressive.											
9	A	PRESTON		4	W	1-0	0-0	Gallagher 76	Simonsen	Buxton	Broomes	Hoefkens	Duberry	Chadwick*	Russell	Brammer	Sidibe^	Gallagher	Kolar	Harper/Dyer
	16/9		*12,453*	*7*	16				*Nash*	*Alexander*	*Davidson*	*Lucketti*	*Davis*	*O'Neil**	*Sedgwick^*	*McKenna*	*Agyemang"*	*Nugent*	*Jones*	*Nowland/Anyinsah/Dichio*
								Ref: G Laws	After a quiet start Agyemang misses when Brammer and Simo get in a muddle. Simo makes a double save from Jones and Agyemang. Kolar robs Alexander and sets up Gallagher to net. The defence stands sold in the face of a late flurry from Billy Davies' side. 'I like' says Boskamp.											
10	H	WOLVERHAMPTON		6	L	1-3	0-1	Buxton 90	Simonsen	Buxton	Broomes	Hoefkens	Duberry	Chadwick*	Russell	Brammer^	Sidibe	Gallagher	Kolar"	Harper/Junior/Dyer
	24/9		18,183	*5*	16			*Cort 42, Miller 48, Naylor 73*	*Oakes*	*Edwards*	*Lescott*	*Naylor*	*Cameron*	*Ricketts*	*Kennedy*	*Gyepes*	*Miller**	*Cort*	*Seol*	*Ndah*
								Ref: M Atkinson	Russell blazes over. Sidibe should have a pen after being bowled over by Gyepes. Wolves take over as City wilt. Seol crosses for Cort to score. Gallagher races clear but spoons over. Miller nods in Seol's cross. Naylor blasts a 30-yard free-kick. Buxton nods in a corner for his first goal.											
11	H	CARDIFF		7	L	**0-3**	0-3		Simonsen	Buxton	Broomes	Hoefkens	Duberry	Chadwick*	Russell	Junior	Sidibe	Gallagher	Harper	Kolar
	27/9		12,240	*9*	16			*Jerome 10, 43, Purse 12,*	*Alexander*	*Weston*	*Barker*	*Purse*	*Loovens*	*Koumas*	*Whitley*	*Ledley*	*Ricketts**	*Jerome*	*Cooper^*	*Lee/Parry*
								Ref: R Beeby	Cameron Jerome nets a second brace in a convincing Cardiff win at the Brit in succession. Poor defending sees hum finish through balls from Koumas and Ledley. Prior nods in as the defence crumbles. Sidibe wastes City's only chance. Six conceded in consecutive home games. Awful.											

No	Venue	Opponent	Att	Pos	Res	Pts	FT	HT	Scorers, Times, and Referees	1	2	3	4	5	6	7	8	9	10	11	Subs used
12	A	PLYMOUTH		10	L		1-2	0-0	Chadwick 47	Simonsen	Buxton	Broomes	Hoefkens	Duberry	Chadwick"	Russell	Junior	Sidibe^	Gallagher	Kolar*	**Sigurdsson**/Dyer/Henry
	1/10		*12,604*	*20*		16			*Russell 50 (og), Buzsacky 77*	*Larrieu*	*Barness*	*Brevett*	*Doumbe*	*Aljofree*	*Wotton*	*Norris*	*Gudjonsson**	*Chadwick^*	*Evans*	*Capaldi*	*Buzsacky/Taylor*
									Ref: M Russell	City are better. Neat passing and good movement, but little end product. Chadwick rounds Larrieu. Simo saves from Capaldi but it rebounds in off Russell. Buzsacky slots home unmarked. Gallagher and Sigurdsson both hit the post. Tony Pulis gains revenge over his former employers.											
13	A	DERBY		14	L		1-2	0-1	Hoefkens 59	Simonsen	Buxton	Broomes	Hoefkens	Duberry	Chadwick^	Russell	Brammer	Sidibe	Gallagher	Sigurdsson*	**Bangoura**/Kolar
	15/10		*22,229*	12		16			*Idiakezs 45, Peschisolido 86*	*Poole*	*Kenna*	*Whittingham*	*Davies*	*Johnson M*	*Bisgaard*	*Johnson S*	*Idiakez*	*Peschiso'o"*	*Smith^*	*El Hamd'ui**	*Tudgay/Jackson/Nyatanga*
									Ref: K Stroud	Rams dominate with Smith and Bisgaard causing problems on the flanks. Simo makes four good stops before Inigo Idiakez nets from 20 yards. Hoefkens scores his first goal off the post. Peschisolido sinks his former club, converting Bisgaard's cross. Incapable of keeping a clean sheet.											
14	H	CREWE		9	W		2-0	1-0	Bangoura 41, Duberry 64	Simonsen	Buxton	Broomes	Hoefkens	Duberry !	Chadwick*	Russell	Brammer	Bangoura	Gallagher^	Sigurdsson"	Sidibe/Henry/**Sweeney**
	18/10		14,080	*23*		19				*Williams*	*Moss*	*Tonkin*	*Foster*	*McCready*	*Lunt*	*Jones B*	*Cochran**	*Varney*	*Vaughan^*	*Rodgers"*	*Roberts/Jones S/Suhaj*
									Ref: N Miller	Gallagher prompts Stoke forward. Simo blocks from Varney with his legs. Broomes plams away a shot but the ref is unsighted. Bangoura cuts inside to thrash low past Williams. Duberry nods in a clinching second. Duberry goes for elbowing Suhaj. Is the new strikeforce coming good?											
15	H	READING		11	L		0-1	0-0		Simonsen	Buxton	Broomes	Hoefkens	Taggart"	Chadwick*	Russell	Brammer	Bangoura	Gallagher	Kolar^	Sidibe/Sweeney/Wilkinson
	22/10		13,484	*2*		19			*Kitson 77p*	*Hahnemann*	*Makin**	*Shorey*	*Sonko*	*Ingimarsson*	*Gunnarsson*	*Little^*	*Harper*	*Kitson*	*Doyle*	*Convey"*	*Sidwell/Oster/Hunt*
									Ref: G Salisbury	Taggart returns to add much needed defensive stability. Steve Coppell's runaway leaders are not tested much at the back. Convey flashes wide. Gunnarsson wastes two good chances. Dave Kitson scores the winner again, picking himself up after being floored by Buxton to score the pen.											
16	A	SOUTHAMPTON		14	L		0-2	0-1		Simonsen	Halls	Broomes !	Hoefkens	Wilkinson	Junior	Russell	Brammer	Sidibe	Gallagher*	Sigurdsson^	Paterson/Sweeney
	29/10		*24.095*	*7*		19			*Walcott 16, Belmadi 90*	*Niemi*	*Delap*	*Svensson*	*Lundekvam*	*Higginbot'm*	*Wise*	*Belmadi*	*Quashie*	*Fuller**	*McCann*	*Walcott*	*Jones*
									Ref: R Oliver	Halls submits a transfer request. Defensive frailties bring yet another red card as Broomes elbows 16-year-old Theo Walcott. Boskamp is also dismissed as he races onto the pitch to protest. Walcott nets Quashie's pass. Belmadj kills it in injury-time. 'It was never a red' rages Boskamp.											
17	A	COVENTRY		12	W		2-1	1-1	Taggart 37, Gallagher 55	Simonsen	Halls	Buxton	Hoefkens	Taggart	Sigurdsson	Russell	Brammer	Sidibe	Gallagher*	Bangoura	Henry
	2/11		*16,617*	*21*		22			*Nalis 12*	*Fulop*	*Hall*	*Page*	*Hughes*	*Duffy*	*Doyle*	*Heath*	*Impey**	*Adebola*	*Scowcroft*	*Nalis^*	*Davis/Thornton*
									Ref: L Probert	A frantic game sees Lilian Nalis net after another defensive cock up. A storm brews between the management after John Rudge's intervention from the stands helps the team reorganise to turn things around. Taggart hammers home a peach of a volley. Gallagher curls a 25-yard pearler.											
18	H	BRIGHTON		9	W		**3-0**	1-0	Bangoura 35, 75, Russell 68	Simonsen	Halls	Buxton	Hoefkens	Duberry	Sigurdsson*	Russell	Brammer	Sidibe	Gallagher^	Bangoura"	Chadwick/Henry/Junior
	5/11		15,274	*22*		25				*Blayney*	*Hart*	*Reid*	*McShane*	*Butters*	*Carole*	*Nicolas*	*Hammond*	*Frutos*	*Robinson**	*Kaz'-Rich's^*	*McPhee/Turienzo*
									Ref: K Wright	In a poor first half Simo tips over a Frutos free-kick. Bangoura nicks a goal from Gallagher's pass. Chadwick's introduction allows City to gel. Gallagher curls onto the bar from 25 yards. Russell celebrates a new contract by ramming in a loose ball. Bangoura nods in Chadwick's cross.											
19	A	CREWE		8	W		2-1	1-0	Bangoura 16, Gallagher 89	Simonsen	Halls	Buxton	Hoefkens	Duberry	Chadwick*	Russell	Brammer	Sidibe	Gallagher^	Bangoura	Sigurdsson/Henry
	18/11		*8,942*	*19*		28			*Johnson 90*	*Williams*	*Moss*	*Tonkin*	*Foster*	*Walker*	*Lunt*	*Jones B*	*Roberts G'y^*	*Jones S*	*Vaughan**	*Higdon*	*Rivers/Johnson*
									Ref: A Woolmer	City dominate for long periods. Williams saves from Chadwick and Russell. Bangoura races onto Brammer's ball to net. Higdon heads against the post as defensive frailties continue. Chadwick creates and Gallagher curls in a beauty. Alex miss three good chances but Johnson volleys in.											
20	H	DERBY		11	L		1-2	1-0	Bangoura 33	Simonsen	Halls	Buxton	Hoefkens	Duberry	Chadwick	Russell	Henry	Sidibe	Gallagher*	Bangoura	Sigurdsson
	22/11		13,205	17					*Smith 64, Nyatanga 69*	*Camp*	*Edworthy*	*Jackson*	*Davies*	*Nyatanga*	*Tudgay^*	*Thirlwell*	*Idiakez**	*Johnson S*	*Smith*	*Blackstock*	*Bolder/Doyle*
						28			Ref: M Jones	On a freezing cold night Bangoura nips in to prod in Sidibe's back-header. Camp twice saves Gallagher free-kicks. Rams turn it around with two quick goals. Smith flicks in a cross. Nyatanga nods in unmarked. Rams' second win in 16 games under Phil Brown. Both against City.											
21	A	SHEFFIELD WED		7	W		2-0	1-0	Bangoura 17, Sidibe 86	Simonsen	Halls	Broomes	Hoefkens	Duberry	Chadwick^	Russell	Brammer	Sigurdsson*	Gallagher	Bangoura"	Sidibe/Henry/Buxton
	26/11		*21,970*	*20*		31				*Weaver*	*Simek*	*Heckingb'm^*	*Coughlan*	*Diallo*	*Partridge**	*Whelan*	*Rocastle*	*Murphy*	*Graham"*	*Brunt*	*Agbonl'r/O'Brien/McGovern*
									Ref: A Hall	Third consecutive away win. Simo produces a world class save to deny the clean through Daryl Murphy and then tips round Brunt's free-kick as Paul Sturrock's men start well. Bangoura nips in to flick a long punt past Weaver. City soak up pressure, Sidibe converts Gallagher's cross.											
22	H	QP RANGERS		11	L		1-2	1-1	Bangoura 26	Simonsen	Halls !	Broomes	Hoefkens	Duberry	Chadwick	Henry	Brammer	Sidibe	Bangoura	Sweeney*	Sigurdsson
	3/12		15,367	*13*		31			*Furlong 2, Langley 52p*	*Royce*	*Bignot*	*Bean*	*Santos*	*Milanese*	*Rowlands*	*Ainsworth^*	*Langley*	*Furlong*	*Moore"*	*Dyer**	*Evatt/Cook/Baidoo*
									Ref: A Marriner	Stoke don't clear an early free-kick and Furlong nets. Bangoura nods in Sweeney's free-kick. Controversy as Bangoura's shirt is pulled but the ref doesn't blow. He then dismisses Halls and gives a pen for an innocuous tackle. Royce is hit by a fan at the final whistle. A 6th home defeat.											
23	H	LEICESTER		6	W		3-2	1-1	Gallagher 36p, Sidibe 75, Bangoura 78	Simonsen	Buxton	Broomes	Hoefkens	Duberry	Russell	Gallagher^	Brammer	Sidibe	Bangoura	Sweeney*	Sigurdsson/Henry
	9/12		11,125	*16*		34			*Gudjonsson 21, Hammond 48*	*Douglas*	*Maybury*	*Stearman**	*Gerrbrand*	*Dublin*	*Kisnorbo*	*Gudjonsson*	*Sylla*	*Hammond^*	*Hume*	*Smith*	*Willams/De Vries*
									Ref: I Williamson	Friday night kick-off for Sky. The defensive frailties show again. Gudjonsson fires in unchallenged and Hammond converts after Broomes's error. The pen is for Douglas's foul on Bangoura. Gudjonsson shudders the bar. Bangoura and Sidibe both head home tasty Brammer crosses.											

No	Date		Att	Pos	Pt	F-A	H-T	Scorers, Times, and Referees	SQUAD	NUMBERS	IN	USE								subs used
24	A	LUTON		5	W	3-2	1-1	Gallagher 45, 83, Coyne 90 (og)	Simonsen	Henry	Buxton	Hoefkens	Duberry	Russell	Chadwick*	Brammer	Sigurdsson^	Sidibe	Gallagher	Harper/Sweeney
	17/12		*8.296*	*10*	37			*Brkovic 21, Nicholls 88p*	*Brill*	*Foley*	*Underwood*	*Coyne*	*Heikkenen*	*Nicholls*	*Brkovic*	*Edwards*	*Howard*	*Vine**	*Robinson^*	*Feeney/Showumni*
								Ref: T Kettle	Topsy-turvy game on a choppy pitch. Brkovic converts Nicholls' cross. Simo claws Brkovic's back-heel off the line. Gallagher nets two Sidibe crosses which leave him with open goals. The penalty is for Herny's foul on Howard. Coyne clips the ball past Brill while trying to clear.											
25	A	BURNLEY		6	L	0-1	0-0		Simonsen	Halls	Broomes	Hoefkens	Duberry	Russell	Chadwick	Brammer	Bangoura	Sidibe	Gallagher	
	26/12		*17,912*	*5*	37			*Akinbiyi 56*	*Jensen*	*Duff*	*Harley*	*McGreal*	*Sinclair*	*Elliott*	*Hyde*	*O'Connor*	*Noel-Wi'ams*	*Akinbiyi*	*Branch**	*Thomas*
								Ref: N Miller	Four ex-Stokies in Burnley's line up, plus Cotterill as manager. One, Akinbiyi, makes the difference as he bundles in the ball from close range as City's defence fails to clear again. He doesn't celebrate. Nothing much for Stokies to cheer either. Aside from Gallagher, little goal threat.											
26	H	LEEDS		9	L	0-1	0-0		Simonsen	Halls*	Broomes^	Hoefkens	Duberry	Russell	Chadwick	Brammer	Bangoura	Sidibe	Gallagher	Buxton/Sigurdsson
	28/12		**20,408**	*3*	37			*Lewis 69*	*Sullivan*	*Kelly*	*Harding*	*Butler*	*Kilgallon*	*Douglas*	*Derry*	*Lewis*	*Healy**	*Cresswell*	*Blake^*	*Miller/Hulse*
								Ref: M Halsey	City are ruthlessly mugged by Kevin Blackwell's team. City dominate. Brammer fires wide. Bangoura volleys over. Sidibe is felled by Kelly. Sullivan palms away Gallagher's pen (18). Chadwick's runs promise much but deliver little. A right-wing cross isn't cleared and Lewis pounces.											
27	A	SHEFFIELD UTD		12	L	1-2	0-1	Sidibe 57	Simonsen	Buxton	Broomes	Hoefkens	Duberry	Russell	Chadwick^	Brammer	Bangoura	Sidibe	Gallagher*	Sigurdsson/Henry
	31/12		*21,279*	*2*	37			*Montgomery 18, Morgan 90*	*Kenny*	*Geary*	*Unsworth**	*Bromby*	*Morgan*	*Montgom'y"*	*Jagielka*	*Quinn*	*Shipperley*	*Kabba^*	*Webber*	*Kozluk/Ifill/Tonge*
								Ref: L Mason	City play well. Kenny denies Chadwick, Gallagher and Bangoura. Simo drops a cross, the defence fails to clear and Montgomery rifles in. Chadwick's shot is deflected to Sidibe to net. More agony as Chris Morgan rises above City's defence to head the winner deep in injury-time.											
28	H	IPSWICH		12	D	2-2	1-2	Russell 27, Sidibe 73	Simonsen	Buxton	Broomes*	Hoefkens	Duberry	Russell	Chadwick"	Brammer	Bangoura	Sidibe	Gallagher"	Henry/Harper/**Kopteff**
	2/1		14,493	*15*	38			*De Vos 7, Wilnis 18*	*Supple*	*Wilnis*	*Barren*	*De Vos*	*Naylor*	*Magilton**	*Williams*	*Westlake*	*Currie*	*Richards*	*McDonald"*	*Juan/Proudlock*
								Ref: L Probert	City start woefully with Broomes struggling. De Vos heads in a corner unmarked. Wilnis converts Currie's low cross at the second attempt. City fight back. Bangoura sets up Russell. Sidibe soars to head in. New signing winger Peter Kopteff beats two men and rips in a shot. Supple saves.											
29	A	WATFORD		13	L	0-1	0-0		Simonsen	Henry	Broomes	Hoefkens	Duberry	Junior	Chadwick	Brammer	Sidibe	Harper*	Gallagher	Dyer
	14/1		*12,247*	*4*	38			*Eagles 54*	*Foster*	*Stewart*	*Doyley*	*DeMerit*	*Mackay*	*Mahon*	*Spring*	*McNamee**	*Henderson^*	*King*	*Eagles*	*Bangura/Bouazza*
								Ref: P Crossley	Stoke lack Bangoura at the African Nations Cup. They are toothless in attack. Simo denies King. Another costly defensive ricket as Hoefkens slices a clearance and Eagles gobbles it up. Coach Gerry Taggart is sent off as tempers fray. Stoke are own worst enemies. No verve or thrust.											
30	H	HULL		13	L	**0-3**	0-1		Simonsen	Buxton	Broomes	Hoefkens	Duberry	Henry	Chadwick*	Russell	Sidibe	Gallagher	Sweeney	Harper^/Rooney
	21/1		13,444	*17*	38			*Russell 7 (og), Parkin 55, Duffy 81*	*Myhill*	*France*	*Delaney*	*Cort*	*Collins*	*Price**	*Andrews*	*Welsh*	*Fagan^*	*Parkin*	*Elliott"*	*Duffy/Wiseman/Ellison*
								Ref: A D'Urso	The Icelanders have put the club up for sale. City capitulate sorrowfully. Broomes clears off the line but it rebounds in off Russell. Two missed pens by Gallagher (48) and Chadwick (64). Parkin beats two to net. Duffy scores unmarked. Fighting breaks out amongst Stokies in the stands.											
31	H	PRESTON		13	D	0-0	0-0		Simonsen	Buxton	Broomes	Hoefkens	Duberry	Henry	Chadwick	Russell !	Sidibe	Gallagher*	Sweeney^	Sigurdsson/Junior
	4/2		14,218	*6*	39				*Nash*	*Alexander**	*Mears*	*Mawene*	*Davis*	*Sedgwick"*	*McKenna*	*O'Neil^*	*Nugent*	*Ormerod*	*Davidson*	*Neal/Luckett/Agyemang*
								Ref: B Curson	PNE are unbeaten in 21. Russell fells Nugent inside the box but the ref gives a free-kick. Alexander, PNE's penalty-taker, departs injured (25). Sidibe fluffs a howler. Russell kicks out at McKenna and sees red (55). Broomes trips Mears, but Simo saves McKenna's penalty. Guts at last.											
32	A	CARDIFF		16	L	**0-3**	0-2		Simonsen	Buxton	Broomes^	Hoefkens	Duberry	Henry	Brammer"	**Skoko**	Sidibe	Sigurdsson	Sweeney*	Kopteff/Hill/Junior
	11/2		*10,780*	*7*	39			*Cooper 18, Cox 30, 68*	*Alexander*	*Barker*	*Scimeca*	*Purse*	*Cox*	*Ardley*	*Boland*	*Cooper*	*Ndumbu-Ns'*	*Jerome*	*Ledley*	
								Ref: M Jones	Bangoura has gone missing after his jaunt to the African Nations Cup with Guinea. City play like they want to be with him. Cooper flashes in a 25-yarder. Sidibe slips clearing a corner and Cox rattles in. City give up. Simo tips over a Cooper drive. Cox nods in Ardley's free-kick. Grim.											
33	H	PLYMOUTH		16	D	0-0	0-0		Simonsen	Hoefkens	Broomes	Hill	Duberry	Chadwick	Brammer	Skoko	Sidibe*	Bangoura	Kopteff^	Sigurdsson/Sweeney
	14/2		10,242	*15*	40				*Larrieu*	*Connolly*	*Barness*	*Doumbe*	*Ward*	*Wotton*	*Norris*	*Nalis*	*Pericard*	*Chadwick**	*Capaldi*	*Evans*
								Ref: M Riley	Bangoura finally returns but looks disinterested. A warm welcome for the visiting boss as Boskamp appears to be losing his grip. Sidibe leaves on a stretcher after Doumbe's challenge (25). TP's men miss two open goals. Bangoura has a drive tipped aside by Larrieu. Nalis fires just over.											
34	H	MILLWALL		16	W	2-1	1-1	Hoekfens 15p, Gallagher 57	Simonsen	Hoefkens	Broomes	Hill	Duberry	Chadwick	Brammer	Skoko^	Sidibe	Sigurdsson	Sweeney*	Gallagher/Russell
	25/2		11,340	*22*	43			*May 8*	*Marshall*	*Lawrence*	*Robinson*	*Whitbread*	*Dunne*	*Craig*	*Elliott*	*Livermore*	*Dyer*	*May**	*Asaba^*	*Powell/Williams*
								Ref: C Webster	Another bad start as unmarked May nods in Craig's cross. In sub-zero temperatures City fight back for once. Hoefkens is felled in the area and slots the pen himself. Sweeney's back injury recurs. Gallagher's clinical finish from 20 yards wins it. Hill is imperious. First league win of 2006.											

No	Date	Opponent	Att	Pos	Res	Pts	FT	HT	Scorers, Times, and Referees	1	2	3	4	5	6	7	8	9	10	11	subs used
35	A	NORWICH		16	L		1-2	0-0	Gallagher 58	Simonsen	Buxton	Broomes	Hill	Duberry	Chadwick	Russell	Skoko	Gallagher*	Bangoura	Junior	Sweeney
	4/3		**24,223**	*10*		43			*McKenzie 52, Johansson 89*	*Green*	*Fleming*	*Charlton*	*Shackell*	*Doherty*	*Robinson*	*McVeigh*	*Hughes**	*Huckerby*	*McKenzie^*	*Earnshaw*	*Etuhu/Johansson*
									Ref: P Crossley	Gallagher's first shot clears the stand. It doesn't get much better. McKenzie hammers home. A hardy 300 travelling fans at least see Gallagher net a free-kick. Huckerby gives Buxton a torrid time. Bangoura heads at Green from 6 yards, Johansson slips his shot under Simo to win it.											
36	A	WOLVERHAMPTON		15	D		0-0	0-0		Simonsen	Hoefkens	Broomes	Hill	Duberry	Brammer	Russell	Skoko^	Gallagher	Bangoura	Chadwick*	Sidibe/Junior
	7/3		*22,439*	*7*		44				*Postma*	*Naylor*	*Ross*	*Lescott*	*Edwards*	*Rosa^*	*Kennedy*	*Anderton**	*Aliadiere*	*Miller*	*Cort"*	*Ince/Ricketts/Frankowski*
									Ref: B Curson	A dull stalemate sees City the happier. Glenn Hoddle's promotion-chasers press hard, but create few chances. Aliadiere's overhead drifts wide. Skoko heads just wide. Hill rattles the bar from Gallagher's cross. Bangoura fails to connect with Brammer's cross. Boos ring round Molineux.											
37	H	CRYS PALACE		15	L		1-3	0-1	Skoko 47	Simonsen	Hoefkens*	Broomes	Hill	Duberry	Brammer	Russell	Skoko	Sidibe	Bangoura	Gallagher^	Buxton/Sigurdsson
	13/3		**10,121**	*5*		44			*Sidibe 30(og), McAnuff 48, Johnson 58*	*Kiraly*	*Boyce*	*Borrowdale*	*Ward*	*Hall*	*Watson**	*Hughes*	*Riihilahti*	*Johnson*	*Morrison*	*McAnuff^*	*Leigertwood/Soares*
									Ref: A Leake	Stoke are taken apart by Iain Dowie's play-off chasers. Sidibe turns in Boyce's cross as the defence backs off. Skoko lifts spirits with a fluke goal as he loops in a flick on. Palace retaliate as McAnuff's shot deflects in off Hill. Johnson sears past the defence to lash past Simo. Awful.											
38	H	BURNLEY		15	W		1-0	0-0	Gallagher 52	Simonsen	Hoefkens	Broomes*	Hill	Duberry	Brammer	Russell^	Skoko	Sidibe	Bangoura"	Gallagher	Buxton/Chadwick/Sigurds'n
	18/3		12,082	*18*		47				*Jensen*	*Bardsley*	*Harley*	*Duff*	*Thomas*	*O'Connor G**	*O'Connor J*	*McCann^*	*Ricketts*	*Gray*	*Branch"*	*Elliott/Noel-Williams/Spicer*
									Ref: M Fletcher	A poor game in high winds. McCann heads over. Bangoura shoots wide. Gallagher produces the one moment of class when he clinically nets Brammer's cross from the left edge of the box. 6th consecutive defeat for Burnley. A City win at least, but no sign of promised great football.											
39	A	LEEDS		15	D		0-0	0-0		Simonsen	Hoefkens	Buxton	Hill	Duberry	Junior"	Russell	Paterson	Sidibe	Bangoura*	Gallagher^	Sigurds'n/Brammer/Sweeney
	25/3		*21,452*	*4*		48				*Sullivan*	*Kelly*	*Crainey*	*Butler*	*Gregan*	*Derry*	*Miller*	*Douglas^*	*Hulse*	*Healy**	*Lewis"*	*Beckford/Blake/Griffiths*
									Ref: K Stroud	Leeds dominate. Hulse nods over. Hill leads the resistance. Simo saves from Hulse and Griffiths when clean through. Leeds are poor in front of goal. City have one chance. Sullivan's stunning save denies Russell. Boskamp vows to blood youngsters for the future. But where will his be?											
40	A	QP RANGERS		13	W		2-1	0-1	Hoefkens 73p, Sigurdsson 79	Simonsen	Hoefkens	Wilkinson	Broomes	Duberry	Brammer	Russell	Chadwick"	Sigurdsson	Bangoura^	Sweeney*	Gallagher/Sidibe/Buxton
	29/3		*10,918*	*14*		51			*Nygaard 7*	*Jones*	*Bignot*	*Evatt*	*Shittu*	*Milanese*	*Bircham^*	*Ainsworth"*	*Lomas*	*Youssouf**	*Nygaard*	*Cook*	*Moore/Langley/Furlong*
									Ref: P Walton	Boskamp is 'ill' or has the hump, depending on which version you believe. Simo's goal is peppered as the makeshift defence creaks. 6ft 7ins Nygaard hammers home a shot. Simo saves Cook's pen (16). Russell is felled. Hoefkens nets the pen. Sigurdsson rams in his first for the club.											
41	H	SHEFFIELD UTD		13	D		1-1	1-0	Skoko 16	Simonsen	Hoefkens	Dickinson	Broomes	Hill*	Skoko	Russell	Junior^	Sidibe	Gallagher"	Chadwick	Buxton/Brammer/Sigurds'on
	1/4		17,544	*2*		52			*Webber 83*	*Kenny*	*Kozluk*	*Unsworth*	*Morgan*	*Short*	*Ifill**	*Jagielka*	*Armstrong*	*Shipperley^*	*Webber*	*Tonge*	*Kabba/Akinbiyi*
									Ref: A Marriner	Six changes again, but Stoke have the better against Neil Warnock's men. Hoefkens fires over. Kenny flaps at a long ball and Skoko nods in. Sidibe misses when clean through. Skoko hits a post. Danny Webber nicks a point by rolling the ball past Simo after Buxton's error lets him in.											
42	A	IPSWICH		11	W		4-1	0-0	Wilnis 51 (og), Bang'a 82, Chadw'k 90, [Russell 90]	Simonsen	Hoefkens^	Wilkinson	Duberry	Hill	Junior	Russell	Brammer"	Bangoura	Gallagher	Kopteff*	Chadwick/Broomes/**Garrett**
	8/4		*23,592*	*13*		55			*Haynes 67*	*Supple*	*Wilnis*	*Richards*	*De Vos*	*Naylor*	*Casement**	*Garvan"*	*Currie*	*Bowditch^*	*Lee*	*Juan*	*Sito/Haynes/Magilton*
									Ref: P Miller	Town have two good pen appeals waved away. Wilnis turns Brammer's cross in under pressure from Hoefkens. Gallagher misses a sitter and Russell peppers Supple's goal. Haynes turns in Juan's shot. Bangoura rams home. Chadwick and Russell race clear to score as Town fall apart.											
43	H	SOUTHAMPTON		12	L		1-2	0-2	Gallagher 83	Simonsen	Hoefkens	Wilkinson^	Duberry	Broomes	Junior	Russell"	Brammer	Bangoura	Gallagher	Chadwick*	Sweeney/Dickinson/Rooney
	15/4		16,501	*15*		55			*Raziak 24p, 31*	*Miller*	*Baird*	*Powell*	*Lundekvam*	*Brennan*	*Wright*	*Chaplow**	*Potter*	*Raziak*	*Fuller*	*Belmadi^*	*Ostlund/Dyer*
									Ref: J Robinson	Boskamp's future is under a cloud as is the future of the club. Grzegorz Raziak, on loan from Spurs, destroys City. He rams in a pen after being felled by Duberry, then lashes home Wright's cross. Gallagher's peach from 30 yards is scant consolation. Another home defeat. Grim times.											
44	A	READING		13	L		1-3	0-1	Rooney 59	Simonsen	Hoefkens	Dickinson	Duberry	Hill	Junior	Russell	Brammer	Bangoura"	Sweeney^	Kopteff*	Rooney/Gallagher/Henry
	17/4		*22,119*	*1*		55			*Sidwell 25, Doyle 56p, Halls 62*	Stack	Halls	Shorey^	Ingimarsson	Sonko	Hunt	Sidwell*	Gunnarsson	Doyle"	Long	Makin	*Dobson/Golbourne/Cox*
									Ref: S Mathieson	Stoke struggle. Simo smothers clean through Sidwell. The same man nods in unmarked. Hoefkens fells Doyle for the pen. Rooney hooks past Stack. Halls prods in Hunt's cross. Steve Coppell's Royals break the 100 point barrier. Boskamp refuses to speak to the media. Club in turmoil.											
45	H	COVENTRY		14	L		0-1	0-0		Simonsen	Hoefkens	Dickinson	Duberry	Hill	Paterson^	Russell	Brammer*	Sidibe	Rooney	Gallagher	Henry/**Hazley**
	22/4		13,385	*11*		55			*Adebola 85*	*Fulop*	*Whing*	*Hall*	*Heath*	*Giddings*	*Doyle*	*Hughes*	*Hutchison**	*John"*	*McShef'ey^*	*Thornton*	*Adebola/Morrell/Turner*
									Ref: P Walton	Stoke's season in microcosm. Flowing passing, little midfield creativity, no goal threat. Adebola's shot from 12 yards, after being set up by Kevin Thornton wins a dull game in which Sidibe wastes the best chance, shooting wide when through. Russell and Brammer also go close.											
46	A	BRIGHTON		13	W		**5-1**	3-0	Rooney 6, 22, 63, Sidibe 40, Sween' 82	Simonsen	Buxton	Dickinson	Duberry	Hill	Junior	Russell	Brammer*	Sidibe	Rooney^	Skoko"	Garrett/Sweeney/Kopteff
	30/4		***5,859***	*24*		58			*Loft 84*	*Henderson*	*Reid*	*Lynch**	*Butters*	*Hinshelwood*	*Carole*	*Carpenter*	*Nicolas*	*Noel-Wil'ms*	*Kazim-Rich's*	*Frutos*	*Loft*
	Home		Away						Ref: K Wright	Adam Rooney becomes the youngest ever scorer of a hat-trick in a Stoke shirt. Three clinical finishes are rounded off by a perfect curling shot from 20 yards. Sidibe slots after Russell hits the bar. Sweeney skips round Reid to net. Biggest away win for 6 years. Some light in the darkness.											
Average	14,432		16,763																		

Carling Cup			Att	F-A	H-T	Scorers, Times, and Referees	SQUAD	NUMBERS	IN	USE							subs used
1	A	MANSFIELD	9	1-1	1-1	Brammer 11p	Simonsen	Halls*	Broomes	Hoefkens	Duberry	Henry	Harper	Brammer	Sidibe	Dyer"	Kolar^	Buxton/Gudjonsson/Russell
23/8			*2,799 2:14*			*Jelleyman 16*	*White*	*Peers*	*Uhlenbeek*	*Jelleyman*	*Day*	*Barker*	*Coke**	*Baptiste*	*Tipton*	*Beardsley^*	*Talbot"*	*Dawson/Brown/Birchall*
						Ref: G Salisbury	Jason White brings down Sidibe. Brammer hammers in the pen. Town are the better side. Broomes struggles with Uhlenbeek, whose cross is											
						(Stoke lose 0-3 on penalties)	converted by Jelleyman. City's crossing is woeful. Town can't convert their chances. Brammer, Hoefkens and Duberry miss in the shoot out.											

FA Cup																	
3	H	TAMWORTH	12	0-0	0-0		Simonsen	Henry	Broomes	Hoefkens	Buxton	Russell	Chadwick"	Brammer	Gallagher^	Sidibe	Kopteff*	Sweeney/Sigurdsson/Harper
7/1			9,366 *C:20*				*Bevan*	*Touhy*	*Anaclet*	*Smith*	*Redmile*	*Bampton^*	*Melton*	*Ward*	*Turner*	*Wright**	*Edwards*	*Storer/Cooper*
						Ref: P Taylor	Stoke are lethargic. Mark Cooper's men smother them, double-teaming the wingers with defenders. City create few chances, although Kopteff,											
							Sidibe and Russell go close. Tamworth nearly become superheroes, but Jake Edwards wastes a last-minute chance when clean through on goal.											
3R	A	TAMWORTH	12	1-1	0-1	Gallagher 80	Simonsen	Buxton	Broomes"	Hoefkens	Duberry	Henry	Chadwick^	Brammer*	Gallagher	Sidibe	Harper	Junior/Kopteff/**Rooney**
17/1			*3,812 C:20*	*aet*		*Jackson 42*	*Bevan*	*Touhy*	*Anaclet*	*Smith*	*Redmile*	*Bampton*	*Melton^*	*Ward"*	*Hegg*	*Wright**	*Jackson*	*Turner/Storer/Stamps*
						Ref: P Joslin	Close to embarrassing after Nathan Jackson sends the capacity Lamb crowd wild as he bundles in Hegg's cross. City twice hit a post. 17-year-											
						(Stoke win 5-4 on penalties)	old Adam Rooney flicks on a corner for Gallagher to net an overhead. Few chances in tense injury-time. Simo saves Touhy's penalty to win it.											
4	H	WALSALL	13	2-1	1-0	Sidibe 45, Chadwick 49	Simonsen*	Buxton	Broomes	Hoefkens	Duberry	Henry	Chadwick^	Brammer	Gallagher"	Sidibe	Sweeney	DeGoey/Kopteff/Sigurdsson
28/1			8,834 *1:16*			*James 51*	*Oakes*	*Pead*	*Fox*	*Westwood*	*Gerrard*	*Wright^*	*Smith*	*Leary*	*McDermott**	*Timm*	*James*	*Nicholls/Standing*
						Ref: K Stroud	Paul Merson's men succumb to a good spell in the middle of the game. Sidibe nets after Gerrard clears Henry's rasper off the line. Chadwick											
							cuts inside to curl a left-footed shot inside the far post. James converts Wright's cross. Nicholls hits a post. De Goey's tips over from Nicholls.											
5	H	BIRMINGHAM	16	0-1	0-0		Simonsen	Hoefkens	Broomes^	Hill	Duberry	Junior	Chadwick	Brammer	Bangoura	Sidibe	Sweeney*	Sigurdsson/Rooney
19/2			18,768 *P:18*			*Forssell 47*	*Taylor*	*Melchiot*	*Gray*	*Bruce*	*Latka*	*Butt*	*Pennant^*	*Johnson*	*Heskey*	*Forssell**	*Clemence*	*Jarosik/Clapham*
						Ref: M Dean	A great cup-tie atmosphere at least sees Stoke give it a go. Maik Taylor twice keeps Steve Bruce's Blues in it. First saving from Hoekfens, then											
							from Duberry's header. Forssell forces in Latka's header from a corner from 2 yards. Bangoura heads a great chance wide from 6 yards. Nearly.											

		Home					Away					
	P	W	D	L	F	A	W	D	L	F	A	Pts
1 Reading	46	19	3	1	58	14	12	10	1	41	18	106
2 Sheff Utd	46	15	5	3	43	22	11	7	5	33	24	90
3 Watford*	46	11	7	5	39	24	11	8	4	38	29	81
4 Preston	46	11	10	2	31	12	9	10	4	28	18	80
5 Leeds	46	13	7	3	35	18	8	8	7	22	20	78
6 C Palace	46	13	6	4	39	20	8	6	9	28	28	75
7 Wolves	46	9	10	4	24	18	7	9	7	26	24	67
8 Coventry	46	12	7	4	39	22	4	8	11	23	43	63
9 Norwich	46	12	4	7	34	25	6	4	13	22	40	62
10 Luton	46	11	6	6	45	31	6	4	13	21	36	61
11 Cardiff	46	10	7	6	32	24	6	5	12	26	35	60
12 Southampton	46	9	10	4	26	17	4	9	10	23	33	58
13 STOKE	46	7	5	11	24	32	10	2	11	30	31	58
14 Plymouth	46	10	7	6	26	22	3	10	10	13	24	56
15 Ipswich	46	8	8	7	28	32	6	6	11	25	34	56
16 Leicester	46	8	9	6	30	25	5	6	12	21	34	54
17 Burnley	46	11	6	6	34	22	3	6	14	12	32	54
18 Hull	46	8	8	7	24	21	4	8	11	25	34	52
19 Sheff Wed	46	7	8	8	22	24	6	5	12	17	28	52
20 Derby	46	8	10	5	33	27	2	10	11	20	40	50
21 QP Rangers	46	7	7	9	24	26	5	7	11	26	39	50
22 Crewe	46	7	7	9	38	40	2	8	13	19	46	42
23 Millwall	46	4	8	11	13	27	4	8	11	22	35	40
24 Brighton	46	4	8	11	21	34	3	9	11	18	37	38
	1104	234	173	145	762	579	145	173	234	579	762	1483

* promoted after play-offs

Odds & ends

Double wins: (3) Crewe, Luton. Millwall.
Double losses: (7) Cardiff, Palace, Derby, Reading, South'pton, Watford.

Won from behind: (6) Coventry (a), Leicester (h), Luton (h), Luton (a), Millwall (h), QPR (a).
Lost from in front: (2) Plymouth (a), Derby (h).

High Spots: Superb performance to defeat Norwich in August.
Adam Rooney's hat-trick at Brighton.
Youth given its chance towards the end of the season.
10 away wins for the first time since season 1999-2000.

Low spots: The spat between Boskamp and John Rudge which splits the camp.
Dreadful defending all season.
The refusal of the Icelandic board to commit to the future, which leads eventually to the club going up for sale.
Losing 11 home games, which incensed the crowd, leading to trouble against Hull.
A fan striking QPR keeper Simon Royce after Rangers won at the Brit.

Ever-presents: (0).
Hat-tricks: (1) Adam Rooney (a) v Brighton.
Leading Scorer: (12) Paul Gallagher.
Player of the Year: Carl Hoefkens.

	Appearances						Goals			
	Lge	*Sub*	LC	*Sub*	FAC	*Sub*	Lge	LC	FAC	Tot
Bangoura, Sammy	**23**	*1*			1		**9**			**9**
Brammer, Dave	**38**	*2*	1		4		**1**	1		**2**
Broomes, Marlon	**36**	*1*	1		4		**2**			**2**
Buxton, Lewis	**25**	*7*		*1*	3		**1**			**1**
Chadwick, Luke	**33**	*3*			4		**2**		1	**3**
De Goey, Ed	**1**	*1*				*1*				
Dickinson, Carl	**4**	*1*								
Duberry, Michael	**41**		1		3		**1**			**1**
Dyer, Bruce	**2**	*9*	1							
Gallagher, Paul	**32**	*5*			3		**11**		1	**12**
Garrett, Rob		*2*								
Gudjonsson, Thordur				*1*						
Halls, John	**13**		1				**2**			**2**
Harper, Kevin	**5**	*9*	1		1	*1*	**1**			**1**
Hazley, Matt		*1*								
Henry, Karl	**11**	*13*	1		3					
Hill, Clint	**12**	*1*			1					
Hoefkens, Carl	**44**		1		4		**3**			**3**
Junior	**16**	*6*			1	*1*				
Kolar, Martin	**12**	*2*	1				**1**			**1**
Kopteff, Peter	**3**	*3*			1	*2*				
Paterson, Martin	**2**	*1*								
Rooney, Adam	**2**	*3*				*2*	**4**			**4**
Russell, Darel	**35**	*2*		*1*	1		**3**			**3**
Sidibe, Mamady	**37**	*5*	1		4		**6**		1	**7**
Sigurdsson, Hannes	**10**	*13*				*3*	**1**			**1**
Simonsen, Steve	**45**		1		4					
Skoko, Josip	**9**						**2**			**2**
Sweeney, Peter	**8**	*9*			2	*1*	**1**			**1**
Taggart, Gerry	**3**						**1**			**1**
Wilkinson, Andy	**4**	*2*								
(own-goals)							**2**			**2**
31 players used	**506**	***102***	**11**	***3***	**44**	***11***	**54**	**1**	**3**	**58**

No	Date	Att	Pos	Pt	F-A	H-T	Scorers, Times, and Referees	SQUAD	NUMBERS	IN	USE								subs used
1	A SOUTHEND			L	0-1	0-1		Simonsen	Hoefkens	**Higginb'am**	Duberry	Hill	Brammer	Russell	Chadwick*	Sidibe	**Pericard**	Sweeney^	Sigurdsson/Eustace
	5/8	*8,971*		0			*Eastwood 14p*	*Flahavan*	*Francis*	*Hammell*	*Prior*	*Barrett*	*Gower^*	*Maher*	*Gutteridge"*	*Eastwood*	*Bradbury*	*C'mp'-Ryce**	*Paynter/Hunt/Clarke*
							Ref: M Russell	TP's second coming sees Luke Chadwick carried off in a oxygen mask and Peter Sweeney break his wrist. Freddie Eastwood's contentious pen is given for Simo's foul on Bradbury after Duberry allows a long ball to bounce. Pericard misses a sitter. Sidibe and Sigurdsson waste chances.											
2	H DERBY		11	W	2-0	1-0	Pericard 18, Russell 58	Simonsen	Hoefkens	Higginbo'm^	Duberry	Hill	Brammer	Russell	Chadwick*	Sidibe	Pericard"	Sweeney	Paterson/Dickinson/Sigurds'n
	8/8	20,013	*16*	3				*Grant*	*Edworthy*	*Jackson*	*Nyatanga*	*Moore*	*Smith T*	*Oakley"*	*Johnson S**	*Howard*	*Smith R^*	*Barnes*	*Pesch'lido/Bisgaard/Idiakez*
							Ref: M Clattenburg	In front of a noisy crowd, City give Billy Davies' Rams a bloody nose. Vincent Pericard opens his account, poking home past Grant from close in. Darel Russell dives to head in after Grant saves Pericard's effort. Sidibe misses anther sitter. Rams have pressure but few clear-cut chances.											
3	H BIRMINGHAM		11	D	0-0	0-0		Simonsen	Hoefkens	Dickinson	Duberry	Hill	Brammer	Russell	Chadwick*	Sidibe	Pericard	Sweeney	Paterson
	12/8	12,347	*4*	4				*Taylor Maik*	*Kelly*	*Sadler*	*Tebily*	*N'Gotty*	*Johnson*	*Nafti*	*Muamba^*	*Forssell"*	*Bendtner*	*Larsson**	*Dunn/Dans/Clemence*
							Ref: R Beeby	Promotion favourites Brum lack Cameron Jerome and DJ Campbell, and consequent teeth in attack. Their first shot on goal comes on 32 mins. Brammer trips Muamba but Simo saves Forssell's spot-kick (57). Stoke have plenty of ball, but Sweeney's cross is too high for Pericard. Tight.											
4	A LUTON		13	D	2-2	1-0	Sweeney 10, Chadwick 70	Simonsen	Hoefkens	Dickinson	Duberry	Hill	Brammer	Russell	Chadwick*	Sidibe	Pericard	Sweeney	**Whitley**
	19/8	*7,727*	*5*	5			*Barnett 54, Langley 60p*	*Beresford*	*Foley*	*Edwards*	*Davis*	*Barnett*	*Coyne*	*Langley*	*Holmes*	*Emmanuel*	*Vine*	*Feeney**	*Morgan*
							Ref: G Sutton	Sweeney lashes home from 25 yards as Stoke begin brightly, and are on top when Leon Barnett turns Emanuel's cross in. Barnett hauls down Pericard but nothing is given. Straight down the other end and a pen is awarded as Sidibe scythes down Morgan. Chadwick prods in a rebound.											
5	H PLYMOUTH		14	D	1-1	1-0	Sidibe 39	Simonsen	Hoefkens	Higginbot'm	Duberry	Hill	Brammer	Russell	Chadwick*	Sidibe	Pericard	Sweeney^	Whitley/Harper
	26/8	**11,626**	*8*	6			*Hayles 78*	*McCormack*	*Hodges*	*Connolly*	*Doumbe*	*Aljofree*	*Norris*	*Wotton*	*Nalis*	*Hayles*	*Chadwick**	*Capaldi^*	*Ebanks-Blake/Reid*
							Ref: E Ilderton	Simo keeps City in the game with a host of early saves, the best flying low to tip round from Nick Chadwick. Sidibe nets after Pericard squares a cross in from a tight angle. City seem to be capable of holding on, but Barry Hayles ends a spell of prolonged pressure by hooking past Simo.											
6	A BARNSLEY		14	D	2-2	2-0	Hill 3, Chadwick 23	Simonsen	**Griffin**	Higginbot'm	Duberry	Hill	Brammer	Russell	Chadwick*	Sidibe	Pericard	Sweeney^	Whitley/Harper
	9/9	*10,464*	*12*	7			*Wright 73, Hayes 76*	*Colgan*	*Williams*	*Tonge*	*Hassell*	*Reid P*	*Devaney*	*Howard^*	*Togwell*	*Richards**	*Hayes*	*McIndoe*	*Wright/Healy*
							Ref: C Webster	Another lead lost. This time two goals. Hill clatters in a header. Chadwick slots after a great passing move. But Stoke then drop back to try to defend for 70 mins. Simo tips Hayes's shot aside. Wright nets with his first touch. Hayes steers home Devaney's cross. Anger on the terraces.											
7	A SHEFFIELD WED		14	D	1-1	1-1	Paterson 34	Simonsen	Griffin	Higginbot'm	Duberry	Hill	Brammer	Russell	Chadwick^	Sidibe	Pericard*	Sweeney"	Paterson/Hoefkens/Pulis
	12/9	*19,966*	*18*	8			*Brunt 40p*	*Jones*	*Simek*	*Spurr*	*Bougherra*	*Coughlan*	*Sam"*	*Whelan**	*O'Brien*	*Tudgay^*	*Burton*	*Brunt*	*Lunt/Bullen/McAllister*
							Ref: A Wiley	Simo saves Bougherra's point-blank header. Martin Paterson scores his first senior goal, slotting Brammer's pass past Jones. Griff is adjudged to have handled. Brunt sends Simo the wrong way from the spot. Brunt fizzes two shots just wide. Tudgay misses an open goal. Solid point.											
8	H BURNLEY		19	L	0-1	0-1		Simonsen	Griffin	Higginbot'm	Duberry	Hill	Brammer	Russell	Chadwick"	Sidibe	Bangoura*	Sweeney^	Paterson/Hoefkens/Rooney
	16/9	12,247	*3*	8			*Gray 1*	*Jensen*	*Duff*	*Harley*	*Thomas*	*McGreal*	*Elliott"*	*Hyde*	*O'Connor J*	*N'l-Wil'ams**	*Gray*	*Jones^*	*McCann/Lafferty/Sinclair*
							Ref: C Foy	Calamity as Andy Gray slots Micah Hyde's pass before a Stoke player has touched the ball. Try as they might, Stoke cannot get back into the game. Bangoura is ineffective and limps off before half-time. Burnley's ex-City contingent hold a vice-like grip. Stoke lack tempo and fluency.											
9	A WOLVERHAMPTON		21	L	0-2	0-1		Simonsen	Griffin	Higginbot'm	Duberry	Hill !	Brammer	Russell	Chadwick*	Sidibe	**Fuller"**	Sweeney^	Hoefkens/Paterson/Rooney
	23/9	*19,489*	*6*	8			*Clarke 25, Olofinjana 68*	*Murray*	*Edwards*	*Mulgrew*	*Breen*	*Craddock*	*Potter*	*Olofinjana*	*Henry*	*Clarke**	*Johnson^*	*Ricketts*	*Davies/Gobern*
							Ref: M Dean	Stoke are the better side, with Fuller impressive, until Leon Clarke scores a great individual goal out of nothing. City capitulate as frustration sets in. Johnson is a handful. Olofinjana nods in Ricketts' cross to seal it. Hill walks for a second yellow (85). Something really has to be done.											
10	H PRESTON		20	D	1-1	1-0	Fuller 41	Simonsen	Hoefkens	Higginbot'm	Duberry	Hill	Brammer	Russell	**Hendrie**	Sidibe	Fuller*	Sweeney^	Bangoura/Paterson
	30/9	14,342	*3*	9			*Agyemang 63*	*Nash*	*Alexander*	*Hill**	*Chilvers*	*St Ledger*	*Sedgwick*	*Whaley^*	*McKenna*	*Agyemang"*	*Nugent*	*Pugh*	*Dichio/Neal/McCormack*
							Ref: A Woolmer	A planned red-card protest by some fans is shouted down, but feelings are running high. Stoke's best display so far sees loanee Lee Hendrie (Villa) clip the bar with a free-kick. Fuller nets Sweeney's pass against his former club. Agyemang scores against the run of play. Positive.											
11	A LEEDS		18	W	4-0	1-0	Hendrie 7, Griffin 58, Higginbotham 62, [Fuller 88]	Simonsen	Hoefkens	Griffin	Duberry	Higginbot'm	**Diao^**	Russell	**Delap**	Sidibe	Pericard*	Hendrie"	Fuller/Brammer/Chadwick
	14/10	*18,173*	*24*	12				*Sullivan*	*Kelly*	*Wright*	*Butler*	*Kilgallon*	*Douglas*	*Derry*	*Westlake^*	*Horsfield**	*Healy"*	*Lewis*	*Cresswell/Stone/Blake*
							Ref: T Kettle	Leeds have just sacked manager Kevin Blackwell. City take advantage. Loanee Salif Diao (Liverpool) impresses. Hendrie curls in a stunning free-kick. Griff hammers in from 25 yards. Higgy nods in a corner-kick. Simo saves Blake's pen (65). Fuller curls in a peach from 20 yards.											

12	H	SUNDERLAND		14	W	2-1	0-1	Hendrie 50, Pericard 54	Simonsen	Hoefkens	Griffin	Duberry	Higginbot'm	Diao	Russell	Delap*	Sidibe^	Pericard	Hendrie"	Chadwick/Fuller/Brammer
		17/10	14,482	*19*	15			*Yorke 28*	*Ward*	*Nosworthy*	*Elliott**	*Varga*	*Collins*	*Whitehead"*	*Leadbitter*	*Miller L*	*Yorke*	*Connolly*	*Wallace^*	*Clarke/Murphy/Brown*
								Ref: P Walton	Delap breaks a leg in a tackle with Elliott (12). It stuns Stoke and Yorke nets a rebound. After the break, City overwhelm Roy Keane's men. Hendrie slots Sidibe's pass. Pericard crashes in a header from Griff's perfect cross. Simo makes two stunning saves. Stirring stuff.											
13	A	SOUTHAMPTON		9	L	0-1	0-0		Simonsen	Griffin	Hill*	Duberry	Higginbot'm	Diao	Russell	Hoefkens	Fuller	Pericard^	Hendrie	Sweeney/Bangoura
		21/10	*20,531*	*18*	15			*Licka 54*	*Davis*	*Wright*	*Bale*	*Baird*	*Lundekvam*	*Skacel**	*Licka*	*Idiakez*	*Rasiak*	*Jones*	*Surman*	*Dyer*
								Ref: L Probert	City are tepid in a flat game. Russell's weak header is easily saved by Davis. Hendrie has a shot tipped round by the keeper. The defence stand off Mario Licka, whose speculative 25-yarder sneaks past Simo, who dives late. Burley's Saints had three defeats in a row, so shut up shop.											
14	H	NORWICH		14	W	**5-0**	2-0	Hendrie 22, Fuller 38, Higginbotham 54p,	Simonsen	Hoefkens	Griffin	Duberry	Higginbot'm	Diao^	Russell	Chadwick	Sidibe	Fuller*	Hendrie"	Pericard/Brammer/Sweeney
		28/10	13,444	*17*	18			[Chadwick 79, Russell 90]	*Ashdown !*	*Colin*	*Drury*	*Shackell*	*Fleming**	*Robinson"*	*Etuhu*	*Hughes^*	*Dublin*	*Doherty*	*Croft*	*Thorne/Eagle/Gallacher*
								Ref: P Robinson	Rampant Stoke are inspired by Hendrie again. He slots Sidibe's pass. Fuller turns to lash in from close range. Ashdown brings down Chadwick and walks. Higgy hammers in the pen after an argument with Hoefkens. Chadwick nets a rebound and Russell's shot goes in off a post. Superb.											
15	A	LEICESTER		17	L	1-2	1-1	Fuller 42	Simonsen	Hoefkens	Griffin	Duberry	Hig'inbot'm*	Diao	Russell	Chadwick^	Sidibe	Fuller	Hendrie	Hill/Pericard
		31/10	*21,107*	*12*	18			*Hume 45, Hughes 64*	*Logan*	*Stearman*	*Johansson*	*McCarthy*	*Kenton*	*Sylla*	*Johnson*	*Hughes*	*Hume*	*Hammond**	*Tiatto*	*Fryatt*
								Ref: G Laws	Foxes are undefeated in seven. City show their Achilles heel in failing to hold onto a lead away from home. Fuller hooks the ball back over his head and into the corner. Hume nets a half-cleared free-kick. Hughes's right-foot shot beats Simo. Fuller hits the bar. Not consistent enough.											
16	H	COVENTRY		14	W	1-0	0-0	Griffin 60	Simonsen	Hoefkens	Griffin	Duberry	Higginbot'm	Diao	Russell	Chadwick*	Sidibe^	Fuller !	Hendrie	Brammer/Pericard
		6/11	19,055	*11*	21				*Marshall*	*Duffy*	*Hall"*	*Page*	*Ward*	*Clarke*	*Birchall**	*Hughes*	*McKenzie*	*John*	*Doyle^*	*Tabb/Adebola/Hutchinson*
								Ref: C Boyeson	The Brit is shrouded in fog for this TV game. It dampens the match into a midfield stalemate. Griffin lifts the gloom with a 30-yard rocket that flies into the top corner. Fuller walks for elbowing Doyle, who had fouled him first (63). Stoke hang on. McKenzie nets a header but is offside.											
17	A	CRYSTAL PALACE		10	W	1-0	1-0	Russell 38	Simonsen	Hoefkens	Griffin	Duberry	Higginbot'm	Diao	Russell	Chadwick*	Sidibe	Pericard	Hendrie	Brammer
		11/11	*18,868*	*20*	24				*Kiraly*	*Butterfield*	*Granville*	*Cort*	*Hudson*	*Hughes*	*Kennedy*	*Soares**	*Morrison*	*Scowcroft^*	*McAnuff*	*Freedman/Kuqi*
								Ref: I Williamson	Stoke are solid in defence and offer more in attack then Iain Dowie's Eagles. Russell's left-footer on the run flies in. Stoke defend manfully with the back four ensuring Simo doesn't have a shot to save. Higgy defies a thigh injury to star. First win at Selhurst for 20 years. Good stuff.											
18	A	HULL		7	W	2-0	1-0	Higginbotham 2, Russell 80	Simonsen	Hoefkens	Griffin"	Duberry	Higginbot'm	Diao	Russell	**Lawrence^**	Sidibe	Pericard*	Hendrie	Brammer/Bangoura/Hill
		18/11	*16,940*	*21*	27				*Myhill*	*Ricketts*	*Dawson**	*Turner*	*Coles*	*Delaney*	*Jarrett*	*Marney*	*Fagan*	*Forster"*	*Elliott^*	*Barmby/Yates/Bridges*
								Ref: G Hegley	A tenacious display as Stoke defend Higgy's header after 79 secs from Hendrie's cross. Liam Lawrence, recruited yesterday from Sunderland, impresses. Stoke resist Hull's second-half pressure. Simo denies Elliott. Russell plays a one-two with Bangoura on the edge of the box to fire in.											
19	H	WEST BROM		6	W	1-0	1-0	Higginbotham 40p	Simonsen	Hoefkens	Griffin	Duberry	Higginbot'm	Diao	Russell	Lawrence	Sidibe	Pericard*	Hendrie^	**Berger**/Hill
		25/11	18,282	*8*	30				*Hoult*	*Robinson*	*Albrechts'n**	*Davies*	*Perry*	*Carter*	*Greening*	*Quashie*	*Kamara^*	*Phillips*	*Koumas*	*Gera/Ellington*
								Ref: M Thorpe	Hoult tips away Hendrie's shot. Russell is felled by Perry in the act of shooting. Higgy and Hoefkens argue over the pen again. Higgy wins and belts it into the corner. Simo tips Phillips' shot over the bar. Berger crosses but no one can convert. City defend resolutely for the final 10 mins.											
20	H	CARDIFF		6	W	3-0	0-0	Fuller 60, Lawrence 63, Sidibe 65	Simonsen	Hoefkens	Griffin	Duberry	Higginbot'm	Diao	Russell	Lawrence^	Sidibe	Pericard*	Hendrie"	Fuller/Berger/Brammer
		28/11	15,039	*2*	33				*Alexander*	*McNaughton*	*Wright*	*Purse*	*Johnson*	*Scimeca*	*Parry*	*McPhail !*	*Chopra*	*Thompson^*	*Ledley**	*Kamara/Campbell*
								Ref: M Riler	Fuller returns from suspension to spark a devastating 5-min spell to knock Dave Jones's side off the top of the table. He fires in a left-foot shot. Lawrence lashes in during a melee. Sidibe taps in Fuller's cross. McPhail walks for hitting Hendrie. Berger lasehs over. A perfect November.											
21	A	COVENTRY		7	D	0-0	0-0		Simonsen	Hoefkens	Griffin	Duberry	Higginbot'm	Diao	Russell	Berger^	Sidibe	Fuller*	Hendrie	Pericard/Brammer
		2/12	*19,073*	*12*	34				*Marshall*	*Duffy*	*Hall*	*Page*	*Ward*	*Clarke*	*Cameron**	*Currie*	*Adebola*	*McKenzie^*	*Doyle*	*John/Birchall*
								Ref: N Miller	Two mean defences dominate a tight encounter. Mickey Adams' men have the better of the first half. Adebola nods over when well placed and then crashes a header against the post. Marshall sprawls to deny Fuller, twice, Hendrie and Sidibe. Now over nine hours without conceding.											
22	H	QP RANGERS		5	W	1-0	1-0	Higginbotham 17p	Simonsen	Hoefkens	Griffin	Duberry	Higginbot'm	Diao^	Russell	Lawrence	Sidibe	Fuller*	Hendrie"	Pericard/Brammer/Berger
		9/12	16,487	*20*	37				*Royce*	*Bignot*	*Milanese*	*Rehmann*	*Mancienne*	*Rowlands^*	*Gallen*	*Smith*	*Blackstock**	*Nygaard"*	*Bailey*	*Furlong/Ward/Baidoo*
								Ref: M Atkinson	Hendrie fires at Royce when clean through. Milanese brings down Fuller and Higgy lashes the pen down the middle. Stoke are less fluent and Fuller is caught offside too often. Blackstock heads narrowly over his own bar. Duberry volleys high. Berger almost tees up Pericard. Clinical.											
23	A	COLCHESTER		7	L	**0-3**	0-2		Simonsen	Hoefkens	Griffin	Duberry	Higginbot'm	Brammer*	Russell"	Lawrence	Sidibe^	Fuller	Hendrie	Berger/Pericard/Eustace
		16/12	***5,345***	*6*	37			*Cureton 2, 17, Garcia 63*	*Gerken*	*Halford*	*Barker*	*Brown*	*Baldwin*	*Duguid*	*Watson^*	*Izzett*	*Iwelumo"*	*Cureton*	*Garcia**	*Ephraim/Jackson/Guy*
								Ref: K Wright	The clean sheet record goes in ignominious fashion. Cureton's shot spins up and over Simo after 75 secs. His second is a deft finish to Izzett's flick. Fuller has a goal wrongly ruled out for a foul on Gerken. Garcia heads in Duguid's centre. Gerken flies to tip round Berger's piledriver.											

No	Date		Att	Pos	Pt	F-A	H-T	Scorers, Times, and Referees	SQUAD	NUMBERS	IN	USE								subs used
24	A	IPSWICH		4	W	1-0	0-0	Lawrence 71	Simonsen	Hoefkens	Buxton*	Hill	Higginbot'm	Diao	Russell	Lawrence	Sidibe	Fuller	Hendrie^	Dickinson/Brammer
	23/12		*20,369*	*16*	40				*Price*	*Bruce^*	*Harding*	*De Vos*	*Naylor*	*Williams*	*Legwinski*	*Garvan*	*Lee**	*Macken*	*Roberts"*	*Haynes/Peters/Walton*
								Ref: U Rennie	Buxton is recalled after 5 months out with a back injury to fill the gap left by Duberry's suspension. City have the better of a tight game. Fuller is denied by Price's legs. Hendrie's backheel deflects into Lawrence's path and the loanee scores. Garvan fizzes just over. Price denies Fuller.											
25	H	SHEFFIELD WED		8	L	1-2	0-1	Sidibe 60	Simonsen	Hoefkens	Higginbot'm	Hill*	Duberry	Diao	Russell	Lawrence	Sidibe	Fuller	Hendrie	Dickinson
	26/12		23,003	*12*	40			*MacLean 35, Burton 79*	*Crossley*	*Bullen*	*Spurr*	*Bougherra*	*Simek*	*Lunt*	*Whelan*	*Andrews**	*Tudgay*	*MacLean*	*Brunt^*	*Burton/O'Brien*
								Ref: C Foy	An end-to-end game livens the chilled spirits. Hill bravely blocks MacLean's shot. Andrews squares for MacLean to net. Andrews pushes over Hendrie but no red is produced. Sidibe heads in Diao's cross. Stoke's 2002 play-off hero Deon Burton scores after Simo saves from Tudgay.											
26	H	LEEDS		7	W	3-1	1-1	Sidibe 12, Ehiogu 54 (og), Fuller 77	Simonsen	Hoefkens	Higginbot'm	Hill	Duberry	Diao	Russell	Lawrence	Sidibe	Fuller^	Hendrie*	Berger/Pericard
	30/12		18,128	*24*	43			*Moore 41*	*Warner*	*Richardson*	*Lewis*	*Heath*	*Ehiogu*	*Douglas*	*Derry*	*Howson*	*Westlake**	*Healy*	*Moore*	*Kandol*
								Ref: A D'Urso	Last game of Hendrie's loan spell. He picks up an injury and limps off, but not before his corner is headed in by Sidibe. Moore nods in Healy's cross. Berger's shot hits Ehiogu and flies in. Fuller robs Ehiogu and leaves Warner stranded outside the area to score. Could this be the year?											
27	H	WOLVERHAMPTON		7	D	1-1	0-0	Hill 85	Simonsen	Hoefkens^	Higginbot'm	Hill	Duberry	Diao	Russell	Lawrence	Sidibe	Fuller	Pericard*	Sweeney"/Wilkinson/Rooney
	13/1		15,882	*10*	44			*Collins 63*	*Murray*	*Little*	*McNamara**	*Breen*	*Collins*	*Kightly*	*Olofinjana*	*Henry*	*Davies C*	*McIndoe^*	*Potter*	*Clapham/Edwards*
								Ref: P Walton	Fuller crashes a shot against the post. Kightly rattles the bar. Lawrence's cross is cleared off the line by Collins. The Scottish defender scores a rare goal, rising in front of Simo to glance in a corner. Lawrence toe-pokes just past the post. Hill crashes home a header from Duberry's flick.											
28	A	PRESTON		9	L	2-3	2-0	Lawrence 2, Sidibe 7	Simonsen	Wilkinson*	Griffin	Higginbot'm	Duberry	Hoefkens	**Matteo**	Lawrence	Sidibe	Pericard^	Russell	Brammer/Rooney
	20/1		*15,151*	*3*	44			*McKenna 65, Nugent 74, Wilson 89*	*Nash*	*Alexander*	*Hill*	*Chilvers*	*Wilson*	*Sedgwick**	*Neal*	*McKenna*	*Ormerod^*	*Nugent*	*Pugh*	*Whaley/Ricketts*
								Ref: R Beeby	A whirlwind start sees Lawrence drills in from 10 yards. Sidibe slots after Nash and Hill collide. Stoke are comfortable, but fall back and back until PNE dominate. McKenna lashes in from 25 yards. Nugent converts Whaley's cross. Simo misses a corner and Wilson scores. Gutting.											
29	A	BURNLEY		6	W	1-0	1-0	Sidibe 24	Simonsen	Wilkinson	Griffin	Higginbot'm	Duberry	Hoefkens	Matteo	Lawrence	Sidibe	Fuller	Russell	
	23/1		*12,109*	*13*	47				*Pollitt*	*Duff*	*Harley*	*Thomas*	*Sinclair*	*Elliott"*	*Djemba-Dj"^*	*O'Connor J*	*N'I-Williams*	*Akinbiyi*	*McCann**	*Laf'rty/Gudjons'n/O'Connor G*
								Ref: M Pike	Rearranged from New Year's Day. GNW twice goes close against his old club. Sidibe nets Fuller's cross after a mazy run. Wilkinson hacks GNW's shot off the line. Sidibe draws a good save from Pollitt, Russell fires just too high. Pollitt denies Matteo and Fuller hits the side-netting.											
30	H	IPSWICH		7	D	0-0	0-0		Simonsen	Hoefkens	Griffin	Higginbot'm	Duberry	Diao	Russell	Lawrence	Sidibe	Fuller	Martin*	Rooney
	30/1		11,812	*14*	48				*Price*	*Sito*	*Harding*	*Wright*	*Wilnis*	*Peters^*	*Legwinski*	*Garvan*	*Walters*	*Williams**	*Roberts*	*O'Callaghan/Haynes*
								Ref: C Webster	A subdued performance as Stoke have lost their verve. Simo is the busier of the two keepers, turning Walters' header round the post. Fuller bears down on goal, but Price smothers. Stoke cannot break down Jim Magilton's stubborn defence. Higgy has a header cleared off the line.											
31	H	SOUTHEND		8	D	1-1	1-0	Fuller 31	Simonsen	Hoefkens	Griffin*	Higginbot'm	**Fortune**	Diao	Russell	Lawrence	Sidibe	Fuller	Hendrie	Wilkinson
	3/2		**23,017**	*23*	49			*Eastwood 86*	*Flahavan*	*Francis*	*Hammell**	*Clarke*	*Sodje*	*Gower*	*Maher*	*Hunt*	*Eastwood*	*Bradbury^*	*Camp'l-Ryce*	*Foran/Harrold*
								Ref: A Taylor	Hendrie is back and a huge crowd, tempted by a £5 ticket offer, turn up. In a scrappy game, Fuller races onto Sidibe's flick to lash a rising shot into the roof of the net. Eastwood pounces to convert a Foran cross as Southend apply late pressure. Duberry has joined Reading for £800,000.											
32	A	BIRMINGHAM		10	L	0-1	0-0		Simonsen	Hoefkens	Griffin	Higginbot'm	Fortune	Eustace	Matteo	Lawrence	Sidibe^	Fuller	Martin*	Rooney/Harper
	11/2		*15,854*	*2*	49			*McSheffrey 71*	*Doyle*	*N'Gotty*	*Sadler*	*Taylor Mar'*	*Jaidi*	*Johnson*	*Clemence**	*Muamba*	*Jerome^*	*Bendtner*	*McSheffrey*	*Larsson/Vine*
								Ref: J Moss	An 11.30am Sunday start on police insistence kills this vital game as a spectacle. Devoid of goalmouth action, the match is a turgid tussle on an uneven surface. Martin tests Doyle. The keeper then misses a through ball but Sadler clears. McSheffrey nets a far-post cross from Bendtner.											
33	H	LUTON		10	D	0-0	0-0		Simonsen	Hoefkens	Griffin"	Higginbot'm	Fortune	Diao	Russell^	Lawrence	Sidibe*	Fuller !	Hendrie	Rooney/Martin/Dickinson
	17/2		12,375	*19*	50				*Beresford*	*Foley*	*Davis !*	*Heikkenen*	*Perrett^*	*Bell"*	*Robinson*	*Spring*	*Boyd**	*Runstrom*	*Morgan*	*Emanuel/Keane/Langley*
								Ref: T Kettle	The tension is mounting as Stoke cannot find the fluency or consistency from before Christmas. Fuller lets it get to him. On 29 mins he clashes with Sol Davis and is shown red. Davis then clatters Sidibe by the corner flag and walks himself (37). Russell wastes City's best chance.											
34	A	DERBY		9	W	2-0	2-0	Higginbotham 15p, Matteo 26	Simonsen	Hoefkens	Griffin	Higginbot'm	Zakuani	Diao	Russell	Lawrence	Sidibe"	Hendrie^	Matteo*	Eustace/Dickinson/Rooney
	21/2		24,897	*1*	53				*Bywater*	*Edworthy*	*McEveley*	*Leacock**	*Johnson M*	*Jones^*	*Oakley*	*Teale*	*Howard*	*Fagan*	*Macken"*	*Mears/Pearson/Lupoli*
								Ref: K Stroud	Fuller is out, suspended. Leacock handles a corner. Higgy cracks in the pen. The next teasing corner is headed in powerfully by Matteo for his first Stoke goal. Howard heads over. Billy Davies' leaders pressure City, but the defence holds firm. Simo flicks Lupolis' shot round the post.											

No	Ven	Opponent	Att	Pos	Res	F-A	H-T	Scorers, Times, and Referees	1	2	3	4	5	6	7	8	9	10	11	Subs used
35	H	BARNSLEY		9	L	0-1	0-1		Simonsen	Hoefkens	Griffin	Higginbot'm	Fortune	Diao	Russell^	Lawrence"	Sidibe	Hendrie	Matteo*	Eustace/Rooney/Martin
	26/2		13,114	*19*	53			*Ferenczi 43*	*Colgan*	*Austin*	*Heck'gbot'm*	*Nyatanga*	*Reid P*	*Devaney*	*Howard*	*Togwell*	*Ferenczi*	*Rajczi**	*McCann*	*Reid K*
								Ref: P Joslin	City struggle to make an impression on Tykes who have lost 13 of 17 games, and let in 37 goals away from home. Devaney nearly scores in the first min. Hungarian striker Ferenczi beats Simo with a precise curling shot. Sidibe is fouled when clear but only yellow is shown. No Fluency.											
36	A	PLYMOUTH		9	D	1-1	0-1	Russell 55	Simonsen	Hoefkens*	Griffin	Higginbot'm	Zakuani	Diao	Russell	Lawrence"	Sidibe	Hendrie^	Eustace	Dickinson/Martin/Paterson
	3/3		*12,539*	*12*	54			*Ebanks-Blake 40p*	*McCormack*	*Sawyer*	*Connolly*	*Seip*	*Timar*	*Summerf'ld**	*Hodges*	*Halmosi*	*Ebanks-B'ke^*	*Gallen*	*Sinclair*	*Gosling/Fallon*
								Ref: M Russell	Sidibe misses with a header from 3 yards. Simo claws away Halmosi's close-range effort. Heofkens brings down Halmosi and Ebanks-Blake converts the spot-kick. Seip blocks Sidibe's shot on the line. Lee Martin produces a lovely piece of skill on the wing to tee up Russell to net.											
37	H	SOUTHAMPTON		9	W	2-1	1-1	Fortune 34, Martin 72	Simonsen	Hoefkens	Griffin	Higginbot'm	Fortune	Diao	Russell	Lawrence"	Sidibe	**Parkin***	Martin^	Paterson/Eustace/Rooney
	10/3		13,404	*8*	57			*Saganowski 17*	*Davis*	*Baird*	*Bale*	*Powell*	*Lundekvam*	*Guthrie^*	*Wright**	*Viafra*	*Rasiak"*	*Saganowski*	*Surman*	*Pele/Skacel/Wright-Phillips*
								Ref: N Swarbrick	Loanee Jon Parkin (Hull) arrives. Saganowski nets after Simo can't hold Baird's shot. Fortune cracks in a corner. Viafra goes down injured, but play continues and Martin is put through to prod in past Davis. Simo fingertips away Viafra's stinging shot. First home win since 30 Dec.											
38	A	SUNDERLAND		9	D	2-2	2-1	Russell 22, Hoefkens 45	Simonsen	Zakuani^	Griffin	Higginbot'm	Fortune	Diao	Russell	Lawrence	Sidibe"	Parkin*	Hoefkens	Fuller/Dickinson/Eustace
	13/3		**31,358**	*3*	58			*Whitehead 24, Murphy 90*	*Ward*	*Simpson*	*Nosworthy*	*Evans**	*Collins*	*Whitehead*	*Leadbitter*	*Yorke"*	*John^*	*Connolly*	*Hysen*	*Wallace/Murphy/Miller L*
								Ref: M Jones	A topsy-turvy game sees Russell slam in from 25 yards, beating Ward on the greasy surface. Whitehead slams in Connolly's knockdown. Both teams are at full throttle. Hoefkens cracks a neat half-volley. Sidibe hits a post. Murphy nets in a scramble. Another failure to hold onto a lead.											
39	A	NORWICH		9	L	0-1	0-1		Simonsen	Zakuani^	Griffin !	Higginbot'm	Fortune	Diao"	Russell	Lawrence	Sidibe	Parkin*	Hoefkens	Fuller/Martin/Eustace
	17/3		*24,293*	*15*	58			*Huckerby 31*	*Warner*	*Lappin*	*Drury**	*Shackell*	*Doherty*	*Safri*	*Etuhu*	*Hughes*	*Martin"*	*Huckerby*	*Croft^*	*Foth'gham/Chadwick/Dublin*
								Ref: P Taylor	Teenager Chris Martin nods just wide as Canaries dominate. Huckerby tests Simo, but then lashes home after a one-two with Martin. Peter Grant's men snuff out Stoke's threat. Shackell hits the post. Fuller lashes over. Griffin sees red for violet conduct (88). 5 points off play-offs.											
40	H	LEICESTER		9	W	4-2	2-1	Parkin 18, Fuller 29p, Sidibe 79,	Simonsen	Hoefkens	Zakuani	Higginbot'm	Fortune	Eustace	Russell*	Lawrence	Fuller	Parkin^	Martin"	Dickinson/Sidibe/Hendrie
	31/3		13,303	*17*	61			*Kenton 16, Ham'ond 58* [Lawrence 90]	*Henderson*	*Stearman*	*Maybury"*	*Kisnorbo*	*Kenton*	*Newton*	*Johnson**	*Jarrett*	*Hume*	*Hammond*	*Tiatto^*	*Hughes/Porter/Fryatt*
								Ref: E Ilderton	Stoke's last chance saloon to gain momentum appears to be halted when Simo is fouled but the ref allows Kenton's goal. Parkin slots from 12 yards. Fuller slams in a pen after being brought down himself. Hammond's scuffed shot trickles in. Sidibe and Lawrence convert Fuller passes.											
41	A	WEST BROM		8	W	3-1	3-0	Fuller 14, Greening 20 (og), Parkin 22	Simonsen	Zakuani	Dickinson	Higginbot'm	Fortune	Eustace	Hoefkens	Lawrence	Sidibe*	Fuller"	Matteo	Parkin^/Hendrie/Martin
	7/4		*20,386*	*5*	64			*Koumas 74*	*Kiely*	*Robinson*	*Albrechtsen*	*McShane*	*Sodje**	*Chaplow*	*Greening^*	*Koren*	*Ellington*	*Phillips"*	*Koumas*	*Hogkiss/Carter/Macdonald*
								Ref: P Taylir	Fuller's pace destroys Albion's rickety defence. First he converts after a woeful Sodje miskick, then hares down the wing to cross for Greening to bundle the ball into his own net. A carbon copy move sees Parkin slam in on the run. Carnage in the away end. Koumas nets a deflection.											
42	H	CRYSTAL PALACE		7	W	2-1	2-1	Parkin 20, Fuller 27	Simonsen	Zakuani	Dickinson	Higginbot'm	Fortune	Eustace	Hoefkens	Lawrence	Parkin	Fuller^	Hendrie*	Martin/Pericard
	9/4		13,616	*12*	67			*Zakuani 30 (og)*	*Kiraly*	*Hudson*	*Borrowdale*	*Cort*	*Lawrence*	*Ifill**	*Kennedy"*	*Soares^*	*Morrison*	*Kuqi*	*Fletcher*	*Grabban/Martin/Scowcroft*
								Ref: R Booth	The injury list grows as Sidibe and Matteo are sidelined. Parkin swivels deftly to slam home a waist-high volley. Fuller wriggles between two defenders to lash a shot past Kiraly. Zakuani dives to head clear Cort's header but turns the ball in. Kiraly turns aside Hendrie's volley. Easy.											
43	A	CARDIFF		7	D	1-1	1-0	Hoefkens 30	Simonsen	Zakuani	Dickinson	Higginbot'm	Fortune*	Eustace	Hoefkens	Lawrence	Pericard^	Fuller	Matteo"	Griffin/Paterson/Russell
	14/4		*11,664*	*12*	68			*Chopra 90*	*Forde*	*McNaughton*	*Gunter*	*Purse^*	*Johnson*	*Whittingham*	*Parry**	*McPhail*	*Chopra*	*Thompson*	*Ledley*	*Flood/Gilbert*
								Ref: G Laws	Parkin has been recalled. Fuller outpaces Purse but Pericard cannot convert. Parry fires over. Hoefkens picks up Pericard's layback to lash in. Higgy's free-kick hits Forde's legs. Paterson misses an open goal from Fuller's cross. Chopra makes City pay after the defence fails to clear.											
44	H	HULL		8	D	1-1	1-0	Lawrence 45	Simonsen	Hoefkens	Griffin	Higginbot'm	Fortune	Eustace*	Matteo	Lawrence	Sidibe^	Fuller	Hendrie"	Russell/Pericard/Martin
	21/4		17,109	*21*	69			*Barmby 90*	*Myhill*	*Ricketts*	*Dawson*	*Turner*	*Delaney*	*Parlour"*	*Ashbee*	*Peltier**	*Windass*	*Forster*	*McPhee^*	*Marney/Barmby/Parkin*
								Ref: A D'Urso	Tension is mounting as the league is too tight to call. Both sides go whisker close before Lawrence's left-foot shot loops up and over Myhill to land in the goal. City just want the game to finish. Parkin returns to haunt Stoke, winning a header which drops for Barmby to steal in to level.											
45	H	COLCHESTER		7	W	3-1	0-1	Russell 53, Sidibe 57, Higginbotham 62	Simonsen	Hoefkens	Griffin	Higginbot'm	Fortune	Diao^	Russell	Lawrence*	Sidibe	Fuller"	Hendrie	Eustace/Martin/Pericard
	28/4		20,108	*9*	72			*Iwelumo 38p*	*Gerken*	*Duguid*	*Barker !*	*Brown*	*Baldwin*	*Garcia**	*Watson*	*Izzett*	*Iwelumo*	*Cureton"*	*Ephraim^*	*McLeod/Guy/Elokobi*
								Ref: G Salisbury	'Winner takes all' game. Big Chris Iwelumo returns to the Brit to net a pen after Diao fells him as Geraint Williams' men hold the upper hand. City sweep Us aside. Russell pokes in. Sidibe cracks home from 15 yards. Higgy nets a diving header. Barker walks for elbowing Hendrie (78).											
46	A	QP RANGERS		8	D	1-1	0-1	Sidibe 84	Simonsen	Zakuani	Griffin	Higginbot'm	Fortune	Diao^	Hoefkens	Matteo	Sidibe	Fuller	Hendrie*	Martin/Russell
	6/5		*16,741*	*18*	73			*Rowlands 6*	*Cole*	*Bignot*	*Timoska !*	*Shimmin*	*Stewart*	*Smith*	*Bailey*	*Bolder^*	*Blackstock**	*Nygaard"*	*Rowlands*	*Furlong/Bircham/Jones R*
	Home		Away					Ref: T Kettle	Disastrous start to the do-or-die mission as Rowlands curls a soft free-kick inside Simo's near post. Martin rattles the bar as Stoke pile forward. Timoska departs for a second yellow as Rangers resort to a series of bad fouls. Sidibe nets Pericard's pull back, but it's far too little too late.											
Average	15,749		17,044																	

League Cup		Att		F-A	H-T	Scorers, Times, and Referees	SQUAD	NUMBERS	IN	USE							subs used
1	H	DARLINGTON	13	1-2	1-1	Pericard 29	Simonsen	**Pulis**	Dickinson	Duberry	Hill	Whitley^	Russell	Harper*	Sidibe"	Pericard	Sweeney	Paterson/Eustace/Sigurds'n
	22/8	3,573	*2:10*			*Logan 45, Joachim 54*	*Stockdale*	*Close*	*James !*	*Holloway*	*Collins*	*Cummins*	*Ngoma*	*Duke*	*Joachim"*	*Logan**	*Johnson^*	*Rowson/Giallanza/Wainwr't*
						Ref: R Booth	Stoke play 80 mins against 10 men after Craig James walks for elbowing Harper. Pericard converts Dicko's cross. City sit back. Collins heads against the bar. The defence backs off Carlos Logan who lashes in from 20 yards. Joachim hammers in a 20 yard screamer. Embarrassed again!											

FA Cup																	
3	H	MILLWALL	7	2-0	0-0	Elliott og 84, Fuller 87	Simonsen	Hoefkens	Hill	Duberry	Higginbot'm	Diao*	Russell	Eustace^	Sidibe	Pericard	Sweeney"	Fuller/Brammer/Rooney
	5/1	8,024	*1:19*				*Pidgley*	*Senda*	*Ross"*	*Robinson*	*Shaw*	*Williams^*	*Ardley*	*Elliott*	*May**	*Byfield*	*Zebroski*	*Hubert/z/Fuseini/Bakayogo*
						Ref: G Laws	The Friday night kick-off indicates how little either of these teams want this game. In a scrappy affair, shots whistle just past both of Pidgley's posts. Shaw thwarts Fuller when through. Sidibe's shots is blocked on the line. Higgy's drive goes in of Elliott. Fuller chips Pidgley to seal it.											
4	A	FULHAM	6	0-3	0-2		Simonsen	Hoefkens	Griffin*	Duberry	Higginbot'm	Matteo^	Russell	Lawrence	Sidibe	Fuller"	**Martin**	Wilkinson/Diao/Rooney
	27/1	*11,059*	*P:15*			*Montella 11, McBride 39, Radzinski 54*	*Lastuvka*	*Volz*	*Bocanegra*	*Christanval*	*Queudrue*	*Rosenior^*	*Brown*	*Routledge*	*McBride"*	*Radzinkski*	*Montella**	*Dempsey/Davies/Jensen*
						Ref: M Atkinson	On-loan Lee Martin (Man Utd) adds some bite to an otherwise dulled attack.Montella taps in Radzinski's cross. Fuller nods just wide. McBride finishes off Queudrue's clever pass. Radzinski kills it by finishing Volz's throughball. City claim offside. TP not really that bothered to go out.											

		Home					Away					
	P	W	D	L	F	A	W	D	L	F	A	Pts
1 Sunderland	46	15	4	4	38	18	12	3	8	38	29	88
2 Birmingham	46	15	5	3	37	18	11	3	9	30	24	86
3 Derby *	46	13	6	4	33	19	12	3	8	29	27	84
4 West Brom	46	14	4	5	51	24	8	6	9	30	31	76
5 Wolves	46	12	5	6	33	28	10	5	8	26	28	76
6 Southampton	46	13	6	4	36	20	8	6	9	41	33	75
7 Preston	46	15	4	4	38	17	7	4	12	26	36	74
8 STOKE	46	12	8	3	35	16	7	8	8	27	25	73
9 Sheff Wed	46	10	6	7	38	36	10	5	8	32	30	71
10 Colchester	46	15	4	4	46	19	5	5	13	24	37	69
11 Plymouth	46	10	8	5	36	26	7	8	8	27	36	67
12 C Palace	46	12	3	8	33	22	6	8	9	26	29	65
13 Cardiff	46	11	7	5	33	18	6	6	11	24	35	64
14 Ipswich	46	13	2	8	40	29	5	6	12	24	30	62
15 Burnley	46	10	6	7	35	23	5	6	12	17	26	57
16 Norwich	46	10	5	8	29	25	6	4	13	27	46	57
17 Coventry	46	11	4	8	30	25	5	4	14	17	37	56
18 QP Rangers	46	9	6	8	31	29	5	5	13	23	39	53
19 Leicester	46	6	8	9	26	31	7	6	10	23	33	53
20 Barnsley	46	9	4	10	27	29	6	1	16	26	56	50
21 Hull	46	8	3	12	33	32	5	7	11	18	35	49
22 Southend	46	6	6	11	29	38	4	6	13	18	42	42
23 Luton	46	7	5	11	33	40	3	5	15	20	41	40
24 Leeds **	46	10	4	9	27	30	3	3	17	19	42	36
	1104	266	123	163	827	612	163	123	266	612	827	1523

* promoted after play-offs

** deducted 10 points

Odds & ends

Double wins: (4) C Palace, Derby, Leeds, West Brom.
Double losses: (0).

Won from behind: (4) Colchester (h), Leicester (h), Southampton (h), Sunderland (h).
Lost from in front: (3) Darlington (h LC), Leicester (a), Preston (a).

High spots: coming so close to the play-offs.
Hammering West Brom at the Hawthorns.
Setting a new clean-sheet record in November and December.
Great use of the loan system.

Low spots: failing to make the play-offs.
Huge splits between fans when Coates and Pulis return.
Too many petulant red cards.
Dismal exit from the League Cup at home to 10-man Darlington.

Ever-presents: (1) Steve Simonsen.
Hat-tricks: (0).
Leading Scorer: (11) Ricardo Fuller.
Player of the Year: Danny Higginbotham.

	Appearances						Goals			
	Lge	Sub	LC	Sub	FAC	Sub	Lge	LC	FAC	Tot
Bangoura, Sammy	1	3								
Berger, Patrik	1	5								
Brammer, Dave	11	11				1				
Buxton, Lewis	1									
Chadwick, Luke	13	2					3			3
Delap, Rory	2									
Diao, Salif	27				1	1				
Dickinson, Carl	5	8	1							
Duberry, Michael	29		1		2					
Eustace, John	7	8		1	1					
Fortune, Jonathan	14						1			1
Fuller, Ricardo	25	5			1	1	10		1	11
Griffin, Andy	32	1			1		2			2
Harper, Kevin		3	1							
Hendrie, Lee	26	2					3			3
Higginbotham, Danny	44				2		7			7
Hill, Clint	15	3	1		1		2			2
Hoefkens, Carl	42	3			2		2			2
Lawrence, Liam	27				1		5			5
Martin, Lee	4	9			1		1			1
Matteo, Dominic	9				1		1			1
Parkin, Jon	5	1					3			3
Paterson, Martin		9		1			1			1
Pericard, Vincent	17	10	1		1		2	1		3
Pulis, Anthony		1	1							
Rooney, Adam		10				2				
Russell, Darel	40	3	1		2		7			7
Sidibe, Mamady	42	1	1		2		9			9
Sigurdsson, Hannes		2		1						
Simonsen, Steve	46		1		2					
Sweeney, Peter	10	3	1		1		1			1
Whitley, Jim		3	1							
Wilkinson, Andy	2	2				1				
Zakuani, Gabriel	9									
(own-goals)							2		1	3
34 players used	**506**	111	**11**	3	**22**	6	**62**	**1**	**2**	**65**

No	Date		Att	Pos	Pt	F-A	H-T	Scorers, Times, and Referees	SQUAD	NUMBERS	IN	USE								subs used
1	A	CARDIFF			W	1-0	1-0	Shawcross 27	Simonsen	**Wright**	Dickinson	Higginbot'm	**Shawcross**	Matteo	Lawrence	Delap	Sidibe	Fuller*	**Cresswell**	Eustace
	11/8		*18,840*		3				*Turnbull*	*McNaughton*	*Capaldi*	*Loovens*	*Johnson*	*Rae*	*Sinclair*	*Ledley*	*MacLean*	*Feeney**	*McPhail*	*Parry*
								Ref: S Tanner	City start with a bang. Ryan Shawcross on season loan from Man U hammers in Lawrence's corner on the volley. Turnbull denies Fuller. Simo parries Sinclair's shot. Stoke hold on until the 88th minute. MacLean is brought down, but Simo saves his spot-kick and a follow-up brilliantly.											
2	H	CHARLTON	12,649	1	W	2-1	0-0	Fuller 57, Parkin 78	Simonsen	Wright*	Dickinson	**Craddock**	Shawcross	Matteo	Lawrence"	Delap	Sidibe	Fuller^	Cresswell	Buxton/Parkin/Eustace
	18/8			*16*	6			*Reid 55*	*Weaver*	*Mouta'akil"*	*Thatcher*	*Bougherra*	*Fortune*	*Semedo*	*Sam**	*Reid*	*Bent*	*McLeod^*	*Ambrose*	*Thomas/Iwelumo/McCarthy*
								Ref: G Laws	Jody Craddock (loan from Wolves) impresses as City dominate. Matteo nods wide. Sidibe slices horribly past an open net. Alan Pardew's men take a surprise lead when Reid curls in a free-kick. Fuller turns to curl in his own pearler from 20 yards. Parkin neatly converts a through ball.											
3	A	SOUTHAMPTON		3	L	2-3	1-1	Fuller 10, Parkin 82	Simonsen	Wilkinson	Hill	Craddock	Shawcross	Matteo"	Lawrence^	Delap	Sidibe*	Fuller	Cresswell	Parkin/Pulis/Eustace
	25/8		*20,300*	*21*	6			*Surman 36, Rasiak 71, Viafara 75*	*Davis*	*Wright*	*Skacel**	*Thomas*	*Powell*	*Dyer*	*Safri*	*Viafara*	*Rasiak*	*W't-Phillips^*	*Surman*	*Ostlund/Saganowski*
								Ref: R Beeby	Hill returns from suspension. Lawrence only just makes it following the birth of his daughter. Fuller turns to fire in. Surman hammers into the bottom corner. Simo is brilliant, making three world-class saves, but he can't stop Rasiak and Viafara scoring from close range. Parkin nods in.											
4	H	WOLVERHAMPTON	17,135	8	D	0-0	0-0		Simonsen	**Zakuani**	Dickinson	Hill	Shawcross	Matteo	Lawrence*	Delap	Sidibe^	Fuller	Cresswell	Parkin/Eustace
	1/9			*6*	7				*Hennessey*	*Foley*	*Collins N*	*Ward D*	*Breen*	*Henry*	*Olofinjana*	*Kightly*	*Keogh*	*Eastwood**	*Ward S*	*Elliott*
								Ref: L Mason	Zakuani returns on loan. Craddock can't play against his parent club. In a tense, rugged match, Fuller's effort deflects over the bar off Breen. Simo denies Darren Ward from a corner. Lawrence shoots tamely went put clear. Delap races through and is felled, but no spot-kick is given.											
5	A	HULL		7	D	1-1	1-0	Delap 44	Simonsen	Zakuani	Hill	Craddock	Shawcross	Matteo	Lawrence^	Delap	Sidibe	Fuller*	Cresswell	Parkin/Eustace
	15/9		*19,642*	*20*	8			*Livermore 87*	*Myhill*	*Delaney*	*Ricketts*	*Brown*	*Turner*	*Marney**	*Hughes^*	*Ashbee*	*Windass*	*Folan*	*Garcia"*	*Okocha/Bridges/Livermore*
								Ref: C Webster	A huge crowd to see Jay-Jay Okocha's debut. They have to wait as Phil Brown starts him on the bench. Stoke pressure and Delap slides in to convert at the far post. City drop further back as Hull press forward, Okocha to the fore. Livermore ghosts in to nod home Folan's knock-back.											
6	H	BARNSLEY	13,071	10	D	0-0	0-0		Simonsen	Wright	Dickinson*	Craddock	Shawcross	Matteo	Lawrence	Delap	Parkin	Fuller	Cresswell^	Zakuani/Sweeney
	18/9			*13*	9				*Muller*	*Kozluk**	*Werling*	*Foster*	*Souza*	*Howard*	*Anderson*	*Camp'l-Ryce^*	*Odejayi*	*Ferenczi*	*McCann*	*Nyatanga/Devaney*
								Ref: N Swarbrick	In a quiet first hour, Simo saves from McCann. Odejayi heads wide and Parkin fires straight at Muller. The pace picks up in the last 20 mins. Fuller hits the bar. Muller tips away Wright's drive. Cresswell blazes over from 4 yards. Anderson and Sweeney both fire just over the bar.											
7	H	PLYMOUTH	12,533	5	W	3-2	1-0	Seip 10 (og), Lawrence 66, Fuller 73	Simonsen	Wright	Hill*	Zakuani	Shawcross	Matteo	Lawrence	Delap	Sidibe"	Fuller	Cresswell^	Wilkinson/Sweeney/Parkin
	22/9			*13*	12			*Seip 52, Fallon 59*	*McCormick*	*Connolly*	*Sawyer"*	*Seip*	*Timar*	*Norris*	*Nalis*	*Buzsaky*	*Chadwick**	*Fallon^*	*Halmosi*	*Ebanks-Blake/Hayles/Hodges*
								Ref: N Miller	A quick free-kick leads Seip to turn in Lawrence's cross. Fuller fires at McCormick. Seip makes amends with a header from a corner. Fallon forces the ball in after a mix-up between Simo and Zakuani. Lawrence nets a flick on from Delap's prodigious throw in. Fuller lobs the keeper.											
8	A	LEICESTER		5	D	1-1	1-0	Fuller 15	Simonsen	Wright	Wilkinson	Zakuani	Shawcross	Matteo	Lawrence	Delap*	Parkin	Fuller	Cresswell	Eustace
	29/9		*23,654*	*20*	13			*Fryatt 47*	*Fulop*	*Chambers*	*McAuley*	*N'Gotty*	*Kisnorbo*	*Stearman*	*Clemence*	*Mattock*	*De Vries**	*Cort"*	*Campbell^*	*Fryatt/Hume/Kishishev*
								Ref: K Hill	Shawcross's volley is cleared off the line. Fuller curls a screamer round two defenders to deceive Fulop. Foxes turn Stoke's dominance around. Simo palms McAuley's header over. Within a minute of coming on, Fryatt swivels to flash a drive home. Lawrence is tripped but no pen given.											
9	A	WEST BROM		7	D	1-1	1-0	Shawcross 27	Simonsen	Wright	Wilkinson	Zakuani*	Shawcross	Matteo	Lawrence	Eustace	Sidibe^	Fuller	Cresswell	Dickinson/Parkin
	3/10		*20,048*	*3*	14			*Barnett 73*	*Kiely*	*Hoefkens**	*Robinson*	*Barnett*	*Albrechtsen*	*Morrison*	*Greening*	*Beattie^*	*Miller*	*Teixeira"*	*Koren*	*Gera/Brunt/MacDonald*
								Ref: C Oliver	Pericard is on the bench 4 days after his release from prison on driving offences. Shawcross powers in Lawrence's cross. City have backs to the wall and resort to time-wasting which riles Baggies fans. Barnett scrambles the ball home. Morrison fires over. Simo saves at the feet of Miller.											
10	H	COLCHESTER	12,395	5	W	2-1	1-0	Shawcross 8, Lawrence 73	Simonsen	Wright	Wilkinson*	Matteo	Shawcross	Delap	Lawrence"	Eustace	Sidibe^	Fuller	Cresswell	Dickinson/Parkin/Sweeney
	6/10			*17*	17			*Platt 58*	*Gerken*	*Dugui*d*	*Elokobi*	*Baldwin*	*Virgo*	*Yeates*	*Izzett*	*Jackson*	*Platt*	*Lisbie*	*Granville^*	*Balogh/Guy*
								Ref: C Penton	Matteo has to play centre-back due to injuries. Shawcross heads in Lawrence's corner. The defensive problems mount when Wilkinson limps off (42). Against the run of play Clive Platt nods in Granville's cross. Fuller frees Lawrence, who fires in from 15 yards. Parkin volleys over.											
11	H	SHEFFIELD WED	14,019	8	L	2-4	2-2	Fuller 12, 41	Simonsen	Zakuani	Wilkinson	Matteo	Shawcross	Delap	Lawrence	Eustace	Parkin*	Fuller	Cresswell	Sweeney
	20/10			*22*	17			*Johnson J 16, Tudgay 23, 85, Burton 87*	*Grant*	*Bullen^*	*Johnson M*	*Wood*	*Spurr*	*Johnson J"*	*O'Brien*	*Whelan*	*Tudgay*	*Jeffers**	*Kavanagh*	*Burton/Hinds/Sodje*
								Ref: L Mason	Stoke self-destruct. Fuller slots under Grant. Owls fight back with Jemal Johnson lashing in on the run. Tudgay nods in after Jeffers' shot hits the post. Fuller nods a poor back-pass past Grant and finishes. Tudgay and Burton convert chances on the break as City leave too many gaps.											

No	H/A	Opponent	Pos	Res	F-A	H-T	Scorers, Times, Referees	1	2	3	4	5	6	7	8	9	10	11	Subs used
12	A	CRYSTAL PALACE	5	W	3-1	0-0	Cresswell 49, 59, Shawcross 74	Simonsen	Wilkinson	Dickinson	Zakuani	Shawcross	Delap	Lawrence	Eustace	Cresswell^	Fuller*	Matteo	Parkin/Hill
23/10		*14,237*	*20*	20			*Freedman 51*	*Speroni*	*Lawrence*	*Craig*	*Hudson*	*Cort*	*Martin^*	*Fletcher*	*Watson*	*Scowcroft*	*Morrison*	*Dickov**	*Freedman/Green*
							Ref: M Thorpe	Cresswell start up front for the first time and scores twice. First he nods in Lawrence's inswinging free-kick, then he follows up after Lawrence hits a post. Freedman beats Shawcross and prods under Simo on the run. Scowcroft volleys over. Delap hits the crossbar and Shawcross nets.											
13	A	BRISTOL CITY	6	L	0-1	0-1		Simonsen	Wilkinson"	Dickinson	Zakuani	Shawcross	Delap	Lawrence^	Eustace	Pericard*	Fuller	Matteo	Parkin/Sweeney/Wright
3/11		*15,012*	*2*	20			*Elliott 35*	*Basso*	*Orr*	*McAllister*	*Fontaine*	*Carey*	*Sproule^*	*Johnson*	*Elliott*	*Noble**	*Trundle"*	*McIndoe*	*Byfield/Skuse/McCombe*
							Ref: R Shoebridge	With Cresswell suspended, Pericard starts after being released from jail again. Fuller volleys wide. Trundle fires just past. Elliott rams a pearler into the top corner from 30 yards. Stoke can't get into the game. Simo produces a great stop to deny Byfield. Dicko tackles Sproule when clear.											
14	H	COVENTRY	9	L	1-3	0-0	Lawrence 72p	Simonsen	Wright*	Wilkinson	**Cort**	Shawcross	Delap	Lawrence	Eustace	Cresswell	Fuller	**Pugh**	Parkin
10/11		13,488	*7*	20			*Mifsud 58, 79, Adebola 63*	*Konstant'los*	*McNamee*	*Hall*	*De Zeeuw*	*Turner*	*Doyle*	*Osbourne*	*Tabb*	*Simpson**	*Mifsud*	*Best^*	*Adebola/Kyle*
							Ref: A Marriner	Stoke are defensively poor. Adebola gives Cort the runaround. Sprightly Michael Mifsud twice races onto through-balls to lash home. Adebola nods in Best's cross. Shawcross looks to have scored, but the ball is clawed off the line. Lawrence's pen is for a trip on him. Mifsud hits a post.											
15	A	SCUNTHORPE	7	W	3-2	1-1	Cressw'l 26, Hayes 88 (og), Lawrence 90	Simonsen	Zakuani*	Dickinson	Cort	Shawcross	Delap	Lawrence	Eustace	Cresswell	Fuller	Pugh	Wright
6/11		***5,521***	*11*	23			*Hayes 31, Goodwin 85*	*Murphy*	*Byrne**	*Youga*	*Crosby*	*Butler*	*Taylor*	*Goodwin*	*Hurst*	*Hayes*	*Paterson*	*Cork*	*Williams*
							Ref: L Probert	An end-to-end tussle. Cresswell's shot is blocked on the line. He then diverts Eustace's effort into the net. Paul Hayes pounces on Shawcross's error to score. Goodwin hammers home from 15 yards. Stoke fight back dramatically, converting two crosses on the breakaway. Superb fight.											
16	H	SHEFFIELD UTD	9	L	0-1	0-1		Simonsen	Wright"	Wilkinson"	Cort	Shawcross	Delap	Cresswell	Eustace	Sidibe*	Fuller	Pugh	Parkin/Phillips/Pericard
10/11		12,158	*12*	23			*Cahill 43*	*Bennett*	*Bardsley*	*Naysmith*	*Kilgallon*	*Cahill*	*Montgomery*	*Gillespie*	*Carney"*	*Beattie*	*Webber**	*Armstrong*	*Lucketti/Tonge*
							Ref: K Stroud	Delap's throws cause chaos, but City cannot force them home. Fuller curls over. Carney whacks the post. Cahill, on loan from Villa, heads in Webber's cross with aplomb. Bennett saves Fuller's deflected shot on the line. Cresswell heads Phillips' cross straight at Bennett at the death.											
17	A	BURNLEY	10	D	0-0	0-0		Simonsen	Wright	Pugh	Cort	Shawcross	Delap	Cresswell	Eustace	Sidibe	Pericard*	Matteo	Parkin
24/11		*11,758*	*13*	24				*Kiraly*	*Alexander*	*Harley*	*Carlisle*	*Unsworth*	*Elliott*	*McCann*	*Mahon^*	*Lafferty**	*Blake"*	*Gray*	*Akinbiyi/Gudjonsson/Jones*
							Ref: L Mason	A tepid first half sees just one shot on target, when Mahon hammers a shot from 3 yards and Simo palms onto a post. Parkin is almost in, but is tackled as he shoots. Lafferty fires over. Delap and Blake hit speculative efforts. Stoke down to halfway after a poor run. Have they blown it?											
18	H	QP RANGERS	8	W	3-1	2-0	Cresswell 5, Lawrence 19, Cort 77	Simonsen	Wright^	Pugh	Cort	Shawcross	Delap	Lawrence	Eustace	Sidibe*	Fuller"	Cresswell	Parkin/Wilkinson/Phillips
27/11		**11,147**	*22*	27			*Vine 63*	*Camp*	*Stewart*	*Barker*	*Timoska*	*Mancienne**	*Rowlands"*	*Leigertwood*	*Buzsaky*	*Blackstock !*	*Vine^*	*Sinclair*	*Malcolm/Nygaard/Bolder*
							Ref: U Rennie	Fuller flicks on a Delap throw for Cresswell to score. Lawrence curls in a perfect free-kick to send the supporters wild. Luigi Di Canio's men are reduced to ten when Blackstock lunges at Shawcross (67). Fuller rounds the keeper but skies. Cort rises to head his first goal for the club.											
19	H	NORWICH	7	W	2-1	0-1	Cort 46, Cresswell 89	Simonsen	Wright*	Pugh	Cort	Shawcross	Delap	Lawrence	Eustace	Sidibe^	Fuller	Cresswell	Wilkinson/Parkin
1/12		19,285	*24*	30			*Huckerby 5*	*Marshall*	*Doherty*	*Shackell*	*Taylor*	*Camara*	*Russell*	*Croft^*	*Pattison**	*Huckerby*	*Dublin*	*Fothering'm*	*Evans/Cureton*
							Ref: L Probert	Veteran Dion Dublin sets up Huckery to net. Marshall denies Lawrence from Delap's throw. Pulis goes mad when the ref turns down two pen claims and is sent to the stands. Cort nods in Pugh's cross. Fuller is booked for diving. In a mad finish the ball flies around and Cresswell nets.											
20	A	SHEFFIELD UTD	5	W	**3-0**	3-0	Cressw'l 2, Beattie 7 (og), Shawcr's 19	Simonsen	Wilkinson*	Pugh	Cort	Shawcross	Delap"	Lawrence	Eustace	Sidibe^	Fuller	Cresswell	Zakuani/Parkin/Dickinson
4/12		*23,378*	*13*	33				*Kenny*	*Bardsley"*	*Naysmith^*	*Kilgallon*	*Cahill*	*Montgom'y**	*Gillespie*	*Tonge*	*Beattie*	*Carney*	*Armstrong*	*Stead/Quinn/Sharp*
							Ref: S Tanner	City rampage into United. Cresswell converts Lawrence's drilled cross. Cort flicks on and the ball flicks in off Beattie. Cort's header is cleared off the line and Shawcross nets. Bryan Robson's men are at sea as Stoke sit back. Kenny is the busier keeper, denying both Fuller and Parkin.											
21	H	WATFORD	5	D	0-0	0-0		Simonsen	Wright^	Dickinson	Cort	Zakuani	Delap	Lawrence	Pugh	Sidibe*	Fuller	Cresswell	Parkin/Buxton
9/12		15,516	*1*	34				*Lee*	*Doyley*	*Jackson*	*DeMerit*	*Stewart*	*Smith**	*Williamson*	*O'Toole*	*King*	*Priskin^*	*McAnuff*	*Ellington/Francis*
							Ref: C Webster	A bore draw as both teams cancel each other out and are happy to accept a point. Ady Boothroyd's runaway leaders go close as King lashes just wide. DeMerit clears Sidibe's shot off the line. Lee palms Pugh's effort around the post. Fuller chips Lee but DeMerit clears the danger.											
22	A	BLACKPOOL	4	W	3-2	2-1	Fuller 37, 61, Cort 41	Simonsen	Wilkinson	Pugh	Cort	Shawcross	Delap	Lawrence	Eustace	Sidibe*	Fuller^	Cresswell	Parkin/Dickinson
15/12		*9,123*	*18*	37			*Flynn 13, Barker 89*	*Rachubka*	*Barker*	*Crainey*	*Gorkss*	*Evatt*	*Tay'-Flet'r"*	*Jorgensen**	*Flynn*	*Burgess*	*Slusarksi^*	*Hoolahan*	*Morrell/Fox/Welsh*
							Ref: P Joslin	Simo saves from Burgess. Flynn cracks the ball home from 20 yards. Stoke dominate and Wilkinson and Shawcross go close. Fuller pounces when Rachubka palms out Lawrence's free-kick. Cort heads in a corner. Fuller races clear to net Lawrence's pass. Barker heads in at the death.											
23	H	WEST BROM	4	W	3-1	2-0	Fuller 5, 38, 66	Simonsen	Wilkinson	Pugh	Cort	Shawcross	Delap	Lawrence	Eustace	Sidibe*	Fuller^	Cresswell	Dickinson/Parkin
22/12		18,420	*2*	40			*Bednar 72*	*Kiely*	*Hoefkens*	*Robinson*	*Cesar"*	*Pele*	*Greening*	*Gera*	*Koren*	*Bednar*	*Teixeira**	*Brunt^*	*Miller/Phillips/Albrechtsen*
							Ref: M Halsey	Ricardo Fuller's one-man demolition job starts with a cool conversion of Sidibe's clever pass. Then he lashes in a loose ball after a free-kick. Cesar has a nightmare against the Jamaican. He is left sprawling as Fuller's swift run lays waste to the defence. Bednar nods in as City relax.											

No	Date	Opponent	Att	Pos	Pt	F-A	H-T	Scorers, Times, and Referees	SQUAD	NUMBERS	IN	USE									subs used
24	A	BARNSLEY		3	D	3-3	1-1	Lawrence 31p, 84, 90p	Simonsen	Wilkinson	Pugh	Cort	Shawcross	Delap	Lawrence	Eustace	Sidibe*	Fuller	Cresswell	Parkin
	26/12		*12,398*	*12*	41			*Howard 23p, Macken 66, 85*	*Muller*	*Foster !*	*Van Homoet*	*Souza*	*Nyatanga*	*Devaney^*	*Togwell*	*Howard*	*Macken*	*Ferenczi**	*McCann*	*Odejayi/Hassell*
								Ref: T Kettle	Cresswell climbs on Howard, who nets the pen. Fuller is felled by Souza. Lawrence scores from the spot. Sidibe fires wide. Shawcross clears off the line but Macken nets. Lawrence one-twos with Fuller to score. In a frantic end, Macken scores. Foster fouls Fuller and sees red. Classic.											
25	A	PLYMOUTH		4	D	2-2	1-1	Cresswell 8, Shawcross 57	**Hoult** !	Wilkinson*	Pugh	Cort	Shawcross	Delap	Lawrence	Eustace	Sidibe^	Fuller	Cresswell	Zakuani/Parkin"/Simonsen
	29/12		*13,692*	*6*	42			*Ebanks-Blake 44, Timar 67*	*Larrieu*	*Connolly*	*Hodges*	*Seip*	*Timar*	*Martin**	*Norris*	*Nalis*	*Ebanks-Bl'ke*	*Easter*	*Halmosi*	*Abdou*
								Ref: S Tanner	Delap's long throw evades everyone but Cresswell, who scores. Fuller fires wide. Shawcross blocks Martin's shot with his hand. Hoult saves the pen but can't stop the rebound. Shawcross and Timar both head in corners. Hoult goes for bringing down Ebanks-Blake (82). City cling on.											
26	H	HULL		4	D	1-1	1-0	Cort 33	Simonsen	Wright"	Pugh	Cort	Shawcross	Delap	Lawrence	Eustace	Sidibe*	Parkin^	Cresswell	Dickinson/Zakuani/Pericard
	1/1		15,788	*9*	43			*Folan 61*	*Myhill*	*Ricketts*	*Dawson*	*Brown*	*Turner*	*Livermore*	*Hughes^*	*Ashbee*	*Windass**	*Folan*	*Garcia*	*Barmby/Elliott*
								Ref: N Swarbrick	Windass skies from 4 yards as Phil Brown's men start well. Cort bullets in a header from a corner against the run of play. He then mistimes a copycat header with Myhill nowhere. Windass crosses for Folan to net a header. Pericard is tripped but no pen is given. Ten games unbeaten.											
27	A	IPSWICH		4	D	1-1	1-1	Fuller 33	Simonsen	Wilkinson*	Dickinson^	Cort	Shawcross	Delap	Lawrence	Eustace	Cresswell	Fuller	Pugh	Zakuani/Parkin
	12/1		*20,346*	*7*	44			*Haynes 19*	*Alexander*	*Sito*	*Wright*	*De Vos*	*Bruce*	*Haynes*	*Miller**	*Garvan*	*Lee*	*Walters*	*Counago^*	*Legwinski /Clarke*
								Ref: K Stroud	Town have dropped only four home points all season. Simo denies Haynes, but can't stop the pacy striker, who beats Dickinson to score. Pugh squares for Fuller to net. Eustace and Miller fire over from distance. Fuller goes round Alexander, but De Vos gets back to clear. Great point.											
28	H	PRESTON		4	W	3-1	2-0	Cort 16, 72, Cresswell 28	Simonsen	Wilkinson	Dickinson	Cort	Shawcross	Delap	Lawrence*	Eustace	Cresswell	Fuller^	Pugh"	Diao/Pericard/Parkin
	19/1		15,011	*22*	47			*Brown 68*	*Lonergan*	*St Ledger*	*Chilvers*	*Mawene*	*Davidson*	*Whaley*	*McKenna*	*Chaplow^*	*Brown*	*Hawley**	*Neal*	*Mellor/Carter*
								Ref: S Attwell	New signing Chris Brown provides a Preston spark, but Delap's throw is flicked in by Cort at the near post. Cresswell converts after Lonergan drops a cross on his foot. He makes amends by turning Mawene's flick aside. Brown slots from close range. Cort slams another header home.											
29	A	CHARLTON		4	L	0-1	0-0		Simonsen	Griffin	Dickinson*	Cort	Shawcross	Delap	Lawrence	Eustace	Cresswell	Fuller	Pugh	Parkin
	29/1		*22,108*	*5*	47			*Sam 83*	*Weaver*	*Moutaouakil*	*McCarthy*	*Bougherra*	*Youga*	*Sam"*	*Holland*	*Zhi*	*Iwelumo**	*Gray*	*Ambrose^*	*Varney/Thomas/Semedo*
								Ref: M Haywood	The unbeaten run is over after 12 games. Shawcross hooks Sam's shot off the line. Iwelumo fires over as Alan Pardew's men dominate. Fuller fires over. Iwelumo misses an open goal. Stoke almost escape but Lloyd Sam nods in Varney's cross. Parkin misses a sitter with his first kick.											
30	H	CARDIFF		4	W	2-1	1-0	Johnson 39 (og), Fuller 57p	Simonsen	Griffin	Pugh	Cort	Shawcross	Delap	Lawrence	Diao	Sidibe*	Fuller	Cresswell	**Whelan**
	2/2		15,045	*9*	50			*Hasselbaink 63*	*Oakes*	*McNaughton*	*Capaldi*	*Loovens*	*Johnson*	*Rae*	*Ledley*	*McPhail*	*Hasselb'nk**	*Parry*	*McPhail*	*Thompson*
								Ref: S Bennett	John Eustace has joined Watford for £250,000. Sidibe is back after Mali's defeat in the African Nations Cup. His shot is saved by Oakes's legs. Johnson slices Lawrence's cross into the net. McNaughton fouls Fuller who nets the pen. Hasselbaink slides in Parry's header. Stoke hang on.											
31	A	WOLVERHAMPTON		4	W	4-2	1-1	Delap 4, Lawrence 49, Cort 74, Fuller 90	Simonsen	Zakuani	Pugh	Cort	Shawcross	Delap	Lawrence^	Diao	Sidibe	**Gallagher***	Whelan	Fuller/Dickinson
	9/2		**25,373**	*12*	53			*Edwards 45, Keogh 47*	*Hennessey*	*Foley*	*Gray*	*Ward*	*Edwards*	*Keogh**	*Henry*	*Edwards^*	*Ebanks-Bl'ke*	*Kyle*	*Jarvis*	*Eastwood/Elliott*
								Ref: A Marriner	Sidibe rounds Hennessey to set up Delap. Gallagher is felled but no pen. Edwards taps in Keogh's centre. Ebanks-Blake sets up Keogh to net. City storm back. In a frenetic half, Lawrence cracks in from 20 yards. Cort slides in from 4 yards. Fuller races the length of the field to fire in.											
32	H	SOUTHAMPTON		3	W	3-2	3-0	Powell 27 (og), Shawcross 35, Sidibe 44	Simonsen	Griffin	Pugh	Cort	Shawcross	Delap	Lawrence*	Diao	Sidibe	Fuller	Whelan	Zakuani
	12/2		19,481	*18*	56			*John 46, 54*	*Davis*	*Davies**	*Wright*	*Powell*	*Ostlund*	*Viafara*	*Surman*	*Saganowski*	*Euell*	*John*	*Idiakez^*	*Wright-Phillips/McGoldrick*
								Ref: N Miller	A Stoke whirlwind takes managerless Saints by storm. Powell turns Lawrence's corner into his own net. Shawcross and Sidibe both power headers past Davis to give City an unassailable lead. Stern John tries his best to claw back the deficit, netting two stunning strikes from range.											
33	H	SCUNTHORPE		1	W	3-2	0-2	Lawrence 53, 67, Cresswell 63	Simonsen	Griffin	Pugh	Cort	Shawcross	Delap	Lawrence	Diao*	Sidibe	Fuller^	Whelan	Cresswell/Zakuani
	15/2		20,979	*24*	59			*Paterson 7, Hobbs 23*	*Murphy*	*Butler*	*Williams*	*Hobbs*	*Crosby*	*Sparrow"*	*Goodwin*	*Cork*	*Horsfield**	*Paterson*	*Morris^*	*Hayes/Forte/May*
								Ref: G Laws	Paterson waltzes through to score. Hobbs turns the ball in during a scramble. City have a mountain to climb. After a half-time roasting from TP they begin the task as Lawrence bursts through to score, and then pokes in Fuller's pull back. Cresswell shoots and Murphy lets the ball slip in.											
34	H	IPSWICH		1	W	1-0	1-0	Lawrence 42	Simonsen	Griffin	Dickinson	Cort	Shawcross	Delap	Lawrence	Whelan	Sidibe*	Fuller	Cresswell	Diao
	23/2		23,563	*7*	62				*Bywater*	*Bruce*	*Harding*	*De Vos*	*Naylor*	*Norris"*	*Miller*	*Quinn**	*Lee^*	*Walters*	*Shumulik'ski*	*Haynes/Counago/Garvan*
								Ref: M Jones	A tight, tense game with little to choose between the teams. City's superior mental reserves see them come out on top. Lawrence cracks a free-kick over. Lee misses from 5 yards. Lawrence slams in a 30-yard belter. Town boss Jim Magilton is sent to the stands. Sidibe fires just wide.											

No	Date	Opposition	Att	Pos	Res	Pts	F-A	H-T	Scorers, Times, and Referees	1	2	3	4	5	6	7	8	9	10	11	Subs used
35	A	PRESTON		1	L		0-2	0-2		Simonsen	Griffin	Pugh	Cort^	Shawcross	Delap	Lawrence	Whelan"	Sidibe*	Fuller	Cresswell	Parkin/Wilkinson/Gallagher
	26/2		10,347	21		62			Chaplow 22, 33	Lonergan	St Ledger	Chilvers	Mawene	Davidson	Whaley	McKenna	Chaplow*	Brown	Hawley^	Neal	Carter/Mellor
									Ref: M Oliver	Alan Irvine's struggling Preston run the whole game. Stoke miss an early opportunity when Cresswell fails to capitalise on defensive errors. Richard Chaplow nods in a free-kick, then he hammers home from distance. Fuller and Shawcross crack against the woodwork. Disappointing.											
36	A	QP RANGERS		2	L		**0-3**	0-2		Simonsen	Griffin !	Pugh	Cort	Shawcross	Diao^	Lawrence"	Whelan	Sidibe*	Fuller	Cresswell	Wilkinson/Buxton/Gallagher
	2/3		13,398	15		62			Leigertwood 12, 21, Buzsaky 56	Camp	Mancienne	Delaney	Hall^	Connolly	Rowlands"	Leigertwood	Buzsaky	Vine*	Agyemang	Ephraim	Blackst'k/Stewart/Ainsworth
									Ref: A D'Urso	Fuller and Sidibe both hit the post early on. Mikele Leigertwood nets two quickfire strikes from the edge of the box. Griffin is incorrectly sent off and his suspension is revoked. It means City can't hit back. Buzsaky fires home from 20 yards. Camp tips round Whelan's 25-yard curler.											
37	H	BURNLEY		2	D		1-1	0-1	Lawrence 90p	**Nash**	Griffin	Pugh	Cort	**Riggott**	Diao^	Lawrence	Delap	Sidibe*	Fuller	Cresswell	Gallagher/Parkin
	8/3		18,342	10		63			Lafferty 2	Kiraly	Alexander	Harley	Carlisle	Varga	O'Connor	Elliott	Randall*	Akinbiyi"	Lafferty^	Blake	Mahon/Spicer/Cole
									Ref: H Webb	Lafferty steals in to net at the far post. City shudder, but gather themselves. Cort clears Elliott's dangerous cross. Fuller fires wide when clean through. Kiraly parries Pugh's free-kick. Nash denies Cole. Cresswell is fouled. Lawrence's pen goes in off a post and Kiraly's head. Relief.											
38	A	NORWICH		2	W		1-0	0-0	Sidibe 58	Nash	Griffin	Dickinson	Cort^	Riggott	Diao*	Lawrence	Delap	Sidibe"	Cresswell	Pugh	Fuller/Shawcross/Gallagher
	11/3		23,471	17		66				Marshall	Otsemobor	Camara*	Shackell	Pearce	Fothering'm	Croft	Pattison	Dublin	Cureton	Bertrand	Evans
									Ref: A Woolmer	Cort blocks Cureton's shot bravely. Delap is brought down but the shouts for a pen are waved away. A dour game is settled when Delap's long throw is met by Sidibe, whose looping header beats Marshall. Cureton misses an open goal. Bertrand and Pattison both waste shots. Crucial.											
39	A	WATFORD		1	D		0-0	0-0		Nash	Riggott	Griffin	Cort*	Shawcross	Cresswell	Dickinson^	Delap	Fuller	Whelan	**Bothroyd"**	Gallagher/Pugh/Diao
	15/3		18,338	3		67				Lee	Bromby	Sadler	Shittu	DeMerit	Smith	Eustace !	O'Toole	Henderson	John*	McAnuff	Williamson
									Ref: R Styles	Eustace is sent off (20) for a two-footed lunge on Cresswell. Lee tips away two Fuller rapiers. Shawcross nods a trademark Delap long throw inches wide. Griffon handles (47). Henderson takes the kick but sees it saved for the second successive game. The game peters out. Solid point.											
40	H	BLACKPOOL		1	D		1-1	0-1	Cort 47	Nash	Griffin	Dickinson	Cort^	Riggott	Diao*	Whelan	Delap	Sidibe	Cresswell	Gallagher	Wilkinson"/Zakuani/Bothroyd
	22/3		20,019	16		68			Burgess 37	Rachubka	Crainey	Barker	Evatt	Gorkss	Hoolahan	Flynn	Jorgensen	Burgess	McPhee	Tay-Fletc'r*	Holt
									Ref: M Pike	Simon Grayson's Blackpool arrive late due to a crash on the M6. Kick-off is delayed. It subdues City. Burgess latches on to McPhee's flick on and nets via a deflection off Cort. Stoke waste several countless chances. Cort finally fires in 'We should have kicked off on time,' moans TP.											
41	A	SHEFFIELD WED		2	D		1-1	1-0	Cresswell 21	Nash	Griffin	Dickinson	Cort	Riggott	Whelan	Lawrence	Delap	**Ameobi^**	Cresswell	**Pearson***	Bothroyd/Pugh
	29/3		21,857	22		69			Songo'o 82	Grant	Hinds*	Spurr	Wood	Beevers	McAllister	Kavanagh	Small^	Songo'o	Burton	Sahar"	Watson/Johnson/Showumni
									Ref: P Taylor	Loanees Ameobi (Newcastle) and Pearson (Derby) arrive. Pearson's low shot is deflected in by Cresswell. City defend deep. Burton fires over. Songo'o breaks the resistance, cutting inside Griffin to curl home. It's discovered Weds fielded too many loanees, but they only receive a fine.											
42	H	CRYSTAL PALACE		2	L		1-2	0-2	Whelan 85	Nash	Griffin	Pugh	Cort	Riggott	Whelan	Cresswell	Delap	Ameobi	Sidibe*	Pearson^	Fuller/Bothroyd
	7/4		15,756	6		69			Soares 23, Fonte 45	Speroni	Lawrence	Hill	Hudson	Fonte	Sinclair"	Soares^	Watson	Morrison	Derry	Moses*	Reid/Scannell/Fletcher
									Ref: M Clattenburg	In front of Sky cameras Neil Warnock's young Palace shine in the first half. Soares rises to head in Sinclair's cross at the far post. Centre-half Jose Fonte hits a dipping volley into the far corner. City press after the break but only have Whelan's volley to show for it. Are City bottling it?											
43	A	COVENTRY		1	W		2-1	0-1	Fuller 55p, Lawrence 79	Nash	Griffin^	Dickinson	Cort	Riggott	Pugh	Cresswell	Delap	Ameobi*	Fuller	Pearson"	Sidibe/Shawcross/Lawrence
	12/4		20,249	20		72			Ward 31p	Schmeichel	Osbourne	Fox	Ward	Dann	Hughes	Tabb	Doyle	Best^	Mifsud*	Thornton	Hines/Simpson
									Ref: U Rennie	Thornton hits the bar and Doyle a post as Coventry dominate. Dickinson trips Best in a scramble. Ward lashes in the pen. Enforced changes through injury change the game. Fuller is felled for the pen. Lawrence is a whirlwind.He slots after Fuller goes clear but is halted. Wonderful.											
44	H	BRISTOL CITY		2	W		2-1	2-0	Sidibe 14, 36	Nash	Riggott	Dickinson	Cort	Shawcross	Whelan	Lawrence"	Delap	Sidibe^	Fuller	Cresswell*	Pearson/Ameobi/Wilkinson
	19/4		24,475	4		75			Adebola 67	Basso	Orr	McAllister	McCombe	Carey	Wilson*	Elliott"	Skuse	Adebola	Byfield^	McIndoe	Noble/Trundle/Vasko
									Ref: M Riley	Pottermouth's battlecry inspires Stoke before kick-off. Mama Sidibe doubles his goal-tally for the season by heading in a corner and racing on to Fuller's pass to beat Basso. Adebola scores his usual goal against City, but it doesn't matter. Potters hold out easily. Only 4 points needed.											
45	A	COLCHESTER		1	W		1-0	1-0	Cresswell 45	Nash	Riggott	Dickinson	Cort	Shawcross	Whelan	Lawrence	Delap	Sidibe*	Fuller	Cresswell	Ameobi
	26/4		6,300	24		78				Gerken	Ifill	White	Coyne	Virgo*	Duguid"	Jackson	Hammond	Lisbie	Elito	Vernon^	Balogh/Sheringham/Platt
									Ref: K Friend	Already relegated Us are saying goodbye to Layer Road. 10,000 are watching on a screen at the Brit. Gerken palms over Cort's header. Fuller and Sidibe fire just wide. Cresswell touches in Lawrence's pullback. News of Hull's late winner dampens the party, but only one point needed.											
46	H	LEICESTER		2	D		0-0	0-0		Nash	Wilkinson*	Dickinson	Cort	Shawcross	Whelan	Lawrence"	Delap	Sidibe^	Fuller	Cresswell	Buxton/Ameobi/Pugh
	4/5	·	**26,609**	22		79				Henderson	Stearman	Mattock	McAuley	N'Gotty	Bell^	Worley*	Oakley	Howard	Hayles	Hume	Fryatt/Chambers
	Home		Away						Ref: M Dean	Party time as Ipswich score against Hull. Fuller is felled but no pen given. Stoke focus on not conceding. Hayles fires wide. McAuley smacks a post. Nash denies Howard, Hayles and Hume. The draw relegates Foxes. Thousands invade the pitch to celebrate with a chorus of 'Delilah'.											
Average	16,823		17,037																		

League Cup		Att		F-A	H-T	Scorers, Times, and Referees	SQUAD	NUMBERS	IN	USE								subs used
1 A ROCHDALE			D	2-2	1-0	Shawcross 4, Cresswell 120	Hoult	Wright	Dickinson	Shawcross	Higginbot'm*	Delap^	Pulis	Eustace	Sidibe	Parkin"	Lawrence	Wilkinson/Sweeney/Cressw'l
14/8		*2,369*		*aet*		*Perkins 83, Prendergast 101*	*Spencer*	*Ramsden*	*Kennedy*	*McArdle*	*D'Laryea*	*Muirhead*	*Jones*	*Perkins*	*Rundles^*	*Murray*	*Dagnall**	*Fondre/Prendergast*
						Ref: M Haywood (Stoke lose 2-4 on penalties)	Shawcross heads in Lawrence's free-kick. City resort to hanging on far too early. Muirhead fires narrowly past. Rundle hits the post. Perkins plays a one-two with le Fondre and hammers in. Prendergast nets a half-volley. City level when Cresswell slots, but he and Dicko miss pens.											

FA Cup																		
3 H NEWCASTLE	4		D	0-0	0-0		Simonsen	Wilkinson	Dickinson	Shawcross	Cort	Eustace^	Lawrence	Pugh	Sidibe*	Fuller"	Cresswell	Parkin/Pulis/Pericard
6/1		22,861 *P:11*					*Given*	*Rozenhal*	*Enrique*	*Taylor*	*Faye*	*Butt*	*Smith*	*Duff^*	*Viduka**	*Owen*	*N'Zogbia*	*Lua Lua/Carroll*
						Ref: S Bennett	Fireworks greet the teams for Stoke's first ever live BBC match. Simo denies Owen. Lawrence hits the side-netting. Duff crosses but Owen and Taylor miss the open goal. Parkin's shot is cleared of the line by Faye. Cresswell's effort is kicked off the line. Fuller's shot deflects wide.											
3R A NEWCASTLE	4		L	1-4	0-2	Lawrence 89	Simonsen	Zakuani	Pugh	Shawcross	Cort	Eustace"	Lawrence	Delap^	Cresswell	Fuller	Parkin*	Diao/Pulis/Dickinson
16/1		*35,108 P:11*				*Owen 8, Cacapa 31, Milner 68, Duff 76*	*Given*	*Carr*	*Enrique*	*Taylor*	*Cacapa**	*Milner*	*Emre !*	*Duff*	*Viduka^*	*Owen*	*N'Zogbia"*	*Rozenhal/Carroll/Lua Lua*
						Ref: U Rennie	Kevin Keegan's second coming sees a rejuvenated Toon pulverise City. Even when Emre is sent off for a lunge on Eustace, Stoke wilt. Owen taps in Duff's cross, Cacapa nods in a corner. Milner fires in from 20 yards. Duff converts N'Zogbia's cross. Lawrence curls in a 20 yarder.											

	P	W	D	L	F	A	W	D	L	F	A	Pts
		Home					Away					
1 West Brom	46	12	8	3	51	27	11	4	8	37	28	81
2 STOKE	46	12	7	4	36	27	9	9	5	33	28	79
3 Hull *	46	13	7	3	43	19	8	5	10	22	28	75
4 Bristol C	46	13	7	3	33	20	7	7	9	21	33	74
5 C Palace	46	9	9	5	31	23	9	8	6	27	19	71
6 Watford	46	8	7	8	26	29	10	9	4	36	27	70
7 Wolves	46	11	6	6	31	25	7	10	6	22	23	70
8 Ipswich	46	15	7	1	44	14	3	8	12	21	42	69
9 Sheff Utd	46	10	8	5	32	24	7	7	9	24	27	66
10 Plymouth	46	9	9	5	37	22	8	4	11	23	28	64
11 Charlton	46	9	7	7	38	29	8	6	9	25	29	64
12 Cardiff	46	12	4	7	31	21	4	12	7	28	34	64
13 Burnley	46	7	9	7	31	31	9	5	9	29	36	62
14 QP Rangers	46	10	6	7	32	27	4	10	9	28	39	58
15 Preston	46	11	5	7	29	20	4	6	13	21	36	56
16 Sheff Wed	46	9	5	9	29	25	5	8	10	25	30	55
17 Norwich	46	10	6	7	30	22	5	4	14	19	37	55
18 Barnsley	46	11	7	5	35	26	3	6	14	17	39	55
19 Blackpool	46	8	11	4	35	27	4	7	12	24	37	54
20 Southampton	46	9	5	9	26	27	4	10	9	30	45	54
21 Coventry	46	8	8	7	25	26	6	3	14	27	38	53
22 Leicester	46	7	7	9	23	19	5	9	9	19	26	52
23 Scunthorpe	46	7	8	8	31	33	4	5	14	15	36	46
24 Colchester	46	4	8	11	31	41	3	9	11	31	45	38
	1104	234	171	147	790	604	147	171	234	604	790	1485

* promoted after play-offs

Odds & ends

Double wins: (5) Cardiff, Colchester, Norwich, Scunthorpe, West Brom.
Double losses: (0).

Won from behind: (8) Charlton (h), Plymouth (h), Scunthorpe (a), Norwich (h), Blackpool (a), Wolves (a), Scunthorpe (h), Coventry (a).
Lost from in front:(2) Southampton (a), Sheff Wed (h).

High Spots: Promotion to the top flight for the first time in 23 years.
The emergence of the Delap long throw.
The side's incredible mental strength.
Liam Lawrence, the Actim Player of the Season for the Championship.

Low spots: Six games without a win over Christmas.
Some fans' nonsensical criticisms of Richard Cresswell.
The home defeat by Crystal Palace, which seemed to land Stoke in the play-offs.

Ever-presents: (0).
Hat-tricks: (2) Ricardo Fuller, West Brom (h); Liam Lawrence v Barnsley (a).
Leading Scorer: (15) Ricardo Fuller, Liam Lawrence.
Player of the Year: Liam Lawrence.

	Appearances						Goals			
	Lge	*Sub*	LC	*Sub*	FAC	*Sub*	**Lge**	LC	FAC	**Tot**
Ameobi, Shola	**3**	*3*								
Bothroyd, Jay	**1**	*3*								
Buxton, Lewis		*4*								
Cort, Leon	**33**				2		**8**			**8**
Craddock, Jody	**4**									
Cresswell, Richard	**42**	*1*		*1*	2		**11**	1		**12**
Delap, Rory	**44**		1		1		**2**			**2**
Diao, Salif	**8**	*3*				*1*				
Dickinson, Carl	**20**	*7*	1		1	*1*				
Eustace, John	**20**	*6*	1		2					
Fuller, Ricardo	**39**	*3*			2		**15**			**15**
Gallagher, Paul	**2**	*5*								
Griffin, Andy	**14**									
Higginbotham, Danny	**1**		1							
Hill, Clint	**4**	*1*								
Hoult, Russell	**1**		1							
Lawrence, Liam	**40**	*1*	1		2		**14**		1	**15**
Matteo, Dominic	**14**									
Nash, Carlo	**10**									
Parkin, Jon	**4**	*25*	1		1	*1*	**2**			**2**
Pearson, Stephen	**3**	*1*								
Pericard, Vincent	**2**	*3*				*1*				
Phillips, Demar		*2*								
Pugh, Danny	**26**	*2*			2					
Pulis, Anthony		*1*	1			*2*				
Riggott, Chris	**9**									
Shawcross, Ryan	**39**	*2*	1		2		**7**	1		**8**
Sidibe, Mamady	**33**	*1*	1		1		**4**			**4**
Simonsen, Steve	**35**	*1*			2					
Sweeney, Peter		*5*		*1*						
Whelan, Glenn	**13**	*1*					**1**			**1**
Wilkinson, Andy	**17**	*7*		*1*	1					
Wright, Stephen	**14**	*2*	1							
Zakuani, Gabriel	**11**	*8*			1					
(own-goals)							**5**			**5**
34 players used	**506**	***101***	**11**	***3***	**22**	***6***	**69**	**2**	**1**	**72**

No	Date		Att	Pos	Pt	F-A	H-T	Scorers, Times, and Referees	SQUAD	NUMBERS	IN	USE								subs used
1	A	BOLTON			L	1-3	0-3	Fuller 90	**Sorensen**	Wilkinson$	Griffin	Shawcross	Cort	**Olofinjana**	Delap*	Whelan	Sidibe^	**Kitson**	Cresswell	Lawrence/Fuller/Dickinson
	16/8		*22,717*		0			*Steins'n 34, Davies K 41, Elmander 45*	*Jaaskel'nen*	*Steinsson*	*Samuel*	*Cahill*	*O'Brien A*	*O'Brien J*	*Nolan*	*Muamba*	*Davies K*	*Elmander**	*Taylor*	*McCann*
								Ref: C Foy	The harsh reality of life at the top begins to dawn after Steinsson's mishit cross curls in. Davies outmuscles Cort to nod in. Elmander heads in Joey O'Brien's cross. Stoke are not at the races. The second half is better. Fuller heads in Lawrence's cross. But TP has much to think about.											
2	H	ASTON VILLA		14	W	3-2	1-0	Lawrence 30p, Fuller 80, Sidibe 90	Sorensen	Griffin	Dickinson	**Faye AD**	Cort	Olofinjana	Delap	**Faye A***	Fuller$	Kitson^	Lawrence	Diao/Sidibe/Cresswell
	23/8		*27,500*	*6*	3			*Carew 63, Laursen 84*	*Friedel*	*Young*	*Shorey**	*Laursen*	*Davies*	*Petrov*	*Reo-Coker*	*Barry*	*Carew*	*Agbonlahor*	*Young*	*Routledge*
								Ref: M Halsey	A fabulous game. Lawrence lashes in a pen after Laursen trips Delap. Carew rounds off a great Villa move to crash in. Fuller nets MoTD Goal of the Month, flicking the ball over Laursen to net. Laursen nets in a scramble. Sidibe rises to back-head Delap's long throw into the far corner.											
3	A	MIDDLESBROUGH		16	L	1-2	0-1	Hoyte 71 (og)	Sorensen	Griffin	Dickinson*	Faye AD	Cort	Olofinjana	Delap	Faye A !	Fuller^	Kitson$	Lawrence	Wilkinson/Sidibe/Cresswell
	30/8		*27,627*	*5*	3			*Alves 38, Tuncay 85*	*Turnbull*	*Hoyte^*	*Pogatetz*	*Huth*	*Wheater*	*Shawky**	*Aliadiere*	*O'Neil*	*Alves$*	*Tuncay*	*Downing*	*Digard/Taylor/Mido*
								Ref: M Dean	Stoke are the better side till Amdy Faye sees red for a tackle on Shawky. Alves curls the free-kick in off the bar. Downing hits a pen against the bar. City's 10 play well on the break. Kitson forces Hoyte to net a Lawrence cross. City cope till Wilkinson sleeps in. Tuncay takes advantage.											
4	H	EVERTON		19	L	2-3	0-1	Olofinjana 55, Jagielka 63 (og)	Sorensen	Griffin	Higginbot'm	**Sonko**	Cort	Olofinjana	Delap	Faye AD*	Fuller	Kitson^	Lawrence$	**Tonge**/Sidibe/Cresswell
	14/9		27,415	*10*	3			*Yakubu 41, Anichebe 51, Cahill 77*	*Howard*	*Neville*	*Lescott*	*Yobo*	*Jagielka*	*Fellaini*	*Anichebe^*	*Cahill**	*Yakubu*	*Arteta*	*Castillo*	*Rodwell/Vaughan*
								Ref: A Wiley	Yakubu finishes coolly from 15 yards. Anichebe flicks in Arteta's peach of a cross. City fight back. Olly lashes in a stunning volley. Jagielka flicks in a Delap throw. David Moyes is sent to the stand after Wiley refuses a cast-iron pen. Cahill nods in a near post corner. Fabulous game.											
5	A	LIVERPOOL		18	D	0-0	0-0		Sorensen	Griffin	Higginbot'm	Sonko*	Faye AD	Olofinjana	Delap	Diao	Sidibe	Kitson$	Lawrence^	Cort/Cresswell/Fuller
	20/9		*43,931*	*2*	4				*Reina*	*Arbeloa*	*Dossena*	*Carragher*	*Skrtel*	*Alonso*	*Gerrard*	*Kuyt*	*Keane^*	*Torres*	*Rieira**	*Babel/Benayoun*
								Ref: A Marriner	Gerrard's free-kick drifts into the net and Reds celebrate his 100th goal, but ref Marriner disallows it correctly for Kuyt's offside. Stoke throw their bodies in front of shots and crosses like heroes. Cort is almost decapitated by a Gerrard piledriver. Sorenseon denies Keane and Rieira.											
6	H	CHELSEA		18	L	0-2	0-1		Sorensen	Griffin	Higginbot'm	Cort	Faye AD	Olofinjana	Lawrence^	Diao	Sidibe$	Kitson*	Cresswell	Fuller/Tonge/Faye A
	27/9		27,500	*1*	4			*Bosingwa 36, Anelka 76*	*Cech*	*Bosingwa*	*Cole*	*Alex*	*Terry*	*Mikel*	*Lampard*	*Ballack$*	*Drogba^*	*Malouda*	*Kalou**	*Anelka/Belletti/Ferreira*
								Ref: M Atkinson	Big Phil Scolari's table-toppers are a class act. City chase shadows in the heat. Sorensen turns away shots from Drogba and Ballack. Bosingwa rifles in from the right edge of the box. Anelka fires in after Cort slips over. Even the watching Sugar Ray Leonard must have been impressed.											
7	A	PORTSMOUTH		19	L	1-2	0-1	Fuller 48	Simonsen	Griffin	Higginbot'm	Cort	Faye AD	Olofinjana	Faye A	Delap$	Fuller	Kitson*	Tonge^	Sidibe/**Soares**/Cresswell
	5/10		19,248	*7*	4			*Crouch 25, Defoe 51*	*James*	*Johnson*	*Belhadj*	*Campbell*	*Distin*	*Diop*	*Davis*	*Hughes*	*Crouch*	*Defoe*	*Traore**	*Hreidarsson*
								Ref: A Marriner	In pouring rain, Pompey score two quality goals. Crouch flashes in an overhead kick. Fuller nods in a Delap throw that was flicked on at the near post by Kitson. Jermain Defoe nets off a post from 18 yards. Harry Redknapp's men play keepball thereafter. City are not up to speed.											
8	H	TOTTENHAM		18	W	2-1	1-1	Higginbotham 19p, Delap 53	Sorensen^	Griffin	Higginbot'm	Sonko$	Faye AD	Olofinjana	Soares	Diao	Sidibe	Kitson*	Delap	Fuller/Simonsen/Shawcross
	19/10		27,500	*20*	7			*Bent 25*	*Gomes*	*Hutton*	*Bale !*	*Woodgate*	*Corluka^*	*Zokora*	*Lennon*	*Jenas*	*Bent*	*Modric*	*Bentley**	*Pavlychenko/Dawson !*
								Ref: L Mason	Bale walks for felling Soares. The 10 men are the better side. Bent slides home from 10 yards. Delap nets an Olofinjana cross. Corluka departs in an ambulance. Dawson sees red for an awful lunge on Sidibe. Fuller's pen hits both posts (90). Delap smashes the follow up against the bar.											
9	A	MANCHESTER C		18	L	0-3	0-1		Sorensen	Griffin	Higginbot'm	Shawcross	Faye AD	Olofinjana	Soares^	Diao$	Sidibe*	Fuller	Delap	Kitson/Cresswell/Whelan
	26/10		*44,624*	*8*	7			*Robinho 14, 47, 72*	*Hart*	*Richards*	*Garrido^*	*Dunne$*	*Ben-Haim*	*Kompany*	*Ireland*	*W't-Phillips*	*Evans**	*Robinho*	*Elano*	*Sturridge/Onuoha/Fernandes*
								Ref: S Tanner	Stoke fall foul of the genius of £32m Robinho, Billionaire Blues' signing from Real Madrid. He converts Evans' cross and rounds off two slick moves. Olly and Higgy both fail to net good chances. Hart saves a Diao piledriver. Shawcross heads straight at Hart from 3 yards. Well beaten.											
10	H	SUNDERLAND		15	W	1-0	0-0	Fuller 73	Sorensen	Griffin	Higginbot'm	Shawcross	Faye AD	Olofinjana^	Soares*	Diao	Sidibe	Fuller$	Delap	Tonge/Faye A/Kitson
	29/10		26,731	*10*	10				*Fulop*	*Bardsley*	*McCartney*	*Ferdinand*	*Collins*	*Whitehead*	*Malbranque$*	*Yorke**	*Cisse^*	*Diouf*	*Richardson*	*Jones/Chopra/Reid*
								Ref: C Foy	Stoke suffocate Roy Keane's Black Cats. Their impotent strikeforce fail to get a shot on target. Cisse is anonymous. Faye dominant. Finally, City break through when Fuller is left unmarked to nod in a Delap throw from 8 yards. Fulop denies Fuller. Sorensen saves from Jones late on.											
11	H	ARSENAL		12	W	2-1	1-0	Fuller 11, Olofinjana 73	Sorensen	Griffin	Higginbot'm	Shawcross	Faye AD	Olofinjana	Faye A	Diao *	Sidibe$	Fuller^	Delap	Whelan/Cresswell/Kitson
	1/11		26,704	*4*	13			*Clichy 90*	*Almunia*	*Sagna**	*Clichy*	*Toure*	*Silvestre*	*Denilson^*	*Fabregas*	*Song*	*Adebayor$*	*Bendtner*	*Diaby*	*Walcott/van Persie !/Vela*
								Ref: R Styles	Fuller flicks in a Delap howitzer. City play rough with the Gunners, who can't cope. Olofinjana breasts in a Delap throw. Robin van Persie sees red for elbowing Sorensen. Walcott departs injured. Clichy nets a deflected shot from 22 yards in injury-time. Wenger's whingeing is comical.											

No	Venue	Opponent	Att	Pos	Res	Pts	F-A	H-T	Scorers, Times, and Referees	1	2	3	4	5	6	7	8	9	10	11	Subs used
12	A	WIGAN		11	D		0-0	0-0		Sorensen	Griffin	Higginbot'm	Shawcross	Faye AD	Olofinjana$	Faye A^	Diao	Sidibe*	Fuller	Delap	Kitson/Cresswell/Whelan
	8/11		15,881	15		14				Kirkland	Melchiot	Figueroa	Bramble	Boyce	Valencia	Cattermole	Palacios	Heskey*	Zaki	Koumas	Camara
									Ref: M Riley	Thomas Sorensen frustrates Wigan with a string of fine saves. Palacios fires over. Heskey, Zaki and Koumas all fire just wide. Kirkland saves Shawcross's header. Shawcross then clears Melchiot's header off the line. Little other action on a freezing day. Last match shown on MoTD!											
13	A	MANCHESTER U		14	L		0-5	0-2	[Welbeck 84]	Sorensen	Griffin$	Higginbot'm	Shawcross	Faye AD	Olofinjana*	Faye A	Diao	Sidibe	Fuller^	Delap	Cresswell/Kitson/Wilkinson
	15/11		75,369	3		14			Ronaldo 3, 89, Carrick 45, Berbatov 49,	Van der Sar	O'Shea	Evra	Vidic	Evans	Carrick	Ronaldo	Fletcher*	Tevez$	Berbatov	Park^	Gibson/Welbeck/Manucho
									Ref: P Walton	From the moment Sorensen loses Ronaldo's free-kick and it flashes past him, City are second best. It's Ronaldo's 100th United goal. Another free-kick rounds off the rout. Carrick's 18-yard shot and Berbatov's finish kill the game. Danny Welbeck lashes in on the run. Heads go down.											
14	H	WEST BROM		13	W		1-0	0-0	Sidibe 84	Sorensen	Griffin	Higginbot'm	Shawcross$	Faye AD	Faye A	Soares^	Diao	Sidibe	Kitson*	Delap	Cresswell/Tonge/Cort
	22/11		26,613	20		17				Carson	Zuiverloon	Robinson	Olsson	Meite	Valero^	Greening	Kim*	Miller	Koren	Brunt	Teixeira/Bednar
									Ref: L Mason	Stoke are head and shoulders the best side but struggle to make an attacking impact. Delap's throws cause havoc but with no result. Finally the pressure pays off. Higgy gets to the byeline after a flowing move and Sidibe soars to power in a header. Tony Mowbray's men have no answer.											
15	H	HULL		13	D		1-1	0-1	Fuller 73p	Sorensen	Griffin	Higginbot'm	Cort	Faye AD	Faye A	Soares*	Diao	Sidibe	Fuller	Delap	Tonge
	29/11		27,500	6		18			King 45	Myhill	McShane	Ricketts	Zayatte	Turner	Boateng^	Marney	Barmby*	King	Geovanni$	Ashbee	Halmosi/Garcia/Cousin
									Ref: K Stroud	Phil Brown's Hull have a plan to deal with Delap. Windass is booked whilst warming up for standing in front of him at throw-ins. Marlon King swivels to lash high into the net. Fuller is upended by Myhill and strokes in the pen. Fuller, Sidibe and Cort are foiled by Myhill. A fair result.											
16	A	NEWCASTLE		13	D		2-2	0-2	Sidibe 60, Faye AD 90	Sorensen	Griffin	Higginbot'm	Sonko	Faye AD	Faye A$	Pugh	Diao*	Sidibe	Cresswell	Delap^	Whelan/Fuller/Tonge
	6/12		47,422	16		19			Owen 9, 24	Given	Beye	Enrique	Coloccini	Bassong	Geremi$	Guthrie*	N'Zogbia	Martins^	Owen	Gutierrez	Taylor/Viduka/Cacapa
									Ref: M Riley	Toon overwhelm City with Michael Owen steering in two poachers' strikes. Fuller's introduction changes everything. His run sets up Sidibe to sidefoot in. City pulverise Toon's shaky defence. Abdy Faye nets in a scramble. His first goal against his ex-club. One of *the* great fight-backs.											
17	H	FULHAM		13	D		0-0	0-0		Sorensen	Wilkinson	Higginbot'm	Sonko	Faye AD	Faye A	Pugh$	Whelan	Sidibe*	Fuller	Delap^	Cresswell/Tonge/Pericard
	13/12		25,287	10		20				Schwarzer	Pantsil	Konchesky	Hangeland	Hughes	Bullard	Davies	Murphy	Dempsey	Johnson	Gera	
									Ref: S Attwell	Stoke start well but Sidibe's knee goes as he lands from a jump and he is out for the season. Lawrence and Kitson also are long-term injured. A stalemate sees Fulham dominate possession but rarely cross halfway. City lack a plan B with no one to take advantage of Delap's throws. Dull.											
18	A	BLACKBURN		14	L		0-3	0-3		Sorensen	Sonko	Higginbot'm	Shawcross	Faye AD	Faye A$	Cresswell	Whelan	Pericard^	Fuller	Delap*	Tonge/Soares/Olofinjana
	20/12		23,004	19		20			McCarthy 9p, 27, Roberts 18	Robinson	Ooijer	Warnock	Samba	Nelson	Andrews	Emerton$	Dunn*	McCarthy^	Roberts	Pederson	Tugay/Derbyshire/Simpson
									Ref: P Walton	A vital game starts badly when Sonko trips Pedersen. McCarthy nets the pen. Sam Allardyce's first match in charge of Rovers continues well, when Roberts taps in Shawcross's errant clearance and McCarthy scores after Sorensen saves from Roberts. Dreadful showing. TP worried.											
19	H	MANCHESTER U		18	L		0-1	0-0		Sorensen	Wilkinson !	Higginbot'm	Shawcross	Faye AD	Faye A^	Pugh	Whelan	Cresswell$	Fuller	Delap*	**Davies**/Olofinjana/Pericard
	26/12		27,500	3		20			Tevez 83	Van der Sar	Neville	O'Shea*	Vidic	Evans	Scholes^	Ronaldo	Fletcher	Tevez	Rooney	Giggs	Berbatov/Carrick
									Ref: C Foy	Stoke give as good as they get. Ronaldo should be dismissed for kicking out, but the ref takes no action. Ronaldo then draws Wilko into a silly foul and Wilko walks for a second yellow. City defend stoutly with Faye magnificent but Berbatov gets free inside the box to square for Tevez.											
20	A	WEST HAM		18	L		1-2	1-0	Faye AD 5	Sorensen	Griffin^	Higginbot'm	Shawcross	Faye AD	Olofinjana	Pugh*	Whelan	Cresswell	Fuller !	Delap	Pericard/Davies
	28/12		34,477	10		20			Cole 51, Tristan 88	Green	Faubert	Ilunga	Collins	Upson	Behrami	Parker*	Collison^	Cole	Di Michele$	Boa Morte	Mullins/Tristan/Spector
									Ref: M Jones	Abdoulaye Faye slams in a header as Stoke begin brightly. Griffin is allowed to carry on injured by TP and fails to clear, allowing Cole to net. Fuller loses it with his skipper, slaps him and is sent off. The ten men cling on, but Diego Tristan latches onto a wayward shot for the winner.											
21	H	LIVERPOOL		17	D		0-0	0-0		Sorensen	Wilkinson	Higginbot'm	Shawcross	Faye AD	Faye A	Delap	Whelan	Kitson^	Cresswell	**Ethering'n***	Lawrence/Pugh
	10/1		27,500	1		21				Reina	Carragher	Aurelio	Hyypia	Skrtel	Mascherano	Gerrard	Benayoun^	Kuyt	Lucas	Rieira*	Babel/Torres
									Ref: L Mason	Delap slams against the bar as Stoke take the game to Rafa Benitez's men. Torres is left on the bench and Liverpool lack zest, ideas and threat. Kuyt heads wide. Kitson flicks a header over. Gerrard hits a post late on as Liverpool finally make an attempt to win the game. A great point.											
22	A	CHELSEA		18	L		1-2	0-0	Delap 60	Sorensen	Wilkinson	Hig'inbot'm^	Shawcross	Faye AD	Faye A*	Delap	Whelan	**Beattie**	Cresswell	Etheringt'n$	Pugh/Griffin/Kitson
	17/1		41,788	3		21			Belletti 88, Lampard 90	Cech	Bosingwa^	Cole	Alex	Carvalho	Mikel$	Lampard	Ballack	Drogba	Malouda*	Kalou	Di Santo/Belletti/Stoch
									Ref: P Walton	City contain a Chelsea side struggling for form, with a manager under pressure. Delap races through onto Beattie's pass to flick past Cech. City defend in depth. Amdy Faye is subbed before he is dismissed. Belletti nods in at the far post. Lampard lashes in from 18 yards to break hearts.											
23	A	TOTTENHAM		19	L		1-3	0-3	Beattie 57	Sorensen	Wilkinson*	Higginbot'm	Shawcross	Faye AD^	Faye A$	Delap	Whelan	Beattie	Cresswell	Etherington	Griffin/Sonko/Fuller
	27/1		36,072	13		21			Lennon 8, Defoe 21, Dawson 25	Cudicini	Corluka	Assou-Ekoto	Woodgate	Dawson	Zokora	Lennon*	Modric	Pavlych'ko^	Defoe	Bentley	Huddlestone/Campbell
									Ref: M Riley	Rampant Spurs put City to the sword in a devastating 20-minute spell. Lennon crashes in on the run. Defoe lashes home Modric's sublime ball. Dawson heads in a corner. Abdy Faye is ill and replaced at half-time. Stoke fare better. James Beattie scores his first, cracking in Ethers' pass.											

No		Date		Att	Pos	Pt	F-A	H-T	Scorers, Times, and Referees	SQUAD	NUMBERS	IN	USE								subs used
24	H		MANCHESTER C		16	W	1-0	1-0	Beattie 45	Sorensen	Wilkinson	Pugh	Shawcross	Faye AD	Faye A^	Delap !	Whelan	Beattie	Fuller*	Etheringt'n$	Cresswell/Griffin/Sonko
		31/1		27,236	*10*	24				*Hart*	*Richards*	*Bridge*	*Onuoha*	*Kompany*	*De Jong^*	*Zabaleta**	*W't-Phillips*	*Bellamy*	*Robinho*	*Ireland*	*Elano/Caicedo*
									Ref: M Atkinson	The game explodes when Delap kicks the ball at SWP after the winger's foul on Ethers. He walks. Backed by a vociferous crowd, Ethers' cross is finished by Beattie. Despite 75% possession, Blues fail to create a clear-cut chance. Robinho and Bellamy kept outside the area. A huge win.											
25	A		SUNDERLAND		17	L	0-2	0-0		Sorensen	Wilkinson*	**Kelly**	Shawcross^	Faye AD	Diao	Cresswell	Whelan	Beattie	Fuller$	Etheringt'n !	Pugh/Sonko/Camara
		7/2		*38,350*	*11*	24			*Jones 78, Healy 90*	*Fulop*	*Bardsley*	*McCartney*	*Ferdinand*	*Collins*	*Whitehead*	*Malbranque**	*Reid^*	*Cisse$*	*Jones*	*Richardson*	*Edwards/Murphy/Healy*
									Ref: R Styles	Pugh handles on the line, but ref Styles misses it. City are marginally the better side until Ethers sees red for kicking out at Collins after being pulled back. After losing 3 players to injury in the first half, City succumb. Jones nods past Sorensen, who misjudges the header. Healy taps in.											
26	H		PORTSMOUTH		17	D	2-2	0-0	Beattie 78p, 80	Sorensen	Wilkinson	Higginbot'm	Shawcross	Faye AD	Diao	Faye A	Lawrence*	Beattie	Sidibe^	Pugh	Tonge/Cresswell
		21/2		26,354	*14*	25			*Kranjcar 75, Shawcross og 90*	*James*	*Johnson*	*Hreidarsson*	*Campbell*	*Distin*	*Bassinas**	*Pennant*	*Davis*	*Crouch*	*Nugent^*	*Kranjcar$*	*Mullins/Kanu/Belhadj*
									Ref: M Jones	The stalemate is broken by a sweeping Pompey move which Niko Kranjcar flashes in from 15 yards. City storm back. Johnson is adjudged to handle, although it looks iffy. Beattie nets his second by flicking in Pugh's shot. City can't hold on. Shawcross deflects in Hreidarsson's shot.											
27	A		ASTON VILLA		19	D	2-2	0-1	Shawcross 88, Whelan 90	Sorensen*	Shawcross	Wilkinson	Sonko	Higginbot'm	Diao	Faye A$	Lawrence	Beattie	Sidibe	Pugh^	Simonsen/Fuller/Whelan
		1/3		*39,641*	*4*	26			*Petrov 45, Carew 79*	*Friedel*	*Cuellar*	*Young*	*Knight*	*Davies*	*Petrov*	*Milner*	*Barry*	*Heskey**	*Agbonlahor*	*Young*	*Carew*
									Ref: H Webb	TP selects 3 centre-halves, but City fail to function. Milner fires over. Petrov lashes in from 25 yards. Carew curls in a belter from 20 yards and City seem down and out. TP reorganises. Whelan hits a post. Shawcross nods in Beattie's cross. Whelan lashes in from 20 yards to spark joy.											
28	H		BOLTON		15	W	2-0	1-0	Beattie 14, Fuller 73	Sorensen	Wilkinson$	Higginbot'm	Shawcross	Faye AD	Diao^	Whelan	Lawrence	Beattie	Sidibe*	Delap	Fuller/Faye A/Sonko
		4/3		26,319	*11*	29				*Jaaskel'nen*	*Steinsson^*	*Samuel*	*Cahill*	*O'Brien A*	*Davies M*	*Muamba**	*McCann*	*Davies K*	*Elmander*	*Taylor*	*Gardner/Makukula*
									Ref: M Dean	Beattie latches on to Whelan's header to crash in confidently on the run. Bolton play well, but rarely threaten. Wilkinson fires narrowly wide. Sorensen denies Taylor. Sonko nods against the bar. City finally take one of their chances when Fuller lashes in during a scramble. A vital win.											
29	A		EVERTON		18	L	1-3	0-2	Shawcross 52	Sorensen	Wilkinson	Higginbot'm	Shawcross	Faye AD	Diao	Whelan	Lawrence$	Beattie	Sidibe*	Delap^	Fuller/Etherington/**Camara**
		14/3		*36,396*	*6*	29			*Jo 18, Lescott 24, Fellaini 90*	*Howard*	*Jagielka*	*Baines*	*Yobo*	*Lescott*	*Osman*	*Neville*	*Cahill**	*Jo^*	*Fellaini*	*Pienaar*	*Saha/Rodwell*
									Ref: A Marriner	David Moyes' injury-depleted men dominate with their 5-man midfield in the ascendancy. Jo beats Sorensen, who then parries Cahill's header to Lescott who nets. Shawcross powers home Lawrence's corner and then almost converts Higgy's flick to level. Fallaini scores from 8 yards.											
30	H		MIDDLESBROUGH		16	W	1-0	0-0	Shawcross 84	Sorensen	Wilkinson*	Higginbot'm	Shawcross	Faye AD	Diao^	Whelan	Lawrence$	Beattie	Fuller	Delap	Kelly/Etherington/Sidibe
		21/3		26,442	*19*	32				*Jones*	*McMahon^*	*Taylor$*	*Huth*	*Wheater*	*Shawky*	*Pogatetz*	*O'Neil*	*King**	*Tuncay*	*Downing*	*Alves/Hoyte/Johnson*
									Ref: L Mason	Gareth Southgate's team arrive for a crucial relegation six-pointer. They play keepball but make little impression on City's massed defence, aside from a couple of long range efforts. City turn the screw. Shawcross times his run beautifully to nod in a Delap throw. The belief is total.											
31	A		WEST BROM		13	W	2-0	1-0	Fuller 2, Beattie 49	Sorensen	Wilkinson	Higginbot'm	Shawcross	Faye AD	Delap	Whelan	Lawrence^	Beattie*	Fuller$	Etherington	Cresswell/Pugh/Olofinjana
		4/4		*26,277*	*20*	35				*Carson*	*Zuiverloon*	*Robinson**	*Olsson*	*Martis*	*Valero*	*Greening^*	*Morrison*	*Fortune*	*Simpson$*	*Brunt*	*Koren/Bednar/Teixeira*
									Ref: M Atkinson	Fuller leaves Shelton Martis for dead and fires a shot under the awful Carson. Baggies fans show their displeasure at Tony Mowbray's men's continued defensive failings, as another lapse allows Beattie to crash in left-footed from 12 yards. Stoke win easily. Travelling fans go wild.											
32	H		NEWCASTLE		13	D	1-1	1-0	Faye AD 33	Sorensen	Wilkinson$	Higginbot'm	Shawcross	Faye AD	Delap	Whelan	Lawrence	Beattie*	Fuller	Etherington"	Cresswell/Pugh/Kelly
		11/4		24,862	*18*	36			*Carroll 81*	*Harper*	*Edgar*	*Taylor*	*Beye*	*Bassong*	*Nolan*	*Guthrie**	*Butt*	*Ameobi"*	*Owen*	*Duff*	*Gutierrez/Carroll*
									Ref: C Foy	Alan Shearer is the focus as desperate Toon need three points. Abdoulaye Faye scores another header from a corner against his old club. Toon struggle but Carroll's introduction gives them focus and he rises to net a classic centre-forward's header. A draw leaves Toon 6 points behind.											
33	H		BLACKBURN		11	W	1-0	0-0	Lawrence 75	Sorensen	Wilkinson*	Higginbot'm	Shawcross	Faye AD	Delap	Whelan	Lawrence	Beattie^	Fuller	Etheringt'n$	Kelly/Cresswell/Sonko
		18/4		27,500	*17*	39				*Robinson*	*Ooijer*	*Givet*	*Samba*	*Nelson*	*Andrews*	*Diouf*	*Mokoena^*	*McCarthy**	*Pedersen*	*Warnock*	*Villanueva/Dunn*
									Ref: H Webb	Another relegation tussle goes City's way as the players' and fans' belief propels them towards safety. Rovers struggle to make any attacking impact, but nullify Stoke's long ball and throw, until Beattie flicks on for Lawrence to turn Givet inside out and lash left-footed past Robinson.											
34	A		FULHAM		12	L	0-1	0-1		Sorensen	Kelly*	Pugh$	Shawcross	Faye AD	Delap	Whelan	Lawrence	Cresswell^	Fuller	Etherington	Sonko/Camara/Dickinson
		25/4		*25,069*	*7*	39			*Nevland 29*	*Schwarzer*	*Pantsil*	*Konchesky$*	*Hangeland*	*Hughes*	*Etuhu*	*Dempsey*	*Murphy*	*Zamora**	*Johnson^*	*Gera*	*Nevland/Kamara/Baird*
									Ref: L Mason	Roy Hodgson's men lose both strikers, but sub Erik Nevland finishes a sublime breakaway for the only goal. City bombard the Fulham box in the second half but nothing drops for them. Fuller flashes a header wide. Shawcross nods over Camara's cross. Still need two points for safety.											

No	Date	Opponent	Att	Pos	Res	F-A	H-T	Scorers, Times, and Referees	1	2	3	4	5	6	7	8	9	10	11	subs used
35	H	WEST HAM		13	L	0-1	0-1		Sorensen	Wilkinson$	Pugh^	Shawcross	Faye AD	Delap	Whelan	Lawrence	Beattie*	Fuller	Etherington	Camara/Olofinjana/Sonko
	2/5		27,500	*7*	39			*Tristan 33*	*Green*	*Neill*	*Ilunga*	*Tomkins*	*Upson*	*Stanislas*	*Noble^*	*Kovac*	*Tristan*	*Di Michele$*	*Boa Morte**	*Collison/Lopez/Sears*
								Ref: P Walton	Gianfranco Zola's men are chasing Europe. They play neat, incisive football with Noble at its heart. City are not quite up to speed, but it takes a sublime free-kick from Tristan to break the deadlock. Noble nods off the line from Faye. Are Stoke crumbling before the finishing line?											
36	A	HULL		12	W	2-1	1-0	Fuller 41, Lawrence 73	Sorensen	Wilkinson	Cort	Shawcross	Faye AD	Delap	Whelan	Lawrence	Beattie*	Fuller$	Etherington^	Cresswell/Pugh/Kelly
	9/5		*24,932*	*17*	42			*Dawson 90*	*Myhill*	*Ricketts*	*Dawson*	*Zayatte$*	*Turner*	*Boateng*	*Garcia**	*Kilbane*	*Fagan*	*Cousin^*	*Barmby*	*Mendy/Manucho/Geovanni*
								Ref: H Webb	Crunch time. Both sides need the points, but Stoke dominate from the moment Fuller turns to fire home during a scramble. City soak up Hull's pressure and play on the break. Lawrence roams freely and crashs in a superb 30-yarder. Dawson's late free-kick is immaterial. Stoke are safe!											
37	H	WIGAN		11	W	2-0	0-0	Fuller 69, Beattie 76	Sorensen	Wilkinson	Cort*	Shawcross	Faye AD	Delap	Whelan	Lawrence	Beattie$	Fuller	Etherington^	Pugh/Diao/Cresswell
	16/5		25,641	*12*	45				*Kingson*	*Melchiot*	*Figueroa$*	*Bramble*	*Boyce*	*Scharner*	*Cho^*	*Brown**	*Rodallega*	*Cattermole*	*N'Zogbia*	*Watson/Mido/Edman*
								Ref: L Probert	City sign off at the Brit with a dominant display against Steve Bruce's Latics. Faye almost gives away a penalty in tripping Rodallega. Fuller finishes off his own run with a shot at the third time of asking. Beattie nods in after Ethers' shot is saved. Stoke right at home in the top flight.											
38	A	ARSENAL		12	L	1-4	1-4	Fuller 31p *[Diaby 18]*	Simonsen*	Wilkinson	Dickinson	Shawcross	Faye AD	Diao^	Whelan	Lawrence	Beattie	Fuller$	Delap	Sorensen/Pugh/Cresswell
	24/5		*60,082*	*4*	45			*Beattie 10 (og), van Persie 16p, 41,*	*Mannone*	*Sagna^*	*Gibbs*	*Toure*	*Song*	*Denilson*	*Diaby*	*Fabregas*	*van Persie*	*Arshavin$*	*Walcott**	*Bendtner/Eboue/Vela*
		Home	Away					Ref: M Atkinson	Bad day as Beattie slices Walcott's cross into his own net. Shawcross fells van Persie for the pen. Diaby nods past Simo, who has to be subbed. Fuller is fouled for Stoke's pen. Van Persie takes advantage of Delap's error to net. Revenge for Wenger's Gunners. City already on the beach.											
Average		26,954	35,939																	

League Cup			Att			F-A	H-T	Scorers, Times, and Referees	SQUAD	NUMBERS	IN	USE								subs used
2	A	CHELTENHAM		14	W	3-2	0-0	Whelan 51, Cresswell 54, Parkin 78	Simonsen	Wilkinson$	Dickinson^	Buxton	Shawcross	Diao*	Whelan	Cresswell	Parkin	Pericard	Pugh	Matteo/Phillips/Shotton
26/8			*3,600*	*1:21*				*Vincent 57, Russell 90*	*Higgs*	*Gill*	*Wright*	*Townsend*	*Duff**	*Lindegard*	*Armstrong*	*Gill^*	*Connor*	*Vincent$*	*Russell*	*Gallinagh/Ledgister/Caines*
								Ref: D Deadman	Stoke's first visit to Whaddon Road is an entertaining run out for the second string. Whelan curls home an exquisite free-kick. Cresswell drills in from 12 yards. Ashley Vincent nets via a post, but Parkin lashes in a stunner. Alex Russell slots late on. First time in third round for 8 years.											
3	H	READING		18	D	2-2	1-1	Pericard 9, Sidibe 50	Simonsen	Wilkinson	Dickinson	Higginbo'm$	Shawcross	Buxton	Lawrence	Whelan	Sidibe*	Pericard	Cresswell^	Phillips/Fuller/Cort
23/9			9,141	*C:6*		*aet*		*Henry 45p, 75*	*Federici*	*Kelly*	*Golborne*	*Bikey*	*Ingimarsson*	*Henry*	*Gunnars'on**	*Cisse^*	*Lita*	*Long*	*Convey$*	*Sigurds'on/Pearce/Mooney*
								Ref: L Probert (Stoke win 4-3 on penalties)	Pericard's bullet header is levelled by James Henry's pen after Higgy trips Bikey. Sidibe finishes Whelan's off target shot with a finish from a tight angle. Steve Coppell's side equalise again through Henry's shot from the edge of the box. Pericard nets City's fifth pen. Lita blazes over.											
4	H	ROTHERHAM		11	W	2-0	1-0	Whelan 21, Pugh 59	Simonsen	Wilkinson	Dickinson	Cort	Shawcross	Olofinjana*	Pugh	Whelan	Kitson	Pericard^	Cresswell	Fuller/Faye A
11/11			15,458	*2:21*					*Warrington*	*Mills*	*Nicholas*	*Sharps*	*Fenton*	*Rhodes*	*Harrison**	*Cummins*	*Broughton^*	*Reid*	*Tonge*	*Taylor/Yates*
								Ref: M Halsey	City canter to victory. Whelan's free-kick curls in from 25 yards. Tricky Alex Rhodes threatens down the left for Mark Robins' Millers. Reid is denied by Simo. Shawcross and Pericard fire over. Pugh smashes in an astute Kitson pass. Simo saves Tonge's 40-yarder. A comfortable win.											
QF	H	DERBY		13	L	0-1	0-0		Simonsen	Griffin	Higginbot'm	Cort	Sonko	Olofinjana*	Delap	Whelan	Sidibe	Fuller	Cresswell	Pugh
2/12			22,034	*C:15*				*Ellington 90p*	*Carroll*	*Connolly*	*Stewart*	*Powell*	*Tomkins*	*Green^*	*Addison*	*Kazmierczak*	*Hulse**	*Ellington*	*Commons*	*Villa/Teale*
								Ref: R Styles	A first quarter-final in 30 years is a dull affair. Carroll keeps Paul Jewell's Rams in it. Rob Styles disallows a Cresswell strike for a dubious handball. Tomkins clears off the line from Sidibe. In steps Styles, who adjudges Griffin to have handled. Ellington cheekily rolls in the penalty.											

FA Cup																				
3	A	HARTLEPOOL		18	L	0-2	0-0		Simonsen	Davies$	Dickinson	Sonko	Shawcross	Olofinjana*	Soares^	Whelan	Pericard	Delap	Tonge	Kitson/Lawrence/Wilkinson
3/1			*5,367*	*1:15*				*Nelson 49, Foley 76*	*Lee-Barrett*	*Sweeney**	*Humphreys*	*Nelson*	*Collins*	*Liddle*	*Jones$*	*Clark*	*Mackay^*	*Jones*	*Porter*	*McCunnie/Foley/Monkhouse*
								Ref: M Halsey	Stoke's second string are never at the races. Lee-Barrett palms Sonko's early header away, but Davies tackles Porter in as he is about to tap in. Michael Nelson glances in a free-kick. David Foley unleashes a 30-yard rocket over Simonsen. Little attacking threat. Are City falling apart?											

	P	W	D	L	F	A	W	D	L	F	A	Pts
		Home					Away					
1 Manchester U	38	16	2	1	43	13	12	4	3	25	11	90
2 Liverpool	38	12	7	0	41	13	13	4	2	36	14	86
3 Chelsea	38	11	6	2	33	12	14	2	3	35	12	83
4 Arsenal	38	11	5	3	31	16	9	7	3	37	21	72
5 Everton	38	8	6	5	31	20	9	6	4	24	17	63
6 Aston Villa	38	7	9	3	27	21	10	2	7	27	27	62
7 Fulham	38	11	3	5	28	16	3	8	8	11	18	53
8 Tottenham	38	10	5	4	21	10	4	4	11	24	35	51
9 West Ham	38	9	2	8	23	22	5	7	7	19	23	51
10 Manchester C	38	13	0	6	40	18	2	5	12	18	32	50
11 Wigan	38	8	5	6	17	18	4	4	11	17	27	45
12 STOKE	38	10	5	4	22	15	2	4	13	16	40	45
13 Bolton	38	7	5	7	21	21	4	3	12	20	32	41
14 Portsmouth	38	8	3	8	26	29	2	8	9	12	28	41
15 Blackburn	38	6	7	6	22	23	4	4	11	18	37	41
16 Sunderland	38	6	3	10	21	25	3	6	10	13	29	36
17 Hull	38	3	5	11	18	36	5	6	8	21	28	35
18 Newcastle	38	5	7	7	24	29	2	6	11	16	30	34
19 Middlesbro	38	5	9	5	17	20	2	2	15	11	37	32
20 West Brom	38	7	3	9	26	33	1	5	13	10	34	32
	760	173	97	110	532	410	110	97	173	410	532	1043

Odds & ends

Double wins: (1) West Brom.
Double losses: (4) Chelsea, Everton, Manchester United, West Ham.

Won from behind: (0).
Lost from in front: (2) Chelsea (a), West Ham (a).

High spots: Clinching safety in blazing sunshine at Hull's KC Stadium.
The paranoia surrounding Rory Delap's long throws.
Media nonsense about Stoke's physical style of play.
Defeating Arsenal, Aston Villa and Manchester City at home.
A decent cup run at last in the League Cup.

Low spots: Ricardo Fuller slapping captain Andy Griffin at West Ham.
The 0-5 hammering at Old Trafford.
Slumping out of the FA Cup at League One Hartlepool.
Losing at home in the last minute to Derby in the League Cup quarter-final.

Ever-presents: (0).
Hat-tricks: (0).
Leading Scorer: (11) Ricardo Fuller.
Player of the Year: Abdoulaye Faye.

	Appearances						Goals			
	Lge	*Sub*	LC	*Sub*	FAC	*Sub*	Lge	LC	FAC	Tot
Beattie, James	**16**						7			7
Buxton, Lewis			2							
Camara, Henri		4								
Cort, Leon	**9**	2	2	1						
Cresswell, Richard	**11**	19	4					1		1
Davies, Andrew		2			1					
Delap, Rory	**34**		1		1		2			2
Diao, Salif	**18**	2	1							
Dickinson, Carl	**3**	2	3		1					
Etherington, Matthew	**12**	2								
Faye, Abdoulaye	**36**						3			3
Faye, Amdy	**18**	3		1						
Fuller, Ricardo	**25**	9	1	2			11			11
Griffin, Andy	**17**	3	1							
Higginbotham, Danny	**28**		2				1			1
Kelly, Stephen	**2**	4								
Kitson, Dave	**10**	6	1	1		1				
Lawrence, Liam	**18**	2	1			1	3			3
Matteo, Dominic				1						
Olofinjana, Seyi	**14**	4	2	1	1		2			2
Parkin, Jon			1					1		1
Pericard, Vincent	**1**	3	3		1			1		1
Phillips, Demar				2						
Pugh, Danny	**9**	8	2	1				1		1
Shawcross, Ryan	**28**	1	3		1		3			3
Shotton, Ryan				1						
Sidibe, Mamady	**17**	5	2				3	1		4
Simonsen, Steve	**2**	2	4		1					
Soares, Tom	**5**	2			1					
Sonko, Ibrahima	**7**	7	1		1					
Sorensen, Thomas	**36**	1								
Tonge, Michael	**1**	9			1					
Whelan, Glenn	**21**	5	4		1		1	2		3
Wilkinson, Andy	**20**	2	3	1		1				
(own-goals)							2			2
34 players used	**418**	***109***	**44**	***12***	**11**	***3***	**38**	**7**		**45**

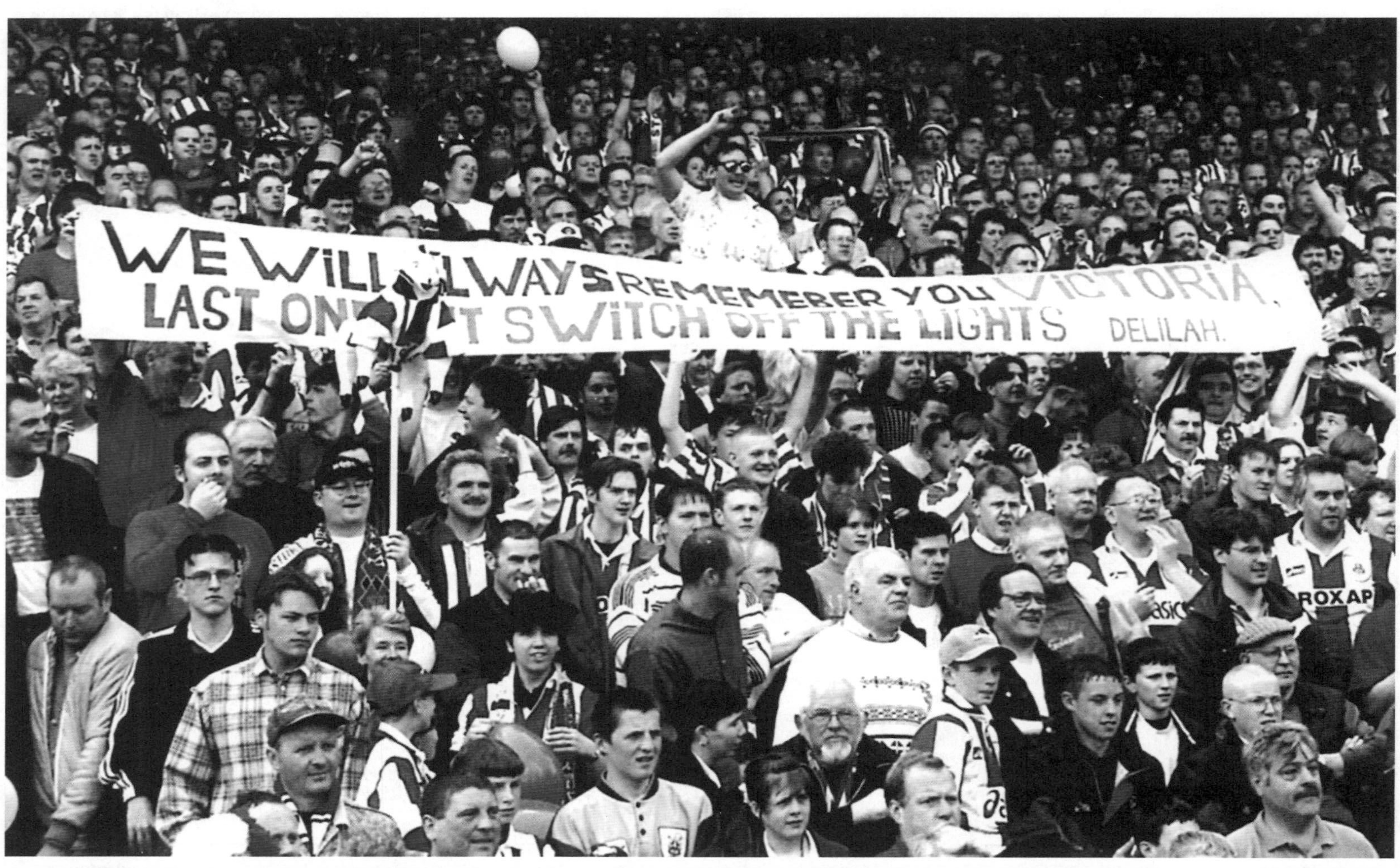
WE WiLL LWAYS REMEMERER YOU VICTORIA.
LAST ON T SWiTCH OFF THE LIGHTS DELILAH.
ROXAP